OXFORD STUDIES IN EUROPEAN LAW

Series Editors

PAUL CRAIG

Professor of English Law at St John's College, Oxford

GRÁINNE DE BÚRCA

Professor of Law at New York University School of Law

Enhanced Cooperation and European Tax Law

OXFORD STUDIES IN EUROPEAN LAW

Series Editors

Paul Craig, Professor of English Law at St John's College, Oxford and
Gráinne de Búrca, Professor of Law at New York University School of Law

The aim of this series is to publish important and original research on EU law. The focus is on scholarly monographs, with a particular emphasis on those which are interdisciplinary in nature. Edited collections of essays will also be included where they are appropriate. The series is wide in scope and aims to cover studies of particular areas of substantive and of institutional law, historical works, theoretical studies, and analyses of current debates, as well as questions of perennial interest such as the relationship between national and EU law and the novel forms of governance emerging in and beyond Europe. The fact that many of the works are interdisciplinary will make the series of interest to all those concerned with the governance and operation of the EU.

OTHER TITLES IN THIS SERIES

Legal Pluralism in European Contract Law
Vanessa Mak

Europe's Passive Virtues
Deference to National Authorities in EU Free Movement Law
Jan Zglinski

Accountability in EU Security and Defence
The Law and Practice of Peacebuilding
Carolyn Moser

Accountability in the Economic and Monetary Union
Foundations, Policy, and Governance
Menelaos Markakis

Official Secrets and Oversight in the EU
Law and Practices of Classified Information
Vigjilenca Abazi

Risk Regulation in the Internal Market
Lessons from Agricultural Biotechnology
Maria Weimer

EU Health Law & Policy
The Expansion of EU Power in Public Health and Health Care
Anniek de Ruijter

The Horizontal Effect of Fundamental Rights in the European Union
A Constitutional Analysis
Eleni Frantziou

EU Powers Under External Pressure
How the EU's External Actions Alter its Internal Structures
Christina Eckes

Frontex and Human Rights
Responsibility in 'Multi-Actor Situations' under the ECHR and EU Public Liability Law
Melanie Fink

EU Equality Law
The First Fundamental Rights Policy of the EU
Elise Muir

Subnational Authorities in EU Law
Michèle Finck

Accessing Asylum in Europe
Violeta Moreno-Lax

National Parliaments after the Lisbon Treaty & the Euro Crisis
Davor Jančić

Environmental Integration in Competition and Free-Movement Laws
Julian Nowag

EU Agencies
Legal and Political Limits to the Transformation of the EU Administration
Merijn Chamon

Enhanced Cooperation and European Tax Law

CAROLINE HEBER
Senior Research Fellow at the Max Planck Institute for Tax Law and Public Finance, Munich

OXFORD
UNIVERSITY PRESS

OXFORD
UNIVERSITY PRESS

Great Clarendon Street, Oxford, OX2 6DP,
United Kingdom

Oxford University Press is a department of the University of Oxford.
It furthers the University's objective of excellence in research, scholarship,
and education by publishing worldwide. Oxford is a registered trade mark of
Oxford University Press in the UK and in certain other countries

First Edition published in 2021

Impression: 1

Published in the United States of America by Oxford University Press
198 Madison Avenue, New York, NY 10016, United States of America

British Library Cataloguing in Publication Data

Data available

Library of Congress Control Number: 2021931818

ISBN 978–0–19–289827–2

DOI: 10.1093/oso/9780192898272.001.0001

Printed and bound by
CPI Group (UK) Ltd, Croydon, CR0 4YY

To Dominik

Series Editors' Preface

Despite the commitment of the EU in recent decades to providing a form of differentiated integration—'closer cooperation' which would permit groups of member states who are willing to move ahead together on legislative initiatives which other member states prefer not to join, the Treaty provisions on closer cooperation have been little used in practice. This is not because there have not been policy areas or specific issues on which groups of states would have liked to move forward, but rather because the conditions which must be satisfied in order to use the Treaty provisions on closer cooperation appear both onerous and vague. Further, on some of the few occasions on which the provisions on closer cooperation have been invoked and used, they have been challenged before the Court of Justice by the non-participating member states.

In this interesting and informative book, Caroline Heber brings together two important subjects in EU law: that of enhanced cooperation on the one hand, and EU tax law on the other hand. In a clear and cogent way, the book explores the history, the varieties and the purpose of mechanisms of differentiation within EU law, examining in particular detail the current Treaty mechanism of closer cooperation. She outlines the uses and attempted uses that have so far been made of this enhanced cooperation procedure, as well as the potential tensions the mechanism creates for competition and non-protectionism in the EU's internal market. More specifically, she explores the attempts that have been made to use the provisions on closer cooperation in the field of taxation law, and the reasons why these have so far failed.

Drawing on her understanding of the tensions and difficulties created by closer cooperation attempts, Heber then provides a very detailed and thorough account of what would be required in order for closer cooperation in taxation to be successfully pursued in compliance with all of the principles and requirements of the Treaty and without damaging the interests of the non-participating states or undermining the interests of the participating states. In a series of substantial chapters, she outlines the procedural and substantive conditions which would have to be fulfilled to this end, and concludes that despite the rather thin and vague provisions of the Treaty on enhanced cooperation, they do and can—properly understood—allow for effective closer cooperation in taxation which includes the necessary safeguards to protect both participating and non-participating states.

The book thus contains a meticulous, detailed and insightful depiction of the history and use of the EU's closer cooperation procedure, drawing on the experience of attempts in the area of tax law, as well as a comprehensive and thorough account of the ways in which and the conditions under which this little-used procedure could effectively and usefully be operationalized in this field in compliance with the Treaty's requirements.

It should be of considerable interest to legal scholars, practitioners and institutional actors who are concerned with flexibility and differentiated integration in the EU, as well as to EU tax scholars and all those who are interested in the harmonization of taxation law in the EU.

Paul Craig
Gráinne de Búrca

Preface

The idea of dedicating my habilitation thesis to enhanced cooperation and European tax law came to me during a conference in February 2014 in Madrid. The conference dealt with widely diverse aspects of a European financial transaction tax. But whenever questions concerning enhanced cooperation were raised, the room fell silent. Nobody quite knew how to deal with the mechanism and character of enhanced cooperation law, including the most pressing question of whether and to what extent enhanced cooperation law must comply in the same way as purely national rules with primary EU law (in particular the fundamental freedoms and competition law) or competing secondary law. This issue was, in my opinion, only answered reflexively according to gut feeling. I found the responses inadequate, because they failed to take sufficient account of the institutional framework of the European treaties and the objective of partially deepened integration via enhanced cooperation. This became my motivation to examine more closely whether enhanced cooperation law does after all have a privileged role within the framework of the European treaties, that is whether it lies hierarchically above Member State legislation but below generally binding directives and regulations.

Searching for the possibilities and the limits of enhanced cooperation lawmaking has not been easy, and I am therefore all the more grateful for the unconditional support I have received during this period. First and foremost, I would like to thank my academic mentors Michael Lang and Wolfgang Schön, who never ceased to encourage me and believe in me, and who were always eager to discuss my new propositions with me. I am extremely grateful to them for all their support. I would also like to thank Erich Vranes for his valuable suggestions and for providing a second expert opinion on my text. While writing a large part of this book during my Emile Noël fellowship at the Jean Monnet Center of NYU Law School, Joseph HH Weiler put my propositions to the test and always challenged me to go one step further. Gráinne de Burca's exacting questions have always provided me with new food for thought, and it is also thanks to her that I decided to submit my book to this collection.

While writing my book, I met many impressive people and was able to learn from them all. I would like to mention three people in particular because their friendship and their tireless spirit have been a great help to me over the past few years. Thank you Vasiliki Kosta, Christian Sternberg, and Kasper Dziurdź.

I would also like to thank my current and former colleagues at the Max Planck Institute for Tax Law and Public Finance for the wonderful and inspiring time I have enjoyed here. My special thanks go to Birke Häcker, Christine Osterloh-Konrad, Erik Röder, and Johanna Stark.

Caroline Heber
Munich, November 2020

Table of Contents

List of Abbreviations

AG	Advocate General
Art	Article
ATAD	Anti-Tax Avoidance Directive
BEPS	Base Erosion and Profit Shifting
CCCTB	Common Consolidated Corporate Tax Base
CFC	Controlled Foreign Corporation
CJEU	Court of Justice of the European Union
CUP	Cambridge University Press
DST	Digital Service Tax
EC	European Community
EEA	European Economic Area
EEC	European Economic Community
eg	exempli gratia (for example)
EPO	European Patent Office
et al	et alii (and others)
et seq	et sequens (and the following)
EU	European Union
EuroHPC	European High Performance Computing Joint Undertaking
fn.	Footnote
FTT	Financial Transaction Tax
GAAR	General Anti-Abuse Rule
GATT	General Agreement on Tariffs and Trade
GSM	Global System for Mobile Communications
ibid	ibidem (in the same place)
ie	id est (that is)
IFRS	International Financial Reporting Standards
km	kilometres
MFN	Most-Favoured-Nation
OECD	Organisation for Economic Co-operation and Development
OEEC	Organisation for European Economic Co-operation
OJ	Official Journal of the European Union
OUP	Oxford University Press
para/paras	paragraph(s)
s/ss	section(s)
TEU	Treaty on European Union
TFEU	Treaty on the Functioning of the European Union
ToA	Treaty of Amsterdam
UK	United Kingdom of Great Britain and Northern Ireland

US	United States of America
v	versus
VAT	Value-Added Tax
VCLT	Vienna Convention on the Law of Treaties
WTO	World Trade Organization

1
Introduction

A. The Enhanced Cooperation Procedure—A Way Forward

A European Union (EU) of almost thirty Member States, in which all should be allowed to keep their national identities and peculiarities, is a project that can encounter severe difficulties. The most notable issue lies in the European legislative procedure. On the one hand, sensitive legislative matters such as European tax measures should be based on the consent of all Member States, ensuring that no Member State is outvoted or forced to implement policy objectives which are contrary to the Member State's aims; on the other hand, a unanimous vote in the Council may easily provoke a lengthy process, which may even lead to a legislative deadlock. The Member States may disagree on both the question of whether an action is necessary and the content of a possible action. Despite the onerous requirement of unanimity within the Council, it is the only way of ensuring that the fundamental interests of each Member State are recognised at a European level and that Member States do not fear that Brussels dictates the legislative framework with which the Member States have to comply. Increasingly 'dictated' uniformity may even destroy the identities of the Member States and, subsequently, the idea of a European Union consisting of united yet diverse Member States.[1]

To cope with the various challenges posed by a Union made up of united but diverse Member States,[2] the Member States decided to introduce a mechanism of flexibility within the European Union: the enhanced cooperation procedure.[3] The

[1] Art 4 Subsection 2 of the TEU; Jukka Snell, 'Still United despite Diversity?' (2018) 43 European Law Review 801 revealing the concept of united in diversity based on the current happenings and arguing that in cases in which there is a clash between national European values the function of European law is to 'transform naked clashes to processes governed by procedures and rules'.

[2] Leonard FM Besselink, 'Does EU Law Recognise Legal Limits to Integration? Accommodating Diversity and Its Limits' in Thomas Giegerich, Oskar Josef Gstrein, and Sebastian Zeitzmann (eds), *The EU between 'An Ever Closer Union' and Inalienable Policy Domains of Member States*, vol 80 (Nomos 2014) 60 et seq explaining the 'recalibration of the relation between unity and diversity'; Christine Kaddous, 'The European Union's Common Values and National Identities: Convergence or Contradiction?' in Thomas Giegerich, Oskar Josef Gstrein, and Sebastian Zeitzmann (eds), *The EU between 'An Ever Closer Union' and Inalienable Policy Domains of Member States*, vol 80 (Nomos 2014) 91 et seq.

[3] Bruno S Frey, 'European Unification Based on Flexibility and Diversity' (2019) 75 FinanzArchiv 93 arguing that the European Union is capable of achieving its core goals through flexibility; Adrienne Héritier, *Policy-Making and Diversity in Europe: Escape from Deadlock* (CUP 1999) 8 arguing that '[t]he very extent of heterogeneity, characteristic of the fifteen-member Union makes diversity, and the concomitant need for reconciliation, overwhelmingly important principles in European policy-making'.

Enhanced Cooperation and European Tax Law. Caroline Heber, Oxford University Press. © Caroline Heber 2021.
DOI: 10.1093/oso/9780192898272.003.0001

procedure enables a minimum of nine Member States to make use of European institutions to introduce secondary EU law which is only binding amongst these Member States. Initially, the flexibility mechanism was incorporated into the European legal framework by the Amsterdam Treaty as the 'closer cooperation' procedure,[4] which aimed to bring together the various partial international agreements established between some, but not all of the Member States into the European legal framework. In other words, the Member States of the European Union achieved differentiated integration among themselves long before the enhanced (or closer) cooperation procedure was implemented into the European treaties.[5] They simply used international agreements, a tool outside the purely European framework, to establish differentiation. To grant Member States the desired flexibility under the protective hand of EU law which guards deeper integration between some Member States, the European flexibility mechanism has been introduced.

Accordingly, Member States have always found ways to constitute differentiation, and enhanced cooperation has therefore not introduced an entirely new concept into the EU's legal framework. However, enhanced cooperation has changed European integration as it allows the establishment of blocs within the European Union and it is a clear political statement by the Member States to enable differentiated integration within the European Union by embedding flexibility within the European legal framework.

Under the enhanced cooperation procedure, a group of at least nine Member States is allowed to introduce secondary EU law. The only difference between enhanced cooperation law and ordinary secondary EU law is the scope of application.[6] Enhanced cooperation law only binds the participating Member States and does not form part of the *acquis communautaire*, allowing acceding Member States to decide whether to join enhanced cooperation. For all participating Member States, enhanced cooperation law has both direct effects (meaning that individuals and companies can rely on enhanced cooperation law before national courts and public bodies) and absolute supremacy over all national laws.[7] There is also

[4] Stefan Griller and others, *The Treaty of Amsterdam: Facts, Analysis, Prospects* (Springer 2000) 206 et seq. Wolfgang Wessels, 'Verstärkte Zusammenarbeit: Eine neue Variante flexibler Integration' in Mathias Jopp, Andreas Maurer, and Otto Schmuck (eds), *Die Europäische Union nach Amsterdam. Analysen und Stellungnahmen zum neuen EU-Vertrag* (Europa Union Verlag 1998) 197 et seq.

[5] '[T]he EC/EU constitution has always acknowledged flexibility ... ever since the adoption of the Treaties of Rome': Jacques Ziller, 'Flexibility in the Geographical Scope of EU Law: Diversity and Differentiation in the Application of Substantive Law on Member States' Territories' in Gráinne de Búrca and Joanne Scott (eds), *Constitutional Change in the EU: From Uniformity to Flexibility?* (Hart Publishing 2000) 113.

[6] Ulrich Becker, 'Differenzierungen der Rechtseinheit durch "abgestufte Integration"' in Jürgen Schwarze and Peter-Christian Müller-Graff (eds), *Europäische Rechtseinheit durch einheitliche Rechtsdurchsetzung* (Nomos 1998) 54 arguing that the nature of the law cannot change because the law is not enacted by all Member States and is not binding on all Member States.

[7] For the concept of direct effects and supremacy of EU law see Alan Dashwood and others (eds), *Wyatt and Dashwood's European Union Law* (6th edn, Hart Publishing 2011) 235 et seq. For the impact of the doctrine of direct effect and supremacy on the European integration process see Erich Vranes,

no doubt that the law enacted under the enhanced cooperation procedure falls within the scope of Art 267 of the Treaty on the Functioning of the European Union (TFEU), and thus is subject to interpretation by the Court of Justice of the European Union (CJEU).

Any permission for group formation within the European Union has an intrinsic impact on competition between Member States because it allows them to build blocs of like-minded Member States, and thus competition between single Member States changes to competition between different blocs of Member States. At the same time, competition between Member States within a bloc may be eliminated through unification or harmonisation of the law. To prevent any harmful effects of rival groups, the European treaties brought several safeguarding measures into effect. The constitutional framework of enhanced cooperation protects the European Union in particular by prohibiting any harm to the European internal market, harm which may result from enhanced cooperation creating barriers to trade between Member States or distortion of competition between them.[8] The framework also protects non-participating and participating Member States. The former are protected from any disproportionate burdens resulting from enhanced cooperation law, and the latter are sheltered from potential disloyal behaviour of non-participating Member States impeding the implementation of enhanced cooperation.

The wording used to describe the requirements for the establishment of enhanced cooperation is familiar to any lawyer specialised in EU law. Like any national law, enhanced cooperation law has to comply with European non-discrimination and free competition rules. Therefore, one may wonder whether a group of Member States is only allowed to do what a single Member State is able to implement on a stand-alone basis in line with fundamental freedoms and state aid law. In other words, it is far from clear whether a group of Member States is allowed to introduce European laws under the enhanced cooperation procedure, which they would typically not be allowed to implement on their own, because these rules either contradict the fundamental freedoms or contradict state aid law.

With regard to the protection of non-participating Member States, the fundamental question points in the same direction: do non-participating Member States need more protection from a joint legislative agenda of Member States, in contrast to the legislative priorities of a single Member State? More protection may be required because the non-participating Member States may be exposed to stronger negative effects if the legislative measure is pursued by a group of at least nine Member States, rather than an individual Member State.

'The Dynamics of European Economic Integration: A Legal Perspective' in Harald Badinger and Volker Nitsch (eds), *Routledge Handbook of the Economics of European Integration* (Routledge 2016) 479 et seq.

[8] See Art 326 of the TFEU.

Aside from the demand to protect 'outsiders', the participating Member States may also need a shelter to be able to pursue enhanced cooperation. Only once it is ensured that non-participating Member States cannot impede the implementation of enhanced cooperation will the establishment of these safeguarding mechanisms be complete. A mechanism of flexibility only functions if the participating Member States are protected from the unwillingness and potential anger of the non-participating Member States, and if the non-participating Member States are sufficiently protected from any potential collusion of fellow Member States. Otherwise, the non-participating Member States may be exploited through the alliance of participating Member States.

The enhanced cooperation procedure does not establish an entirely new framework for incorporating secondary EU law within a group of Member States. The procedure uses the existing framework but sets rules for the authorisation to establish enhanced cooperation in the first place. In other words, if a group of Member States has passed the requirements of authorisation, they are entitled to use the European institutions, the European competences, and the ordinary legislative framework to establish secondary EU law which is only binding on the participating Member States. Of course, some amendments are necessary due to the fact that only participating Member States are allowed to vote in the Council, but leaving that aside, the procedure remains the same. Thus, authorised enhanced cooperation forms a mini-Union within the European Union which is entitled to enact laws under the same procedure as the whole European Union.

The procedural framework for enhanced cooperation involves the willing Member States, the European Commission, the Council, and the European Parliament. The right of initiative rests with the willing Member States; they have to issue a request to the Commission. The Commission then reveals whether the requirements set by the European treaties are satisfied. If this is the case, the Commission may entrust the Council with that matter. The Council can authorise enhanced cooperation with a qualified majority vote after the European Parliament has granted its consent.

Despite the political decision of the Member States to allow differentiated integration within the European Union, the requirements set for establishing enhanced cooperation by the European treaties grant a clear preference to unify European actions over enhanced cooperation. Enhanced cooperation can only be established if the legislative attempt cannot be attained within a reasonable period by the European Union as a whole.[9] The requirement that any enhanced cooperation must be open to all Member States at any time is another indicator that a uniform European approach is still the favoured option, despite the existence of the enhanced cooperation procedure.

[9] Art 20 Subsection 2 of the TEU.

The provisions enshrined in the European treaties on the enhanced cooperation procedure touch on the protection of the European internal market, the non-participating and participating Member States, and the priority of all-binding European measures. However, the provisions are drafted vaguely, and thus leave much room for interpretation as well as misinterpretation. The vague drafting of the constitutional framework for enhanced cooperation is particularly problematic, since the decision on whether or not to establish enhanced cooperation is purely political.[10] Thus, the legal requirements may be misinterpreted and in turn prevent the establishment of enhanced cooperation.[11] This already indicates the particular importance of clearly distinguishing between the political and legal dimension of enhanced cooperation. The latter is provided for by the provisions of the European treaties; the former is, however, a decision which has to be taken by the Member States on a case-by-case basis, and which may not be open to a clear 'yes or no' answer, as is the case with the legal requirements.

B. Political versus Legal Issues

The enhanced cooperation procedure has two important dimensions: a legal and a political one. The political aspect is enshrined in Art 20 Subsection 1 of the Treaty on European Union (TEU) and demands that any '[e]nhanced cooperation shall aim to further the objectives of the Union, protect its interests and reinforce its integration process'. Accordingly, enhanced cooperation must not undermine the integration process or harm the interests and objectives of the European Union. It is however questionable whether the need to foster European integration forms a legal requirement and, if so, how one should decide on whether enhanced cooperation does more harm than good. The question thus arises: should enhanced cooperation be allowed? The search for the turning point at which enhanced cooperation is more harmful than useful reminds us of the work of a doctor who constantly acts under the premise 'first, do no harm' ('*primum non nocere*').[12] In that respect, one may argue that an additional piece of legislation only adds complexity, and if it does not even bind all the Member States, the complexity factor (in particular between the Member States inside enhanced cooperation—the insiders—and the Member State outside the enhanced cooperation—the outsiders) prevails, and thus, enhanced cooperation should only be an option for very small technical

[10] Carole Lyons, 'Flexibility and the European Court of Justice' in Gráinne De Búrca and Joanne Scott (eds), *Constitutional Change in the EU: From Uniformity to Flexibility?* (Hart Publishing 2000) 106.

[11] The CJEU has the power to interpret these requirements: Carole Lyons, 'Flexibility and the European Court of Justice' in Gráinne de Búrca and Joanne Scott (eds), *Constitutional Change in the EU: From Uniformity to Flexibility?* (Hart Publishing 2000) 97 et seq. Jo Shaw, 'The Treaty of Amsterdam: Challenges of Flexibility and Legitimacy' (1998) 4 European Law Journal 63, 79 et seq.

[12] The comparison has been drawn by Adam Zalasinski during a private conversation with the author.

agreements between Member States, which do not harm, but on the other hand, also do not help much.

Such a view of enhanced cooperation conflicts with its aim and objectives. It was introduced to bring the whole European Union forward by strengthening integration.[13] The only way forward requires one to focus on the explicit legal requirements for establishing enhanced cooperation.[14] The need to 'further the objectives of the Union, protect its interests and reinforce its integration process' has to be understood as the umbrella overarching the entire enhanced cooperation procedure, and thus provides guidance for the interpretation of the legal conditions explicitly set out in the European treaties. The progress of integration is not, however, a 'hard' legal requirement. On the contrary, if all the legal conditions (covering both procedural and substantial conditions) are met, enhanced cooperation law does not harm the European integration process, and arguments claiming that the differentiation within the law between participating and non-participating Member States has negative effects on the European integration process can be rejected because the European integration model precisely allows for such a differentiation. It is therefore suggested that the '*primum non nocere*' requirement is met if all (strict) legal conditions are satisfied. In such cases, inaction is unacceptable for three reasons.

First of all, it has to be acknowledged that all the Member States have decided to allow differentiated integration within the EU's framework.[15] During the Amsterdam Treaty negotiations,[16] they all agreed to introduce a mechanism which allows willing Member States to implement secondary EU law, and such law is only binding among them.[17] Thus, it was their choice to give up the mandate of

[13] Helmut Kortenberg, 'Closer Cooperation in the Treaty of Amsterdam' (1998) 35 Common Market Law Review 833, 833 et seq. Guy Verhofstadt, 'A Vision of Europe' (Brussels, 21 September 2000) <https://www.cvce.eu/content/publication/2005/7/22/e1570f15-55ae-4b60-b9e7-861ccc6876ad/publishable_en.pdf> accessed 3 February 2021 'It is an instrument to strengthen the Union from within, an instrument of integration, not exclusion.'

[14] Fabian Amtenbrink and Dimitry Kochenov, 'Towards a More Flexible Approach to Enhanced Cooperation' in Andrea Ott and Ellen Vos (eds), *50 Years of European Integration: Foundations and Perspectives* (Asser 2009) 185 arguing that 'much points towards the view that the decision on the application of the substantive conditions for enhanced cooperation is essentially of a political nature'.

[15] And still do: 'the European Council noted that the concept of ever closer union allows for different paths of integration for different countries, allowing those that want to deepen integration to move ahead, while respecting the wish of those who do not want to deepen any further', Council, 27 June 2014, European Council Meeting 26 and 27 June, General Secretariat of the Council, EUCI 79/14, para 27.

[16] Eric Philippart and Geoffrey Edwards, 'The Provisions on Closer Co-Operation in the Treaty of Amsterdam: The Politics of Flexibility in the European Union' (1999) 37 Journal of Common Market Studies 87, 96–97 arguing that 'the price for overcoming the reservations of Member States wanting to insulate pillar I completely was high: the set of enabling conditions has been deliberately designed to make its implementation very difficult; after each round of negotiations at the IGC, choices were made in favour of more conditions and the most restrictive wording'.

[17] '[F]lexibility was no longer seen as an *ad hoc* pragmatic answer to the difficulty of reaching agreement on common rules': Nick Bernard, 'Flexibility in the European Single Market' in Catherine Barnard and Joanne Scott (eds), *The Law of the Single European Market: Unpacking the Premises* (Hart Publishing 2002) 101; see also Jo Shaw, 'Constitutionalism and Flexibility in the EU: Developing a

the uniformity[18] of European law to allow for more flexibility within the European Union.[19] From this it follows that the concept of differentiated integration is enshrined within the European treaties. Any arguments which merely attack the non-uniform nature of enhanced cooperation law can thus simply be rejected on the grounds of the Member States' choice of the differentiated integration model.

Secondly, the use of the enhanced cooperation procedure is subject to a wide set of legal conditions[20] which have to be met to allow some Member States to establish deeper integration just amongst each other. The legal conditions cover both procedural and substantive requirements. The procedural framework guarantees that European institutions such as the European Commission, the European Parliament, and the Council are involved in the law-making process,[21] that enhanced cooperation is only to be pursued if an agreement between all the Member States cannot be reached,[22] and that any non-participating Member State is free to join enhanced cooperation at any time.[23] The substantive conditions, on the other hand, ensure that achievements at a common European level are not endangered by enhanced cooperation. In that vein, any enhanced cooperation must not diminish competition or establish trade barriers between the Member States or provide for any form of discrimination.[24] Furthermore, the rights, competences, and obligations of non-participating Member States are explicitly protected by the European treaties.[25]

Thirdly, the constitutional framework for enhanced cooperation defines the criteria for establishing enhanced cooperation, and enhanced cooperation law can only be tested against these criteria. Clear conditions for establishing enhanced cooperation are important to provide certainty for the application of the mechanism. If one wants to transpose the purely political dimension into a legal requirement, the entire mechanism of enhanced cooperation would be unstable, unclear, and ineffective. Of course, a political decision has to be made, but it is as simple as asking

Relational approach' in Gráinne de Búrca and Joanne Scott (eds), *Constitutional Change in the EU: From Uniformity to Flexibility?* (Hart Publishing 2000) 331.

18 Giorgio Gaja, 'How Flexible Is Flexibility Under the Amsterdam Treaty?' (1998) 35 Common Market Law Review 855, 857.

19 Jo Shaw labelled the flexibility 'constitutionally tolerable': Shaw, 'The Treaty of Amsterdam' (n 11) 69; Nicolas Bernard, 'The Future of European Economic Law in the Light of the Principle of Subsidiarity' (1996) 33 Common Market Law Review 633, 71 arguing that 'closer cooperation as "in-built"' no longer requires 'to permit it [differentiation] on a case-by-case basis'.

20 Which are supposed to be 'as strict as Cinderella's step-mother': Steve Peers, 'Enhanced Cooperation: The Cinderella of Differentiated Integration' in Bruno de Witte, Andrea Ott, and Ellen Vos (eds), *Between Flexibility and Disintegration—The Trajectory of Differentiation in EU Law* (Edward Elgar 2017) 77.

21 In particular, Art 329 of the TFEU.

22 Art 20 Subsection 2 of the TEU.

23 Art 20 Subsection 1 of the TEU.

24 Art 326 of the TFEU.

25 Art 327 of the TFEU.

the following question: do we want to form a group and establish laws which are only binding within that group, or would we rather keep the dichotomy of unilateral Member States' measures and uniform European laws? This decision is a purely political one which cannot be transposed into a legal framework.[26]

Given the three arguments outlined above, it becomes very clear that the political dimension of enhanced cooperation has to be understood as a general guide for the interpretation of the explicit legal conditions.

C. Methodology and Problem Set

The legal requirements explicitly set out by the European treaties for establishing enhanced cooperation are highly familiar concepts to European lawyers. The distortion of competition, discrimination, and trade barriers are ideas which shape the EU's framework and have been judicially interpreted and developed by the CJEU. However, the concepts related to competition, trade barriers, and discrimination, in particular, have become safeguarding measures against national protectionist measures for the European internal market. There are hundreds of published cases on the interplay between national tax laws and the fundamental freedoms,[27] and an increasing number of cases dealing with the interaction between national taxation and European state aid law. On the other hand, there is a fairly small number of court cases which deal with the interplay between secondary EU law and the fundamental freedoms. Both the outcome and reasoning of the rulings are very different from the ones which test purely domestic rules against the fundamental freedoms. In state aid law, the rules are not even applicable to directives and regulations, as their effects cannot be attributed to a single Member State but instead to the European Union as a whole.

Enhanced cooperation law lies somewhere between unilateral legal measures taken by a single Member State and uniform EU laws binding all Member States. In some cases, enhanced cooperation law may mirror a uniform EU law more closely, as only two Member States are not part of the group, as is the case in the field of the European unitary patent. On the other hand, enhanced cooperation law of a group of nine Member States may be much closer to unilateral actions of a Member State than to uniform European actions.

Against this background, it is necessary to develop a concept for the interpretation of the legal requirements which brings together both determining elements of cooperation and incomplete unity. It might be necessary to acknowledge that

[26] In that vein see Daniel Thym, *Ungleichzeitigkeit und europäisches Verfassungsrecht* (Nomos 2004) 64.

[27] See for a list of all CJEU cases in direct tax law matters <https://ec.europa.eu/taxation_customs/sites/taxation/files/20191212_court_cases_direct_taxation_en.pdf> accessed 3 February 2021.

the law of enhanced cooperation is not the law of a single Member State because it reflects the objectives of at least nine Member States and is therefore unlikely to be of a merely protectionist nature. At the same time, it may not be feasible to grant enhanced cooperation law the same power as ordinary secondary EU law because otherwise enhanced cooperation law would be able to interfere with the core pillars of the European internal market concept.

The concept to be developed uses the general aim and purpose of enhanced cooperation—the deepening of integration between some Member States—as a way of identifying whether a group of Member States is allowed to implement certain legal measures which a single Member States would be prevented from doing under the concept of the fundamental freedoms or state aid law. Accordingly, the deeper the degree of integration, the more the Member States pursue the aim of enhanced cooperation, which may allow them to protect their commonly established values via protective trade obstacles introduced towards non-participating Member States. Where enhanced cooperation merely aims to foster trade between the participating Member States, guidance from another trade-enhancing discipline is sought: the law of the World Trade Organization.

As will be explained, enhanced cooperation has only been implemented a few times since it was introduced into the framework of the European Union by the Amsterdam Treaty. Despite the small number of enhanced cooperation attempts, non-participating Member States brought two of these cases before the CJEU and claimed that the legal conditions had not been met. The willingness of non-participating Member States to fight enhanced cooperation law clearly shows that bloc building has, so far, often been perceived as a threat towards the non-participating Member States.[28] The European treaties address the situation of the non-participating Member States by forcing any enhanced cooperation to 'respect the competences, rights and obligations' of the Member States outside the group.[29] In that respect, it is important to analyse whether a non-participating Member State can (only) fight negative effects following from enhanced cooperation if these negative effects overcome a certain threshold and account for legal infringements, or whether non-participating Member States can also refuse to accept negative factual effects, such as locational effects. The answer rests on the fundamental principle of enhanced cooperation: the value of tolerance. A mechanism of differentiated integration can only work if the Member States inside enhanced cooperation accept that some fellow Member States have chosen to remain outside the group, and if the non-participating Member States accept that some Member States wish to pursue a joint legislative cause.

[28] '[N]on-participating Member States seem deeply wary of... being one of the countries left behind in important policy initiatives', 'Editorial: What Do We Want? "Flexibility! Sort-of..." When Do We Want It? "Now! Maybe..."' (2013) 50 Common Market Law Review 673, 675.

[29] Art 327 of the TFEU.

D. Course of Investigation

The following book is divided into seven chapters. Following this introductory chapter, Chapter 2 explores different forms of flexibility and their relationship to one another. Differentiation between the Member States existed long before the enhanced cooperation procedure was introduced into the European legal framework by the Amsterdam Treaty. The Member States have used and still use mechanisms outside the EU framework, in particular international agreements, to establish a legally binding concept among them. The chapter not only discusses the differences between enhanced cooperation law and partial international agreements but also the relationship between each other. Differentiation within the European Union can, however, also be established through primary and secondary EU law. The former may allow that one or more Member States are not bound by a particular set of legal provisions. In the latter case, explicit carve outs are less likely, but secondary EU law may provide the Member States with alternatives, or even provide them with tailor-made exceptions. However, differentiation established through primary or secondary EU law also fundamentally deviates from differentiation established through enhanced cooperation. The analysis of flexibility through differentiation is followed by an analysis of a recently proposed alternative to flexibility: the qualified majority voting system. The analysis shows that qualified majority voting within the Council must not be introduced in the area of taxation.

Chapter 3 explores the successes and failures of enhanced cooperation. A comparison between the legislative initiatives which were successfully pursued under the enhanced cooperation procedure and the ones which failed (because the Member States either did not issue the necessary request to the European Commission or did not find the needed consent between them to enact secondary EU legislation) identifies the areas which are likely to be regulated by enhanced cooperation law.

Chapter 4 is dedicated to the law-making process, which is predominantly procedural. The first part (subsections B and C) of this chapter reveals the involvement of the European institutions, namely the European Commission, the European Parliament, and the Council and their respective particular roles within the legislative process. The second part (subsection D) analyses the requirement protecting the uniformity of European law: the enhanced cooperation law's last resort character. The third part (subsection E) explores ways for non-participating Member States to enter into enhanced cooperation, and ways in which participating Member States may leave the group. The last part (subsections F and G) of this chapter is dedicated to a more general question, that of legislative power. Since the constitutional framework of enhanced cooperation only sets out the authorisation process for a group of Member States to use both the European institutions and the power of the European Union, the question of which laws can be enacted under the enhanced cooperation procedure, in particular with respect to the scope and content, depends on the ordinary competence framework. This part of the chapter provides an analysis of both the European internal market competence and the subsidiarity principle, and subsequently reveals what the Member States can accomplish in European taxation.

Chapter 5 explores how the enhanced cooperation procedure interacts with the European internal market. The chapter is divided into three Parts: Part I discusses the relationship between the fundamental freedoms and the differentiation established between the Member States. There is a particular focus on the question of whether or not participating Member States are allowed to protect their harmonised values by way of protective obstacles against non-participating Member States. In the case of trade liberalisation or trade-enhancing measures, we will explore whether the principle of reciprocity can be used to align trade-hampering effects of enhanced cooperation law with the fundamental freedoms. Part II addresses state aid law issues. The plain wording of the European treaties on the prohibition of state aid may give the impression that any form of secondary EU law does not fall within its scope. Since enhanced cooperation law does not bind all Member States, state aid law has to be applied to protect competition between participating and non-participating Member States. Part III explores the compliance of enhanced cooperation law with the European acquis. A particular focus is drawn to the potential conflict between ordinary secondary EU law and enhanced cooperation law.

Chapter 6 develops the most important value inherent to enhanced cooperation: the value of tolerance. The notion of tolerance is not a one-way street: Member States within enhanced cooperation have to respect fellow Member States outside enhanced cooperation as well as their wish to pursue the European objectives on a unilateral path. Likewise, the Member States outside enhanced cooperation have to respect that some Member States will pursue a legislative act jointly. The precise ramifications this has for enhanced cooperation will be discussed in detail.

Chapter 7 provides an outlook and a conclusion. The outlook is based on an analysis of the legal requirements for establishing enhanced cooperation and in particular addresses the question of whether the existing provisions in the European treaties require amendments to the European treaties to allow the enhanced cooperation procedure to fully succeed, or whether the existing framework suffices in allowing the willing Member States to progress with enhanced cooperation and deepen integration among them.

2
Various Forms of Differentiation and Majority Voting as an Alternative

A. Different Forms of Flexibility

Enhanced cooperation is a form of flexibility within the context of European Union (EU) law. The important question is, however, whether enhanced cooperation is one form of flexibility within the EU's framework, allowing the use of other flexibility mechanisms, or whether enhanced cooperation is the only form of flexibility to be used within the EU legal context, and is thereby an exclusive source of flexibility. Enhanced cooperation is beyond doubt the most obvious form of flexibility because it is directly provided for by the European treaties, and not merely the result of law-making at European level, as in the case of differentiation by primary or secondary EU law. Examining the European treaties and secondary EU law provisions more closely, it becomes quite clear that the European legislature has often used forms of flexibility to respect the needs and concerns of Member States and overcome their blocking minority within the legislative process, thereby meeting the willing Member States' desire(s). Accordingly, allowing the Member States of the European Union to refrain from the general claim to walk jointly on the same path of integration, and thus develop together in the same direction, is not an entirely new approach to the European Union introduced by the enhanced cooperation procedure.[1]

Despite the different forms of flexibility within the European legal framework, flexibility can also be achieved through international agreements, and thus inherently outside the European Union's legal concept. Accordingly, primary EU law, secondary EU law but also international treaties signed between (all or some) Member States may be the source of differentiation between Member States. These legal measures achieve flexibility by either allowing the willing Member States to pursue their common goal without engaging the unwilling Member States, or by granting them exemptions from EU law, or by allowing them to apply different (in comparison to the other Member States) legal consequences to certain

[1] '[T]his approach towards the future of the EU is not new but it has received a more legally grounded dimension under the ToA [Treaty of Amsterdam], being now constitutionally embedded in the Treaties': Carole Lyons, 'Flexibility and the European Court of Justice' in Gráinne de Búrca and Joanne Scott (eds), *Constitutional Change in the EU: From Uniformity to Flexibility?* (Hart Publishing 2000) 103.

Enhanced Cooperation and European Tax Law. Caroline Heber, Oxford University Press. © Caroline Heber 2021.
DOI: 10.1093/oso/9780192898272.003.0002

circumstances.[2] The difference between the two modes of flexibility rests with the scope of application of the law. In the former case, the Member States are not subject to the law, and thus the differentiation follows from the division between insiders (the Member States bound by the law) and outsiders (the Member States not subject to the law). In the latter case, however, all Member States fall within the scope of the law; the law, however, allows one or several Member States to apply legal consequences which are different from the consequences applied by the other Member States.

The differentiation established by enhanced cooperation is based on the territorial scope of the law. The law introduced under the enhanced cooperation procedure only binds the members of the group (ie insiders). The outsiders, that is the non-participating Member States, are not subject to enhanced cooperation law, and thus cannot be forced to comply with any of these rules. But that particular form of differentiation is also not an entirely new concept within the EU law framework. Partial international agreements (treaties between some Member States), but also primary EU law, have achieved differentiation based on the scope of the legal claim.

Any differentiation in the law between the Member States can also be categorised by other means such as their scope or approach towards achieving differentiation. The latter concerns the question of whether the differentiation mechanism is defined positively, meaning that it allows the willing Member States to progress without excluding some Member States. Thus, the differentiating law is open for other Member States. The differentiation mechanism can, however, also be defined negatively, meaning that some Member States are explicitly excluded.[3] The scope of differentiation depends on the openness of the differentiating law. In other words, it is a question of whether all the Member States can invoke differentiation (eg where EU law provides the Member States with options) or whether it is only open to some Member States.[4] Furthermore, one could also distinguish between original and subsequent differentiation, which would raise the question of whether the differentiation has been established at the time when the law was originally enacted or at a later point in time. In the academic literature, it has also been suggested that any differentiation in the law can be characterised by time, space, and subject.[5] These factors inevitably overlap and thus should be rejected for lack of clarity.[6]

[2] Daniel Thym, *Ungleichzeitigkeit und europäisches Verfassungsrecht* (Daniel Thym 2004) 23 et seq.

[3] See for an analysis of positive and negative differentiation Filip Tuytschaever, *Differentiation in European Union Law* (Hart Publishing 1999) 121 et seq.

[4] ibid 120–21.

[5] Alexander CG Stubb, 'A Categorization of Differentiated Integration' (1996) 34 Journal of Common Market Studies 283.

[6] For the overlap between time and space see Eberhard Grabitz, 'Community Law and Differentiation between the Member States' in Asser Instituut Colloquium Europees Recht (ed), *Gedifferentieerde integratie en Gemeenschapsrecht* (TMC Asser Instituut 1985) 21.

This short overview already reveals that flexibility can possess many aspects and is not solely achieved by using the enhanced cooperation mechanism. The following subsection aims to describe the different forms of differentiation in more detail and, in particular, discuss the characteristics of the mechanisms of differentiation. With regard to the various legal tools for establishing differentiation (exemptions and options in primary and secondary EU law and international treaties), whether the implementation of the enhanced cooperation into the European treaties has had any impact on the legitimacy of using other flexibility mechanisms will be discussed.

The first subsection reveals differentiation which can be achieved through international treaties signed between some, but not all, Member States (see subsection I). Enhanced cooperation and partial international agreements are in competition with each other because their scope overlaps, and thus it may be up to the Member States to decide whether they wish to pursue their goals within the EU legal framework by using the enhanced cooperation procedure, or whether they wish to employ international agreements. The latter is more flexible in the sense that the conditions are less onerous than the requirements for intra-EU cooperation, and when acting under international law, Member States preserve complete control over the negotiation process, the implementation, and the enforcement of the law.[7] Subsections II and III proceed to discuss the different forms of flexibility within the European legal framework, apart from enhanced cooperation. The analysis starts with differentiation in primary EU law, which is usually achieved by excluding some Member States from the scope of the law (see subsection II). Secondary EU law, on the other hand, often achieves differentiation by providing exemptions and options for parts of the directive or regulation (see subsection III). Before the different forms of flexibility are compared with the enhanced cooperation procedure (see subsection V), subsection IV discusses the possibility of post-differentiation, in other words, differentiation which is not established at the time at which the law is enacted, but later (see subsection IV). Post-differentiation would grant the Member States an exit route which may facilitate their willingness to pass secondary EU law.

I. International Agreements between Member States

When the European Economic Community was founded, it was clear that its Member States retained sovereignty to conclude international treaties not only between each other but also with third parties. The fact that international agreements

[7] Bruno de Witte, 'Chameleonic Member States: Differentiation by Means of Partial and Parallel International Agreements' in Bruno de Witte, Dominik Hanf, and Ellen Vos (eds), *The Many Faces of Differentiation in EU Law* (Intersentia nv 2001) 239.

have remained an alternative to European law-making was particularly evident in the fact that the European treaties did not terminate any international treaties which Member States had previously ratified.[8] Moreover, after the European Economic Community had been established, the Member States concluded agreements under international law, for example the Benelux Economic Union.[9] These treaties are undeniable proof that the Member States have preserved their treaty-making powers, at least in areas outside the European Union's exclusive competence and areas which are not determined by secondary EU law.[10] Thus, the EU framework does not exclusively determine the relationship between the Member States.[11]

Relevant reasons for using international law mechanisms instead of pursuing the European legislative path may include the preservation of complete control over the negotiation process, the implementation, and the enforcement of the law.[12] The Court of Justice of the European Union (CJEU) has, however, tried to counteract such attempts by applying the European standards of interpretation and application of the law to international treaties signed between the Member States.[13]

International treaties between Member States can either account for a parallel (to the EU law) agreement, meaning an international agreement signed between all the Member States, or a partial agreement, referring to an international agreement between only some Member States.[14] Parallel agreements do not raise differentiation issues based on the validity claim because all the Member States are within the scope of the treaty, but may establish differentiation by allowing some treaty partners exemptions or other alternative routes. These agreements raise severe legitimacy issues because the Member States '"switch" from the ... EU track to

[8] Art 351 of the TFEU; Paul P Craig and Gráinne de Búrca, *EU Law: Text, Cases, and Materials* (6th edn, OUP 2015) 359 on the relevant CJEU case law.

[9] Treaty establishing the Benelux Economic Union.

[10] Bruno de Witte and Thibault Martinelli, 'Treaties between EU Member States as Quasi-Instruments of EU Law' in Marise Cremona and Claire Kilpatrick (eds), *EU Legal Acts: Challenges and Transformations*, vol XXV/4 (OUP 2018) 158.

[11] Bruno de Witte, 'Chameleonic Member States: Differentiation by Means of Partial and Parallel International Agreements' in Bruno de Witte, Dominik Hanf, and Ellen Vos (eds), *The Many Faces of Differentiation in EU Law* (Intersentia nv 2001) 232.

[12] For the pros and cons of choosing the international path over the European see Daniel Thym, 'Flexible Integration: Garant oder Gefahr für die Einheit und die Legitimation des Unionsrechts?' (2013) Europarecht Beiheft 32.

[13] The Court has explicitly done so via the 1968 Brussels Convention on jurisdiction and recognition of judgments in civil and commercial matters, which, however, covered an area which should—as explicitly mentioned by the European treaties—be subject to deeper cooperation by the Member States through international treaties, Bruno de Witte, 'Old-Fashioned Flexibility: International Agreements between Member States of the European Union' in Gráinne de Búrca and Joanne Scott (eds), *Constitutional Change in the EU: From Uniformity to Flexibility?* (Hart Publishing 2000) 248–49.

[14] Robert Schütze, 'EC Law and International Agreements of the Member States—An Ambivalent Relationship?' (2007) 9 Cambridge Yearbook of European Legal Studies 387, 408–25; Allan Rosas, 'The Status in EU Law of International Agreements Concluded by EU Member States' (2010) 34 Fordham International Law Journal 1304, 1317–20; Steve Peers, 'Towards a New Form of EU Law?: The Use of EU Institutions Outside the EU Legal Framework' (2013) 9 European Constitutional Law Review 37, 41–42.

the international law track, while by-passing the institutional balance established by the founding Treaties'.[15]

1. Partial International Agreements within the European Union

Partial treaties establish differentiation within the European Union because they are only signed between some Member States. Accordingly, differentiation follows, as in the case of enhanced cooperation, from the division between the group of Member States which is subject to the international agreement (insiders) and the group of Member States which is not bound by the treaty (outsiders).[16] Only the former Member States are bound by the treaty obligations, and thus, there is a differentiation between the Member States based on the validity claim of the international treaty.

An important partial agreement, which has already been mentioned, is the Benelux Economic Union. The Benelux partnership has not, however, been the only form of regional grouping within and even beyond the European borders.[17] The partnership between neighbours formed the ground for closer cooperation between some Member States outside the EU framework, especially in the mid-1990s. The coming together of Member States through the use of public international law was seen as a threat to European integrity, raising claims to implement flexibility mechanisms inside the European treaties.[18] Flexibility within the European Union would not remove differentiation, but it could provide for safeguarding measures, ensuring that no 'schism would progressively emerge within the Community',[19]

[15] Witte, 'Old-Fashioned Flexibility' (n 13) 42.

[16] An international treaty cannot impose legal obligations or bestow legal right upon third parties. The fundamental principle of customary international law '*pacta tertiis nec nocent nec prosunt*' is now enshrined in Art 34 of the Vienna Convention on the Law of Treaties (VCLT). Thus, a non-treaty party, an outsider, cannot have obligations or burdens imposed on it through an international treaty.

[17] Helen Wallace, 'Flexibility: A Tool of Integration or a Restraint on Disintegration?' in Karlheinz Neunreither and Antje Wiener (eds), *European Integration After Amsterdam: Institutional Dynamics and Prospects for Democracy* (OUP 2000) 176. Recently, Germany and France signed both the Aachen Treaty, a renewal of the Élysée Treaty, and German-French-Parliament Treaty. Both treaties aim to strengthen the Franco-German relationship.

[18] For the same threat in the US context and a reason for introducing a ban on any State to enter into a treaty, alliance, or confederation, and the compact clause, allowing a State to enter into an agreement with another State or foreign power, in the US Constitution (see for the compact clause Chapter 6, subsection C.II) 'the prospect of separate, unsupervised agreements among its member-states and between a member-state and a foreign nation must constitute a cause for alarm. One obvious threat is dissolution through sedition and secession—which, as we have learned, states are more likely to commit collectively than individually' Michael S Greve, 'Compacts, Cartels, and Congressional Consent' (2003) 68 Missouri Law Review 285, 296. According to Amtenbrink and Kochenov the threat still remains if the EU does not succeed in making the European flexibility mechanism work, Fabian Amtenbrink and Dimitry Kochenov, 'Towards a More Flexible Approach to Enhanced Cooperation' in Andrea Ott and Ellen Vos (eds), *50 Years of European Integration: Foundations and Perspectives* (Asser 2009) 182.

[19] Helmut Kortenberg, 'Closer Cooperation in the Treaty of Amsterdam' (1998) 35 Common Market Law Review 835. Likewise, the European Commission stated that the European framework 'must ensure that Member States wishing to cooperate more closely together do not do so outside the institutional framework laid down by the Treaties, as happened for example with the Schengen Agreement before the Treaty offered them an alternative', 26 January 2000, Commission Opinion in accordance with Article 48 of the Treaty on European Union on the calling of a Conference of Representatives

and guaranteeing that the standards of democracy, judicial control, and solidarity are met.[20]

Against this background, some scholars have argued that since the European treaties provide for a flexibility mechanism which permits some Member States to cooperate, they are no longer allowed to use the non-EU tools,[21] these being international agreements, as the basis for cooperation.[22] Others have accepted that the Member States remain competent to sign international agreements between them but argued that, at least, they must try using enhanced cooperation.[23] The truth is, however, that the primary EU law provisions on enhanced cooperation do not deprive the Member States of their treaty-making powers.[24] Of course, the European treaty provisions could force the Member States to use enhanced cooperation for subject matters covered by the European framework. This, however, would require an explicit agreement between the Member States[25] because an exclusive European flexibility mechanism would restrict the Member States' treaty-making power, a power every sovereign State holds within the international community.[26] Art 20

of the Governments of the Member States to amend the Treaties, COM(2000) 34, 32. In this vein see also Federico Fabbrini, 'Enhanced Cooperation under Scrutiny: Revisiting the Law and Practice of Multi-Speed Integration in Light of the First Involvement of the EU Judiciary' (2013) 40 Legal Issues of Economic Integration 197, 206.

[20] European Parliament, European Parliament resolution on closer cooperation (2000/2162(INI)), OJ, 12 July 2001, C 197, 191.

[21] Vlad Constantinesco, 'Les clauses de "coopération renforcée". Le protocole sur l'application des principes de subsidiarité et de proportionnalité' (1997) 33 Revue trimestrielle de droit europeen 751, 47.

[22] Paul Craig, 'Pringle and Use of EU Institutions Outside the EU Legal Framework: Foundations, Procedure and Substance' (2013) 9 European Constitutional Law Review 263, 274 arguing that enhanced cooperation 'is the preferred mechanism for fostering integration while protecting EU values, where the requisite agreement among states cannot be secured. The default assumption must then surely be that where the contracting states have not used enhanced cooperation this should incline the EU institution against participation in such an inter-state agreement. This default position may be defeasible if, for example, there is some good objective reason for not using enhanced cooperation. This does not however alter the default position, which should be regarded as especially strong if the states have not even considered in good faith whether they might attain their objectives within the Lisbon Treaty via enhanced cooperation.'

[23] Deirdre Curtin, 'Emerging Institutional Parameters and Organised Difference in the European Union' in Bruno de Witte, Dominik Hanf, and Ellen Vos (eds), *The Many Faces of Differentiation in EU Law* (Intersentia nv 2001) 350 et seq.

[24] View of Advocate General Kokott, 26 October 2012, C-370/12, *Pringle*, ECLI:EU:C:2012:675, para 174; the CJEU's ruling is not as explicit: 'In those circumstances [in circumstances in which the Treaties on which the Union is founded do not confer on the Union a specific competence], Article 20 TEU does not preclude either the conclusion by the Member States whose currency is the euro of an agreement such as the ESM Treaty or their ratification of it', CJEU, 27 November 2012, C-370/12, *Pringle*, ECLI:EU:C:2012:756, para 169; Anzhela Cédelle, 'Enhanced Cooperation: A Way Forward for Tax Harmonization in the European Union?' in Joachim Englisch (ed), *International Tax Law: New Challenges to and from Constitutional and Legal Pluralism* (IBFD 2016) 196 questioning whether that the Court would 'follow this reasoning even in those instances where the use of enhanced cooperation is available as an alternative'.

[25] The principle of conferral also applies to the external powers of the European Union: Alan Dashwood, 'The Relationship between the Member States and the European Union' (2004) 41 Common Market Law Review 355, 357 et seq.

[26] From an international law perspective, every State is allowed to sign international treaties (Art 6 of the VCLT: 'Every State possesses capacity to conclude treaties'). Within the European Union, the

of the Treaty on European Union (TEU) cannot be regarded as such an explicit agreement because it states that the Member States *may* make use of the European Union's institutions for establishing closer cooperation between them. The wording of the provision clearly shows that enhanced cooperation is designed as an alternative for the Member States to cooperate,[27] and thus the Member States are still[28] allowed to use 'old-fashioned' tools to achieve flexibility, even when complying with their duties of sincere cooperation[29].[30]

2. Partial Treaties beyond the European Union

Some particular policy areas may not give rise to mere intra-European problems which can be addressed by European legislation or international treaties between Member States, but instead call for a global approach because of increased globalisation. Environmental issues, data protection, but also conflict of law rules are matters which would demand agreements stretching far beyond the European Union's borders. In this regard, Jan-Jaap Kuipers raised the question of whether the Member States should (be allowed to) use the enhanced cooperation procedure to address problems which are not purely European, or whether they should pool their strength and push for international agreements between each other and towards third countries which may provide for a global response to the problem.[31] This line of question is mistaken because it suggests that it is an either/or relationship between a European legislative measure (being enhanced cooperation) and international agreements, yet this is certainly not the case. The European Union has already introduced a tax regime for interest and royalty payments through secondary EU law which required international agreements signed between the European Union and 'key third countries', such as Switzerland, Liechtenstein, and Monaco in order for the regime to succeed and for the European financial market

Member States are no longer able to enter into international treaties when the European Union is competent to conclude the international treaty. According to Art 3 Subsection 2 of the TFEU, the European Union enjoys exclusive competence for the conclusion of an international treaties 'when its conclusion is provided for in a legislative act of the Union or is necessary to enable the Union to exercise its international competence, or in so far as its conclusion may affect common rules or alter their scope'. Art 3 Subsection 2 of the TFEU reflects the broad case law of the CJEU on the EU's ancillary competence to sign international treaties. See ibid 369 et seq. Christophe Hillion and Ramses A Wessel, 'Competence Distribution in EU External Relations after ECOWAS: Clarification or Continued Fuzziness?' (2009) 46 Common Market Law Review 551.

[27] In this vein see Amtenbrink and Kochenov (n 18) 185.

[28] Art 4 Subsection 3 of the TEU.

[29] See for the term Witte, 'Old-Fashioned Flexibility' (n 13).

[30] In this vein see Giorgio Gaja, 'How Flexible Is Flexibility under the Amsterdam Treaty?' (1998) 35 Common Market Law Review 855, 870; Claus-Dieter Ehlermann, 'Differenciation, flexibilite, cooperation renforcee: les nouvelles dispositions du traite d'Amsterdam' (1997) Revue du Marche Unique Europeen 53, 66.

[31] Jan-Jaap Kuipers, 'The Law Applicable to Divorce as Test Ground for Enhanced Cooperation' (2012) 18 European Law Journal 201, 213–15.

to remain competitive.[32] Combining both international and European measures has the clear advantage of maintaining strong European rules between the Member States and a broadening of the involved countries by international agreements. The rules are 'strong' because they impose direct effects, and conflicting national provisions have to be disapplied in their favour.[33] The relationship between the European Union and third countries is, however, determined by international agreements.

In cases in which not all the Member States can agree on secondary EU legislation and the enhanced cooperation procedure is used to overcome the legislative deadlock, enhanced cooperation law can also be combined with international agreements between the mini Union (the group of participating Member States) and third countries. With regard to the EU's implicit power to sign the international agreement, no distinction should be made between ordinary secondary EU law and enhanced cooperation laws. *AETR*[34] and the fourth alternative of Art 216 of the Treaty on the Functioning of the European Union (TFEU), which is based on this case law,[35] show that the EU's power to enter into international agreements with foreign powers may flow 'from measures adopted ... by the Community institutions'. This may be the case where the secondary EU law's policy requires a treaty making power of the European Union. If any steps taken outside the framework of the European institutions would be incompatible with the unity of the European internal market, the EU's treaty-making power may even exclude the possibility of concurrent powers of Member States.[36] The CJEU case law shows that the implicit treaty-making power of the European Union can only flow from the objective of secondary EU law. In other words, the EU's implicit treaty-making power is tied to the aim and scope of the secondary EU law act. If the secondary EU law only applies to the participating Member States, the European Union may only have the power to enter into international agreements which bind the participating Member States. The limitation to participating Member States can be achieved by a territorial restriction of the international treaty.

Now, the joint undertaking on supercomputing seems an example of a joint force of some Member States of the European Union and third countries. So far, almost all Member States of the European Union and Switzerland have signed the European High Performance Computing Joint Undertaking (EuroHPC)

[32] Commission, 19 July 2001, Proposal for a Council directive to ensure effective taxation of savings income in the form of interest payments within the Community, COM(2001) 400 final, explanatory memorandum.

[33] Alan Dashwood and others (eds), *Wyatt and Dashwood's European Union Law* (6th edn, Hart Publishing 2011) 235 et seq.

[34] CJEU, 31 March 1971, 22/70, *AETR*, ECLI:EU:C:1971:31, para 16.

[35] For an analysis of the CJEU case law and the provisions within the European treaties see Caroline Heber, 'Die Kompetenzverteilung Im Rahmen Der Austrittsverhandlungen Nach Art. 50 EUV Unter Besonderer Berücksichtigung Bestehenden Sekundärrechts' (2017) 52 Europarecht 581, 595.

[36] CJEU, 31 March 1971, 22/70, *AETR*, ECLI:EU:C:1971:31, para 31; see Art 3 Subsection 2 of the TFEU.

declaration.[37] In that vein, the willing Member States have expressed their desire to establish enhanced cooperation between them. Since Switzerland is also going to be partner to this joint undertaking, the legal framework provided by enhanced cooperation would necessarily have to be supplemented by an international treaty. Whether the latter is only signed by the European Union or by the European Union and all participating Member States is not yet clear. As indicated above, the law introduced under the enhanced cooperation procedure is, however, a sufficient tool for the Member States to grant the European Union the power it needs to sign the relevant international agreement, without any participation of the participating Member States.

II. Primary EU Law

Primary EU law is another source of legal differentiation between Member States. Differentiation established through primary EU law may take different forms. Accession treaties, for example, often include transition provisions which grant the new Member States some time to align their national laws with European Union law.[38] Transition provisions are temporary and do not exclude the Member State from an entire subject matter; they only defer the legal effectiveness of the law until a time at which the new Member State is capable of complying with the rules.[39] On the other hand, primary EU law can establish permanent differentiation between the Member States by granting exceptions to an entire subject area to one or more Member States.[40] If the Member States are excluded from an entire subject area they do not have a say in the legislative process, and thus are not represented by the European institutions for that particular matter. From this it follows that an opt-out impacts the composition and functioning of the European institutions, affecting not only the legal but also the institutional unity of the European Union as a whole.[41]

The most prominent example of differentiation at the primary EU law level may be the Economic and Monetary Union, which provides an opt-out for the United Kingdom and a quasiopt-out for Denmark.[42] Another example of differentiation at

[37] Declaration, Cooperation framework on High Performance Computing, 23 March 2017, <http://ec.europa.eu/newsroom/dae/document.cfm?doc_id=43815> accessed 3 February 2021.

[38] See in that vein Stefan Griller and others, *The Treaty of Amsterdam: Facts, Analysis, Prospects* (Springer 2000) 199.

[39] Thym, *Ungleichzeitigkeit und europäisches Verfassungsrecht* (n 2) 25–26.

[40] Ulrich Becker, 'Differenzierungen der Rechtseinheit durch "abgestufte Integration"' in Jürgen Schwarze and Peter-Christian Müller-Graff (eds), *Europäische Rechtseinheit durch einheitliche Rechtsdurchsetzung* (Nomos 1998) 26 et seq.

[41] Bernd Martenczuk, 'Die differenzierte Integration nach dem Vertrag von Amsterdam' (1998) Zeitschrift für Europarechtliche Studien 447, 356.

[42] Rebecca Adler-Nissen, 'The Diplomacy of Opting Out: A Bourdieudian Approach to National Integration Strategies' (2008) 46 Journal of Common Market Studies 663, 663 defining Denmark and the United Kingdom as the 'two opt-out champions'; see in that vein Maya Sion-Tzidkiyahu,

the primary EU level would be in the area of freedom, security, and justice, which consists of incorporation of the Schengen treaty into the EU framework and its advancement. Primary EU law still provides an explicit opt-out for the United Kingdom and one for Ireland, which prior to Brexit allowed them to only participate in specific measures if they wished to do so (voluntary opt-in).[43] Denmark is also granted an opt-out, because 'Denmark shall not take part in the adoption by the Council of proposed measures pursuant to Title V of Part Three of the TFEU'.[44] Moreover, differentiation was a necessary tool to overcome the UK's blocking minority when European social policy was established.[45]

The next two subsections examine the primary EU law differentiation in the Economic and Monetary Union, and the area of freedom, security, and justice more closely. The former introduces the concept of differentiation into the European framework by introducing a three-step plan for achieving the goals of an Economic and Monetary Union, but also allows clear opt-outs. The latter finds its origin in an international agreement between Member and non-Member States, the Schengen treaty, and thus the area of freedom, security, and justice does not end at the EU's borders, but nor does it cover the entire European Union as some Member States are granted an opt-out.

1. The Economic and Monetary Union

Since the meeting of the heads of State in The Hague in December 1969, it has become clear that the Community aims to establish an Economic and Monetary Union.[46] The Council and the European Commission were entrusted to 'work out a plan in stages' which has the completion of the Economic and Monetary Union as its goal.[47] The subsequent Werner Report emphasised the need to proceed in stages because such a union would not be realisable without a transition period.[48] The proposed steps should be independent of and reinforce each other.[49] Likewise, the

'Comparing Opt-Outs: How Different Is Differentiated Integration' in Thomas Giegerich, Desirée Schmitt, and Sebastian Zeitzmann (eds), *Flexibility in the EU and Beyond: How Much Differentiation can European Integration Bear?* (Nomos 2017) 111 et seq.

[43] Art 3 of the Protocol on the position of the United Kingdom and Ireland, OJ, 10 November 1997, OJ, C 340, 99.

[44] Protocol No 22, On the position of the Denmark, security and justice, OJ, 7 June 2016, OJ, C 202, 298; for the original version see Art 5. of the Protocol on the position of Denmark, OJ, 10 November 1997, OJ, C 340, 101–02.

[45] Catherine Barnard, 'Flexibility and Social Policy' in Gráinne de Búrca and Joanne Scott (eds), *Constitutional Change in the EU: From Uniformity to Flexibility?* (Hart Publishing 2000); Griller and others (n 38) 200.

[46] 'Meeting of the Heads of State or Government, The Hague Summit 1-2 December 1969' (1970) 3 Bulletin of the European Communities 7, 9.

[47] ibid.

[48] 'Report to the Council and the Commission on the Realisation by Stages of Economic and Monetary Union in the Community - Werner Report' (1970) 3 Bulletin of the European Communities 1, 14.

[49] ibid.

Tindemans Report stated that 'achieving Economic and Monetary Union ... will be a lengthy business' and should be undertaken in steps. The first 'positive steps which can be taken in the immediate future ... will lead to a degree of integration which is doubtless imperfect but which will make it easier to take the "large steps"'.[50]

The model for achieving an Economic and Monetary Union sets out three consecutive steps which allow for a sufficient transition period. Every Member State should endeavour to achieve the objectives set out at each step within a specific time frame. The readily compliant States can then take the next steps towards Economic and Monetary Union. The concept provides for an early idea of a Europe of different speeds. The differentiation should, however, be temporal because it ends automatically when all Member States have crossed the finishing line.

However, the concrete implementation of the step-by-step approach not only provided for a temporal differentiation due to the failure to meet the convergence criteria but also provided for permanent differentiation within the European Union. The Maastricht Treaty granted the United Kingdom and Ireland the right to decide whether or not they wished to become a part of the Monetary Union, by moving to the third stage.[51] Without such an opt-out, the necessary changes to the European treaties would have been blocked, and thus permanent differentiation was considered a necessary compromise. During the treaty negotiations for the Maastricht Treaty, the Danish government took the view that the Danish Constitution required an additional referendum before a final decision could be taken on Denmark's participation in stage three of the Monetary Union.[52] Against this background, Denmark was also granted the possibility of only entering into phase three after notifying the Council, which also constitutes an opt-out.[53]

Sweden was not granted an official opt-out, unlike the United Kingdom and Denmark, but Sweden still refuses to comply with some of the convergence criteria, and thus prevents itself from having to move to the third stage. The outcome is quite odd because Sweden fulfils all economic and fiscal convergence criteria but it does not take part in the European exchange rate mechanism, which is one of the convergence criteria for entering into stage three of the Monetary Union. Sweden could easily join the mechanism but it refuses to do so and subsequently prevents the pursuit of closer monetary coherence. The Council seems to accept the Swedish approach and has allowed it to remain outside of the Eurozone.[54]

[50] Leo Tindemans, 'Report on the European Union' (1976) 9 Bulletin of the European Communities 11, 23.

[51] Protocol to the Maastricht Treaty on certain provisions relating to the United Kingdom of Great Britain and Northern Ireland, OJ, 29 July 1992, C 191, 87.

[52] Thym, *Ungleichzeitigkeit und europäisches Verfassungsrecht* (n 2) 135.

[53] Protocol to the Maastricht Treaty on certain provisions relating to Denmark, OJ, 29 July 1992, C 191, 89.

[54] Council decision, 3 May 1998, OJ, 11 May 1998, 34.

From all of this, it logically follows that the model for achieving a Monetary Union introduces differentiation within the European Union, which is, on the one hand, only temporary (until the Member States comply with the convergence criteria), and, on the other hand, permanent because Denmark and apparently Sweden are allowed to remain outside the Eurozone by not moving forward to the third stage of the integration process.

2. Area of Freedom, Security and Justice

The European Union shall, according to Art 3 Subsection 2 of the TEU, 'offer its citizens an area of freedom, security and justice without internal frontiers, in which the free movement of persons is ensured in conjunction with appropriate measures concerning external border controls, asylum, immigration and the prevention and combating of crime'. An area of freedom, security and justice is the necessary step for achieving a true European internal market, an area without internal frontiers. After the heads of States conference in Paris in December 1974, it became clear that the Member States wanted to enhance the free movement of persons between their territories, and thus discussed the possibility of establishing a passport Union.[55] A draft paper exemplifying a stage-by-stage harmonisation of legislation, concerning foreigners and the abolition of passport control, should be provided to the Member States before the next summit.[56] In this vein, the European Commission issued a report to the Council proposing immediate and long-term goals.[57] Initially, the first strand referred to a uniform passport being created, and, secondly, that identity checks at Community internal frontiers should be abolished. The abolition of intra-Community checks makes the reorganisation of the checks at external frontiers of the Community important because these checks are 'carried out by each Member State on behalf of all others'. In 1982, the Commission issued a draft for a Council declaration setting out the key parameters for establishing the passport union.[58] The Member States, however, could only agree insofar as taking the appropriate measures to reduce waiting times and the duration of checks.[59]

The little progress made at the Community level was not enough for the French President, François Mitterrand, and the German Chancellor, Helmut Kohl. They agreed to enhance the Franco-German cooperation and abolish all border checks between their respective countries.[60] Inspired by these efforts, the European

[55] 'Report on the Results of the Conference of Heads of Government Held in Paris on 9 and 10 December 1974' (175AD) 436/74 <http://aei.pitt.edu/1459/> accessed 3 February 2021.

[56] ibid 9.

[57] European Commission, 'Towards European Citizenship - Implementation of Point 10 of the Final Communiqué Issued at the European Summit Held in Paris on 9 and 10 December 1974' (1975) 8 Bulletin of the European Communities 7.

[58] Commission, 9 July 1982, Draft Council resolution on the easing of the formalities relating to checks on citizens of Member States at the Community's internal frontiers, OJ, 31 July 1982, C 197, 6–7.

[59] Council, Resolution, OJ, 19. June 1984, C 159, 1.

[60] Abkommen zwischen Frankreich und der BRD über den schrittweisen Abbau der Kontrollen an der deutsch-französischen Grenze, Saarbrücken, 13. July 1984, BGBl. 1986 II 767 et seq.

Commission made another attempt and proposed further steps to ease controls and formalities applied to the crossing of intra-Community borders.[61] Soon, however, it became clear that any further endeavours would be blocked by the United Kingdom, Ireland, and Denmark.[62] Since some Member States did not want to let the idea of a European area without intra-EU border controls fade away, the governments of the States of the Benelux Economic Union, the Federal Republic of Germany, and the French Republic signed a convention on the gradual abolition of checks at their common borders (Schengen I).[63] The Schengen Convention was, without any doubt, a treaty outside the European legal framework but with a clear connection to the aims of the Community. The first recital explicitly stated that being aware of 'the ever closer union of the peoples of the Member States of the European Communities should find its expression in the freedom to cross internal borders for all nationals of the Member States and in the free movement of goods and services'. In 1990, the existing and acceding Member States signed the convention implementing the Schengen Agreement of 14 June 1985,[64] which integrated EU law and the Schengen acquis more greatly.[65] Through the Amsterdam Treaty, the Schengen acquis was finally introduced into the framework of the European Union.[66] The price that the Schengen Member States had to pay for the required[67] signatures of the United Kingdom, Ireland, and Denmark was their total opt-out.[68] The Member States are, however, allowed to opt in for particular legislative initiatives voluntarily. The combination of a complete opt-out with a voluntary opt-in provides an *à la carte* solution.[69] The governments of Ireland, the United Kingdom

[61] Commission, 23 January 1985, Proposal for a Council Directive on the easing of controls and formalities applicable to nationals of the Member States when crossing intra-Community borders, COM(84) 749, OJ, 19 February 1985, C 47, 5–7.

[62] Hans Claudius Taschner, *Schengen: die Übereinkommen zum Abbau der Personenkontrollen an den Binnengrenzen von EU-Staaten* (Nomos 1997) 12 et seq. Claude Blumann, 'L'Europe des citoyens' Revue du Marche commun et de l'Union européenne 1991, 286 et seq.

[63] Convention, 14 June 1985, now reprinted in OJ 22 September 2000, L 239, 19–62.

[64] Reprinted in OJ 22 September 2000, L 239, 19–62.

[65] Astrid Epiney, 'Das zweite Schengener Abkommen: Entstehung, Konzept und Einbettung in die Europäische Union' in Alberto Achermann and others (eds), *Schengen und die Folgen: der Abbau der Grenzkontrollen in Europa* (Beck Verlag 1995) 30.

[66] See in particular the protocol integrating the Schengen acquis into the framework of the European Union, OJ, 10 November 1997, C 340, 93 et seq. See for more details Thym, *Ungleichzeitigkeit und europäisches Verfassungsrecht* (n 2) 82 et seq. Daniel Thym, 'The Schengen Law: A Challenge for Legal Accountability in the European Union' (2002) 8 European Law Journal 218.

[67] Since it is becoming a part of the acquis, see Kortenberg (n 19) 841–42.

[68] Protocol on the position of the United Kingdom and Ireland, OJ, 10 November 1997, OJ, C 340, 99; Protocol on the position of the Denmark, OJ, 10 November 1997, OJ, C 340, 101–02; Protocol on the application of certain aspects of Article 7a of the Treaty establishing the European Community to the United Kingdom and to Ireland, OJ, 10 November 1997, C 340, 97–98; see for a deeper analysis Martin Hedemann-Robinson, 'The Area of Freedom, Security and Justice with Regard to the UK, Ireland and Denmark: The "Opt-in Opt-Outs" under the Treaty of Amsterdam' in David O'Keeffe and Patrick Twomey (eds), *Legal Issues of the Amsterdam Treaty* (Hart Publishing 1999) 291 et seq.

[69] For a general discussion of this integration model see Daniel Thym, 'Competing Models for Understanding Differentiated Integration' in Bruno de Witte, Andrea Ott, and Ellen Vos (eds), *Between Flexibility and Disintegration: The Trajectory of Differentiation in EU Law* (Edward Elgar Pub 2017) 34 et seq with further references.

(prior to Brexit), and Denmark can pick and choose which legislative actions they wish to partake in and which they would rather not.

III. Secondary EU Law

Differentiation can also be established through secondary EU law.[70] A directive or regulation may, however, not be as far reaching in establishing differentiation as primary EU law or treaty law, as secondary EU laws usually do not exclude Member States entirely from their scope.[71] Differentiation through secondary EU law is most fundamental when the directive or regulation sets the legal framework but grants each Member State the choice of whether or not to introduce the framework. In taxation, the directive may set out the basic features or even details of a tax, such as a financial transaction tax, and each Member State has the right to choose whether to levy a financial transaction tax or restrain from imposing a burden on financial transaction. However, if a Member State wishes to tax financial transactions, it has to do so in accordance with the framework set out by the directive. The Capital Duty Directive provides for such a facultative framework.[72] The Directive prohibits an introduction of new indirect taxes on the raising of capital. If, however, Member States wish to maintain their capital duties, the taxes have to comply with the circumstances defined in the Directive.[73] Likewise, the Value-Added Tax (VAT) Directive grants the Member States the option of introducing VAT grouping. Accordingly, the Member States comply with the VAT Directive if they do not introduce VAT grouping, but if they implement VAT grouping in their national VAT system they have to do so in accordance with the framework set by Art 11 of the VAT Directive.[74]

An optional framework directive grants Member States wide discretion as they can decide whether or not they wish to introduce the legal framework set by the directive. At the same time, an optional framework directive facilitates the

[70] For a detailed analysis of differentiation within secondary EU law see Gráinne de Búrca, 'Differentiation within the Core: The Case of the Common Market' in Gráinne de Búrca and Joanne Scott (eds), *Constitutional Change in the EU: From Uniformity to Flexibility?* (Hart Publishing 2000) 138 et seq.

[71] One could argue that the so-called Maltese clause (Art 7a of Rome III) could be understood as an entire exclusion of Malta from the secondary EU law framework. The clause explicitly states that '[n]othing in this Regulation shall oblige the courts of a participating Member State whose law does not provide for divorce or does not deem the marriage in question valid for the purposes of divorce proceedings to pronounce a divorce by virtue of the application of this Regulation'. Since Malta does not provide for divorce law, Malta does not have to apply 99% of the secondary EU law, Kuipers (n 31) 222.

[72] Council, 12 February 2008, Directive 2008/7/EC, concerning indirect taxes on the raising of capital, OJ, 21 February 2008, L 46, 11.

[73] Art 8-14 of the Capital Duty Directive.

[74] CJEU, 25 April 2013, C-480/10, *Commission v Sweden*, ECLI:EU:C:2013:263, para 34; CJEU, 9 April 2013, C-85/11, *Commission v Ireland*, ECLI:EU:C:2013:217; CJEU, 16 July 2015, *Minerva*, ECLI:EU:C:2015:496.

functioning of the European internal market because Member States only have the option of not introducing the regulative approach at all or introducing the framework as provided in the directive. Thus, no Member State has the power to choose a unilateral option which may be different from what all other Member States may choose. In other words, an optional framework directive in the area of a tax on financial transactions would allow the Member States to decide whether or not to tax financial transactions, but it would prevent Member States from designing their individual financial transaction tax.

However, in the vast majority of cases secondary EU law provides for differentiation on the level of legal consequences, meaning that some Member States may be allowed to apply legal consequences to a particular bundle of facts which are different from the legal consequences applied to the same facts in another Member State. Secondary EU tax law is a particularly good example of such a form of differentiation. The VAT Directive provides for multiple VAT exemptions which are only allowed to apply in a particular Member State.[75]

Despite granting the right to apply different legal consequences in order to attain consent in the legislative negotiation process, the European institutions are required to take into account the differences in the development of the Member States when imposing provisions concerning the establishment and functioning of the European internal market. The differences between the Member States may allow for the proposition of 'appropriate provisions'.[76] Differentiation in secondary EU law, which is based on the Member States' different levels of development, has to be temporary and must not contradict the European internal market. This provision has, in particular, been put into force after German reunification.[77]

Primary EU law also explicitly allows for the temporary derogation of secondary EU law falling within the EU's environmental policy if the EU law imposes disproportionate costs upon the public authorities of a Member State.[78] The derogation of the law establishes differentiation within the European Union, since the secondary EU law is not applied in all of the Member States.

Within the scope of secondary EU law differentiation is, however, predominantly created by the Member States' leeway when applying the law or transposing it into national laws. Since the European legislature is bound by the principle of subsidiarity,[79] secondary EU law often only provides for minimum harmonisation.

[75] See Title XIII, Chapter 1, Sections 1 and 2 of the VAT Directive. Greece, for example, is still allowed to exempt the supply of water by a public body by public law (Art 376 in conjunction with Annex X Part B lit. 8 of the VAT Directive); or Portugal is allowed to exempt the transport of passengers (Art 377 in conjunction with Annex X Part C lit.10 of the VAT Directive).

[76] Art 27 of the TFEU.

[77] Becker, 'Differenzierungen der Rechtseinheit' (n 40) 38.

[78] Art 192 Subsection 5 of the TFEU.

[79] Art 5 Subsection 3 of the TEU; see Chapter 4, subsection G.VI.

This allows each Member State to apply a higher level of protection. In taxation, the Anti-Tax Avoidance Directive (ATAD) forms an example of minimum harmonisation,[80] and thus allows the Member States to use provisions ensuring a higher level of protection than that which secondary EU law introduces (within the boundaries of the fundamental freedoms).

From this it follows that differentiation established by secondary EU law is, in most cases, the result of granting a Member State the right to deviate from the general path. Only by granting exceptions on a piecemeal basis was it possible to introduce a common VAT system and other major legislative initiatives. So far, however, secondary EU law has not entirely excluded one or some Member States, which may, at least in the case of a directive, be possible.[81] Art 288 of the TFEU explicitly states that '[a] directive shall be binding, as to the result to be achieved, upon each Member State *to which it is addressed*', and thus a directive may not lack legal force if it does not apply to all Member States, even outside the use of the enhanced co-operation procedure.[82]

IV. Flexibility through Post-differentiation

So far, all sources of flexibility establish differentiation from the beginning, meaning that the differentiation is introduced by the newly enacted law, and thus there has not been a moment in which all Member States have been bound by the law. Flexibility could, however, also work in the opposite direction: it may be established at a later stage, such as when the Member States have 'tested' the secondary EU law, and some Member States conclude that the law leads to undesired outcomes, whereas other Member States want to stick to it. The existence of an exit route for Member States may convince hesitant Member States to join the legislative action in the first place[83] because if they find that the law functions badly, they can still free themselves from any obligations imposed by that particular law.[84]

[80] Recitals 2 and 3 of the Council Directive, 12 July 2016, 2016/1164/EU, laying down rules against tax avoidance practices that directly affect the functioning of the internal market, OJ, 19 July 2016, L 193, 1–2.

[81] Koen Lenaerts and Marlies Desomer, 'Towards a Hierarchy of Legal Acts in the European Union? Simplification of Legal Instruments and Procedures' (2005) 11 European Law Journal 744, 746.

[82] Wolfgang Schön, 'Facilitating Entry by Facilitating Exit: New Paths in EU Tax Legislation' (2018) 46 Intertax 339, 341; Stefan Korte, 'AEUV Art. 115' in Christian Calliess and Matthias Ruffert (eds), *EUV/AEUV* (5th edn, Beck Verlag 2016) para 16. See in this vein also CJEU, 15 December 1982, 211/81, *Commission v Denmark*, ECLI:EU:C:1982:437, para 28 et seq.

[83] Schön, 'Facilitating Entry by Facilitating Exit' (n 82) 341.

[84] Wolfram Richter, 'Mehrheitsbeschlüsse in der europäischen Steuerpolitik?' (2019) Ökonomenstimme <https://www.oekonomenstimme.org/artikel/2019/05/mehrheitsbeschluesse-in-der-europaeischen-steuerpolitik/> accessed 3 February 2021.

The possibility for post-differentiation through opting out of this specific piece of legislation has the advantage that it may persuade the Member States to join a particular legislative action. At the point at which they could choose to take the exit route, they may, however, still not leave if the secondary EU law turns out to achieve positive outcomes. If secondary EU law allows the Member States to opt out at a certain point, it is necessary to determine the conditions for the remaining Member States. It would perhaps be possible to argue that the Member States have implicitly accepted a later differentiation by introducing the right to leave into the secondary EU law. In the case of a directive, the restricted territorial scope of the law would not prevent its force.[85] Aside from the possibility of restricting the scope of a directive to certain Member States, the relationship between the Member States bound by secondary EU law and the Member States that chose to exit is unclear. It is particularly unclear whether the Member States bound by secondary EU law are allowed to treat the exiting Member States like third countries in cases where secondary EU law distinguishes between Member States of the European Union and third countries. If not, there may be little incentive for any Member State to retain the legal instrument. One could, however, argue that the remaining Member States automatically establish enhanced cooperation. The Council's vote on the secondary EU law could then be understood in terms of an automatic authorisation of the Council to establish enhanced cooperation some time in the future. Yet problems may arise if the basic requirements of enhanced cooperation, such as the number of participating Member States, are not met.

Beyond any doubt, post-differentiation has its charms, but it is far from being a straightforward and unproblematic approach. In particular, the relationship between the Member States that are still bound by the secondary EU law, and the Member States that have chosen the exit route, is unclear. The implementation of secondary EU law should therefore be facilitated by an exit option; which would in turn, however, provide an exit for all Member States.[86] Those Member States who do not wish to exit should have to pursue the ordinary way to establish enhanced cooperation. Forcing the Member States to pursue the legislative path to introduce enhanced cooperation may be a death sentence for that particular law, but an entirely uncoordinated interaction between participating and non-participating Member States would cause confusion, anger, and dissatisfaction, leading to more harm to European integration than a joint legislative action of all Member States could ever provide.

[85] Art 288 of the TFEU, see this chapter subsection A.III.

[86] This can either be achieved by a sunset clause, or by the possibility of voting on whether or not the secondary EU law should be repealed, but such a vote would only be a true exit route if the Member States were allowed to take that decision by a qualified or simple majority voting.

V. Differences and Advantages between Compromise-based Differentiation in Primary and Secondary EU Law, Differentiation through International Treaties, and Enhanced Cooperation

The European framework provides for different forms of flexibility allowing the establishment of differentiation between the Member States, even outside the enhanced cooperation procedure. Beyond the European context, differentiation between Member States may be established by partial, and in some cases parallel, international agreements. Now one may perhaps wonder why the existing canon of flexibility has been supplemented by the enhanced cooperation procedure.

The first apparent reason, which has already been mentioned above,[87] came out of the fear that the need for flexibility within the European Union would drag the Member States of the European Union into international agreements outside the European framework, and their intensive use would threaten European integrity.[88] A European flexibility mechanism would not reduce differentiation within the European Union but would safeguard the interests of the European Union and its integrity.

The use of international agreements has certain advantages[89] but also severe disadvantages because the key elements of European supranationalism, such as the supervisory function of the European Commission and the CJEU, supremacy over national laws, and direct effect of the law do not apply to treaty laws.[90] The lack of priority and control makes it more challenging to ensure compliance.[91] Enhanced cooperation provides an answer to the dilemma because it offers both the advantages of European supranationalism and flexibility.

Differentiation between Member States following from ordinary secondary or primary EU law provides the advantages of European supranationalism,[92] but the law-making process has a severe shortcoming: the Member States blocking the legislative attempt accompany the entire negotiation process, and thus the discussions are dominated by their unwillingness to cooperate. That particular setting

[87] See this chapter subsection A.

[88] Kortenberg (n 19) 835. Also in this vein Fabbrini (n 19) 206.

[89] See this chapter subsection A.I.

[90] Hans Claudius Taschner, *Richtlinie oder internationale Übereinkommen?: Rechtsinstrumente zur Erreichung der Ziele der Europäischen Union* (Zentrum für Europäisches Wirtschaftsrecht 1996) 21 et seq highlighting the differences in the binding effects: an international treaty can be terminated by the parties especially in cases in which the other parties do not comply with their obligations under the treaty. A breach of secondary EU law by on Member State does not allow the other Member States to refrain from their EU law obligations.

[91] Alec Stone Sweet, 'The European Court of Justice' in Paul P Craig and Gráinne de Búrca (eds), *The Evolution of EU Law* (2nd edn, OUP 2011) 124; Thym, 'Flexible Integration' (n 7) 32.

[92] Ulrich Becker, 'Art. 20 EUV' in Hans von der Groeben, Jürgen Schwarze, and Armin Hatje (eds), *Europäisches Unionsrecht* (7th edn, Nomos 2015) para 64 for secondary EU law enacted under the enhanced cooperation procedure.

limits Member States' possibility to engage in a process which leads to a shaping and forming of shared values.[93] Therein lies the uniqueness of the enhanced cooperation procedure. The procedure allows willing Member States to engage in a law-making process undisturbed by the unwilling Member States. Of course, the non-participating Member Stats can join the meetings of the participating Member States[94] but they do not have a say in the final voting, and thus their opinion may be heard but does not dominate the procedure.[95] However, the enhanced cooperation procedure not only provides the grounds for introducing deeper harmonisation between some of the Member States, it also sets out the foundation for protecting their shared values.[96] The framework of enhanced cooperation also protects the value of reciprocity which may underlie a common trade-fostering mechanism.[97]

The protection of the achievements of the group is, however, not unconditional. The rights of the non-participating Member States are sufficiently protected to ensure both the right to participate in enhanced cooperation and the right to remain outside enhanced cooperation.[98] The balancing of the interests of both participating and non-participating Member States is unique within the European legal framework.

B. Majority Voting as an Alternative

From quite early in its life, it was suggested that an alternative to flexibility would be qualified majority voting within the European Union.[99] The appeal of differentiated integration is supposed to lie primarily in the reluctance to allow qualified majority voting, and flexibility would fade if such voting were to become the rule.[100]

Subsection I sets out the political initiatives for a (slow) move from unanimity to qualified majority voting in many fields of the law except for some, including taxation. Subsection II outlines the recent initiative for qualified majority voting in taxation. Subsection III suggests that the European Union, as it stands today, is not ready for majority voting in taxation, and thus flexibility in taxation should be the relevant tool to overcome a legislative deadlock.

[93] See for more details on that particular issue Chapter 5, Part I, subsections E.III and E.VI.

[94] Art 20 Subsection 3 of the TEU: 'All members of the Council may participate in its deliberations.'

[95] Art 20 Subsection 3 of the TEU: 'but only members of the Council representing the Member States participating in enhanced cooperation shall take part in the vote'.

[96] See Chapter 5, Part I, subsection E, Chapter 6, subsection F.

[97] See Chapter 5, Part I, subsections E.VII and E.VIII.

[98] See Chapter 6.

[99] Even if the use of qualified majority voting is allowed, 'both the possibility that a 'blocking minority' of states (rather than simply an individual veto) could impede the desired progress of others, and the implications of ever wider policy and geographical expansion have ensured that the notion of differentiated integration remains as salient as ever': Búrca, 'Differentiation' (n 70) 142.

[100] Claus-Dieter Ehlermann, 'How Flexible Is Community Law? An Unusual Approach to the Concept of "Two Speeds" ' (1984) 82 Michigan Law Review 1274.

I. Unanimity Voting: A Relic in some Policy Areas—Including Taxation

When the Communities only consisted of their six founding fathers, it was clear that all Member States should approve of decisions taken at a European level. Accordingly, unanimous voting was the starting point for all European legislative actions. After further States joined the Community, the unanimity requirement was no longer taken for granted. On the contrary, as early as 1976, the Tindemans Report suggested that the majority voting in the Council 'should become normal practice in the Community field'.[101] In the same vein, the German and Italian ministers for foreign affairs, Hans-Dietrich Genscher and Emilio Colombo, also pushed for a structural reform of the existing European legislative system, including the introduction of majority voting in the Council, in an attempt to make the European Union more efficient and effective.[102] The various attempts to introduce majority voting were based on the idea that no-one could imagine how the Community should remain capable of acting if more Member States were joining.[103]

Despite the serious push for structural reform, including the introduction of majority voting in the Council, some Member States were keen to retain the unanimity requirement, allowing them to veto any legislative action which failed to comply with their own national policy goals. The lack of progress pushed the European Council towards implementing an ad-hoc committee, the Dooge Committee, to put forward ideas for improving the operation of the Community system and to propose ways of enhancing European political cooperation. With regards to the principle of majority voting, the Committee was quite clear and suggested the implementation of a 'new general principle that decisions *must* be taken by a qualified or simple majority'.[104] Despite the suggestion of moving towards majority voting, the Committee accepted that particular fields of the law need the consent of all Member States, and thus '[u]nanimity will still be required in certain *exceptional cases*, which will have to be distinctly fewer in number in relation to the present Treaties'.[105]

[101] Tindemans (n 50) 31.

[102] Hans-Dietrich Genscher, *Erinnerungen* (2nd edn, Siedler 1995) 362 et seq. Ulrich Rosengarten, *Die Genscher-Colombo-Initiative: Baustein für die Europäische Union* (Nomos 2008) 50. For a general link of efficient law making and majority voting see Matthias Ruffert, 'Rechtserzeugung und Rechtsdurchsetzung im Europäischen Raum' in Eva Schumann (ed), *Hierarchie, Kooperation und Integration im Europäischen Rechtsraum: 17. Symposion der Kommission 'Die Funktion des Gesetzes in Geschichte und Gegenwart'* (Walter de Gruyter 2015) 100.

[103] Mathias Jopp and others (eds), 'Entscheidungseffizienz und Handlungsfähigkeit nach Nizza: die neuen Anwendungsfelder für Mehrheitsentscheidungen', *Das Vertragswerk von Nizza und die Zukunft der Europäischen Union* (Europa Union 2001) 81.

[104] Dooge Committee, 'Report from the Ad Hoc Committee on Institutional Affairs to the European Council' (1985) 27 emphasis added.

[105] ibid emphasis added.

After tough negotiations, the Dooge Committee's recommendations were implemented by the Single European Act,[106] which is why the Member States extended qualified majority voting in the Council in this Act. Art 18 of the Single European Act introduced Art 100a into the European Economic Community (EEC) Treaty (today Art 114 of the TFEU), which allowed the Council to act by qualified majority when adopting measures for the approximation of the provisions laid down by law, regulation, or administrative action in Member States which aim at fostering the internal market.[107] Art 100a of the EEC Treaty was drafted as a derogation from Art 100 of the EEC Treaty (the standard harmonisation clause) and included exceptions in Subsection 2. According to Art 100a Subsection 2 of the EEC Treaty, fiscal provisions, provisions relating to both the free movement of persons, and the rights and interests of employed persons were (and still are)[108] subject to unanimous voting in the Council. Aside from this major achievement in the area of internal market harmonisation, the abolition of unanimous voting did not go as far as one might have wished, and thus the discussion also overshadowed the negotiations of the Maastricht, Amsterdam, Nice, and Lisbon Treaties.[109]

In the course of the negotiations for the Amsterdam Treaty, a breakthrough seemed to be within reach because provisions on culture, industry, and the professions, as well as substantial parts on the freedom of movement, were plausible candidates for qualified majority voting.[110] At the last moment, however, Germany backed down and could not agree to extend majority voting to any of these fields.[111] In the aftermath of this disappointing outcome, eliminating the unanimity requirement was a top priority in the negotiation process of the Nice Treaty. Both the European Commission[112] and Germany (which is quite surprising, considering it blocked the attempt to extend the majority voting procedure under the Amsterdam Treaty) pushed for a fundamental transfer to majority voting. According to Joschka Fischer, Germany's minister of foreign affairs at that time, the enlarged European Union could only remain capable of action if qualified majority

[106] Single European Act, OJ, 20. June 1987, L 169, 1.

[107] ibid 8.

[108] Art 114 Subsection 2 of the TFEU.

[109] For more details on each subject matter see House of Commons, 'The Extension of Qualified Majority Voting from the Treaty of Rome to the European Constitution' (2004) Research Paper 04/54. After the Treaty of Lisbon, qualified majority voting replaced unanimity in every policy area, Europäische Union and Rat, *The European Council and the Council of the EU through Time Decision- and Law-Making in European Integration* (2016) 32 <https://doi.org/10.2860/10651> accessed 9 May 2019.

[110] Andreas Maurer, 'Reformziel Effizienzsteigerung und Demokratisierung: Die Weiterentwicklung der Entscheidungsmechanismen' in Mathias Jopp and Otto Schmuck (eds), *Die Reform der Europäischen Union—Analysen, Positionen, Dokument* (Bundeszentrale für politische Bildung 1996) 31.

[111] Michel Petite, 'The Treaty of Amsterdam' (1998) Harvard Jean Monnet Chair Working Paper 24 <http://www.jeanmonnetprogram.org/archive/papers/98/98-2-.rtf> accessed 3 February 2021.

[112] See also a report commissioned by the European Commission: Richard von Weizsäcker, Jean-Luc Dehaene, and David Simon, 'The Institutional Implications of Enlargement—Report to the European Commission' (1999) 8.

voting was the rule and not the exception, and thus he advocated a rule-exception approach.[113] Exceptions should only be allowed according to strict criteria, such as constitutional or defence issues.[114] The preparatory works for the intergovernmental conference in Helsinki, however, already pointed in another direction. Similar to the Amsterdam Treaty, a case-by-case approach was taken. Every subject was discussed and weighed up as to whether or not it should be subject to qualified majority voting in future.[115]

In this vein, the Portuguese Presidency put forward a list of subject matters (the shortened version included twenty-five provisions) which may be subject to qualified majority voting. The list also included taxation, which was subject to strong reservations from certain Member States.[116] The strong reservations were the reason for not discussing the idea to extend majority voting to the area of taxation any further under the French presidency.

During the negotiations for the Constitutional Treaty, it had been discussed that a more precise demarcation of the Union's authority should, in some cases, enable unanimous voting to be dispensed with (e.g. taxation in connection with the operation of the internal market, i.e. modernising and simplifying existing legislation, administrative cooperation, combating fraud or tax evasion, measures relating to tax bases for companies, but not including tax rates; the aspects of free circulation of capital linked to the fight against fraud; taxation in respect of the environment; certain aspects of social security; certain measures concerning passports; and the European public prosecutor's role in safeguarding the Union's financial interests).[117]

Since then, the unanimity requirement has given way to qualified majority voting in all subject areas, except for some particular sensitive policy areas including taxation,[118] social security or social protection, the accession of new

[113] The rule and exception approach had the backing of the European Parliament and a number of delegation, see 'Summary of the Proceedings of the Intergovernmental Conference between 14 February and 6 June 2000 on the Eve of the Feira European Council to Be Held on 19 and 20 June' (2000) PE 286.924 2.

[114] Joschka Fischer, 'Rede Des Bundesministers Des Auswärtigen, Joschka Fischer, Vor Dem Belgischen Parlament' (Brussels, 14 November 2000) <https://www.bundesregierung.de/breg-de/service/bulletin/rede-des-bundesministers-des-auswaertigen-joschka-fischer--786446> accessed 3 February 2021.

[115] Council of the European Union, 'Presidency Report: Efficient Institutions After Enlargement—Options For The Intergovernmental Conference' (1999) 13636/99 5; see also 'Summary of the Proceedings of the Intergovernmental Conference between 14 February and 6 June 2000 on the Eve of the Feira European Council to Be Held on 19 and 20 June' (n 113) 2.

[116] 'Summary of the Proceedings of the Intergovernmental Conference between 14 February and 6 June 2000 on the Eve of the Feira European Council to Be Held on 19 and 20 June' (n 113) 3.

[117] Commission, 17 September 2003, Opinion of the Commission, pursuant to Article 48 of the Treaty on European Union, on the Conference of representatives of the Member States' governments convened to revise the Treaties, COM(2003) 548, 7.

[118] Many see the unanimity requirement as the reason for the lack of legislative progress: Otmar Thömmers, 'Corporate Taxation in the European Union in the Year 2002—A Single Currency and Fifteen Different Tax Jurisdictions' (2002) 30 Intertax 123, 123.

Member States, foreign and common defence and operational police cooperation between the Member States of the European Union.

II. New Initiative to Achieve Majority Voting in Taxation

It took almost twenty years until the discussion of majority voting in taxation was back on the table. Jean-Claude Juncker, the former president of the European Commission, put forward his strong wish to extend qualified majority voting to decisions in the area of taxation in his State of the Union Address before the European Parliament in 2017.[119] He indicated that he was aiming to change the existing European treaties by using the 'passerelle clause' which allows one to change parts of the European treaties in a simplified manner.

The idea of removing the unanimity requirement in taxation was not a flash in the pan. The European Commission followed up on the idea and issued its working programme for the upcoming future in which the Commission reveals its agenda for a more united, stronger, and more democratic Europe.[120] Several events motivated the programme, including the United Kingdom's referendum in favour of leaving the European Union and the subsequent triggering of Art 50 of the TEU,[121] the blocking of legislative attempts by some Member States over years,[122] and the rising threat of nationalist and populist actions and movements within the Member States.[123] To fight the negative developments, the Commission proposed an ambitious agenda which provided for systemic changes intended to make the European Union more united, stronger, and more democratic.[124] An essential part is devoted to the change from unanimous decision-making in taxation to decision-making by

[119] Jean-Claude Juncker, 'State of the Union Address 2017' (European Parliament, Brussels, 12 September 2017) <http://europa.eu/rapid/press-release_SPEECH-17-3165_en.htm> accessed 3 February 2021.

[120] European Commission, 'Commission Work Programme 2018—An Agenda for a More United, Stronger and More Democratic Europe' (2017) COM(2017) 650 final 11–12.

[121] European Council, 29 April 2017, Guidelines following the United Kingdom's notification under Article 50 TEU, EUCO XT 20004/17.

[122] A good example is the Common Consolidated Corporate Tax Base. The European Commission issued its first proposal in 2011 (Commission, 15 March 2011, Proposal for a Council Directive on a Common Consolidated Corporate Tax Base (CCCTB), COM(2011) 121/4 final), and relaunched the project in 2015/2016 (Commission, 25 October 2016, Proposal for a Council Directive on a Common Corporate Tax Base, COM(2016) 685 final). Yet, the proposal did not make it into hard law. For an overview of all the (failed) initiatives in the tax law area see Carlo Garbarino, 'Harmonization and Coordination of Corporate Taxes in the European Union' (2016) 25 EC Tax Review 277, 277–78.

[123] Marco Bassini, 'Rise of Populism and the Five Star Movement Model: An Italian Case Study' (2017) Jean Monnet Working Paper; Silvia Suteu, 'The Populist Turn in Central and Eastern Europe: Is Deliberative Democracy (Part of) the Solution?' (2017) Jean Monnet Working Paper; On the current European crisis see Gurminder K Bhambra, 'The Current Crisis of Europe: Refugees, Colonialism, and the Limits of Cosmopolitanism' (2017) 23 European Law Journal 395.

[124] For a critical analysis, in particular of the democratic aspect, see Ana Paula Dourado, 'The Commission Proposal to Replace Unanimity with a Qualified Majority in the Case of Tax Matters' (2019) 47 Intertax 341.

qualified majority voting.[125] However, the programme does not reveal more than the simple wish to change, and the attempt to use the 'passerelle clause' to achieve the necessary changes to the European treaty.

At the beginning of 2019, the European Commission issued a more concrete proposal to the European Parliament, the European Council, and the Council, in order to acquaint them with its plans to achieve changes to the European treaty on the voting requirements in the area of taxation.[126] In that document, the Commission begins by explaining the importance of taxation and its potential impact on the European internal market. Particular emphasis is given to the need to find a common approach in taxation to master the challenges of digitalisation and globalisation, and the consequential possibility of some taxpayers to structure their business arrangements in a way which reduces or even avoids taxation. The Commission also refers to legislative proposals blocked by some Member States, such as the Common (Consolidated) Corporate Tax Base, which has been on the Commission's agenda for a long time and gone through amendments, but still without any likelihood of being accepted by all Member States.[127] The VAT Directive forms another example in which the European legislature is incapable of acting. Today the law is outdated and no longer capable of dealing with new economic realities and while amendments to the VAT Directive have been proposed, hardly any have passed the unanimity threshold.[128]

[125] The unanimity requirement has often been blamed as the cause of a lack of European tax integration. See for example Eric CCM Kemmeren, 'Sources of EU Law for European Tax Integration: Well-Known and Alternative Legal Instruments' in Dennis Weber (ed), *Traditional and Alternative Routes to European Tax Integration: Primary Law, Secondary Law, Soft Law, Coordination, Comitology and their Relationship* (IBFD 2010) 33; Frans Vanistendael, 'A Personal View' in Ary Lans Bovenberg and others (eds), *Harmonization of Company Taxation in the European Community: Some Comments on the Ruding Committee Report* (1992) 29; Pasquale Pistone, 'Expected and Unexpected Developments of European Integration in the Field of Direct Taxes' (2007) 35 Intertax 70, 70 arguing that '[t]he need for unanimous Council decisions has almost paralysed positive integration of direct taxes. By contrast, negative integration kept developing and establishing limits on cross-border direct taxation, thus showing the need for positive integration. The friction between these two forces gave rise to a hectic and unstable process of legal development, which has turned European tax law into an area of high legal uncertainty and (in some cases of) inconsistency.' Frans Vanistendael, 'On Democratic Legitimacy of European Tax Law and the Role of the European Parliament' in Pasquale Pistone (ed), *European Tax Integration: Law, Policy and Politics* (IBFD 2018) also claiming that the current law-making procedure shows a lack of democratic legitimacy. Malcolm Gammie, 'The Compatibility of National Tax Principles with the Single Market' in Frans Vanistendael (ed), *EU Freedoms and Taxation* (IBFD 2006) 163–64 doubting whether the qualified majority voting in taxation would provide a change because there is no general consensus between the Member States on how taxes on capital, including company taxes should look like (which is very different from the situation in the field of consumption taxes).

[126] Commission, 15 January 2019, Communication from the Commission to the European Parliament, the European Council and the Council—Towards a more efficient and democratic decision-making in EU tax policy, COM(2019) 8 final.

[127] For example the Commission's proposal for a Common Corporate Tax Base, see Hanno Kube, Ekkehart Reimer, and Christoph Spengel, 'Tax Policy: Trends in the Allocation of Powers Between the Union and Its Member States' (2016) 25 EC Tax Review 247, 253.

[128] The VAT treatment of vouchers raised several problems with respect to the timing. Should the supply of a voucher already be subject to VAT; or should the redemption of the voucher be taxed? Accordingly, the VAT treatment of vouchers did need some form of coordination, but it did not change the fundaments underlying the European VAT system. Nonetheless, it took the Member States four

As already intended by Jean-Claude Juncker's speech and the European Commission's working programme, the necessary amendments to the European treaty should be achieved by using the 'passerelle clause'. According to Art 48 Subsection 7 of the TEU, the European Council may adopt a decision authorising the Council to act by qualified majority in a given area or case when the European treaties would require the Council to act by unanimity. Such a decision by the European Council would require notification of the national parliaments in the first place. The European Council is only entitled to adopt the decision if they do not make their opposition known within six months. For this decision, the European Council has to act unanimously after obtaining the consent of the European Parliament, which is granted by a majority of its members. Importantly, Art 48 Subsection 7 of the TEU does not change the distribution of competences between the Member States and the European Union, it 'only' impacts the procedure the European institutions have to follow when exercising their existing powers.[129]

The European Commission is proposing a roadmap which consists of four steps.[130] First, unanimity should be dismissed for introducing measures which have no direct impact on the Member States' taxing rights, bases, or rates, but are nonetheless critical for combatting tax fraud, evasion, and avoidance and in facilitating tax compliance from businesses in the European internal market.[131] Secondly, unanimity should be replaced by qualified majority voting for measures primarily of a fiscal nature designed to support other policy goals such as the fight against climate change, or environmental protection. Thirdly, qualified majority voting should cover measures that amend outdated existing secondary EU law, such as in the field of the VAT Directive. Fourthly, qualified majority voting should be allowed for other initiatives in taxation which are necessary for the European internal market and fair and competitive taxation in Europe; this step would allow the Common (Consolidated) Corporate Tax Base to be passed with a qualified majority voting.

years to agree on the amendments to the VAT directive (Commission, 10 May 2012, Proposal for a Council Directive amending Directive 2006/112/EC on the common system of value-added tax, as regards the treatment of vouchers, COM(2012) 206 final; Council, 27 June 2016, 2016/1065/EU, Directive amending Directive 2006/112/EC, as regards the treatment of vouchers, OJ, 1 July 2016, L 177, 9.

[129] Hans-Joachim Cremer, 'Art. 48' in Christian Calliess and Matthias Ruffert (eds), *EUV/AEUV* (5th edn, Beck Verlag 2016) para 12.

[130] COM(2019) 8 final, 11 et seq.

[131] Recent trends of positive integration show that Member States are willing to enact legislative measures which pursue the goal of protecting the European internal market against base erosion and profit shifting. Anti-BEPS measures 'have indeed taken precedence over other legislative initiatives aimed at boosting or enhancing the internal market', Mario Tenore, 'Trends and Facts in European Tax Integration: Harmonization and Coordination' in Pasquale Pistone (ed), *European Tax Integration: Law, Policy and Politics* (IBFD 2018) 4 et seq.

III. Is the European Union Ready for Majority Voting in Taxation?

The question of whether or not the European Union is ready for majority voting in taxation can be addressed from different angles. On the one hand, one could ask whether lowering the threshold for passing secondary EU law in the field of taxation is beneficial to improve the free movement of goods, services, persons, and capital between the Member States. Here the answer would be yes. Taxation has a severe impact on the level playing field, and thus affects the efficient allocation of resources within the European internal market. If all taxpayers were to face an equal tax burden regardless of where they conduct their economic activity, it would facilitate an optimal allocation of resources.

On the other hand, one could analyse the impact of majority voting in taxation on the stability within the European Union. The stability question is triggered by the fact that the minority is subject to the decision taken by the majority.[132] Even if the power to overrule blocking minorities may not have been used much in the Council,[133] it may occur in the future, and thus requires some Member States to follow rules which may contradict their policy objectives.[134] The acceptance of being overruled and having to introduce policy choices of the majority depends on the materiality of the decision and the depth of the division between Member States.

[132] Majority voting can only apply in areas in which the minority is willing to accept the decision of the majority: Ulrich Everling, 'Zur Mehrheit und Einstimmigkeit in der verfaßten Europäischen Union' in Reinhard Hendler, Martin Ibler, and José Martínez Soria (eds), *Für Sicherheit, für Europa: Festschrift für Volkmar Götz zum 70. Geburtstag* (Vandenhoeck & Ruprecht 2005) 127.

[133] A VoteWatch Europe report on the Council's voting behaviour clearly shows that during the period of 2009 and 2012 65% of Council decisions were taken unanimously, despite the fact that only a qualified majority voting was needed (VoteWatch Europe, 'Agreeing to Disagree: The Voting Records of EU Member States in the Council since 2009' (2012) <https://www.votewatch.eu/blog/wp-content/uploads/2012/07/votewatch-annual-report-july-2012-final-7-july.pdf> accessed 3 February 2021). According to the report, 'Member States prefer to shape the policy in such a way that every participant can agree with the final output' (p 8). In many cases, a legislative proposal is not brought to a vote, not because the qualified majority was not reached, but because some Governments do not want to be seen to be out-voted (Daniel Naurin, 'The Councils of the EU: Intergovernmental Bargaining in a Supranational Polity' in Jeremy Richardson and Sonia Mazey (eds), *European Union: Power and Policy-making* (4th edn, Routledge 2015) 144.). The Member States' take on being outvoted differs widely. France, for example, may rather accept a compromise than be outvoted, whereas others, like Germany, have fewer complexes about being outvoted (Stéphanie Novak, 'Qualified Majority Voting from the Single European Act to Present Day: An Unexpected Permanence' Notre Europe—Research Paper 7). See also Holly Cullen and Andrew Charlesworth, 'Diplomacy by Other Means: The Use of Legal Basis Litigation as a Political Strategy by the European Parliament and Member States' (1999) 36 Common Market Law Review 1243, 1257 et seq. For the 'shadow of the vote' discussion, see Jonathan Golub, 'In the Shadow of the Vote? Decision Making in the European Community' (1999) 53 International Organization 733.

[134] For communicative action in international taxation see Cees Peters, *On the Legitimacy of International Tax Law*, vol 31 (IBFD 2014) 331 Peters argues that 'states and individuals and other actors do not only follow the norms of international tax law because they (intrinsically) 'try do "do the right thing"' but also because they have been actively part of the establishment of these norms in open and inclusive deliberations.

The following subsections analyse the impact majority voting may have on the European Union's stability in more detail. For that purpose, the principles and justification for majority voting, especially within a nation State, will be discussed, because within the Member States majority voting is the rule, including taxation (see subsection 1). The generally accepted dogma that majority voting is required to grant the State the capability of acting may not apply to multi-ethnic nation States (see subsection 2). In cases of severe divergence between the people, majority voting would not facilitate peace within the State. On the contrary, the tyranny of the majority would become unbearable and would destroy the unity of the State. The existing scholarship on how to deal with a State consisting of different and divergent groups within a democratic system will be used to decide on the impact majority voting has on the EU's stability. A definitive answer to the question can, however, only be provided once the general capability of national tax laws to establish national policy objectives has been revealed (see subsection 3).

1. Principles and Justifications for Majority Voting

In constitutional law, majority voting is generally understood as an inevitable component of any democratic order because if the people are to rule, they must do so on an equal basis, meaning that each vote has equal weight and more votes must thus count for more weight.[135] On the other hand, one could also disentangle democratic decision-making from majority voting, allowing the argument to be made for majority voting individually.[136] Thus, a democratic system can be established without being committed to majority rules[137] because the government by the people can be achieved by different means. The only fundamental requirement is that the people agree on the decision-making process, regardless of whether this is a form of majority voting or voting by a certain group of people (eg only the ones affected by the law to be enacted should be allowed to vote, or their vote should carry more weight than the other votes).[138] In terms of majority voting only, philosophical scholarship has put forward different arguments[139] for its justification,

[135] Wojciech Sadurski, *Equality and Legitimacy* (OUP 2008) 18 et seq. Christian Hillgruber, '§ 61 Mehrheitsprinzip' in Hanno Kube and others (eds), *Die Leitgedanken des Rechts in der Diskussion: Symposion aus Anlass des 70. Geburtstages von Professor Dr. Dr. h.c. mult. Paul Kirchhof, Band I* (CF Müller Wissenschaft 2013) 661 et seq.

[136] Ben Saunders has shown that democracy does not automatically require majority voting regardless of whether the argument for democracy is based on its intrinsic fairness, conduciveness to better decisions, or valuable by-products, Ben Saunders, 'Democracy, Political Equality, and Majority Rule' (2010) 121 Ethics 148.

[137] ibid 163; see for the requirement of unanimity Emmanuel-Joseph Sieyès, *Préliminaire de la Constitution françoise* (1789) 38 <https://gallica.bnf.fr/ark:/12148/bpt6k41690g/f6.image.texteImage> accessed 13 May 2019.

[138] Harry Brighouse and Marc Fleurbaey, 'Democracy and Proportionality' (2010) 18 Journal of Political Philosophy 137, 138 et seq.

[139] In the following the main arguments will be discussed, it should however be mentioned that some scholars have found these arguments to be insufficient: Mathias Risse, 'Arguing for Majority Rule' (2004) 12 Journal of Political Philosophy 41.

such as the perversity of minority rules,[140] maximisation of people exercising self-determination, respect, the Condorcet's Jury Theorem, May's Theorem, and compromise.[141]

In scholarly legal work, however, majority voting is mainly supported by the idea of guaranteeing the nation State's ability to act. A minority of people should not be able to block actions,[142] but they are protected, in particular, by fundamental rights which ensure that the majority cannot take actions in exploitation of the minority.[143] Accordingly, majority voting is a tool to ensure the effectiveness and efficiency within the State.[144] A lack of ability to act may damage the State's unity and provoke a split of the parts which disagree with each other.

2. Limits of Majority Decision Making

History tells us that majority voting does not always work as a vehicle to safeguard effectiveness and efficiency within the nation State. In cases where severe gaps exist between members of the population, in particular concerning their ethnic background, majority voting may cause conflicts.[145] The more a nation State's society is fragmented by political, cultural, or ethnic means, the more critical it becomes to give every fraction of that society a voice. Otherwise, a stable unity may not be achievable.[146]

In constitutional legal theory, scholars analyse the possibility of turning a fragmented political culture into a stable democracy under the heading of 'consociational democracy'.[147] National attempts at power-sharing in multi-ethnic nation States deeply influence the discussion, such as Canada (in 1849),[148] the

[140] Jack Lively argued for the possibility of such an approach but under the presumption that such a minority approach would lead to the prevailing of the majority: see Jack Lively, *Democracy* (Blackwell 1975) 13–14. This approach, however, has severe shortcomings, especially when there are more than two alternatives, see for a general analysis of the impact of multiple alternatives on majority voting Frances Myrna Kamm, 'Equal Treatment and Equal Chances' (1985) 14 Philosophy & Public Affairs 177, 182 et seq.

[141] Risse (n 139) 44–45; Saunders (n 136) 164–69.

[142] For the importance of blocking legislative actions and for its ineffectiveness: 'A United States congressman has two principal functions: to make law and to keep laws from being made. The first of these he and his colleagues perform only sweat, patience and a remarkable skill in the handling of creaking machinery; but the second they perform daily, with ease and infinite variety. Indeed, if that government is best that governs least, then Congress is one of the most perfect institutions of government.' Robert Bendiner, *Obstacle Course on Capitol Hill* (McGraw-Hill 1964) 15.

[143] Philippe C Schmitter and Terry Lynn Karl, 'What Democracy Is... and Is Not' (1991) 2 Journal of Democracy 75, 79.

[144] Bernard Manin, 'On Legitimacy and Political Deliberation' (1987) 15 Political Theory 338, 341.

[145] Rudy B Andeweg, 'Consociational Democracy' (2000) Annual Review of Political Science 509.

[146] Gabriel A Almond, 'Comparative Political Systems' (1956) 18 The Journal of Politics 391.

[147] Arend Lijphart, 'Consensus and Consensus Democracy: Cultural, Structural, Functional, and Rational-Choice Explanations' (1998) 21 Scandinavian Political Studies 99.

[148] In Canada, Part V of the Constitution Act 1982 still reflects the diversity within the diversity between the provinces, as substantial changes to the constitution require the consent of every province (Subsection 41); see also Fritz W Scharpf, 'Was man von einer europäischen Verfassung erwarten und nicht erwarten sollte' (Darmstadt, 7 November 2002).

Netherlands (in 1917), Austria (in 1945),[149] Czechoslovakia (in 1989), and South Africa (in 1994), and their historical responses.[150] Consociational democracy explains the stability of a deeply fragmented society by incorporating minorities into the political decision-making process, which majority voting fails to achieve.[151] A majority voting process is incapable of achieving stability in a society which is divided by sharp divisions between their subcultures, because the leaders of one subculture may give priority to the needs and demands of those who are part of that particular subculture.[152] In the absence of a representation of all subcultures some may be left behind. Thus, all significant leaders shall be stakeholders in the decision-making process and bind them to the commonly achieved agreements.[153]

According to Arend Lijphart, successful consociational democracy requires four elements:[154] first, the decisions must be taken by a 'grand coalition', meaning a group of people representing the most influential ethnic groups in the society. Second, the ethnic groups should enjoy autonomy allowing them to deal with issues only vital to them. Third, political representation should be allocated proportionally. Fourth, the minority should enjoy the right to veto decisions to protect their vital interests.

Consociational democracy rests on a firm belief in achieving stability within a highly diverse group by granting any subgroup a say in the decision-making process, and by allowing any minority to veto decisions contradicting their fundamental interests. The veto power of minorities is restricted to fundamental legislative decisions, such as changes to the constitutional law.[155]

3. Consocionationalism and European Taxation

In light of the aims of majority voting and its limits in a heterogeneous society, one may be hesitant to export majority voting to the EU level in the field of taxation because it may not lead to a more united, stronger, and more democratic European Union but to a European Union plagued by internal frustration and conflicts.[156]

[149] See for more details Kurt Richard Luther and Wolfgang C Müller, *Politics in Austria: Still a Case of Consociationalism?* (Psychology Press 1992).

[150] Lijphart, 'Consensus and Consensus Democracy' (n 147) 101.

[151] Ian Lustick, 'Stability in Deeply Divided Societies: Consociationalism versus Control' (1979) 31 World Politics 325, 327 et seq.

[152] Arend Lijphart, 'Consociational Democracy' (1969) 21 World Politics 207, 211–12.

[153] Pippa Norris, 'Stable Democracy and Good Governance in Divided Societies: Do Powersharing Institutions Work?' (2005) Harvard University Faculty Research Working Papers Series 4.

[154] Arend Lijphart, 'The Power-Sharing Approach' in Joseph V Montville (ed), *Conflict and Peacemaking in Multiethnic Societies* (Lexington Books 1990) 494–95.

[155] See for example the Canadian Constitution which requires the blessing of every province if substantial amendments are at stake. If the change in the Constitution affects one province directly, it has to agree to the amendment. Ordinary amendments (only) require the agreement of seven provinces whose population totals more than half of Canada's at the last census (the 7/50 rule); Part V of the Canadian Constitution.

[156] Richter (n 113). For a different view see Pasquale Pistone, 'A Plea for Qualified Majority Voting and the Ordinary Legislative Procedure in European Tax Law' in Servaas van Thiel, Piergiorgio Valente, and Stella Raventós-Calvo (eds), *CFE Tax Advisers Europe: 60th Anniversary Liber Amicorum* (IBFD 2019) 11; Edoardo Traversa and Alice Pirlot, 'The UK Brexit Referendum: A Catalyst to Reform the

Unlike many other subject areas, taxation is a vehicle to pursue sensitive national policy objectives.[157] Taxation is not only a revenue raiser, it is also a nuanced tool to steer taxpayers' behaviour,[158] achieve justice and equal opportunities through redistribution,[159] and address economic needs.[160] Accordingly, secondary EU law on taxation not only aligns technical formalities which are designed differently in the Member States, it may have a severe impact on the Member States' policy objectives. Take a tax on financial transaction as an example; it is true that such a tax provides the Member States with additional revenue, but it is also a rigid mechanism to regulate the financial market, and thus a clear statement of intent to prioritise a stable financial market over the pure economic attractiveness of the marketplace.[161] Another example would be a Common Corporate Tax Base which could either boost investment, such as through considering current value depreciation of shares, or could in fact encourage taxpayers to invest equity if the taxpayers are allowed to deduct notional interest for their capital.

On the other hand, the Member States are heterogeneous in their policy objectives, due to their social, cultural, historical, and economic differences. These differences are the reason why consent is sometimes hard to achieve at an EU level.[162] But these differences should not be eliminated for the sake of a perfect single market. On the contrary, the European Union should be understood as a

European Union Institutional Architecture in Tax Matters?' (2016) 44 Intertax 878, 879–80 arguing that more tax harmonisation would foster Member State tax sovereignty, because currently integration in taxation takes place through negative harmonisation 'without any explicit consent from the side of the Member States'. Massive negative integration may have some severe shortcomings. However, there is no doubt that the Member States have committed themselves to fostering the free movement of goods, services, persons, and capital within the internal market and that whether the CJEU overstepped its competences by interpreting primary EU law is a completely other story. For an analysis of the question of whether the CJEU takes political decisions which should be left to the legislature see Frans Vanistendael, 'General Report on the Fundamental Freedoms and National Sovereignty in the European Union' in Frans Vanistendael (ed), *EU Freedoms and Taxation* (IBFD 2006) 213 et seq.

157 Bruno Peeters and Herwig Verschueren, 'The Impact of European Union Law on the Interaction of Members States' Sovereign Powers in the Policy Fields of Social Protection and Personal Income Tax Benefits' (2016) 25 EC Tax Review 262, 263.

158 OECD, *Taxation, Innovation and the Environment* (2010); Deborah Gordon, *Steering a New Course: Transportation, Energy, and the Environment* (Island Press 1991) 180 et seq.

159 Thomas Piketty, *Le capital au XXIe siècle* (Éditions du Seuil 2013); Thomas Piketty, *Capital in the Twenty-First Century* (Harvard University Press 2014); Beverly Moran, 'Wealth Redistribution and the Income Tax' (2009) 53 Howard Law Journal 319; Paul L Caron and James R Repetti, 'Occupy the Tax Code: Using the Estate Tax to Reduce Inequality and Spur Economic Growth' (2012) 40 Pepperdine Law Review 1255; Liam Murphy and Thomas Nagel, *The Myth of Ownership: Taxes and Justice* (OUP 2002); Christine Osterloh-Konrad, 'Zur Legitimation steuerlicher Umverteilung' (2017) Steuer und Wirtschaft 305.

160 Jennifer E Farrell, *The Interface of International Trade Law and Taxation* (IBFD 2013) 7 et seq.

161 Caroline Heber and Christian Sternberg, 'Over-the-Counter Derivative Markets in the Light of EMIR Clearing Obligations and the Financial Transaction Tax' (2014) 16 Derivatives & Financial Instruments 107; Caroline Heber and Christian Sternberg, 'Market Infrastructure Regulation and the Financial Transaction Tax' (2016) 8 World Tax Journal 3.

162 See in this vein also Richter (n 84).

Union of all its Member States, which are different and diverse but united under one European roof.[163]

Both the differences between the Member States in social, economic, and cultural means and the power of steering behaviour and expressing values are political reasons for rejecting any attempts at abandoning the requirement of a unanimous decision in the Council in favour of qualified majority voting. European tax laws which are not based on the consent of all Member States may allow one to take a swift step towards the goal of uniformity, but these laws will not achieve a steady deepening of the integration between the Member States.[164] Being outvoted in the area of taxation may cause serious alienation within the European Union.[165] If Member States fear that they can no longer follow their intrinsic interests and national values, they may no longer be proud and willing to be a member of the European Union. Thus, unanimity in European taxation should not be abandoned. The lack of progress on legislative actions should be addressed by the use of measures of differentiation.[166] Extending differentiation diminishes uniformity, which is far less dangerous than the instability which follows from uniform laws being dictated over some Member States in particularly sensitive areas.

[163] Art 4 Subsection 2 of the TEU; Armin von Bogdandy and Stephan Schill, 'Die Achtung der nationalen Identität unter dem reformierten Unionsvertrag: Zur unionsrechtlichen Rolle nationalen Verfassungsrechts und zur Überwindung des absoluten Vorrangs' (2010) 70 Zeitschrift für ausländisches öffentliches Recht und Völkerrecht 701; 'argument for self-determination' Floris de Witte, 'Sex, Drugs & EU Law: The Recognition of Moral and Ethical Diversity in EU Law' (2013) 50 Common Market Law Review 1545, 1546; Deakin Simon, 'Legal Diversity and Regulatory Competition: Which Model for Europe?' (2006) 12 European Law Journal 440, 441 et seq. For more details on the national identity clause see Elke Cloots, *National Identity in EU Law* (OUP 2015) 134 et seq.

[164] Majority voting can only apply in areas in which the minority is willing to accept the decision of the majority: Everling (n 132) 127.

[165] Richter (n 84); Marquardsen, *Einstimmigkeit in Steuerfragen—Reformbedarf?*, vol 534 (2020) 30.

[166] In this vein also Curtin (n 23) 349.

3

Experience with Enhanced Cooperation—Success and Failure

A. Experience of Success

Since the Amsterdam Treaty introduced the mechanism of enhanced cooperation, it has successfully been used for five legislative acts. Two of these acts can be summarised under the heading of divorce law and related issues and regulation in that field was the first legislative act introduced under the enhanced cooperation procedure.[1] Enhanced cooperation law establishes a common formula for deciding which Member State's legal order should be applied for a divorce of an international couple. A separate and much later enacted regulation determines the property regimes of international couples in case of divorce or death. The second legislative act under the enhanced cooperation procedure, and most likely the most familiar one, has been the unitary patent which provides for uniform patent protection in the territory of all participating Member States. Despite these three acts, the enhanced cooperation procedure has also been used to introduce the European public prosecutor and the permanent structured cooperation in the area of defence and security within the European legal framework.

The latter cooperation is unique since it deals with cooperation of the Member States in the area of defence through concrete projects and commitments. For that particular purpose, the Lisbon Treaty has introduced a legal basis.[2] However, it took almost a decade until it was used. A Council decision in December 2017 established permanent structured cooperation;[3] in March 2018, the list of joint projects was adopted.[4] Permanent structured cooperation will not be analysed in more detail since its special scope and content would not allow one to form conclusions on any general characteristics for the use of the enhanced cooperation procedure.

[1] The first enhanced cooperation law was introduced in 2010, which is why, in 2009, Amtenbrink and Kochenov claimed that '[e]nhanced cooperation seems to have failed the "field-test"', Fabian Amtenbrink and Dimitry Kochenov, 'Towards a More Flexible Approach to Enhanced Cooperation' in Andrea Ott and Ellen Vos (eds), *50 Years of European Integration: Foundations and Perspectives* (Asser 2009) 182.

[2] See Art 42 Subsection 6, and Art 46 of the TEU.

[3] Council, 11 December 2017, 2017/2315/EU, establishing permanent structured cooperation (PESCO) and determining the list of participating Member States, OJ, 14 December 2017, L 331, 57.

[4] Council, 6 March 2018, 2018/340/EU, establishing the list of projects to be developed under PESCO, OJ, 8 March 2018, L 65, 24.

Enhanced Cooperation and European Tax Law. Caroline Heber, Oxford University Press. © Caroline Heber 2021.
DOI: 10.1093/oso/9780192898272.003.0003

The following subsections reveal the success stories of establishing enhanced cooperation, these being enhanced cooperation in divorce law and related issues (see subsection I), the European unitary patent (see subsection II), and the European Public Prosecutor (see subsection III). This subsection will describe the scope and content of the law, the reason why the enhanced cooperation procedure was chosen to enact the law, address why a common action between all the Member States could not be achieved, and analyse whether the non-participating Member States promote or oppose enhanced cooperation.

I. Divorce Law and Related Issues

1. Historical Developments in Divorce Law

The establishment of a European internal market with free movement rights not only allowed European citizens to perform economic activities in another Member State but it also meant that individuals developed a personal life there. International romances lead to international marriages, and since not all of them are destined to last forever, thousands of divorces with an international character are pronounced by Member State courts every year.[5] Both the substantive law and the conflict of law rules vary fundamentally from Member State to Member State.[6] In Malta, for example, a marriage could not be dissolved at this time,[7] whereas in Sweden and Finland, a divorce will easily be granted even without adducing any reasons to support the divorce claim.[8] In the latter Member States the right to divorce even accounts for a fundamental right.[9] Concerning the conflict of law rules, some Member States practice the *lex fori* rule, and thus apply national law to any divorce matters; others, on the other hand, aim to apply the law of the closest connection such as the law of their habitual residence.[10] These differences may seem particularly odd considering that there has been the 'free movement' of divorce orders

[5] See for more detailed numbers Commission, 17 July 2006, Impact Assessment to the proposal for a Council Regulation (EC) Ni 2201/2003 as regards jurisdiction and introducing rules concerning applicable law in matrimonial matters, COM(2006) 399 final.

[6] Aude Fiorini, 'Rome III—Choice of Law in Divorce: Is the Europeanization of Family Law Going Too Far' (2008) 22 International Journal of Law, Policy and the Family 178, 179.

[7] Lemoine Bérénice, 'Rome III Regulation: Getting Divorced in Europe' in Thomas Giegerich, Desirée Schmitt, and Sebastian Zeitzmann (eds), *Flexibility in the EU and Beyond: How Much Differentiation can European Integration Bear?* (Nomos 2017) 255.

[8] Masha Antokolskaia, 'Objectives and Values of Substantive Family Law' in Johan Meeusen and others (eds), *International Family Law for the European Union* (Intersentia 2007) 49; Nynke A Baarsma, *The Europeanisation of International Family Law* (TMC Asser Press 2011) 149.

[9] Katharina Boele-Woelki, 'To Be, Or Not to Be: Enhanced Cooperation in International Divorce Law within the European Union Wider Perspectives' (2008) 39 Victoria University of Wellington Law Review 779, 785.

[10] ibid 781.

since the Brussels II regulation entered into force.[11] The Brussels II regulation was the first secondary EU law in the process of unifying the Member States rules in divorce law. In 1998, it started as a convention—the Brussels II Convention—containing rules on jurisdiction and the enforcement of judgments in matrimonial matters,[12] but the convention did not comprise rules on applicable law. The convention was transformed into secondary EU law, the Brussels II regulation.[13] Soon after the regulation entered into force, Brussels II was amended by Brussels IIa, which did not substantially change the legal situation for divorces.[14] A few months later, more fundamental changes to the regulation had been announced, and in 2006 the European Commission issued the proposal for the amendments. The new proposal aimed to harmonise conflict of law rules, and thereby address 'shortcomings of the present situation'.[15] The shortcomings are particularly triggered by the differences between the conflict of law rules of the Member States and the subsequent legal uncertainty and the lack of flexibility. The harmonisation of the conflict of law rule not only strengthened legal certainty, predictability, and flexibility for the spouses, it was also supposed to facilitate the mutual recognition of judgments because the 'fact that courts of the Member States apply the same conflict-of-law rules to determine the law applicable to a given situation reinforces the mutual trust in judicial decisions given in other Member States'.[16]

Despite these good reasons for harmonising the conflict of law rules for divorces, the legal status quo of the Member States was too different, and the proposal was too ambitious to find the necessary compromise. The Rome III proposal included choice of forum rules, as well as conflict of law rules.[17] The latter should have been applied when the spouses did not choose the applicable law, and when determined by the element of close connection. The multi-stage conflict of law rules could have led to the application of foreign law, 'not only of the divorce law of another Member State but also of the law of other jurisdictions'.[18] The fundamental differences between the substantive law and its underlying values in the Member States made some Member States hesitant to vote for the new regulation. However, some

[11] Council Regulation, 29 May 2000, 1347/2000/EC, Council regulation on the jurisdiction, recognition and enforcement of judgements in matrimonial matters and in matters of parental responsibility for children of both spouses, OJ, 30 June 2000, L 160, 19.

[12] Council, 28 May 1998, the Convention on Jurisdiction and the Recognition and Enforcement of Judgments in Matrimonial Matters, OJ, 16 July 1998, C 221, 1.

[13] Boele-Woelki (n 9) 781.

[14] Commission, 14 March 2005, Green Paper on applicable law and jurisdiction in divorce matters, COM(2005) 82 final, 2.

[15] Commission, 14 March 2005, Green Paper on applicable law and jurisdiction in divorce matters, COM(2005) 82 final, 3.

[16] Commission, 17 July 2006, Proposal for a Council Regulation amending Regulation 2201/2003/EC as regards jurisdiction and introducing rules concerning applicable law in matrimonial matters, COM(2006) 399 final.

[17] Jan-Jaap Kuipers, 'The Law Applicable to Divorce as Test Ground for Enhanced Cooperation' (2012) 18 European Law Journal 201, 208 et seq.

[18] Boele-Woelki (n 9) 784.

Member States[19] were keen to pursue the harmonisation of the conflict of law rules further and thus started the legislative process under the enhanced cooperation procedure.[20] On 24 March 2010, the European Commission followed the request of the willing Member States[21] and submitted a proposal for a Council authorisation of enhanced cooperation.[22] The Council authorised enhanced cooperation by its decision on 12 July 2010,[23] after the European Parliament had granted its consent,[24] and only a few months later, the regulation was implemented between the participating Member States.[25]

Since the Rome III regulation entered into force, three Member States have joined the group—Lithuania, Greece, and Estonia—but there are still many which are not bound by the Rome III regulation and, as it seems today, it is quite unlikely that the situation is going to change in the near future.

2. Property Regimes for International Couples in Europe

A related issue to the conflict of law rules in the area of divorce and legal separation is the question of the applicable law in matters concerning matrimonial property regimes. In 2006, the European Commission issued a green paper on conflict of law rules concerning matrimonial property regimes.[26] The Green Paper highlighted that the implementation of the principle of mutual recognition of decisions relating to matrimonial property had been a priority on the Council's and Commission's agenda since 1998.[27] Despite various attempts to introduce the principle of mutual recognition, the Green Paper shows that further steps are necessary to overcome practical and legal difficulties which frequently occur when distributing and managing the property of a separated or divorced international couple.

[19] In the beginning, it was Austria, Greece, Hungary, Italy, Luxembourg, Romania, Slovenia, and Spain.

[20] Council of the European Union, 24 and 25 July 2008, Press Release of the 2887th Council meeting, Justice and Home Affairs, Brussels, 11653/08, 23.

[21] Greece, Spain, Italy, Hungary, Luxembourg, Austria, Romania, and Slovenia by letters dated 28 July 2008; Bulgaria by letter dated 12 August 2008, France by letter dated 12 January 2009. On 3 March 2010, Greece withdrew its request, but Germany joint the request by a letter dated 15 April 2010, Belgium by a letter dated 22 April 2010, Latvia by a letter dated 17 May 2010, Malta by a letter dated 31 May 2010, and Portugal joined the request during the Council meeting of 4 June 2010.

[22] Commission, 24 March 2010, Proposal for a Council decision authorising enhanced cooperation in the area of the law applicable to divorce and legal separation, COM(2010) 105 final.

[23] Council, 12 July 2010, 2010/405/EU, authorising enhanced cooperation in the area of the law applicable to divorce and legal separation, OJ, 22 July 2010, L 189, 12.

[24] European Parliament, 10 June 2010, on the draft Council decision authorising enhanced cooperation in the area of the law applicable to divorce and legal separation (09898/2010—C7-0145/2010—2010/0066(NLE)).

[25] Council, 20 December 2010, 1259/2010/EU, Regulation implementing enhanced cooperation in the area of the law applicable to divorce and legal separation, OJ, 29 December 2010, L 343, 10.

[26] Commission, 17 July 2006, Green Paper on conflict of laws in matters concerning matrimonial property regimes, including the question of jurisdiction and mutual recognition, COM(2006) 400 final.

[27] Action Plan of the Council and the Commission on how best to implement the provisions of the Treaty of Amsterdam on an area of freedom, security and justice, OJ, 23 January 1999, C 19, 1; see also Draft programme of measures for implementation of the principle of mutual recognition of decisions in civil and commercial matters, OJ, 15 January 2001, C 12, 1.

These problems are often triggered by the great disparity between both substantive law and private international law governing the property effects of marriage and other forms of unions in the Member States.[28]

For the European Commission, it was clear that the harmonisation of substantive law was not an option at the time, and thus, the Commission focused solely on the rules governing conflict of law. However, the Commission's work ultimately did not lead to a proposal for secondary EU law. The Commission only adopted proposals for a regulation on the jurisdiction, applicable law, and the recognition and enforcement of decisions in matters of property of international couples in 2011,[29] after further steps towards extending the principle of mutual recognition were undertaken.[30] During the meeting in December 2015, the Council concluded that a unanimous political agreement could not be established on the proposals relating to matrimonial property regimes and property consequences of registered partnerships.[31] Some Member States,[32] however, wished to pursue the legislative action further and thus issued a request to the Commission indicating their willingness to establish enhanced cooperation among them. The Commission followed the request,[33] and subsequently the European Parliament granted its consent,[34] and the Council authorised enhanced cooperation.[35] On 24 June 2016, the participating Member States were able to establish an agreement on both regulations.[36]

[28] Commission, 17 July 2006, Green Paper on conflict of laws in matters concerning matrimonial property regimes, including the question of jurisdiction and mutual recognition, COM(2006) 400 final, 4.

[29] Commission, 16 March 2011, Proposal for a Council regulation on jurisdiction, applicable law and the recognition and enforcement of decisions in matters of matrimonial property regimes, COM(2011) 126 final; Commission, 16 March 2011, Proposal for a Council regulation on jurisdiction, applicable law and the recognition and enforcement of decisions regarding the property consequences of registered partnerships, COM(2011) 127.

[30] The Stockholm Programme—An open and secure Europe serving and protecting citizens, OJ, 4 May 2010, C 115, 1.

[31] Council, 3 and 4 December 2015, Outcome of the 3433rd Council Meeting, Justice and Home Affairs, 14937/15, 5.

[32] Belgium, Bulgaria, the Czech Republic, Germany, Greece, Spain, France, Croatia Italy, Luxembourg, Malta, the Netherlands, Austria, Portugal, Slovenia, Finland, and Sweden.

[33] Commission, 2 March 2016, Proposal for a Council decision authorising enhanced cooperation in the area of jurisdiction, applicable law and the recognition and enforcement of decisions on the property regimes of international couples, covering both matters of matrimonial property regimes and the property consequences of registered partnerships, COM(2016) 108 final.

[34] European Parliament, 21 August 2013, on the proposal for a Council regulation on jurisdiction, applicable law and the recognition and enforcement of decisions in matters of matrimonial property regimes, A/-0253/2013; European Parliament 10 September 2013, Texts adopted, A7-0254/2013.

[35] Council, 9 June 2016, Decision authorising enhanced cooperation in the area of jurisdiction, applicable law and the recognition and enforcement of decisions on the property regimes of international couples, covering both matters of matrimonial property regimes and the property consequences of registered partnerships, OJ, 16 June 2016 L 159, 16.

[36] Regulation, 24 June 2016, 2016/1103/EU, implementing enhanced cooperation in the area of jurisdiction, applicable law and the recognition and [e]nforcement of decisions in matters of matrimonial property regimes, OJ, 8 July 2016, L 183, 1; Regulation, 24 June 2016, 2016/1104/EU, implementing enhanced cooperation in the area of jurisdiction, applicable law and the recognition and enforcement of decisions in matters of the property consequences of registered partnerships, OJ, 8 July 2016, L 183, 30.

II. The European Unitary Patent

1. Historical Developments

The idea of introducing a unitary patent within the EU legal framework arose within the Community when it only consisted of its six founding Member States. Soon after the Rome Treaty entered into force, it became clear that the existence of six national intellectual property rights systems was not consistent with the objectives of the European Economic Community. The individual systems of the Member States, each being restricted to the State's territorial borders, hindered the free movement of goods within the European internal market and, therefore, in addition to the dismantling of customs barriers and quotas, efforts also have to be made to remove national borders on property rights.[37] The first attempts to introduce a European patent can be dated back to the beginning of the 1960s, but the Member States at that time could not reach a consensus on which States should cooperate; either only the members of the European Community or all States which wished to join.[38] Over the years, several proposals for a European patent were launched; the major acts were proposed in 1975 (first community patent convention),[39] 1989 (second community patent convention),[40] 1997 (green paper on the Community patent),[41] 2000 (first proposal for a European patent regulation),[42] 2004 (second proposal for a European patent regulation),[43] and 2007 (European Commission's strategy paper)[44].[45] Despite many attempts to find a European answer to securing intellectual property rights, no initiative received the approval of all the Member States, and thus none of these proposals entered into force. What seems striking is that the Member States did not fundamentally disagree on the core features of patent law. Instead, they disagreed over formal issues such as language requirements, the relationship between the unitary patent and the national rights, and the court enforcement structure.[46]

[37] Friedrich-Karl Beier, 'Stand und Aussichten der europäischen Rechtsvereinheitlichung auf dem Gebiete des gewerblichen Rechtsschutzes' (1969) Gewerblicher Rechtsschutz und Urheberrecht Internationaler Teil 145, 145–46.

[38] Justine Pila, 'The European Patent: An Old and Vexing' (2013) 62 International & Comparative Law Quarterly 917, 918 et seq.

[39] Convention for the European patent for the common market, 76/76/EEC, OJ, 26 January 1976, L 17, 1.

[40] Council, 15 December 1989, Agreement relating to community patents, 89/695/EEC, OJ, 30 December 1989, L 401, 1.

[41] Commission, 24 June 1997, Promoting innovation through patents—Green Paper on the Community patent and the patent system in Europe, COM(1997) 314 final.

[42] Commission, 28 November 2000, Proposal for a Council Regulation on the Community patent, OJ, 28 November 2000, C 337E, 278.

[43] Commission, Proposal for a Council regulation on the Community patent, Annex I to the Council of the European Union document, 8 March 2004, 7119/04.

[44] Commission, 3 April 2007, Enhancing the patent system in Europe, COM(2007) 165 final.

[45] See for more details Thomas Jaeger, 'The EU Patent: Cui Bono et Quo Vadit?' (2010) 47 Common Market Law Review 63, 63–64.

[46] ibid 64.

Since the Member States could not agree on a unitary patent, they were stuck with an inefficient and costly multi-layered system.[47] Protection was provided through national laws; however, the framework of the European Patent Convention made it easier to receive protection in multiple Member States. A European patent, under the European Patent Convention, is a bundle of national rights, and only facilitates the validation in each Member State.[48] It became quite obvious that the European patent framework showed severe competitive disadvantages for the European technology-related businesses,[49] because protection in all Member States was quite expensive,[50] in particular compared with the US patent.[51] Despite the general acceptance that innovation cannot possibly flourish without sufficient protections, the Member States could not agree on a Community patent which would exist alongside the national systems and the system introduced by the European Patent Convention. Even numerous amendments to the first proposal did not lead to success. In the end, there were two main factors which prevented a unanimous vote on the European patent: the translation arrangement and the judicial system.[52] Concerning the former, the Member States could not agree on the number of languages into which the patent specifications would have to be translated. The majority was in favour of the working languages of the European Patent Office, namely English, French, and German. However, Spain and Italy favoured the official languages of the Office of Harmonization for the Internal Market, namely German, English, French, Italian, and Spanish. To facilitate the negotiation process, the EU patent was split into two separate regulations, one addressing the translation arrangements only, but both should enter jointly into force.

During the Council meeting in December 2010, it was confirmed that a unanimous vote on the European patent could not be reached, not then and not in the foreseeable future, and thus the only way forward would be to align those Member States which could agree on the European Commission's proposal for a unitary

[47] Hanns Ullrich, 'Patent Protection in Europe: Integrating Europe into the Community or the Community into Europe?' (2002) 8 European Law Journal 433, 435.

[48] Matthias Lamping, 'Enhanced Cooperation—A Proper Approach to Market Integration in the Field of Unitary Patent Protection?' (2011) 42 International Review of Intellectual Property and Competition Law 879, 899–900.

[49] As early as 1995, the Commission issued a green paper on innovation which aimed at a genuine European strategy for the promotion of innovation. It became clear that Europe has an excellent scientific base but is still less successful than the other regions in the world at converting existing skills into new products, especially in the high-technology sector: Commission, 20 December 1995, Green Paper on Innovation, COM(1995) 688 final.

[50] For a linking of innovation and patent protection, see Commission, 24 June 1997, Promoting innovation through patents—Green Paper on the Community patent and the patent system in Europe, COM(1997) 314 final.

[51] Enrico Bonadio, 'The EU Embraces Enhanced Cooperation in Patent Matters: Towards A Unitary Patent Protection System' (2011) 2 European Journal of Risk Regulation 416, 416.

[52] Matthias Lamping, 'Enhanced Cooperation—A Proper Approach to Market Integration in the Field of Unitary Patent Protection?' (2011) 42 International Review of Intellectual Property and Competition Law 879, 900.

patent through the use of the enhanced cooperation procedure.[53] In that vein, the willing delegates asked the Commission to prepare a proposal for a unitary patent introduced under the enhanced cooperation procedure.

On 14 December 2010, the European Commission submitted a proposal for a Council decision, authorising enhanced cooperation in the area of the creation of unitary patent protection.[54] The European Parliament gave its consent for a common European patent to be created under the enhanced cooperation procedure in February 2011,[55] and the Council authorised enhanced cooperation on the 10 March 2011.[56] Based on the authorisation of both the Council and the European Parliament, the Commission issued a proposal for a regulation implementing enhanced cooperation in the area of the creation of unitary patent protection on 13 April 2011.[57] The Commission's proposal relied on its previous work on a unitary patent within the entire European Union, its main feature being its unitary effect. Accordingly, the 'unitary patent should be of autonomous nature and provide equal protection throughout the territories of the participating Member States. It may only be granted, transferred, revoked or may lapse in respect of those territories as a whole.'[58] Concerning the language issues, the 'unitary effect should be granted only in one of the official languages of the EPO [European Patent Office]'[59].

On 27 June 2011, the participating Member States reached an agreement on the European patent. Commissioner Michel Barnier and Minister of States Zoltán Cséfalvay called the agreement 'a crucial step in improving the European patent system'.[60] In the end, all Member States except for Italy and Spain joined enhanced cooperation and agreed on the two regulations for implementing a unitary patent system. In 2016, Italy joined enhanced cooperation. Since Croatia did not join enhanced cooperation after becoming a member of the European Union, there are still two non-participating Member States: Spain and Croatia.

In light of the time needed to implement the unitary patent based on the enhanced cooperation procedure, the application of enhanced cooperation was quite a success. In December 2010, it was found that an agreement between all the

[53] Council, 10 December 2010, 3057th Council meeting, Competitiveness (Internal Market, Industry, Research and Space), press release, 17668/10.

[54] Commission, 14 December 2010, a proposal for a Council decision authorising enhanced cooperation in the area of the creation of unitary patent protection, COM(2010) 790 final.

[55] European Parliament, EU patent: Parliament gives go-ahead for enhanced cooperation, press release, 15 February 2011.

[56] Council, 10 March 2011, 2011/167/EU, authorising enhanced cooperation in the area of the creation of unitary patent protection, OJ, 22 March 2011, L 76, 53.

[57] Commission, 13 April 2011, Proposal for a regulation of the European Parliament and of the Council implementing enhanced cooperation in the area of the creation of unitary patent protection, COM(2011) 215 final.

[58] ibid 6.

[59] ibid 21.

[60] Press release, 27 June 2011, MEMO11/463.

Member States is not likely to be achieved, and thus any further legislative attempts should be based on the enhanced cooperation procedure. Only a few months later, the group reached a compromise and was able to enact two regulations. The story of the unitary patent is quite common at the European legislative level: a majority of Member States can agree on a legislative approach but a few are unwilling to give up their policy agenda (either for protectionist or legitimate reasons), and thus block the entire legislative move at EU level.

2. Resistance of Non-participating Member States

The non-participating Member States, Italy and Spain, felt that their rights were affected by the joint initiative under the umbrella of the enhanced cooperation procedure so they brought an action before the Court of Justice of the European Union (CJEU), which can be summarised in five legal arguments. It was claimed first that the Council lacked the competence to establish enhanced cooperation in the area of unitary patent; second, that power had been misused; third, that conditions for the decision to authorise enhanced cooperation had been breached, in particular, the requirement of last resort; fourth that Art 20 Subsection 1 of the TEU, Art 118 of the TFEU, Art 326 of the TFEU, and Art 327 of the TFEU had been infringed; and fifth, that the European Union's judicial system had been disregarded.[61]

The Court rejected all claims raised by Italy and Spain that doubted the legitimacy of the Council's authorisation decision. At first, the CJEU ruled on the competence framework and found that the Council had the competence to authorise enhanced cooperation because the unitary patent falls within the scope of the competences shared between the European Union and the Member States, and subsequently does not form part of the EU's exclusive competence framework.[62]

Secondly, and more importantly for present purposes, the Court ruled that the Council has not misused its power by circumventing the requirement of unanimity required by Art 118 of the TFEU. Enhanced cooperation cannot only be established as a last resort if one Member State declares that it is not yet ready for the proposed measure. As provided by Art 20 Subsection 2 of the TEU, 'the situation that may lawfully lead to enhanced cooperation is that in which "the objectives of such cooperation cannot be attained within a reasonable period by the Union as a whole"'. The impossibility needed to switch to the path of enhanced cooperation is not explicitly defined by the European treaties and thus can stem from some Member States' lack of interest or inability to participate.[63]

Thirdly, the Court had to rule on the requirement of last resort, which, according to the CJEU, can best be determined by the Council.[64] The use of the enhanced

[61] CJEU, 16 April 2013, C-271/11 and C-295/11, *Kingdom of Spain v Council*, ECLI:EU:C:2013:240, para 9.

[62] ibid paras 25–26.

[63] ibid para 36.

[64] ibid para 53.

cooperation procedure may not be legitimate if the Member States have demonstrated a willingness to compromise and reach an agreement between all the Member States in the foreseeable future.[65]

Fourthly, the CJEU rejected the claim that the enhanced cooperation did not create a higher level of integration compared with the current situation. The European patent, which is based on the European Patent Convention, does not confer uniform protection on the participating States. In contrast, the unitary patent under enhanced cooperation would confer uniform protection in the territory of all participating Member States, and thus enhances the status quo.[66]

Further to the point of the legal requirements set by the European treaties, the Court could not find any reasons why the competences, rights, or obligations of the non-participating Member States should be infringed by the enhanced cooperation.[67] Finally, the information on the content of the enhanced cooperation provided by the Council was sufficient,[68] it is thus not the task of the Council to describe every detail of the law to be enacted by the enhanced cooperation procedure.

Two observations emerge from this. First, the non-participating Member States may be easily offended by the use of the enhanced cooperation procedure because it excludes them and allows the other Member States to pursue their common policy objective jointly. The fear of exclusion may encourage the non-participating Member States to fight against the law introduced under the enhanced cooperation procedure before the CJEU.[69]

Secondly, the ruling of the Court indicates that the Court wants to give the enhanced cooperation procedure a fighting chance. The CJEU granted the Council broad discretion in deciding whether or not enhanced cooperation would be a measure of last resort. The Court would only review whether the Council has seriously considered all the facts and has put enough thought into its decision. With regard to the integration progress, the Court rightly did not address the relationship between integration and differentiation following on from the use of the enhanced cooperation procedure. As already proposed above,[70] the fact that the enhanced cooperation procedure has been introduced into the European treaties is a clear manifestation of the EU's choice in allowing a differentiated integration model. Thus, the fact that enhanced cooperation establishes differentiation cannot possibly be challenged with regard to the negative impact on integration. A lack of integration progress could only follow from the substantive law introduced by the enhanced cooperation procedure. In the case of the unitary patent, however, it

[65] ibid.
[66] ibid paras 62–63.
[67] ibid paras 82–83.
[68] ibid para 92.
[69] The question of how the rights and interests of non-participating Member States are best protected to avoid fights before the CJEU is in particular subject to Chapter 4.
[70] See Chapter 1, subsection B.

achieves a definite step forward because it establishes unitary protection in all the participating Member States, a legal situation which could not possibly be reached under the existing law. Therefore, the CJEU did not hesitate to characterise enhanced cooperation law in the field of the unitary patent as a boost to integration and thus compliant with the requirements set by the European treaties.

III. European Public Prosecutor

The Lisbon Treaty introduced the possibility of establishing a European public prosecutor to combat crimes affecting the financial interests of the European Union into the European legal framework.[71] Prosecuting offences against the EU's budget rests on the competence of the Member States,[72] but the European Commission witnessed that, despite the significant damage of these offences, they are not always investigated and prosecuted properly by the national authorities. To overcome the lack of institutional background and to allow law enforcement also in cross-border settings, the Commission issued a proposal for the establishment of the European Public Prosecutor's Office in 2013.[73]

The proposal aimed to vest the European Public Prosecutor's Office with the mandate to investigate, prosecute, and bring to justice the perpetrators of offences against the EU's financial interests.[74] The European Public Prosecutor's Office was supposed to operate as a single office across all Member States combining European and national law enforcement efforts. Despite the lack of a specialised prosecution office at the European level which is explicitly committed to protecting the budgetary interests of the European Union, and fight offences such as cross-border VAT fraud, the Member States were not all in favour of such a European institution vested with such wide competences.

At the meetings of the Working Party on Cooperation in Criminal Matters, it became evident that most delegations seemed to support the principle of establishing a European Public Prosecutor's Office, 'but have raised many questions and concerns regarding various aspects of the proposal'.[75] In that vein, the Council

[71] Art 86 section 1 of the TFEU; Katalin Ligeti and Michele Simonato, 'The European Public Prosecutor's Office: Towards a Truly European Prosecution Service?' (2013) 4 New Journal of European Criminal Law 7, 7 et seq. Ladislav Hamran and Eva Szabova, 'European Public Prosecutor's Office—Cui Bono? The Future of Prosecution after Lisbon' (2013) 4 New Journal of European Criminal Law 40, 41 et seq.

[72] The European Union has no power in the area of criminal law.

[73] Commission, 17 July 2013, Proposal for a Council Regulation on the establishment of the European Public Prosecutor's Office, COM(2013) 534 final.

[74] ibid recital 7.

[75] Council, 7 February 2014, Legal service contribution, 6267/14, 3. Despite the concerns several Member States raised concerning the regulation for a European Public Prosecutor's Office, the United Kingdom, Ireland, and Denmark did not want to opt in, and thus, they wished to not take part in the adoption and application of the regulation on the European Public Prosecutor's Office; for the opt-out and opt-in regime of the United Kingdom, Ireland, and Denmark see Chapter 2, subsection A.II.

registered the absence of unanimity in support of the European Commission's proposal for a European Public Prosecutor's Office during its meeting in February 2017.[76] In contrast to other provisions in the European treaties, Art 86 of the Treaty on the Functioning of the European Union (TFEU) explicitly provides for a procedure to be followed if unanimity cannot be reached in the Council. In the absence of unanimity in the Council, a group of Member States can request to refer the draft regulation to the European Council. If the discussions in the European Council do not achieve consent among all the Member States, Art 86 of the TFEU explicitly offers willing Member States the possibility of establishing enhanced cooperation based on the draft regulation. If the willing Member States wish to do so, they shall notify the European Parliament, the Council, and the Commission. 'In such a case, the authorisation to proceed with enhanced cooperation referred to in [the European treaties] shall be deemed to be granted and the provisions on the enhanced cooperation shall apply.'

Following the procedural framework, seventeen Member States requested that the draft regulation be referred to the European Council on 14 February 2017.[77] Intense discussion on that matter in the European Council also failed to establish an agreement between all Member States, and thus the willing Member States notified the European Parliament, the European Commission, and the Council that they were eager to pursue the matter further under enhanced cooperation. A few months later, the participating Member States agreed on the regulation and established the European Public Prosecutor's Office amongst them.[78]

B. Experience of Failure

The use of the enhanced cooperation procedure has, however, not always been a success. On the one hand, there are several cases in which the use of the enhanced cooperation procedure has been proposed along the lines of the legislative negotiation process, but enhanced cooperation has never been established. On the other hand, there are legislative proposals which did not become secondary EU law, but the alternative route of enhanced cooperation has not been brought forward at all. The following subsections focus on three legislative failures: the European Foundation (see subsection I), secondary EU law on passenger car-related taxes (see subsection II), and procedural rights in criminal proceedings (see subsection III). All three legislative actions failed due to a blocking minority in the Council,

[76] Council, 7 February 2017, Outcome of the 3517th Council meeting, General Affairs, 6035/17, 6.

[77] Regulation, 12 October 2017, 2017/1939/EU, implementing enhanced cooperation on the establishment of the European Public Prosecutor's Office, OJ, 31 October 2017, L 283, 1, recital 6.

[78] Currently, the enhanced cooperation consists of twenty-two Member States: Belgium, Bulgaria, Czech Republic, Germany, Estonia, Greece, Spain, France, Croatia, Italy, Cyprus, Latvia, Lithuania, Luxembourg, Malta, the Netherlands, Austria, Portugal, Romania, Slovenia, Slovakia, and Finland.

and they were not the subject of enhanced cooperation, although the use of the European flexibility mechanism has explicitly been proposed. Aside from these three explicit legislative failures, the Common Consolidated Corporate Tax Base (CCCTB), which has also been a candidate for enhanced cooperation, becomes a tool for combatting base erosion and profit shifting, and such an understanding of the CCCTB may render it unsuitable for enhanced cooperation (see subsection IV).

I. The European Foundation

National foundations play an essential role in the EU's civil society. Their activities contribute to the fundamental values and objectives of the European Union, such as 'the respect for human rights, the protection of minorities, employment and social progress, protection and improvement of the environment or the promotion of scientific and technological advances'.[79] Despite the importance of national foundations, they face serious problems when they engage in cross-border operations. Differences between Member State laws not only arise when it comes to the non-profit character of the entity but also when the channelling of funds in a cross-border setting is characterised by difficulties due to different national regimes. The European Commission explicitly revealed that 'foundations have to spend part of the resources they collect on legal advice and fulfilling legal and administrative requirements laid down by the different national laws'.[80] Against this background, the Commission proposed the introduction of a legal statute for a European foundation.[81] This new European legal form intends to facilitate foundations operating on the (entire) European internal market, by allowing them to channel their funds more efficiently, and thus use their private funds for public benefit purposes.

Another substantial problem concerning foundations operating on a cross-border basis is their tax treatment within each single Member State. Traditionally, national foundations, as well as their beneficiaries, are subject to beneficial tax treatment, for example in the form of tax exemptions (mostly restricted to non-profit organisations), preferential tax rates, or simplified tax regimes.[82] From the beginning, it was clear that it would be impossible to find a common ground between the Member States to harmonise the tax treatment of both national foundations and the proposed European foundation. The lack of European harmonisation should, however, not put a European foundation in a worse position. Thus, the European

[79] Commission, 8 February 2012, Proposal for a Council Regulation on the Statute for a European Foundation, COM(2012) 35 final.
[80] ibid 3.
[81] ibid.
[82] See for a comparative study Sabine Heidenbauer, *Charity Crossing Borders: The Fundamental Freedoms' Influence on Charity and Donor Taxation in Europe* (Kluwer Law International 2011) 7 et seq.

Commission proposed a rather simple yet effective way to allow the new legal form to benefit from beneficial national regimes, but without having to harmonise these rules. Art 49 of the Commission's proposal required that any European foundation should be subject to the same tax treatment as any foundation established in that Member State. Likewise, the tax treatment of donors to the European foundation (Art 50 of the proposal), and the beneficiaries of the European foundation (Art 51 of the proposal), should be the same as the treatment of donors and beneficiaries of a domestic foundation.

The proposal for a European foundation was subject to drawn-out discussions and compromises. In the end, however, the initiative failed because eight Member States—namely Austria, Denmark, Estonia, Germany, the Netherlands, Portugal, Slovakia, and the United Kingdom—rejected the draft. The entire proposal was based on Art 352 of the TFEU, which allows the European Union to supplement competences if an action by the European Union is necessary within the framework of the European treaties' policies. However, the widening of the competence framework demands a unanimous action by the Council. Since it seemed impossible to reach an agreement between all the Member States, the European Commission withdrew the proposal in 2015, acknowledging that 'there are no prospects that an agreement can be reached'.[83]

The scenario described is not an unfamiliar or particularly unusual one; some Member States do not share the same beliefs or have different policy objectives, and thus the necessary consent at the European level cannot be reached. What was, however, striking was that when it was foreseeable that not all the Member States would agree on the proposal for the European foundation, one member of the European Parliament, Mr Pascual de Grandes, highlighted the possibility of using the enhanced cooperation procedure as an alternative way to give the European foundation a fighting chance.[84] This initiative was supported by other members of the European Parliament but never paved the way towards an initiative driven by the Member States.

The use of the enhanced cooperation procedure for establishing a new legal form would not have been an entirely bad idea. Of course, the benefits that the European foundation is supposed to provide would be restricted to the territory of the participating Member States. It would, however, provide an alternative to national foundations, and it would ease the foundation's activity in all intra-group settings. Thus, a European foundation enacted under the enhanced

[83] Commission, 16 December 2014, Annex 2 to the Communication from the Commission to the European Parliament, the Council, the European Economic and Social Committee and the Committee of the Regions, Commission Work Programme 2015, COM(2014) 910, 12; see also Withdrawal of Commission Proposals, OJ, 7 March 2015, C 80, 21.

[84] General Secretariat of the Council, 9 December 2014, Summary record of the meeting of the European Parliament Committee on Legal Affairs, 16715/14, 2.

cooperation procedure would have been an enrichment of foundation law in Europe.[85]

One reason why the Member States may have been hesitant to pursue the European foundation under the enhanced cooperation procedure may have been the European Union's lacking competence in that field. Any legislative act establishing a new legal form could only be based on Art 352 of the TFEU, which would extend the EU's competence for a particular legal act which—due to its nature—has to be performed at the European level. Whether the requirement set by Art 352 of the TFEU would be met if not all of the Member States were bound by the act, but instead only a group of participating Member States, may be highly doubted.[86]

II. Passenger Car-related Taxes

The European Commission's proposal for a directive on passenger car-related taxes[87] is another example of a legislative attempt at the European level which never made it into hard law but which could have taken the alternative way—the enhanced cooperation procedure—to overcome blocking minorities in the Council. The proposal aimed to harmonise the different national tax systems for passenger cars within the European Union. The Commission found that the various national regimes resulted in 'tax obstacles such as double taxation, tax-induced cross-border transfer of cars, distortions and inefficiencies, which impede the proper functioning of the Internal Market'.[88] Additionally, passenger car-related taxes are 'one of the three pillars of the Community's strategy to reduce CO_2 emissions'[89] to meet the standards set by the Kyoto Protocol.[90] A harmonised European approach to passenger car-related tax should ensure the optimal use of the fiscal measure to steer the taxpayer's behaviour towards a more environmentally friendly use of resources. The Commission's proposal for passenger related taxes was therefore twofold: on the one hand, the common approach aimed to improve the functioning of

[85] Stefanie Jung, 'Need for a New Approach in European Company Law?—The European Foundation as a Turning Point' (2015) 21 Trusts & Trustees 625, 629.

[86] With regard to other (shared) competence clauses, a reference to the entire European Union (eg the expressions 'throughout the Union' and 'Union-wide' used in Article 118 TFEU) does not prohibit enhanced cooperation, CJEU, 16 April 2013, C-274/11 and C-295/11, *Spain and Italy v Council*, ECLI:EU:C:2013:240, para 68; see also Anzhela Cédelle, 'Enhanced Cooperation: A Way Forward for Tax Harmonization in the European Union?' in Joachim Englisch (ed), *International Tax Law: New Challenges to and from Constitutional and Legal Pluralism* (IBFD 2016) 196, 181 et seq.

[87] Commission, 5 July 2005, Proposal for a Council Directive on passenger car related taxes, COM(2005) 261 final.

[88] ibid 2.

[89] ibid.

[90] Commission, 20 December 1995, Communication from the Commission to the Council and the European Parliament, A Community strategy to reduce CO_2 emissions from passenger cars and improve fuel economy, COM(1995) 689.

the European internal market, and, on the other hand, the harmonised tax measure was part of a strategy to reduce CO_2 emissions.

The proposal required an elimination of national registration taxes, which would have had a severe impact on the budget of some Member States. To smooth the process, it was proposed to reduce these taxes gradually and to compensate the budgetary losses from other sources, such as an annual circulation tax. Although the proposal was supposed to be revenue neutral, Member States could not agree on the terms of this directive.

In light of the lack of consensus between the Member States, the Rapporteur for the European Parliament, Karin Riss-Jørgensen, proposed that 'the countries favouring the Commission's proposal in question should proceed with the enhanced cooperation procedure, according to Arts 43–45 of the Treaty'.[91]

Instead of overcoming the legislative deadlock by using the enhanced cooperation procedure, as proposed by Rapporteur Karin Riss-Jørgensen, the initiative was abandoned without any reference as to why the alternative route of enhanced cooperation was not a suitable way to progress. It is beyond doubt that a directive binding all Member States would have been more efficient concerning the functioning of the internal market and the aim to reduce CO_2 emissions. However, an agreement on coordinated action between some Member States would have been a step in the right direction by addressing the issues at least within enhanced cooperation.

III. Procedural Rights in Criminal Proceedings

In 2004, the European Commission issued a proposal to set minimum standards for certain procedural rights in criminal law proceedings among the Member States.[92] The proposal stated that fundamental rights should be respected as guaranteed by the European Convention for the Protection of Human Rights and Fundamental Freedoms (ECHR), and as a result of the constitutional traditions of the Member States, and as safeguarded by the Charter of Fundamental Rights of the European Union. Since mutual recognition of judgments should be a core principle within the European Union, it was necessary to safeguard minimum standards of protection in every Member State. The proposal was subject to intense discussion but an agreement on particular issues such as 'whether to adopt a Framework Decision or a non-binding instrument', and how to avoid the 'risk of developing conflicting

[91] European Parliament, 10 July 2006, on the proposal for a Council directive on passenger car-related taxes, A6-0240/2006, Rapporteur's position. European Parliament Report on the proposal of a Council directive on passenger car related taxes, A6-0240/2006.

[92] Commission, 28 April 2004, Proposal for a Council framework decision on certain procedural rights in criminal proceedings throughout the European Union, COM(2004) 328 final.

jurisdictions with the European Court of Human Rights', could not be reached.[93] Ireland, the United Kingdom, Malta, Slovakia, the Czech Republic, and Cyprus believed that the European Convention for Human Rights would be a sufficient legal instrument to ensure the protection of fundamental rights in criminal proceedings within the Member States.[94] Due to the lack of consensus between the Member States, the French delegation indicated that it was in favour of launching enhanced cooperation during the Council's meeting in September 2007.[95] Despite the ambitious attempt to go ahead with enhanced cooperation, the Member States agreed on a step-by-step approach for implementing minimum standards in criminal proceedings.[96]

IV. The Common Consolidated Corporate Tax Base

In 2001, the European Commission announced a 'strategy for providing companies with a consolidated corporate tax base for their EU-wide activities'[97] intended to lead towards an internal market without tax obstacles.[98] The Commission's early work shows that the initial intent for introducing a CCCTB was to allow companies to take full advantage of the European internal market and to enable the European internal market to compete against the US and the Japanese market.[99] In light of the differing national rules and experiences, it became clear that a compromise between all Member States would be hard to reach, and thus the Commission proposed 'the possibility for an enhanced cooperation for the introduction of the Common Corporate Tax base'.[100]

[93] Council, 4 and 5 December 2006, 2768th Council Meeting, Justice and Home Affairs, press release, 15801/06, 12.

[94] Wolfgang Wagner, 'Negative and Positive Integration in EU Criminal Law Co-Operation' (2011) 15 European Integration Online Papers 15; Mar Jimeno-Bulnes, 'The Proposal for a Council Framework Decision on Certain Procedural Rights in Criminal Proceedings throughout the European Union' in Elspeth Guild and Florian Geyer (eds), *Security Versus Justice? Police and Judicial Cooperation in the European Union* (Ashgate Publishing, Ltd 2008) 172.

[95] Council, 12 and 13 September 2007, 2807th meeting of the Council of the European Union, Justice and Home Affairs, 10699/07, 12.

[96] Resolution, 30 November 2009, on a Roadmap for strengthening procedural rights of suspected or accused persons in criminal proceedings, OJ, 4 December 2009, C 295, 1; see also Daniela A Kroll and Dirk Leuffen, 'Enhanced Cooperation in Practice. An Analysis of Differentiated Integration in EU Secondary Law' (2015) 22 Journal of European Public Policy 353, 365.

[97] Commission, 23 October 2001, COM(2001) 582 final.

[98] For a historical overview of trade obstacles imposed by tax laws and the possibility of fighting these obstacles through a CCCTB see Michel Aujean, 'The CCCTB Project and the Future of European Taxation' in Michael Lang and others (eds), *Common Consolidated Corporate Tax Base* (Linde Verlag 2008).

[99] Commission, 7 July 2004, Commission Non-Paper to informal Ecofin Council, 10 and 11 September 2004, A Common Consolidated EU Corporate Tax Base.

[100] Ibid 4; Commission, 23 October 2001, COM(2001) 582 final, 17. See also Charles E McLure Jr, 'Legislative, Judicial, Soft Law, and Cooperative Approaches to Harmonizing Corporate Income Taxes in the US and the EU' (2007) 14 Columbia Journal of European Law 377, 414 et seq. Christiana Panayi, *European Union Corporate Tax Law* (CUP 2013) 81 et seq. Luca Cerioni, *European Union and Direct*

After a decade of preparatory work, the European Commission issued a proposal for a Directive on a CCCTB.[101] The key vision of the proposal was 'to serve the needs of companies that operate across borders'.[102] In concrete terms, the CCCTB aimed to reduce administrative burdens and tax compliance costs for European companies by way of introducing a 'one-stop-shop' principle which would allow companies to apply a single set of tax rules across the European Union and deal with only one tax administration.[103] However, the proposed secondary EU law initially failed due to lack of compromise between Member States.

In light of the Base Erosion and Profit-Shifting (BEPS) discussion, the European Commission relaunched the CCCTB project in October 2016. The relaunch offers a two-step process. At first, the Member States should introduce a common corporate tax base and only at a second step should consolidation be put in place (i.e. C(C)CTB). 'In methodology and rationale, the "reload" process, however, remarkably deviates compared to the one adopted earlier.'[104] The new proposal predominantly focuses on fairness, transparency, and anti-avoidance,[105] and thus should be the main mechanism to prevent base erosion and profit shifting within the European Union.[106] If the C(C)CTB forms a tool to fight both aggressive tax planning of multinational companies and harmful tax competition within the European Union, it no longer makes sense to restrict the scope of the C(C)CTB to the willing Member States. Such an understanding of the C(C)CTB demands secondary EU law legislation which binds all Member States, which is why enhanced cooperation is no longer discussed as an alternative route for a C(C)CTB.

Taxation: A Solution for a Difficult Relationship (Routledge 2015) 215 et seq. Luca Cerioni, 'The Possible Introduction of Common Consolidated Base Taxation via Enhanced Cooperation: Some Open Issues' (2006) 46 European Taxation 187.

[101] Commission, 16 March 2011, Proposal for a Council Directive on a Common Consolidated Corporate Tax Base (CCCTB), COM(2011) 121/4 final.

[102] Recital 8, of the proposal, COM(2011) 121/4 final.

[103] COM(2011) 121/4 final, 5; 'making business easier and cheaper', Press release 16 March 2011, IP/11/319; see also Eric CCM Kemmeren, 'CCCTB: Enhanced Speed Ahead for Improvement' (2011) 20 EC Tax Review 208; Johanna Hey, 'CCCTB—Optionality' in Michael Lang and others (eds), *Common Consolidated Corporate Tax Base* (Linde Verlag 2008) 95 et seq.

[104] Shafi U Khan Niazi, 'Re-Launch of the Proposal for a Common Consolidated Corporate Tax Base (CCCTB) in the EU: A Shift in Paradigm' (2017) 44 Legal Issues of Economic Integration 293, 301.

[105] 'Alongside the anti-tax avoidance function of the CCCTB, the re-launched project would *also* retain its features as a corporate tax system which facilitates cross-border trade and investment in the internal market' (emphasis added), Commission, 25 October 2016, Proposal for a Council Directive on a Common Corporate Tax Base, COM(2011) 685 final, 2. See also Jan Lambertus van de Streek, 'Some Introductory Remarks on the Relaunched CCTB/CCCTB Proposals from a Policy Perspective' in Dennis Weber and Jan Lambertus van de Streek (eds), *The EU Common Consolidated Corporate Tax Base: Critical Analysis* (Kluwer Law International 2018) 4 et seq.

[106] Maarten Floris de Wilde, 'The CCCTB Relaunch: A Critical Assessment and Some Suggestions for Modification' in Pasquale Pistone (ed), *European Tax Integration: Law, Policy and Politics* (IBFD 2018) 38.

C. The European Financial Transaction Tax—Success or Failure?

Today, it is not possible to tell exactly whether the story of the financial transaction tax (FTT) will turn out to be a success or a failure. The current path, however, points to failure; time will tell whether the tide turns.

I. Historical Developments

The story of the European tax on financial transactions begins in the aftermath of the latest financial crisis. In September 2011, the European Commission issued a proposal for a common FTT.[107] According to the explanatory memorandum of the proposal, the common FTT is supposed to facilitate three main objectives. First, the tax should make financial institutions contribute 'more fairly' to the costs of dealing with the last financial crisis. It has been claimed that the financial sector does not provide a fair contribution to covering the costs because of the 'under-taxation of the sector'.[108] Secondly, the common FTT should complement the European regulatory framework and thus steer taxpayers towards less risky behaviour in the financial market.[109] The Commission revealed that some Member States had already taken measures to implement such a tax on a unilateral basis, resulting in distortions in the European internal market. Thus, a common approach would, thirdly, achieve a common level playing field between all financial operators on the European internal market.

As the European Commission's impact assessment shows, there are many ways of levying a tax on financial transactions. The design of a tax on financial transactions is particularly critical because of the transactions' high mobility, and thus the tax's locational effects. To prevent such effects, the Commission explicitly rejected current existing approaches, such as the British stamp duty, which imposes a tax liability on the transfer of securities of British companies, and the Swedish transaction tax, which applies to 'all equity security trades in Sweden using local brokerage services as well as to stock options'.[110] The Commission's proposal aimed for a tax which applies to 'all financial transactions, on the condition that at least one party to the

[107] Commission, 28 September 2011, Proposal for a Council Directive on a common system of financial transaction tax an amending Directive 2008/7/EC, COM(2011) 594.

[108] ibid 2.

[109] For a detailed analysis of the interplay between the proposed financial transaction tax and the European regulatory framework see Caroline Heber and Christian Sternberg, 'Over-the-Counter Derivative Markets in the Light of EMIR Clearing Obligations and the Financial Transaction Tax' (2014) 16 Derivatives & Financial Instruments 107; Caroline Heber and Christian Sternberg, 'Market Infrastructure Regulation and the Financial Transaction Tax' (2016) 8 World Tax Journal 3.

[110] European Commission, 'Impact Assessment Vol. 1—Proposal for a Council Directive on a Common System of Financial Transaction Tax and Amending Directive 2008/7/EC' (2011) SEC(2011) 1102 final 18.

transaction is established in a Member State'.[111] The proposal defines financial transactions in its widest possible sense, including, for example, the purchase and sale of financial instruments, the conclusion of derivatives, and the exchange of financial instruments.[112] The key question within the proposed regime concerns who is established within the territory of a Member State, which is addressed by Art 3 of the Commission's proposal. According to this provision, a financial institution is deemed to be established in the territory of a Member State where (a) it has been authorised by the authorities of that Member State to act as such; (b) it has its registered seat within that Member State; (c) its permanent address or its usual residence is located in that Member State; (d) it has a branch within that Member State; or (e) it is party to a financial transaction with another financial institution established in the territory of that Member State according to one of the previous criteria (counter-party principle). If a financial institution fulfils more than one listed criterion, the first condition fulfilled from the start of the list in descending order shall be relevant for determining the establishment. The proposal also provides for an escape clause, according to which a financial institution shall not be deemed to be established in the territory of a Member State if it provides that there is 'no link between the economic substance of the transaction and the territory of any (participating)[113] Member State'.[114]

The European Commission's proposal uses a far-reaching concept of establishment which is built upon the residence principle and the place of transaction principle.[115] Broadening the tax base is one part of the anti-relocation measures implemented as part of the Commission's proposal. A very low tax rate, taxing both ends of the transaction, and taxation of all financial transactions in financial instruments, in which one party fulfils the criteria of being established, are additional measures to minimise the risk of tax avoidance. During negotiations in the Council, it also became apparent that the Member States' views on a tax on financial transactions were very different. Some Member States felt that the anti-relocation features of the proposal were not powerful enough and they therefore feared massive relocation effects. Others were afraid that a tax on financial transactions would trigger negative knock-on effects on the efficiency of the financial market, but also on the non-financial part of the economy, and on overall growth. Other Member States were in favour of purely national measures with or even without any coordination between the Member States; and some might have accepted a common European approach, but only if the tax had a much narrower scope.[116]

[111] Art 1 Subsection 2 of the proposal COM(2011) 594 final.
[112] Art 2 Subsection 1 Nr. 1 of the Proposal COM(2011) 594 final.
[113] Art 4 Subsection 3 of the proposal COM(2013) 71 final.
[114] Art 3 Subsection 3 of the proposal COM(2011) 594 final.
[115] Joachim Englisch, John Vella, and Anzhela Cédelle, 'The Financial Transaction Tax Proposal under the Enhanced Cooperation Procedure: Legal and Practical Considerations' (2013) British Tax Review 223, 236.
[116] See for more details Commission, 14 February 2013, Commission Staff Working Document, Impact Assessment, COM(2013) 71 final, 9.

The whole initiative for a common tax on financial transactions was based on Art 113 of the TFEU, which requires a unanimous decision in the Council. During the meetings of the working party, however, it became clear that consent between all the Member States was not likely to be achieved. Thus, some Member States who were keen on commonly implementing a tax on financial transactions supported the idea of enhanced cooperation.[117] At their request,[118] the European Commission issued a proposal for a Council decision authorising enhanced cooperation in the area of FTT on 25 October 2010.[119] The Council authorised enhanced cooperation for an FTT but four Member States abstained: the Czech Republic, Luxembourg, Malta, and the United Kingdom.[120]

On 14 February 2013, the European Commission issued a proposal for an FTT based on the enhanced cooperation procedure.[121] The proposal is based significantly on the previous proposal but provides for some amendments concerning the establishment principle. A financial institution is not only established within a participating Member State based on the residency principle or the place of transaction principle but also based on the so-called issuance principle. The issuance principle deems a financial institution to be established within a participating Member State for a financial transaction in structured products or financial instruments issued within that participating Member State.[122] The extensive widening of the scope of the tax may also be triggered by the fear of locational effects which may increase if some Member States, in particular the United Kingdom, do not impose an FTT.

To date, the participating Member States have been unable to find a compromise on the design for a common tax on financial transactions. The French president, Emmanuel Macron, wanted to postpone further discussions until a Brexit deal has been concluded, to ensure that financial transactions do not move towards London.[123] But before the Brexit deal was signed and way before the European Union has negotiated a trade agreement with the United Kingdom, the German Finance Minister, Olaf Scholz, put forward a new proposal for a European financial transaction tax.[124] The scope of the newly proposed transactions tax is much

[117] Council, 22 June 2012, 3178th Council meeting, Economic and Financial Affairs, Press Release 11682/12, 11.

[118] Belgium, Germany, Estonia, Greece, Spain, France, Italy, Austria, Portugal, Slovenia, and Slovakia.

[119] Commission, 25 October 2012, Proposal for a Council decision authorising enhanced cooperation in the area of financial transaction tax, COM(2012) 631 final/2.

[120] Council, 22 January 2013, Press Release, 5555/13; Council, 22 January 2013, 2013/52/EU, Council decision authorising enhanced cooperation in the area of financial transaction tax, OJ, 25 January 2013, L 22, 11.

[121] Commission, 14 February 2013, Proposal for a Council Directive implementing enhanced cooperation in the area of financial transaction tax, COM(2013) 71 final.

[122] Art 4 Subsection 1 lit. g of the proposal, COM(2013) 71 final.

[123] 'Macron Says European Financial Transaction Tax Must Make Sense' Reuters (13 July 2017) <https://uk.reuters.com/article/us-france-tax-ftt-idUKKBN19Y1B7> accessed 3 February 2021.

[124] <https://www.bundesfinanzministerium.de/Content/DE/Standardartikel/Themen/Schlaglichter/Steuergerechtigkeit/2019-12-10-Gesetzesvorschlag-Finanztransaktionsteuer.html> accessed 3 February 2021.

smaller than the FTT proposed by the European Commission, as the tax should be levied at a minimum standard rate of 0.2% and should only apply to financial transactions that mainly involve the acquisition of shares which are issued by a listed company with a market capitalisation above €1 billion and located in a participating Member State.[125] The proposal also excludes particular transactions (ie internal public offerings, intra-group transactions, and repurchase agreements) from the FTT net.[126]

Under the new proposal, derivatives are not subject to tax and the proposal was therefore dismissed by the Austrian Finance Minister, Gernot Blümel. According to Blümel, Austria wants 'a common, broad financial transaction tax'.[127] Today, it is far from clear whether the participating Member States can find a compromise on the old, the new, or an alternative proposal for a European financial transaction tax.

II. The UK's Fight against the European Financial Transaction Tax

On 18 April 2013, the United Kingdom applied to the CJEU to annul the Council's authorisation decision. The application was based on two substantial pleas. First, it was claimed that Art 327 of the TFEU, as well as customary international law, would be infringed if the FTT introduced under the enhanced cooperation procedure contained the counter-party principle and the issuance principle as proposed by the European Commission. In other words, the United Kingdom felt that the extraterritorial reach of the FTT would infringe its rights as a non-participating Member State as guaranteed under the European treaties, and would contradict customary international law, as there is no sufficient connection[128] between the Member State levying the tax and the financial transaction.[129] The second plea concerns the costs associated with the application of the FTT. The United Kingdom feared that since it is required to assist mutually in the recovery of claims related to the tax, it would be burdened with costs it should not bear. Under the current framework of mutual assistance, recovery of the costs is not guaranteed.

[125] ibid.

[126] <https://home.kpmg/xx/en/home/insights/2019/12/etf-420-german-finance-minister-issues-amended-financial-transaction-tax-proposal.html> accessed 3 February 2021.

[127] <https://www.bloomberg.com/news/articles/2020-01-21/eu-financial-tax-faces-new-trouble-as-austria-threatens-to-quit> accessed 3 February 2021.

[128] See for more details on the requirement Rutsel S Martha, *The Jurisdiction to Tax in International Law: Theory and Practice of Legislative Fiscal Jurisdiction* (Kluwer Law International 1989) 46 et seq. Manfred Mössner, 'Source versus Residence—an EU Perspective' (2006) 60 Bulletin for International Taxation 501; Ian Brownlie, *Principles of Public International Law* (6th edn, OUP 2003) 297 et seq. Malcolm N Shaw, *International Law* (8th edn, CUP 2017) 486.

[129] Christiana Panayi, 'The EU's Financial Transaction Tax, Enhanced Cooperation and the UK's Challenge—IBFD' (2013) 53 European Taxation 358; Englisch, Vella, and Cédelle (n 115).

The CJEU ruled that the application for an annulment of the Council's decision was premature.[130] At a stage at which the Council has authorised enhanced cooperation, but the Member States have not yet agreed on the wording of the directive in the form of a unanimous vote in the Council, it is not possible to analyse the effects the tax may have on institutions, persons, and transactions situated in a non-participating Member State.[131] The Council decides to authorise the participating Member States to engage further in negotiations concerning an FTT, and thus, any detailed principles of such a tax, like the counter-party principle or the issuance principle are not a constituent element of the Council's decision.[132] At this stage of the process, the Court would only be able to review whether the procedural framework laid down by the European treaties, such as the involvement of the European institutions, is satisfied.[133]

From this it follows that any legal or factual effects imposed on non-participating Member States by enhanced cooperation can only be reviewed by the CJEU when the law has been formally introduced. If the Council has only authorised the procedure, but the participating Member States have not agreed on the final law, the Court only reviews its compliance with the procedural framework set out by the European treaties.

D. Sleeping Beauty or Non-starter?

The current experience of the enhanced cooperation mechanism shows that it has been successfully used in five[134] cases and has failed as many times. To be clear, if the experience of the enhanced cooperation procedure is understood as almost equally failing and succeeding, then failing would only refer to cases in which the idea of using the enhanced cooperation procedure to overcome a legislative deadlock in the Council has been suggested but has not worked out either because the Member States which were willing to find a compromise for the legislative attempt did not want to use enhanced cooperation for that particular matter, and thus have not issued the necessary request to the European Commission,[135] or because the

[130] CJEU, 30 April 2014, C-209/13, *United Kingdom of Great Britain and Northern Ireland v Council*, ECLI:EU:C:2014:282.

[131] The story of the unitary patent clearly shows that one has to distinguish between challenging the Council's authorisation (CJEU, 16 April 2013, C-274/11 and C-295/11, *Spain and Italy v Council*, ECLI:EU:C:2013:240) and challenging enhanced cooperation law (CJEU, 5 May 2015, C-146/13, *Spain v Parliament and Council*, ECLI:EU:C:2015:298; CJEU, 5 May 2015, C-147/13, *Spain v Council*, ECLI:EU:C:2015:299).

[132] CJEU, 30 April 2014, C-209/13, *United Kingdom of Great Britain and Northern Ireland v Council*, ECLI:EU:C:2014:282, para 36.

[133] ibid para 33.

[134] Adding together the enhanced cooperation on jurisdiction, applicable law, and the recognition and enforcement of decisions regarding the property consequences of both marriages and registered partnerships, see this chapter subsection A.I.2.

[135] See for the procedural requirements Chapter 4, subsection B.I.

participating Member States have not found a compromise within the group on the final legislation.[136] Failure does not, however, include the many cases in which a legislative attempt did not reach the necessary consent within the Council over the years, and the Commission withdrew its proposal without having anyone thought about the use of the enhanced cooperation procedure. However, the question is whether the latter cases should not also determine the story of the enhanced cooperation procedure; if so, it would be a story of complete failure.

It goes without saying that a solution at a European level covering all Member States is the preferred option. The differences between the Member States' policies, their different economic development, but also their different needs often do not allow for a compromise between all the Member States.[137] The enhanced cooperation procedure provides an alternative route for cases in which at least nine Member States can agree on certain policy objectives and are willing to move forward within the group. The latter condition—the willingness to move forward with some but not all the Member States—is one, if not the most important factor that decides between success and failure. The enhanced cooperation procedure can only succeed if some Member States are willing to act within the group, and thus accept that the other Member States are outside the group and that they pursue a different path, and if the unwilling Member States respect that some Member States cooperate, and thus jointly follow a legislative path.

The willingness to pursue a particular legislative action with some but not all Member States depends upon the necessity to act jointly. The need to work together may be triggered by three separate and distinct concerns: incapability, fear, and simplification.

We shall first consider the incapability issue. A single Member State may be unable to address a particular issue properly, and thus may be willing to be part of enhanced cooperation.[138] The incapability may be caused by different reasons. It may either be the subject matter that asks for common actions, such as environmental issues. In that field, it may also be necessary to find an additional international agreement with non-EU States to achieve the policy objective properly.[139] Or the legislative framework to be introduced may require a common effort because it relies on coordinated actions between the Member States, such as a framework which allows the Member States to comply with their obligations under the European treaties jointly.[140]

[136] So far this scenario can only be witnessed for the FTT: see this chapter subsection C.I.

[137] For a realistic view on compromises see Katerina Sideri, 'The European Commission and the Law-Making Process: Compromise as a Category of Praxis' (2005) 1 International Journal of Law in Context 155, 174 arguing that often for a legal proposal it 'becomes less about saying the right thing and more about reflecting a temporary equilibrium, which is bound to change again'.

[138] For the question of how this correlates with the principle of subsidiarity see Chapter 4, subsection G.VI.

[139] See for an analysis of the possibility of combining the enhanced cooperation procedure with international treaties Chapter 2, subsection A.I.2.

[140] See Chapter 5, Part I, subsection E.VIII.

Fear may determine a common legislative action of some Member States, if the law imposes negative effects upon the Member States, such as dislocation effects. A tax on mobile factors, such as financial transactions, may make financial transactions be traded in another Member State, or financial institutions be established outside the territory of the Member State levying the tax. If the tax is sufficiently high, taxpayers may also adjust their behaviour by moving to another jurisdiction with immobile factors. A joint Member State action would minimise diversity and subsequently the possibility of taxpayers being able to circumvent taxation through adjusting their behaviour. This mainly works if all (Member) States with equal market conditions impose the tax since in such a scenario the transaction costs for the taxpayer to circumvent taxation are high, reducing the possibility of leaving.[141]

From this it follows that the levying of some taxes may have quite negative effects on the Member States, leading them to decide either to introduce the tax jointly with other Member States, which decreases the negative effects, or simply not implement them at all. The FTT is a perfect example. Every Member State is allowed to implement a tax on financial transactions at the national level, as Sweden and Italy have already done.[142] However, there are some serious incentives not to walk the path alone, such as negative locational effects. If just one Member State within the European Union levies a tax on financial transactions or other equally mobile factors, it is very likely that taxpayers will adjust their behaviour by moving to the other Member States which do not collect an equal tax. If, however, a critical mass of Member States collaborates on that matter, the locational effects may decrease because there are more benefits associated with trading or producing within one of these Member States than negative effects associated with paying the tax.

Simplification is, so far, the only real concern which has bound some Member States together and has led to the use of the enhanced cooperation procedure. Simplification is achieved by a unified framework which is built on recognition. The legislative action in divorce law and related issues sets common standards for identifying the applicable law. Conflict of law rules aim to smooth the interplay between the laws of the Member States involved in an international couple setting. Likewise, the unitary patent provides for unitary protection within all participating Member States, but merely by aligning the registration and enforcement procedure for all participating Member States, and not adding much value to the scope of protection. Accordingly, what has been established at the EU level, under

[141] Johanna Stark, *Law for Sale: A Philosophical Critique of Regulatory Competition* (OUP 2019) 17 et seq.

[142] For the Swedish transaction tax see Lagen (1983:1053) om skatt på omsättning av vissa värdepapper, see for an overview of the tax Lena Hiort af Ornäs and Magnus Wiberg, 'Beskattning av finanssektorn, ett ämne på den internationella agendan' (2011) Kkattenytt 497. For the Italian financial transaction tax: Legge 24 dicembre 2012, n. 228 Disposizioni per la formazione del bilancio annuale e pluriennale dello Stato (Legge di stabilita' 2013). (12G0252) (GU Serie Generale n.302 del 29-12-2012—Suppl. Ordinario n. 212), art 1, paras 491–500.

enhanced cooperation, are mere coordination provisions which ease the application of national laws in cross-border settings, or which make it easier to gain protection in various Member States. None of the existing joint actions, however, establish harmonised material values between the Member States.

Harmonisation of values is achieved by unifying substantive national laws. The unification of substantive rules requires a common set of values and not just rules with identical wording.[143] Thus, the Member States have to weigh up contradicting values against each other and have to find compromises which then establish a particular (new) value judgement. This approach fosters and deepens integration between the Member States because it not only provides rules for solving conflicts between their laws but also provides for a unified and common solution. An obvious question remains: why have the Member States not yet used enhanced cooperation to grow together by harmonising their values?

In taxation, the answer may be a potential competitive disadvantage. If enhanced cooperation law widens the tax base, increases the tax rate, or introduces an entirely new tax, the participating Member States may be exposed to a competitive disadvantage even when acting jointly with the other Member States. Non-participating Member States may allow economic players to remain on the European internal market but without being subject to increased taxes. The competitive disadvantage may be intensified if the non-participating Member States set countermeasures to the law of enhanced cooperation, such as lowering their tax rates in cases in which enhanced cooperation law increases the rates, reducing of the scope of their tax in cases in which enhanced cooperation law widens the tax base, or rejecting the introduction of new taxes which are implemented between the participating Member States based on enhanced cooperation law.

Thus, the enhanced cooperation procedure must not only form the ground to allow a group of Member States to create a common value among them but must also protect the commonly established value from being exploited by the non-participating Member States. Herein lies the problem of the existing enhanced cooperation procedure: attention is sometimes only given to the protection of non-participating Member States—they should not be exploited by colluding Member States. If, however, the participating Member States have no chance to protect their joint achievements and to protect themselves from being exploited by the non-participating Member States, they have no reason to cooperate outside the mere establishing of simplification rules. Without any safeguarding measures, the common values of the participating Member States could be exploited by non-participating Member States and thereby make any true harmonisation of Member States' values extremely unlikely.

[143] See Chapter 5, Part I, subsection E.III.

Against this background, this book, and in particular Chapters 5 and 6, reveals how the existing legal framework for establishing enhanced cooperation has to be interpreted to grant both the participating and the non-participating Member States sufficient protection from exploitation. Only if neither the participating nor the non-participating Member States fear to be harmed by enhanced cooperation does the procedure have a chance of succeeding.

4

The Law-making Procedure

A. Overview of the Procedural Framework for Establishing Enhanced Cooperation

Where a joint action of the European Union as a whole cannot be attained within a reasonable period, the European treaties allow a group of Member States to enhance the integration process further through cooperation.[1] The Member States who wish to establish enhanced cooperation between themselves shall, as a first step, address a request to the European Commission. In this request, the Member States have to specify the scope and objectives of their joint initiative. The requirement that the willing Member States have to make the first step to establish enhanced cooperation ensures that none of the participating Member States are forced into enhanced cooperation but are instead free to join the group.[2] However, the procedure differs if the common foreign and security policy is concerned.[3]

Based on the Member States' request, the European Commission may submit a proposal to the Council.[4] The Commission enjoys some leeway in deciding whether or not the Council is entrusted with this matter. In cases in which the Commission does not want to pursue the issue any further and therefore does not provide the Council with a proposal for enhanced cooperation, the Commission should inform the Member States who wish to cooperate more closely of the reasons for doing so.

With regards to the requirements set by the European treaties, Member States are not entitled to cooperate more closely under the concept of enhanced cooperation in the field of the exclusive competence of the European Union. Furthermore, the provisions of the European treaties require Member States to restrict any enhanced cooperation to areas covered by the European treaties. This requirement excludes areas which remain in the exclusive competence of the Member States from the scope of enhanced cooperation.[5] From this it follows that the Member

[1] Art 20 Subsection 2 of the TEU.

[2] Daniel Thym, *Ungleichzeitigkeit und europäisches Verfassungsrecht* (Daniel Thym 2004) 48; Christian von Buttlar, 'Rechtsprobleme der "verstärkten Zusammenarbeit" nach dem Vertrag von Nizza' (2011) Zeitschrift für Europarechtliche Studien 649, 672.

[3] Art 329 Subsection 1 TFEU.

[4] ibid.

[5] Hermann-Josef Blanke, 'Art. 20' in Hermann-Josef Blanke and Stelio Mangiameli (eds), *The Treaty on European Union (TEU)—A Commentary* (2013) para 31.

Enhanced Cooperation and European Tax Law. Caroline Heber, Oxford University Press. © Caroline Heber 2021.
DOI: 10.1093/oso/9780192898272.003.0004

States are free to engage in enhanced cooperation in areas which do not fall in the exclusive competence of either the European Union or the Member States. Thus, the Member States may use the enhanced cooperation procedure in the area falling within the scope of the competences shared between the European Union and the Member States.

In cases in which the European Commission decides to submit a proposal for enhanced cooperation to the Council, the Council may authorise the Member States to proceed with enhanced cooperation with a qualified majority voting. The Council can, however, only do so after obtaining the consent of the European Parliament. This might not be true for enhanced cooperation in the field of common foreign and security policy since in this area the Council can only grant authorisation to proceed with enhanced cooperation if the Council reaches a unanimous decision.

The procedure following the authorisation by the Council depends upon the competence clause underlying the proposal. Thus, the majority by which the Council acts and how the European Parliament is involved in the law-making process differs widely. However, all procedural rules of the European treaties assume the participation of all Member States. Where they are applied in the framework of enhanced cooperation, they have to be understood as rules which only apply to the participating Member States. Only these Member States are entitled to take part in the vote, and thus unanimity has to be constituted by the votes of the representatives of the participating Member States.[6] In cases in which the procedural rules require a qualified majority vote, the exact percentage that has to be satisfied must be determined concerning the number of participating Member States and according to the general rule of Art 238 of the Treaty on the Functioning of the European Union (TFEU). Despite the restriction on voting, all non-participating Member States are allowed to participate in the deliberations for enacting enhanced cooperation law.[7] Throughout the law-making process, and even after enhanced cooperation law has been introduced, any non-participating Member State is free to join.[8]

According to this framework, the enhanced cooperation procedure does not create an entirely new regime for a group of Member States who wish to participate more closely; the procedure merely sets out the authorisation process for granting a group of Member States the right to use the general framework of the European Union for enacting laws which are only binding among them. The authorisation process particularly involves the willing Member States and the European

[6] Art 330 of the TFEU.
[7] Art 20 Subsection 3 of the TEU.
[8] Art 328 of the TFEU.

Commission as well as the Council and can be compared with the entitlement to establish a mini-Union within the European Union.[9]

The brief overview of the procedural framework already highlights the problems which may occur when applying the enhanced cooperation procedure. The procedure should only be applied if a uniform action of the European Union as a whole cannot be attained in the foreseeable future. But what does it mean to be a measure of last resort? Does it mean that a proposal on the relevant objectives has already failed to make it into binding law for all Member States? Or does it suffice that some Member States have indicated that they will not support attempts for joint actions in a particular area? And what if all the Member States could agree on minor harmonisation measures?

Furthermore, the European Commission is entrusted with the decision of whether or not to forward a proposal for enhanced cooperation to the Council. But on which grounds does the Commission have to decide? Does the Commission only have to verify the requirements set by the European treaties, such as the prohibition to undermine the European internal market,[10] or does the Commission have the power to reject Member State requests on the ground that such an action may be harmful to the entire harmonisation process because some Member States are not likely to join, despite the fact that the law may be in line with all substantive conditions set by the European treaties?

The European treaties explicitly state that any enhanced cooperation shall be open to all non-participating Member States, but it does not say anything on the right of the participating Member States to leave. Does this automatically imply that all participating Member States are trapped until they can agree to dissolve enhanced cooperation, and are the Member States allowed to do so?

The following subsections systematically answer these questions. Subsection B analyses the requirements the European Commission has to consider in its decision. Subsection C is dedicated to the Council's authorisation decision which forms the constitutional backbone of the whole enhanced cooperation. Subsection D defines the requirement of being a measure of last resort. In other words, this section sets out the necessary steps which have to be taken before a group of Member States is allowed to walk the path of enhanced cooperation. Subsection E deals with the ins and outs—accordingly, the joining of the non-participating Member States and the leaving of participating Member States. Ultimately, subsection F looks to the (ordinary) competence framework and subsection G defines the limits for European legislative actions in the area of taxation.

[9] 'Editorial Comments: Enhanced Cooperation: A Union à Taille Réduite or à Porte Tournante?' (2011) 48 Common Market Law Review 317, 323.

[10] Art 326 Subsection 1 of the TFEU.

B. The Role of the European Commission within the Enhanced Cooperation Procedure

Within the procedural framework for establishing enhanced cooperation, the European treaties assign a key role to the European Commission.[11] The Commission has the power to decide whether or not it submits a proposal to the Council. Accordingly, if a group of Member States is genuinely willing to go forward and establish enhanced cooperation, the Commission is the first instance which decides upon the success or failure of the joint initiative. Despite the critical role the Commission has in the proceedings, the European treaties do not specify any criteria which the Commission explicitly has to consider when deciding on the proposal for enhanced cooperation.

The primary EU law framework can be interpreted in two ways. First, the European Commission may only be allowed to verify the substantive requirements set by the European treaties, such as the requirement that the joint initiative does not fall within the scope of the exclusive competence of the European Union. Secondly, the Commission may also be allowed to test and judge the joint initiative in the light of the EU's integration process. Such a reading of the provision would grant the Commission the power to abstain from entrusting the Council with the proposal for enhanced cooperation because the legal requirements set by the EU treaties are not met, but also because the Commission considers the project to be harmful to the European integration process.[12]

The following subsections will answer the question of which factors the European Commission has to consider (see subsection II), but will first assess the Commission's role within the proceedings for enhanced cooperation, in particular the Member States' right of initiative, in the light of the Commission's general role assigned by the European treaties (see subsection I).

I. The Right of Initiative Lies with the 'Willing' Member States

The starting point for any enhanced cooperation lies with an initiative by the Member States willing to establish enhanced cooperation and thus differs from the ordinary law-making process at the European level. Under the ordinary

[11] José Martín Y Pérez De Nanclares, 'La flexibilidad en el Tratado de Amsterdam: especial referencia a la noción de cooperación reforzada' (2007) Revista de Derecho Comunitario Europeo 205, 224; Helmut Kortenberg, 'Closer Cooperation in the Treaty of Amsterdam' (1998) 35 Common Market Law Review 833, 849.

[12] See for such an interpretation of the European treaties Thym, *Ungleichzeitigkeit und europäisches Verfassungsrecht* (n 2) 49; Francisco Javier Quel López, 'Análisis de las reformas en el Espacio de Libertad, Seguridad y Justicia en el Tratado de Niza' (2007) Revista de Derecho Comunitario Europeo 117, 138; Par Florence Chaltiel, 'Le traité d'Amsterdam et la coopération renforcée' (1998) Revue du Marche commun et de l'Union européenne 289, 291.

procedure, the right of initiative lies with the European Commission enabling it to play its role as guardian of the European treaties.[13] There are, however, good reasons for not entrusting the Commission with the right of initiative within the framework of enhanced cooperation. As the enhanced cooperation procedure only works as a measure of last resort, the Commission must have made some efforts to achieve a uniform measure for the European Union as a whole.[14] If the Commission held the right to start the proceeding for enhanced cooperation, the Commission would need to determine the point in time at which it is no longer sensible to work on a uniform solution for the entire European Union and start with separate negotiations within a smaller group of Member States. The European treaties do not provide any guidance on the 'right' moment to switch from the ordinary law-making track to the enhanced cooperation procedure because the constitutional framework of enhanced cooperation only requires that the objects of the legislative attempt cannot be attained within a reasonable period by the European Union as a whole. The Commission could run the risk of failing to take account both of the interests of the European Union as a whole since it provides the impetus too early to establish enhanced cooperation, and of the interest of differentiated integration. The interests of differentiated integration may be damaged because the Commission may submit the proposal for a joint action of the group at a time at which the Member States have already gone through many rounds of negotiations with all the Member States and frustration can hardly be overcome. Therefore, some even argue that the shifting of the right of initiative from the Commission to the willing Member States is the least the procedural framework could do because the former is, first of all, committed to the interests of the European Union as a whole.[15] The interests of the European Union will always favour an action by the European Union as a whole over enhanced cooperation, and thus the Commission may miss the point at which it is necessary to push for enhanced cooperation. To overcome the problem of missed opportunities, the French president went so far as to urge the establishment of an independent secretariat in order to relieve the Commission of its dual function within the enhanced cooperation procedure. The independent secretariat was intended (instead of the Commission) to be entrusted with the verification of the requirements to pursue enhanced cooperation.[16] However, the creation of an autonomous body to focus solely on

[13] CJEU, 4 September 2018, C-57/16 P, *ClientEarth*, ECLI:EU:C:2018:660, para 87; Daniel Wyatt, 'Is the Commission a Lawmaker? On the Right of Initiative, Institutional Transparency and Public Participation in Decision-Making: ClientEarth' (2019) 56 Common Market Law Review 825, 825.

[14] For the *ultima ratio* requires, see this chapter subsection D.

[15] Bernhard Zepter, 'Zukunft und Aufgaben der Europäischen Kommission' (2000) 23 Integration 260, 262; Thomas Wiedmann, 'Der Vertrag von Nizza—Genesis einer Reform' (2001) Europarecht 185, 210.

[16] ibid.

examining the conditions for establishing enhanced cooperation would be an exaggeration. In any case, the trick of granting the willing Member States the right of initiative has (sufficiently) relieved the Commission of the pressure to always balance the interests of the European Union as a whole along with the interests of the individual Member States willing to compromise and pursue a common action.

However, the current procedure forces Member States, as an initial step, to form alliances and coordinate with each other. This hurdle can certainly be understood as an obstacle to differentiated integration through enhanced cooperation.[17] If the Commission were to submit the project to the Member States and they would only have to agree to it, the difficult start-up phase during which the Member States who are in principle willing to pursue a joint action would also have to meet with confidence, would be alleviated. However, the practice has shown that the Commission stands by the willing Member States and supports them as soon as they give indications that they wish to use the enhanced cooperation mechanism to overcome a legislative deadlock.[18]

As soon as it is clear that some Member States are willing to establish enhanced cooperation, the European Commission is the right institution to verify whether the requirements set by the European treaties are satisfied, as well as to allow or reject the pursuit of enhanced cooperation. The Commission is capable of functioning as an arbitrator between the interests of the European Union, the interests of the willing Member States, and the interests of non-participating Member States.[19]

From this it follows that the European treaties officially grant the Member States the right of initiative to relieve the Commission of its dual function: watching the interests of the European Union as a whole and watching the interest of the Member States willing to move forward with enhanced cooperation. The Commission, however, supports the Member States, and thus the hurdle to initiate enhanced cooperation does not reveal itself to be a significant obstacle to enhanced cooperation.

[17] Thomas Wiedmann, 'Der Vertrag von Nizza—Genesis einer Reform' (2001) Europarecht 185, 210.

[18] See for example Commission, 24 March 2010, Proposal for a Council decision authorising enhanced cooperation in the area of the law applicable to divorce and legal separation, COM(2010) 105 final; Commission, 2 March 2016, Proposal for a Council decision authorising enhanced cooperation in the area of jurisdiction, applicable law and the recognition and enforcement of decisions on the property regimes of international couples, covering both matters of matrimonial property regimes and the property consequences of registered partnerships, COM(2016) 108 final; Commission, 14 December 2010, a proposal for a Council decision authorising enhanced cooperation in the area of the creation of unitary patent protection, COM(2010) 790 final.

[19] Giulia Tiberi, '"Uniti nella diversita'": l'integrazione differenziata e le cooperazioni rafforzate nell'Union europea' in Franco Bassanini and Giulia Tiberi (eds), *Le nuove istituzioni europee. Commento al trattato di Lisbona* (Il Mulino 2010) 318; Filip Tuytschaever, *Differentiation in European Union Law* (Hart Publishing 1999) 58 et seq. Daniel Thym, 'Competing Models for Understanding Differentiated Integration' in Bruno de Witte, Andrea Ott, and Ellen Vos (eds), *Between Flexibility and Disintegration: The Trajectory of Differentiation in EU Law* (Edward Elgar Pub 2017) 47.

II. Political Requirements

The European treaties do not specify whether, and if so to what extent, the European Commission has to consider political requirements in the process of deciding on the entitlement to pursue enhanced cooperation. To that effect, it is not clear whether the Commission should (only) consider the substantive conditions set by the European treaties, such as the requirement that any enhanced cooperation must not undermine the internal market and the requirement that the objects of enhanced cooperation do not fall within the scope of the European Union's exclusive competence, or whether the Commission is entrusted with a wider mandate, which would also allow it to examine the impact of enhanced cooperation on the European integration process.

The prevailing academic opinion attributes a far-reaching right of scrutiny to the European Commission so that the Commission cannot only assess the legal conditions but also the influence of enhanced cooperation on the integration process of the European Union.[20] Even if the Commission is allowed to consider the impact of enhanced cooperation on the European integration process, the mere fact that enhanced cooperation establishes differentiation between Member States cannot be a ground for rejecting a joint initiative. The Member States have endorsed a differentiated integration model by introducing the enhanced cooperation procedure into the European treaties, and thus differentiation is not per se a threat to European integration.[21] The threat to European integration may, however, follow from the underlying reason of having to choose the path of differentiated integration. It may be one thing to allow some Member States to establish enhanced cooperation and commonly pursue a policy object if the non-participating Member States want to join at a later point but are just not yet ready to do so. It is, however, a completely different matter if the non-participating Member States have an alternative view on the particular policy area (either on the question of whether to act or how to act) or are unwilling to pool their sovereignty in that particular field,[22] and thus it may be likely that they will not join in the foreseeable future.

Of course, it is impossible to know in advance that a legislative initiative will never find the consent of all Member States. The political will within a Member State can dramatically change after new elections, or new factual circumstances

[20] Thym, 'Competing Models' (n 19) 46; Chloé Lignier and Anton Geier, 'Die Verstärkte Zusammenarbeit in der Europäischen Union—Politischer Hintergrund, Bestandsaufnahme und Zukunftsperspektiven' (2015) 79 Rabels Zeitschrift für ausländisches und internationales Privatrecht (RabelsZ) 546, 562 et seq. Jo Shaw, 'The Treaty of Amsterdam: Challenges of Flexibility and Legitimacy' (1998) 4 European Law Journal 63, 75.

[21] See Chapter 1, subsection B.

[22] Federico Fabbrini, 'Enhanced Cooperation under Scrutiny: Revisiting the Law and Practice of Multi-Speed Integration in Light of the First Involvement of the EU Judiciary' (2013) 40 Legal Issues of Economic Integration 197, 206; Giorgio Gaja, 'How Flexible Is Flexibility under the Amsterdam Treaty?' (1998) *35 Common Market Law Review* 855, 858.

may require a shift in public policy. However, there is still a fundamental difference between Member States unwilling to cooperate because they do not share the policy objective and Member States who agree on the policy but are not ready to join the initiative because of financial, social, or economic constraints. In the first case, the non-participating Member States only join after a political turning point, which is highly unpredictable and depends upon circumstances which cannot be influenced by the participating Member States. In cases in which the Member States are simply not ready but in line with the policies pursued under enhanced cooperation, the participating Member States can influence the time of joining by support the non-participating Member States to overcome the financial or economic hurdles which do not allow them to join.

If there are no economic or financial reasons (accordingly constraints which can be overcome and can be addressed by the participating Member States) for not joining, there is a chance that the non-participating Member States are never going to join. In such a case, the use of the enhanced cooperation procedure does not introduce different speeds within the European Union but instead a permanent division between the Member States. Considering the Commission's decision, would the Commission be entitled to reject the request of some Member States to establish enhanced cooperation if there are no objective criteria which indicate when the non-participating Member States are going to join (eg reducing the unemployment rate or digitising the financial authorities)?

The following subsection examines the political discussions on whether or not to introduce differentiated integration within the European Union, which purpose it should serve, and its supposed impact on the integration process. The historical intent for implementing more flexibility through the enhanced cooperation procedure within the European treaties may provide some guidance on the relevant factors the European Commission has to consider in its decision, as the scenarios in which differentiated integration was needed and to which the enhanced cooperation procedure should apply were well defined in the political discussion. The historical intent may not be reflected in the plain wording of the provisions on the enhanced cooperation procedure and may not be appreciated by the Court of Justice of the European Union's (CJEU) interpretation of these rules. The following subsections reveal both the historical background and the CJEU's understanding of the law to define the relevant factors the Commission has to consider in its decision.

1. Historical Intent for Implementing Differentiated Integration within the European Treaties

The discussion over the various forms of differentiated integration is almost as historical as the process of European integration itself.[23] The first political claims

[23] Luisa Antoniolli, '"United in Diversity"? Differentiated Integration in an Ever Diverse European Union' in Luisa Antoniolli, Luigi Bonatti, and Carlo Ruzza (eds), *Highs and Lows of European*

for a more flexible Europe were made against the background of a rising number of Member States,[24] all possessing different levels of political, social, and—most importantly—economic development.[25] Accordingly, the idea of a multi-speed Europe was always sold as a mechanism for allowing Member States which are willing and able to achieve deeper integration amongst them to progress. Some have even called it a duty of Member States to go forward if they are ready.[26] The Member States who are not yet ready to participate should join when they are capable of doing so.[27] The integration process is therefore a gradual process: the Member States who are willing shall precede, and the other Member States shall follow if and when they are in a position to do so.[28] The differentiation between the Member States was only supposed to exist for a certain time because it was expected that, at some point, all Member States are ready to join.[29]

Integration: Sixty Years After the Treaty of Rome (Springer International Publishing 2019) 84; Claus-Dieter Ehlermann, 'How Flexible Is Community Law? An Unusual Approach to the Concept of "Two Speeds"' (1984) 82 Michigan Law Review 1274; Christian von Buttlar (n 2) 650 et seq. Heiko Beck, *Abgestufte Integration im Europäischen Gemeinschaftsrecht unter besonderer Berücksichtigung des Umweltrechts: Bestandsaufnahme und Perspektiven* (Peter Lang 1995) 39 et seq. Dominik Hanf, 'Flexibility Clauses in the Founding Treaties, from Rome to Nice' in Bruno de Witte, Dominik Hanf, and Ellen Vos (eds), *The Many Faces of Differentiation in EU Law* (Intersentia nv 2001).

24 For the different integration models see Ulrich Becker, *EU-Erweiterung und differenzierte Integration: zu beitrittsbedingten Übergangsregelungen am Beispiel der Arbeitnehmerfreizügigkeit* (Nomos Verlag 1999) 45 et seq.

25 Anja Riedeberger, *Die EU zwischen einheitlicher und differenzierter Integration* (Springer 2016) 57 et seq. Maurizio Bach, 'The Enlargement Crisis of the European Union: From Political Integration to Social Disintegration?' in Maurizio Bach, Christian Lahusen, and Georg Vobruba (eds), *Europe in Motion: Social Dynamics and Political Institutions in an Enlarging Europe* (Nomos 2006) 21; Georg Vobruba, *Die Dynamik Europas* (Springer 2007) 16 et seq. Peter-Christian Müller-Graff, 'Differenzierte Integration: Konzept mit sprengender oder unitarisierender Kraft für die Europäische Union?' (2007) 30 Integration 129, 138; Thomas Giegerich, 'Introduction: Trying to Fathom the Shallows of European Unification' in Thomas Giegerich, Oskar Josef Gstrein, and Sebastian Zeitzmann (eds), *The EU between 'An Ever Closer Union' and Inalienable Policy Domains of Member States*, vol 80 (Nomos 2014) 39 arguing that differentiated integration 'may be the price that must after all be paid for the many enlargement rounds which have turned the closely-knit original Community of the six founding Member States into a necessarily much looser Union of twenty-eight'. For a more historical perspective see Ulrich Derpa, *Die verstärkte Zusammenarbeit im Recht der Europäischen Union: Dogmatik Interpretation und Praxis eines alternativen Integrationskonzeptes* (Boorberg Verlag 2003) 53 et seq; Hans-Eckart Scharrer, 'Abgestufte Integration—Eine Einführung' in Eberhard Grabitz (ed), *Abgestufte Integration: Eine Alternative zum herkömmlichen Integrationskonzept* (NP Engel Verlag 1984) 6 et seq.

26 Already included in the Tindemans Report 'those States which are able to progress have a duty to forge ahead', Leo Tindemans, 'Report on the European Union' (1976) 9 Bulletin of the European Communities 11; Martin Westlake, *The European Union beyond Amsterdam: New Concepts of European Integration* (Routledge 1998) 3; Alexander CG Stubb, *Negotiating Flexibility in the European Union—Amsterdam, Nice and Beyond* (Palgrave Macmillan 2002) 34; Andreas H Hvidsten and Jon Hovi, 'Why No Twin-Track Europe? Unity, Discontent, and Differentiation in European Integration' (2015) 16 European Union Politics 3, 5 et seq.

27 For an overview of the debate Thym, 'Competing Models' (n 19) 30.

28 Jean-Claude Piris, *The Future of Europe: Towards a Two-Speed EU?* (CUP 2011) 66 et seq.

29 The Reflection Group recommended that flexibility within the European Union should only be pursued of 'differences in the degree of integration should be temporary' and provisions are in place 'for ad hoc measures to assist those who want to take part in given action or policy but are temporarily unable to do so', 'Reflection Group's Report' (1995) 6–7; Gunilla Herolf (eds), 'Enlargement and Flexibility—Recurrent Items on the Agenda', *EU Enlargement and Flexibility* (Utrikespolitiska Institute

Such a form of differentiated integration would solve the problem of a legislative deadlock which is the consequence of different economic, financial, and technical abilities of the Member States. If, for example, one Member State does not possess the financial and technical power to nationally implement the definitive Value-Added Tax (VAT) system, which requires the Member State of origin to transfer VAT to the Member State of destination, the Member State would not be in a position to approve the legislative proposal in the Council. To allow the Member States who are ready to engage in a cross-border transfer of VAT to move forward, it would be necessary to exclude the Member States which are not capable of providing the relevant technical measure. It is clear, however, from the outset that the outsiders will join the common framework as soon as they are ready.

From this it follows that the political discussion was mainly[30] based on the assumption that any cooperation of some Member States, being either the core Europe[31] or an undefined group of willing and ready Member States, was only a transitional solution and that a uniform standard of integration would be achieved by the later joining of fellow Member States.[32] However, a uniform standard of integration can only be achieved if the policy underlying the legislative approach is shared by all Member States. Concerning the case at hand, all Member States must, therefore, be in favour of the implementation of the definitive VAT system.

One could even read the first European provisions on differentiated integration, as introduced by the Amsterdam Treaty,[33] as a manifestation of the idea that all the

1998) 8 emphasising that those two requirements are not included in the general flexibility measure (the closer cooperation procedure). However, some may argue that the participating Member States have a duty to help (which goes beyond mere financial support) those Member States which are willing but unable to join under Art 4 Subsection 3 of the TEU: Claus-Dieter Ehlermann, 'Engere Zusammenarbeit nach dem Amsterdamer Vertrag: Ein neues Verfassungsprinzip?' (1997) Europarecht 362, 379.

[30] It is, of course, true that some, in particular the United Kingdom, wished for an even more flexible Europe—a Europe à la carte. For the Europe à la carte concept see Thym, 'Competing Models' (n 19) 34 et seq.

[31] The idea of a core Europe was in particular popular among French and German politicians, see for more details Karl Lamers and Wolfgang Schäuble, 'Reflections on European Policy' (1994) European Documents 1895/96; Thym, 'Competing Models' (n 19) 32 et seq. For an overview of the Fischer initiative see Theodore Konstadinides, *Division of Powers in European Union Law: The Delimitation of Internal Competence between the EU and the Member States* (2009) 258. However, we will see that the enhanced cooperation procedure does not favour a going forward of particular Member States and thus 'it is perfectly possible that different combinations of States will be in or out, depending on the subject matter in issue' which 'offers the prospect of less friction and diversion between the "ins" and the "outs"', Stephen Weatherill, '"If I'd Wanted You to Understand I Would Have Explained It Better": What Is the Purpose of the Provisions on Closer Co-Operation Introduced by the Treaty of Amsterdam?' in David O'Keeffe and Patrick Twomey (eds), *Legal Issues of the Amsterdam Treaty* (Bloomsbury Publishing PLC 1999) 24.

[32] Jo Shaw, 'Flexibility in a "Reorganized" and "Simplified" Treaty' (2003) 40 Common Market Law Review 279, 285 et seq. Some authors even criticise the use of forms of differentiated integration in cases in which all the Member States can agree on the policy objectives, but not all are yet ready to implement the chosen measure due to technical, social, or financial reasons. Their fear is that flexibility undermines social and political solidarity, and the equality of sovereign governments: Ben Hall, 'How Flexible Should Europe Be?' (2000) Centre for European Reform Working Paper, London 2.

[33] See in particular Art K.12 and Arts K.15–K.17 of the Amsterdam Treaty.

Member States have to favour the objectives of the legislative proposal. The initial framework for establishing a 'closer' (now enhanced) cooperation required the consent of all Member States of the European Union in the Council. The Member States did not hold an explicit veto power because the vote on the authorisation of the closer cooperation was taken by qualified majority voting, yet every Member State was able to request that the matter should be referred to the European Council because of 'important stated reasons of national policy'.[34] Such a claim of a Member State did not per se block the establishing of the enhanced cooperation[35] but required a unanimous decision by the European Council.[36]

The hurdle of the quasi veto power in the Council has been removed,[37] but it has still been argued that the idea of mere temporary differentiation within the European Union remains part of enhanced cooperation.[38] If that were true, then the enhanced cooperation procedure must not be applied in fields in which the Member States cannot agree on the 'whether' or the 'how' to regulate a certain subject matter, as a different take on the 'whether' or the 'how' to regulate will most likely lead to a situation in which the non-participating Member States would not join the enhanced cooperation. 'Enhanced cooperation would then not lead to a two-speed Europe, but rather push Europe into two directions.'[39]

The historical background indicates that enhanced cooperation was supposed to establish only temporary differentiation. If the enhanced cooperation procedure was a mechanism allowing different speeds within the European Union but no division, the use of the enhanced cooperation procedure would only be allowed for legislative attempts which are supported by all Member States. The plain wording of the provisions on the enhanced cooperation procedure in the European treaties does not limit differentiation established through enhanced cooperation to temporary differentiation. In light of the historical developments, one may ask whether the primary EU law provisions have to be interpreted restrictively only allowing different speeds within the European Union. If the provisions needed to

[34] ibid.

[35] Paul Craig, *The Lisbon Treaty: Law, Politics, and Treaty Reform* (OUP 2013) 439.

[36] If objections were raised, the Council could, acting with a qualified majority, request that the matter be referred to the European Council for decision by unanimity. For more details on the procedure concerning the first and third pillar see Anzhela Cédelle, 'Enhanced Cooperation: A Way Forward for Tax Harmonization in the European Union?' in Joachim Englisch (ed), *International Tax Law: New Challenges to and from Constitutional and Legal Pluralism* (IBFD 2016) 171.

[37] Daniel T Murphy, 'Closer or Enhanced Cooperation: Amsterdam or Nice' (2003) 31 Georgia Journal of International and Comparative Law 265, 315 arguing that 'this [the elimination of the national veto] is one of the most important revisions made to the closer cooperation procedures by the Treaty of Nice'.

[38] See for a broader analysis of temporal differentiation Klaus H Goetz, 'The Temporal Dimension' in Kenneth Dyson and Angelos Sepos (eds), *Which Europe? Differentiated Integration* (Palgrave Macmillan 2010).

[39] Jan-Jaap Kuipers, 'The Law Applicable to Divorce as Test Ground for Enhanced Cooperation' (2012) 18 European Law Journal 201, 213; Federico Fabbrini, 'The Enhanced Cooperation Procedure: A Study in Multispeed Integration' Centro Studi Sul Federalismo—Research Paper 13–14.

be interpreted in such a way, it would be the European Commission's task to reject all requests for establishing enhanced cooperation which might provide for a permanent differentiation.

The following subsection examines the CJEU case law and reveals the Court's view on the question of whether different policy beliefs of the Member States are reasons for denying the implementation of enhanced cooperation between some Member States, or whether the differentiation established between the Member States through enhanced cooperation can also be of a potentially permanent nature, allowing the use of the enhanced cooperation even if the Member States disagree on the 'whether' and the 'how' to regulate.

2. CJEU Case Law on the Requirement of a Unified Political Belief

In *Spain and Italy v Council*,[40] the Grand Chamber of the CJEU addressed the question of whether Member States are allowed to use enhanced cooperation to overcome a legislative deadlock in cases in which some Member States are capable of taking part in further integration but disagree on how to design the legislative framework. The case concerned the implementation of a unitary patent. The implementation of such a tool has long remained on the EU decision-makers' agenda,[41] and while the Member States could generally agree on the legal framework, they had difficulties in agreeing on the language issue.[42] Most Member States agreed to a trilingual regime—which allowed the registration of patents in English, French, and German. Italy and Spain, however, wanted the number of legitimate languages to be extended to five to include Italian and Spanish. The Member States who could agree on a common framework and the use of three legitimate languages wanted to move forward with the unitary patent and wished to establish enhanced cooperation between them.[43] Spain and Italy brought the issue before the CJEU, questioning the legitimacy of using the enhanced cooperation procedure—amongst other things—when the non-participating Member States are not only incapable but unwilling to implement the framework because of its design.[44]

[40] CJEU, 16 April 2013, C-274/11 and C-295/11, *Spain and Italy v Council*, ECLI:EU:C:2013:240.

[41] For the background of the European unitary patent see Steve Peers, 'The Constitutional Implications of the EU Patent' (2011) 7 European Constitutional Law Review 229, 230 et seq.

[42] See Chapter 3, subsection A.II.1.

[43] 'Having regard to the requests made by the Kingdom of Belgium, the Republic of Bulgaria, the Czech Republic, the Kingdom of Denmark, the Federal Republic of Germany, the Republic of Estonia, Ireland, the Hellenic Republic, the French Republic, the Republic of Cyprus, the Republic of Latvia, the Republic of Lithuania, the Grand Duchy of Luxembourg, the Republic of Hungary, Malta, the Kingdom of the Netherlands, the Republic of Austria, the Republic of Poland, the Portuguese Republic, Romania, the Republic of Slovenia, the Slovak Republic, the Republic of Finland, the Kingdom of Sweden and the United Kingdom of Great Britain and Northern Ireland', Council, 10 March 2011, 2011/167/EU, Decision authorising enhanced cooperation in the area of the creation of unitary patent protection, OJ, 22 March 2011, L 76, 53.

[44] CJEU, 16 April 2013, C-274/11 and C-295/11, *Spain and Italy v Council*, ECLI:EU:C:2013:240, para 9, 42 et seq.

The CJEU ruled that 'contrary to what is maintained by the Kingdom of Spain and the Italian Republic, Article 20 TEU and Articles 326 TFEU to 334 TFEU do not circumscribe the right to resort to enhanced cooperation solely to the case in which at least one Member State declares that it is not yet ready to take part in a legislative act of the Union in its entirety. As provided in Article 20(2) TEU, the situation that may lawfully lead to enhanced cooperation is that in which 'the objectives of such cooperation cannot be attained within a reasonable period by the Union as a whole'. *The impossibility referred to in that provision may be due to various causes*; for example, a lack of interest on the part of one or more Member States or the inability of the Member States, who have all shown themselves interested in the adoption of an arrangement at Union level, to reach a consensus on the content of that arrangement.'[45]

The CJEU did not try to interpret the rule in light of the historical debate and the initial political wish to not divide the European Union and to grant the Member States the possibility of pursuing legislative action at a different speed. Rather, the Court considered the plain wording of the provisions, and since there was no explicit restriction to be found, the CJEU allowed the establishment of enhanced cooperation despite the fact that those on the outside—Spain and Italy—could not agree on the framework of the unitary patent, at least when it came to the legitimate languages, and thus may likely never join.[46]

3. Findings and Appraisal

From the CJEU's ruling, it follows that the European Commission does not have the power to reject the initiative of some Member States to establish enhanced cooperation simply based on the grounds that the incapability to find a consensus between all the Member States is triggered by a fundamental disagreement on the legislative framework between participating and non-participating Member States. In other words, enhanced cooperation can be established if the need for differentiation lies in a disagreement on 'how' to regulate. The CJEU went further and also declared the general lack of interest on the issue of some Member States as a reason for the impossibility of finding common ground between all Member States, which allows establishing enhanced cooperation. Accordingly, there are different reasons behind the inability to reach an agreement between all Member States, all of which paved the way for establishing enhanced cooperation between the willing Member States. Paragraph 36 of the judgment reads as if the CJEU did

[45] CJEU, 16 April 2013, C-274/11 and C-295/11, *Spain and Italy v Council*, ECLI:EU:C:2013:240, para 36, emphasis added.

[46] See also CJEU, 16 April 2013, C-274/11 and C-295/11, *Spain and Italy v Council*, ECLI:EU:C:2013:240, para 82: 'While it is, admittedly, essential for enhanced cooperation not to lead to the adoption of measures that might prevent the non-participating Member States from exercising their competences and rights or shouldering their obligations, it is, in contrast, *permissible for those taking part in this cooperation to prescribe rules with which those non-participating States would not agree if they did take part in it*' (emphasis added.

not want to rule out enhanced cooperation between the Member States simply because some Member States were not prepared to compromise or simply because they did not care. However, in both cases despite the lack of interest and disagreement on how to regulate, there is still a chance that the non-participating Member States may be convinced to join at a later stage because they see that the system or framework works[47] or because they see that the disadvantages of the law are outweighed by its advantages. In the same vein, a disagreement on the subsidiarity question, accordingly the question of whether EU actions are required or whether the Member States are perfectly capable of solving the issue on their own, would similarly not entitle the Commission to reject an initiative for enhanced cooperation. The fear of a loss of sovereignty, which leaves some Member States hesitant to join, may be overcome at some point.[48]

But all these reasons for a lack of consensus between all the Member States do not refer to a situation in which the outsiders fundamentally disagree on the policy objective, such as the question of whether or not to implement a unitary patent, a Financial Transaction Tax (FTT) or a Common Consolidated Corporate Tax Base (CCCTB).

In case certain Member States fundamentally disagree on policy objectives, they may not be convinced by the well-functioning of the system to join; it would require a political change triggered by elections or a radical factual development. If some Member States are of the firm belief that the financial sector should not be burdened by an FTT because they want to boost their financial economy, it may be less likely that these Member States ever join, even if the tax under enhanced cooperation functions quite well. Such Member States may only join if the political view towards the financial sector changes, which may be the case if a newly elected government promises to even out income inequalities and thus make the financial sector contribute more heavily to the common welfare system. However, without such a dramatic political turning point, it is quite likely that these Member States will never join, and the European Union will be divided into two blocs: the one establishing enhanced cooperation, and the other Member States opposing the policy decision.[49]

47 See in this vein Commission, 23 May 2001, Tax policy in the European Union—Priorities for the years ahead, COM(2001) 260 final 23: 'The enhanced co-operation could be targeted so as to produce such benefits for the participating countries that non-participants would be motivated to become involved.'

48 The Schengen Zone may work as a good example: Roland Bieber, 'Schlußbetrachtung: Schengen als Modell zukünftiger Integration?' in Alberto Achermann and others (eds), *Schengen und die Folgen: der Abbau der Grenzkontrollen in Europa* (Stämpfli [u.a] 1995); Klaus-Peter Nanz, 'Das Schengener Übereinkommen: Personenfreizügigkeit in integrationspolitischer Perspektive' (1994) Integration 92.

49 Accordingly, differentiation is not only temporary as proposed by the early works on the 'two-tier system' (Eberhard Grabitz and Bernd Langeheine, 'Legal Problems Related to a Proposed "Two-Tier System" of Integration within the European Community' (1981) 18 Common Market Law Review 33; Bernd Langeheine, 'Abgestufte Integration' (1983) Europarecht 227.). The permanent differentiation was, however, discussed under the heading 'variable geometry': Nina Ost, 'Flexibilitat des

But is such a division automatically a bad thing? To put it differently, does enhanced cooperation on policy objectives, which are subject to different views within the Member States, harm the European integration process if it is guaranteed that enhanced cooperation fulfils all substantive conditions set by the European treaties? Accordingly, one may ask whether it is better for the European integration process to disallow joint actions in particularly sensitive policy areas, which are characterised by the fundamentally different beliefs of the Member States, and subsequently, leave Member States with their unilateral regulatory actions. In the case of burdensome taxes, such as a tax on financial transactions, the Member States can implement such taxes on a unilateral basis if it is not already contained within their existing tax framework. Such a situation would also provide for a division between the one group of Member States levying a tax on financial transactions and another group of Member States not imposing such a tax. The Member States imposing the tax would, however, do so in an uncoordinated manner. The different design and scope of the national tax systems may lead to double taxation and increased compliance costs. As long as Member States do not agree on policy objectives, the division into two blocs with contradicting views will remain, regardless of allowing the one bloc to cooperate. Without the right to cooperate, the differences between the unilateral tax systems may, however, provide for additional trade obstacles within the European internal market. From this perspective, nothing has been gained in favour of the European integration process if the Member States which can, for example, agree on the taxation of the financial sector are prevented from even establishing enhanced cooperation.

Now, one may argue that bloc building may become more dangerous to the European integration process if one side is united under the roof of enhanced cooperation because it essentially brings bloc building to the next level: the insiders versus the outsiders, that is the Member States levying a common (European) FTT versus the Member States not levying the tax. However, the building of a bloc under a unifying roof can also occur outside enhanced cooperation. It has already been stressed[50] that enhanced cooperation is not in itself a self-contained regime, which grants the European flexibility mechanism exclusivity for all attempts of Member States to work together jointly. In other words, the existence of the enhanced cooperation mechanism in the European treaties does not prevent Member States from using other tools to coordinate and align their legislative actions. They are still allowed to enter into international agreements which, beyond any doubt, are capable of establishing differences between the Member States being a party to the treaty and the Member States not having signed the international agreement. From

Gemeinschaftsrechts—Vom Notantrieb zum Vertragsprinzip?' (1997) Die Öffentliche Verwaltung 495, 496, 501.

[50] See Chapter 2, subsection A.I.

this it follows that the Member States are capable of establishing blocs within the European Union in the absence of the use of the enhanced cooperation procedure.

Against this background, the use of the enhanced cooperation is beneficial, even in cases of deviating policy interests of all the Member States, as it allows the removal of trade obstacles within the group following from the differences of the national tax systems. Bloc building within the European Union could also follow from different unilateral actions of the Member States, as well as from the use of international agreements to coordinate and align the actions of the members of one bloc. The fact that bloc building could also be a consequence of joint actions outside the enhanced cooperation procedure is, however, not the determining factor. The determining factor for allowing bloc building precisely through the use of the enhanced cooperation procedure is the set of safeguarding mechanisms for non-participating Member States and the European internal market. Unlike in the case of the use of international agreements, the mechanism of enhanced cooperation ensures that the competences, rights, and obligations of non-participating Member States are explicitly protected,[51] and that the European internal market is not undermined.[52] Chapters 5 and 6 reveal the requirement of not undermining the internal market and respecting the rights, competences, and obligations of non-participating Member States. These safeguarding clauses are sufficient ways of ensuring that the groups of Member States following different policies do not become rival blocs. Thus, if these requirements are truly satisfied, there is no room left for a denial of collective actions of some Member States under the enhanced cooperation procedure on the grounds of negative implications on the European integration process.[53]

From all this it follows that the European Commission's power to allow or reject the pursuit of enhanced cooperation between some Member States is restricted to a thorough examination of the legal requirements set by the European treaties. The reason that some Member States do not want to participate must not influence the Commission's decision on whether or not it supports the request to establish enhanced cooperation. However, in light of the historical developments,

[51] Art 327 of the TFEU, see Chapter 6 and in particular Chapter 6, subsection B.IV.

[52] Art 326 of the TFEU; the Member States have to comply with the requirements set out by the European treaty with respect to the internal market when entering into international agreements. CJEU, 8 September 2009, C-478/07, *Rudolf Ammersin*, ECLI:EU:2009:521, para 98; CJEU, 20 May 2003, C-469/00, *Ravil*, ECLI:EU:C:2003:295, para 37; CJEU, 10 November 1992, C-3/91, *Exportur*, ECLI:EU:C:1992:420, para 8; CJEU, 27 September 1988, 235/87, *Annunziata Matteucci*, ECLI:EU:C:1988:460, para 22; see also Paul Craig and Gráinne de Búrca, *EU Law: Text, Cases, and Materials* (6th edn, OUP 2015) 358–59. In the case of an enhanced cooperation, the question of whether or not the internal market suffers from the cooperation is tested before the law is enacted.

[53] A different perspective is only possible if the European integration process is understood as the creation of perfect uniformity. However, the historical developments of the European Community and later of the European Union show that the primacy of uniformity cannot be fully maintained: von Buttlar (n 2) 680; Martin Hedemann-Robinson, 'The Area of Freedom, Security and Justice with Regard to the UK, Ireland and Denmark: The "Opt-in Opt-Outs" under the Treaty of Amsterdam' in David O'Keeffe and Patrick Twomey (eds), *Legal Issues of the Amsterdam Treaty* (Hart Publishing 1999).

one may argue that enhanced cooperation should only be established when all the Member States support the policy decision and the differentiation is only temporal. The wording of the primary EU law provisions does not require such an interpretation, and thus the CJEU allows the establishment of enhanced cooperation even if a different level of development of the Member States is not the reason for differentiation. Even beyond the scope of existing CJEU case law, the Member States should be entitled to establish enhanced cooperation if the participating and the non-participating Member States fundamentally disagree on the policy objectives. Without a change in the political landscape or a dramatic change of factual circumstances, the fundamental disagreement may cause a permanent differentiation within the European Union. However, the European treaties provide for safeguarding clauses ensuring that the bloc formation does not harm the European internal market. Accordingly, the Commission must not reject any request for establishing enhanced cooperation on the grounds that some Member States may likely not join, and thus enhanced cooperation may cause a permanent division between participating and non-participating Member States.

4. The European Commission's Role after Blessing Enhanced Cooperation

After the European Commission has granted its blessing by submitting a proposal to the Council, the Commission is still involved in the law-making process and required to monitor compliance with the substantive requirements set by the European treaties. First and foremost, the Commission may issue a proposal for the secondary EU law act which has to comply with all substantive conditions laid down in primary EU law after the Council has authorised enhanced cooperation. During negotiations in the Council over the design and content of the law, the Commission has to monitor any amendments made by the Council.[54] If the amended proposal no longer meets the substantive conditions set by the constitutional framework of enhanced cooperation and if the participating Member States are not willing to undo their changes or find an agreement which complies with the primary EU law framework, the Commission may withdraw the proposal.

The Commission derives the power of withdrawal from the power of legislative initiative. Within the enhanced cooperation procedure, the right of initiative lies with the willing Member States because they have to address a request to the Commission in the first place. Yet, the willing Member States' right of initiative only relieves the Commission of its dual function: monitoring the interests of the European Union as a whole and monitoring the interest of the Member States willing to move forward and establish enhanced cooperation. Thus, the

[54] According to Art 291 Subsection 1 of the TFEU, where the Council acts on a proposal from the Commission, the Council may amend the proposal by acting unanimously. In the area of enhanced cooperation, the provision has to be applied in an analogous manner, meaning that the participating Member States within the Council can amend the proposal from the Commission.

Commission's power to withdraw a proposal does not change within the enhanced cooperation procedure simply because the ultimate right of initiative lies with the willing Member States. However, the Commission's power to withdrawal does not vest the Commission with a general veto power.[55] Any withdrawal must be based on objective grounds which are subject to judicial review.[56] Accordingly, if the amendments to the proposal by the Council do not satisfy the substantive conditions as set by the European treaties, the Commission is entitled to withdraw its proposal.

C. The Council's Authorisation

The Council's authorisation to establish enhanced cooperation law is a fundamental part of the procedural framework. The decision is taken by all Member States and the Council acts by qualified majority, except in the area of common foreign and security policy.[57] Whether the Council should authorise enhanced cooperation through a qualified majority voting or whether a unanimous decision should be required was subject to a fundamental debate before the mechanism of closer cooperation was introduced into the European treaties by the Amsterdam Treaty. The primary law provisions, as introduced by the Amsterdam Treaty, already allowed the Council to act by a qualified majority[58] but also granted each Member State represented in the Council the right to request that the matter is referred to the European Council because of 'important stated reasons of national policy'.[59] Such a Member State claim did not per se block the establishment of enhanced cooperation,[60] but demanded a unanimous decision by the European Council. The quasi veto power of a single Member State was repealed by the Nice Treaty, which now restricts the requirements for the Council's decision to a qualified majority voting.[61] Some commentators still find the enhanced cooperation procedure too inflexible and thus claim that the authorisation by the Council to pursue enhanced cooperation should be granted by a simple majority voting.[62]

[55] CJEU, 14 April 2015, C-409/13, *Council v Commission*, ECLI:EU:C:2015:217, para 75.

[56] ibid para 76.

[57] Art 329 Subsections 1 and 2 of the TFEU.

[58] 'The authorisation referred to in paragraph 1 shall be granted by the Council, acting by a qualified majority', Art K.12, Treaty of Amsterdam amending the Treaty on European Union, the Treaties establishing the European Communities and certain related acts, OJ, 10 November 1997, C 340, p 1; Art 40a of the Treaty of Nice amending the Treaty on European Union, the Treaties establishing the European Communities and certain related acts, OJ, 10 March 2001, C 80, p 1.

[59] ibid.

[60] Paul Craig, *The Lisbon Treaty: Law, Politics, and Treaty Reform* (OUP 2013), 439.

[61] See for the discussions on the 'emergency brake' Stubb (n 26) 111, 112, 116 et seq.

[62] Eric Philippart, 'Un nouveau mécanisme de coopération renforcée pour l'Union européenne élargie' (2003) Notre Europe 24.

The Council's authorisation to establish enhanced cooperation between some Member States is the real starting point for the joint legislative process because the authorisation grants the willing Member States the right to engage in a bargaining and negotiation process to find an adequate agreement to enact the law. As the Council's authorisation turns out to be the foundation for enhanced cooperation between Member States, one may be tempted to define it as being of a constitutional nature.[63]

The (constitutional) foundation for a joint legislative action—the Council's authorisation—defines both the personal and the material scope of enhanced cooperation. The personal scope is defined by the participating Member States and is characterised by openness,[64] meaning that any non-participating Member State is free to join.[65] The material scope of enhanced cooperation law is set out without much detail because the true design and shape of the law are still open for debate between the participating Member States. The Council's authorisation can only lay out the principles the law of enhanced cooperation may follow, which the Member States may have defined in their notification, demonstrating their willingness to establish enhanced cooperation. Apart from the political intent and the general cornerstones of the common legislative initiative, none of the involved parties can provide more details on the material scope, because only the further legislative process can show on what points the participating Member States are willing to agree.[66]

In that vein, the CJEU ruled that the UK's claim to nullify the Council's authorisation for enhanced cooperation in the field of a common tax on financial transactions was premature. Any negative effects the United Kingdom fears may prove not to be true because the Member States have not yet designed the scope of the tax.[67] From this it follows that the CJEU qualifies the Council's authorisation as an indication of what the group of Member States is aiming for, but the group is free to enter into an open debate and may end up with laws which have a different scope than initially expected. Thus, the Member States are only bound by the political intention underlying their request and the Council's subsequent authorisation.

Accordingly, the participating Member States have a wide leeway with respect to the actual design and the material scope of the law introduced under enhanced cooperation. However, the fundamentals are set by the Council's authorisation

[63] 'Editorial Comments: Enhanced Cooperation: A Union à Taille Réduite or à Porte Tournante?' (n 9) 317.

[64] Whether the enhanced cooperation is based on an inherent bias for a reduction of the Member States will be subject to more in-depth analysis; see this chapter subsection E.II.

[65] Art 328 of the TFEU.

[66] For a critical view see Anzhela Cédelle and John Vella, 'Differentiated Integration in the EU: Lessons from the Financial Transaction Tax' in Panos Koutrakos, and Jukka Snell (eds), *Research Handbook on the Law of the EU's Internal Market* (Edward Elgar Publishing 2017) 364–65.

[67] CJEU, 30 April 2014, C-209/13, *United Kingdom of Great Britain and Northern Ireland v Council*, ECLI:EU:C:2014:282, para 36.

and have to be accepted. In other words, if the Council grants a group of Member States the authorisation to pursue enhanced cooperation in the field of a common FTT, the Member States are not allowed to introduce financial regulations for the banking sector based on the authorisation. Likewise, if the Council's authorisation is granted for an FTT which aims to prevent under-taxation of the financial sector,[68] that is a mere fiscal tax, the Member States are not allowed to design and shape the tax in a way which best achieves a steering goal, for example a stable financial market. Restricting the binding nature of the Council's authorisation to the cornerstones and political intention of the intended law balances both the needed flexibility of the participating Member States to enter into a negotiation process, and predictability for non-participating Member States. Some non-participating Member States might have joined the legislative initiative if they had known that the participating Member States would agree on entirely different laws than initially expected. The non-participating Member States can always join later, but they may no longer be able to influence the negotiation process. Therefore, the Member States are bound by the political intent underlying the Council's authorisation, yet they remain free to design and shape the law to achieve these policy objectives.

D. Mechanism of Last Resort

Art 20 Subsection 2 of the Treaty on European Union (TEU) states that the decision authorising enhanced cooperation shall be adopted by the Council as *a last resort* when it has been established that the objectives of such cooperation cannot be attained within a reasonable period by the Union as a whole. The requirement to use the mechanism of enhanced cooperation as an *ultima ratio* raises various questions. First of all, is the Council the only institution to determine whether or not it is possible to reach a consensus among all Member States at the European level? Should the European Commission wait until the Council explicitly finds that a common action between all Member States cannot be taken in the foreseeable future to issue a proposal for establishing enhanced cooperation? Such a Council decision would be separate and distinct from an authorisation to act under the enhanced cooperation procedure. Or should the Commission instead evaluate the possibility of finding an agreement between all the Member States on its own, and subsequently submit a proposal to the Council after the Member States have notified the Commission that they are willing to establish enhanced cooperation and if the Commission finds that all the Member States will not be able to reach a compromise in the near future?

68 See for more details Pablo A Hernández González-Barreda, 'On the European Way to a Financial Transaction Tax under Enhanced Cooperation: Multi-Speed Europe or Shortcut?' (2013) 41 Intertax 208, 218 et seq.

Despite the question of who is responsible for identifying whether enhanced cooperation is used as an *ultima ratio* in a given situation, questions arise on the actual notion of last resort. Are some Member States allowed to establish enhanced cooperation to achieve deeper harmonisation among them, although all Member States can agree on a compromise that creates a lower level of integration, but integration between all Member States? And what is the nature of the relationship between enhanced cooperation and other mechanisms which may be able to overcome the issues related to unanimous decision-making, such as the passerelle clause?

The following subsections systematically address all questions. Subsection I considers the relationship between enhanced cooperation and the passerelle clause enshrined in the European treaties . Subsection II answers the question of who has to decide on whether enhanced cooperation is a mechanism of last resort in a given situation. Subsection III examines whether a legislative attempt must have failed at the European level to allow the use of enhanced cooperation. The policy implications of the last resort requirement are discussed in subsection IV. Subsection V examines whether enhanced cooperation can be established if all the Member States can agree on secondary EU law providing for a lower level of integration.

I. The Passerelle Clause: A Preferred Alternative?

Jan-Jaap Kuipers raised the question of whether enhanced cooperation in the area of divorce law was 'really a measure of last resort', since the Lisbon Treaty introduced the passerelle clause for family law with cross-border implications.[69] The passerelle clause of Art 81 Subsection 3 of the TFEU for cross-border family law issues is not the only provision in the European treaties which allows for a change to the decision-making rules outside the ordinary procedure for changing the European treaties. Art 153 Subsection 2 of the TFEU provides a bridging clause for matters of social policy, Art 192 Subsection 2 of the TFEU for certain matters of employment policy, and Art 312 Subsection 2 of the TFEU on the multiannual financial framework.[70] A more general bridging clause has been introduced by the Lisbon Treaty in Art 48 Subsection 7 of the TEU;[71] it grants the European Council the right to 'adopt a decision authorising the Council to act by a qualified majority' in an area or case which would generally require a unanimous vote. The passerelle clause is capable of changing the European treaties with respect

[69] Kuipers (n 39) 216. For the legal procedure see Art 81 Subsection 3 of the TFEU.

[70] Robert Böttner, 'The Treaty Amendment Procedures and the Relationship between Article 31(3) TEU and the General Bridging Clause of Article 48(7) TEU' (2016) 12 European Constitutional Law Review 499, 510.

[71] Art 48 Subsection 7 of the TEU applies to the entirety of the TFEU plus Title V of the TEU: Steve Peers, 'The Future of EU Treaty Amendments' (2012) 31 Yearbook of European Law 17, 43–44.

to the voting requirements, but they do not change the allocation of powers between the European Union and the Member States.[72] In other words, the passerelle clause may change how the European institutions enact the law concerning voting and participation requirements, but it cannot change which areas can be regulated through European legislation. There are several areas excluded from the application of the bridging clauses, such as decisions with military implications.[73] Taxation, however, falls within the scope of Art 48 section 7 of the TEU.[74]

The application of Art 48 Subsection 7 of the TEU allows one to move from unanimous decision-making in the Council to a qualified majority voting, which of course simplifies and advances the decision-making process.[75] The change is, however, subject to a process of control by national parliaments. Each national parliament is allowed to veto an initiative under Art 48 Subsection 7 of the TEU within six months without being required to state reasons.[76] The procedure provides some simplification, as the national parliaments do not have to ratify or approve the decision; they approve it if they do not veto the initiative.[77]

Against the background of the procedural framework of Art 48 Subsection 7 of the TEU, it becomes evident that the provision aims to ease the change from unanimity to qualified majority voting. In case the Member States are ready to give up their veto power in certain areas of the law, they should not be required to wait until the negotiations over an entire range of treaty changes have been settled. Thus, Art 48 Subsection 7 of the TEU should be applied before negotiations over a certain legislative act start. If the negotiation process has already started, and if it turns out that some Member States have a completely different view on the particular matter (whether and how the subject should be regulated by European law), the application of Art 48 Subsection 7 of the TEU would be a non-starter. The Member States who take a contrary view on the matter in the Council and thus block a unanimous decision are very likely to veto an initiative to change from unanimity to qualified majority voting in that particular field. The only situation in which the national parliament will not veto the initiative is when the minister's decision is not backed by the majority of the national parliament. But the provision is not built to circumvent a Member State's vote in the Council. It is a provision which should extend majority voting in case the Member States are ready, and thereby enhance and advance the European legislative process.

In this vein, it is striking that Art 333 of the TFEU allows a change from a unanimous vote to qualified majority voting within enhanced cooperation. The change

[72] Eileen Denza, 'Art. 48' in Hermann-Josef Blanke and Stelio Mangiameli (eds), *The Treaty on European Union (TEU)—A Commentary* (Springer 2013) para 47.

[73] See also explicit exceptions listed in Art 353 of the TFEU.

[74] See Chapter 2, subsection B.II.

[75] For the effects qualified majority voting may have in the area of taxation see Chapter 2, subsection B.III.

[76] Böttner (n 70) 506–07.

[77] Peers, 'EU Treaty Amendments' (n 71) 43.

in the decision-making requires a unanimous vote of the Council, and the voting will take place at a time when the key elements of the law have already been discussed.[78] The passerelle clause would only make sense if it were argued that the design of the law is fully open to discussion between the participating Member States, and none of the Member States have already made up their minds on the design and scope of the law. The legal framework for establishing enhanced cooperation would allow such a view because the Council's authorisation only determines the material scope of the law in a very vague manner.[79] In practice, however, the Member States know what every Member State is aiming for, and thus if one fears being outvoted on sensitive subject matters such as taxation, the Member State would not be likely to agree on a changing from unanimity to qualified majority voting in these areas. This includes enhanced cooperation.

From this it follows that the passerelle clause of Art 48 Subsection 7 of the TEU should not be understood as a measure for overcoming a legislative deadlock in a particular situation. If a specific proposal for European legislation is on the table, and a unanimous vote in the Council cannot be reached, an initiative to change from unanimous to qualified majority voting in the Council fails. Thus, enhanced cooperation may be characterised as a measure of last resort even if a change from unanimity to qualified majority voting under the passerelle clause has not been initiated.

II. Who has to Decide on the *Ultima Ratio* Issue?

According to the plain wording of the provision, enhanced cooperation shall only be authorised *by the Council* if a legislative action cannot be attained by the European Union as a whole within a reasonable period of time. In other words, the Council has to evaluate whether a compromise between all the Member States is truly impossible when it is asked to authorise enhanced cooperation. The question of whether enhanced cooperation is adopted as a measure of last resort has to be asked within the Council's authorisation approval process. However, before the Council is entrusted with this question, other parties which are involved in the enhanced cooperation procedure have to decide on the *ultima ratio* issue: first, the Member States which are willing to pursue the legislative action and which address a request to the European Commission for the establishing of enhanced cooperation;[80] secondly, the Commission, which submits a proposal for enhanced cooperation to the Council;[81] thirdly, the European Parliament, which approves

[78] Robert Böttner, 'Eine Idee lernt laufen—zur Praxis der Verstärkten Zusammenarbeit nach Lissabon' (2016) 19 Zeitschrift für europarechtliche Studien 501, 528.

[79] In that vein CJEU, 30 April 2014, C-209/13, *United Kingdom of Great Britain and Northern Ireland v Council*, ECLI:EU:C:2014:282, para 36; see for more details this chapter subsection C.

[80] Art 329 Subsection 1 of the TFEU.

[81] ibid.

the proposal;[82] and fourthly, the Council, which takes the final decision in authorising the enhanced cooperation.[83] It should be remembered that the 'Council, in taking that final decision, is best placed to determine whether the Member States have demonstrated any willingness to compromise and are in a position to put forward proposals capable of leading to the adoption of legislation for the [European] Union as a whole in the foreseeable future'.[84]

Despite the fact that the Council takes the final decision on the *ultima ratio* question, the other institutions—these being the European Commission and the European Parliament—and also the Member States initiating enhanced cooperation are influenced by the requirement that enhanced cooperation is only an option if not all Member States can agree on a compromise.

Every attempt to launch a legislative initiative at a European level will start with negotiations between all the Member States and the effort to find common ground on the particular matter. The preliminary negotiations will already show whether the necessary majorities will be found for a joint initiative, or whether the views of the Member States fundamentally clash, preventing any uniform actions of the Member States, or whether some level of agreement may be reached, which allows for niggling harmonisation. Since enhanced cooperation will only be authorised as a last resort measure, the Member States which agree on policy objectives will only propose enhanced cooperation if they are convinced that a general agreement between all Member States cannot be reached in the foreseeable future.

Likewise, the European Commission will only issue a proposal to the Council if the Commission is convinced that all requirements, including the *ultima ratio* requirement, are met. It would be a waste of effort for the Commission to work on a proposal on establishing enhanced cooperation if a requirement for the granting of authorisation by the Council is (definitely) not met. Accordingly, the Commission will follow the discussions in the Council and decide whether or not to engage in endorsing the use of the enhanced cooperation procedure after some Member States have issued their request.[85] However, the monitoring of the negotiation

[82] ibid.

[83] CJEU, 16 April 2013, C-274/11 and C-295/11, *Spain and Italy v Council*, ECLI:EU:C:2013:240, para 52.

[84] CJEU, 16 April 2013, C-274/11 and C-295/11, *Spain and Italy v Council*, ECLI:EU:C:2013:240, para 53.

[85] See for the proposal of a Council decision authorising enhanced cooperation in the area of financial taxation: 'The proposal and variants thereof were extensively discussed in the meetings of the Council . . . but failed to get the required unanimous support because of fundamental and un-bridgeable differences amongst Member States', 23 October 2012, COM(2012) 631 final, p 3; within the proposal for a Council decision authorising enhanced cooperation in the area of the creation of unitary patent protection the Commission highlighted the different stages in the negotiation process where the proposal failed to reach the required unanimity, 14 December 2010, COM(2010) 790 final, p 2 et seq; within the proposal for a Council decision authorising enhanced cooperation in the area of jurisdiction, applicable law, and the recognition and enforcement of decisions on the property regimes of international couples, covering both matters of matrimonial property regimes and the property consequences of registered partnerships the Commission explicitly referred to the Council's conclusions at the meeting of 3 December 2015 according to which 'it would not be possible to reach an EU-wide agreement for

process in the Council does not demand an official Council decision stating that the necessary majorities for the adoption of European legislation are not in place.[86] In other words, even if there is no official opinion from the Council on the failure of the negotiations, the Commission can form an opinion on whether to submit a proposal for authorising enhanced cooperation to the Council.

From all of this it follows that the Council takes the final decision on whether the enhanced cooperation in a particular field is truly the *ultima ratio*. The actions of other institutions involved—predominantly the European Commission and the willing Member States—will be influenced by the requirement of enhanced cooperation as being a mechanism of last resort. However, it does not require a separate decision by the Council stating that an agreement between all the Member States will not be reached in the foreseeable future for the Commission to act, but a clear indication from the negotiation process is required to find enhanced cooperation to be the measure of last resort.

III. The Council's Decision in Authorising Enhanced Cooperation

In *Spain and Italy v Council*, the unitary patent case, the CJEU ruled that '[t]he Council, in taking the final decision, is best placed to determine whether the Member States have demonstrated any willingness to compromise and are in a position to put forward proposals capable of leading to the adoption of legislation for the Union as a whole in the foreseeable future'.[87] The Court's ruling refers to the Council's authorisation: the final decision in the process of allowing some Member States to establish enhanced cooperation. In that regard, the Court does not judge on the requirement of 'last resort' but ascertains 'whether the Council has carefully and impartially examined those aspects that are relevant to this point and whether adequate reasons have been given for the conclusion'.[88]

From this it follows that the final decision on the last resort measure rests with the Council. In the past, however, the Council has not only implicitly ruled on the last resort measure by authorising the enhanced cooperation, the Council has

the adoption of the two regulations within a reasonable period of time', 2 March 2016, COM(2016) 108 final, p 3; within the proposal for a Council decision authorising enhanced cooperation in the area of the law applicable to divorce and legal separation, the Commission referred to the conclusions of the Council according to which 'there was no unanimity to go ahead with the proposed Regulation and that insurmountable difficulties existed, making a decision requiring unanimity impossible now and in the foreseeable future', 24 March 2010, COM(2010) 104 final, pp 2–3.

[86] Sebastian Reinhard Johannes Cloppenburg, *Eine Finanztransaktionssteuer im 'kleinen Kreis'* (Peter Lang 2018) 190–91.

[87] CJEU, 16 April 2013, C-274/11 and C-295/11, *Spain and Italy v Council*, ECLI:EU:C:2013:240, para 53.

[88] ibid para 54.

also issued a statement on the progress of the negotiations, which may conclude that an agreement among all the Member States is not achievable in the near future.[89] When it becomes clear that consent in the Council will not be reached, some Member States reveal their ambition to establish enhanced cooperation, and subsequently issue their (common or separate) requests to the European Commission. Thus, the starting point for any existing enhanced cooperation is based on the conviction that an agreement between all the Member States will probably not be reached in the foreseeable future, which is reflected in the Council's statements. Aside from the preliminary findings of the Council, the decision on the last resort requirement is taken by the Council by authorising enhanced cooperation.

IV. Aim and Purpose

The aim and purpose underlying the last resort requirement is quite clear. Enhanced cooperation rejects the general European principle of uniformity. However, uniformity within the European Union should not be lightly abandoned.[90] Therefore, the possibility of joint action by all Member States should be explored before allowing some Member States to establish enhanced cooperation.[91] The *ultima ratio* requirement also reveals that secondary EU law binding all Member States should be the rule and enhanced cooperation the exception. The clear preference for uniform European law must not be confused with the clear choice of the Member States to introduce differentiated integration into the European legal framework.[92] Differentiated integration may have become a clear characteristic of European Union law but it must only be pursued if uniform legislative action cannot be established.

The European treaties do not specify how much time has to pass before it is certain that a common legislative action of all Member States may not be achievable,[93] and thus some Member States are allowed to establish enhanced cooperation. Recently, the European Parliament proposed that enhanced cooperation should be open for the Member States if a proposal by the European Commission 'did not manage to reach an agreement through the regular

[89] See for the progress on the European financial transaction tax Commission, 23 October 2012, MEMO, Enhanced Cooperation on Financial Transaction Tax—Questions and Answers, MEMO/12/799 ('Member States concluded that they would not be able to agree upon it unanimously within a reasonable period').

[90] In this vein see also Cédelle (n 36) 198–99.

[91] In that vein see Cloppenburg (n 86) 188.

[92] See Chapter 1, subsection B.

[93] According to Advocate General Bot, 'it is clear that [the last resort] condition is not necessarily the fact that a legislative proposal has been rejected by a vote, but rather the fact that there is a genuine deadlock, which could arise at all levels of the legislative process and which demonstrates that it is impossible to arrive at a compromise', Opinion of Advocate General Bot, 11 December 2012, C-274/11 and C-295/11, *Spain and Italy v Council*, ECLI:EU:C:2012:782, para 111.

decision-making procedure within the mandate of two consecutive Council presidencies'.[94] The European Parliament is also in favour of a 'fast-track authorisation of enhanced cooperation in fields of high political salience to be accomplished within a shorter timeframe'.[95] The advantage of a fixed period would be that the Member States may automatically consider using enhanced cooperation as an alternative path. A 'fast-track' authorisation procedure would not be necessary because the enhanced cooperation procedure is, and should be, a mechanism of last resort; however, this does not mean that the Member States are not allowed to pursue the path of differentiated integration even before the proposed period of two consecutive Council presidencies. If it is certain that some Member States have a very different view on a particular policy matter, and thus would not accept any secondary EU law heading into a different direction, the willing Member States are immediately allowed to take the necessary steps to implement enhanced cooperation. 'Immediately' should not be taken literally, as the Commission's first proposal for secondary EU law should always address all the Member States. It is only possible to discuss potential legislative actions and get an idea of the Member States' willingness to further the legislative initiative if there is a concrete proposal on the table.

V. Reasonability of Integration at a Lower Level

The European treaties only allow enhanced cooperation to be implemented when 'the objectives of such cooperation cannot be attained ... by the Union as a whole'.[96] The phrase 'objectives of the cooperation' may be subject to a quite narrow or a very wide interpretation. The difference of both interpretative methods comes to light when all the Member States can agree on a common legislative action which, however, only provides for a (very) low level of integration between the Member States, and only some Member States can agree on a deeper form of integration. If the 'objective' of enhanced cooperation is defined in a very narrow way, the willing Member States may not be hindered from establishing enhanced cooperation. If, however, one takes a broader perspective, the fact that a compromise can be reached between all Member States, regardless of the lower level of integration, may prevent enhanced cooperation.

If a decision between lower-level and deeper integration is at stake, it may be possible to combine both ordinary secondary EU law and enhanced cooperation

[94] European Parliament, 28 January 2019, on the implementation of the Treaty provisions concerning enhanced cooperation, 2018/2112(INI).
[95] ibid.
[96] Art 20 Subsection 2 of the TEU.

law because minimum harmonisation at a European level grants Member States substantive leeway to establish supplementing enhanced cooperation law. We shall assume, for example, that all the Member States can agree on the need for closer cooperation in the field of audits of taxpayers engaging in cross-border economic activities. At present, Member States can enter into joint audits based on the Mutual Assistance Directive.[97] Some Member States may, however, introduce a more standardised framework for pursuing joint audits. In this case, secondary EU law defining the limits, the scope, and the precise procedure of such joint audits would build an additional layer of regulation for some Member States.[98]

However, in most cases, the decision between the ordinary secondary EU law and enhanced cooperation law is based on preferences and does not truly reflect a lower or deeper level of integration. We shall assume, for example, that all Member States can agree on the need to tax the financial sector more heavily so that financial institutions contribute more fairly to the costs of the last financial crisis. We shall further assume that some Member States are in favour of introducing a fully fledged FTT which taxes every financial transaction involving a resident or a deemed resident financial institution, as has been proposed by the European Commission.[99] All the Member States could, however, agree on introducing a stamp duty, following the British example. The combination of both taxes would lead to over-taxation and a lack of competitiveness amongst these Member States. A decision which lies between a fully fledged FTT and a stamp duty is not a decision between lower-level and deeper integration; it is a decision of preferences, in essence, concerning one's aims with regard to a tax on financial transactions.

From this it follows that a decision between lower-level integration between all Member States and a deeper integration between some Member States may sometimes be resolved by introducing minimum harmonisation between all the Member States, and an additional layer of regulation by enhanced cooperation law. A decision between a legislative act for all the Member States and a legislative act under the enhanced cooperation procedure cannot be made when the different approaches are based on different preferences, such as in the example of the taxation on financial transactions. However, such a decision is not a decision between lower-level or deeper harmonisation; it is a decision on the design and shape of the law.

[97] Directive, 15 February 2011, 2011/16/EU, on administrative cooperation in the field of taxation and repealing Directive 77/799/EEC, OJ, 11 March 2011, L 64, 1; for more information on that matter see Isabella Zimmerl, *Joint Tax Audits als Ausgangspunkt zur Effektuierung des Verständigungsverfahrens - Eine Analyse möglicher dogmatischer Entwicklungen unter besonderer Berücksichtigung der deutsch-italienischen Verwaltungszusammenarbeit* (2019).

[98] See this chapter subsection G.V.1.b.

[99] For more details on the FTT see Chapter 3, subsection C.I.

E. Going in and Going out: Joining and Leaving Enhanced Cooperation

The personal scope of enhanced cooperation is not set in stone. The European treaties demand that any enhanced cooperation consists, at any time, of at least nine Member States, but the exact number can vary because some Member States may join after enhanced cooperation has been established, and some may leave throughout the process of establishment. Whilst the ability of non-participating Member States to join after enhanced cooperation has been established is explicitly allowed by the European treaties, a participating Member State's right to leave can only be determined by the principles of EU law and the enhanced cooperation procedure.

I. Non-participating Member States Joining Enhanced Cooperation

Any enhanced cooperation must be open to all non-participating Member States.[100] The procedural framework for joining an existing group at any stage of the process is explicitly determined by Art 331 of the TFEU. The procedure is pretty straightforward and requires the non-participating Member State which wishes to participate in enhanced cooperation to notify both the Council and the European Commission. Subsequently, the Commission has to investigate whether or not the willing Member State is ready and fit to join within four months.[101] The wording of Art 331 of the TFEU precisely reflects the situation of a Member State which was, at the time enhanced cooperation was founded, unable to join due to the status of its political, social, or economic development, but later reached the level of the other Member States, and thus wishes to join.[102] Importantly, an acceding Member State also has to undergo the procedure of Art 331 of the TFEU if it wishes to become a participating Member State. An automatic accession is prevented by the European treaties, since any enhanced cooperation is not part of European acquis.[103]

The European Commission can either conclude that the willing Member State has fulfilled the conditions of participation, and thus is entitled to join, or is not

[100] Art 328 of the TFEU.

[101] Fabian Amtenbrink and Dimitry Kochenov, 'Towards a More Flexible Approach to Enhanced Cooperation' in Andrea Ott and Ellen Vos (eds), *50 Years of European Integration: Foundations and Perspectives* (Asser 2009) 190 arguing that the 'need to be ready to comply with the legal framework established within the existing enhanced cooperation project they intent to join' narrows down the principle of openness; see also Eric Philippart and Geoffrey Edwards, 'The Provisions on Closer Co-Operation in the Treaty of Amsterdam: The Politics of Flexibility in the European Union' (1999) 37 Journal of Common Market Studies 87, 91 emphasising that the 'open door' principle is 'based on objective criteria and acceptance of an acquis established by others'.

[102] Art 331 of the TFEU explicitly states: 'the conditions of participation have been fulfilled'.

[103] Art 20 Subsection 4 of the TFEU.

yet ready to become a member of the group. In the latter case, the Commission has to 'indicate the arrangements to be adopted' to comply with the conditions necessary to enter, and the Commission has to set a deadline for re-examining the request. On expiry of the deadline, the Commission has to re-examine the situation. If the Commission is still of the opinion that the willing Member State is unable to join, the Member State is allowed to refer the matter to the Council, which has to decide on the request. Accordingly, the Council has the power to outvote the Commission's decision.

The new participating Member State enjoys all rights and is bound by all obligations at the moment it joins enhanced cooperation. As soon as the Member State becomes a part of enhanced cooperation, no differentiation between the founding members and member which joined at a later point in time is allowed.

II. Participating Member States Leaving Enhanced Cooperation

For different reasons, a Member State may wish to leave enhanced cooperation throughout the different stages of the law-making process. A Member State may have indicated its interest in being part of a joint initiative, but never addressed an official request to the European Commission (see subsection 1). Moreover, Member States may want to leave the joint initiative after they addressed an official request to the Commission (see subsection 2), or after the Council issues its authorisation to pursue with enhanced cooperation (see subsection 3), or even after the law has been introduced under the enhanced cooperation procedure and has been adopted by the participating Member States (see subsection 4). The different stages of the law-making process may deal differently with the Member State's claim to leave the enhanced cooperation. Therefore, the following subsections will be split into the different stages of the process of leaving and will also propose necessary reforms to the current constitutional framework of the enhanced cooperation procedure to provide certainty for the process of leaving (see subsection 5).

1. 'Leaving' after Indicating One's Interest

Given that some Member States indicate their willingness to establish enhanced cooperation before they officially issue a request to the European Commission, one may ask whether the mere statement of intent can already bind the Member States. This question is particularly relevant if the Member States entered into negotiations to be able to issue a joint request to the Commission. Such negotiations would be necessary if all the willing Member States had to issue one (joint) request because such a request already needs some form of specification on the scope and the object of enhanced cooperation. If, however, the Member States are allowed to address an individual request to the Commission disclosing their point of views and what they are individually aiming for, no explicit prior coordination between the Member States is needed. It would then be up to the Commission to decide whether there is sufficient consensus between the Member States to pursue the establishment of enhanced cooperation.

Examining the practical experience with the enhanced cooperation procedure, it becomes evident that each Member State wishing to participate in enhanced cooperation should address an individual request to the European Commission.[104] The request will typically be no more than a declaration of intent to support the pursuing of a legislative endeavour which is stuck in a legislative deadlock. This would give the Member States the possibility of (only) referring to the Commission's work and would free them from defining in detail what they are aiming for. An alternative is hardly possible because enhanced cooperation can only be a measure of last resort which presupposes that the European institutions, and in particular the Commission, have put some serious effort in trying to achieve a consensus among all the Member States.[105] Such an effort would at least demand a proposal for the legislative initiative.

From this it follows that there is no bond between the willing Member States before each of them issues a request to the European Commission indicating their willingness to participate in enhanced cooperation. If a Member State has already indicated that it is willing to support the establishment of enhanced cooperation but later changes its opinion and abstains from issuing a request to the Commission, the Member States which stand by their words and address a request to the Commission cannot force that Member State to participate.

2. Leaving after Addressing a Request to the European Commission

The question of entitlement to leave becomes more interesting when the Member State has already issued a request to the European Commission indicating its willingness to join enhanced cooperation. If a Member State is no longer willing to be a part of enhanced cooperation after submitting its request, the Member State's right

[104] For the European unitary patent: '12 Member States, namely Denmark, Germany, Estonia, France, Lithuania, Luxembourg, the Netherlands, Poland, Slovenia, Finland, Sweden and the United Kingdom, addressed requests to the Commission by letters dated 7, 8 and 13 December 2010 indicating that they wished to establish enhanced cooperation between themselves in the area of the creation of unitary patent protection on the basis of the existing proposals supported by these Member States during the negotiations and that the Commission should submit a proposal to the Council to that end. The requests were confirmed at the meeting of the Council on 10 December 2010. In the meantime, 13 more Member States, namely Belgium, Bulgaria, the Czech Republic, Ireland, Greece, Cyprus, Latvia, Hungary, Malta, Austria, Portugal, Romania and Slovakia have written to the Commission indicating that they also wish to participate in the envisaged enhanced cooperation. In total, 25 Member States have requested enhanced cooperation', Council, 10 March 2011, 2011/167/EU, decision authorising enhanced cooperation in the area of the creation of unitary patent protection, OJ, 22. March 2011, L 76/53; for an enhanced cooperation in the area of a financial transaction tax: '10 Member States, namely Belgium, Germany, Greece, Spain, France, Italy, Austria, Portugal, Slovenia and Slovakia, addressed requests to the Commission by letters received between 28 September and 22 October 2012 indicating that they wished to establish enhanced cooperation between themselves in the area of FTT', Commission, 23 October 2012, COM(2012) 631.

[105] See this chapter subsection D.

to leave depends on the legal nature of the request. The issue becomes particularly relevant where the remaining Member States no longer reach the minimum threshold of nine Member States, as prescribed by the primary EU law rules.

As has been revealed in the above,[106] each Member State submits its request to the European Commission without any intense prior negotiations between the willing Member States. Accordingly, a binding effect cannot follow from any coordination between the Member States, but from submitting the request. There may be different views on the binding effect of a Member State's request to the Commission for pursuing enhanced cooperation. On the one hand, the fact that, at this stage, the Member States do not know what the Commission's proposal ultimately looks like militates against the binding effect, as the Commission may not consider all claims and demands of the Member States within its proposal. On the other hand, in most cases, the Member States will rely on the previous work of the Commission and declare their willingness to support enhanced cooperation for a legislative attempt which could not find the consent of all the Member States. If the Commission does not change fundamental parts of the legislative proposal, the Member States issuing a request know what to expect. But, of course, the Member States could have relied on the previous work of the Commission and could have requested changes or amendments, which the Commission may or may not consider.

Returning to the right of initiative, it has been revealed that a request by the Member States ensures that every Member State freely joins an enhanced cooperation, and relieves the European Commission from the dual function of having to recognise the interests of the European Union as a whole (which would prefer a compromise between all the Member States), as well as the interests of willing Member States. The dual function would require the Commission to find the moment at which it is no longer sensible to work on a uniform solution for the entire European Union, and not too late to commence separate negotiations within a smaller group of Member States.[107] If the request of the willing Member States is only to safeguard the principle that the right of initiative lies with the Member States, then it is justified to understand the request of the Member States as a mere request to act without imposing any binding effects upon the Member States requesting the Commission's action. Even from a purely interest-driven perspective, it would not make much sense to oblige Member States to join the enhanced cooperation because they have issued a request. If they were bound by their request without a way out, the Member States might hesitate to issue the request, contradicting the aim of enhanced cooperation, which should provide the Member States with a feasible alternative to a compromise between all the Member States.

From all of this it follows that the request of a willing Member State does not tie that Member State to the joint legislative initiative without giving it the possibility

[106] See this chapter subsection E.II.1.
[107] See this chapter subsection B.I.

to leave. The request of willing Member States should be understood as a simple invitation of the European Commission to pursue the legislative attempt within a smaller group of Member States. Just as the Commission is not bound to act by the willing Member States' request, the requesting Member States are not obliged to remain a part of the legislative initiative. If a Member State no longer supports the legislative initiative, despite having issued a request to the Commission, the Member State would need to inform the Commission of its changed opinion, but it is not obliged to stay within the group.

3. Leaving after the Council's Authorisation

The next milestone within the enhanced cooperation procedure is the authorisation granted by the Council. The authorisation is based on both the proposal for enhanced cooperation of the European Commission and the (number of) Member States willing to establish enhanced cooperation. The number of potential participating Member States influences the decision of the Council, not only with regard to the need to satisfy the requirement of having at least nine Member States on board but also concerning the suitability of such enhanced cooperation with respect to the objectives of the joint legislative initiative. Against this background, there are good reasons for restricting the right of participating Member States to withdraw from their obligation to participate in enhanced cooperation once the Council has given its consent to pursue the legislative attempt within the group. If, however, it is foreseeable that the Member State will block the legislative initiative, it would be better for all parties to allow the one Member State to leave. Moreover, if one Member State only wanted to participate in order to sabotage the establishment of enhanced cooperation, the willing Member States may wish to exclude that Member State from the legislative process.

As a consequence, there are different reasons triggering a Member State's departure after the Council has authorised the pursue of enhanced cooperation. First, the Member State may unilaterally decide that it wants to leave, but the remaining Member States disagree and do not want it to leave (see subsection a). Secondly, all the Member States agree that it is better for that one Member State to leave the group (see subsection b). And, thirdly, the Member States may wish to exclude one Member State which only joined the group to hamper the legislative attempt (see subsection c)

a) Unilateral Leaving of the Group

In the above,[108] it has already been revealed that the authorisation by the Council sets both the personal and the material scope of enhanced cooperation. The personal scope is determined by the participating Member States, and thus the

[108] See this chapter subsection C.

number of the Member States participating in enhanced cooperation, as well as which Member States form part of the group, have an impact on the Council's decision. The number of participating Member States may change in future because any enhanced cooperation is open to all non-participating Member States.[109] If, however, the non-group member wants to join the enhanced cooperation, the process is subject to a 'unionized'[110] procedure, which involves the European institutions implicated in the founding procedure of enhanced cooperation.[111]

From this it follows that the unilateral departure of a participating Member State, after Council authorisation, contradicts both the procedural framework and the nature of enhanced cooperation. The procedural framework establishes that the Council's authorisation builds the constitutional fundament of any enhanced cooperation,[112] and thus the authorising decision and the subsequent substantive enhanced cooperation laws have to have an identical personal scope.[113] Perhaps the Council's decision would have been different from the outset if fewer Member States wished to establish enhanced cooperation, for example because the number of Member States is incapable of achieving the objectives.

With respect to the nature of enhanced cooperation, one may be tempted to understand the whole mechanism as being based on the voluntary act of each participating Member State,[114] which would allow each Member State to change its will throughout the legislative process.[115] Yet such a view would misinterpret the entire enhanced cooperation procedure and, in particular, the authorisation decision by the Council. The Council's authorisation grants a particular group of Member States the right to use the institutions of the European Union to enact a law which is binding among them. Accordingly, the Council's decision is the starting point for a negotiation and bargaining process amongst willing Member States. Giving each participating Member State the right to pull out of the legislative process because the Member State does not agree with the legislative evolution would dramatically affect the stability of the legal framework, and would not be in line with the aim and purpose of the enhanced cooperation procedure.[116] This is

[109] Art 328 of the TFEU.

[110] 'Editorial Comments: Enhanced Cooperation: A Union à Taille Réduite or à Porte Tournante?' (n 9) 324.

[111] Art 331 of the TFEU.

[112] See this chapter subsection C.

[113] 'Editorial Comments: Enhanced Cooperation: A Union à Taille Réduite or à Porte Tournante?' (n 9) 324.

[114] In this vein see House of Commons European Scrutiny Committee, 'Withdrawal from Enhanced Cooperation: The Committee's Evidence Session with Baroness Wilcox' Thirty-ninth Report of Session 2010–12 16 (oral evidence). The Council did not explicitly react to Estonia's withdrawal from enhanced cooperation in the field of financial transactions, but it can be extrapolated from the subsequent Council meeting that the Member States did not consider 'this step to be of any significance for the future progress of enhanced cooperation', Cédelle and Vella (n 66) 368. See the Outcome of the Council Meeting, 3435th Council meeting, Economic and Financial Affairs, 15068/15.

[115] 'Editorial Comments: Enhanced Cooperation: A Union à Taille Réduite or à Porte Tournante?' (n 9) 325.

[116] See also in this vein, ibid.

of particular concern when enhanced cooperation only consists of nine Member States. In such a scenario, the Member State threatening to leave would gain a disproportionate negotiating power because that departure would lead to the failure of the entire enhanced cooperation. For a level playing field all willing Member States need to be locked in without giving any Member State the power to decide unilaterally to pull out.

To make the point clear, any Member State which is part of the group of willing members when the Council issues its authorisation to pursue enhanced cooperation is bound insofar as it can no longer unilaterally pull out of the process.[117] Otherwise, a level playing field between all participating Member States cannot exist. Besides the threat to leave, a Member State could also abuse its negotiating power in cases in which the law requires the unanimous approval of the participating Member States.[118] If the one Member State only joined to put pressure on the other Member States to enact enhanced cooperation law in its favour, the other Member States may be able to exclude that disloyal Member State from the group. Besides disloyal behaviour, there may be good reasons to allow one Member State to leave the group, for example because the negotiation process reveals that all participating Member States except for one can agree on far-reaching integration. Whether there is also an opportunity to leave the group when the other group members allow the one member to pull out is subject to discussion in the following subsection.

b) Common Agreement on Leaving the Group

If the entire group thinks it would be better for both the group and one particular Member State if the latter leaves the group, the Member State may be allowed to withdraw from the legislative procedure. The difference between a common agreement between all participating Member States and a unilateral decision to leave rests on the possibility of amending the constitutional foundation of enhanced cooperation because the remaining participating Member States are willing to continue their legislative initiative without the one Member State aiming to leave. Of course, primary EU law provisions do not provide for a 'unionized' procedure as in the case of joining enhanced cooperation, but there are good reasons for allowing a Member State to leave the group, especially when other participating Member States are willing to let the Member State go.

Even if all participating Member States are on the same page and allow the withdrawal of one Member State, the constitutional foundation of enhanced cooperation—the Council's authorisation—needs to be amended. The amending procedure requires the involvement of the European Commission, as the 'Guardian

[117] So also the findings of the European Scrutiny Committee of the House of Commons: House of Commons European Scrutiny Committee, (n 114) paras 28–30.

[118] See for a disloyal attack by Malta this chapter subsection E.II.3.c.

of the Treaty'. To align the founding procedure with the leaving procedure it would be necessary for the Commission to submit a request to the Council allowing the one Member State to leave. Then the Council has to act again by a qualified majority voting, on the one hand allowing the Member State to withdraw from enhanced cooperation, and on the other hand, allowing the participating Member States to continue their joint legislative endeavours.

c) Excluding One Member State from the Group

The Member States of the group aiming to establish enhanced cooperation amongst them may wish to exclude a Member State which only chose to become a part of the group to sabotage the legislative initiative. It may be particularly easy to sabotage legislative endeavours concerning tax law, which calls for a unanimous decision of the participating Member States to pass the law. If just a single Member State led the others to believe that it is truly willing to be a part of enhanced cooperation, but only wants to prevent it, the law would never see the light of day. The primary EU law provisions do not provide for a procedural framework to exclude a participating Member State in the event of severe breaches of loyalty. Since no specific rules on the exclusion of Member States can be found within the constitutional framework of enhanced cooperation, one may find it necessary to start over and establish a new group of truly willing Member States. But even then, the disloyal Member State may again wish to join the group. Thus, one may be pleased to grant the truly willing Member States the chance to protect their joint legislative initiative from '*chevaux de Troie*'.[119]

The negotiating process of Rome III was characterised by a disloyal attack by Malta. At that time, Maltese national law did not provide for a divorce procedure. Upon Malta's accession to the European Union in 2004, however, it became bound by Brussels IIa,[120] a regulation concerning conflict of law issues in family law matters (including divorce proceedings), which was negotiated between Member States which all recognised divorce,[121] and thus the regulation did not include any carve-outs. Malta chose to join the legislative initiative aiming to amend the regulation. At the outset, it may have looked like a big success because Malta was the biggest objector of the regulation, but it abused its strong negotiating power. Unanimous agreement between Member States was required to pass the law, and thus any amendments to the text required Maltese consent. Malta made the group implement Art 7a in Rome III[122] (known as the 'Maltese clause'), which permitted

[119] Philippart (n 62) 27.

[120] Council Regulation, 29 May 2000, 1347/2000/EC, on jurisdiction and the recognition and enforcement of judgments in matrimonial matters and in matters of parental responsibility for children of both spouses, OJ, 30 June 2000, L 160, p 19.

[121] See Chapter 3, subsection A.I.1.

[122] Council Regulation, 20 December 2010, 1259/2010/EU, of implementing enhanced cooperation in the area of the law applicable to divorce and legal separation, OJ, 29 December 2010, L 343, p 10.

Malta not to apply the regulation.[123] Now, one may wonder whether the participating Member States or the European Commission could have excluded Malta from the procedure, since Malta was only onboard to change its obligations and duties to both accept and implement the EU's acquis communautaire.[124]

The answer to the question of whether or not the participating Member States or the European Commission could exclude one Member State from enhanced cooperation based on their dishonest and disloyal conduct may be answered differently depending on the perspective taken. On the one hand, the primary EU law provisions do not provide for a procedural framework which would entitle either the participating Member States or the Commission to exclude one member from the group, indicating that a participating Member State cannot be excluded from the joint action. On the other hand, one may argue that the European constitutional framework commits all Member States to mutual respect and loyalty,[125] and any breach of the bond of trust by sabotaging the legislative attempt of a group of Member States may allow those wounded in their trust to combat disloyalty through exclusion.[126] Of course, if the right to exclude is based on the wrongdoings of one Member State, a discussion will begin on which behaviour has to be considered disloyal (and thus allows an exclusion) and which behaviour simply has to be accepted because it represents the intrinsically honest motivation of one Member State. But to be frank, it is possible to distinguish a disloyal behaviour of one Member State which only aims to sabotage the legislative action from a truly honest negotiation process which does not achieve the level of integration an even smaller group of Member States would have achieved. If a Member State joins enhanced cooperation despite its fundamental reservations against the objectives of the joint initiative, and if the Member State then vetoes all compromises, the intention of that Member State is quite clear.

Even if it is possible to identify disloyal conduct of a participating Member State and separate it from a mere restrictive policy strategy, the constitutional framework for enhanced cooperation does not provide for a right to exclude disloyal Member States. However, primary EU law demands that non-participating Member States do not impede the implementation of enhanced cooperation between the participating Member States.[127] If a Member State joins enhanced cooperation with the intention of sabotaging the law-making process, the Member State may be a fictitious participating Member State. The fact that the fictitious participating Member State officially joined enhanced cooperation must not undermine the primary EU law safety net for the willing Member States. The disloyal Member State should be seen as a non-participating Member State because the constitutional framework

[123] See for a clear overview Kuipers (n 39) 211 et seq.
[124] ibid 223.
[125] Art 4 Subsection 3 of the TEU.
[126] Thym, *Ungleichzeitigkeit und europäisches Verfassungsrecht* (n 2) 57.
[127] Art 327 of the TFEU: see on the value of tolerance Chapter 6.

for enhanced cooperation divides all Member States into willing Member States (participating Member States) and unwilling Member States (non-participating Member States). Member States with disloyal intention should be considered non-participating Member States for the purpose of applying the safeguards for willing participating Member States introduced in primary EU law.

Art 327 of the TFEU explicitly demands that non-participating Member States shall not impede the establishment of enhanced cooperation. The prohibition on impeding the implementation of enhanced cooperation laws includes the worst form of impediment: sabotage of the law-making process. Against the background of Art 327 of the TFEU, the willing Member States may be allowed to address a request to the European Commission to exclude a particular Member State from enhanced cooperation because of its disloyal behaviour. The Commission may issue a proposal to the Council concerning necessary amendments to the initial authorisation of enhanced cooperation. If the Council agrees on the amendments to the authorisation, the foundation for enhanced cooperation is changed, excluding the disloyal Member State from enhanced cooperation.

To conclude, Art 327 of the TFEU and the procedure for establishing enhanced cooperation may grant the willing Member States the right to exclude disloyal Member State from enhanced cooperation. As in the case of a common agreement between all the Member States,[128] the foundation for enhanced cooperation—the Council's authorisation—needs to be amended to ensure that the willing Member States are allowed to pursue their joint legislative initiative without the disloyal Member State.

4. Leaving after Adopting the Law

Some participating Member States may wish to leave enhanced cooperation after the substantive law has been adopted. The desire to leave the group may not arise immediately after the law has been introduced but over time, when one or more Member States realise that the law is no longer fit to cope with economic realities, or simply because the Member State has changed its own policy. Under a traditional approach, the participating Member States can only free themselves from the obligations imposed upon them by enhanced cooperation laws if they commonly revoke the law.[129] In the field of tax law, this would require a unanimous decision by all participating Member States. In the case of ordinary secondary EU law, the

[128] See in this chapter subsection E.II.3.b.

[129] 'Editorial Comments: Enhanced Cooperation: A Union à Taille Réduite or à Porte Tournante?' (n 9) 326. However, a different point of view has been put forward based on Art 50 of the TEU. Since Member States are allowed to withdraw from the European Union as a whole, they must be allowed to leave enhanced cooperation whenever they wish to do so (see Christoph Thun-Hohenstein, *Der Vertrag von Amsterdam: die neue Verfassung der EU* (Manz Verlag 1997) 126). Such a view is particularly problematic as Member States would be allowed to cherry-pick enhanced cooperation initiatives. They could join enhanced cooperation and withdraw from it at any time. Such an understanding of enhanced cooperation would weaken the entire integration process, as every Member State would be allowed to back down from its commitment. Art 50 of the TEU grants Member States the right to withdraw

lock-in effect concerning the Interest and Royalties Directive is particularly notable. It prohibits taxation at source, and thus facilitates any base eroding and profit shifting practices of companies.[130] If not all (participating) Member States agree to either revoke the directive or amend it, all (participating) Member States are stuck with the law without having any chance to change it.

One way of preventing a petrifaction effect would be to implement a sunset clause into enhanced cooperation laws. Sunset clauses have a natural expiration date, which would force the participating Member State to come together to evaluate the law and decide whether or not they wish to retain it. The evaluating process would allow amendments to the law, but also the departure of some Member States, because the renegotiating of the terms involves the setting up of new enhanced cooperation which has to satisfy the primary EU law requirements.

If, however, the enhanced cooperation does not include sunset clauses, the participating Member States may have introduced a special procedure for revoking the law, or for allowing a participating Member State to leave. The Member States could implement a provision within enhanced cooperation law which allows the repeal of the law with a qualified or simple majority voting of the participating Member States.[131] Such a clause would ensure that, in areas in which unanimity is required, one Member State is not capable of preventing all participating Member States from moving on and either amending the law (and allowing the participating Member States which do not agree on the amendments to leave) or abolishing it. A clause allowing the ability to revoke secondary EU law in the area of taxation with a qualified majority voting (and not by a unanimous decision) does not contradict the European Union's competence framework as the clause would have found its way into the directive through a unanimous decision of the participating Member States and is only likened to that secondary EU law act. Accordingly, simplified revoking rules do not circumvent the unanimity clause in tax law, they merely ensure that Member States are not stuck with enhanced cooperation laws even though reform is required because the political climate has changed, or the law operates in a way which the Member States do not want it to.

If enhanced cooperation law permits a single Member State to leave the group after introducing the law, it does not necessarily require a change of the Council's authorisation, as is the case when a participating Member State leaves the group

altogether from the European Union, but if a Member State makes use of that particular clause, the Member State is out and there is no further need to strengthen the integration between the departing Member State and the remaining Member States. The only outstanding issue is to find a way forward in trade relations in the form of trade agreements. Accordingly, one cannot deduce any arguments from Art 50 of the TEU for the withdrawal from enhanced cooperation.

[130] See for more details especially on the countermeasures taken by the European Union Wolfgang Schön, 'Facilitating Entry by Facilitating Exit: New Paths in EU Tax Legislation' (2018) 46 Intertax 339, 339–40.

[131] With respect to ordinary secondary EU law, see ibid 340.

throughout the law-making process. The Council's authorisation does not need to be amended because it is the constitutional foundation of the legislative process of enhanced cooperation. At the moment, the participating Member States have passed the law, the foundation enabling some Member States to act jointly has fulfilled its purpose, and the participating Member States can deduce their right to leave directly from enhanced cooperation law.

From this it follows that the Member States are well advised to provide for some safeguarding clauses which allow them to either exit or revoke enhanced cooperation laws. If, however, the participating Member States have not introduced clauses which allow them to repeal the law with a smaller quorum, or which make the law expire after a certain time (and if the participating Member States have not chosen to extend its legal force), or which allows a single Member State to leave, the Member States have to either revoke the law with the ordinary voting requirement in the Council (ie unanimity or qualified majority voting) or be stuck with it until the political climate changes.[132]

5. Withdrawal from Enhanced Cooperation *De Lege Ferenda*

Recently, the European Parliament criticised the framework of the enhanced cooperation procedure for not providing rules on the withdrawal of a participating Member State from enhanced cooperation in cases in which the Member State 'no longer wishes to participate', or on the expulsion of a participating Member State who 'no longer fulfils the conditions of the enhanced cooperation'.[133] The latter scenario may be solved by way of interpretation of the primary EU law rules; whereas the former would require treaty changes.[134] An analysis of the historical background of the enhanced cooperation procedure shows that the European flexibility mechanism was supposed to allow the Member States to act in accordance with their level of development and thus allow the Member States to introduce legislative measures at different times.[135] Such an enhanced cooperation mechanism would be built on the desire to make non-participating Member States join[136] and not advertise the withdrawal from enhanced cooperation because as soon as all Member States are ready, each of them should join. The wording of the primary EU

[132] Ordinary secondary EU tax law also cannot be repealed by qualified majority voting. However, there are good reasons for facilitating an easy way out: see for more details ibid et seq; see also Chapter 2, subsection A.IV.

[133] European Parliament, 28 January 2019, on the implementation of the Treaty provisions concerning enhanced cooperation, 2018/2112(INI).

[134] The European Parliament proposes amendments and specification through a regulation based on Art 352 of the TFEU. Such an attempt should be rejected, see Chapter 7, subsection C.

[135] Riedeberger (n 25) 57 et seq; Bach (n 25) 21; Vobruba (n 25) 16 et seq; Müller-Graff, 'Differenzierte Integration' (n 25) 138. For a more historical perspective see Derpa (n 25) 53 et seq; Scharrer (n 25) 6 et seq.

[136] Art 20 TFEU: 'cooperation shall be open at any time to all Member States'; Art 328 of the TFEU: 'The Commission and the Member States participating in enhanced cooperation shall ensure that they promote participation by as many Member States as possible.'

law provisions does not only permit the application of the enhanced cooperation procedure in cases in which some Member States are not ready,[137] and the CJEU has not interpreted the provisions in light of historical developments either.[138] Accordingly, the European flexibility mechanism may allow for long-lasting differentiation, and thus the inclusion of a standardised exit route for participating Member States would not change the concept of flexibility within the European legal framework.

As has already been discussed above,[139] the possibility of withdrawing from secondary EU law, regardless of whether it is established under the ordinary EU law-making process or the enhanced cooperation procedure, may relax the Member States' decision to participate. If the Member States know that there is an exit route, they may be less risk averse. If the law turns out to bring more harm than good, the Member States can withdraw and introduce laws which suit their needs better. In the vast majority of cases, however, the Member States may wish to retain the law since it provides a robust legal and regulatory framework.

If the Member States conclude that they wish to make the enhanced cooperation procedure even more flexible by introducing a standardised exit route which grants each participating Member State the possibility of withdrawing, they can do so by amending the European treaty. As in the case of entry, it would be wise to involve the European Commission in the process in order to ensure a well-ordered procedure. Accordingly, a Member State who wishes to leave enhanced cooperation should notify the Commission and should also state the reasons for its decision. The reasons for leaving should not influence the authorisation for withdrawal, but they may help the remaining participating Member States to improve the law. The Commission should set a date upon which the Member State will cease to be part of the enhanced cooperation. The period should be sufficient to allow the exiting Member State and the remaining participating Member States to take necessary (legal and logistical) steps.

The changes to the European treaties also need to regulate the legal consequences for no longer fulfilling the requirement of at least nine participating Member States after a Member State withdraws from enhanced cooperation. It might be possible to allow the remaining Member States to retain enhanced cooperation. However, the more plausible and systemic approach would be to force a termination of the joint initiative. In such a case, the European Commission would not set the date on which the Member State leaves the group, but the date on which the enhanced cooperation shall terminate. Likewise, the Commission should grant

[137] According to Art 20 Subsection 2 of the TEU, the situation that may lawfully lead to enhanced cooperation is that in which 'the objectives of such cooperation cannot be attained within a reasonable period by the Union as a whole'.

[138] CJEU, 16 April 2013, C-274/11 and C-295/11, *Spain and Italy v Council*, ECLI:EU:C:2013:240, para 36.

[139] See Chapter 2, subsection A.IV.

the participating Member States enough time to adapt their national legal framework to prepare for termination of enhanced cooperation laws.

F. Competence Clauses

The primary EU law framework for establishing enhanced cooperation consists of a set of rules granting a group of Member States the right to use the ordinary procedural framework for enacting laws which are only binding amongst the participating Member States. As soon as enhanced cooperation is established by the Council's authorisation, the law-making process has to comply with the ordinary European legislative framework,[140] and thus the joint initiative has to be based upon the right competence clause. The choice of legal basis in the legislative process is a constitutional matter and should 'rest on objective factors amenable to judicial review'.[141] The CJEU ruled that the principle of conferred powers requires the legal basis to be determined before the European legislature takes any actions, and has to appear in the measure taken.[142]

The following subsections will give an overview of the EU's competence framework (see subsection I) by elaborating on its structure and design (see subsection II) and explaining how a conflict of competence rules can be resolved (see subsection III). A conflict of competences arises when more than one rule can form the legal basis for legislative action. In taxation, a conflict of competences may occur in particular when steering taxes are at stake. Secondary EU law may not only explicitly harmonise national tax laws to erode harmful differences between them but may incidentally harmonise national taxes in cases in which the European legislature is aiming to introduce European measures to steer taxpayers' behaviour, for example towards more environmentally friendly conduct. Thus, the legislative attempt may be based on two competence clauses: first, the EU's internal market competence (Art 115 of the TFEU) which may be applicable to harmonise unilateral steering taxes in the Member States thus ensuring the proper functioning of the European internal market, and secondly, the relevant competence clause of

[140] Some necessary amendments are made with respect to the voting process within the Council: only the vote of the participating Member States counts, Art 330 of the TFEU.

[141] Päivi Leino, 'The Politics of Efficient Compromise in the Adoption of EU Legal Acts' in Marise Cremona and Claire Kilpatrick (eds), *EU Legal Acts: Challenges and Transformations*, vol XXV/4 (1st edn, OUP 2018) 33. See also CJEU, 6 December 2001, Opinion 2/00, ECLI:EU:C:2001:664, para 5 'The choice of the appropriate legal basis has constitutional significance'; for the requirement of objective factors for judicial review: CJEU, 11 June 1991, C-300/89, *Commission v Council*, ECLI:EU:C:1991:244, para 10; CJEU, 29 April 2004, C-338/01, *Commission v Parliament*, ECLI:EU:C:2004:253, para 54; CJEU, 8 September 2009, C-411/06, *Commission v Parliament and Council*, ECLI:EU:C:2009:518, para 45; CJEU, 6 November 2008, *Parliament v Council*, ECLI:EU:C:2008:605, para 34.

[142] CJEU, 21 January 2003, C-378/00, *Commission v Parliament and Council*, ECLI:EU:C:2003:41, para 66; in this vein also CJEU, 16 June 1991, C-325/91, *France v Commission*, ECLI:EU:C:1993:245, para 26.

the field which should be influenced by the steering tax, such as the EU's competence in environmental matters. A proper explanation of how to solve a conflict of competences also requires a definition of the scope of the EU competences, and in particular, the scope of the EU's competence to align national laws, including national tax laws (Art 114 and Art 115 of the TFEU). The need to define the limits of the competence clause in more detail follows from its vague drafting, it allows the harmonisation of unilateral tax measures if the differences between the laws in each Member State directly affect the establishing and functioning of the European internal market.

I. Overview of the Competence Framework within the European Treaties

The framework of the EU's legislative power is built on the fundamental principle of conferral,[143] which only allows the European Union to act where the European treaties confer the competence on it. Any competence which is not conferred upon the European Union remains with the Member States.[144] The same holds for the legislative power of enhanced cooperation; the European legislature only has the power to enact laws under the enhanced cooperation procedure where the European Union holds legislative power, but with the exception of the EU's exclusive competences.[145]

The European competence clauses, vesting the European Union with the legislative power, are spread along within the European treaties and describe both its scope and the procedural framework which has to be satisfied for enacting secondary EU law based on that particular competence clause.[146] The procedural framework of a competence clause determines the involvement of the European institutions, and precisely defines the quorums which have to be satisfied both in the Council and in the European Parliament.

Aside from the principle of conferral, the subsidiarity principle[147] and, to a certain extent, the proportionality clause protect the sovereignty of the Member States. The subsidiarity requirement is only met when the objects of the legislative attempt 'cannot be sufficiently achieved by the Member States ... but can rather, by reason of the scale or effects of the proposed action, be better achieved at Union

[143] Art 5 Subsection 2 of the TEU; Craig and Búrca (n 52) 74.
[144] Art 4 Subsection 1 of the TEU.
[145] Art 20 Subsection 1 of the TFEU.
[146] Armin von Bogdandy and Jürgen Bast, 'The Federal Order of Competence' in Armin von Bogdandy and Jürgen Bast (eds), *Principles of European Constitutional Law* (2nd edn, Hart Publishing 2010) 278 et seq; Martin Nettesheim, 'Kompetenzen' in Armin von Bogdandy and Jürgen Bast (eds), *Europäisches Verfassungsrecht: theoretische und dogmatische Grundzüge* (2nd edn, Springer 2009) 391 et seq.
[147] See this chapter subsection G.VI.

level'.[148] The proportionality clause, on the other hand, requires the European institutions to restrict their actions to 'what is necessary to achieve the objectives of the Treaties'.[149] The legislative actions of enhanced cooperation must satisfy both the subsidiarity requirement and the proportionality test.

II. The Framework of the Competence Clauses

The European competence framework offers different types of competence clauses. Some, in particular those relating to the European internal market, are defined with respect to the purpose they aim to achieve.[150] Other clauses are designed based on individual subject matter, such as environmental competence.[151] The former grants the European institutions wide discretion as to the measures and rules required to achieve the objectives laid down in the competence clause. The requirements necessary to harmonise Member States' unilateral laws are precisely defined in a later subsection of the study. It will be analysed whether any differences between Member State laws already create an obstacle to intra-EU trade, and thus allow the harmonising of legislative actions at the European level.[152]

III. Conflict of Competence Clauses

Purpose-oriented competence clauses are particularly wide in scope, and thus, they may be applicable for a legislative initiative which could, however, easily be based on another competence clause. Thus, it may be very likely that for one legislative action, more than one clause may be suitable as a legal basis. If more than one competence clause is potentially applicable and they are not procedurally complementary,[153] the European legislature has to choose between the relevant competence clauses based on 'objective factors which are amenable to judicial review'.[154]

[148] Art 5 Subsection 3 TFEU.
[149] Art 5 Subsection 5 TFEU.
[150] See this chapter subsection G.V.
[151] Arts 191 and 192 of the TFEU.
[152] See this chapter subsection G.
[153] In cases in which both competence clauses provide for the same procedural framework (engagement of the European institutions and the majorities in the Council) and where the use of a single legal basis proves impossible, the European legislature is bound to adopt the European legal act on the basis of both competence clauses: CJEU, 27 September 1988, 165/87, *Commission v Council*, ECLI:EU:C:1988:458, para 10.
[154] CJEU, 11 June 1991, C-300/89, *Commission v Council*, ECLI:EU:C:1991:244, para 10; CJEU, 9 November 1995, C-426/93, *Germany v Council*, ECLI:EU:C:1995:367, para 29; CJEU, 13 September 2005, C-176/03, *Commission and European Parliament v Council*, ECLI:EU:C:2005:542, para 45; CJEU, 23 October 2007, C-440/05, *Commission v European Parliament and Council*, ECLI:EU:C:2007:625, para 61; CJEU, 3 September 2008, C-402/05 P and C-415/05 P, *Kadi*, ECLI:EU:C:2008:461, para 182; CJEU, 6 May 2014, C-43/12, *Commission v European Parliament and Council*, ECLI:EU:C:2014:298,

These factors include, in particular, 'the aim and content' of the legislative act.[155] The aim and the content of the legal act may be capable of indicating the relevant competence clause;[156] in some cases, however, both the aim and content are vague and broad so that it may still be possible to base the legislative act on more than one competence clause. If the aim and purpose of the law allows the application of two or more competence clauses and the use of one single competence clause proves impossible, the European legislature is allowed to base its actions on more than one single competence clause, if both or all of them are required to satisfy the same legal procedure.[157] If, however, the applicable competence clauses demand a different procedure for introducing secondary EU legislation, the European legislature has to choose one legal base for its legislative action because it is not possible to split the procedure and comply with both procedural frameworks.

The procedural framework of each competence clause reflects a balancing of Member States' interests (in particular their sovereignty) and the EU's interests. Depending on the intensity of the European intervention through legislative action, different participation rights and quorums, especially in the Council, have to be recognised and satisfied. In tax law, for example, the Council requires a unanimous vote of the Member States,[158] whereas a qualified majority vote is sufficient to harmonise other areas of Member States' national laws.[159] If the European legislature were to combine the requirements set by the individual competence clauses, the interests of the Member States and the interests of the European Union would no longer be balanced in the way as supposed by the European constitutional framework.[160]

The different majority voting requirements in the Council not only influence the balancing of the interest of both the European Union and the Member States but they also affect the negotiation and bargaining process at a European level,[161] and thus, the question 'with regard to the correct legal basis is not a purely formal

para 29; CJEU, 10 September 2015, C-363/14, *European Parliament v Council*, ECLI:EU:C:2015:579, para 41.

[155] ibid.

[156] Leino (n 141) 35.

[157] CJEU, 27 September 1988, 165/87, *Commission v Council*, ECLI:EU:C:1988:458, para 11; CJEU, 11 June 1991, C-300/89, *Commission v Council*, ECLI:EU:C:1991:244, para 17.

[158] Art 115 of the TFEU; for the reasons underlying the unanimity requirement. See Chapter 2, subsection B.III.

[159] Art 114 of the TFEU.

[160] CJEU, 11 June 1991, C-300/89, *Commission v Council*, ECLI:EU:C:1991:244, para 19; for the principle of institutional balance see Jean-Paul Jacqué, 'The Principle of Institutional Balance' (2004) 41 Common Market Law Review 383; Leino (n 141) 38 et seq with further references to the CJEU case law.

[161] Ben Smulders and Katharina Eisele, 'Reflections on the Institutional Balance, the Community Method and the Interplay between Jurisdictions after Lisbon' (2012) 31 Yearbook of European Law 112, 114 arguing that the concept of institutional balance, as a legal principle, forces the EU institutions to act within the limits of their respective powers as provided by the European treaties protecting individuals against any abuse of power.

one, inasmuch as … [the competence clauses] of the Treaty entail different rules regarding the manner in which the Council may arrive at its decision. The choice of the legal basis could thus affect the determination of the content of [the legislative act]'.[162] In other words, if the European legislature were to combine two competence clauses, in the sense that it would comply with the stricter requirements set by one of the clauses, for example the Council would take a unanimous decision although some parts of the secondary EU law may be covered by a competence clause which only requires a qualified majority voting, then the opinion-forming process would be confused. It makes a big difference whether the legislative action requires the consent of all Member States or whether it 'only' requires a qualified majority voting in the Council. Member States may be more generous in their willingness to compromise if they know that they can be outvoted when the going gets tough. But if they know that they can block any legislation, they will be less willing to compromise. It is precisely these different dynamics which are characteristic of the individual policy areas, and therefore should not be confused.

In cases where the recourse to a dual legal basis is excluded since both competence rules set out different procedural requirements, the CJEU determines the appropriate legal basis based on the main purpose and content of the act.[163] In its case law, the Court first acknowledges that one legislative act might satisfy different aims, but concludes that each legislative act has only one main purpose and content,[164] which may be determined in an objective manner through a thorough analysis of the contested act.[165] The main purpose and content of a legislative act form the 'centre of gravity' for solving conflicts between competence clauses.[166] The 'centre of gravity' theory does not prevent the legislative act from having incidental

[162] CJEU, 23 February 1988, 131/86, *UK v Council*, ECLI:EU:C:1988:86, para 11.

[163] CJEU, 17 March 1993, C-155/91, *Commission v Council*, ECLI:EU:C:1993:98, para 20; CJEU, 11 June 1991, C-300/98, Titanium Dioxide, ECLI:EU:C:1991:244, para 10 et seq; René Barents, 'The Internal Market Unlimited: Some Observations on the Legal Basis of Community Legislation' (1993) 30 Common Market Law Review 85, 102 criticising that the method of selecting the legal basis 'offers a considerable flexibility for subjecting the choice of a legal basis to the political preferences of the institution concerned' which may conflict with the guarantee function of the legal basis.

[164] See in that vein Bruno Simma, Joseph HH Weiler, and Markus C Zöckler, *Kompetenzen und Grundrechte: Beschränkungen der Tabakwerbung aus der Sicht des Europarechts* (Duncker & Humblot 1999) 29 et seq. See for a critical analysis Armin von Bogdandy, 'Der rechtliche Rahmen der Zugangsregeln' in Eberhard Grabitz, Armin von Bogdandy, and Martin Nettesheim (eds), *Europäisches Außenwirtschaftsrecht: der Zugang zum Binnenmarkt: Primärrecht, Handelsschutzrecht und Außenaspekte der Binnenmarktharmonisierung* (Beck Verlag 1994) 20.

[165] Ronald van Ooik, 'Cross-Pillar Litigation before the ECJ: Demarcation of Community and Union Competences' (2008) 4 European Constitutional Law Review 399, 408; Siegfried Breier, 'Der Streit Um Die Richtige Rechtsgrundlage in Der Rechtsprechung Europäischen Gerichtshofes' (1995) Europarecht 46, 52 criticising the CJEU's approach as the process for determining the legal basis becomes politically controllable.

[166] Annegret Engel, *The Choice of Legal Basis for Acts of the European Union: Competence Overlaps, Institutional Preferences, and Legal Basis Litigation* (Springer 2018) 13 et seq. In a more recent case, the CJEU merely relied on the content of the legislative act: CJEU, 10 February 2009, C-301/06, *Ireland v Parliament and Council*, ECLI:EU:C:2009:68; Bart Van Vooren, *EU External Relations Law and the European Neighbourhood Policy: A Paradigm for Coherence* (Routledge 2012) 136 arguing that 'the "aim" component serves little purpose in the final outcome of deciding the correct legal base'.

effects, such as positive effects on the European internal market through a harmonising of market conditions, or (positive) effects on environmental or health standards;[167] however, these auxiliary effects are not relevant for determining the legal basis of the European legislative act.[168] The main purpose and content of the act is the only factor for determining the relevant competence clause which also covers all auxiliary effects of the legislative act.

G. Fostering the European Internal Market by Harmonising National Laws at the European Level

The European treaties grant the European institutions the power to harmonise the national law rules of the Member States if the differences between the national rules directly affect the establishment and functioning of the European internal market.[169] The secondary EU laws have to have as 'their object the establishing and functioning of the internal market'.[170] The European treaties lay out in Art 115 of the TFEU a harmonisation clause for national tax laws. The rule is tightly linked with the general harmonisation clause of the European treaties, but in taxation unanimity is required. Art 115 of the TFEU ensures that European tax laws can only be introduced when all Member States are on board.[171] The unanimity requirement makes it particularly hard to find compromises at the European level and to introduce European tax laws.[172] Likewise, within the procedural framework of enhanced cooperation, all participating Member States must agree on the harmonising measure in taxation because a unanimous vote in the Council (consisting of the participating Member States only) is required if Art 115 of the TFEU constitutes the legal basis of the legislative act.

[167] Even if they achieve very high standards. In the tobacco advertising cases, the CJEU explicitly ruled that if the 'conditions for recourse to Article 100a [now Art 114 of the TFEU] as a legal basis are fulfilled, the Community legislature cannot be prevented from relying on that legal basis on the ground that public health protection is a decisive factor in the choices to be made', CJEU, 5 October 2000, C-376/98, *Germany v European Parliament and Council*, ECLI:EU:C:2000:544, para 88; CJEU, 10 December 2002, C-491/01, *British American Tobacco*, ECLI:EU:C:2002:741, 62.

[168] Simma, Weiler, and Zöckler (n 164) 30 et seq.

[169] Art 114 of the TFEU.

[170] Art 114 of the TFEU.

[171] Art 114 Subsection 2 and Art 115 of the TFEU; see Chapter 2, subsection B.III.

[172] Hanno Kube, Ekkehart Reimer, and Christoph Spengel, 'Tax Policy: Trends in the Allocation of Powers Between the Union and Its Member States' (2016) 25 EC Tax Review 247, 252–53; Eric CCM Kemmeren, 'Sources of EU Law for European Tax Integration: Well-Known and Alternative Legal Instruments' in Dennis Weber (ed), *Traditional and Alternative Routes to European Tax Integration: Primary Law, Secondary Law, Soft Law, Coordination, Comitology and Their Relationship* (IBFD 2010) 33; Frans Vanistendael, 'A Personal View' in Ary Lans Bovenberg and others (eds), *Harmonization of Company Taxation in the European Community: Some Comments on the Ruding Committee Report* (1992) 29; Pistone, 'Expected and Unexpected Developments of European Integration in the Field of Direct Taxes' (2007) 35 Intertax 70. For more details and the European Commission's proposal to move towards qualified majority voting in European taxation see Chapter 2, subsection B.

The provisions on the harmonisation of the (national) laws are often referred to as the European internal market competence clauses because they are defined without any restrictions on the subject matter.[173] However, Art 114 and Art 115 of the TFEU do not vest the European legislature with 'a general power to regulate the internal market', which would not impose any limits for the harmonisation of the national laws.[174] Any harmonising legislative action has to facilitate the establishment and the functioning of the European internal market and thus has to facilitate intra-EU trade.[175] With regard to the emergence of conflicts with other competence clauses, it has already been demonstrated that the competence clause has to be determined against the main purpose and content of the legislative act.[176] The main purpose and content has to be identified in an objective manner through a thorough analysis of the contested act.[177] Accordingly, if the law serves another, more dominant purpose than facilitating the functioning of the European internal market, the European institutions have to base their actions on the more appropriate legal basis.

Speaking of the main purpose, the purpose of the European internal market competence is to introduce secondary EU legislation which harmonises Member State laws in cases in which the differences between national laws create trade obstacles within the European internal market. The improvement for the internal market may predominantly follow from the uniform approach established by the secondary EU law in all the Member States. But even if the wording of the primary law provisions is specified to the need to improve the European internal market, many open questions remain. For example, an improvement could require an outcome which is, in economic terms, more beneficial for all intra-EU transactions, but it could also mean an improvement for the European internal market from a European integration point of view. We shall assume for example that the CJEU case law, by way of negative integration, has already removed a particular trade obstacle resulting from differences in the national tax laws, such as forcing the source Member State to grant family deductions if the home Member State is unable to do so.[178] Is the European legislature allowed to introduce a directive based on Art 115 of the TFEU which would codify this principle? From the perspective of European integration, one may clearly answer in the affirmative because the Member States establish positive integration by determining which Member State has to recognise

[173] Frans Vanistendael, 'On Democratic Legitimacy of European Tax Law and the Role of the European Parliament' in Pasquale Pistone (ed), *European Tax Integration: Law, Policy and Politics* (IBFD 2018) 106 referring to it as the 'catch-all clause'.

[174] See in that vein Stephen Weatherill, 'The Limits of Legislative Harmonization Ten Years after Tobacco Advertising: How the Court's Case Law Has Become a Drafting Guide' (2011) 12 German Law Journal 827, 831.

[175] CJEU, 5 October 2000, C-376/98, *Germany v European Parliament and Council*, ECLI:EU:C:2000:544, para 83.

[176] See this chapter subsection F.III.

[177] Ooik (n 165) 408; Engel (n 166) 13 et seq.

[178] CJEU, 14 February 1995, C-279/93, *Schumacker*, ECLI:EU:C:1995:31.

the personal deductions when a person earns all their income in the host Member State and no income in the home Member State. From a purely economic point of view, the person engaging in an economic activity in another Member State is not granted any additional benefits through secondary EU law because the negative integration (the CJEU case law) already forces the host Member State to grant family deductions.

Despite the interplay between negative and positive integration, the need to improve the European internal market also raises the question of whether an improvement requires less regulation on the market. In other words, is it enough for an improvement of the functioning of the European internal market to establish common and unified laws within the European Union, or do they necessarily also have to impose a softer regulatory framework?

The following analysis defines the scope of the EU's internal market competence and begins with an overview of the European internal market concept, which will in particular address the issue of whether the European internal market aims for a true single market between the Member States or whether the European internal market consists of the national markets of the Member States of the European Union (see subsection I). Subsection II describes how the concept of the European internal market influences European law-making. The third subsection argues that the European treaties provide the European legislature with a true regulatory power (see subsection III.1), which does not demand a pitching to optimal economic efficiency (see subsection III.2) and which allows the European legislature to incidentally follow policy objectives not conferred upon the European Union by the European treaties (see subsection III.3). Subsection IV transposes the findings to the European legislature's power to introduce steering taxes. The analysis of what it means for secondary EU laws to facilitate the internal market is then divided into two parts. The first discusses secondary EU law measures facilitating intra-EU trade by eliminating existing trade obstacles (see subsection V.1), accordingly obstacles that cannot be removed by applying the fundamental freedoms, either because the obstacles are justified (legal restriction) or because they do not fall within the scope of the fundamental freedoms (economic restriction). The second part focuses on the interplay between negative and positive harmonisation, but with a particular focus on the possibility of using Art 114 and Art 115 of the TFEU to introduce a coordinative framework between the Member States for complying with their European treaty obligations (see subsection V.2). Such a framework may deepen integration between the Member States but may not change the status quo for intra-EU trade from an economic point of view. Against this background, the principles of subsidiarity (see subsection VI) and proportionality (see subsection VII) and their impact on European law-making is revealed. Lastly, it is examined whether action by the European legislature is always required to achieve harmonisation of the national laws or whether both the fundamental freedoms and the European competition rules already put (enough) pressure on the Member State to find common ground for their national laws (see subsection VIII).

I. The European Internal Market Concept

Art 26 of the TFEU defines the European internal market as an 'area without frontiers in which the free movement of goods, persons, services and capital is ensured'.[179] Accordingly, goods, services, persons, and capital should flow freely irrespective of any Member States' borders and should thus be used where they are of the greatest benefit.[180] An efficient allocation[181] of resources beyond a Member State's territory exposes goods, services, persons, and capital to serious competition improving the welfare of the people.[182] Such a market model requires an entire opening of Member State national borders for goods, services, persons, and capital to allow the free play of market forces, and neither the Member States nor the market players must have the possibility of interfering with the optimal allocation of resources.[183]

From this it follows that the European internal market requires more than an opening of the national borders for goods, services, persons, and capital; it also requires a level playing field for all market players which allows them to operate under equal conditions and engage in undistorted competition.[184] The European treaties, more precisely the fundamental freedoms,[185] prohibit any restrictive or discriminatory treatment of foreign goods, services, persons, and capital or cross-border

[179] Stephen Weatherill, 'The Competence to Harmonise and Its Limits' in Panos Koutrakos and Jukka Snell (eds), *Research Handbook on the Law of the EU's Internal Market* (Edward Elgar Publishing 2017) 83 emphasising that '[t]he "internal market" is a slippery concept and it is wide and deep in its reach'.

[180] For the economic perspective of uniformity and effectiveness of the European internal market see Michael Dougan, *National Remedies before the Court of Justice: Issues of Harmonisation and Differentiation* (Hart Publishing 2004) 70 et seq.

[181] The European treaties (especially Art 120 of the TFEU) refer to an economic concept: See Hal R Varian, *Intermediate Microeconomics: A Modern Approach* (9th edn, 2014) 605; Kenneth J Arrow and Gerard Debreu, 'Existence of an Equilibrium for a Competitive Economy' (1954) 22 Econometrica 265.

[182] 'Report of the Heads of Delegation to the Foreign Ministers (Spaak Report)' (1956) 5; Eric CCM Kemmeren, 'Double Tax Conventions on Income and Capital and the EU: Past, Present and Future' (2012) 21 EC Tax Review 157, 158–60; Eric CCM Kemmeren, 'The CJEU and the Internal Market Concept in Direct Taxation' in Werner Haslehner, Georg Kofler, and Alexander Rust (eds), *EU Tax Law and Policy in the 21st Century* (Kluwer Law International 2017) 56–57. See also Art 120 of the TFEU; Udo Di Fabio, 'Europa am Wendepunkt: Wirtschaftsregierung oder Subsidiarität' in Handwerkskammer Düsseldorf (ed), *Welche Chancen hat Subsidiarität in Europa?*, vol 5 (Verlagsanstalt Handwerk 2014) 27 et seq arguing for the positive effects of competition. For the general free trade theory: Martin Raible, *Protektionismusverbote im Recht der Wirtschaftsintegration: eine vergleichende Untersuchung der Regelung des Freihandels im Recht der USA, der EU und der WTO* (Nomos 2006) 41.

[183] Wolfgang Schön, 'Tax Competition in Europe—the Legal Perspective' (2000) 9 EC Tax Review 89, 91.

[184] Michael Dougan, 'Minimum Harmonization and the Internal Market' (2000) 37 Common Market Law Review 853, 857; Johanna Hey, *Harmonisierung der Unternehmensbesteuerung in Europa* (Verlag Dr Otto Schmidt 1997) 85.

[185] Vassilios Skouris, 'Fundamental Rights and Fundamental Freedoms: The Challenge of Striking a Delicate Balance' (2006) 17 European Business Law Review 225, 226 referring to the fundamental freedoms as the 'essence of the internal market'.

economic activities, and thus prevent a shielding of the Member States' national markets. As soon as the national markets are open, and national laws do not hinder or harm intra-EU trade, European competition law ensures equal market conditions for all economic subjects by preventing them from colluding, and by prohibiting Member States from providing state aid to some undertakings.[186]

At some point, the fundamental freedoms and competition law may, however, not be able to establish a level playing field, and thus the European internal market demands European legislation. Thus, the European treaties vest the European institutions with the power to harmonise Member State laws which directly affect the establishment or functioning of the internal market.

The European internal market is, however, not as clear cut as one might think.[187] The European treaties respect fundamental rights[188] and allow the Member States (also) to follow values which interfere with rather than serve the economic demands of a true single market.[189] Primary EU law provisions do so by allowing an restriction of the fundamental freedoms to be justified by an overriding reason of public interest, and by allowing the European legislature to harmonise common values of the Member States which do not simply satisfy the economic claims of a single market. Accordingly, the European internal market is not purely efficiency driven; it still allows the Member States to protect their national values against competing market efficiency claims.[190]

[186] Title VII, Chapter 1 of the TFEU.

[187] Stephen Weatherill, *The Internal Market as a Legal Concept*, vol XXV/1 (OUP 2017) 24 arguing that the fundamental aim of the European treaties 'should not be taken as a claim that the internal market, or the EU generally, is solely about economic concerns. In fact, … the internal market as a legal concept … is more than narrowly economic in character and purpose.' See also CJEU, 11 December 2007, C-438/05, *Viking*, ECLI:EU:C:2007:772, para 79; CJEU, 18 December 2007, C-341/05, *Laval*, ECLI:EU:C:2007:809, para 105.

[188] There are two situations in which fundamental freedoms and fundamental rights can intervene: first, any derogation from the fundamental freedoms must comply with fundamental rights (CJEU, 18 June 1991, C-260/89, *Elliniki Radiophonia Tiléorassi AG*, para 43; CJEU, 30 April 2014, C-390/12, *Pfleger*, ECLI:EU:C:2014:281, para 35; CJEU, 11 June 2015, C-98/14, *Berlington Hungary*, ECLI:EU:C:2015:386, para 74; see in this vein also CJEU, 26 June 1997, C-368/95, *Vereinigte Familiapress Zeitungsverlags- und vertriebs GmbH*, ECLI:EU:C:1997:325, para 18). Second, fundamental freedoms have to be balanced with fundamental rights (which indicates that there is not a hierarchy between them): CJEU, 12 June 2003, *Schmidberger*, ECLI:EU:C:2003:333.

[189] For example, CJEU, 14 October 2004, C-36/02, *Omega*, ECLI:EU:C:2004:614; CJEU, 22 December 2010, C-208/09, *Sayn-Wittgenstein*, ECLI:EU:C:2010:805; one may argue that these cases concern fundamental rights, such as the personal dignity; however, it is the Member State's individual interpretation of the fundamental right which reflects the value which the Member State follows, see in that vein Christine Kaddous, 'The European Union's Common Values and National Identities: Convergence or Contradiction?' in Thomas Giegerich, Oskar Josef Gstrein, and Sebastian Zeitzmann (eds), *The EU between 'An Ever Closer Union' and Inalienable Policy Domains of Member States*, vol 80 (n 25) 97 et seq; see also Leonard FM Besselink, 'Does EU Law Recognise Legal Limits to Integration? Accommodating Diversity and Its Limits' in Thomas Giegerich, Oskar Josef Gstrein, and Sebastian Zeitzmann (eds), *The EU between 'An Ever Closer Union' and Inalienable Policy Domains of Member States*, vol 80 (Nomos 2014) 65 et seq.

[190] Joseph HH Weiler, 'The Transformation of Europe' (1991) 100 The Yale Law Journal 2403, 2478 et seq.

II. Market Regulation and European Law Harmonisation

Following up on the 'economic sharpness' of the European internal market and Member States' possibility to prioritise certain values over market efficiency, the opportunity to grant a certain non-market value priority over efficiency concerns is not only important to individual Member States for the question of whether a restriction of the fundamental freedom is justified, it also influences the common actions of Member States in the form of European legislation, because it addresses the question of whether secondary EU laws introduced under Art 114 or Art 115 of the TFEU have to reduce regulation on the European market. A demand for less regulation would foster the free play of the market forces.[191]

Early US Supreme Court case law clearly demanded the free play of the market forces for the US market, and thus the Court followed its economic due process approach until 1937. Under this approach, full market freedom was desired and thus statutes which, for example, restricted the working hours to a maximum of sixty hours per week and ten hours per day were nullified.[192] The US Supreme Court abandoned its economic due process approach in 1937,[193] and now follows an approach which allows States to interfere with economic freedom.[194]

Contrary to the US experience, the CJEU has always accepted that the European internal market is not a pure single market, and thus the Court never intended to follow an economic due process approach.[195] The CJEU allowed the European internal market to be a market which is made up of more than trade and economic freedoms.[196] The harsh application of the fundamental freedoms to Member State national laws is not a sign that the CJEU wishes to eliminate regulation. On the contrary, the Court wishes to encourage Member States to find a common approach at the European level which reinforces regulation and eliminates differences between

[191] See in that vein Bastiaan van Apeldoorn, *Transnational Capitalism and the Struggle over European Integration* (Routledge 2009) 1.

[192] Poulson Bany, 'Substantive Due Process and Labor Law' (1982) 6 The Journal of Libertarian Studies 267.

[193] Frank Easterbrook, 'The Constitution of Business' (1988) 11 George Mason University Law Review 53, 53.

[194] Whether the Supreme Court has again ruled towards an 'economic due process' approach, see Want William, 'Economic Substantive Due Process: Considered Dead Is Being Revived by a Series of Supreme Court Land-Use Cases' (2014) 36 University of Hawai'i Law Review 455.

[195] Miguel Poiares Maduro, *We the Court: The European Court of Justice and the European Economic Constitution* (Hart Publishing 1998) 77; Pedro Caro de Sousa, *The European Fundamental Freedoms: A Contextual Approach* (OUP 2015) 99 et seq; Miguel Poiares Maduro, 'Reforming the Market or the State Article 30 and the European Constitution: Economic Freedom and Political Rights' (1997) European Law Journal 55, 60 et seq. José Luis da Cruz Vilaça and Nuno Piçarra, *Are There Material Limits to the Revision of the Treaties on the European Union?: Referat Im Rahmen Der Vortragsreihe 'Das Wirtschaftsrecht Der Europäischen Union', Bonn, 17. Oktober 1994* (Zentrum für Europäisches Wirtschaftsrecht 1995) 13–14 arguing that the fundamental freedoms protect an economic activity 'from any interference'. See also on the question of whether the fundamental freedoms have to be understood as economic due-process clauses Opinion of Advocate General Tesauro, 27 October 1993, C-292/92, *Hünermund*, ECLI:EU:C:1993:863, para 1, see also 10, 11, and 28.

[196] CJEU, 7 February 1985, 240/83, *ADBHU*, ECLI:EU:C:1985:59, para 12, emphasis added.

the national regimes. Regulatory burdens imposed by secondary EU legislation have not been eliminated by the CJEU since it is not the regulation which harms the European internal market but the different approaches taken by Member States, yet these differences are eliminated by secondary EU legislation.

The European internal market is not meant to be an area free from any legislative interference, whose absence guarantees the free play of economic forces. The economic freedom is not the only value which determines the European internal market, and thus European legislation can be influenced by other factors such as health safety or environmental protection.[197] An elimination of market regulation is not what Art 114 and Art 115 of the TFEU aim for, but they do aim to improve the European internal market by establishing a common regulatory framework between all the Member States. Common regulatory rules facilitate the free movement of goods, services, persons, and capital within the European internal market. A rejection of the need to reduce market regulation through European legislation is also in line with Art 114 Subsection 3 of the TFEU, which requires the European institutions to guarantee a high level of health, safety, consumer and environmental protection.

III. The European Internal Market and the Harmonisation of the Member States' Laws

The European internal market aims for an efficient allocation of resources,[198] but not at any price. Values which are important to Member States can be pursued despite contradicting the economic demands of a true single market. This market model influences the European legislative actions undertaken to ensure both its establishment and its functioning, since the harmonisation attempt may not only be influenced by market efficiency concerns but also by values which are common to the Member States.[199] Allowing, or in some field even requiring, the European legislature to consider values which are important to the Member States and to weigh them against pure efficiency considerations has three implications. First, it requires a true regulatory power of the European legislature (see subsection 1). Secondly, it means that the European legislature will not be solely concerned with

[197] CJEU, 5 October 2000, C-376/98, *Germany v European Parliament and Council*, ECLI:EU:C:2000:544, para 88; CJEU, 10 December 2002, C-491/01, *British American Tobacco*, ECLI:EU:C:2002:741, 62.

[198] Ferdinand Wollenschläger, *Grundfreiheit ohne Markt: die Herausbildung der Unionsbürgerschaft im unionsrechtlichen Freizügigkeitsregime* (Mohr Siebeck 2007) 19 et seq.

[199] Stephen Weatherill, 'Pre-Emption, Harmonisation and the Distribution of Competence to Regulate the Internal Market' in Catherine Barnard and Joanne Scott (eds), *The Law of the Single European Market: Unpacking the Premises* (Hart Publishing 2002) 53 highlighting that 'legislative harmonisation provides a classic example of the way in which trade integration "spills over" to confront and infuse even more complex areas of regulatory policy'.

optimising economic efficiency (see subsection 2). Thirdly, it means that the line between legitimate European harmonisation measures and European legislation which uses the cover of harmonisation to smuggle measures of policy areas outside the European competences into the European framework becomes blurred (see subsection 3).[200]

1. The European Legislature's True Regulatory Power

With regard to the first claim, the nature of the harmonisation action at the European level can be understood very differently. First, it would be feasible to explain the competence of the European Union to align Member State laws which have a direct effect on the European internal market as the European legislature's power to liberalise the national rules which hamper intra-EU trade. An attempt by the European legislature to reduce market regulation would not aim to develop a common understanding of the underlying values; it would only attempt to find the least common denominator between Member State policies. But the European internal market model and the wording of Art 114 and Art 115 of the TFEU make it quite clear that the European institutions should aim to harmonise the values underlying the law and not only to implement a uniform wording for the national rules.[201] Establishing common values between the Member States requires the European legislature to balance all contradicting (fundamental) rights or interests.[202] If fundamental rights are at stake, the European legislature is required to seriously balance the rights against the market needs[203] or the contradicting rights against each other.[204] We shall assume, for example, that the European institutions are aiming to introduce a minimum share capital for limited liability companies. Such a legislative attempt requires two contradictory fundamental rights to be balanced against each other: the freedom to conduct business on the one hand, and the protection from economic exploitation on the other. The balancing act allows the establishment of a common value between the Member States which determines the design of the regulatory framework introduced by secondary EU law.

[200] Weatherill, 'The Limits of Legislative Harmonization Ten Years after Tobacco Advertising' (n 174) 829.

[201] See also Weatherill, 'The Competence to Harmonise' (n 179) 85.

[202] See in that vein Vasiliki Kosta, *Fundamental Rights in EU Internal Market Legislation* (Hart Publishing 2015) 23–24.

[203] Opinion of Advocate General Fennelly, 15 June 2000, C-376/98, *Germany v European Parliament and Council*, ECLI:EU:C:2000:324, para 65.

[204] The CJEU did not oblige the European legislature to establish a common approach in the form of adopting the highest level of protection which can be found in a particular Member State. The European legislature is free to balance internal market interests and non-economic interests which may, from the perspective of a single Member State, lead to a higher or lower protection of certain public interest concerns, but the Europeanised standard must achieve a considerable improvement in the protection of non-economic interests within the European Union (CJEU, 13 May 1997, C-233/94, *Germany v European Parliament and Council*, ECLI:EU:C:1997:231, para 48); see also Isidora Maletič, *The Law and Policy of Harmonisation in Europe's Internal Market* (2013) 23. See Chapter 5, Part I, subsection D.III.

In the field of taxation, the balancing of Member States' interests becomes particularly important because secondary EU law may aim to establish a common approach for the taxation of cross-border economic activities. Cross-border economic activities may run the risk of being taxed twice without being able to claim a worse treatment of the cross-border economic activity compared to the purely domestic one in any of the involved Member States.[205] If a legislative act at a European level coordinates and allocates the taxing rights between the Member States, it would require a balancing of the fiscal interests of the Member States. The setting of a common value in taxation would also be possible but would require deep harmonisation, it would need to go so far as to touch on the fundaments of taxation, accordingly the determining factors of how and why to tax.

From this it follows that Art 114 and Art 115 of the TFEU vest the European Union with the power to develop European values, and thus European legislation does not only have to reduce market regulation. These Europeanised values form the basis of the establishment of a common framework in a particular field of the law, and the uniform application of the regulatory framework facilitates the European internal market.

2. No Pitching to Optimal Economic Efficiency

Concerning the second claim, the power of the European Union to establish Europeanised values allows the European legislature to design secondary EU laws based on these values and not only on the aim of reducing market regulation. A value-oriented harmonisation approach may not achieve a level playing field at a rank conducive to optimal economic efficiency.[206] The efficiency loss may be triggered by the fact that the outcome of the balancing exercise at the European level may be fundamentally different than what the Member States are providing for within their national regulatory framework. Thus, it may be possible that the secondary EU law implements a much stronger regulatory framework than that which the Member States require on a purely domestic basis, and thus the secondary EU law would counteract rather than facilitate a Europe-wide reduction of market regulation.[207] To argue that such a secondary legislative attempt cannot possibly be based on Art 114 or Art 115 of the TFEU because the law does not achieve any trade liberalisation would be mistaken. The European internal market needs may not be an explicit part of the balancing exercise, but the fact that the law between the Member States becomes uniform already removes obstacles to intra-EU trade

[205] Wolfgang Schön, 'Neutrality and Territoriality—Competing or Converging Concepts in European Tax Law?' (2015) 69 Bulletin for International Taxation 271, 274 et seq; Jukka Snell, 'Non-Discriminatory Tax Obstacles in Community Law' (2007) 56 International & Comparative Law Quarterly 339, 365. See also Chapter 5, Part I, subsection C.I.2.

[206] Dougan, 'Minimum Harmonization' (n 184) 860.

[207] For example, the strong regulatory framework in the financial market: Directive, 25 May 2014, 2014/65/EU, on markets in financial instruments an amending Directive 2002/92/EC and Directive 2011/61/EU, OJ, 12 June 2014, L 173, 349.

following from the different regulatory approaches taken by the Member States.[208] Only in very rare cases will the secondary EU law introduce obstacles to intra-EU trade, like the secondary EU law provisions on crystal glass, which require the product description to only be in the language or languages used in the Member State in which the crystal glass is sold or marketed.[209] The secondary EU law required the producer to change the description on the packaging depending on the Member State in which the crystal glass should be sold or marketed. In the vast majority of cases, however, the unification of the law between the Member States will eliminate trade obstacles regardless of the intensity of the regulation with which the market players have to comply. Since the European internal market does not require a specific level of protection, but a unified regulatory approach between the Member States,[210] the European legislature is allowed to base their legislative action on Europeanised values to create a unified legal framework on Art 114 or Art 115 of the TFEU.

3. Smuggling of Non-market Policies into the European Harmonisation Framework

The third claim touches on the question of 'how much' non-market policy considerations can influence the harmonisation process at the European level to allow the secondary EU law to be covered by the European internal market competence. This question has been discussed, in particular, in light of the EU's regulatory approach on tobacco products and their advertising. The European Union issued several legislative pieces on tobacco products, determining the maximum limits for the tar yield of cigarettes,[211] banning tobacco for oral use (so-called snus),[212] and prohibiting tobacco advertising and sponsorships.[213] The European legislature

[208] Markus Möstl, 'Grenzen der Rechtsangleichung im europäischen Binnenmarkt—Kompetenzielle, grundfreiheitliche und grundrechtliche Schranken des Gemeinschaftsgesetzgebers' (2002) Europarecht 318, 327, 335.

[209] See Chapter 5, Part I, subsection D.I.

[210] Renaud Dehousse, 'Integration v. Regulation? Social Regulation in the European Community' (1992) EUI Working Paper LAW 5.

[211] Directive, 17 May 1990, 90/239/EEC, on the approximation of the laws, regulations and administrative provisions of the Member States concerning the maximum tar yield of cigarettes, OJ, 30 March 1990, L 137, 36; confirmed by Directive, 5 June 2001, 2001/37/EC, on the approximation of the laws, regulations and administrative provisions of the Member States concerning the manufacture, presentation and sale of tobacco products, OJ, 18 July 2001, L 194, 26; now in force Directive, 3 April 2014, 2014/40/EU, on the approximation of the laws, regulations and administrative provisions of the Member States concerning the manufacture, presentation and sale of tobacco and related products and repealing Directive 2001/37/EC, OJ, 29 April 2014, L 127, 1.

[212] Directive, 13 November 1989, 89/622/EEC, on the approximation of the law, regulations and administrative provisions of the Member States concerning the labelling of tobacco products, OJ, 8 December 1989, L 359, 1; confirmed by Directive, 5 June 2001, 2001/37/EC (Fn. 549); now in force Directive, 3 April 2014, 2014/40/EU (Fn. 549).

[213] Directive, 6 July 1998, 98/43/EC, on the approximation of the laws, regulations and administrative provisions of the Member States relating to the advertising and sponsorship of tobacco products, OJ, 30 July 1998, L 213, 9, now in force Directive, 26 May 2003, 2003/33/EC, on the approximation of the laws, regulations and administrative provisions of the Member States relating to the advertising and sponsorship of tobacco products, OJ, 20 June 2003, L 152, 16.

introduced these legislative acts under the heading of approximating the national laws. The different health restrictions on tobacco products would not allow a free movement of these products within the European internal market, and thus a uniform approach was needed at the European level. Several Member States, however, were of the opinion that legislative action on the uniform regulation of tobacco products was not covered by the EU's competences since the law was not driven by the aim of harmonising national regulatory approaches in tobacco products but of introducing public health policy standards into the European legal framework.[214] In that vein, Germany challenged the directive prohibiting all forms of tobacco advertising and sponsorship before the CJEU.[215]

The subsequent Court ruling was the first and only judgment invalidating a secondary EU law provision due to a lack of competence. The reason why the CJEU found that the directive went too far is decisive in understanding why the Court has not invalidated many other secondary EU law acts which also follow certain policy objectives which may not be covered by the European competence framework.

The first Directive on tobacco advertising and sponsorship prohibited the advertising of tobacco products on posters, parasols, ashtrays, and other products hotels, restaurants, and cafés usually use, and it also prohibited advertising spots in cinemas. The ban was excessive and did not serve the European internal market for two main reasons. First, parasols and ashtrays, in the form of advertising material, are not traded on the European internal market like newspapers and magazines, which are prohibited from including advertising for tobacco products. However, a ban on advertising on certain products only makes sense from an internal market perspective if the products are traded on the internal market, and thus may be subject to different regulatory regimes. In the case of parasols and ashtrays, however, they are provided to hotels, restaurants, and cafés as advertising material, and no trading on the market occurs. Advertising on posters and in cinemas was also characterised as purely domestic, and thus the ban on advertising on these products does not facilitate the trade between the Member States either.

Second, according to Art 5 of the directive, the Member States are allowed to introduce 'stricter requirements concerning the advertising or sponsorship of tobacco products' if the stricter standard is necessary to guarantee the health protection of the individuals. A stricter standard on the advertising of products traded on the European internal market would introduce trade barriers, and thus the ban on tobacco advertising and sponsorship as set out in the directive does not facilitate any cross-border movement of goods within the European internal market.

[214] Germany's claim for annulment of the directive on advertising and sponsorship of tobacco products was supported by the French Republic, the United Kingdom, and the European Commission: see CJEU, 5 October 2000, C-376/98, *Germany v European Parliament and Council*, ECLI:EU:C:2000:544.

[215] CJEU, 5 October 2000, C-376/98, *Germany v European Parliament and Council*, ECLI:EU:C:2000:544. For the arguments see Opinion of Advocate General Fennelly, 15 June 2000, C-376/98, *Germany v European Parliament and Council*, ECLI:EU:C:2000:324, paras 37–38.

A free-movement clause is particularly important in the field of product standard harmonisation as such a clause ensures that any product complying with the requirements set by the secondary EU law can be traded in any Member State. The reason for such a high threshold lies in the CJEU case law. The Court has developed the concept of mutual recognition particularly for the area of free movement of goods,[216] which has to be recognised by any secondary EU law act. However, secondary EU law may not always demand a ceiling.[217] Aside from product standards, minimum harmonisation measures are allowed, for example in the area of taxation, which do not include a free-movement clause but nonetheless comply with the requirements set by Art 114 or Art 115 of the TFEU.

All other secondary EU laws which have been challenged over time before the CJEU on the grounds of the EU's lack of competence may aim to ensure health, safety, or environmental protection, but they fulfil the requirements of Art 114 of the TFEU by regulating items traded between the Member States, and thereby easing intra-EU trade.[218] Accordingly, when the European legislature harmonises national laws based on Art 114 or Art 115 of the TFEU, the legislature cannot be denied the possibility of introducing secondary legislation which also safeguards other general interests recognised by the European treaties.[219] The non-market objectives may even outweigh the market aims,[220] and the European legislature may still be allowed to base the European legislation on Art 114 or Art 115 of the TFEU because the secondary EU legislation fosters intra-EU trade.[221] The European

[216] The principle of mutual recognition acknowledges diversity between the regulatory approaches of the Member States, but at the same time facilitates intra-EU trade: Besselink (n 189) 65; '[T]he principle of mutual recognition is a mechanism of allocation of regulatory competence to the Country of origin ('home Country control principle'), designed to avoid goods being subject to a dual burden of regulation by home and the host county': Nicolas Bernard, 'La libre circulation des marchandises, des personnes et des services dans le Traité CE sous l'angle de la compétence' (1998) 34 Cahiers de droit européen 11.

[217] Weatherill, *The Internal Market* (n 187) 210.

[218] Such as a directive aiming at harmonising the national regulation on food supplements, Directive, 10 June 2002, 2002/46/EC, on the approximation of the laws of the Member States relating to food supplements, OJ, 12 July 2002, L 183, 51; CJEU, 12 July 2005, C-154/04, *Alliance for Natural Health*, ECLI:EU:C:2005:449; or all the other directives on tobacco products CJEU, 10 December 2002, C-491/01, *British American Tobacco*, ECLI:EU:C:2002:741; for the amended directive on tobacco advertising and sponsorship (Directive, 26 May 2003, 2003/33/EC, on the approximation of the laws, regulations and administrative provisions of the Member States relating to the advertising and sponsorship of tobacco products, OJ, 20 June 2003, L 152, 16) CJEU, 12 December 2006, C-380/03, *Germany v European Parliament and Council*, ECLI:EU:C:2006:772; and concerning the right to privacy Directive, 24 October 1995, 95/46/EC, on the protection of individuals with regard to the processing of personal data and on the free movement of such data, OJ, 23 November 1995, L 281, 31; CJEU, 20 May 2003, C-465/00, C-138/01, and C-139/01, *Österreichischer Rundfunk*, ECLI:EU:C:2003:294.

[219] CJEU, 5 October 2000, C-376/98, *Germany v European Parliament and Council*, ECLI:EU:C:2000:544, para 78; CJEU, 10 December 2002, C-491/01, *British American Tobacco*, ECLI:EU:C:2002:741, para 78.

[220] Bruno de Witte, 'A Competence to Protect—The Pursuit of Non-Market Aims through Internal Market Legislation' in Phil Syrpis (ed), *The Judiciary, the Legislature and the EU Internal Market* (CUP 2012) 36 arguing that secondary EU laws must also adequately contribute to improve the conditions for the establishment and functioning of the internal market.

[221] In that vein also Kosta, *Fundamental Rights* (n 202) 19 et seq. '[I]nternal market legislation . . . must satisfy a specific internal market test, in the sense that the authors of the act must make a plausible

legislature only exceeds its competences if a provision within the secondary EU law act does not facilitate any intra-EU trade whatsoever. Moreover, if the European Union holds the power to regulate a particular policy matter which may even outweigh the aim of legal harmonisation, it is necessary to apply the centre of gravity test.[222] Using the main purpose and content test, it is possible to identify which of the competence clauses is the primary one and has to form the legal basis for the secondary EU law act.[223]

From this it follows that European legislation harmonising the laws of the Member States can follow particular policy objectives, such as public health safety, environmental protection, or privacy protection. The European legislature is allowed to 'smuggle' policy objectives into the EU legal framework which are not covered by the EU's competences if these objectives are the guiding factors for harmonisation. In these cases, the non-market aims may even outweigh internal market needs. But as long as all provisions within the secondary EU law act (also) facilitate intra-EU trade, the European legislature is allowed to base the harmonisation measure on the EU's internal market competence. If, however, the European Union also holds the power to regulate the policy objectives driving European harmonisation, the main purpose and content test has to be applied to identify which of the competence clauses is the relevant one, and subsequently which procedural framework has to be followed.

IV. Identifying the 'Right' Competence for Steering Taxes

It is common ground that Member States use taxes not only for the sake of raising revenue but also to achieve certain policy objectives. Accordingly, taxes form a tool to influence behaviour, and Member States may find it more appropriate to steer people's behaviour indirectly, through taxation, which leaves them with the option of maintaining their behaviour but paying for it. Excise duties and financial transaction taxes are good examples of taxes attempting to influence behaviour. Duties on tobacco and alcohol aim to reduce the use of these health-damaging substances,[224] and the transaction taxes in the financial sector aim to prevent

case that the act either helps to remove disparities between national provisions that hinder the free movement of goods, services or persons, or helps to remove disparities that cause distorted conditions of competition... Such legislation also invariably and legitimately pursues other public policy objectives ... Internal market legislation is always also about "something else" ....' Bruno de Witte, 'Non-Market Values in Internal Market Legislation' in Niamh Nic Shuibhne (ed), *Regulating the Internal Market* (Edward Elgar Publishing 2006) 75.

[222] Engel (n 166) 13 et seq.

[223] Opinion of Advocate General Fennelly, 15 June 2000, C-376/98, *Germany v European Parliament and Council*, ECLI:EU:C:2000:324, para 58. See for the conflict of competence rules this chapter subsection F.III.

[224] See recital 2 of the Directive, 21 June 2011, 2011/64/EU, on the structure and rates of excise duty applied to manufactured tobacco, OJ, 5 July 2011, L 176, 24.

high-frequency trading which is supposed to have negative effects on the financial market. In the area of environmental protection, some Member States have decided to levy a carbon tax,[225] whereas others debate extensively whether they should introduce such a tax as an element of their climate protection strategy. A carbon tax would not prohibit the emission of carbon dioxide; however, it would make these emissions more costly.

Even at the national level, steering taxes have a dual purpose. On the one hand they influence the behaviour of consumers and entrepreneurs. On the other hand, these taxes contribute to the Member States' budgets like any other tax even if the tax is successful in reducing the unwanted behaviour, such as the emission of carbon dioxide. Likewise, at the European level, secondary EU law may harmonise national steering taxes to smooth intra-EU trade but, at the same time, may introduce new tools to protect the environment or public health and safety. To determine which competence clause forms the legal basis for the legislative act and determines the procedural framework, it depends on whether the European Union holds the power to enact European laws for both fields (eg harmonising national taxes and the competence to introduce environmental or consumer protection laws or public safety standards). In cases in which the European Union holds the power in both areas (conflict of competences),[226] the main purpose and content test has to be applied. This means that the main purpose and content of the legislative action has to be determined based on the objectives, the wording, and substance of the law.[227] If the protection of the environment or public health is the predominant driver for the legislative initiative, the positive impact on the European internal market through harmonisation is only a positive reflex, and in cases in which the harmonisation of national laws is the predominant goal, the European legislature nevertheless has to ensure a high level of environmental[228] or human health protection.[229]

If, however, the European legislature only holds the internal market competence and is not allowed to enact laws in the fields which are affected by the steering effect of the tax, it needs to be determined whether the steering effects are covered by

[225] For an overview see Elke Asen, 'Where Is Carbon Taxed in Europe?' (Tax Foundation, 14 November 2019) <https://taxfoundation.org/carbon-taxes-in-europe-2019/> accessed 14 December 2019.

[226] See this chapter subsection F.III.

[227] CJEU, 11 June 1991, C-300/89, *Commission v Council*, ECLI:EU:C:1991:244, para 10; CJEU, 9 November 1995, C-426/93, *Germany v Council*, ECLI:EU:C:1995:367, para 29; CJEU, 13 September 2005, C-176/03, *Commission and European Parliament v Council*, ECLI:EU:C:2005:542, para 45; CJEU, 23 October 2007, C-440/05, *Commission v European Parliament and Council*, ECLI:EU:C:2007:625, para 61; CJEU, 3 September 2008, C-402/05 P and C-415/05 P, *Kadi*, ECLI:EU:C:2008:461, para 182; CJEU, 6 May 2014, C-43/12, *Commission v European Parliament and Council*, ECLI:EU:C:2014:298, para 29; CJEU, 10 September 2015, C-363/14, *European Parliament v Council*, ECLI:EU:C:2015:579, para 41. See also Ooik (n 165) 408.

[228] Art 11 TFEU.

[229] Art 168 of the TFEU.

the internal market competence. As CJEU case law shows,[230] the European legislature can follow any non-market policy objective as long as any provision of the legislative act (also) facilitates the functioning of the European internal market. We shall assume for example that there is a common agreement between the Member States that particularly violent computer games have a negative impact on the social development of minors. Some Member States already impose a tax on those games aiming at reducing the sale of these computer games for the sake of protecting minors. The uncoordinated approach of the national laws hinders the intra-EU trade in violent computer games.[231] A European initiative to introduce secondary EU law establishing the framework for imposing taxes on violent computer games could aim to facilitate the European internal market or protect minors. The European legislature has the power to harmonise these laws on the basis of the European internal market competence; however, the European treaties do not vest the European Union with the competence to introduce secondary EU law in the field of the protection of minors.[232] Against the background of the division of powers between the European Union and the Member States, no main purpose and content test needs to be applied because the European legislature has no choice other than using the European internal market competence to harmonise the taxes on violent computer games. Under Art 115 of the TFEU, the European legislature has the power to use the protection of minors as the driving factor for establishing the tax framework but also has to ensure that any provision within the secondary EU law framework aims to facilitate trade between the Member States. The demand to facilitate trade within the European Union presupposes, for example, that one Member State accepts and recognises the levying of these taxes in a fellow Member State. If the directive does not include free movement clauses, in the sense that any computer game which was already subject to tax can freely be traded within the European Union without being taxed again, the secondary EU law would not meet the requirements set by Art 115 of the TFEU, and thus the European legislature would exceed its competences.

V. Secondary EU Law Facilitating the Establishment and Functioning of the European Internal Market

1. Economic and Legal Trade Obstacles

From the previous subsections it has become clear that any legislative action at the European level, which is based on either Art 114 or Art 115 of the TFEU, aims

[230] See this chapter subsection G.III.3.

[231] These duties are not levied when the goods are finally consumed but on upstream transactions. The differences between the domestic excise duties harms intra-EU trade in these goods.

[232] See Art 6 (e) of the TFEU.

to eliminate existing obstacles to intra-EU trade. Trade obstacles can either fall within or outside[233] the scope of the fundamental freedoms. Obstacles imposed by national laws of the Member States which fall within the scope of the fundamental freedoms can be defined as legal restrictions. Such restrictions are either lawful or unlawful depending on whether the Member State can justify the restriction with an overriding reason of public interest. From the perspective of the fundamental freedoms, justified legal restrictions are allowed to stand, but they nevertheless hamper trade between the Member States. On the other hand, trade obstacles not falling within the scope of the fundamental freedoms, because the trade hampering effect does not follow from a worse treatment of foreigners or cross-border economic activities, can be defined as economic obstacles. In taxation, economic obstacles are imposed by the disparities of the national tax law systems and their uncoordinated application.[234] The best example is double taxation.[235] It goes without saying that double taxation negatively affects cross-border economic activity because any economic player will think twice about whether or not to engage in a cross-border economic activity if such an activity exposes the entrepreneur to being taxed twice.[236] However, the fundamental freedoms are not able to catch these obstacles because the national tax laws do not treat cross-border economic activities worse than purely domestic activities.[237]

From this it follows that intra-EU trade may be hampered by different kinds of obstacles: on the one hand, there may be legal restrictions which are covered by the fundamental freedoms, and which any market player can thus litigate against. On the other hand, there are obstacles which negatively affect the functioning of the European internal market, but which cannot be addressed by the fundamental freedoms.

The following subsections will be divided into two. Subsection a) will address the legal issues on harmonising national laws which hamper intra-EU trade by imposing legal restrictions. Subsection b) will address economic obstacles. It will be identified which of these legal and economic obstacles to intra-EU trade can be eliminated by a European harmonisation measure.

[233] For example, double taxation: Pater J Wattel, Otto Marres, and Hein Vermeulen (eds), *Terra/Wattel European Tax Law*, vol I General Topics and Direct Taxation (7th edn, Kluwer Law International 2018) 51 et seq.

[234] Wolfgang Schön, 'Taxing Multinationals in Europe' in Bettina Banoun, Ole Gjems-Onstad, and Arvid Aage Skaar (eds), *Høyt skattet: festskrift til Frederik Zimmer på 70-årsdagen 28. Mars 2014* (Universitetsforl 2014) 478.

[235] Sjoerd Douma, 'The Three Ds of Direct Tax Jurisdiction: Disparity, Discrimination and Double Taxation' (2006) 46 European Taxation 522, 524 et seq.

[236] Daniel Gutmann, 'How to Avoid Double Taxation in the European Union?' in Isabelle Richelle, Wolfgang Schön, and Edoardo Traversa (eds), *Allocating Taxing Powers within the European Union* (Springer 2013) 67.

[237] Georg W Kofler, 'Double Taxation and European Law: Analysis of the Jurisprudence' in Alexander Rust (ed), *Double Taxation within the European Union* (Kluwer Law International 2011) 98 et seq. For a deeper analysis and the question of why the concept of mutual recognition cannot be applied in the field of taxation, see Chapter 5, Part I, subsection C.I.2.

a) *Eliminating Legal Restrictions through Harmonisation*

Member States impose (justified) legal restrictions to protect certain overriding public interests. The right to justify trade restrictions allows the Member States to give important (national) values priority over market efficiency. It has already been stressed that the European internal market does not ask for an optimal allocation of resources at any price.[238] The internal market may, however, demand a uniform approach of the Member States not to burden cross-border economic activities more heavily than purely domestic activities.[239] The European internal market competence can be used to align the national provisions protecting certain values.[240] In this case, the unified approach removes the trade hampering effect following from the differences of the Member States' national regimes, all of which aim to protect the same value.[241] Unification aiming to facilitate the functioning of the European internal market can be achieved either only for the cross-border situation or for the entire regulatory framework, covering both the purely domestic and the cross-border situation.

The principle of subsidiarity may force the European legislature to restrict European legislation to what is necessary to facilitate cross-border trade. Concerning the elimination of legal restrictions to intra-EU trade, the harmonising European law measures may only regulate the cross-border situation and would grant the national legislature the freedom to determine the regulatory framework for the purely domestic situation, if the cross-border and the purely domestic situation can be sufficiently separated.[242]

b) *Eliminating Economic Obstacles through Harmonisation and Coordination*

Member States' national tax laws often impose obstacles to intra-EU trade which cannot be addressed by the fundamental freedoms.[243] The trade hampering effects follow from differences between the Member States' tax regimes and their parallel application.[244] The Member States' tax regimes can differ in their design and scope,

[238] See this chapter subsection G.I.

[239] See this chapter subsection G.II.

[240] The policy concerns underlying the Member States' derogations can, and have to be, addressed by the act of European harmonisation, and thus the European legislature is allowed to pursue those non-market values under Art 114 of the TFEU, see Witte, 'A Competence to Protect' (n 220) 32 et seq.

[241] In that vein, CJEU, 24 February 2000, C-168/98, *Luxembourg v European Parliament and Council*, ECLI:EU:C:2000:100, para 32; CJEU, 13 May 1997, C-233/94, *Germany v European Parliament and Council*, ECLI:EU:C:1997:2331, para 17, 'Member States may, subject to certain conditions, impose national measures pursuing a legitimate aim compatible with the Treaty and justified on overriding public interest grounds, which include the protection of consumers. They may thus, in certain circumstances, adopt or maintain measures constituting a barrier to freedom of movement. Article 57(2) of the Treaty authorises the Community to eliminate obstacles of that kind in order to make it easier for persons to take up and pursue activities as self-employed persons.'

[242] For the subsidiarity issue see this chapter subsection G.VI.2.

[243] For this line of arguments in the field of double taxation see Gutmann (n 236) 67.

[244] Paul Farmer and Adam Zalasinski, 'General Report' in Xenios L Xenopoulos (ed), *Direct Tax Rules and the EU Fundamental Freedoms: Origin and Scope of the Problem; National and Community Responses and Solutions: FIDE 2006 National Reports; Topic 1* (Theopress 2006) 402.

for example different definitions of the income tax base. But differences can also occur because the Member States have introduced entirely different tax systems. The obstacles to intra-EU trade follow from the constant need to comply with the different tax rules of the Member States. We shall assume, for example, that a taxpayer has to comply with the tax law rules of both the home and the host Member State, and the former entirely follows the International Financial Reporting Standards (IFRS) for calculating the domestic tax base, whereas the latter requires significant amendments to the profits calculated under commercial law (which may or may not entirely follow the IFRS standards) for tax law purposes. Beyond any doubt, the amendments required to comply with the tax jurisdiction of both the home and the host Member State hamper intra-EU trade.[245]

The differences between the Member States' tax laws are not always of a systematic nature; differences may follow from the leeway for justifying legal restrictions. In other words, Member States may use the leeway for justified restrictions of the fundamental freedoms differently. In the pre-Anti-Tax Avoidance Directive (ATAD) world,[246] the CJEU case law on exit taxes, for example, granted some leeway with respect to the time frame for the instalment payments.[247] Thus, the Member States may have imposed exit taxes which are all subject to a different framework, one allowing instalment payments over five years, others require a one-off tax payment after ten years.[248] Whereas the subject matter—the exit tax—falls within the scope of the fundamental freedoms, and thus accounts for a (justified) legal restriction;[249] the obstacles following from the differences between the

[245] Economic obstacles following from different definitions of the tax base in different Member States 'are not controlled by the ECJ', Schön, 'Taxing Multinationals' (n 234) 478.

[246] Council Directive, 12 July 2016, 2016/1164/EU, laying down rules against tax avoidance practices that directly affect the functioning of the internal market, OJ, 19 July 2016, L 193, 1.

[247] The CJEU found it proportionate to grant the taxpayer the choice between an immediate payment of the amount of tax due on the unrealised capital gains relating to the assets held by that person, or a deferred payment of that tax, possibly together with interest (CJEU, 29 November 2011, C-371/10, *National Grid Indus BV*, ECLI:EU:C:2011:785, para 73; CJEU, 6 September 2012, C-38/10, *Commission v Portugal*, ECLI:EU:C:2012:521, paras 31 and 32). The Court also acknowledged that the risk of non-recovery increases with the passing of time, and thus, the ability to spread payment of the tax owing before the capital gains are actually realised over a period of five years constitutes a 'satisfactory and proportionate measure for the attainment of the objective of preserving the balanced allocation of the power to impose taxes between the Member States' (CJEU, 23 January 2014, C-164/12, *DMC*, ECLI:EU:C:2014:20, para 62. If the national law does not allow any deferral, the law contradicts the fundamental freedoms: CJEU, 23 November 2017, *A Oy*, ECLI:EU:C:2017:888. According to the ATAD, the taxpayer should be given the right to defer the payment of an exit tax by paying the tax in instalments over five years (Art 5 Subsection 2).

[248] For an overview of the different approaches Member States may take in the area of exit taxation see Frank PG Pötgens and others, 'The Compatibility of Exit Tax Legislation Applicable to Corporate Taxpayers in France, Germany, Italy, The Netherlands, Portugal, Spain and The United Kingdom with the EU Freedom of Establishment—Part 1' (2016) 44 Intertax 163; Frank PG Pötgens and others, 'The Compatibility of Exit Tax Legislation Applicable to Corporate Taxpayers in France, Germany, Italy, The Netherlands, Portugal, Spain and The United Kingdom with the EU Freedom of Establishment—Part 2' (2016) 44 Intertax 247.

[249] CJEU, 29 November 2011, C-371/10, *National Grid Indus BV*, ECLI:EU:C:2011:785; CJEU, 21 May 2015, C-657/13, *Verder*, ECLI:EU:C:2015:331.

national frameworks for imposing the justified tax are outside the scope of the fundamental freedoms.[250]

The third category of economic obstacles to intra-EU trade arises due to a parallel application of Member States' tax laws. An uncoordinated application may trigger taxation in more than one Member State, and it is obvious that double taxation makes trade between Member States far less attractive.

There is no question that a unified approach of the Member States towards taxation, for example a unified tax system on financial transactions or, at least, minimum rules for the corporate tax base,[251] would facilitate intra-EU trade. The Common Corporate Tax Base (CCTB)would prevent market players from additional burdens following from the need to calculate the tax bases autonomously in each Member State according to that Member State's national rules.[252] Accordingly, the taxpayer would be allowed to use the calculations on the tax base of the source Member State in the home Member State without needing to adjust them. There can also be no doubt that coordination between the Member States' tax regimes would facilitate what the internal market is aiming for: an efficient allocation of resources. Double taxation distorts competition within the internal market and thus may prevent an optimal allocation of resources.[253]

Despite the truly negative effects economic obstacles have on the free movement of goods, services, persons, and capital, it is not entirely clear whether they fall within the scope of Art 115 of the TFEU, and thus can be addressed by European legislation.[254] Some scholars reject a wide interpretation of Art 115 of the TFEU because they fear that extensive European tax legislation means uniformity of the national tax systems.[255] Uniformity of the entire national tax systems of the Member States is not required by the European internal market. However, Art 115

[250] Stephen Weatherill, 'Viking and Laval: The EU Internal Market Perspective' in Mark R Freedland and Jeremias Prassl (eds), *Viking, Laval and Beyond* (Hart Publishing 2014) 29 emphasising that harmonisation is only required where the CJEU refuses to apply the fundamental freedoms. For a very narrow interpretation of the European internal market competence see Daniel Blum and Andreas Langer, 'At a Crossroads: Mandatory Disclosure under DAC-6 and EU Primary Law—Part 1' (2019) 59 European Taxation 282, 284 et seq reducing the European mandatory disclosure rules to a mechanism to fight aggressive tax planning. However, the European mandatory disclosure rules go beyond that; they also harmonise the different national approaches of the Member States and ensure that a fruitful and standardised exchange of information is possible in that field.

[251] Frans Vanistendael, 'Comments on the Ruding Committee Report' (1992) 1 EC Tax Review 3, 11; Vanistendael, 'A Personal View' (n 172) 28–29. See also the European Commission's proposal for a Common Corporate Tax Base: Commission, 25 October 2016, COM(2016) 685 final.

[252] Bruno Peeters, 'EUCIT: For How Much Longer Will Political Objections Outweigh the Advantages?' (2015) 24 EC Tax Review 128 arguing that the European internal market would need not only a CCCTB but a European Corporate Income Tax which also harmonises the tax rate between the Member States.

[253] See in that vein Anzhela Cédelle, 'Double Taxation and the Internal Market: No Simple Fix?' in Pasquale Pistone (ed), *European Tax Integration: Law, Policy and Politics* (IBFD 2018) 696.

[254] Adam Zalasiński, 'Tax Rules Applicable without Distinction and the EU Internal Market Freedoms—An Analysis of Recent Case Law Regarding Taxation of Investment Income' 57 European Taxation 11, 541.

[255] Hey, *Harmonisierung der Unternehmensbesteuerung* (n 184) 77 et seq, 108.

of the TFEU vests the European legislature with the power to issue directives[256] for the harmonisation of the Member State tax laws which apply to cross-border economic activities because their differences may hamper intra-EU trade. Even if one restricts the power to align the law to laws regulating cross-border situations, the EU's legislative power is far-reaching in taxation, because the vast majority of tax rules may apply to both an economic cross-border activity and a purely domestic economic activity.

Art 115 of the TFEU grants the European Union a wide competence to eliminate any trade obstacles within the European internal market through the harmonisation of the national laws.[257] The European internal market needs and the interests of the Member States in particularly sensitive fields such as taxation, are balanced within Art 115 of the TFEU, not only by determining the European Union's competence but also through the procedural framework. Any legislative act which is based on Art 115 of the TFEU requires unanimous voting in the Council. The unanimity requirement does not change the far-reaching scope of the competence of the European Union but grants each Member State a veto power. In other words, the Member States conferred a far-reaching internal market competence upon the European Union to grant the European legislature flexibility: any trade obstacle can be addressed by European legislation. On a second level (the procedural level), however, the Member States ensured that no legislative act will see the light of the day without their blessing.

From all of this it follows that the European institutions should be allowed to take any legislative measures necessary to eliminate economic trade obstacles within the European internal market. The fundamental freedoms may not be able to address these obstacles but nonetheless, economic trade obstacles are capable of distorting competition on the market[258] and thus preventing an optimal allocation of resources. European legislation can address these obstacles because the legislative power of the European institutions goes beyond the scope of the fundamental freedoms. However, particularly sensitive areas, such as taxation, are carved out by Art 114 of the TFEU, and the procedural framework of Art 115 of the TFEU

[256] Exceptions to the restriction to only use directives as a harmonising tool can be found in the area of customs and implementing legislation. According to Art 291 Subsections 2 and 3 of the TFEU, the European Parliament and the Council can enact regulations to ensure uniform conditions for implementing legally binding secondary EU law. In that vein, Art 397 of the VAT Directive explicitly provides for the possibility of an implementation regulation requiring a unanimous decision in the Council (see Regulation, 15 March 2011, laying down implementing measures for Directive 2006/112/EC on the common system of value added tax, OJ, 23 March 2011, L 77, 1.

[257] Gareth Davies, 'The Competence to Create an Internal Market: Conceptual Poverty and Unbalanced Interests' in Sacha Garben and Inge Govaere (eds), *The Division of Competences between the EU and the Member States: Reflections on the Past, the Present and the Future* (Hart Publishing 2017) 78 criticising the broad scope because it suggests that 'the internal market will be 'complete' when there are no differences in law left . . . it is not a worthy goal for the European Union'.

[258] Ulrich Immenga and others (eds), 'Über Privatrechtsvereinheitlichung und Marktintegration', *Festschrift für Ernst-Joachim Mestmäcker: zum siebzigsten Geburtstag* (Nomos 1996) 353.

ensures that European tax laws can only be introduced when all Member States are onboard. Accordingly, every Member State can veto European tax legislation if it is not ready to sacrifice national values for the establishment of a true single market.

2. Framing the Member States' Obligations for the Establishment and Functioning of the European Internal Market

There is another category of secondary EU law which may fall within the scope of Art 114 and Art 115 of the TFEU. The law of this category may not primarily achieve less market regulation or facilitate intra-EU trade by enhancing the economic status quo. The Member States may, however, want to introduce secondary EU laws which allow the Member States to comply with the fundamental freedoms, but through common efforts of the Member States. In other words, the fundamental freedoms may force the Member States to grant certain benefits not only to purely domestic economic activities or resident taxpayers but also to cross-border economic activities, or non-resident taxpayers. The CJEU case law thereby already eliminates existing trade obstacles by way of negative integration. The granting of the benefit, as required by the fundamental freedoms, may not be in line with the fundamental structure of the national tax system, and thus the Member States may wish to introduce a cooperative framework between them, which on the one hand guarantees the free movement rights, but on the other allocates the burden for achieving free movement between the Member States. Take personal deductions as an example. According to CJEU case law, the home Member State is required to consider the personal circumstances of a taxpayer when calculating the tax due.[259] The home Member State is not allowed to reduce the personal deductions if the taxpayer earns income in another Member State, which is also (only)[260] taxable in the other Member State.[261] The Member States may find it more appropriate to link the personal allowance with the right to tax. Accordingly, any Member State, being the home and host Member State, has to grant personal deductions in accordance with the income taxable in that very Member State. Such an approach leads to a proportional granting of personal deductions in the home and host Member States determined by the proportion of income taxable in that Member State. Of course, the framework requires an assessment by the home Member State stating the individual distribution of the taxpayer's income and subsequently the host Member State's duty to grant a proportion of the personal deductions.

A framework coordinating the granting of personal allowances may, in some cases, be beneficial for the taxpayer,[262] in particular when the taxpayer is not able to

[259] CJEU, 14 February 1995, C-279/93, *Schumacker*, ECLI:EU:C:1995:31, paras 32–33; CJEU, 18 June 2015, C-9/14, *Kieback*, ECLI:EU:C:2015:406, para 22; CJEU, 9 February 2017, C-283/15, *X*, ECLI:EU:C:2017:102, para 30.

[260] Due to a tax treaty signed between the Member States.

[261] CJEU, 12 December 2002, C-385/00, *de Groot*, ECLI:EU:C:2002:750.

[262] Peter J Wattel, 'Red Herrings in Direct Tax Cases before the ECJ' (2004) 31 Legal Issues of Economic Integration 81, 85.

exhaust the entire allowance in the home Member States but is not entitled to claim the allowance in the host Member State, according to the *Schumacker* doctrine.[263] In the vast majority of cases, however, the framework will provide for a result which also would have been achieved by applying the national rules in conformity with the fundamental freedoms and the subsequent CJEU case law. In these cases, the secondary EU law framework does not provide for an additional benefit for the European internal market. But nonetheless, the European legislature should be allowed to base such a legislative attempt on Art 115 of the TFEU because it ensures the functioning of the European internal market by deepening integration between the Member States. A coordinated framework establishes standards at the European level which the fundamental freedoms are not able to create on a stand-alone basis.[264] Secondary EU law, which is based on harmonised standards or values, is able to counterbalance the unprincipled application of the fundamental freedoms and allow the Member States to align the needs of the European internal market and their national legislation.[265] In the case of personal deductions, it would be the linking of the right to tax and the need to provide personal allowances. The sharing of the burden of granting the personal allowances between the Member States may be considered more appropriate, or even more legitimate, and thus the introduction of such a system may be capable of compensating for the rough and one-sided application of the fundamental freedoms.[266] In other words, a coordinative framework may allow one to overcome shortcomings following from the fundamental freedoms single country perspective, which hardly considers a compensatory treatment in another Member State.[267] A framework implemented at the European level, however, would give Member States more flexibility to cope with the requirements set by the fundamental freedoms.

From all of this it follows that the European legislature should not only be allowed to introduce secondary EU law legislation which eliminates obstacles to intra-EU trade but also to preserve the status quo established by negative integration but according to the standards or values the Member States have agreed on. Cooperative secondary EU laws allow the Member States to comply with their duty under the free movement rights in a more legitimate, or more manageable way. In tax law, the only possible competence clause is Art 115 of the TFEU, and it should be open to introduce a framework not directly enhancing the status quo for

[263] CJEU, 14 February 1995, C-279/93, *Schumacker*, ECLI:EU:C:1995:31, para 32 et seq.

[264] See Chapter 5, Part I, subsection E.VIII.

[265] Fritz W Scharpf, 'Negative and Positive Integration in the Political Economy of European Welfare States' in Martin Rhodes and Yves Mény (eds), *The Future of European Welfare: A New Social Contract?* (Palgrave Macmillan 1998) 160 et seq. Floris de Witte, 'Transnational Solidarity and the Mediation of Conflicts of Justice in Europe' 18 European Law Journal 694, 702 et seq.

[266] Kees van Raad, 'Non-Residents—Personal Allowances, Deduction of Personal Expenses and Tax Rates' (2010) 2 World Tax Journal 154, 158 et seq.

[267] For a detailed analysis of the case law see Chapter 5, Part I, subsection E.VIII.2.

intra-EU trade but preserving what has been accomplished by way of negative integration through the setting of common standards at the European level.

VI. Subsidiarity Concerns

The legislative procedure at the European level is not only determined by the question of whether the European Union holds the power to act but also by the subsidiarity principle which adds another layer and asks whether 'the objectives of the proposed action cannot be sufficiently achieved by the Member States'.[268] In other words, if it is clear that the European Union can act because the European treaties transpose the necessary competence upon it, the subsidiarity principle would beg the question of whether the Member States could not also have achieved the objectives on their own.[269] Under a plain reading of the provision, the subsidiarity principle grants a clear preference to Member States' legislative actions over EU actions, and thus any legislative action would require an explicit justification if pursued on the European and not the national level.[270] The true content and scope of the subsidiarity principle can best be revealed when examining the genesis of the principle of subsidiarity and the related CJEU case law more closely.

1. The Genesis of the Principle of Subsidiarity

Today, the preamble of the TEU demands that the Member States shall 'continue the process of creating an ever-closer union among the peoples of Europe, in which decisions are taken as closely as possible to the citizen in accordance with the principle of subsidiarity'.[271] This statement clearly reveals the balancing act performed by the drafters of the European treaties: on the one hand, deeper integration between the Member States would demand 'an unprecedented extension of the powers conferred upon the European [Union]', but on the other hand, the confidence of the Member States would demand a 'solemn guarantee of the proximity of government'.[272] The obligation to balance both the needs of integration and the

[268] Art 5 Subsection 3 of the TEU.

[269] Peter-Christian Müller-Graff and Werner Weidenfeld, 'Die Kompetenzen in der Europäischen Union', *Europa Handbuch: Band I: Die Europäische Union - Politisches System und Politikbereiche* (4th edn, Verlag Bertelsmann Stiftung 2006) 149; Thomas Köster, 'Subsidarität als Lebenselixier für Europa - Statement' in Handwerkskammer Düsseldorf (ed), *Welche Chancen hat Subsidiarität in Europa?*, vol 5 (Verlagsanstalt Handwerk 2014) 18 et seq. Criticising that the European legislature has not always lived up to the demands the principle of subsidiarity poses, but acknowledging that the principle is vague and hard to frame in concrete terms.

[270] Antonio Goucha Soares, 'Pre-Emption, Conflicts of Powers and Subsidiarity' (1998) 23 European Law Review 132, 143.

[271] For a historical point of view see Alan Dashwood, 'The Limits of European Community Powers' (1996) 21 European Law Review 113, 115.

[272] Koen Lenaerts, 'The Principle of Subsidiarity and the Environment in the European Union: Keeping the Balance of Federalism' (1993) 17 Fordham International Law Journal 846, 847–48.

independence of the Member States has characterised all significant amendments to the Rome Treaty. The balancing act was particularly evident in the Maastricht Treaty, which introduced the principle of subsidiarity as a general principle into the European treaties.[273] But even before subsidiarity became a general principle of European Union law, it determined European legislative power both explicitly and implicitly.[274] The implicit face of subsidiarity has first been expressed in a European Commission's 'Report on the European Union' in 1975, which reads that 'the European Union is not to give birth to a centralizing super-state. Consequently, and in accordance with the *principe de subsidiarité*, the Union will be given responsibility only for those matters which the Member States are no longer capable of dealing with efficiently'.[275] After the Single European Act, the subsidiarity principle has found its explicit expression in the newly inserted provision on the EU's legislative power in environmental matters, which stated that the European legislature is restricted to those actions whose objectives could 'be attained better at the Community level than at the level of the individual Member States'.[276]

The introduction of the principle of subsidiarity as a general principle of European law was required during the negotiations of the Maastricht Treaty because the Member States feared an extensive use of legislative power by Brussels.[277] Art 3b of the Treaty Establishing the European Community stated that outside the EU's exclusive competences, the European Union 'shall take action, in accordance with the principle of subsidiarity, only if and insofar as the objectives of the proposed action cannot be sufficiently achieved by the Member States and can, therefore, by reason of the scale or effects of the proposed action, be better achieved by the [European Union]'. Subsidiarity was perceived as a threshold the European Union has to overcome to be allowed to act. The subsidiarity threshold was not meant to relate to or call into question the powers conferred upon the European Union;[278] it was, however, understood as a way of 'alleviating the competence problem'.[279] From this perspective, the subsidiarity principle was a tool designed

[273] Art 3b, Maastricht Treaty, OJ, 29 July 1992, C 191, 6.

[274] See for a detailed overview Robert Schütze, *Cooperative Federalism Constitutionalized* (OUP 2009) 247 et seq.

[275] European Commission, 'Report on the European Union, 25 June 1975' (1975) 8 Bulletin of the European Communities.

[276] Art 130r Subsection 4 of the European treaty in the version of the Single European Act, OJ, 29 June 1987, L 169, 12.

[277] Deborah Z Cass, 'The Word That Saves Maastricht? The Principle of Subsidiarity and the Division of Powers within the European Community' (1992) 29 Common Market Law Review 1107, 1109.

[278] Council, 11–12 December 1992, Conclusions of the Presidency in Edinburgh, Overall approach to the application by the Council of the subsidiarity principle and Article 3b of the Treaty on European Union, 16; 'the *distribution of competences* between the Union and the Member States is based on [the relevant competence provision in the European treaties], while the principle of subsidiarity lays down legally binding guidelines for the EU institutions in *using their competences*', Opinion of Advocate General Kokott, 23 December 2015, C-358/14, *Poland v European Parliament and Council*, ECLI:EU:C:2015:848, para 144.

[279] Paul Craig, 'Subsidiarity: A Political and Legal Analysis' (2012) 50 JCMS: Journal of Common Market Studies 72, 73.

to address disputes related to the division of competence between the European Union and the Member States by ensuring respect for the national identities of Member States and safeguarding their powers.[280]

The subsidiarity principle affects both the decision on whether the European Union should act,[281] and the decision on the appropriate measure to be taken. Concerning the latter, the decision on introducing European regulations or directives, establishing full or partial harmonisation, and granting the Member States a certain leeway may be influenced by the principle of subsidiarity.[282] Since the practical application of the subsidiarity principle raised several questions, a detailed protocol on subsidiarity as part of the Amsterdam Treaty has incorporated specific guidelines for applying the principle which, in particular, supplements the Edinburgh guidelines.[283]

Even though the principle of subsidiarity is subject to legal review by the CJEU,[284] the Court has limited its scrutiny to a review of the reasoning of the European Commission and the Council on subsidiarity matters, and so far, no legislative action has been declared invalid because it violated the principle of subsidiarity.[285] The Court has thus far always accepted the Council's assessment that the aims were best achieved by EU legislation. The CJEU was criticised for

[280] Council, 11–12 December 1992, Conclusions of the Presidency in Edinburgh, Overall approach to the application by the Council of the subsidiarity principle and Article 3b of the Treaty on European Union, 13. In this vein also see Mark A Pollack, 'The End of Creeping Competence? EU Policy-Making since Maastricht' (2000) 38 Journal of Common Market Studies 519, 525; Kees van Kersbergen and Bertjan Verbeek, 'The Politics of International Norms: Subsidiarity and the Imperfect Competence Regime of the European Union' (2007) 13 European Journal of International Relations 217, 225; Claudio Sacchetto, 'Member States Tax Sovereignty: Between the Principle of Subsidiarity and the Necessity of Supranational Coordination' in Philippe Hinnekens and Luc Hinnekens (eds), *A Vision of Taxes Within and Outside the European Borders: Festschrift in Honor of Prof. Dr. Frans Vanistendael* (Kluwer Law International 2008) 805.

[281] The all-or-nothing decision: Robert Schütze, 'Subsidiarity after Lisbon: Reinforcing the Safeguards of Federalism?' (2009) 68 The Cambridge Law Journal 525, 532; Schütze, *Cooperative Federalism Constitutionalized* (n 274) 263; see also Tuytschaever (n 19) 240.

[282] See for regulatory failures relating to a high level of generality of the European law Craig, 'Subsidiarity' (n 279) 75.

[283] Protocol on the application of the principle of subsidiarity and proportionality, OJ, 10 November 1997, C 340, 105; Edinburgh guidelines: Council, 11–12 December 1992, Conclusions of the Presidency in Edinburgh, Overall approach to the application by the Council of the subsidiarity principle and Article 3b of the Treaty on European Union; Gráinne de Búrca, 'The Principle of Subsidiarity and the Court of Justice as an Institutional Actor' (1998) 36 Journal of Common Market Studies 217, 218–19. For the different view of the Member States and the European institutions on the impact of these developments see Ivo E Schwartz, *EG-Kompetenzen für den Binnenmarkt: exklusiv oder konkurrierend/subsidiär?* (Zentrum für Europäisches Wirtschaftsrecht 1995) 3 et seq.

[284] Council, 11–12 December 1992, Conclusions of the Presidency in Edinburgh, Overall approach to the application by the Council of the subsidiarity principle and Article 3b of the Treaty on European Union, 16; CJEU, 12 November 1996, C-84/94, *United Kingdom of Great Britain and Northern Ireland v Council*, ECLI:EU:C:1996:431, paras 47, 55; CJEU, 13 May 1997, C-233/94, *Germany v European Parliament and Council*, ECLI:EU:C:1997:231.

[285] Katarzyna Granat, *The Principle of Subsidiarity and Its Enforcement in the EU Legal Order: The Role of National Parliaments in the Early Warning System* (Hart Publishing 2018) 30–31.

not taking the subsidiarity principle seriously,[286] but the Court has good reasons for not scrutinising European laws on the basis of subsidiarity claims, such as the political nature of the subsidiarity principle,[287] its lack of clear content,[288] and its anti-integration character.[289] The scholarly works were also not hesitant to provide their views on the subsidiarity principle, which cover a federal proportionality interpretation,[290] mere competence related argumentation,[291] and approaches combining the two.

After the Lisbon Treaty, it was expected that the CJEU would fulfil its role as guardian of the subsidiarity principle because the changes to the European treaty lead to a broadening of the competences of the European Union and an extension of majoritarian decision-making.[292] The Court did not change its ruling concerning the cautious assessment of the subsidiarity principle, but more recent judgments reveal two trends relevant for deciding on the subsidiarity concerns: the cross-border nature of the legislative act, and evidence provided by an impact assessment.[293]

The importance of the cross-border nature of the legislative framework to justify European legislative actions has already been established by the Edinburgh guidelines and was again emphasised in the protocol to the Amsterdam Treaty. The subsidiarity requirement is fulfilled if 'the issue under consideration has *transnational aspects* which cannot be satisfactorily regulated by action by Member States'.[294] Advocate General Maduro followed up on the cross-border element in the *Vodafone* case and argued that:

[286] Which sometimes includes a fundamental critique on the subsidiarity principle: Gareth Davies, 'Subsidiarity: The Wrong Idea, in the Wrong Place, at the Wrong Time' (2006) 43 Common Market Law Review 63.

[287] Búrca, 'The Principle of Subsidiarity' (n 283) 225; Takis Tridimas, 'The Rule of Reason and Its Relation to Proportionality and Subsidiarity' in Annette Schrauwen (ed), *Rule of Reason: Rethinking Another Classic of EC Legal Doctrine* (Europa Law Publishing 2005) 120; Schütze, 'Subsidiarity after Lisbon' (n 281) 527; George A Bermann, 'Taking Subsidiarity Seriously: Federalism in the European Community and the United States' (1994) 94 Columbia Law Review 331, 336.

[288] Antonio Estella de Noriega, *The EU Principle of Subsidiarity and Its Critique* (OUP 2002) 96, 136.

[289] ibid 7.

[290] Schütze, 'Subsidiarity after Lisbon' (n 281) 532; Schütze, *Cooperative Federalism Constitutionalized* (n 274) 263.

[291] 'We should remember that subsidiarity applies to the reaching of a *measure*'s objective, in other words to the question at which level an aim can better be reached with which is set out in the measure itself', Philipp Kiiver, *The Early Warning System for the Principle of Subsidiarity: Constitutional Theory and Empirical Reality* (Routledge 2012) 75.

[292] The qualified majority vote is of particular relevance because in these cases the Member States have no power to veto a legislative act if they find a European response to the particular matter inappropriate, Lenaerts, 'The Principle of Subsidiarity' (n 272) 851.

[293] Granat (n 285) 32.

[294] Council, 11–12 December 1992, Conclusions of the Presidency in Edinburgh, Overall approach to the application by the Council of the subsidiarity principle and Article 3b of the Treaty on European Union, 19; Protocol on the application of the principle of subsidiarity and proportionality, OJ, 10 November 1997, C 340, 106, emphasis added.

> [t]he decisive argument [for complying with the subsidiarity principle] derives, however, from the cross-border nature of the economic activity to be regulated... [O]ne may legitimately believe that Community may be in a better position than Member States to address the problem of roaming retail prices. Due to the transnational character of the economic activity in question (roaming), the Community may be both more willing to address the problem and in a better position to balance all the costs and benefits of the intended action for the internal market.[295]

In this vein, Advocate General Kokott argued that the 'removal of obstacles to cross-border trade in the European internal market... is a prime example of action which cannot, as a rule, be sufficiently realised at national level'[296] because there will always be a disparity between the national laws of the Member States, thereby causing obstacles to trade. If, however, national, regional, or local features are central to the legislative issue, or if the legislative action should address problems of a purely regional or local dimension, it is quite likely that the matter can be sufficiently realised at national level.[297]

From this it may follow that in cases in which a framework for transnational interactions between the Member States need to be established which asks for a balance between the interests of the Member States, the European Union may be in a better position to achieve an appropriate and fair outcome because each Member State follows its own interests and may not consider the interests of their fellow Member States.

The impact assessment has become an important tool for determining whether, and if so to what extent, the European Union should be involved in pursuing particular policy objectives since the beginning of the new millennium.[298] To date, the European Commission has not issued a single proposal for a European legislative action without previously working out an impact assessment which provides evidence for political decision-makers on the advantages and disadvantages of possible policy options.[299] An impact assessment typically includes an analysis of the following: the nature and scale of the problem, how it is evolving and who is most affected, the stakeholders concerned, whether the Union should be involved, likely economic, social, and environmental concerns, the different policy options,

[295] Opinion of Advocate General Maduro, 1 October 2009, C-58/08, *Vodafone*, ECLI:EU:C:2009:596; para 33.

[296] Opinion of Advocate General Kokott, 23 December 2015, C-358/14, *Poland v European Parliament and Council*, ECLI:EU:C:2015:848, para 154.

[297] Opinion of Advocate General Kokott, 23 December 2015, C-358/14, *Poland v European Parliament and Council*, ECLI:EU:C:2015:848, paras 152, 153.

[298] Commission, 5 June 2002, Communication from the Commission on Impact Assessment, COM(2002) 276 final; Commission, 15 January 2009, Impact Assessment Guidelines, SEC(2009) 92; Craig, 'Subsidiarity' (n 279) 77.

[299] Commission, 15 January 2009, Impact Assessment Guidelines, SEC(2009) 92, 4, 6.

a comparison of these options with respect to effectiveness, efficiency, and coherence.[300] Both the Advocate Generals and the CJEU have made references to the impact assessment carried out by the Commission when analysing the legitimacy of the European legislative act from the perspective of the subsidiarity principle.[301]

2. Degree and Scope of the Harmonisation Framework

The principle of subsidiarity particularly influences the scope and the degree of the harmonising secondary EU law. The degree of the harmonisation measure refers to the question of whether the secondary EU law provides for full, partial or minimum harmonisation. If secondary EU law establishes full harmonisation, the Member States' right to regulate is displayed by the secondary EU law. The law determines the entire regulatory framework for that area, and since the law claims to be exhaustive and comprehensive, the Member States are not granted any leeway. Since full harmonisation entirely represses the regulatory power, it can only be applied where a Member State's leeway would contradict the laws' objectives.[302] So far, there are only some legislative pieces at the European level that establish full harmonisation.[303] In European (direct) tax laws, partial harmonisation is the standard, meaning that certain (cross-border) situations are determined by secondary EU law.[304] Since the law does not claim to be exhaustive, the Member States

[300] ibid 4; for the effectiveness test and efficiency test see also Stefan Griller and others, *The Treaty of Amsterdam: Facts, Analysis, Prospects* (Springer 2000) 104.

[301] CJEU, 4 May 2016, C-358/14, *Poland v European Parliament and Council*, ECLI:EU:C:2016:323, para 123; Opinion of Advocate General Maduro, 1 October 2009, C-58/08, *Vodafone*, ECLI:EU:C:2009:596; Opinion of Advocate General Kokott, 23 December 2015, C-358/14, *Poland v European Parliament and Council*, ECLI:EU:C:2015:848, para 182.

[302] The subsidiarity requirement requires one to follow a least interventionist approach: Phil Syrpis, 'Theorising the Relationship between the Judiciary and the Legislature in the EU Internal Market' in Phil Syrpis (ed), *The Judiciary, the Legislature and the EU Internal Market* (Intersentia 2012) 18; Nina Boeger, 'Minimum Harmonisation, Free Movement and Proportionality' in Phil Syrpis (ed), *The Judiciary, the Legislature and the EU Internal Market* (CUP 2012) 65 et seq. Sean van Raepenbusch and Dominik Hanf, 'Flexibility in Social Policy' in Bruno de Witte, Dominik Hanf, and Ellen Vos (eds), *The Many Faces of Differentiation in EU Law* (Intersentia 2001) 75 et seq.

[303] See for example the directive on unfair business-to-consumer commercial practices (2005/29/EG): CJEU, 10 July 2014, C-421/12, *Commission v Belgium*, ECLI:EU:C:2014:2064; CJEU, 9 November 2010, C-540/08, *Mediaprint Zeitungs- und Zeitschriftenverlag GmbH & Co. KG*, ECLI:EU:C:2010:660, para 27; CJEU, 14 Januar 2010, C-304/08, *Zentrale zur Bekämpfung unlauteren Wettbewerbs e.V.*, ECLI:EU:C:2010:12, para 41.

[304] See for cross-border mergers Directive, 19 October 2009, 2009/133/EC, on the common system of taxation applicable to mergers, divisions, partial divisions, transfers of assets and exchanges of shares concerning companies of different Member States and to the transfer of the registered office of an SE or SCE between Member States, OJ, 25 November 2009, L 310, 34; or cross-border dividend flows between the parent and the subsidiary: Directive, 30 November 2011, 2011/96/EU, on the common system of taxation applicable in the case of parent companies and subsidiaries of different Member States, OJ, 29 December 2011, L 345, 8. See also Paul Farmer, 'Direct Taxation and the Fundamental Freedoms' in Anthony Arnull and Damian Chalmers (eds), *The Oxford Handbook of European Union Law* (OUP 2015) 810–11. Shawn W Donnelly, *The Regimes of European Integration: Constructing Governance of the Single Market* (OUP 2010) 22 et seq arguing for the company law regime that '[i]n exchange for [the Member States'] cooperation in opening up the single market, the [company law] regime entrenched the right of national governments to protect politically sensitive institutions and companies form being affected'.

are free to regulate all situations which are not predetermined by secondary EU law. Another common form of harmonisation, in particular in the area of environmental protection or social and welfare interests, grants the Member States the right to go further than what has been accomplished at the European level (minimum harmonisation).[305] In other words, secondary EU legislation only sets a floor and the European treaties, in particular the European non-discrimination clauses, set the ceiling.[306] In taxation, minimum harmonisation has been chosen for the ATAD,[307] which allows the Member States to introduce stronger tax measures in compliance with the fundamental freedoms to prevent tax avoidance.[308]

Concerning the scope of the secondary EU law, the law could either unify the entire regulatory framework (covering both purely domestic and cross-border situations) or could be restricted to cross-border situations. The principle of subsidiarity would require the scope of the secondary EU law to be restricted to what is necessary to achieve the objectives, which may in some cases be only the cross-border situation. Despite subsidiarity claims, a uniform framework covering both the purely domestic and the cross-border situation would be necessary where the regulatory framework addresses preparatory measures, and thus an ad-hoc compliance with the relevant legal framework—being either the one for the cross-border or the purely domestic situation—is impossible. An ad-hoc compliance with the regulatory framework may be particularly impossible in the field of product standards. The market players may not know at the time of production whether they are selling the goods domestically or abroad. The unification of the entire regulatory framework would allow the market players to comply with the domestic and foreign standards, and thus they are not running into the risk of having to adjust their products to comply with the regulatory framework of another Member State. These unified standards may introduce a higher protection, for example for consumers or the environment, as previously provided by the laws of the Member States, and nonetheless facilitate the functioning of the European internal market.[309]

In tax law, comparable situations may likely be found in procedural law. We shall assume, for example, that the legal duties to preserve records vary from Member State to Member State. One Member State may require the taxpayer to keep the original records for ten years, other Member States may allow keeping a digital version of the original record for three years. Secondary EU law unifying the taxpayers' obligation on preserving records would have to cover both the obligations for a purely domestic and a cross-border situation. In the absence of an entire

[305] Dougan, 'Minimum Harmonization' (n 184) 855.

[306] Stephen Weatherill, *The Internal Market as a Legal Concept*, vol XXV/1 (OUP 2017) 210.

[307] Council Directive, 12 July 2016, 2016/1164/EU, laying down rules against tax avoidance practices that directly affect the functioning of the internal market, OJ, 19 July 2016, L 193, 1–2.

[308] 'minimum level of protection'; Member States can 'ensure a higher level of protection'; see recitals of the ATAD.

[309] See this chapter subsection G.II.

framework, the taxpayers would still be required to adjust their behaviour depending on whether they engage in a cross-border economic activity or in a purely domestic one. Of course, in such cases, one could think about introducing secondary EU law which provides for a minimum harmonisation. If the directive only sets the minimum standards with which the taxpayers have to comply within a cross-border situation, the Member States are allowed to require the taxpayer to meet a higher standard in a purely domestic situation. From the perspective of the principle of subsidiarity, one may argue that such a legislative action is more appropriate since it would grant the Member States some regulatory leeway without interfering with the proper functioning of the European internal market. The higher regulatory threshold would only burden the pure domestic activity which does not affect the trade between the Member States. Although the secondary EU law may allow the Member States to introduce stricter rules for a purely domestic setting, the Member States may not make use of the possibility of setting higher standards because of the competitive pressure between the Member States.[310]

In some areas of substantive tax law, unification of the law may facilitate the functioning of the European internal market, even if the law only applies to a cross-border situation. In the field of dividend distribution, for example, the taxpayer distributing the dividends can comply with the framework established for domestic dividends or with the one established for a cross-border situation at the time of distribution. No adjustments to previous actions would be required. Thus, a directive unifying the Member States' approaches for eliminating economic double taxation would be sufficient if only applied in the case of cross-border dividend distributions between the parent and its subsidiaries.[311] A common approach of the Member States towards the elimination of economic double taxation also touches on the elimination of juridical double taxation (an obstacle not covered by the fundamental freedoms),[312] but this seems to be ignored. The Parent-Subsidiary Directive prevents any worse treatment of cross-border dividend flows by unifying the mechanism of preventing multiple levels of taxation (at the level of the parent and the level of the subsidiary). Some Member States may have exempted taxation at the level of the subsidiary, others may have taxed the dividends on the level of the subsidiary but have credited the tax levied at the level of the parent. To ensure no worse treatment of cross-border dividend flows, the Parent-Subsidiary Directive harmonises the framework for eliminating economic double taxation for cross-border dividend distributions between the subsidiary and its parent.

[310] Dougan, 'Minimum Harmonization' (n 184) 867.

[311] Council Directive, 30 November 2011, 2011/96/EU, on the common system of taxation applicable in the case of parent companies and subsidiaries of different Member States, OJ, 29 December 2011, L345, 8. The Directive explicitly argues on the grounds of eliminating economic double taxation: see recitals 3 and 6.

[312] See this chapter subsection G.V.1.b, and Chapter 5, Part I, subsection C.I.2.

From this it follows that the principle of subsidiarity has an impact on European legislation, especially with respect to the degree and scope of the law. Concerning the degree, the European legislature may introduce partial and minimum harmonisation, except the objects demand full harmonisation. With regards to the scope of the law, the legal framework can either only unify the legal situation for cross-border economic activities (eg the Parent-Subsidiary Directive) or develop the legal requirements for the cross-border and the purely domestic situation. From the perspective of the subsidiarity principle, the latter approach can only be applied in cases where an ad-hoc compliance with the different standards is not possible, and thus the differences between the regulatory framework for the purely domestic and the one for the cross-border situation may already hamper the functioning of the European internal market.

3. Subsidiarity in the Field of Enhanced Cooperation

Irrespective of whether one follows a quite radical understanding of subsidiarity, as an all-or-nothing decision between the legislative action of the European Union or of the Member States, or a more balanced approached, when it comes to the establishment of enhanced cooperation, one has to ask how the principle of subsidiarity can and should be applied. The traditional subsidiarity principle may not be applicable because it weighs the sufficiency of an action of a single Member State against an action of the European Union, accordingly an action of all the Member States. Within the field of the enhanced cooperation procedure, however, it will never be an action of the whole European Union; rather, it will be an act of some Member States. Thus, some authors have argued that the enhanced cooperation procedure demands a new form of subsidiarity: 'differentiated subsidiarity'.[313]

If the principle of subsidiarity is interpreted differently in the context of the enhanced cooperation procedure, as an element for deciding whether a group of Member States should be allowed to act instead of the European Union as a whole, the subsidiarity principle would turn into a political instrument. The subsidiarity principle can only remain a legal requirement if it is applied within the enhanced cooperation procedure in the same vein as within the ordinary law-making process at the European level. Thus, the subsidiarity principle asks whether national measures taken by the Member States are sufficient to achieve certain European policy objectives, or whether European actions are required. If certain aims require an EU action, it may either be an action of all the Member States or an action of some Member States in the form of enhanced cooperation. The differentiation between the Member States in the pursuit of objectives within enhanced cooperation and the non-participating Member States individually aiming to achieve the European treaties' objectives is taken care of by other legal requirements for establishing

[313] Hervé Bribosia, 'De la Subsidiarité à la Coopération Renforcée' in Yves Lejeune (ed), *Le traité d'Amsterdam: espoirs et déceptions* (Bruylant 1998); Tuytschaever (n 19) 240 et seq.

enhanced cooperation set out in the European treaties.[314] Accordingly, for the purpose of the subsidiarity requirement, it should be supposed that enhanced cooperation can achieve what the entire European Union can otherwise achieve.

VII. The Principle of Proportionality

The principle of proportionality is another fundamental principle of EU law which influences the law-making process. The principle of proportionality 'has achieved treaty status, after a consistent jurisprudence of the Court of Justice of the European Union has deemed it to be a general principle of EU law'.[315] Aside from the general principle of proportionality, Art 5 Subsection 4 of the TEU sets out a proportionality claim addressing the European legislature. According to this provision, 'the content and form of Union action shall not exceed what is necessary to achieve the objectives of the Treaties'. In more general terms, the core of the principle of proportionality applies when the pursuit of a legitimate objective is not in question,[316] but the measures taken to achieve it conflict with other interests. At the European level, 'other interests' with which actions of the European Union may conflict are, in particular, the sovereignty of the Member States as well as fundamental rights. However, these interests are considered in the rights-based proportionality test of Art 52 Subsection 1 of the Charter of the fundamental rights of the European Union[317] and the subsidiarity-based proportionality test which is embodied in the subsidiarity principle (Art 5 Subsection 3 of the TEU).[318]

Art 5 Subsection 4 of the TEU is frequently used as a principle of economic efficiency.[319] In that vein, any action of the European Union has to stand a cost-benefit

[314] See in particular Chapter 5 and Chapter 6.

[315] Valentina Vadi, 'Proportionality, Reasonableness, and Standards of Review in I Treaty Arbitration' in Andrea K Bjorklund (ed), *Yearbook on International Investment Law & Policy, 2013–2014* (OUP 2015) 207. For the development of the principle of proportionality in European law see Takis Tridimas, 'Proportionality in Community Law: Searching for the Appropriate Standard of Scrutiny' in Evelyn Ellis (ed), *The Principle of Proportionality in the Laws of Europe* (Hart Publishing 1999) 69 et seq; Nicholas Emiliou, *The Principle of Proportionality in European Law: A Comparative Study* (Kluwer Law International 1996) 134 et seq.

[316] It is sometimes argued that the principle of proportionality follows a four-step approach, which addresses the legitimacy of the policy objective at the first step. So far, the Court has given the legislature a wide discretion to decide which policies need to be implemented, see Juliane Kokott and Christoph Sobotta, 'The Evolution of the Principle of Proportionality in EU Law -Towards an Anticipative Understanding?' in Stefan Vogenauer and Stephen Weatherill (eds), *General Principles of Law: European and Comparative Perspectives* (Hart Publishing 2017) 168 et seq.

[317] For a disproportionate law-making see CJEU, 8 April 2014, C-293/12 and C-594/12, *Digital Rights Ireland*, ECLI:EU:C:2014:238; see also Marie-Pierre Granger and Kristina Irion, 'The Court of Justice and the Data Retention Directive in Digital Rights Ireland: Telling off the EU Legislator and Teaching a Lesson in Privacy and Data Protection' (2014) 39 European Law Review 835, 844 arguing that the CJEU applies 'rigorous proportionality testing under the Charter'.

[318] Koenraad Lenaerts and Piet Van Nuffel, *European Union Law* (3rd edn, 2011) ss 7–039. See Chapter 6, subsection E.II.3.a.

[319] Aurelien Portuese, 'Principle of Proportionality as Principle of Economic Efficiency' (2013) 19 European Law Journal 612.

analysis,[320] ensuring that the benefits outweigh the costs.[321] The principle of proportionality should ensure that the European legislative measures do not impose disproportionate costs for the European Union, the Member States, and economic operators.[322] We will return to the principle of proportionality as a measure to prohibit disproportionate burdens when analysing the rights of non-participating Member States, because a burden-based proportionality test may grant non-participating Member States protection from disproportionate burdens following from enhanced cooperation laws.[323]

VIII. Alternatives to European Law Unification

It should not go unmentioned that harmonisation of Member States' national tax laws cannot only be achieved through secondary EU law legislation but also through existing competitive pressure between the Member States. Competition between the Member States is, however, not only a way of achieving unification between national laws, but also a tool with a disciplining function.[324] Free competition is a cornerstone of the European internal market and aims for a free level playing field between the undertakings on the internal market. The concept does not cover competition between the Member States. On the contrary, competition between the Member States is only a reflex of the market opening function of the fundamental freedoms.[325] Since the Member States can no longer shield their national markets through discriminatory or restrictive national rules which prevent foreign goods, services, persons, or capital from entering the market, the Member

[320] For an overview of the cost-benefit analysis in the European Union, the GATT/World Trade Organization system, and in the US federal system see Trachtman, 'Trade And ... Problems, Cost-Benefit Analysis and Subsidiarity' (1998) 9 European Journal of International Law 32.

[321] George A Bermann, 'Proportionality and Subsidiarity' in Catherine Barnard and Joanne Scott (eds), *The Law of the Single European Market: Unpacking the Premises* (Hart Publishing 2002) 80; Anne CM Meuwese, *Impact Assessment in EU Lawmaking* (Kluwer Law International BV 2008) 26.

[322] The second protocol to the Lisbon treaty on the application of the principles of subsidiarity and proportionality suggests with reference to the proportionality test that any European action 'shall take account of the need for any burden, whether financial or administrative, falling upon the Union, national governments, regional or local authorities, economic operators and citizens, to be minimized and commensurate with the objective to be achieved' (Consolidated version of the Treaty on European Union—Protocol No 2 on the application of the principle of subsidiarity and proportionality, OJ, 9.5.2008, 115, pp 206–09).

[323] See Chapter 6, subsection E.II.3.

[324] Wolfgang Schön, 'Playing Different Games? Regulatory Competition in Tax and Company Law Compared' (2005) 42 Common Market Law Review 331, 350.

[325] Kube, Reimer, and Spengel (n 172) 251; Amedeo Arena, 'The Doctrine of Union Preemption in the E.U. Internal Market: Between Sein and Sollen' (2010) Columbia Journal of European Law 477, 507 highlighting that a 'Home State Control model, such as that underlying the TFEU rules on free movement, is conducive to market integration but entails the risk of a "race to the bottom" where companies have an incentive to establish themselves in the Member State whose rules are most lenient and other States are induced to relax their requirements in order to prevent capital drain'.

States are exposed to competition between each other.[326] As has been mentioned, exposing Member States to competition may have some beneficial disciplining effects because it forces them to budget properly to offer taxpayers public goods at fair prices.[327] The positive effects of competition between the Member States are forced by the European internal market concept, but not demanded. Thus, the need to maintain competition between the Member States cannot be used as an argument for rejecting legislative attempts at the European level. However, competition between the Member States supports the process of aligning national tax laws of the Member States to the extent necessary for the functioning of the European internal market.

IX. Findings

To conclude, the European internal market is an area in which all goods, services, persons, and capital can move freely and thus should be used where they are of the greatest benefit. However, the European internal market is not entirely efficiency driven; the Member States are allowed to prioritise important values over market needs. Where the Member States follow identical values, they should commonly implement European legislation to remove trade obstacles following from differences of the national regulatory frameworks but without the need to reduce market regulation. Accordingly, any secondary EU law harmonising the national laws of the Member States facilitates intra-EU trade by eliminating differences between the regulatory systems of the Member States and does not necessarily have to reduce market regulation. The benefit for the European market already follows from unifying the national laws.

The European legislature's power to harmonise Member States' national tax laws is far-reaching, as Art 114 and Art 115 of the TFEU allow both economic and legal obstacles to intra-EU trade to be eliminated by way of legislative harmonisation. The European harmonising measures may fundamentally be influenced by non-market values, such as the protection of consumers, minors, or the environment. If the European legislature is not allowed to regulate these non-market values, the European harmonisation act can be based on the EU's internal market competence as long as all provisions within the secondary EU law act facilitate intra-EU trade.

[326] Ruth Mason and Michael S Knoll, 'A Brief Sur-Reply to Professors Graetz and Warren' 1194 <https://www.yalelawjournal.org/forum/a-brief-sur-reply-to-professors-graetz-and-warren> accessed 15 December 2019. For a definition of the competition between the Member State tax systems, see Markus Müller, *Systemwettbewerb, Harmonisierung und Wettbewerbsverzerrung: Europa zwischen einem Wettbewerb der Gesetzgeber und vollständiger Harmonisierung* (Nomos 2000) 23 et seq.

[327] Geoffrey Brennan and James M Buchanan, 'Towards a Tax Constitution for Leviathan' (1977) 8 Journal of Public Economics 255, 258 et seq; Jeremy Edwards and Michael Keen, 'Tax Competition and Leviathan' (1996) 40 European Economic Review 113; Geoffrey Brennan and James M Buchanan, *The Power to Tax: Analytical Foundations of a Fiscal Constitution* (CUP 2006) 15 et seq.

The predominant aim underlying the legislative act only matters if the European legislature is also allowed to regulate the relevant non-market values, as the main purpose and content test identifies the relevant competence rule. Moreover, the European legislature can use the internal market competence to establish a co-operative framework between the Member States allowing them to comply with their duties set by the European treaties, but in a way which fits the system of their national legal orders better. A cooperative framework between the Member States may not enhance the intra-EU trade because the relevant trade obstacles may have been removed by way of negative integration, but it grants the Member States the possibility of counterbalancing the unprincipled application of the fundamental freedoms.

The European internal market competence vests the European legislature with true regulatory power, meaning that a balancing act between different contradictory rights and interests has to take place at the European level. This balancing act facilitates the establishment of European values and standards, and thus, the European legislature is not restricted to seeking the lowest common denominator between the Member States or the highest level of protection within a Member State.

The European treaties provide important measures ensuring that the wide scope of Art 115 of the TFEU does not contradict the freedom of the Member States to pursue important national values in sensitive political areas: the principles of subsidiarity and proportionality and the requirement of uniform voting in the Council. The principle of subsidiarity poses two important questions: first, it asks whether a legislative action by the Member States would be sufficient to achieve the objective; and, secondly, how the European legislature should act. The latter question refers to the degree and scope of the secondary EU law. The European legislature should only provide for as much European harmonisation as necessary to achieve the objective, and thus ensures the Member States as much freedom to regulate as possible. The principle of proportionality follows and demands that European legislative action does not exceed what is necessary to achieve its objectives. Within the enhanced cooperation procedure, the principles of subsidiarity and proportionality should not be used as elements to decide whether a group of Member States should be allowed to act instead of the European Union as a whole, because both principles would turn into political instruments and would fail their initial aim.

5
Enhanced Cooperation and its Impact on the European Internal Market—Art 326 of the TFEU

A. Setting the Scene

Art 326 of the Treaty on the Functioning of the European Union (TFEU) is one of the core provisions within the constitutional framework for enhanced cooperation, particularly as the provision lays out the relationship between enhanced cooperation law and the European internal market. Despite the importance of this relationship (because it determines substantial boundaries for the creation of enhanced cooperation laws), the provision is drafted in a very vague and open-ended manner which does not provide much guidance for deciding which enhanced cooperation laws is in line with the European internal market concept.

The plain wording of Art 326 of the TFEU demands that '[a]ny enhanced cooperation shall comply with the Treaties and Union law' and 'shall not undermine the internal market or economic social and territorial cohesion. It shall not constitute a barrier to or discrimination in trade between Member States, nor shall it distort competition between them.' The provision refers to well-known concepts of the European treaties: non-discrimination, distortion of competition, and internal legal coherence. The non-discrimination claim refers in particular to the fundamental freedoms which ensure a free movement of goods, services, persons, and capital within the European internal market. An undistorted market is guaranteed by different primary EU law mechanisms. At the legislative level, state aid law is the most relevant one as it forbids the national legislature from drafting the laws in a way which would grant certain undertakings a particular benefit. The coherence claim is a more general legal demand to establish a legal system which is free from contradictions.

From this it already follows that the following chapter will be divided into three main parts. Part I will set out how the fundamental freedoms apply to enhanced cooperation laws. Applying the fundamental freedoms to enhanced cooperation laws becomes particularly challenging as these laws are a hybrid between the law of a single Member State and secondary EU law. These laws represent the policy objectives of more than one Member State, but they do not speak for all Member

Enhanced Cooperation and European Tax Law. Caroline Heber, Oxford University Press. © Caroline Heber 2021.
DOI: 10.1093/oso/9780192898272.003.0005

States within the European Union. An analysis of the current Court of Justice of the European Union (CJEU) case law will show that the Member States are allowed to use secondary EU law to prioritise important non-economic values over pure market efficiency goals, and thus the fundamental freedoms do not apply with the same strength to secondary EU laws as to laws of single Member States. From the outset, it is not entirely clear which benchmark should be applied to enhanced cooperation laws because the law does not establish a uniform regulatory approach for the entire European internal market, but the laws go beyond pure national interests. The current chapter will use the level of integration which enhanced cooperation laws establish between the participating Member States as the determining factor to find the appropriate benchmark for scrutiny under the fundamental freedoms.

Part II will show how state aid law should be applied to enhanced cooperation laws. The hybrid nature of the law enacted under the enhanced cooperation procedure also becomes evident when applying state aid law. According to the plain wording of Art 107 of the TFEU, only the granting of aid by a single Member State or through state resources is prohibited, and one may therefore ask why state aid rules should apply to enhanced cooperation law. It will be argued that enhanced cooperation law may not be attributed to the European legislature in the same fashion as secondary EU law for state aid law purposes because enhanced cooperation law is capable of distorting the competition between the particiating and the non-participating Member States and enhanced cooperation law must not undermine the competence framework set by the European treaties for economic policy-making through the approval of Member State aid.

Part III will in particular elaborate on the relationship between ordinary secondary EU laws and enhanced cooperation laws. Within the European legal framework, derogation rules solve conflicts between overlapping laws which demand different legal consequences. Conflicts between ordinary secondary EU laws may be resolved by applying the *lex specialis* or the *lex posterior* principle[1] or its underlying notion within the interpretation process, as no hierarchical relationship between regulations, directives and decisions exists.[2] By contrast, a conflict between EU law and national laws is always solved in favour of European law because it holds precedence over national conflicting laws.[3] With respect to enhanced cooperation laws, Art 326 of the TFEU demands full compliance with primary and

[1] Rita Szudoczky, *The Sources of EU Law and Their Relationships: Lessons for the Field of Taxation: Primary Law, Secondary Law, Fundamental Freedoms and State Aid Rules* (IBFD 2014) 68; Christian Meurs, *Normenhierarchien im europäischen Sekundärrecht* (Mohr Siebeck 2012) 81 with further references.

[2] On the missing hierarchy between legal forms mentioned in Art 288 of the TFEU see Roland Bieber and Isabelle Salomé, 'Hierarchy of Norms in European Law' (1996) 33 Common Market Law Review 909, 917.

[3] CJEU, 15 July 1964, 6/64, *Costa E.N.E.L.*, ECLI:EU:C:1964:66, p 1269.

secondary EU law. Part III of this chapter will show what full compliance with existing secondary EU law means for the legislative power of the European legislature under the enhanced cooperation procedure and the impact of newly enacted secondary EU law on conflicting enhanced cooperation laws.

Before addressing the legal coherence issue and the application of the fundamental freedoms and state aid law to enhanced cooperation laws, the following subsections will discuss the hybrid nature of enhanced cooperation laws which builds the foundation for the subsequent discussion.

B. A Hybrid between the Law of the Member States and Secondary EU Law

The law introduced under the enhanced cooperation procedure is a hybrid between the law of a single Member State and secondary EU law[4] because it represents the policy objectives of more than one Member State, but it does not speak for all Member States within the European Union. The fact that enhanced cooperation rests somewhere between ordinary secondary EU law and the national law of single Member States puts the functioning of both the fundamental freedoms and state aid law as well as the existing hierarchy of the European legal system under pressure. The general assumption that more specific or more recent secondary EU law derogates conflicting general and older laws may not work in the field of enhanced cooperation laws because under the enhanced cooperation procedure the European legislature cannot use its regulatory power to specify and amend existing secondary EU laws. Moreover, the general assumption that a pure national regulatory approach is likely to hamper competition and the free movement of goods, services, persons, and capital, whereas a coordinated regulatory framework between all the Member States is unlikely to be harmful cannot apply in the realm of enhanced cooperation. Enhanced cooperation law may foster trade between the participating Member States but may harm cross-group trade, meaning trade between the participating and non-participating Member States. Accordingly, the fundamental freedoms and state aid law have to be applied in an area which is dominated by deeper market integration on the one hand, and (in the worst case) trade obstacles on the other hand.

To date, there is hardly any CJEU case law on the interpretation and application of the rules on the enhanced cooperation procedure,[5] and absolutely no judicial guidance on the interplay between enhanced cooperation law on the one hand and the fundamental freedoms and state aid law on the other. However,

[4] Stephen Weatherill, *The Internal Market as a Legal Concept*, vol *XXV/1* (OUP 2017) 9.

[5] CJEU, 16 April 2013, C-271/11 and C-295/11, *Kingdom of Spain v Council*, ECLI:EU:C:2013:240.

there are multiple court cases dealing with the compatibility of national Member States laws and the fundamental freedoms and state aid rules, and some rulings on the relationship and interaction between secondary EU law and the fundamental freedoms. At this point, it can already be said that the CJEU distinguishes between the law of a single Member State and secondary EU law when it comes to the balancing of non-market values and market efficiency. Harmonised non-market values outweigh the value of market integration more easily than non-market values pursued by a single Member State. Enhanced cooperation law may harmonise values between participating Member States but not between all Member States, and the success of integration therefore goes beyond public interest concerns of individual Member States but lags behind European integration through ordinary secondary EU law. Being in between national laws and secondary EU laws makes it clear that a single Member State's freedom to protect national values forms the bottom line for a group of at least nine Member States to protect their common values. However, a strong integration effort by participating Member States in the form of harmonised values or coordination of the national laws may be considered when applying the fundamental freedoms to enhanced cooperation law.

From this it already follows that a serious discussion on how the fundamental freedoms and state aid law should be applied to enhanced cooperation law involves an elucidation of how these two cornerstones of the European internal market concept are applied to national laws and, in the case of the fundamental freedoms, to secondary EU law. It is only possible to develop a concept for the application of the fundamental freedoms and state aid law to the law of enhanced cooperation based on these findings.

Part I: FUNDAMENTAL FREEDOMS

A. The Fundamental Freedoms as a Limit to the Legislative Power

The market freedoms limit the power of the national legislature. Whereas European law-making is only affected insofar as the Member States are prohibited from forming a cartel at European level and thereby agreeing to European legislation which allows the Member States to protect and seal their markets,[6] the national

[6] Wolfgang Schön, 'Tax Issues and Constraints on Reorganizations and Reincorporations in the European Union' (2004) 34 Tax Notes International 197, 202.

legislature has to comply with the negative harmonisation claims following from the fundamental freedoms.

With respect to enhanced cooperation, it is not clear from the outset how the fundamental freedoms could or should be applied. The law enacted under the enhanced cooperation procedure is unique. It is something 'in between' Member States' laws and secondary EU law because it can establish coordination and common values between some Member States but creates differentiation from non-participating Member States. The application of the fundamental freedoms raises the question of whether enhanced cooperation law should be understood as ordinary secondary EU law or as national law of the participating Member States for identifying a restriction of the market freedoms and determining the justification threshold the group has to meet. The CJEU's case law shows that only some national values of the Member States can outweigh market efficiency, and trade-hampering national laws have to meet a very high justification threshold to be allowed to stand. Through secondary EU law, however, Member States can quite substantially push for the prioritisation of non-market values like environmental or social values. Where secondary EU law creates trade obstacles to pursue a non-market value, the law only has to meet a very low justification threshold. Accordingly, a common approach by the Member States in the form of harmonised values and coordination measures may outweigh market efficiency more easily than national values. Enhanced cooperation law can establish deeper harmonisation between participating Member States like ordinary secondary EU law (eg in the form of conflict-solving, mutual recognition, or coordination measures, or even by way of establishing common values), but from the perspective of the non-participating Member States it may be equivalent to domestic laws of another Member State.

The bottom line for the application of the fundamental freedoms to enhanced cooperation law with respect to identifying restrictions and allowing their justification (meaning both the justification threshold and the legitimacy of justification grounds) is set by a Member State's freedom to follow national interests or values.[7] To put it differently, from the perspective of the fundamental freedoms, a group of at least nine Member States is allowed to do what each Member

[7] Anzhela Cédelle and John Vella, 'Differentiated Integration in the EU: Lessons from the Financial Transaction Tax' in Panos Koutrakos and Jukka Snell (eds), *Research Handbook on the Law of the EU's Internal Market* (Edward Elgar Publishing 2017) 372–73 raising the question of whether Art 326 of the TFEU goes further than what the fundamental freedoms demand from national tax laws. This would, for example, lead to a situation where double taxation caused by enhanced cooperation laws would be prohibited under Art 326 of the TFEU. Not eliminating double taxation (as it would be the case within enhanced cooperation) may, at first glance, infringe the fundamental freedoms, even if double taxation would not fall within the scope of the fundamental freedoms. For a detailed analysis of the Member States' entitlement to restrict the group benefit to participating Member States, see this chapter subsection E.VII.7.

State would be allowed to do on a unilateral basis. Where enhanced cooperation law goes beyond national interests and establishes common values, installs coordination, or removes existing trade obstacles, as ordinary secondary EU law does, a group of Member States may also be allowed to protect their common achievements by establishing obstacles towards the non-participating Member States.

The following subsection starts with the different integration levels secondary EU laws may establish between the Member States and their impact on the European internal market (see subsection B). The different integration levels may legitimise the application of different justification thresholds for trade obstacles created by enhanced cooperation laws. The subsequent subsection uncovers the bottom line for the application of the fundamental freedoms to enhanced cooperation law, namely the Member States' freedom to pursue national values. We will see that only some national values are considered when applying the fundamental freedoms to national laws and that national laws have to meet a high justification threshold if they constitute market access restrictions or discriminate against foreign goods, services, persons, or capital (see subsection C). In contrast, secondary EU law allows the Member States to give (almost any) harmonised value priority over market efficiency and it is quite easy to pass the proportionality test (see subsection D). The different application of the fundamental freedoms to on the one hand Member State national laws and on the other hand secondary EU law lays the basis for defining how the free movement rights interfere with enhanced cooperation laws. It will be argued that the European constitutional framework does not allow an automatic differentiation (with respect to comparability, justification, and proportionality) between intra-group situations (economic transactions between participating Member States) and cross-group situations (economic transactions between participating and non-participating Member States) when applying the fundamental freedoms to enhanced cooperation laws (see subsection E.I). However, the fundamental freedoms may honour deeper integration between participating Member States (see subsection E.II). Depending on the enhanced cooperation's integration level (see subsection E.III and E.V), restrictions of the fundamental freedoms (see subsection E.IV) either have to meet the high justification threshold which the national laws of a single Member State usually have to meet, or are allowed to undergo a light-touch justification (with respect to the legitimacy of the justification ground and the proportionality test) as ordinary secondary EU law does (see subsection E.VI). In cases where enhanced cooperation law establishes a strong coordinating bond between the participating Member States, a comparison between an intra-group situation (economic transactions between two participating Member States) and a cross-group situation (economic transaction between a participating and a non-participating Member State) may no longer be justified (see subsections E.VII and E.VIII).

B. Different Integration Levels of Legal Rules and their Impact on the European Internal Market

The European internal market—'an area without internal frontiers in which the free movement of goods, persons, services and capital is ensured'[8] —is subject to regulation at both domestic and European level. Regardless of the subject matter, national and European laws influence the functioning of the internal market either through trade-fostering or trade-hampering rules. Discriminatory national rules discourage foreign market players from providing their services, establishing a permanent economic presence, or investing their capital in that particular Member State. Likewise, non-discriminatory national regulatory rules may make it harder or less attractive for foreign entrepreneurs to gain access to a Member State's market. At the outset, such regulatory rules do not discriminate against foreigners or foreign products, but a market player may think twice about whether he wants to enter the foreign market and comply with this additional layer of regulatory standards. Despite trade-hampering rules, national laws can facilitate intra-EU trade by recognising lower product standards of other Member States or by granting foreign market players benefits for gaining access to the domestic market.[9]

To some extent, the fundamental freedoms are capable of addressing the trade-hampering effects of national rules. However, Member States may be able to justify some discriminatory national rules or market access restrictions. Moreover, some (national) trade obstacles do not even fall within the scope of the fundamental freedoms. When negative integration is no longer capable of abolishing existing trade obstacles,[10] positive integration in the form of secondary EU law is needed to overcome trade impediments.[11] The harmonisation of Member States' national rules facilitates the functioning of the European internal market even without deregulating or liberalising the market.[12]

The level of integration and subsequently the trade-facilitating effects of secondary EU law may vary depending on the types of rules on which Member States

[8] Art 26 Subsection 2 of the TFEU.

[9] The granting of these benefits must pass the state aid test, Art 107 of the TFEU. For more details see this chapter Part II, subsection E.

[10] Peter J Wattel, Otto Marres, and Hein Vermeulen (eds), *Terra/Wattel European Tax Law*, vol *I General Topics and Direct Taxation* (7th edn, Kluwer Law International) 25–26. Thanks to private enforcement of European law, the CJEU was able to remove many trade obstacles; Erich Vranes, 'The Dynamics of European Economic Integration: A Legal Perspective' in Harald Badinger and Volker Nitsch (eds), *Routledge Handbook of the Economics of European Integration* (Routledge 2016) 482.

[11] In this vein Herbert Rosenfeldt and Aike Würdemann, 'Schöpfer des Binnenmarktes im Käfig der Verträge—Die grundfreiheitliche Bindung des EU-Gesetzgebers' (2016) Europarecht 453, 461 et seq. In the area of direct taxation, the export group issued a report on cross-border tax obstacles which individuals are facing and which cannot be addressed by the fundamental freedoms: Expert Group, 'Ways to Tackle Cross-Border Tax Obstacles Facing Individuals within the EU.' (2016) Website <https://publications.europa.eu/en/publication-detail/-/publication/4bfee942-ca41-11e5-a4b5-01aa75ed71a1> accessed 1 July 2019.

[12] In this context, deregulation refers to a reduction of state influence on the economy.

can agree. *Conflict of law* rules form the minimum level of harmonisation of national laws to facilitate the free flow of goods, services, persons, and capital within the internal market. Conflict of law rules are necessary where national Member State laws are not unified and the Member States' decision on which jurisdiction should apply in a cross-border situations fundamentally differs between the Member States. In private law, conflict of law rules are particularly important for finding an agreement between Member States on the application of one jurisdiction over (international) civil and commercial matters or (international) divorces.[13] Further, in social security matters, the European social security coordination system determines the applicable legislation in cross-border situations. These sets of conflict of law rules prohibit the Member States from determining at their discretion the ambit and the conditions for the application of their national laws and the territory within which that legislation takes effect.[14] Contrary to the unification of laws, conflict of law rules do not change the Member States' regulatory framework but they lay down a structure allowing identification of the jurisdiction to be applied to a situation which may legitimately be regulated by the law of more than one Member State. Accordingly, the Member States do not change their regulatory framework but introduce common rules to identify the most appropriate Member State law to apply.

Secondary EU law can go much further than simply introducing conflict of law rules and implement a *mutual recognition* framework. Mutual recognition is, to some extent, already safeguarded by the fundamental freedoms and thus Member States cannot fully ignore the fact that foreign goods or persons have already complied with the regulatory framework of another Member State.[15] However, under the fundamental freedoms Member States may still be allowed to demand compliance with higher national standards. Secondary EU law may ensure that any Member State recognises and accepts compliance with the foreign regulatory standards, even in cases where domestic production has to meet higher standards.

Beyond these two categories of norms facilitating the functioning of the European internal market, Member States can use secondary EU law to establish *coordination* between them. Coordination also requires solving conflicts, as the relevant jurisdiction needs to be identified, but it goes beyond that and demands a change of the existing national framework. Coordinating secondary EU law may restrict national claims or force Member States to behave in a particular way. In

[13] Council, 12 December 2012, 1215/2012/EU, Regulation on jurisdiction and the recognition and enforcement of judgments in civil and commercial matters, OJ, 20 December 2012, L 351/1; Council, 20 December 2010, 1259/2010/EU, Regulation implementing enhanced cooperation in the area of the law applicable to divorce and legal separation, OJ, 29 December 2010, L 343, 10.

[14] Bruno Peeters and Herwig Verschueren, 'The Impact of European Union Law on the Interaction of Members States' Sovereign Powers in the Policy Fields of Social Protection and Personal Income Tax Benefits' (2016) 25 EC Tax Review 262, 265. For the secondary EU law see Regulation, 29 April 2004, 883/2004/EC, on the coordination of social security systems, OJ, 20 April 2004, L 166, 1.

[15] For more details see this chapter Part I, subsection C.I.1.

taxation law, coordination in the form of double tax treaties plays a key role. An uncoordinated application of national tax rules to cross-border economic activities may easily lead to double taxation or double non-taxation.[16] Tax treaties coordinate the taxing rights between the contracting (Member) States by allowing or forcing one (Member) State to tax (which may be differently from what national laws would indicate) and preventing the other (Member) State from taxing or forcing the State to credit the foreign tax.[17]

Secondary EU law also allows the Member States to go a step further and unify their substantive laws. *Unifying national laws* goes far beyond coordination because it harmonises the values underlying the law. Accordingly, unifying secondary EU law not only builds bridges between Member State laws but also harmonises the foundation underlying the laws. Harmonising the values underlying the law provides for the deepest form of integration between the Member States and forces them to give up their purely domestic interests. The proposed European tax on financial transactions provides a good example of a possible unified European law. A European financial transaction tax would not only coordinate and balance the different national approaches, it would also identify European objectives which are independent and distinct from any national aim, and these European objectives would guide the entire framework and structure of the European financial transaction tax.

From the perspective of the internal market, a law enacted under the enhanced cooperation procedure may on the one hand have the same trade-hampering impact as national laws have because enhanced cooperation law may discriminate or restrict the market access for goods, services, persons, or capital of non-participating Member States. These trade-hampering effects may demand an application of the fundamental freedoms to enhanced cooperation law in the same way as they are applied to national Member State laws. On the other hand, the law of enhanced cooperation establishes deeper integration between the participating Member States by way of conflict of law rules, mutual recognition, or coordination measures, or by establishing harmonised values and unified substantive laws. From this it follows that the impact of enhanced cooperation law on the European internal market depends on the perspective one takes. Within the group of participating Member States, the law may deepen integration. Towards the non-participating Member States, the law may discriminate or impose market access restrictions to protect the integration efforts of enhanced cooperation. This already sets out the fundamental question of this Part of the chapter: how does deeper integration between the participating Member States relate to the creation

[16] Ruth Mason and Michael S Knoll, 'What Is Tax Discrimination' (2011) 121 Yale Law Journal 1014, 1026 et seq.

[17] Michael Lang, *Introduction to the Law of Double Taxation Conventions* (2nd edn, Linde Verlag 2013) ss 30, 39; Alexander Rust, 'Double Taxation' in Alexander Rust (ed), *Double Taxation within the European Union* (Kluwer Law International 2011) 8–9.

and potential justification of trade obstacles imposed by enhanced cooperation law towards non-participating Member States?

C. The Fundamental Freedoms and National Tax Laws

The fundamental freedoms aim to integrate national markets into one EU-wide single market: the European internal market. National markets should no longer be isolated or protected by preferential national legislation; they should merge into one big Europe-wide market where the free movement of goods, persons, services, and capital is ensured. The first step towards such a single European market was to abolish all customs barriers.[18] But even in an area without any customs duties, national laws are capable of hindering trade.[19] This is precisely where the fundamental freedoms should apply.

Chapter 4 revealed that the European internal market does not aim for a clear cut efficient single market.[20] Nonetheless, a successful single market demands widespread harmonisation. Standards of production, labour law, social security, taxation, competition, and consumer and environmental protection need to be uniform. Otherwise, the differences within the laws hinder trade, and this harms the single market. A flourishing single market thus provides for uniformity in all those fields and manifests a political decision to prize market efficiency and market-wide neutrality of competition above other competing national values[21].[22] To a certain extent, the European Union seeks uniformity and therefore has the power to enact European laws which bind all Member States and prevent them from enacting specific national laws.[23] On the other hand, there are various fields of law which remain in the Member States' hands. In these areas, the Member States are sovereign and implement national rules which are in line with their national values.[24]

The conflict between having sovereign national lawmakers[25] and the aim of establishing a single European market is solved through the fundamental freedoms

[18] Dennis Swann, *The Economics of the Common Market* (4th edn, Penguin Books 1981) 11–12.

[19] Rene Barents, 'Charges of Equivalent Effect to Customs Duties' (1978) 15 Common Market Law Review 415; Arjen WH Meij and Jan A Winter, 'Measures Having an Effect Equivalent to Quantitative Restrictions' (1976) 13 Common Market Law Review 79; John K Bentil, 'EEC Commercial Law and "Charges Having Equivalent Effect to Customs Duties"' (1975) 9 Journal of World Trade 458; see also Catherine Barnard, *The Substantive Law of the EU: The Four Freedoms* (6th edn, OUP 2019) 9 et seq.

[20] See this chapter subsection G.I.

[21] National (non-market values) are by no means protectionist in nature, see for a differentiation, see Miguel Poiares Maduro, 'Reforming the Market or the State Article 30 and the European Constitution: Economic Freedom and Political Rights' (1997) *European Law Journal* 55, 68 et seq.

[22] Joseph HH Weiler, 'The Transformation of Europe' (1991) *100 The Yale Law Journal* 2403, 2478.

[23] See Chapter 4, subsection G.

[24] Most importantly, the area of taxation.

[25] Which 'almost by default, serve the national interest', Mónika Papp, 'Member State Interests and EU Internal Market Law' in Marton Varju (ed), *Between Compliance and Particularism: Member State Interests and European Union Law* (Springer 2019) 107; see also Ben Clift and Cornelia Woll, 'Economic Patriotism: Reinventing Control over Open Markets' (2012) 19 Journal of European Public Policy 307.

as tools of negative integration.[26] Unlike the European legislature's harmonisation measures,[27] which create new legislative frameworks and standards or modify existing ones (positive integration), the fundamental freedoms try to achieve integration by prohibiting the application of national laws which impose trade impediments[28] without[29] replacing the national laws with European legislation.[30] Accordingly, Art 3 of the EC Treaty states that obstacles to free trade between the Member States need to be abolished. The phrase 'obstacles to free trade' is very broad and could cover any national law or practice which may prevent someone from entering a foreign market.[31] Even differences in the laws between the home and the host Member State (which follow from their different policy choices) may be characterised as obstacles to free trade as they may require adjustments of goods to comply with the regulations of both Member States.[32] The differences in the law may, for example, force entrepreneurs to keep books not only in the home Member State, to pay social security and taxes in two Member States, to pay more for labour in the host Member State, and to comply with different or multiple due diligence rules. All of those burdens can be understood as obstacles to trade and thus would need to be abolished.

It follows from this that the application of the fundamental freedoms to national Member State laws has to balance both the value of deeper market integration and the non-market values underlying the national law.[33] A serious balancing of both

[26] Pedro Caro de Sousa, 'Negative and Positive Integration in EU Economic Law: Between Strategic Denial and Cognitive Dissonance?' (2012) 13 German Law Journal 979; Fritz W Scharpf, 'Negative and Positive Integration in the Political Economy of European Welfare States' in Martin Rhodes and Yves Mény (eds), *The Future of European Welfare: A New Social Contract?* (Palgrave Macmillan 1998) 158 et seq. Robert Schütze, *European Union Law* (CUP 2015) 475 et seq. For the opinion that only the taxpayer is the 'winner' when negative integration takes the upper hand see Sylvia Elwes, 'The Internal Market versus the Right of Member States to Levy Direct Tax-A Clash of Fundamental Principles' (2013) 41 Intertax 15, 24 et seq.

[27] See Chapter 4, subsection G.

[28] 'For many years this landmark judgement [being the *Dassonville* case] has been read as implying that the internal market relies on the principle of removing any Member State *obstacles* to trade, thus going well beyond a mere prohibition on discriminatory domestic regulation', Vranes (n 10) 488.

[29] However, CJEU case law has often been an incentive to find a compromise for introducing secondary EU laws: Karen J Alter, *The European Court's Political Power: Selected Essays* (OUP 2009) 157 arguing that the Court is 'a provider of ideas'.

[30] Hanno Kube, Ekkehart Reimer, and Christoph Spengel, 'Tax Policy: Trends in the Allocation of Powers Between the Union and Its Member States' (2016) 25 EC Tax Review 247, 255 arguing that the CJEU case law in the area of direct taxation has contributed to eliminating obstacles in intra-EU trade, 'but equally weakened the consistency, clarity and predictability of the Member States' tax systems'. The distinction of negative and positive integration goes back to the economic integration theory: Jan Tinbergen, *International Economic Integration* (2nd edn, 1965) 77–78.

[31] Since the Member States also have to respect the fundamental freedoms when exercising competences retained at national level, there is hardly an area of life where the market freedoms do not intrude demanding equal market conditions for intra-EU activities: Gareth Davies, 'Internal Market Adjudication and the Quality of Life in Europe' (2014) Columbia Journal of European Law 289, 292 et seq arguing that the market freedoms are not absolute but broad.

[32] For the analysis of the double burden see this chapter Part I, subsection C.I.1.

[33] Explicitly for a balance between internal market needs and national interests: CJEU, 12 June 2003, C-112/00, *Schmidberger*, ECLI:EU:C:2003:333, paras 81–82. Jotte Mulder, 'Responsive Adjudication and the "Social Legitimacy" of the Internal Market: Social Legitimacy of EU Free Movement

national non-market and market values requires first, the application of the fundamental freedoms to all areas of the law—even to those where the legislative power remains exclusively with the Member States, like in tax law[34]—and, secondly, the possibility to consider national diversities.[35] Only if all national laws can be tested against the fundamental freedoms can the market values be enforced.[36] And only if important national values[37] are capable of preventing the law from being inapplicable because the law discriminates or imposes market access restrictions,[38] or are at

Adjudication' (2016) 22 European Law Journal 597, 604 arguing for two step approach: 'free movement rights are placed as a prima facie right above a public interest concern such as human dignity, merely to then at the justification stage, deal with all the permissible limitations of the free movement right on the basis of human dignity'. However, the following study reveals that the CJEU also takes the values of the Member States into account when determining whether a particular national rule constitutes a restriction of the fundamental freedoms and when finding the right *tertium comparationis*. More substantial on the balancing argument, see Stephen Weatherill, 'Viking and Laval: The EU Internal Market Perspective' in Mark R Freedland and Jeremias Prassl (eds), *Viking, Laval and Beyond* (Hart Publishing 2014) 27 et seq. Leone Niglia, 'Eclipse of the Constitution {Europe Nouveau Siècle}' (2016) 22 European Law Journal 132, 136 et seq. Arguing that the CJEU has never made the balancing act explicit and thus practised a find of 'undisclosed balancing'. Accordingly, the 'Court has pretended to "neutrally" enforce rights as "derived" from the Treaties and consequently has presented its choices in allegedly uncontroversial judicial language, while de facto weighing and balancing the interests and goals at stake'. However, in recent time, the CJEU is more explicit on the balancing act. Ruth Mason, 'Flunking the ECJ's Tax Discrimination Test' (2007) 46 Columbia Journal of Transnational Law 72, 93 claiming that 'tax cases should involve weighing the Member States' interests in retaining tax autonomy against the Community's interests in market integration'.

[34] For example, CJEU, 4 October 1991, C-246/89, *Commission v United Kingdom*, ECLI:EU:C:1991:375, para 12; CJEU, 14 February 1995, C-279/93, *Schumacker*, ECLI:EU:C:1995:31, para 21; some of the CJEU's rulings even struck at the core of national tax system necessitating a fundamental rethinking of the Member State's tax system: Suzanne Kingston, 'The Boundaries of Sovereignty: The ECJ's Controversial Role Applying Internal Market Law to Direct Tax Measures' (2007) 9 Cambridge Yearbook of European Legal Studies 287, 287.

[35] Currently, the CJEU considers the national identity of the Member States to determine whether the national law constitutes a restriction (see this chapter Part I, subsection C.I) or to justify discriminations or restrictions of fundamental freedoms (see this chapter Part I, subsection C.III). In earlier cases, the CJEU also considered national diversity on the level of the comparability test. In these cases, national laws where often not discriminatory because the situations were not comparable (see this chapter Part I, subsection C.II). Thomas Horsley, 'Reflections on the Role of the Court of Justice as the "Motor" of European Integration: Legal Limits to Judicial Lawmaking' (2013) 50 Common Market Law Review 931, 951 arguing that the CJEU enjoys wide discretion when deciding whether the Member States are successful in justifying their policy preferences.

[36] '*Umrahmungsprinzip*': Koen Lenaerts, 'Die gemeinschaftsrechtliche Umrahmung der direkten Besteuerung', *Verhandlungen des 66. Deutschen Juristentages*, vol II/1 (Beck Verlag 2006) Q20–Q21. The fundamental freedoms also apply to tax incentives of the Member States. The Member States are allowed to use their national tax law to steer the behaviour of the taxpayer, but they are not allowed to do so in a discriminatory manner: Edoardo Traversa and Barbara Vintras, 'The Territoriality of Tax Incentives within the Single Market' in Isabelle Richelle, Wolfgang Schön, and Edoardo Traversa (eds), *Allocating Taxing Powers within the European Union* (Springer 2013).

[37] Joseph HH Weiler, 'The Constitution of the Common Market Place: Text and Context in the Evolution of the Free Movement of Goods' in Paul P Craig and Gráinne de Búrca (eds), *The Evolution of EU Law* (OUP 1999) 366.

[38] For the 'dual legal structure' of the fundamental freedoms (covering both discriminatory restrictions and restrictions in a closer sense see Axel Cordewener, 'The Prohibitions of Discrimination and Restrictions within the Framework of the Fully Integrated Internal Market' in Frans Vanistendael (ed), *EU Freedoms and Taxation* (IBFD 2006) 8–9).

least capable of justifying restrictions of the fundamental freedoms,[39] is it possible to ensure that the European Union remains a Union of its Member States, which are united but diverse.[40]

The following subsections seek to give a clear overview of the scope of the fundamental freedoms when applied to the law of a single Member State and the freedom of Member States to prioritise non-market values over market efficiency goals. The individual Member States' ability to hamper intra-EU trade for the sake of non-market values forms the bottom line for a group of Member States engaging in enhanced cooperation. In other words, mechanisms to defend non-market values which a single Member State is allowed to use may also be brought forward by a group of Member States to legitimise their joint trade-harming rules.

A deeper analysis of the extensive case law on the interaction between national laws and the fundamental freedoms reveals that Member States are able to rely on their non-market values and protect them at three different levels: first on the restriction level where non-market values may influence the decision of whether or not Member State national law imposes a market access restriction and thus harms the fundamental freedoms (see subsection I); secondly, on the level of comparison (see subsection II); and thirdly, on the level of justification (see subsection III). Against the background of these rulings, the analysis also reveals that some CJEU decisions provide for a different approach and follow a value set which is neither derived from the law of the Member State nor EU law but is intrinsic to the judges' beliefs (see subsection IV).

[39] Leonard FM Besselink, 'Does EU Law Recognise Legal Limits to Integration? Accommodating Diversity and Its Limits' in Thomas Giegerich, Oskar Josef Gstrein, and Sebastian Zeitzmann (eds), *The EU between 'An Ever Closer Union' and Inalienable Policy Domains of Member States*, vol 80 (Nomos 2014) 65–66.

[40] See Art 4 Subsection 2 of the TEU: 'The Union shall respect the equality of Member States before the Treaties as well as their *national identities*, inherent in their fundamental structures, political and constitutional, inclusive of regional and local self-government' (emphasis added). Koen Lenaerts, '"United in Diversity"—Also in Fiscalibus?' in Philippe Hinnekens and Luc Hinnekens (eds), *A Vision of Taxes Within and Outside the European Borders: Festschrift in Honor of Prof. Dr. Frans Vanistendael* (Kluwer Law International 2008) 625 arguing that '[t]here is indeed room for diversity in direct taxation matters. Beside the diversity which flows from the disparities in the tax legislation of the Member States, the ECJ admits that some tax restrictions may be justified or even that some tax restrictions do not infringe the principle of equal treatment at all.' See for more details on 'diversity' and 'national identity' in the European treaties, Besselink (n 39) 69 et seq. For a detailed analysis of whether this clause has an impact on EU law and the constitutional law of the Member States see Armin von Bogdandy and Stephan Schill, 'Overcoming Absolute Primacy: Respect for National Identity under the Lisbon Treaty' (2011) 48 Common Market Law Review 1417. The European law's dual commitment is reflected by safeguarding a 'core nucleus of shared values where the ECJ must ensure uniformity', while at the same time, the Member States are allowed to accommodate the value diversity that stems from the variegated cultural, historical, and social heritages of the Member States: Koen Lenaerts, 'The Court's Outer and Inner Selves: Exploring the External and Internal Legitimacy of the European Court of Justice' in Maurice Adams and others (eds), *Judging Europe's Judges: The Legitimacy of the Case Law of the European Court of Justice* (Hart Publishing 2013) 29; see also Jotte Mulder, 'Responsive Adjudication and the "Social Legitimacy" of the Internal Market: Social Legitimacy of EU Free Movement Adjudication' (2016) *22 European Law Journal* 597. For an acknowledgement that the Member States can even have a different take on the necessary level of child protection, see CJEU, 14 February 2008, C-244/06, *Dynamic Medien Vertriebs*, ECLI:EU:C:2008:85, para 44.

I. First Step: Market Access Restriction

The understanding of the European internal market as a market of different Member States which preserve their national identities has a serious impact on the scope and application of the fundamental freedoms. If the European internal market allows the protection of national values at the expense of full neutrality within the market, the fundamental freedoms will not address all obstacles to free trade. Some hurdles to free trade may remain because they are simply outside the scope of the fundamental freedoms.

First and foremost, the fundamental freedoms aim to combat national measures which are of a protectionist nature.[41] Protectionist national rules favour domestic goods, services, persons, and capital with the aim of protecting and sealing the national market. The trade-hampering effects of protectionist measures are obvious. However, the CJEU has gone much further than fighting protectionist rules under the market freedoms and has ruled that the fundamental freedoms prohibit Member States from imposing market access restrictions.[42] Such restrictions may exist if the laws prohibit, impede, or render the exercise of a market freedom less attractive.[43] Accordingly, any national law which is not discriminatory but makes it (more) burdensome or simply unattractive for foreign market players to gain access to the national market is in principle prohibited.[44] Thus, it is

[41] Craig and Búrca (n 37) 607 et seq. Maduro, 'Reforming the Market or the State Article 30 and the European Constitution' (n 21) 67 indicating that the Treaty of Rome was a 'trade agreement intended to prevent protectionist policies and reduce barriers to trade'.

[42] To be truly efficient, the CJEU developed the fundamental freedoms from mere anti-discrimination clauses based on nationality to free movement rights protecting almost any cross-border economic activity within the European internal market from discrimination and safeguarding the market player's market access in each Member State. There are hardly any cases where the CJEU found no economic effect and thus no involvement of the fundamental freedoms (eg CJEU, 4 October 1991, C-159/90, *The Society for the Protection of Unborn Children Ireland*, ECLI:EU:C:1991:378, providing information through a students' unions in Dublin about abortions in London). For an overview of the development see Axel Cordewener, *Europäische Grundfreiheiten und nationales Steuerrecht: 'Konvergenz' des Gemeinschaftsrechts und 'Kohärenz' der direkten Steuern in der Rechtsprechung des EuGH* (Dr Otto Schmidt Verlag 2002) 200 et seq.

[43] For the freedom of establishment see CJEU, 29 November, C-371/10, *National Grid Indus*, ECLI:EU:C:2011:785, para 36; CJEU, 5 October 2004, C-442/02, *Caixa Bank France*, ECLI:EU:C:2004:586, para 11. For the free movement of capital see CJEU, 28 September, C-282/04 and 283/04, *Commission v Kingdom of the Netherlands*, ECLI:EU:C:2006:608, para 27; for the free movement of services and the free movement of workers the CJEU directly referred to the hurdle to access the market see CJEU, 10 May 1995, C-384/93, *Alpine Investments*, ECLI:EU:C:1995:126, para 38; CJEU, 15 December 1995, C-415/93, *Bosman*, ECLI:EU:C:1995:463, para 103; CJEU, 27 January 2000, C-190/98, *Graf*, ECLI:EU:C:2000:49, para 23.

[44] Sjoerd Douma calls this the 'disadvantage-test' since according to the CJEU case law 'any "disadvantage" caused by a tax measure constitutes a prima facie infringement of the principle of free movement'. Douma's work is substantially influenced by the idea of 'twofolded neutrality' according to which tax sovereignty and the principle of free movement needs to be balanced in a way that the latter respects direct tax measures, which form the backbone of an income tax system, and national tax rules must be neutral in regard to the exercise of the freedoms of movement (Opinion of AG Maduro, 7 April 2005, C-446/03, *Marks & Spencer*, ECLI:EU:C:2005:201, para 67). As Douma finds this approach still too abstract, he favours a but-for test according to which the general structure of the domestic income tax

no longer necessary to prove that nationals are treated more favourably; any law which makes it harder for entrepreneurs, even national ones,[45] to gain access to another Member State's market can be challenged by the fundamental freedoms. Fully in line with the aim of an effective allocation of resources, the law of a single Member State constitutes a restriction of the fundamental freedoms if the disadvantageous treatment affects the decision of where to invest. This not only covers the choice between a domestic and a foreign investment but also the choice between two foreign investments.[46]

Having said this, the vast majority of market access restrictions nevertheless constitute a form of discrimination[47] because they apply the same treatment to goods, services, persons, and capital which are not in a comparable situation (discriminatory restrictions).[48]Foreign goods, services, persons, and capital may be different from their domestic equivalent[49] because they may, for example, have already complied with the regulatory framework of the home Member State, and the accumulation of the regulatory framework of the home and the host Member State hinders intra-EU trade.[50] Adjusting products or obtaining (another) certification

system is taken for granted and it is tested whether the single tax measure derogates from the general system and leads to a heavier tax burden (Sjoerd Douma, 'Non-Discriminatory Tax Obstacles' (2012) 21 EC Tax Review 67, 71, 82–83; Sjoerd Douma and Frank Engelen, 'Non-Discriminatory Tax Obstacles to Free Movement' in Michael Lang and Christine Weinzierl (eds), *Europäisches Steuerrecht—Festschrift für Friedrich Rödler* (Linde Verlag 2010) 201 et seq). However, this approach uses a technique which is used and should only be used to test national tax measures against state aid law.

[45] Even though the national rules may hinder economic activities within a Member State, only cross-border activities are protected by the fundamental freedoms, and thus the fundamental freedoms allow one to treat a pure national economic activity worse than a cross-border one (reverse discrimination: see for an overview of the case law and some critique Alina Tryfonidou, *Reverse Discrimination in EC Law* (Kluwer Law International 2009); Alina Tryfonidou, 'Reverse Discrimination in Purely Internal Situations: An Incongruity in a Citizens' Europe' (2008) 35 Legal Issues of Economic Integration 43; Dominik Hanf, '"Reverse Discrimination" in EU Law: Constitutional Aberration, Constitutional Necessity, or Judicial Choice?' (2011) 18 Maastricht Journal of European and Comparative Law 29). In those cases, the national constitutional law has to intervene.

[46] CJEU, 30 June 2016, C-176/15, *Riskin and Timmermans*, ECLI:EU:C:2016:488, para 25; it is important to distinguish between the restriction and the comparability (see this chapter Part I, subsection C.II). On the level of comparability, two foreign investments may not be comparable and thus the fundamental freedoms may not be infringed. Nonetheless, the different treatment of two foreign investments may constitute a restriction.

[47] The Court has consistently refused to understand the accumulation of two regulatory frameworks as a form of discrimination and has characterised such trade obstacles as 'restrictions' of the free movement rights; Kingston (n 34) 298–99.

[48] Michael Lang, 'Direct Taxation: Is the ECJ Heading in a New Direction?' (2006) 46 European Taxation 421, 422 arguing for the Futura case that '[a]lthough the ECJ did not make this explicit, it appeared to have assumed that a non-resident taxpayer with its head office outside Luxembourg and only a PE in Luxembourg was not in the same situation as a Luxembourg resident with its head office in Luxembourg'.

[49] In the light of national legislation prohibiting the payment of remuneration on sight accounts, foreign and the domestic market players may not be in a comparable situation because domestic credit institutions have an extensive network of branches and thus greater opportunities to raise capital from the public, CJEU, 5 October 2004, C-442/02, *Caixa-Bank France*, ECLI:EU:C:2004:586, para 13 et seq.

[50] Barnard, *The Substantive Law of the EU* (n 19) 23–24; Schütze, *European Union Law* (n 26) 502 et seq; Craig and Búrca (n 37) 620 et seq.

for the professional skills hampers cross-border economic transactions, at least if the additional regulatory layer of the host Member State follows the same purpose as the regulatory framework of the home Member State. The following analysis shows that the Member States only impose an obstacle to intra-EU trade by requiring the market player to comply with an additional layer of regulatory rules if the rules of the home Member State and the host Member State aim for the same purpose (see subsections 1 and 2). Considering the aim and purpose of the national laws to decide on whether or not they impose an additional burden which infringes the fundamental freedoms clearly shows that the fundamental freedoms respect the regulatory objectives of the Member States. However, at the same time, the fundamental freedoms force the Member States to accept and respect the different approaches of their fellow Member States to achieve the same goal. In other words, Member States are free to decide on the regulatory goals they want to achieve, but they are not allowed to determine an exclusive approach for achieving these goals.

Aside from discriminatory market access restrictions, the CJEU case law has identified some non-discriminatory restrictions. They have in common that the aim and purpose of the national laws is irrelevant for determining their restrictive character. The first category of non-discriminatory market access restrictions covers national laws which place a burden on the very act of movement (see subsection 3). A burden on the action which is necessary to exercise the market freedoms is so fundamental that it constitutes a restriction of the fundamental freedoms regardless of the Member State's underlying motives or aims. However, these aims may, at a later stage, be able to justify the restriction.

The second category of non-discriminatory market access restrictions is formed by rules prohibiting the trade of certain goods and services (see subsection 4). To be frank, these rules do not make it harder for foreign market players to enter the domestic market. Such rules erode the market for certain goods or services, and thus forbid the marketing of goods or services which can be traded on the market of another Member State. If national law prohibits market access entirely, the law is restrictive regardless of its underlying purpose.

The third, and final, category of non-discriminatory market access hindering rules are national laws which render intra-EU trade less attractive (see subsection 5). This category of market access restrictions liberalises domestic Member State markets without considering Member State national values at the outset. A thorough understanding of the doctrine of 'less attractive' may be particularly important in the area of national tax laws because domestic taxes may automatically make cross-border economic activities less attractive. Being exposed to special taxes or charges may be the manifestation of disadvantageous treatment of cross-border economic activities. Subsection 5 will explain how the case law on the requirement of not rendering cross-border economic activities less attractive should be applied to Member State tax laws.

1. Double Burden: Accumulation of Two National Regulatory Regimes of the Same Kind

As early as 1979 the CJEU decided in its groundbreaking decision *Cassis de Dijon*[51] that Member States must allow products which are lawfully produced and marketed in a fellow Member State into their markets. Accordingly, foreign fruit liqueurs can be sold as 'liqueurs' on the national market, even though the alcohol content is below the required national threshold for marketing substances as 'liqueurs'. The Court thereby forced all Member States mutually to recognise the regulatory approaches of their fellow Member States[52] which aim for the same regulatory goal as the domestic approaches.[53] The mutual recognition principle is not restricted to a certain set of norms but to rules influencing the market access of a foreigner or foreign products.[54] Any national, even-handed regulatory rule of a host Member State which hinders foreigners or foreign products from accessing the Member State's market[55] because its application imposes a regulatory[56] or administrative[57] double burden[58] can be tested against the fundamental freedoms.

[51] CJEU, 20 February 1979, 120/78, *Rewe-Zentral AG*, ECLI:EU:C:1979:42.

[52] The principle of mutual recognition balances the internal market needs and the Member States' right to safeguard national, regional, and local identities and traditions: see Alfonso Mattera, 'The Principle of Mutual Recognition and Respect for National, Regional and Local Identities and Traditions' in Fiorella Kostoris Padoa Schioppa (ed), *The Principle of Mutual Recognition in the European Integration Process* (Palgrave Macmillan 2005) 5 et seq.

[53] Koen Lenaerts, 'The Principle of Subsidiarity and the Environment in the European Union: Keeping the Balance of Federalism' (1993) *17 Fordham International Law Journal* 846, 856; for a fundamental critique on the mutual recognition principle see Stephen Weatherill, 'The Principle of Mutual Recognition: It Doesn't Work Because It Doesn't Exist' (2018) 43 European Law Review 224; Joseph HH Weiler, 'Mutual Recognition, Functional Equivalence and Harmonization in the Evolution of the European Common Market and the WTO' in Fiorella Kostoris Padoa Schioppa (ed), *The Principle of Mutual Recognition in the European Integration Process* (Palgrave Macmillan 2005) 25–26 arguing that ‚[t]he principle of mutual recognition is an intermediate device which may help in reconciling the basic tension created by regulatory diversity in a single or liberalized marketplace'.

[54] CJEU, 20 February 1979, 120/78, *Rewe-Zentral AG*, ECLI:EU:C:1979:42, para 16.

[55] In the legal literature, authors make a distinction between the market access and equal competition on the market: Wulf-Henning Roth, 'Die Niederlassungsfreiheit zwischen Beschränkungs- und Diskriminierungsverbot' in Wolfgang Schön (ed), *Gedächtnisschrift für Brigitte Knobbe-Keuk* (Dr Otto Schmidt Verlag) 737–39.

[56] Examples of a regulatory double burden are the requirement to comply with national product standards (Kenneth Armstrong, 'Mutual Recognition' in Catherine Barnard and Joanne Scott (eds), *The Law of the Single European Market: Unpacking the Premises* (Hart 2002).), the need to have a national degree (CJEU, 28 April 1977, 71/76, *Thieffry*, ECLI:EU:1977:65; CJEU, 1 February 1996, C-164/94, *Aranitis*, ECLI:EU:1996:13; CJEU, 7 May 1991, C-340/89, *Vlassopoulou*, ECLI:EU:C:1991:193; CJEU, 7 May 1992, C-104/91, *Aguirre Borrell*, ECLI:EU:C:1992:202) or the demand to keep books according to national accounting standards (CJEU, 15. May 1997, C-250/95, Futura Participation, ECLI:EU:C:1997:239.).

[57] If the regulatory framework of a Member State sets out the obligation to contract in the motor insurance sector, foreign market players wishing to enter the Member State's market 'will be required to re-think their business policy and strategy'. Market access involves changes and costs for foreign entrepreneurs which may reduce their ability to compete effectively with domestic entrepreneurs, and thus the obligation to contract restricts the fundamental freedoms, CJEU, 28 April 2009, C-518/06, *Commission v Italy*, ECLI:EU:C:2009:270, paras 69–71.

[58] The notion of double burden can be explained as a form of discrimination because the host Member State does not recognise the efforts taken in the home Member States, and thus the host Member State treats two situations which are not alike in a like manner: Barnard, *The Substantive Law*

Member States are thus no longer allowed to ignore the qualification of a person or lawfully produced products. If goods or services can be marketed in one Member State—since they comply with the regulations of that Member State—they can be marketed in all other Member States as well.[59] This development not only helped to open up national markets and to allow foreign qualifications to be recognised and foreign products to be traded within the internal market without having to comply with several regulatory regimes, but the wide application of the fundamental freedoms also entailed a far-reaching deregulation of the national markets due to regulatory competition.[60]

As already indicated above, the principle of mutual recognition can only be applied in cases where the regulatory purpose of the national rule belonging to the home and the host Member State are equivalent.[61] The trade-hampering differences between the rules lie in the design of the regulatory measure. There are multiple ways of ensuring that products do not harm people's health, that consumers and shareholders are protected, or that entrepreneurs have a sufficient professional qualification. The European internal market does not prevent any Member State from protecting their national values or from choosing the most suitable way of protecting these values.[62] However, the European internal market forbids Member States from failing to respect foreigners' and foreign products' compliance with rules which have the same purpose as the national ones.[63] The market access of goods, persons, or services which already complied with even-minded foreign regulatory rules do not threaten national values.

of the EU (n 19) 23–24; Michael Lang, 'Kapitalverkehrsfreiheit, Steuerrecht und Drittstaaten' (2011) Steuer und Wirtschaft 209, 216.

[59] Christine Osterloh-Konrad, Caroline Heber, and Tobias Beuchert, 'Anzeigepflichten für Steuergestaltungen in Deutschland' (Springer 2017), 65–66; Susanne Schmidt, 'Mutual Recognition as a New Model of Governance' (2007) 14 Journal of European Public Policy 667, 667.

[60] Simon Deakin, 'Legal Diversity and Regulatory Competition: Which Model for Europe?' (2006) *12* European Law Journal 440; Niamh Dunne, 'Liberalisation and the Pursuit of the Internal Market' (2018) 43 European Law Review 803, 810; Catherine Barnard and Simon Deakin, 'Market Access and Regulatory Competition' in Catherine Barnard and Joanne Scott (eds), *The Law of the Single European Market: Unpacking the Premises* (Bloomsbury Publishing PLC 2002).

[61] Armstrong (n 56) 226. Ekkehart Reimer, 'Taxation—an Area without Mutual Recognition?' in Isabelle Richelle, Wolfgang Schön, and Edoardo Traversa (eds), *Allocating Taxing Powers within the European Union* (Springer 2013) 197.

[62] Jacques Pelkmans, 'Mutual Recognition in Goods and Services: An Economic Perspective' (2012) Bruges European Economic Research Papers 2 <https://www.ceps.eu/publications/mutual-recognition-goods-and-services-economic-perspective> accessed 18 March 2018. However, in the *Säger* case, the CJEU went beyond an evaluation of the impact a German regulatory rule has on the freedom to access the German market. The law required market players to obtain a licence for pursuing legal affairs on behalf of third parties. In the case at hand, a market player monitored patents for his clients via a computerised system and advised the patent holders when the fees for renewing the patents became due. The CJEU ruled that the need to obtain a licence and show one's ability goes beyond what is necessary to protect the interests of the clients and is 'disproportionate to the needs of the recipients'. CJEU, 25 July 1991, C-76/90, *Säger*, ECLI:EU:C:1991:331, para 17.

[63] For the recognition of foreign entities see CJEU, 9 March 1999, C-212/97, *Centros*, ECLI:EU:C:1999:126; CJEU, 5 November 2002, C-208/00, *Überseering*, ECLI:EU:C:2002:632; CJEU, 30 September 2003, C-167/01, *Inspire Art*, ECLI:EU:C:2003:512. For the recognition of a driving licences

2. Double Burden: Accumulation of Two National Rules of a Different Kind

Without a doubt, any form of double burden harms intra-EU trade. If access to another Member State's market is associated with a second layer of regulatory burdens, entrepreneurs will think twice about whether or not it is worth accessing the foreign market. To prevent the double regulatory burden from hampering intra-EU trade, the principle of mutual recognition builds on the notion that every good, service, or person which is traded on a Member State's market already complies with the regulations of that very Member State, and therefore should not be subject to an additional layer of regulations which has the same goal in mind. But precisely this fact shows the limits of the principle of mutual recognition.[64] Any efforts undertaken in one Member State can only be recognised in another Member State if these efforts aim for the same objectives as the regulatory rule of the home Member State.[65] Accordingly, the fundamental freedoms stretch to their limits where the national rules do not have the same purpose.[66] If the host Member State's second burden has a different purpose, complying with these rules may not be called redundant or superfluous and in any case not protectionist. Since the aim and purpose of the national rules has not already been satisfied by complying with foreign national rules (most likely in the home Member State), a demand to satisfy the national rules (in the host Member State) cannot be understood as an attempt by the Member State to protect and isolate its national market.

Substantive tax law is an example where the principle of mutual recognition cannot be applied precisely due to the idea that the law of the home and host Member State have different objectives:[67] '[t]he collection of revenue by one Member State in no way protects the revenue interest of another'[68] Member State.[69]

see for example CJEU, 13 October 2011, C-224/10, *Apelt*, ECLI:EU:C:2011:655; CJEU, 22 November 2011, C-590/10, *Köppl*, ECLI:EU:C:2011:765.

64 For the limits of mutual recognition with respect to different policy choices see Nick Bernard, 'Flexibility in the European Single Market' in Catherine Barnard and Joanne Scott (eds), *The Law of the Single European Market: Unpacking the Premises* (Hart Publishing 2002) 109.

65 Ekkehart Reimer (n 61) 197 et seq. Craig and Búrca (n 37) 623 et seq.

66 Bernard, 'Flexibility' (n 64) 104 claiming that '[t]rue mutual recognition would require going on step further and recognising not just different ways of satisfying the regulatory objectives of the host State but also accepting the regulatory choices of the home State themselves'.

67 CJEU, 14 November 2006, C-513/04, *Kerckhaert*, ECLI:EU:C:2006:713, para 20; CJEU, 12 February 2009, C-67/08, *Block*, C-67/08, ECLI:EU:C:2009:92, para 31; CJEU, 16 July 2009, *Damseaux*, C-128/08, ECLI:EU:C:2009:471, paras 32–33.

68 Jukka Snell, 'Non-Discriminatory Tax Obstacles in Community Law' (2007) 56 *International & Comparative Law Quarterly* 339, 365. Despite this Snell qualifies the different application of the fundamental freedoms as an inconstancy in the case law of the CJEU: Jukka Snell, 'The Legitimacy of Free Movement Case Law: Process and Substance' in Maurice Adams and others (eds), *Judging Europe's Judges: The Legitimacy of the Case Law of the European Court of Justice* (Hart Publishing 2013) 115.

69 Wolfgang Schön, 'Neutrality and Territoriality—Competing or Converging Concepts in European Tax Law?' (2015) 69 Bulletin for International Taxation 271, 274. Reimer (n 61) 204; Szudoczky, *The*

What is true for substantive tax law is not necessarily true for procedural tax law.[70] In this area of the law, it makes perfect sense to look at the obligations a taxpayer already had to fulfil in a fellow Member State, such as bookkeeping and disclosure requirements,[71] to determine what can still be required under domestic rules.[72]

The CJEU has been heavily criticised for applying the fundamental freedoms differently to the various branches of national law.[73] Applying different standards to the same situations would contradict the Court's own principles.[74] The inconsistency is especially apparent when comparing CJEU case law on double taxation and social security. In the latter, the Court consistently ruled that market freedoms preclude the host Member State from levying a social security fee if the person already participates in the social security system of the home Member State.[75] Looking closer at the line of reasoning, the Court finds that the second layer of social security payments does not provide for any additional social protection. The social net is already provided for by the system of the home Member State. In this respect, the mutual recognition argument is applicable because the second burden—the social security levy in the host Member State—does not provide for anything which is not already covered by the security net of the home Member State. The aim of protecting workers is thus already achieved through the payment of a social security contribution in the home Member State. The difference between social security and tax law cases simply lies in the fact that the aim and purpose of the social security system in the host Member State can be fulfilled by the social security net of the home Member State. The home Member State's social security net also protects the insured person outside the territory of the home Member State. However, within the territory of the host Member State, services may be provided by a social security institution, which, in

Sources of EU Law (n 1) 352; Georg W Kofler, 'Double Taxation and European Law: Analysis of the Jurisprudence' in Alexander Rust (ed), *Double taxation within the European Union* (Kluwer Law International 2011) 124.

[70] CJEU, 15. May 1997, C-250/95, *Futura Participation*, ECLI:EU:C:1997:239, para 26; CJEU, 9 October 2014, C-326/12, *van Caster*, ECLI:EU:C:2014:2269.

[71] Kofler, 'Double Taxation and European Law' (n 69) 113–14.

[72] Christine Osterloh-Konrad, Caroline Heber, and Tobias Beuchert, *Anzeigepflichten für Steuergestaltungen in Deutschland: verfassungs- und europarechtliche Grenzen sowie Überlegungen zur Ausgestaltung* (Springer 2017) 63 et seq.

[73] Georg W Kofler and Ruth Mason, 'Double Taxation: A European Switch in Time' (2007) 14 Columbia Journal of European Law 63, 80. Frans Vanistendael, 'The Compatibility of the Basic Economic Freedoms with the Sovereign National Tax Systems of the Member States' (2003) 12 EC Tax Review 136, 137 et seq.

[74] CJEU, 21 March 1972, 82/71, *Pubblico Ministero Italiano*, ECLI:EU:C:1972:20, para 5; CJEU, 1 July 1993, C-20/92, *Hubbard*, ECLI:EU:C:1993:280, para 19.

[75] CJEU, 3 February 1982, 62/81 and 63/81, *Seco and Desquenne & Giral*, ECLI:EU:C:1982:34; CJEU, 15 February 1996, C-53/95, *Kemmler*, ECLI:EU:C:1996:58; CJEU, 28 March 1996, C-272/94, *Guiot*, ECLI:EU:C:1996:147; CJEU, 23 November 1999, C-369/96 and C-376/96, *Arblade*, ECLI:EU:C:1999:575.

return, may seek compensation for its services from the social insurance carrier in the person's home Member State. The financial needs of a Member State can, however, be satisfied neither by the levying of a tax in another Member State nor by the Member States claiming compensation for their 'services' (in the form of public goods). This difference explains why taxation does not constitute a double burden which would fall within the scope of the fundamental freedoms. There is, however, no doubt that double taxation hinders intra-EU trade as it leads to a tax burden which exceeds the burden a market player would face if it only engaged in domestic trade. Yet the fundamental freedoms, as they stand today, are simply not capable of removing these trade obstacles. However, these obstacles may be removed by laws enacted under the enhanced cooperation procedure.

3. Hindering the Exercise of the Market Freedoms by Burdening or Restricting the Act of Moving

National rules may also hinder market access of foreigners or foreign goods without imposing a second regulatory layer[76] by directly linking the exercise of a market freedom with negative implications.[77] Such national rules can either be applied by the home Member State as a restriction on leaving or by the host Member State as a restriction on entry. Both forms hinder access to a 'foreign' EU market.

To date, the CJEU has ruled in a handful of cases on infringements of the fundamental freedoms by hindering entry or exit without making any reference to the aim and purpose of the law. Since the national law directly hinders the exercise of the market freedoms, the trade-hampering effects are so fundamental that there is no need to analyse the purpose of the law for determining the restrictive character of the national law. However, the purpose of the law may help to justify the trade obstacle but is not needed to show the restrictive nature of the law.

The first relevant CJEU ruling concerned a French rule which allowed advocates to establish chambers in one place only (within and outside France). The rule was found to infringe the fundamental freedoms because a lawyer, once established in a Member State, 'would be able to enjoy the freedom of the Treaty to establish himself in another Member State *only* at the price of abandoning the establishment he already had'.[78] In that particular case, the national rule hindered foreign lawyers from entering the national market (restriction on entry). On the other hand, it might have also prevented a French lawyer from establishing a second chamber in

[76] See this chapter Part I, subsection C.I.1.

[77] '[D]iscrimination is not a necessary feature of the market access principle': Malcolm Gammie, 'The Compatibility of National Tax Principles with the Single Market' in Frans Vanistendael (ed), *EU Freedoms and Taxation* (IBFD 2006) 115.

[78] CJEU, 12 July 1984, 107/83, *Klopp*, ECLI:EU:C:1984:270, para 18, emphasis added.

another Member State because it would have required him to give up his national (French) chamber (restriction on exit). The French rule hindered the exercise of the freedom of establishment insofar as it did not allow advocates to have two or more chambers. Having one chamber automatically disallowed the exercise and enjoyment of the freedom of establishment.

The CJEU had to rule on a quite similar restriction in the *Bosman* case.[79] The transfer rules of a professional national football league only allowed the transfer of a professional player from one club to another if the latter club paid the former a transfer, training, or development fee. Accordingly, whether or not a player was allowed to transfer depended upon the payment of a fee from the club he was to join to the club he was to leave. The requirement to pay a certain fee was directly linked to the exercise of a football player's right of free movement of workers, and such a restriction of free movement infringes the rights of workers to move as they wish.[80] If the host club is not willing to pay the fee, the professional football player is stuck and is not allowed to transfer.[81]

Another free movement restriction was found in Greek law. The law prescribed a mandatory legal form of employment relationship between tourist and travel agencies, and tourist guides licensed to pursue the profession of guide in Greece.[82] The law applied to all tourist guides licensed in Greece regardless of their nationality or their place of residence. The CJEU ruled that the regulatory framework deprives a tourist guide from another Member State of the possibility of working in Greece as a self-employed person. Foreign (but also domestic) tourist guides have to enter into an employment relationship with tourist or travel agencies to be allowed to offer their services. In other words, foreign tourist guides are not allowed to provide their services as self-employed persons in Greece if they do not enter into a contractual relationship with a Greek tourist or travel agency. Such a burden on the offering of services constitutes an infringement of the freedom of tourist guides to provide services of that kind as self-employed persons.[83]

[79] CJEU, 15 December 1995, C-415/93, *Bosman*, ECLI:EU:C:1995:465.

[80] ibid para 103.

[81] See for this line of argument also CJEU, 13 April 2000, C-176/96, *Lehtonen*, ECLI:EU:C:2000:201. In contrast, organisation and selection rules in judo may have the effect of limiting the number of participants in a tournament, but these rules do not prohibit athletes from accessing the market. They may not be allowed to participate in a particular tournament but they do not govern access to the labour market by professional sportsmen, CJEU, 11 April 2000, C-51/96 and C-191/97, *Deliège*, ECLI:EU:C:2000:199, para 61 et seq. Douma (n 44) 75 arguing that these rules 'actually make the market'; see also Jukka Snell, 'Notion of Market Access: A Concept or a Slogan, The' (2010) 47 Common Market Law Review 437, 462; Eleanor Spaventa, 'The Outer Limit of the Treaty Free Movement Provisions: Some Reflections on the Significance of Keck, Remoteness and Deliège' in Catherine Barnard and others (eds), *The Outer Limits of European Union Law* (Bloomsbury Publishing PLC 2009). Other rules 'making the market' are the prohibition of resale at a loss (CJEU, 24 November 1993, *Keck and Mithouard*, ECLI:EU:C:1993:905), the prohibition of Sunday trading (CJEU, 23 November 1989, C-145/88, *Torfaen Borough Council*, ECLI:EU:C:1989:593), and the prohibition of night-time production (CJEU, 14 July 1981, *Oebel*, ECLI:EU:C:1981:177).

[82] CJEU, 5 June 1997, C-398/95, *SETTG*, ECLI:EU:1997:282.

[83] ibid paras 17–19.

In these cases, the national rules directly hindered the exercise of the free movement rights. Thus, the finding that the law imposes a restriction to the fundamental freedoms required neither a thorough analysis of the aim and purpose of the national law nor an assessment of a worse treatment of the cross-border scenario. The trade-hampering effects of the law are evident on an isolated basis.

In tax law, there is one prominent example which also hinders the exercise of the market freedoms, namely exit taxation. Exit taxes are typically designed in a discriminatory manner, but they would also contradict the fundamental freedoms if the domestic setting were treated in the same unfavourable manner. In the case of exit taxation, the Court has argued on the grounds of discrimination or has used a comparison to the purely domestic situation without finding the exit tax explicitly discriminatory.[84] This line of argument is possibly easier to sell. But even if the national legislature decided to treat national cases alike, a domestic exit tax would have to be qualified as a restriction of the market freedoms, which may under certain circumstances be justified. It is the exercise of the freedom (that being the move from one Member State to another one) which triggers taxation. Therefore, the tax is not problematic per se, but the fact that it puts a burden on the free movement of taxpayers clashes with the free movement rights. Whether or not moving within the Member State would also be subject to tax does not change the picture.[85] In the words of Advocate General Jacobs: '[i]f an obstacle to inter-State trade exists, it cannot cease to exist simply because an identical obstacle affects domestic trade'.[86] The European legislature has now harmonised exit taxation at a European level. The Anti-Tax Avoidance Directive (ATAD) allows the Member States to levy an exit tax under certain circumstances.[87] The common legislative approach may allow the outweighing of market values to a greater extent than Member States are allowed to do within their unilateral measures,[88] and thus the European legislature may go beyond a codification of the CJEU case law.

[84] CJEU, 11 May 2004, C-9/02, *Hughes de Lasteyrie du Saillant*, ECLI:EU:C:2004:138, para 46; CJEU, 7 September 2006, C-470/04, N, ECLI:EU:C:2006:525, paras 35–37; CJEU, 29 November 2011, C-371/10, *National Grid Indus*, ECLI:EU:C:2011:785, para 37.

[85] Hanns Hügel, 'Grenzüberschreitende Umgründungen, Sitzverlegung und Wegzug im Lichte der Änderung der Fusionsrichtlinie und der neueren EuGH-Judikatur' in Elisabeth König and Walter Schwarzinger (eds), *Körperschaften im Steuerrecht: Festschrift für Werner Wiesner zum 65. Geburtstag* 193. This may also be indicated by some parts of the CJEU case law: CJEU, 11 May 2004, C-9/02, *Hughes de Lasteyrie du Saillant*, ECLI:EU:C:2004:138, para 45; CJEU, 12 July 2012, C-269/09, *Commission v Spain*, ECLI:EU:C:2012:439, para 56.

[86] Opinion of Advocate General Jacobs, 24 November 1994, C-412/93, *Leclerc-Siplec*, ECLI:EU:C:1994:394, para 39.

[87] Art 5 of the Council Directive, 12 July 2016, 2016/1164/EU, laying down rules against tax avoidance practices that directly affect the functioning of the internal market, OJ, 19 July 2016, L 193, 1.

[88] See this chapter Part I, subsection D.

4. Prohibiting Market Access through a Total Ban on Services, Goods, or Establishments

Accessing a new market is prohibited in cases where the trade in certain goods or services is forbidden, such as through the prohibition of lotteries, the ban on the sale of drugs, or the existence of a statutory monopoly. The CJEU accepts that Member States disallow the selling of particular substances such as drugs and that they enter into a common agreement to prevent illicit drug trafficking.[89] Less stringent regulations of some Member States on 'soft' drugs do not make a soft drug per se marketable.[90] However, if a general agreement or understanding between the Member States on the illegitimacy of certain products does not exist, the total ban of services or products, for example not granting the authorisation to run a laser drome, constitutes a restriction of the fundamental freedoms.[91]

In this vein, the Court ruled that national laws may restrict the fundamental freedoms if the trading of particular services or goods is not prohibited per se, but the services or goods may only be provided by a particular institution, such as the national lottery. In the *Schindler* case, the CJEU ruled that lotteries may be subject to particularly strict regulations and close control by the public authorities; however, 'they are not totally prohibited'[92] and thus a restriction of these services to national entities infringes on the market freedoms.

From this it follows that Member States can commonly agree or find a common understanding that certain goods or services are not marketable. A total ban of these products from a Member State's market does not restrict the fundamental freedoms even if one Member State softens its regulatory framework for those goods and services. Accordingly, Member States are allowed to decide jointly that certain goods or services have to be considered harmful to the society and thus should not be allowed to be traded on the national market or on the European internal market as a whole. However, if only a single Member State imposes a total ban on goods or services, the ban restricts the free movement of these goods and services. The CJEU does not consider the aim and purpose of the ban for the purpose of ruling on the restrictive nature. However, the aim and purpose may be considered at the justification stage. Likewise, if the trade in some particular services or goods is not prohibited in full, but only allowed for some agencies or market player, the fundamental freedoms are infringed.

Likewise, the CJEU found that national rules delaying the distribution of films by means of video-cassettes during the first month following their release in the cinema to protect their exploitation do not per se constitute obstacles to intra-EU

[89] Council, 25 October 2004, Framework decision 2004/757/JHA, laying down minimum provisions on the constituent elements of criminal acts and penalties in the field of illicit drug trafficking, OJ, 11 November 2004, L 335, 8.

[90] CJEU, 16 December 2010, C-137/09, *Josemans*, ECLI:EU:C:2010:774, para 41.

[91] CJEU, 14 October 2004, C-36/02, *Omega*, ECLI:EU:C:2004:614, para 28.

[92] CJEU, 24 March 1994, C-275/92, *Schindler*, ECLI:EU:C:1994:119, para 31.

trade. This is because all Member States have such rules in place and they do not have the 'purpose of regulating trade patterns' as the rules apply to both video-cassettes manufactured in the national territory and to imported video-cassettes.[93] However, 'the application of such a system may create barriers to intra-Community [intra-EU] trade in video-cassettes because of the disparities between the systems operated in the different Member States and between the conditions of the release of cinematographic works in the cinemas of these States'.[94]

A slight variation of these examples is the Austrian needs test for granting a licence to open a pharmacy.[95] This needs test is a survey on how many pharmacies exist in a particular area and how many people live therein. The law stipulates that a pharmacy is needed if there are more than 5,500 permanent inhabitants in a particular area. Accordingly, market access is only allowed if and to the extent that there is a need for a pharmacy in a particular area. The national rule does not ban particular goods or services from the market. It does, however, restrict the right to establish a pharmacy in a certain area if there is a lack of a qualified need for it.

5. Rendering Intra-EU Trade Less Attractive—Far-reaching Liberalisation of National Markets

Besides these two categories of non-discriminatory market access restrictions (rules hindering the exercise of the free movement rights[96] and a total ban on certain goods and services[97]), the CJEU has held that some national regulatory rules constitute a restriction of the market freedoms because they render the exercise of free movement less attractive.[98] National rules constitute a market access restriction of the foreign market if they forbid the contacting of new clients via phone both at home and in all other Member States (cold calling),[99] if the national company law allows granting some shareholders specific control rights (golden shares),[100] or if collective redundancies are restricted to specific circumstances.[101] These national rules do not differentiate between a purely domestic situation and a cross-border setting. Nor do they impose a second regulatory layer on the market player when accessing the market, burden the act of moving, or ban certain goods

[93] CJEU, 11 July 1985, *Cinéthèque SA*, ECLI:EU:C:1985:329, para 21.

[94] ibid para 22.

[95] CJEU, 13 February 2014, C-367/12, *Sokoll-Seebacher*, ECLI:EU:C:2014:68.

[96] See this chapter Part I, subsection C.I.3.

[97] See this chapter Part I, subsection C.I.4.

[98] This emphasises the efficiency objective of undistorted decision-making internal market: Gammie (n 77) 141 et seq.

[99] CJEU, 10 May 1995, C-384/92, *Alpine Investments*, ECLI:EU:C:1995:126, para 2.

[100] CJEU, 6 December 2007, C-463/04 and C-464/04, *Federconsumatori*, ECLI:EU:C:2007:752; CJEU, 26. March 2009, C-326/07, *Commission v Italy*, ECLI:EU:C:2009:193; CJEU, 8 July 2010, C-171/08, *Commission v Portugal*, ECLI:EU:C:2010:412; CJEU, 11 November 2010, *Commission v Portugal*, ECLI:EU:C:2010:669; CJEU, 10 November 2011, C-212/09, *Commission v Portugal*, ECLI:EU:C:2011:717. In this vein see also CJEU, 13 May 2003, C-98/01, *Commission v United Kingdom*, ECLI:EU:C:2003:273, para 47.

[101] CJEU, 21 December 2016, C-201/15, *AGET Iraklis*, ECLI:EU:C:2016:972.

and services entirely from the market. However, the strict regulation may prevent foreign market players from accessing the market and the CJEU has therefore found these rules to restrict the fundamental freedoms.[102]

Against this background, national rules can constitute market access restrictions if they have particularly deterrent effects. If the limited possibility of collective redundancies, the prohibition of cold calling, and the reservation of special participation rights constitute a restriction of the fundamental freedoms, one may wonder whether the levying of taxes or special charges also renders the exercise of the market freedoms less attractive and thus constitutes a restriction of the fundamental freedoms.[103] Any special tax or charge burdens foreign goods, services, persons, or capital and thus may prevent market players to access the market.

Initially, CJEU case law did not give a clear picture on whether or not the levying of a tax or special charge renders the exercise of a market freedom less attractive. In the *De Coster* case,[104] the CJEU found a Belgian municipal tax on satellite dishes to infringe on the freedom to provide services. The tax aimed to prevent an 'uncontrolled proliferation' of those satellite dishes and was levied on any satellite dish regardless of where it had been produced. It was, however, argued that broadcasters established in Belgium enjoy unlimited access to cable distribution of their programmes and the use of cable was not taxed. Broadcasters from other Member States could only transmit their programmes via satellite. The limited access of foreign broadcasters to cable and the need for satellite dishes to transmit foreign programmes led to indirect discrimination against foreign broadcasters, and thus only the tax on satellite dishes was found incompatible with the freedom to provide services.[105]

Advocate General Colomer argued that regardless of the discriminatory nature of the tax, a tax on satellite dishes must infringe the market freedoms because it 'may discourage viewers or make the conditions for receiving television programmes by satellite more onerous'.[106] He therefore categorised the tax on satellite dishes as a barrier to the freedom to provide services regardless of how national broadcasters are affected. But, as mentioned above, the Court ruled that the tax was only inconsistent with the market freedoms because of its discriminatory nature.

In the *Viacom Outdoor* case,[107] the CJEU could not rely on unlawful discrimination when it was asked whether an Italian municipal advertising tax was in line

[102] Menelaos Markakis, 'Can Governments Control Mass Layoffs by Employers? Economic Freedoms vs Labour Rights in Case C-201/15 AGET Iraklis' (2017) 13 European Constitutional Law Review 724, 733 argues that the 'common thread running through the case law in this area is the Court's embrace of the Säger "market access"'.

[103] For a critical view see Juliane Kokott and Hartmut Ost, 'Europäische Grundfreiheiten und nationales Steuerrecht' (2011) Europäische Zeitschrift für Wirtschaftsrecht 496, 496.

[104] CJEU, 29 November 2001, C-17/00, *De Coster*, ECLI:EU:C:2001:651.

[105] ibid paras 35 and 38.

[106] Opinion of Advocate General Colomer, 28 June 2001, C-17/00, *De Coster*, ECLI:EU:C:2001:366, para 134.

[107] CJEU, 17 February 2005, C-134/03, *Viacom Outdoor*, ECLI:EU:C:2005:94.

with the freedom to provide services. This tax was levied on bill-posting services. First, the Court found that the tax did not discriminate against any foreign service provider, and thus the tax did not draw 'any distinction based on the place of establishment of the provider or recipient of the bill-posting service or on the place of origin of the goods or services that form the subject-matter of the advertising messages disseminated'.[108] The Court went on to argue that the tax was levied at a fixed amount 'which may be considered *modest* in relation to the value of the services provided'.[109] Therefore, the CJEU ruled that the tax on bill posting did not infringe the freedom to provide services.[110]

In the aftermath of the *Viacom Outdoor* case, it was unclear whether the tax was in line with the market freedoms because it did not discriminate against foreigners and cross-border services or because the tax was considered 'modest'. In the later *Mobistar* case,[111] the Court made it crystal clear that the levying of a tax is not a restriction of the fundamental freedoms per se, even though it may be an obstacle to free trade within the internal market.[112] In *Mobistar*, the CJEU was asked whether imposing a tax on transmission pylons, masts, and antennae for the Global System for Mobile Communications (GSM) infringes the freedom to provide services. First, the Court referred to its settled case law, according to which the market freedoms, in that particular case the freedom to provide services, require both the elimination of all discriminations on the grounds of nationality and the abolition of any restriction.[113] Secondly, the Court referred to its earlier ruling in *de Coster* where the indirect discriminatory treatment of a tax was found to infringe a market freedom. Thirdly, the CJEU stressed that the tax at hand did not directly or indirectly discriminate against foreigners or the providing of cross-border services and thus the tax did not infringe the freedom to provide services. The only effect of taxing transmission pylons, masts, and antennae for GSM is 'to create additional costs in respect of the services in question' and these costs 'affect in the same way the provision of services between Member States and that within one Member State', and thus, these taxes 'do not fall within the scope of Art 59 of the Treaty'.[114]

108 ibid para 37.

109 ibid para 38, emphasis added.

110 More explicit: Opinion of Advocate General Kokott, 28 October 2004, C-134/03, *Viacom Outdoor*, ECLI:EU:C:2004:676, para 62 ('If this approach is adopted and national duties are seen as restrictions of fundamental freedoms, then, in the final analysis, all duties, no matter what kind, would have to be examined against Community law; the Member States would then potentially be required in each individual case to show that their duties were justified for compelling reasons in the general interest, i.e. reasonable, necessary and proportionate with the aims pursued').

111 CJEU, 8 September 2005, C-544/03 und C-545/03, *Mobistar and Belgacom Mobile*, ECLI:EU:C:2005:518.

112 See also Opinion of Advocate General Kokott, 21 December 2011, C-498/10, *X*, ECLI:EU:C:2011:870, para 28; Opinion of Advocate General Kokott, 5 September 2013, C-385/12, *Hervis*, ECLI:EU:C:2013:531, para 83.

113 ibid para 29.

114 ibid para 31.

The *Berlington Hungary*[115] case does not change the outcome. The case concerned a flat tax on the operation of slot machines outside casinos and a proportional tax on the net quarterly revenue from each slot machine. The new taxes on slot machines heavily burdened undertakings in that business area and the taxes were introduced without a transitional period allowing such business operators to adjust their business models. The facts of the case make it quite clear that the national tax on slot machines was a regulatory measure and not an ordinary tax.[116] Therefore, the Court's ruling, according to which the tax constitutes a restriction of the fundamental freedoms, must not be read in a general fashion.

In *Vorarlberger Landes- und Hypothekenbank AG*, the CJEU confirmed its previous ruling by finding the Austrian stability charge compatible with the fundamental freedoms as 'the mere fact that those charges are liable to increase banking transaction costs cannot constitute an impediment to the freedom to provide services'.[117]

6. Conclusions on the Impact of Non-market Values on Market Access Restrictions

The vast majority of market access restrictions have a discriminatory element as the national rules (of the host Member State) do not consider that the foreign goods, services, persons, or capital have already complied with the regulatory regime in the home Member States. The regulatory regimes of the home and the host Member State may be different in substance, but they have the same underlying objective. Ignoring the efforts of complying with the regulatory standards in the home Member State and making the goods, services, persons, and capital comply with the domestic regulatory regime (as a second layer) is not per se necessary to achieve the regulatory objective. In double burden cases, the CJEU necessarily recognises the aim and purpose of the national rules, and only if both regimes aim for the same objectives does the double burden constitutes an infringement of the fundamental freedoms. In other words, if the national regulatory measures aim to protect non-market values which are not yet protected by the regulatory regime of the home Member States, the host Member States are allowed to force compliance with the domestic regime without imposing market access restrictions.

115 CJEU, 11 June 2015, C-98/14, *Berlington Hungary*, ECLI:EU:C:2015:386.

116 For the regulatory character of the tax see para 41 of the ruling: 'That would be the case [the existence of a restriction] if the referring court found that the tax increase provided for by the amending Law of 2011 had the effect of restricting the operation of slot machines to casinos, to which that increase did not apply. Thus, it is claimed, that increase produced an effect comparable to that of prohibiting the operation of slot machines outside casinos, which settled case-law considers to be a restriction on the freedom to provide services' and para 49 'whether national legislation such as the amending Law of 2012 restricts the free movement of goods and the freedom to provide services in so far as it prohibits the operation of slot machines outside casinos'.

117 CJEU, 22 November 2018, C-625/17, *Vorarlberger Landes- und Hypothekenbank AG*, ECLI:EU:2018:939, para 32.

However, national measures may also impose non-discriminatory market access restrictions. Such restrictions hamper intra-EU trade not because they impose a more burdensome treatment on foreign goods, services, persons, and capital, but because they make the market access less attractive. Identifying the 'less attractiveness' does not demand a recourse to the aim and purpose of the law, as it follows from the burdening of the free movement act or an entire ban of certain goods and services. Only in a minor set of cases has the CJEU gone beyond these two categories of non-discriminatory market access restrictions and found national measures to impose market access restrictions because they are not sufficiently liberal.

7. Findings on Market Access Restrictions in the Field of National Tax Laws

Tax sovereignty still rests in the hands of the Member States. They are allowed to impose national taxes and decide what to tax and how to tax it; accordingly, they are free to define the tax event, the tax base, and the tax rate. Despite being sovereign in the field of taxation, the national rules are subject to scrutiny under the fundamental freedoms, and thus every national tax law has to comply with the European guarantees of the free movement of goods, services, persons, and capital.

In that respect, the CJEU has explicitly ruled that the levying of national taxes does not contradict the fundamental freedoms because the mere existence of taxes cannot be understood as making cross-border economic activities less attractive.[118] In the case of double taxation, the second tax layer does not infringe the fundamental freedoms either, as a second layer of regulation might do. The Court has recognised the underlying purpose of national substantive tax law rules, this being the raising of revenue in the absence of any (additional) steering effects. Contrary to regulatory norms, the aim and purpose of substantive tax laws cannot be satisfied through the levying of taxes in a fellow Member State. Taxes have a pure self-serving purpose, and thus, the concept of mutual recognition developed in CJEU case law is not applicable to the field of taxation. This is not the result of a need for a special application of the fundamental freedoms in the field of taxation because of sovereignty concerns, it is simply because the aim and purpose of taxation cannot be achieved by levying taxes in another Member State. In contrast, a regulatory aim such as product safety can be ensured by the regulatory framework of another Member State.

Having said this, substantive Member State tax rules can constitute restrictions of the fundamental freedoms by levying a special charge or a special tax on the very act of moving. If the very act which is necessary to make use of the free movement rights guaranteed by the European treaties is burdened, the fundamental freedoms

[118] See also Douma and Engelen (n 44) 196 et seq.

are infringed regardless of how purely domestic economic activity would be taxed and regardless of the national law's underlying purpose.

Administrative tax laws are different from substantive tax laws; the principle of mutual recognition can be applied because the bookkeeping and information disclosure serve the same purpose in both the home and the host Member State—these tools should provide the tax authorities with the information they need. Accordingly, additional burdens in these areas may very well be addressed by forcing one Member State to recognise the efforts of the taxpayer to comply with the administrative standards of a fellow Member State, and particularly harsh administrative tax law rules of a Member State may make a cross-border economic activity less attractive. This outcome is relevant to the concept of enhanced cooperation in two ways: it shows the necessity of further legislation to improve the internal market and identifies possible limits of such legislation.

II. Second Step: Comparability

The promise of the European Union to unite its Member States but still allow them to be diverse is also honoured in the application of the fundamental freedoms on the comparability level. For this purpose, the aim of the national law builds the framework for finding the *tertium comparationis*, and thus, the objects of the national legislature have a significant impact on deciding whether or not the national laws are in line with the fundamental freedoms.

In the CJEU's earlier case law, the Court used the comparability test to identify whether or not the law of a single Member State restricts or even discriminates cross-border economic activities. A national rule would only constitute a restriction of the free movement of goods, services, persons, or capital if the law treated the comparable purely domestic setting more favourably.[119] In its more recent case law, the Court asks the comparability question when it has already been established that the national rule imposes a restriction on the free movement provisions.[120] There are few cases in which the CJEU does not touch on the comparability question at all.[121] Applying the comparability test at a

[119] For example, CJEU, 25 February 2010, C-337/08, *X Holding*, ECLI:EU:C:2010:89, para 22; CJEU, 27 November 2008, C-418/07, *Société Papillon*, ECLI:EU:C:2008:659, para 27; CJEU, 18 July 2007, C231/05, *Oy AA*, ECLI:EU:C:2007:439, para 38.

[120] CJEU, 6 September 2012, C-18/11, *Philips Electronics*, ECLI:EU:C:2012:532, paras 16–17; CJEU, 21 February 2012, C-123/11, *A Oy*, ECLI:EU:C:2013:84, paras 32–33; CJEU, 30 June 2016, C-176/15, *Riskin and Timmermans*, ECLI:EU:C:2016:488, paras 25 and 28; CJEU, 22 February 2018, C-398/16 and C-399/16, *X BV and X NV*, ECLI:EU:C:2018:110, para 32; Opinion of Advocate General, 5 June 2019, C-641/17, *College Pension Plan of British Columbia*, ECLI:EU:C:2019:463, para 60 et seq.

[121] CJEU, 15 May 2008, C-414/06, *Lidl Belgium*, ECLI:EU:C:2008:278; CJEU, 23 October 2008, C-157/07, *Krankenheim Ruhesitz am Wannsee-Seniorenheimstatt*, ECLI:EU:C:2008:588; CJEU, 4 July 2013, *Argenta Spaarbank NV*, ECLI:EU:C:2013:447. Opinion of Advocate General Kokott, 13 March

later stage has the effect that comparability becomes a part of the justification stage.[122]

At first glance, one might say that it does not make any difference whether national trade obstacles are allowed to stand either because the cross-border situation is not comparable with the purely domestic one or because the obstacle is justified. In both cases, the national rule is in line with the market freedoms regardless of whether it is a justified discrimination or restriction, or not a discrimination or restriction at all. There is, however, one fundamental difference. A discriminatory or restrictive national rule is allowed to stand if it is justified and if the national measure is proportionate. The proportionality test only applies if the rule is found to discriminate or restrict at the outset. This may matter in cases where different national measures are available and the national legislature chooses the most restrictive one.

Either way, the CJEU recognises the legislative goals of the Member States through the comparability test. Whether the comparability test should systematically form a part of the justification stage or should be used beforehand to identify a restriction or discrimination is not within the scope of this study and will therefore not be substantially be discussed.

The following subsections present the case law of the CJEU on whether, and if so to what extent, the CJEU takes the aim and purpose of the national laws into account when finding the *tertium comparationis*, thereby allowing non-market goals of the Member States to influence the application of the fundamental freedoms (see subsection 1). The legitimacy of the CJEU's general approach is scrutinised by showing alternatives which are used more rarely by the CJEU, to find the 'right' *tertium comparationis* (see subsection 2). Against this background it will be argued that the concept of the European internal market demands a comparability test which finds the *tertium comparationis* based on the aim and purpose of the national law and which works as a filter to prevent non-protectionist national laws from being scrutinised (see subsection 3). The aim and purpose of the national law may determine the benchmark for the comparison, but it does not define the scope of the comparability test (see subsection 4). The preceding question of which situations are open to a comparison under the fundamental freedoms is predominantly answered by the aim and purpose of the fundamental freedoms. The fundamental freedoms only consider the legislative framework of a single Member State (single country perspective). An overall approach can only be applied if the Member States explicitly link their national legislative system with the legal treatment in a fellow Member State (see subsection 4.a). Moreover, the

2014, C-48/13, *Nordea Bank*, ECLI:EU:C:2014:153, para 21 et. seq, criticising the CJEU's inconsistent application of the comparability test.

[122] See for example CJEU, 22 November 2018, C-575/17, *Sofia*, ECLI:EU:C:2018:94, para 42 et seq; CJEU, 30 June 2016, C-176/15, *Riskin and Timmermans*, ECLI:EU:C:2016:488, para 27 et seq.

fundamental freedoms allow a horizontal comparison, but the market freedoms honour bilateral agreements between the Member States by accepting a different treatment of cross-border economic activities between different Member States (see subsection 4.b).

1. Comparability in the CJEU Case Law

The identification of two comparable situations may be different if undertaken through the lens of the national legislature or pursued based purely on efficiency considerations. In that respect, CJEU case law is not entirely consistent. It very much depends on which area of national law is tested against the market freedoms. In general, however, the CJEU does not put too much emphasis on finding the equivalent 'purely domestic' setting.[123] In most cases, the Court simply finds that the national rule hinders cross-border trade and thus infringes one of the market freedoms. Then, the Court moves directly on and examines whether the national rules are justified and thus are allowed to stand.

In tax law, the picture is ambiguous. On the one hand, the CJEU follows its usual path and finds a cross-border economic activity or a non-resident taxpayer simply comparable with the equivalent purely domestic undertaking or resident taxpayer. On the other hand, the Court puts a great deal of effort into finding the correct *tertium comparationis*. In the latter cases, the CJEU considers the aim, purpose, or object of the national rule in order to determine what can and cannot be compared.[124] The aim and purpose of the law must, however, not conflict with the internal market as such. Accordingly, the mere aim to protect revenue or the domestic industry (in other words, economic values)[125] is not a legitimate aim[126] and thus cannot be the determining factor to find the *tertium comparationis*.

In the academic literature, there is the attempt to categorise CJEU case law concerning the objectives that might have influenced the Court's decision on whether

[123] Opinion of Advocate General Kokott, 13 March 2014, C-48/13, *Nordea Bank*, ECLI:EU:C:2014:153, para 21 et. seq; Joachim Englisch, 'Comment on ECJ 17.7.2014 (Nordea Bank)' (2014) Highlights & Insights on European Taxation 10; Joachim Englisch, 'Nordea Bank—ein weiterer Meilenstein der EuGH-Judikatur' (2014) Internationales Steuerrecht 561; Joachim Englisch, 'Grundfreiheiten: Vergleichbarkeit, Rechtfertigung und Verhältnismäßigkeit', *Europäisches Steuerrecht*, vol 41 (Dr Otto Schmidt Verlag 2018) 276 et seq. For the application of the fundamental freedoms outside tax law see Craig and Búrca (n 37) 639 et seq.

[124] See for example CJEU, 18 July 2007, C-231/05, *Oy AA*, ECLI:EU:C:2007:439, para 38; CJEU, 25 February 2010, C-337/08, *X Holding*, ECLI:EU:C:2010:89, para 22; CJEU, 20 September 2018, C-685/16, *EV*, ECLI:EU:C:2018:743, para 88; CJEU, 4 July 2018, C-28/17, *NN*, EU:C:2018:526, para 31; CJEU, 12 June 2018, C-650/16, *Bevola*, EU:C:2018:424, para 32; CJEU, 22 June 2017, C-20/16, *Bechtel*, EU:C:2017:488, para 53; CJEU, 12 June 2014, C-39/13, C-40/13, and C-41/13, *SCA Group Holding*, EU:C:2014:1758, para 28, CJEU, 25 February 2010, C-337/08, *X Holding*, EU:C:2010:89, para 22; CJEU, 2 June 2016, C-252/14, *Pensioenfonds Metaal en Techniek*, EU:C:2016:402, para 48; CJEU, 18 June 2015, C-9/14, *Kieback*, EU:C:2015:406, para 21; CJEU, 8 November 2012, C-342/10, *Commission v Finland*, EU:C:2012:688, para 36; CJEU, 10 May 2012, C-39/10, *Commission v Estland*, EU:C:2012:282, para 51.

[125] See this chapter Part I, subsections C.III.1 and D.III.1.

[126] CJEU, 14 November 1995, C-484/93, *Svensson and Gustavsson*, ECLI:EU:C:1995:379, para 15; CJEU, 11 September 2007, C-76/05, *Schwarz*, ECLI:EU:C:2007:492, paras 78–80.

or not the purely domestic and the cross-border situation can be compared.[127] It is true that the CJEU sometimes, like in *Schumacker*, refers to factual circumstances when determining whether or not a resident and a non-resident taxpayer are in a comparable situation.[128] However, the Court always looks at the aim and purpose of the national law to identify whether these factual circumstances allow for equal treatment.

Likewise, in all of the outbound dividend cases, the CJEU has ruled that from the home Member State's perspective of the company which issues the dividends, resident and non-resident shareholders may not per se be in a comparable situation when it comes to the relief of economic double taxation. The Member State may only be forced to apply its national relief mechanism if the Member State taxes the outbound dividends.[129] The economic double taxation is only triggered within one Member State where the Member State decides to tax outbound dividend flows. If this Member State should decide not to tax dividends flowing out of its territory, the Member State cannot be obliged to grant relief from juridical double taxation which follows from levying taxes at a company level in the company's home Member State and the levying of taxes at shareholder level in the home Member State of these shareholders. From the perspective of the company's home Member State, no economic double taxation exists. 'Subject to tax' is the only relevant factor to determine whether or not a purely domestic and a cross-border situation are comparable because the aim and purpose of the national law is to eliminate economic double taxation. If the national rule aims to prevent economic double taxation, the company's resident Member State must tax the outbound dividends both at the company and shareholder level to allow the national relief mechanism to apply. Otherwise, there is no economic double taxation allowing a comparison with economic double taxation in a purely domestic setting.

2. Comparability—Alternatives Routes

Looking at the aim and purpose of the national law for determining comparability allows one to recognise the national non-market values underlying the law but

[127] Peter J Wattel, 'Non-Discrimination à la Court: The ECJ's (Lack of) Comparability Analysis in Direct Tax Cases' in Guglielmo Maisto, Pasquale Pistone, and Dennis Weber (eds), *Non-discrimination in Tax Treaties: Selected Issues from a Global Perspective* (IBFD 2016) 261 et seq. Szudoczky, *The Sources of EU Law* (n 1) 528 et seq. Englisch, 'Grundfreiheiten: Vergleichbarkeit, Rechtfertigung und Verhältnismäßigkeit' (n 123) 278 et seq.

[128] Michael Lang, 'Recent Case Law of the ECJ in Direct Taxation: Trends, Tensions, and Contradictions' (2009) 18 EC Tax Review 98, 101 et seq listing the relevant cases where the Court refers to factual circumstances and providing fundamental critique.

[129] CJEU, 14 December 2006, C-170/05, *Denkavit*, ECLI:EU:C:2006:783, paras 34–36; CJEU, 3 June 2010, C-487/08, *Commission v Spain*, ECLI:EU:C:2010:310, paras 50–51; CJEU, 20 October 2011, C-284/09, *Commission v Germany*, ECLI:EU:C:2011:670, paras 55 56; CJEU, 17 September 2015, C-10/14, C-14/14, and C-17/14, *Miljoen*, ECLI:EU:C:2015:608, para 67. In the *Sofina* case, the CJEU ruled that the Member States taxing outbound dividend flows is also required to grant non-resident companies the same cash-flow advantages as domestic companies: CJEU, 22 November 2018, C-575/17, *Sofia*, ECLI:EU:C:2018:943, para 29 et seq.

simultaneously has some serious shortcomings. First, it may not always be too easy for the CJEU to determine the aim and purpose of a national measure with any precision, particularly in cases where the national rule is an exception to the general system, or even worse, an exception to the exception. Secondly, it may well be that the national rule simply has more than one objective.[130] If this is the case, should both objectives be considered in finding the right *tertium comparationis* or should one prevail over the other? Giving one objective priority over the other may be arbitrary; why should one dominate the other? Or is it possible to ascertain one main object for every national rule? On the other hand, taking both objectives into account may make the analysis unworkable, especially in those cases where the different objectives demand a different comparator.

In light of the difficulties in finding the right *tertium comparationis* the critique on the definitive outcome of the comparability approach becomes even more sophisticated. The outcome of the comparability approach is definitive because in cases where comparability is denied (eg in *Truck Center*),[131] the Member States are free to decide on how differently they want to treat the non-comparable situations.[132] In other words, as soon as two situations are found to be non-comparable, the fundamental freedoms do not determine the extent to which the differences between the situations permit a different treatment. The definitive outcome is particularly challenging when considering the fact that the outcome of what is and what is not comparable depends on the perspective one takes. A different perspective on withholding taxes may allow Member States to apply different procedures of charging tax to resident and non-resident taxpayers,[133] but may create an obstacle to intra-EU trade by imposing an obligation on the recipient of services to make retention at source of the tax on the payment made to the non-resident provider of the service.[134]

There are two alternative routes to the objective-based comparability test. First, the comparator could be found based on a pure competition-based approach, or second, a restriction of the market freedoms could be ascertained without any

[130] CJEU, 6 October 2015, C-66/14, *IFN-Holding AG*, ECLI:EU:C:2015:661, para 32: 'the Austrian legislature intended to create a tax incentive for the creation of groups of companies [first purpose] by ensuring equal treatment between the purchase of the establishment ("asset deal") and the purchase of the holding in the company that owns the establishment ("share deal") [second purpose]'.

[131] CJEU, 22 December 2008, C-282/07, *Truck Center*, ECLI:EU:C:2008:762.

[132] Lang, 'Recent Case Law of the ECJ in Direct Taxation' (n 128) 100–01; Richard Lyal, 'Non-Discrimination and Direct Tax in Community Law' (2003) 12 EC Tax Review 68, 69; Michael Lang, 'Eine Wende in der Rechtsprechung des EuGH zu den direkten Steuern?' in Michael Hebig, Wilhelm H Wacker, and Peter Bareis (eds), *Aktuelle Entwicklungsaspekte der Unternehmensbesteuerung: Festschrift für Wilhelm H. Wacker zum 75. Geburtstag* (Erich Schmidt Verlag 2006) 369; Karin Simader, *Withholding Taxes and the Fundamental Freedoms* (Kluwer Law International 2013) 135; Lang, 'Direct Taxation' (n 48) 422 arguing that '[t]here is no reason why justifications and the principle of proportionality should not be considered if different situations are treated differently'.

[133] CJEU, 22 December 2008, C-282/07, *Truck Center*, ECLI:EU:C:2008:762, para 42 et seq.

[134] CJEU, 3 October 2006, *Scorpio*, ECLI:EU:C:2006:630, paras 33–34; see also Christoph Marchgraber, *Double (Non-)Taxation and EU Law* (Kluwer Law International 2018) 111 et seq.

findings on the objective comparability of the domestic and the cross-border situation.

As regards the first approach, it has been argued in the literature that the fundamental freedoms should not operate as a general anti-discrimination clause, meaning that the question of what should and should not be compared with each other should not be determined by the national rule which is tested against the fundamental freedoms.[135] Supporters of the first approach argue that the market freedoms have their own agenda[136] and thus are capable of finding the right comparator without any reference to the aim and purpose of the national rule. It is the internal market which should build the framework for finding which pure domestic and which cross-border situation could and should be compared. Since a core goal of the internal market is free competition, it is competitive equality which is key.[137]

The opinion of Advocate General Kokott in the *Nordea Bank* case outlines the second approach. According to her, there is 'no need to examine the objective comparability of the situations'[138] and thus the traditional approach on establishing comparability—in particular to examine whether the national rule discriminates, and thus, constitutes a restriction of the fundamental freedoms—is outdated. Advocate General Kokott is particularly critical of the possibility of using the same line of argumentation at the comparability stage and at the justification stage.[139]

[135] Englisch, 'Grundfreiheiten: Vergleichbarkeit, Rechtfertigung und Verhältnismäßigkeit' (n 123) 286 et seq.

[136] Mason (n 33) 93 arguing that '[t]o give the equality principle meaning, the Court's comparisons must make consistent reference to outside standards by which equality can be judged'. However, these standards 'must be determined with reference to the goals underlying the prohibition on tax discrimination'.

[137] Joachim Englisch, *Wettbewerbsgleichheit im grenzüberschreitenden Handel: mit Schlussfolgerungen für indirekte Steuern* (Mohr Siebeck 2008) 293 et seq.

[138] Opinion of Advocate General Kokott, 13 March 2014, C-48/13, *Nordea Bank*, ECLI:EU:C:2014:153, para 28.

[139] The CJEU case law on the different techniques for taxing dividends is not entirely consistent with respect to the comparability and justification stages. In the *Brisal* case, the CJEU found that withholding taxes imposed on non-resident taxpayers constitute a restriction of the fundamental freedoms but may be justified (CJEU, 13 June 2016, C-18/15, *Brisal*, ECLI:EU:C:2016:549, para 22). In *Truck Center* and *Pensioenfonds Metaal en Techniek*, however, the CJEU found the non-resident and the resident shareholder not to be comparable in the light of the aim and purpose of the national law (CJEU, 22 December 2008, C-282/07, *Truck Center SA*, ECLI:EU:C:2008:762, para 47; CJEU, 2 June 2016, C-252/14, *Pensioenfonds Metaal en Techniek*, ECLI:EU:C:2016:401, para 63); Luc de Broe and Niels Bammens, 'Truck Center: Belgian Withholding Tax on Interest Payments to Non-Resident Companies Does Not Violate EC Law: A Critical Look at the ECJ's Judgment in Truck Center' (2009) 18 EC Tax Review 131, 133 criticising the CJEU to deny comparability; in their view, 'the Court should have first confirmed the comparability of the situations as it did in previous judgments on the ground that the source state taxes the resident and the non-resident on the same type of income (interest) and that, from the payer's perspective, the source state treats interest payments to resident and non-resident lenders alike, that is, in both instances, a deduction is allowed ... It should then have concluded that there was a different treatment to the detriment of the non-resident lender. Subsequently, it should have tested whether the administrative burden imposed on the tax authorities of the source state could justify the discrimination'. See in that vein also Giorgio Beretta, 'The Brisal and KBC Finance Decision: Once Again the CJEU Assesses the Compatibility with EU Law of Gross Withholding Taxation of Non-Residents' (2017) 26 EC Tax Review 193, 196. Niels Bammens, *The Principle of Non-Discrimination in International and*

Since the CJEU recognises unwritten grounds of justification there is no longer a need to use the comparability test as a first layer of justification.[140]

3. Comparability—Which Way to Go?

There are several ways of finding a *tertium comparationis* to determine whether or not a national rule infringes the market freedoms. There are very good reasons why there should not be too much emphasis on the comparability test to determine whether the national law constitutes a restriction of the fundamental freedoms: first, a strict comparability test which takes the aim and purpose of the national law into account would not allow the CJEU to weigh the interests of the European internal market and the non-market values of the Member States at the proportionality stage. Secondly, a strict comparability test would be specific to tax law. In all other areas of law, the CJEU does not investigate the aim and purpose of the national law to find the comparator. Accordingly, abolishing the strict comparability test would foster an equal application of the market freedoms in the various fields of the law.

Having said this, there are even better reasons for maintaining a comparability test which considers the aim and purpose of the national rule. The internal market may aim for efficiency and an open market economy with free competition,[141] but at the same time the internal market allows all Member States to preserve their national identities. If this promise is taken seriously, a thoughtful balancing act has to be undertaken between the national values and the internal market needs in all fields of law. However, such a serious balancing cannot be undertaken at the justification stage alone. The comparability stage works as a filter to stop scrutinising non-protectionist national laws. The filter function of the comparability test ensures that regulatory attempts of Member States are not jeopardised as such;[142] Member States are allowed to take regulatory measures if they think they are necessary. An objective comparison which does not consider the aim of the national legislature may, however, be capable of compromising this concession because one can only determine whether or not the national law is truly supposed to be

European Tax Law (2012) 990 et seq arguing that the objectives of the national law can be considered at the comparability level or level of justification; Michael Lang, 'Das EuGH-Urteil in der Rechtssache D.—Gerät der Motor der Steuerharmonisierung ins Stottern?' (2005) Steuer und Wirtschaft International 356, 369; considering the aim and purpose of the law (only) at the comparability level would align the non-discrimination principle in tax treaty law and EU law; for an example on the differences of the two approaches, see Claus Staringer and Hermann Schneeweiss, 'Tax Treaty Non-Discrimination and EC Freedoms' in Michael Lang, Josef Schuch, and Claus Staringer (eds), *Tax Treaty Law and EC Law* (Linde Verlag 2007) 237–38.

[140] Opinion of Advocate General Kokott, 13 March 2014, C-48/13, *Nordea Bank*, ECLI:EU:C:2014:153, para 24.

[141] Art 120 of the TFEU.

[142] If the comparability test is understood as a filter to carve out non-protectionist national laws, then there is no need to apply the principle of proportionality to a different treatment of different situations.

protectionist and trade hampering through the lens of the national legislature,[143] and only such laws should primarily be fought by the fundamental freedoms.[144]

If comparability is established and the national law may therefore have an a priori protectionist nature, the justification stage examines the (secondary) objectives underlying the national law more closely. At the justification stage, all national non-market values may be balanced against market efficiency needs. Since the general framework of the law allows one to compare two unequally treated situations, indicating a protectionist law-making of a Member State, the national values brought forward on the justification level also have to pass the proportionality test.

4. Scope of the Comparability Test

Thus far, we have concluded that the benchmark within the comparability test is set by the aim and purpose of the national law. Accordingly, the aim and purpose of the national law determines whether an EU situation and a purely domestic situation are similar and thus have to be treated alike. However, the benchmark for the comparison does not define the scope of the comparability test. In other words, the aim and purpose of the law can determine whether two situations are comparable, but the aim and purpose of the law cannot identify which situations fall within the scope of the comparability test in the first place. The scope of the comparability test is determined by the fundamental freedoms and their capability to establish market neutrality.

In the field of taxation, neutrality is established by treating foreign and domestic goods, services, persons, and investment alike. Accordingly, every Member State has to first ensure that non-resident taxpayers investing, establishing a permanent economic presence, or offering goods or services in its territory are not treated worse than resident market players and, secondly, that it does not make a difference for the tax burden of a resident taxpayer whether he sells his goods, provides his services, or invests at home or abroad. However, it becomes far more complicated if one also considers the other Member States' legal treatment as either the host or the home Member State. Since taxation occurs both at source and at residence, achieving import or export neutrality does not depend upon just one Member State. But do the fundamental freedoms ask for *overall* tax neutrality or *per-country* neutrality? In other words, should the foreign tax burden be considered within the comparability test?

Besides the question of whether the tax treatment in the other Member State(s) has to be considered in the comparison between the domestic and the cross-border economic activity, it is questionable whether the market freedoms also protect

[143] See also Wattel, Marres, and Vermeulen (n 10) 41–42.

[144] For a different view see Joachim Englisch, 'Dividend Taxation: Outbound and Inbound (Verkooijen and ACT Group Litigation)' in Werner Haslehner, Georg Kofler, and Alexander Rust (eds), *Landmark Decisions of the ECJ in Direct Taxation* (Kluwer Law International 2015) 44–45 arguing that 'the national legislator's intentions should be reserves for the justification analysis'.

cross-border economic undertakings from a tax treatment which is less favourable than the one applied to the same economic cross-border undertaking involving different Member States (*horizontal* comparison). In other words, do the fundamental freedoms allow a Member State to treat cross-border economic activities differently depending on the Member States involved because these two cross-border situations can simply not be compared? Or would such a different treatment of two cross-border situations result in a fragmentation of the internal market which constitutes a restriction of the fundamental freedoms because the fundamental freedoms allow a comparison between two cross-border situations? A different treatment of two cross-border situations could follow either from national law provisions or, as is more likely, from tax treaties signed between different Member States.

a) Per Country or Overall Perspective

It is not clear from the outset whether the fundamental freedoms demand overall tax neutrality (considering taxation in both the home and the host Member State) or a simple per-country tax neutrality (considering taxation only in the home or the host Member State). A fully efficient single market would demand an overall perspective to prevent any trade obstacles following from an uncoordinated application of or disparities between two national (tax) systems.[145]

The fundamental freedoms—on a stand-alone basis—would only be capable of establishing full market neutrality if they forced Member States to consider the tax treatment of a fellow Member State within their tax assessment, and subsequently could prohibit the Member States from discriminating against foreign taxes. Including discrimination of foreign taxes within the scope of the fundamental freedoms would require an overall perspective when it comes to finding the right comparator. This would mean that the national tax burden would, along with the foreign tax burden, have to be compared with the pure national tax burden.

Frans Vanistendael is one of the most influential proponents of the overall approach.[146] He once used the example of a big snooker table, which has since become a famous analogy for the weak spots of the market freedoms, to illustrate what is missing if a simple per-country approach is applied.[147] The internal market will not be able to grow into one big market where economic operators smoothly

[145] Alfredo F García Prats, 'Is It Possible to Set a Coherent System of Rules on Direct Taxation under EC Law Requirements?' in Philippe Hinnekens and Luc Hinnekens (eds), *A Vision of Taxes Within and Outside the European Borders: Festschrift in Honor of Prof. Dr. Frans Vanistendael* (n 40) 432–33 warning that a 'pan-European approach to the compatibility analysis may lead and oblige to different treatment and different consequences in some cases already solved'.

[146] In this vein see also Eric CCM Kemmeren, 'The Internal Market Approach Should Prevail over the Single Country Approach' in Philippe Hinnekens and Luc Hinnekens (eds), *A Vision of Taxes Within and Outside the European Borders: Festschrift in Honor of Prof. Dr. Frans Vanistendael* (Kluwer Law International 2008) (n 40) 561 et seq.

[147] Vanistendael, 'The Compatibility of the Basic Economic Freedoms' (n 73) 139.

move within the market like balls rolling on one big snooker table if double taxation is not addressed by the fundamental freedoms. It is of course true that full efficiency within the internal market may only be achieved by forcing the Member States to credit foreign taxes fully. It is, however, not the task of the market freedoms to do this. They operate to open up national trade borders which allow the markets of the Member States to merge into a single but not uniform market, like several different pieces of fabric stitched together to form a patchwork blanket. Preventing double taxation requires more than the abolition of trade borders; it requires serious coordination of Member States' taxing rights through secondary EU law.[148] Accordingly, full market neutrality cannot be achieved by the fundamental freedoms because it demands coordination and value harmonisation through European legislation.

The limited scope of the fundamental freedoms can be justified on different grounds. First, forcing Member States to adjust their tax system in accordance with that of other Member States may infringe or even erode the tax sovereignty of Member States,[149] and would grant the CJEU competences which are not allocated to the Court by the EU treaties.[150] Secondly, the fundamental freedoms are applied to both inbound and outbound economic activities and both the home and the host Member State could therefore be forced to consider the tax levied in the other Member State depending on which treatment is considered discriminatory and brought before the CJEU. Without any form of coordination between the Member States,[151] such an approach would lead to arbitrary results because it would depend on the taxpayer deciding which tax treatment he concludes to be more burdensome.

Tax coordination between Member States may be established either through secondary EU law or on a bilateral basis by way of tax treaties. At a European level, tax coordination is rare. Some specific directives deal with issues of tax

[148] For the scope of Art 115 of the TFEU see Chapter 4, subsection G.

[149] Georg W Kofler, 'Tax Treaty "Neutralization" of Source State Discrimination under the EU Fundamental Freedoms?' (2011) 65 Bulletin for International Taxation 684, 687; Dennis Weber, 'In Search of a (New) Equilibrium Between Tax Sovereignty and the Freedom of Movement Within the EC' (2006) 34 Intertax 585, 602.

[150] Michael Lang, 'ECJ Case Law on Cross-Border Dividend Taxation - Recent Developments' (2008) 17 EC Tax Review 67, 72.

[151] Neither customary international law nor European Union law provide a framework for an allocation of taxing rights between (Member) States: Schön, 'Neutrality and Territoriality' (n 69) 275; Daniel Gutmann, 'Some Theoretical Thoughts on Judicial Power and Tax Law—with a Particular Focus on the ECJ' in Philippe Hinnekens and Luc Hinnekens (eds), *A Vision of Taxes Within and Outside the European Borders: Festschrift in Honor of Prof. Dr. Frans Vanistendael* (n 40) 490; Johanna Hey, 'Vorrecht des Quellenstaates und binnenmarktkonforme Besteuerung von Kapitalgesellschaften in der Europäischen Union' in Wolfgang Spindler, Klaus Tipke, and Thomas Rödder (eds), *Steuerzentrierte Rechtsberatung: Festschrift für Harald Schaumburg zum 65. Geburtstag* (Dr Otto Schmidt Verlag 2009) 773; Wolfgang Schön, 'International Tax Coordination for a Second-Best World (Part I)' (2009) 1 World Tax Journal 67, 71 et seq. For a different view with respect to customary international law see Eric CCM Kemmeren, 'Double Tax Conventions on Income and Capital and the EU: Past, Present and Future' (2012) 21 EC Tax Review 157, 159.

coordination, such as the Parent-Subsidiary Directive, but a general approach is lacking. The ATAD does not change the absence of tax coordination at European level. It has introduced tools to eliminate double non-taxation in case of hybrid mismatches which require the Member States first to consider the tax treatment of a certain transaction within a fellow Member State (overall approach) and second to subsequently decide on how the transaction should be treated domestically (co-ordination of the tax treatment). If Member States have to consider the fact that the transaction can be deducted in another Member State, the former may equally be able to consider the fact that the income has already been taxed. This line of argument simply ignores some essential facts. First, it ignores the fact that Member States have explicitly restricted the approach to issues of double non-taxation following from hybrid mismatches. Nothing in the ATAD indicates that the Member States are willing to extend this approach to cases of double taxation.[152] On the contrary, the ATAD is supposed to secure taxing rights of Member States and thus does not contain coordinative measures which would prevent double taxation per se. The ATAD may deal with double taxation, but only in those cases where the measures implemented by the ATAD trigger double taxation.[153]

Apart from tax coordination through secondary EU law, Member States quite substantially establish tax coordination on a bilateral basis through tax treaties. According to the CJEU case law, tax treaties do not allow the application of an overall approach to determine whether or not the national measure plus the tax treaty obligations discriminate cross-border economic activities. Rather, the Court finds that compensatory measures of tax treaties,[154] for example the crediting of withholding taxes in the home Member State, justify a discriminatory treatment which follows from national laws of the Member States (eg the levying of a withholding tax in the host Member State). This approach has been criticised because if treaty relief from discriminatory source taxation neutralises the

[152] This is clearly no case of a legislative loophole which would require an analogues application of the law. See for the requirements of such an application Wolfgang Schön, 'Die Analogie im Europäischen (Privat-)Recht' in Marietta Auer and others (eds), Carsten Herresthal, *Privatrechtsdogmatik im 21. Jahrhundert: Festschrift für Claus-Wilhelm Canaris zum 80. Geburtstag* (2017). For a critical analysis of extending the scope of secondary EU law see Joseph HH Weiler, 'Epilogue: Judging the Judges—Apology and Critique' in Maurice Adams and others (eds), *Judging Europe's Judges: The Legitimacy of the Case Law of the European Court of Justice* (2013) 242.

[153] 'Where *the application of those rules* gives rise to double taxation, taxpayers should receive relief through a deduction for the tax paid in another Member State or third country, as the case may be. Thus, the rules should not only aim to counter tax avoidance practices but also *avoid creating other obstacles* to the market, such as double taxation [emphasis added]', recital 5 of the ATAD.

[154] The CJEU only considers compensatory measures following from tax treaty law (CJEU, 19 January 2006, C-265/04, *Margaretha Bouanich*, ECLI:EU:C:2006:51, para 51; CJEU, 12 December 2006, C-374/04, Test Claimants in Class IV of the ACT Group Litigation; ECLI:EU:C:2006:773, para 71; CJEU, 14 December 2006, C-170/05, *Denkavit Internationaal*, ECLI:EU:C:2006:783, para 44 et seq; 17 September 2015, C-10/14, C-14/14, and C-17/14, *Miljoen*, ECLI:EU:C:2015:608, para 80. See also CJEU, 8 November 2007, C-379/05, *Amurta*, ECLI:EU:C:2007:655, para 83); and rejects compensatory measures following from domestic tax laws (CJEU, 8 November 2007, C-379/05, *Amurta*, ECLI:EU:C:2007:655, paras. 84 and 78; CJEU, 11 September 2008, C-43/07, *Arens-Sikken*, ECLI:EU:C:2008:490, para 66).

discriminatory effects of the host Member State's taxation, then there would be no discrimination in the first place.[155] Apart from criticising the approach of finding the national law discriminatory and then justified instead of not discriminatory at all, the 'neutralisation' doctrine indicates a rejection of the per-country approach because the tax treatment in the other Member State is taken into account.[156] However, if one examines the CJEU's case law more closely, it becomes apparent that the Member States are only able to *justify* their discriminatory taxes if their domestic tax treatment is linked with the tax treatment of another Member State through a tax treaty.[157] The linkage of both systems no longer allows one to view the national law in isolation, but at the same time does not extend the scope of the fundamental freedoms to recognise the national laws of another Member State too. The CJEU accepts a neutralising tax treatment of fellow Member States to which the Member State is committed under a bilateral tax treaty because the rights and obligations under a treaty are attributable to both contracting Member States. Recognising the neutralising tax treatment of a fellow Member State does not extend the view to the tax treatment in the other Member States, not even at the justification stage, but respects bilateral bridges between national laws. This, of course, does not explain why the Court qualifies the neutralisation as a justification and does not go as far as to reject the existence of discriminatory treatment. The Court may wish to do so because of the existing two-step approach. First, the Member State levies a tax which has discriminatory effects and, secondly, after the Member State has already levied the tax, a fellow Member State offers relief from discrimination.

The situation is different if the Member State's national law establishes a link to the tax treatment of a particular transaction or payment in another Member State because in such a case the national law establishes and demands an overall approach. In *Schempp*, for example, German income tax law only allowed a deduction of maintenance payments as 'special expenses' from the income tax base if the payments were subject to tax in the hands of the recipient. Accordingly, the law applied the principle of 'correspondence': the debtor is entitled to a deduction if the payment constitutes taxable income for the recipient.[158] Where the recipient is not resident in Germany, the right to deduct maintenance payments depends upon the tax treatment of the recipient's home Member State. In these cases, the Member

[155] Kofler, 'Tax Treaty "Neutralization"' (n 149) 685; Karin Spindler-Simader, 'Dividend Withholding Taxes after Miljoen, X and Société Générale' (2016) 25 EC Tax Review 70, 74; Frederik Zimmer, 'Withholding Taxes in the EU and the EEA' (2008) 52 Tax Notes International 667, 670.

[156] Weber (n 149) 599 et seq. Gerard TK Meussen, 'Denkavit Internationaal: The Practical Issues' (2007) 47 European Taxation 244, 245 et seq.

[157] Alexander Fortuin, 'Denkavit Internationaal: The Procedural Issues' (2007) 47 European Taxation 239, 242 arguing that if the home Member State 'removes an infringement caused by the source state [it is] a question as to whether an infringement can be justified'.

[158] CJEU, 12 July 2005, C-403/03, *Schempp*, ECLI:EU:C:2005:446, para 4.

State law demands that the tax treatment of fellow Member States is taken into account, and thus the tax treatment in the other Member State also influences the comparability of two situations.[159] Such a linkage and subsequent different treatment of the same payment but involving different tax systems of the Member States is accepted by the CJEU. To make the point clear, the link is established by the law of a Member State and not by the fundamental freedoms. However, European non-discrimination law accepts that one Member State's tax law considers the tax treatment in a fellow Member State.

From all of this, it follows that the fundamental freedoms only demand a single country approach. The tax treatment of an economic cross-border activity in another Member State does not influence the comparability of a purely domestic situation and a cross-border one. The single country perspective demands that every Member State treat foreign taxpayers or cross-border economic activities no less favourably than resident taxpayers or purely domestic undertakings.[160] However, the Member States are able to switch from a single country perspective to an overall perspective for the application of the fundamental freedoms if they link their national tax system with the (tax) treatment of a fellow Member State. In such cases, the national laws of the Member States demand an overall approach, and thus the national law goes beyond the single country approach of the fundamental freedoms. The CJEU may find that tax treaties are not intrinsic national laws because tax treaties are not capable of establishing an overall approach on the comparability level, but they are able to justify a discriminatory treatment.

b) *Horizontal versus Vertical Comparison*

The scope of the comparability test also determines the ability of the fundamental freedoms to force Member States to treat domestic and cross-border economic activities alike but also to ensure an equal treatment of two cross-border situations.[161] A horizontal comparison would not contradict the per-country perspective because the focus is still on a single Member State's law which happens to treat

[159] ibid para 35.

[160] Member States are neither required to consider the tax already levied in the other Member State nor obliged to adapt their own system to the different tax system of a fellow Member State: CJEU, 21 November 2013, *X*, ECLI:EU:C:2013:756, para 29; CJEU, 8 December 2011, C-157/10, *Banco Bilbao Vizcaya Argentaria SA*, ECLI:EU:C:2011:813, para 39; CJEU, 1 December 2011, C-253/09, *Commission v Hungary*, ECLI:EU:C:2011:795, para 83; CJEU, 12 February 2009, C-67/08, Block, ECLI:EU:C:2009:92, para 31; CJEU, 6 December 2007, C-298/05, *Columbus Container Services BVBA & Co*, ECLI:EU:C:2007:754, para 51.

[161] Meaning a cross-border situation within the European internal market. A different treatment of two non-Member States (under free movement of capital) can never constitute a comparison because such a different treatment has no effect on the European internal market: CJEU, 10 February 2011, C-436/08 and C-437/08, *Haribo and Salinen*, ECLI:EU:C:2011:61, para 48; Lang, 'Kapitalverkehrsfreiheit' (n 58) 216.

two cross-border situations differently depending on which Member States are involved.

At first glance, the CJEU case law is not fully consistent on the issue of whether a restriction of the market freedoms can follow from a different treatment of two foreign investments,[162] or two cross-border economic activities. Accordingly, it is not clear whether a different treatment of two foreign investments or two cross-border economic activities would pass the comparability test, and thus has to be justified, or whether two cross-border situations are not comparable under the framework of the fundamental freedoms. In some cases, the Court has explicitly denied the possibility of comparing two non-residents or two cross-border scenarios.[163] In others, however, the Court seems to deduce a general prohibition of discrimination between two non-residents or two cross-border economic activities from the market freedoms.[164]

There are three main categories of cases in which the Court discusses the possibility of applying a horizontal comparison. The first one is the comparison between a foreign branch and a foreign subsidiary to test the free choice of legal forms (see subsection (aa). The second line of cases concerns the comparability of two cross-border situations which are subject to different tax treaties (see subsection (bb). And thirdly, the CJEU has scrutinised the law of a single Member State which treats two cross-border situations differently (see subsection (cc).

(aa) Horizontal Comparison and the Free Choice of Legal Forms The CJEU has applied a horizontal comparison to identify whether the Member States treat the establishment of a branch and the setting up of a subsidiary in another Member State alike as required by the freedom to choose the legal form.[165] The different legal forms give each economic entity the possibility of integrating into the host Member State's legal and economic order, to the extent it wishes to be part of this new market.[166] If every economic entity has the right to choose whether to operate

[162] CJEU, 30 June 2016, C-176/15, *Riskin and Timmermans*, ECLI:EU:C:2016:488, para 25; it is important to distinguish between the restriction and the comparability (see this chapter Part I, subsection C.II). On the level of comparability, two foreign investments may not be comparable, and thus the fundamental freedoms may not be infringed. Nonetheless, the different treatment of two foreign investments may constitute a restriction. For the impact of a horizontal comparison on the non-discrimination provisions see Alexander Rust, 'Equality and Non-Discrimination in European Tax Law' in Werner Haslehner, Georg Kofler, and Alexander Rust (eds), *EU Tax Law and Policy in the 21st Century* (Kluwer Law International 2017) 61–62.

[163] CJEU, 30 June 2016, C-176/15, *Riskin and Timmermans*, ECLI:EU:C:2016:488, para 31 et seq; CJEU, 20 May 2008, C-194/06, *Orange European Smallcap Fund*, ECLI:EU:C:2008:289, para 63; CJEU, 12 December 2006, C-374/04, *Test Claimants in Class IV*, ECLI:EU:C:2006:773, para 91; CJEU, 5 July 2005, C-376/03, *D*, ECLI:EU:C:2006:424, para 61.

[164] CJEU, 24 February 2015, C-5112/13, *Sopora*, ECLI:EU:C:2015:108, para 25.

[165] Arne Friese, *Rechtsformwahlfreiheit im Europäischen Steuerrecht* (Dr Otto Schmidt Verlag 2010) 141 et seq.

[166] Wolfgang Schön, 'The Free Choice between the Right to Establish a Branch and to Set-up a Subsidiary—a Principle of European Business Law' (2001) 2 European Business Organization Law Review 339, 346.

through a branch or subsidiary in another Member State, both legal forms need to be treated alike. Preferential treatment of the subsidiary over the branch would automatically encourage the economic entity to set up a subsidiary instead of a branch and vice versa. Subsequently, the CJEU found in its early cases that the freedom of establishment requires not only an equal treatment of foreign and domestic companies but also demands a non-discriminatory treatment of both dependent and independent branches to carry out an economic activity in another Member State. According to the Court, 'the freedom to choose the most appropriate legal form for the pursuit of activities in another Member State, which the second sentence of the first paragraph of Article 52 of the Treaty [now: Art 43 of the TFEU] expressly confers on economic operators'.[167] To identify whether the host Member State treats branches and subsidiaries of a foreign undertaking alike, the scenario of a foreign company setting up a local branch and the scenario of a foreign company establishing a local subsidiary need to be compared. This constitutes a horizontal comparison. In cases of inbound economic activities, such as in the *Avoir fiscal* and *Saint-Gobain* cases, the Court did not engage in a separate analysis of whether branches and subsidiaries of a foreign company are treated differently and whether this accounts for a separate infringement of the freedom of establishment. The Court did, however, rule that '[t]he difference in treatment to which branches of non-resident companies are subject in comparison with resident companies as well as the restriction of the freedom to choose the form of secondary establishment must be regarded as constituting *a single composite infringement* of Article 52 and 58 of the Treaty [now: 43 and 48 of the TFEU]'[168].[169] To distinguish between these two discrimination cases, Wolfgang Schön called the comparison of resident with non-resident companies the 'comparison of the "subject" of the freedom of establishment'; whereas the comparison of the subsidiary with the branch forms 'the "object" of the freedom of establishment'.[170]

In cases of outbound economic activity, the CJEU was more reluctant to secure the free choice of legal forms. In *Columbus Container Services* and *KBC Bank*, the Court found that 'Member States are at liberty to determine the conditions and the level of taxation for different types of establishments chosen by national companies or partnerships operating abroad, on condition that those companies or partnerships are not treated in a manner that is discriminatory in comparison with comparable national establishments'[171].[172]

[167] CJEU, 21 September 1999, C-307/97, *Saint-Gobain*, ECLI:EU:C:1999:438, para 42.

[168] ibid para 43.

[169] For the CJEU's different argumentation in CLT-UFA (CJEU, 23 February 2006, C-253/03, *CLT-UFA*, ECLI:EU:C:2006:129) see Daniela Hohenwarter-Mayr, *Verlustverwertung im Konzern* (LexisNexis Verl ARD ORAC 2010) 105–06.

[170] Schön, 'The Free Choice between the Right to Establish a Branch and to Set-up a Subsidiary' (n 166) 348.

[171] CJEU, 6 December 2007, C-298/05, *Columbus Container Services*, ECLI:EU:C:2007:754, para 53.

[172] CJEU, 4 June 2009, C-439/07 and C-499/07, *KBC Bank and Beleggen, Risicokapitaal, Beheer NV*, ECLI:EU:C:2009, para 80.

(bb) Horizontal Comparison and Tax Treaties The second category of cases in which a horizontal comparison may be applied concerns the most-favoured-nation treatment. The most-favoured-nation treatment refers to a concept in international law and is generally defined as 'treatment accorded by the granting State to the beneficiary State, or to persons or things in a determined relationship with that State, not less favourable than treatment extended by the granting State to a third State or to persons or things in the same relationship with that third State'.[173] The CJEU was confronted with the question of whether or not, in tax law cases, a most-favoured-nation clause is embedded into the market freedoms where the different bilateral tax treaties provided for a different tax outcome depending on which Member States are involved.[174] Tax treaties distribute taxing rights between the contracting parties and provide (tax) benefits to the residents of the treaty partners. These benefits vary from treaty to treaty, even within the European Union.[175] Accordingly, a transnational investment would be subject to a higher or lower total tax burden depending on the tax treaty signed between the host and the home Member State. Member States would thus be capable of granting certain benefits to a resident of another fellow Member State but, because of a different tax treatment, not to a resident of a third Member State.[176]

In more recent CJEU case law,[177] the Court has ruled that a different treatment of two foreign investments,[178] two foreign workers,[179] or two cross-border economic activities has a severe impact on the decision of where to invest or where to operate. The disadvantageous treatment could discourage some investment or some cross-border economic activities within the European internal market and thus constitutes a restriction of the fundamental freedoms. However, if the different treatment follows from different tax treaties the Court accepts market fragmentation because in light of a particular tax treaty, two foreign investments are not in a comparable situation.[180] The benefits granted to the foreign investments subject to that tax treaty 'are an integral part of all the rules under the convention and contribute to the overall balance of mutual relations between the two contracting States'.[181] Thus, the benefit cannot be separated from the tax treaty.[182]

[173] Report of the International Law Commission on the work of its thirtieth session, Document A/33/10, Yearbook of the International Law Commission 1978, Vol. II, 1, 21.

[174] CJEU, 5 July 2005, C-376/03, *D*, ECLI:EU:C:2005:424, para 53 et seq.

[175] Georg W Kofler, 'Most-Favoured-Nation Treatment in Direct Taxation: Does EC Law Provide for Community MFN in Bilateral Double Taxation Treaties?' (2005) 5 Houston Business and Tax Law Journal 1, 6. '[I]t is the rule, rather than the exception, that such benefits vary from treaty to treaty.'

[176] ibid.

[177] For a detailed analysis of all the CJEU 'close-to-cases', see Kofler, 'Most-Favoured-Nation Treatment in Direct Taxation' (n 175) 34 et. seq.

[178] CJEU, 30 June 2016, C-176/15, *Riskin and Timmermans*, ECLI:EU:C:2016:488, para 25.

[179] CJEU, 24 February 2015, C-512/13, *Sopora*, ECLI:EU:C:2015:108.

[180] CJEU, 30 June 2016, C-176/15, *Riskin and Timmermans*, ECLI:EU:C:2016:488, para 31 et seq; see also CJEU, 5 July 2005, C-376/03, *D*, ECLI:EU:C:2005:424, para 61 et seq.

[181] ibid para 31.

[182] CJEU, 20 May 2008, C-194/06, *Orange European Smallcap Fund*, ECLI:EU:C:2008:289, para 63; CJEU, 12 December 2006, C-374/04, *Test Claimants in Class IV*, ECLI:EU:C:2006:773, para 91; CJEU, 5

The non-application of most-favoured-nation treatment has been heavily criticised in the academic literature. Accordingly, a preferential tax treatment which was given to an entrepreneur in one Member State, but not to an entrepreneur in another Member State, was considered 'absolutely unacceptable in the single market'.[183] The individual right of each Member State to negotiate bilateral tax treaties may be generally accepted, but critics claim that each of these treaties must comply with EU law and the market freedoms it guarantees. A different tax treatment may be accepted from a pure national policy perspective but cannot be in line with the market freedoms.[184] Most proponents rely on a textual interpretation of the EU treaties and emphasis that the European treaties prohibit *any* discrimination on the grounds of nationality, which would also cover a most-favoured-nation treatment.[185]

Beyond any doubt, the finding that two cross-border situations which are subject to different tax treaties are not comparable fragments the European internal market. However, all tax treaty rules are subject to negotiations solely between the two contracting parties and are balanced and reciprocal.[186] A tax treaty signed between two Member States only aims to prevent double taxation or double non-taxation between the contracting parties. To protect these treaties and the underlying negotiations between the two Member States, the Court allows certain tax benefits to be granted only to residents of the contracting party, and not to residents of a third fellow Member State. The Court allows the different treatment of two non-resident taxpayers, or two cross-border economic activities involving different Member States, by finding them incomparable.

July 2005, C-376/03, *D*, ECLI:EU:C:2006:424, para 61; see also Opinion of Advocate General Wathelet, 19 September 2017, C-284/16, ECLI:EU:C:2017:699, para 72 arguing that 'FEU Treaty does not contain an MFN clause'. Advocate General Wathelet argued based on Art 18 of the TFEU because the case concerned a dispute settlement mechanism of an investment treaty which may address different free movement rights.

[183] Albert Rädler, 'Tax Treaties and the Internal Market', Report of the Committee of independent experts on company taxation (Ruling Report), Annex 6 (1992) 378. See also Albert Rädler, 'Most-Favoured-Nation Clause in European Tax Law?' (1995) 4 EC Tax Review 66, 66–67.

[184] Malcolm Gammie and Guy Brannan, 'EC Law Strikes at the UK Corporation Tax—The Death Knell of UK Imputation?' (1995) 23 Intertax 389, 402.

[185] Ruud van der Linde, 'Some Thoughts on Most-Favoured-Nation Treatment within the European Community Legal Order in Pursuance of the D Case' (2004) 13 EC Tax Review 10, 12. Franz Wassermeyer, 'Does the EC Treaty Force the Member States to Conclude a Multilateral Tax Treaty?' in Michael Land and others (eds), *Multilateral Tax Treaties* (Kluwer Law International 1998) 18.

[186] CJEU, 21 September 1999, C-307/97, *Saint-Gobain*, ECLI:EU:C:1999:438, para 59; CJEU, 12 December 2006, C-374/04, *Test Claimants in Class IV*, ECLI:EU:C:2006:773, para 91; Moris Lehner, 'The Influence of EU Law on Tax Treaties from a German Perspective' (2000) 54 Bulletin for International Taxation 461, 470; Eric Kemmeren, 'The Termination of the "most Favoured Nation Cause" Dispute in Tax Treaty Law and the Necessity of a Euro Model Tax Convention' (1997) 6 EC Tax Review 146, 148–49.

(cc) Horizontal Comparison and National Tax Laws Over the years, it is possible to discern several CJEU cases in which the Court not only compared a cross-border situation with a purely domestic one but also argued along the line of a discrimination of two non-nationals.[187] Three of these cases are particularly interesting. Throughout all of them, however, the Advocate Generals' opinions focus on the horizontal comparison in particular, which might have had an impact on the CJEU's rulings.

In *Cadbury Schweppes*,[188] a British tax rule on controlled foreign companies was tested against the fundamental freedoms. The national rule provided that the national parent company could be taxed on undistributed gains of its controlled subsidiary in another Member State if the subsidiary is not subject to a substantive tax on its gains. Accordingly, the controlled foreign company rule only kicked in if the other fellow Member State did not substantially tax the gains of the subsidiary. In a purely domestic setting, the parent company was never taxed on the undistributed gains of its controlled subsidiary. Likewise, a tax on foreign gains was not levied under the controlled foreign company rule if the tax in the other fellow Member States was not less than three-quarters of the amount of tax which would have been paid in the United Kingdom.

On the basis of a wide understanding of what 'discrimination' means, Advocate General Léger argued that the situation of a British parent company holding shares in its controlled subsidiary in a low tax jurisdiction, and the situation of a British parent company holding shares in its controlled subsidiary in another fellow Member State, which provides for a less favourable tax regime, should be compared.[189] The CJEU did not use such clear language and focused much more on the vertical comparison.[190] In one paragraph, however, the CJEU compared the tax disadvantage not only with the purely domestic situation but also with 'a subsidiary established outside that Member State [the United Kingdom] which is not subject to a lower level of taxation'.[191]

The wording of the CJEU in *Cadbury Schweppes* was utilised by Advocate General Mengozzi in *Columbus Container Services*.[192] Here, a German national rule was tested against the market freedoms. The national rule stated that the

[187] For an overview of all the relevant cases, see Michael Lang, 'Totgesagte leben länger: Horizontale Vergleichbarkeit und die Verwirklichung des Binnenmarkts' (2016) 26 Steuer und Wirtschaft International 118; Michael Lang, 'There Is Life in the Old Dog Yet: Horizontal Comparability and the Establishment of the Internal Marke' in Reuven S Avi-Yonah, and Michael Lang (eds), *Comparative Fiscal Federalism* (2nd edn, Kluwer Law International 2016) 28 et seq. See also Kofler, 'Most-Favoured-Nation Treatment in Direct Taxation' (n 175) 34 et seq.

[188] CJEU, 12 September 2006, C-196/04, *Cadbury Schweppes*, ECLI:EU:C:2006:544.

[189] Opinion of Advocate General Léger, 2 May 2006, C-196/04, *Cadbury Schweppes*, ECLI:EU:C:206:278, para 77.

[190] CJEU, 12 September 2006, C-196/04, *Cadbury Schweppes*, ECLI:EU:C:2006:544, para 44.

[191] ibid para 45.

[192] Opinion of Advocate General Mengozzi, 29 March 2007, C-298/05, *Columbus Container Service*, ECLI:EU:C:2007:197, paras 113–114.

exemption method should not apply to profits of a foreign permanent establishment if the permanent establishment is subject to low taxation. In those cases, the foreign income tax paid could only be credited against the German income tax. The national rule applied irrespective of the obligation arising out of a bilateral tax treaty to exempt the foreign income.

Columbus Container Services is different from *Cadbury Schweppes* because in the former there is no equivalent purely national setting. The negative tax implications following from applying the credit and not the exemption method are only visible when a German company with a permanent establishment located in a low tax jurisdiction is compared with a German company with a permanent establishment located in a jurisdiction which levies an income tax that corresponds to the German income tax. According to Advocate General Mengozzi, a horizontal comparison needs to be made in such a case because the concept of the internal market requires it. If the Member States were allowed to treat the permanent establishments of national companies different depending on where they are established, the internal market would be at 'risk of fragmentation'.[193]

The CJEU, however, reached a completely different conclusion. The Court found that the application of the credit method instead of the exemption method did not restrict the freedom of establishment because the total tax burden of a German company with a permanent establishment located in a low tax jurisdiction corresponds with the total tax burden of a German company with a domestic permanent establishment.[194] The fact that the total tax burden may be lower if the permanent establishment has been established in another Member State which applies a lower income tax than the German one, but is still sufficient to allow for the application of the exemption method, was—at least implicitly—rejected by the CJEU.

In the more recent *Sopora* case, concerning the free movement of workers, the CJEU may have for the first time applied a horizontal comparison. This case concerned the Dutch 30% flat rate rule, according to which foreign highly skilled experts who relocated to the Netherlands and took up employment there were granted an allowance for exemption of 30% of the employment income without any further proof. The flat rate rule was also available if this amount exceeded the real extraterritorial expenses. This rule was, however, only available to those employees who had their residence outside a radius of 150 kilometres (km) from the Dutch border during twenty-four months before the start of their employment in the Netherlands. If this condition was not fulfilled, the employees were only allowed to deduct their real extraterritorial expenses.

Advocate General Kokott was very clear in her opinion on whether or not any less favourable treatment of non-residents is covered by the market freedoms.

[193] ibid 117.

[194] CJEU, 6 December 2007, C-298/05, *Columbus Container Services*, ECLI:EU:C:2007:754, paras 51–53.

Following the arguments of Advocate Generals Léger and Mengozzi, she argues that there is a serious risk of fragmentation of the internal market 'if the Member States were allowed to give preferences to workers from certain Member States over workers from other Member States'.[195] Therefore, the tax treatment of two non-resident taxpayers taking up employment in the Netherlands should be allowed to be compared.

The CJEU explicitly ruled that the free movement of workers aims to abolish *all* discrimination based on nationality *between workers of the Member States*, and 'read in the light of Article 26 TFEU, the view must be taken that the freedom *also prohibits discrimination between non-resident workers* if such discrimination leads to nationals of certain Member States being *unduly favoured* in comparison to others'.[196] Concerning the national rule, the Court found that the administrative simplification of granting the flat rate allowance only to those workers who lived outside a radius of 150 km from the Dutch border before taking up employment in the Netherlands is in line with the free movement of workers because it does not constitute a restriction. The Court highlighted the fact that all foreign workers are allowed to deduct their extraterritorial expenses regardless of where they lived before relocating to the Netherlands. The fact that the flat rate rule may be more beneficial was, however, not enough to find that the rule contradicted Art 45 of the TFEU.[197]

5. Findings

The fundamental freedoms help to open up national markets by fighting protectionist measures in domestic laws which hinder trade between the Member States. To assess whether national laws are of a protectionist nature, the comparability test works as a filter to prevent non-protectionist national laws from being scrutinised. In that vein, the *tertium comparationis* has to be identified with respect to the aim and purpose of the national law. Only a comparison which considers the attempt of the national legislature can establish whether the national rules are truly protectionist. Furthermore, the use of the aim and purpose of the national rule as a benchmark for the comparability test guarantees that the national values of the Member States are sufficiently considered. For precisely these reasons, the fundamental freedoms do not follow fixed intrinsic values; they use

195 Opinion of Advocate General Kokott, 11 November 2014, C-512/13, *Sopora*, ECLI:EU:C:2014:2375, para 28.

196 CJEU, 24 February 2015, C-512/13, *Sopora*, ECLI:EU:C:2015:108, para 25, emphasis added.

197 Gerard TK Meussen, 'Horizontal Discrimination and EU Law: The Sopora Case' (2014) 54 European Taxation 322, 324 arguing that the 'Netherlands regime is unacceptable discrimination because, in fact, it is a tariff measure that decreases the effective income tax rate of non-resident employees with scarce knowledge or capabilities'; also criticising the outcome Daniel S Smit, 'The 150km Requirement under the Dutch 30% Wage Tax Facility C-512/03 (Sopora)' in Michael Lang and others (eds), *ECJ—Recent Developments in Direct Taxation 2013* (Linde Verlag 2014).

the values underlying national laws regardless of the many shortcomings this approach may have.[198]

The more recent CJEU case law indicates that the fundamental freedoms not only fight protectionism but also prevent Member States from fragmenting the European internal market. A differentiation of national laws between the Member States in the form of a different treatment of goods, services, persons, or capital, depending on the Member States they are coming from or to which they move, distorts the decision on where to invest, where to produce, where to provide services, or where to move. To prevent fragmentation of the European internal market, the CJEU allows a comparison of two non-resident workers from different Member States, and foreign investment in different Member States.[199] However, a horizontal comparison is only allowed if the differentiation follows from the law of a single Member State and against the background of the aim and purpose of the law.

The aim of preventing fragmentation of the European internal market widens the scope of the fundamental freedoms because they demand that Member States not treat cross-border economic activities more adversely than purely domestic economic transactions and not grant any cross-border economic transaction within the European internal market favourable treatment. In other words, if a Member State unilaterally decides to grant goods, services, persons, or capital from a particular Member States benefits, these benefits also have to be granted to goods, services, persons, or capital from any other fellow Member State. We shall assume that one Member States unilaterally decides to credit taxes levied in a particular Member State, Member State A, but denies any tax credits with respect to other Member States. According to CJEU case law, double taxation does not fall within the scope of the fundamental freedoms,[200] because when applying a comparison between a purely domestic situation and a cross-border situation, no worse treatment exists. The allegedly worse treatment follows from the accumulation of taxes in two Member States, but the tax in each Member State is not discriminatory. Under European law, Member States are not required to consider foreign taxes because the fundamental freedoms only ask for simple per-country neutrality. The potential double burden does also not account for a market access

[198] The fact that the CJEU sometimes has severe problems in finding the 'one' aim and purpose of the national law becomes especially visible when the Court qualifies the cross-border economic activity and the pure domestic activity as comparable and uses the different aims that are underlying the national law at the justification stage.

[199] Eric CCM Kemmeren, 'Sopora: A Welcome Landmark Decision on Horizontal Comparison' (2015) 24 EC Tax Review 178, 182 doubting (but still favouring the idea) that the CJEU applies the horizontal approach also to the other free movement rights. Karsten Engsig Sørensen, 'Enhanced Free Movement: Opportunities and Limits for EU Member States Entering into Bilateral Agreements' (2019) 44 European Law Review 319, 330 arguing that 'it must be assumed that the same interpretation applies to the other free-movement rights'.

[200] CJEU, 14 November 2006, C-513/04, *Kerckhaert*, ECLI:EU:C:2006:713, para 20; CJEU, 12 February 2009, C-67/08, *Block*, C-67/08, ECLI:EU:C:2009:92, para 31; CJEU, 16 July 2009, *Damseaux*, C-128/08, ECLI:EU:C:2009:471, paras 32–33.

restriction because the burden in each Member State (the tax) follows a different purpose. In other words, taxes in Member State A do not help to satisfy the revenue needs of Member State B.[201] However, if a Member State unilaterally decides to credit foreign taxes of Member State A but not foreign taxes of Member State C, the argument that the foreign tax does not have to be recognised no longer holds, because the tax of Member State A also does not satisfy the revenue needs of Member State B. Accordingly, the fundamental freedoms do not force Member States to recognise foreign taxes, but they demand foreign taxes be treated alike.

Besides unilateral measures of Member States, a different tax treatment of two non-resident taxpayers may also follow from the application of two different tax treaties. In these cases, fragmentation of the European internal market is accepted because the different treatment is not attributable to a single Member State. Rather, the different treatment follows from a balanced and reciprocal deal between two Member States which denies comparability between these cross-border situations.

III. Third Step: Rule of Reason

Exceptionally, the European treaties allow Member States to maintain trade obstacles which fall within the scope of the fundamental freedoms if they are justified by a legitimate public interest reason and proportionate (the so-called rule of reason doctrine).[202] Accordingly, the justification level is another way to recognise[203] national interests underlying the Member State laws,[204] because under the rule of reason the values of market integration are balanced against other non-market values.[205] However, under the rule of reason doctrine non-market values, which are not explicitly set out in the European treaties as grounds of justification,

[201] See this chapter Part I, subsection, C.I.2.

[202] '[T]he application [of a national measure restricting intra-EU trade] can be justified by a public-interest objective taking precedence over the free movement of goods', CJEU, 24 November 1993, C-267/91 and C-268/91, *Keck*, ECLI:EU:C:1993:905, para 15; CJEU, 26 June 1997, C-368/95, *Familiapress Zeitungsverlags- und vertriebs GmbH*, ECLI:EU:C:1997:325, para 8.

[203] However, it is the duty of the Member States to prove that the national measure pursues the legitimate objects—the public interest concerns, Niamh Nic Shuibhne and Marsela Maci, 'Proving Public Interest: The Growing Impact of Evidence in Free Movement Case Law' (2013) 50 Common Market Law Review 965.

[204] Stephen Weatherill, 'Beyond Preemption? Shared Competence and Constitutional Change in the European Community' in David O'Keeffe and Patrick Twomey (eds), *Legal Issues of the Maastricht Treaty* (Chancery Law Pub 1994) 16 describes it as the CJEU being 'forced to make some difficult assessments in the trade-off between market liberalization and, for example, national initiatives of environmental protection and consumer protection'. For many authors, the justification level seems to be the only way to allow Member States to hold on to their national laws pursuing non-economic values: Catherine Barnard, 'Derogations, Justifications and the Four Freedoms: Is State Interest Really Protected?' in Catherine Barnard (ed), *The Outer Limits of European Union law* (Hart Publishing 2009) 274 claiming that 'for the defendant Member State, every failed justification is another nail in the coffin of its legislative autonomy and, more generally, for the diversity of national rules'.

[205] Wolf Sauter and Harm Schepel, *State and Market in European Union Law: The Public and Private Spheres of the Internal Market before the EU Courts* (CUP 2009) 39.

can only be considered if the national legal measure does not discriminate on the basis of nationality (direct discrimination).[206] In case of direct discrimination, only the explicit derogation grounds laid down in the European treaties can be used to justify unequal treatment.[207]

The following subsections set out how national values influence the rule of reason doctrine. Subsection 1 examines which national interests are capable of functioning as a ground of justification. Subsection 2 demonstrates that the CJEU hardly engages in a true balancing of the values of market integration and the non-market values of the Member States.

1. Overriding Reasons of Public Interest

The CJEU has accepted the need to recognise broader arguments of justification than those explicitly provided in the European treaties.[208] These additional grounds of justification reflect the non-market values of a Member State, in the form of the ethics of its society and the interests of its people.[209] Initially, the CJEU ruled that certain values are 'mandatory requirements' to supplement derogations from free movement explicitly laid down by the European treaties.[210] Now, the Court refers to 'imperative requirements',[211] 'overriding requirements in the public interest',[212] or simply 'public interest requirements'.[213] All these expressions refer to '"good"

[206] Early CJEU case law indicates that the national measure 'must not be applied in a non-discriminatory manner' to allow justification on the grounds of overriding reasons of public interest (CJEU, 30 November 1995, C-55/94, *Gebhard*, ECLI:EU:C:1995:411, para 37). However, more recent case law shows, that a strict approach shall only be applied to direct discriminations. In other words, discrimination on the basis of nationality can only be justified on the basis of derogating provisions expressly provided for in the European treaties; indirect discrimination and restrictions can be justified on overriding reasons of public interest. Elie Roth, 'The Rule of Reason Doctrine in European Court of Justice Jurisprudence on Direct Taxation' (2008) 56 Canadian Tax Journal 67, 73; Axel Cordewener, Georg W Kofler, and Servaas van Thiel, 'The Clash Between European Freedoms and National Direct Tax Law: Public Interest Defences Available to the Member States' (2009) 46 Common Market Law Review 1951, 1952.

[207] The European treaties allow for derogations on the grounds of 'core national interests', see Papp (n 25) 110.

[208] Cordewener, Kofler, and Thiel (n 206) 1955.

[209] The Member States do not enjoy any discretion of defining these grounds, the grounds of justification are to the control and review of the CJEU, Papp (n 25) 110.

[210] CJEU, 20 February 1979, 120/78, *Rewe-Zentral AG*, ECLI:EU:C:1979:42, para 8.

[211] CJEU, 27 October 2005, C-234/03, *Contse SA*, ECLI:EU:C:2005:644, para 39; CJEU, 6 November 2003, C-243/01, *Piergiorgio Gambelli and Others*, ECLI:EU:C:2003:597, para 65; CJEU, 30 September 2003, C-167/01, *Inspire Art*, ECLI:EU:C:2003:512, para 133; CJEU, 12 October 2000, C-314/98, *Snellers Auto's BV*, ECLI:EU:C:2000:557, para 55; CJEU, 9 March 1999, C-212/97, *Centros*, ECLI:EU:C:1999:126, para 34; CJEU, 30 April 1991, C-239/90, *Boscher*, ECLI:EU:C:1991:180, para 17; CJEU, 12 March 1987, 178/84, *Commission v Germany*, ECLI:EU:C:1987:126, para 30.

[212] CJEU, 18 May 2017, C-99/16, *Lahorgue*, ECLI:EU:C:2017:391, para 34; CJEU, 12 June 2014, C-156/13, *Digibet*, ECLI:EU:C:2014:1756, para 23; CJEU, 30 April 2014, C-390/12, *Pfleger*, ECLI:EU:C:2014:281, para 35; CJEU, 19 July 2012, C-470/11, *Garkalns SIA*, ECLI:EU:C:2012:505, para 39; CJEU, 21 October 2010, C-81/09, *Idrima Tipou AE*, ECLI:EU:C:2010:622, para 62; CJEU, 9 July 1997, C-34/95, C-35/95, and C-36/95, *De Agostini*, ECLI:EU:C:1997:344, para 53; CJEU, 25 July 1991, C-288/89, *Stichting Collectieve Antennevoorziening Gouda*, ECLI:EU:C:1991:323, para 13.

[213] CJEU, 1 July 2014, C-573/12, *Ålands Vindkraft AB*, ECLI:EU:C:2014:2037, para 76.

reasons put forward by the Member States to justify their conduct'.[214] Economic reasons are not considered 'good' reasons in the case law of the CJEU[215] because they include an element of protectionist, or self-interested, aim,[216] which protects industries from competition.[217] In that vein, the Court has consistently refused to consider arguments relating to loss of revenue[218] or the need to support the domestic economy.[219] However, Member States have again and again attempted to argue that their imposed trade restrictions are justified because an equal treatment of purely domestic and cross-border economic activities would result in a loss of tax revenue or an erosion of the tax base. The CJEU has always[220] rejected these claims and found that the reduction in tax revenue is not one of the grounds listed in the European treaties and cannot be considered an overriding general interest which may be relied upon to justify unequal treatment.[221]

[214] Barnard, *The Substantive Law of the EU* (n 19) 168.

[215] Cordewener, *Europäische Grundfreiheiten und nationales Steuerrecht* (n 42) 134 et seq arguing that it is hardly impossible to differentiate between non-economic and economic reasons.

[216] Opinion of Advocate General Jääskinen, 16 April 2013, C-105/12 to 107/12, *Essent Nederland BV, Eneco Holding NV and Delta NV*, ECLI:EU:C:2013:242, para 89.

[217] Sue Arrowsmith, 'Rethinking the Approach to Economic Justifications under the EU's Free Movement Rules' (2015) 68 Current Legal Problems 307, 309, 314; Bernard, 'Flexibility' (n 64) 106 criticising the CJEU's approach in Alpine Investments because '[o]ne would have thought that protecting the reputation of a sector of the national economy looked suspiciously like an economic justification'.

[218] Except for tax avoidance and evasion: Luc Hinnekens, 'Basis and Scope of Public Interest Justification of National Tax Measures Infringing Fundamental Treaty Freedoms' in Frans Vanistendael (ed), *EU Freedoms and Taxation* (IBFD 2006) 76 et seq.

[219] However, the CJEU has accepted economic interests where they serve a non-economic end, Jukka Snell, 'Economic Aims as Justification for Restrictions on Free Movement' in Annette Schrauwen (ed), *Rule of Reason: Rethinking Another Classic of EC Legal Doctrine* (Europa Law Publishing 2005) 37, 39, 51; Wulf-Henning Roth, 'Economic Justifications and the Internal Market' in Mielle K Bulterman and others (eds), *Views of European Law from the Mountain: Liber Amicorum Piet Jan Slot* (Wolters Kluwer Law International 2009) 78 et seq. Lenaerts, 'United in Diversity' (n 40) 626. However, in exceptional cases, the CJEU allowed to justify restrictive economic measures based on the need to assure the supply of 'essential public services', CJEU, 10 July 1984, 72/83, *Campus Oil Limited*, ECLI:EU:C:1984:256, para 34. See also Hinnekens (n 218) 75.

[220] However, the CJEU 'has given Member States greater leeway to preserve the integrity of their tax bases by allowing them, first, to combat non-commercial arrangements designed to shift tax bases and, secondly, to preserve a degree of symmetry between taxation and relief', Paul Farmer, 'Striking a Proper Balance between the National Fiscal Interests and the Community Interest—a Perpetual Struggle?' in Dennis Weber (ed), *The Influence of European Law on Direct Taxation: Recent and Future Developments* (Kluwer Law International 2007) 32.

[221] CJEU, 16 July 1998, C-264/96, *Imperial Chemical Industries plc (ICI)*, ECLI:EU:C:1998:370, para 28; CJEU, 21 September 1999, C-307/97, *Compagnie de Saint-Gobain*, ECLI:EU:C:1999:438, para 50; CJEU, 6 June 2000, C-35/98, *B.G.M. Verkooijen*, ECLI:EU:C:2000:294, para 59; CJEU, 8 March 2001, C-397/98 and C-410/98, *Metallgesellschaft Ltd and Others*, ECLI:EU:C:2001:134, para 59; CJEU, 21 November 2002, C-436/00, *X*, ECLI:EU:C:2002:704, para 50; CJEU, 11 March 2004, *Hughes de Lasteyrie du Saillant*, ECLI:EU:C:2004:138, para 60. Although revenue constraints cannot be considered good reasons for restricting free movement, the CJEU has limited the effects of its judgment *ratione temporis*, for example, in the *Dansk Denkavit* case because 'the amount yielded by the contested levy was approximately 7 000 million ECU, or 4% of Denmark's revenue during the period in question', CJEU, 31 March 1992, C-200/90, *Dansk Denkavit*, ECLI:EU:C:1992:152, para 20. Restricting retroactive effects of the decisions of the CJEU becomes increasingly important in the area of direct taxation: Michael Lang, 'Limitation of the Temporal Effects of Judgments of the ECJ' in Dennis Weber (ed), *The Influence of European Law on Direct Taxation: Recent and Future Developments* (Kluwer Law International 2007); Jürgen Lüdicke, 'European Tax Law, Quo Vadis?' (2008) 62 Bulletin for International Fiscal

In this vein, the CJEU has also rejected any claims of the Member States to justify restrictions of free movement aiming at protecting the economy of the country.[222] Therefore, the aim of granting the domestic economy a competitive advantage cannot be understood as an intrinsic interest of the society requiring a balancing against the values of market integration.

The CJEU's case law shows that public interests can have many different angles, and that a public interest concern does not necessarily rise to the level of fundamental right claims. Public interest reflects all non-economic societal needs and demands, and since the public interest claim is open-ended,[223] Member States can react to actual and legal developments which are worthy of protection.[224]

In tax law, the CJEU has qualified different aims of national rules to be in the public interest, such as the concept of coherence, the balanced allocation of taxing rights, the effectiveness of fiscal supervision, and the fight against tax avoidance and evasion. These grounds are all capable of justifying restrictions of the fundamental freedoms, as long as the national rule is proportionate.

All of these public interest concerns in taxation protect the aim and purpose of the national laws. The concept of coherence, for example, acknowledges that any tax system offers tax benefits and tax disadvantages and that, in some cases, the benefit and the advantage are linked.[225] In other words, a taxpayer has to suffer a disadvantage to be entitled to a benefit.[226] If the benefit and the disadvantage build on each other, denying the tax benefits in cross-border cases in which the taxpayer was not subject to a tax disadvantage can be justified.[227] The concept of coherence acknowledges that a national tax system is not simply a concatenation of self-sufficient rules which can be viewed and tested against the fundamental freedoms in an isolated fashion. Some rules only achieve their aim and purpose if they are taken together with other norms. Accordingly, this ground of justification respects the national tax system and its underlying goals.

Documentation 8, 12; Roman Seer, 'The Jurisprudence of the European Court of Justice: Limitation of the Legal Consequences?' (2006) 46 European Taxation 470, 470.

222 CJEU, 5 February 2014, C-385/12, *Hervis Sport*, ECLI:EU:C:2014:47, para 44; CJEU, 6 June 2000, C-35/98, *B.G.M. Verkooijen*, ECLI:EU:C:2000:294, para 47 and 48.

223 Norbert Reich, 'How Proportionate Is the Proportionality Principle? Some Critical Remarks on the Use and Methodology of the Proportionality Principle in the Internal Market Case Law of the ECJ' in Hans-Wolfgang Micklitz and Bruno de Witte (eds), *The European Court of Justice and the Autonomy of the Member States* (Intersentia 2012) 91 et seq, in particular 97; Hinnekens (n 218) 77.

224 Cordewener, *Europäische Grundfreiheiten und nationales Steuerrecht* (n 42) 133.

225 For an analysis of the entire CJEU case law on the coherence of a national tax system see Dennis Weber, 'An Analysis of the Past, Current and Future of the Coherence of the Tax System as Justification' (2015) 24 EC Tax Review 43; for a detailed analysis of the logical symmetry argument underlying the notion of coherence Robert Neyt and Steven Peeters, 'Balanced Allocation and Coherence: Some Thoughts in Light of Argenta and K' (2014) 23 EC Tax Review 64, 68 et seq.

226 Peter J Wattel, 'Red Herrings in Direct Tax Cases before the ECJ' (2004) 31 Legal Issues of Economic Integration 81, 93–94 criticising the narrow coherence concept of the CJEU.

227 Joachim Englisch, 'Fiscal Cohesion in the Taxation of Cross-Border Dividends (Part Two)' (2004) 44 European Taxation 355, 356 et seq.

On the other hand, the effectiveness of fiscal supervision allows the Member State to ask for more information in a cross-border situation in order to assess the taxpayer under the domestic tax rules because of the jurisdictional limits of one Member State's jurisdiction to enforce.[228] According to the International Court of Justice, the enforcement of the law in the territory of another State is considered unlawful.[229] Thus, the Member States can either gather information via an exchange of information with the relevant fellow Member State or by requiring the taxpayer to provide more information (more information than in a purely domestic setting). CJEU case law shows that the Court allows a Member State to choose which form of information gathering it finds more appropriate and efficient.[230]

The Member States' right to justify restrictions on the fundamental freedoms on the grounds of a balanced allocation of taxing rights shows that the CJEU not only examines national laws of the Member States and asks for their aim and purpose, but also allows consideration of bilateral agreements between the Member States to influence the national tax system which may be able to justify restrictions.[231]

From this it follows that the Member States are not able to rely on budgetary constraints or protectionist claims to justify trade restrictions or discrimination through their domestic tax law. Purely economic claims cannot be considered as societal interests which need to be balanced against the value of market integration. In taxation, the public interest claim is a claim to apply the domestic policy decision reflected in the tax burden to intra-EU economic situation. This requires a balanced application of both tax benefits and tax burdens, an overcoming of a lack of information in cross-border situations, and a recognition of reciprocal deals between States balancing their taxing rights.

2. Balancing Act

In cases in which Member States are able to rely on a legitimate public interest concern, the national measure is not automatically justified; it 'must be suitable for securing the attainment of the objective which they pursue; and they must not go beyond what is necessary in order to attain it'.[232] At this stage, the CJEU has

[228] CJEU, 28 October 1999, C-55/98, *Vestergaard*, ECLI:EU:C:1999:533, para 26; CJEU, 3 October 2002, C-136/00, *Danner*, ECLI:EU:C:2002:558, para 49; CJEU, 26 June 2003, C-422/01, *Skandia and Ramstedt*, ECLI:EU:C:2003:380, para 42; CJEU, 8 July 1999, C-254/97, *Baxter*, ECLI:EU:C:1999:368, para 18; CJEU, 10 March 2005, C-39/04, *Laboratoires Fournier SA*, ECLI:EU:C:2005:161, para 24; Lang, 'Kapitalverkehrsfreiheit' (n 58) 220.

[229] PCIJ, 7 September 1927, Collection of Judgments Series A Nr. 10, The Case of S.S. 'Lotus', p 19.

[230] CJEU, 28 October 1999, C-55/98, *Vestergaard*, ECLI:EU:C:1999:533, para 26; CJEU, 3 October 2002, C-136/00, *Danner*, ECLI:EU:C:2002:558, para 49; CJEU, 26 June 2003, C-422/01, *Skandia*, ECLI:EU:C:2003:380, para 42; CJEU, 9 October 2014, C-326/12, *van Caster*, ECLI:EU:C:2014:2269, para 49 et seq.

[231] For a more detailed analysis of this matter see this chapter Part I, E.VIII.2.

[232] CJEU, 30 November 1995, C-55/94, *Gebhard*, ECLI:EU:C:1995:411, para 37; CJEU, 12 December 1996, C-3/95, *Reisebüro Broede*, ECLI:EU:C:1996:487, para 28; CJEU, 9 March 1999, C-212/97, *Centros Ltd*, ECLI:EU:C:1999:126, para 34; CJEU, 15 January 2002, C-439/99, *Commission v Italy*, ECLI:EU:C:2002:14, para 23; CJEU, 11 July 2002, C-294/00, *Gräbner*, ECLI:EU:C:2002:442, para 39; CJEU, 30 September 2003, C-167/01, *Inspire Art Ltd*, ECLI:EU:C:2003:512, para 133; CJEU, 13

to engage in a true balancing of the values of market integration and non-market values.

In a number of cases, the CJEU has stopped at the suitability level and asked whether the measure taken by the Member State can achieve its intended goal, which is considered to be a public interest concern. In other cases, the Court has put a great deal of effort into analysing whether or not the national measure is the least restrictive measure, or whether there are ways to achieve the national value which are less restrictive but equally effective.[233]

In tax law, it has become evident that the CJEU is very strict when it comes to an unequal substantive tax treatment of non-resident and resident taxpayers or cross-border and purely domestic economic activities. In other words, the Court does not accept that a taxpayer has to pay more in taxes just because he makes use of the free movement rights guaranteed by the European treaties. Accordingly, the taxpayer should not be burdened with higher tax rates,[234] should not be denied the possibility to deduct the business expenditure related to the income gained in the Member State,[235] and should above all have access to all national measures to prevent economic double taxation[236] (in the case of outbound dividends only if the Member State chose to tax the dividend flowing outside the country).[237] In all these cases, the CJEU has found that the Member State could have employed less restrictive, but equally effective, ways to achieve the aim underlying the national laws. In particular, lack of information never justifies an unequal treatment in substantive tax law issues; the Court demands an exchange of information between the relevant Member States or a widening of taxpayers' duties which allows the Member State to treat a resident and a non-resident, as well as a domestic economic activity and a cross-border economic activity equally when it comes to the tax base.[238] From this it follows that the CJEU does not take the legal situation

November 2003, C-153/02, *Neri*, ECLI:EU:C:2003:614, para 46; CJEU, 14 February 2008, C-244/06, *Dynamic Medien Vertriebs GmbH*, ECLI:EU:C:2008:85, para 42; CJEU, 25 April 2013, C-212/11, *Jyske Bank Gibraltar Ltd*, ECLI:EU:C:2013:270, para 60; CJEU, 21 September 2017, C-125/16, *Malta Dental Technologists Association*, ECLI:EU:C:2017:707, para 56; CJEU, 14 November 2018, C-342/17, *Memoria Srl*, ECLI:EU:C:2018:906, para 51.

[233] For example CJEU, 13 December 2005, C-446/03, *Marks & Spencer*, ECLI:EU:C:2005:763; CJEU, 12 June 2018, C-650/16, *Bevola*, ECLI:EU:C:2018:424, para 55 et seq. Dominik Freyer, 'The Proportionality Principle under EU Tax Law: General and Practical Problems Caused by Its Extensive Application—Part 1' (2017) 57 European Taxation 384, 385 et seq.

[234] CJEU, 2 April 1988, C-213/96, *Outokumpu Qy*, ECLI:EU:C:1998:155; CJEU, 12 June 2003, *Gerritse*, ECLI:EU:C:2003:340; CJEU, 19 November 2009, C-540/07, *Commission v Italy*, ECLI:EU:C:2009:717; CJEU, 5 February 2014, C-385/12, *Hervis*, ECLI:EU:C:2014:47; CJEU, 22 June 2017, C-20/16, *Bechtel*, ECLI:EU:C:2017:488.

[235] CJEU, 12 June 2003, *Gerritse*, ECLI:EU:C:2003:340; CJEU, 11 October 2007, C-443/06, *Hollmann*, ECLI:EU:C:2007:600; CJEU, 13 June 2016, C-18/15, *Brisal*, ECLI:EU:C:2016:549.

[236] CJEU, 30 June 2011, C-262/09, *Meilicke*, ECLI:EU:C:2011:438; CJEU, 7 September 2004, C-319/02, *Manninen*, ECLI:EU:C:2004:484.

[237] CJEU, 14 December 2006, C-170/05, *Denkavit*, ECLI:EU:C:2006:783; CJEU, 8 November 2007, C-379/05, *Amurta*, ECLI:EU:C:2007:655.

[238] CJEU, 13 June 2016, C-18/15, *Brisal*, ECLI:EU:C:2016:549, para 34 et seq.

(chosen by the Member State) for granted; the Court may force the Member States to do more than they are willing to do (eg gather information via an exchange of information) to allow an equal application of the tax laws to non-resident taxpayers or cross-border economic activities.

IV. Findings on the Impact of Member States' Non-market Values on the Fundamental Freedoms

Non-market values can be considered at three different levels in the process of testing national measures against the fundamental freedoms. First, a trade-hampering market access restriction in the form of a double burden may only exist if the burden imposed by the home and the host Member State aims for the same objective. Accordingly, if the host Member State can prove that the regulatory framework in the home Member State does not sufficiently protect the host Member State's public interest, the application of the regulatory framework in the host Member State does not impose a market access restriction. Some national measures are particularly trade-impeding, like a total ban of certain goods or services and the burden of the very act of exercising the free movement rights, and therefore impose a market access restriction regardless of their underlying aim and purpose.

Secondly, at the comparability level, the aim and purpose of the national law forms the benchmark for determining whether or not a cross-border and a purely domestic situation are comparable. Finding the *tertium comparationis* based on the aim and purpose of the national rule[239] allows non-market values to be taken into account. To a certain extent, Member States are also able to influence the scope of the fundamental freedoms through their national law-making. The scope of the fundamental freedoms defines which situations are generally open to comparison. The fundamental freedoms only seek a simple per-country approach, meaning that only the legal treatment of one Member State is considered at the comparability level. In other words, the legal treatment in the other Member States is not recognised when determining comparability. However, if the Member State's national measure is explicitly linked to the treatment of a particular economic transaction in a fellow Member State, the scope of the fundamental freedoms is widened and includes both the domestic and the foreign treatment. A tax treaty may also provide for a linkage between the domestic and the foreign tax treatment; however, the CJEU does not consider the linkage and a neutralisation of the restriction at the comparability level but at the justification level. Moreover, a horizontal comparison does not apply when Member States

[239] The aim and purpose approach rejects a pure competition-based approach.

enter into tax treaties. The fundamental freedoms honour the bilateral reciprocal agreement between two Member States, and thus do not force the Member States to apply a favourable tax treatment following from one tax treaty to a cross-border situation which is subject to a different tax treaty.

Thirdly, Member States can justify restrictions of the fundamental freedoms based on non-market values at the justification level. The CJEU has accepted the need to recognise broader arguments of justification than those explicitly provided in the European treaties, and thus additional grounds of justification reflecting non-market values of Member States are accepted within the European internal market framework. However, Member States cannot justify restrictions of fundamental freedoms based on economic reasons such as a loss of revenue or the need to support the domestic economy, because these reasons always include an element of protectionist or self-interested aims.

V. Limits of Member States' Value Setting

The fundamental freedoms invalidate protectionist national laws and national measures, causing a fragmentation of the European internal market. This aim requires an examination of the application of national laws because a harsher treatment of foreigners, foreign products, or cross-border economic activities is inimical to free movement. To identify whether foreigners, foreign products, or cross-border economic activities are treated less favourably, it is not necessary to test the national laws against certain external values or principles. A comparison between the treatment of the purely domestic and the cross-border situation would be enough to identify a more adverse treatment in an EU context.

Accordingly, the fundamental freedoms do not need to provide and do not embody any content-based values which Member States have to follow when enacting national laws. Only when it comes to the justification level do the European treaties define the public interest concerns which are capable of justifying a restriction of the fundamental freedoms. Moreover, the existing secondary law in the field of taxation does not establish any principles on what to tax and how to tax it. The Member States are entirely free to decide on tax bases, tax rates, exemptions, and allowances, as long as they do not place non-resident taxpayers and cross-border economic activities in a worse position.

Having said this, the CJEU has gone further in its case law both at the level of comparability (see subsection 1) and the level of justification (see subsection 2) and applied a kind of God-given 'value set'.[240]

[240] Eric Kemmeren, for example, argues that the CJEU followed its own values in *Société Générale SA* because the Court 'develops its own taxable base, as it [the Court] decides that, based on European law, only expenses which are directly linked to the actual *payment* of the dividends must be taken into account for the purpose of comparing the tax burdens of resident and non-resident companies. These

1. CJEU Case Law and its Underlying Value Choice on the Level of Comparability

Some CJEU jurisprudence reveals the Court's bias for applying substantive tax principles to the level of comparability. Accordingly, the CJEU has given a preference on which Member State should be entitled to tax or which Member State has to grant a tax benefit. The following subsections analyse whether or not the Court overstepped its competences.

a) *Taxation of Inbound Dividends*

The taxation of dividends provoked a large number of cases brought before the CJEU. These cases were mostly triggered by the two levels of taxation in a company shareholder scenario. Every Member State has decided to tax the gain of a company first at the level of the company, and then at the level of the shareholders when the gain is distributed. To prevent economic double taxation, Member States implement different mechanisms, such as the dividend imputation system, which allow the shareholders to credit the tax levied at the level of the company against their tax liability. In a cross-border situation, Member States are quite reluctant to grant equal benefits because no Member State is willing to credit a foreign tax against the shareholder's domestic tax liability.

With regards to inbound dividends, the CJEU ruled that a shareholder 'resident in a Member State and receiving dividends from a company established in that State is comparable to that of shareholders who are resident in that State and receive dividends from a company established in another Member State'.[241] The receipt of dividends from a resident company is comparable to the receipt of dividends from a non-resident company because in both situations the income will be taxed twice: at company level and at shareholder level (economic double taxation).[242] The Court fully ignores the fact that in a cross-border situation it is not economic double taxation alone which would be addressed by a credit of the tax levied at company level, but also *juridical* double taxation[243] would also be prevented.[244]

Despite the confusion over what an economic and what a juridical double taxation is, the CJEU not only accepted taxation implicitly at source, the Court also

expenses do not include, for example, interest expenses concerning ownership of the shares *per se*, whereas such expenses are deductible as expenses from dividend received when calculating the taxable base of residents', Eric CCM Kemmeren, 'Gross Withholding Taxes: Is the Court of Justice of the European Union Back on Track with Regard to Deductible Expenses?' (2017) 26 EC Tax Review 2, 5–6.

[241] CJEU, 30 June 2011, C-262/09, *Meilicke*, ECLI:EU:C:2011:438, para 30.

[242] CJEU, 7 September 2004, C-319/02, *Manninen*, ECLI:EU:C:2004:484, paras 35–36.

[243] For a definition of *juridical* double taxation and *economic* double taxation see Rust (n 17) 1.

[244] Weber (n 149) 597–98; Michael J Graetz and Alvin CJr Warren, 'Dividend Taxation in Europe: When the ECJ Makes Tax Policy' (2007) 44 Common Market Law Review 1577, 1602 arguing that the 'ECJ's portfolio investment cases, which involve the intersection of economic and international double taxation, do raise many of those issues, but most of them have simply been ignored by the Court'; Malcolm Gammie, 'Non-Discrimination and the Taxation of Cross-Border Dividends' (2010) 2 World Tax Journal 162, 172.

granted the source Member State the prior taxing right.[245] Priority was given to the source Member State by comparing domestic and foreign dividend flows and the subsequent forcing of the home Member State to consider the foreign tax and grant a credit as it would have done in a purely domestic setting. The favouring of source over residence is not anchored in the European treaties,[246] and is thus a pure value judgment by the Court. The fact that the Court follows pure value judgements in inbound dividend cases is even more evident when one considers that the market freedoms do not prohibit the discrimination of foreign taxes.[247]

b) Personal deductions

The CJEU had to rule on the question of whether or not a non-resident taxpayer is allowed (also) to deduct personal expenses in the host Member State on numerous occasions. Within the (income) tax framework, the taxpayer's personal and family situation shall be considered when determining his individual tax burden. The notion of 'personal and family situation' has to be understood in a very broad way. The idea of personal deductions or allowances, as understood by CJEU case law, therefore covers any tax advantage which is linked to the taxpayer's personal ability to pay tax, regardless of how the national tax codes labels these benefits.[248] The first and probably most famous ruling on personal deduction was *Schumacker*.[249] In this case, the CJEU found that a resident and a non-resident taxpayer are not in a comparable situation when it comes to the granting of personal allowances. The home Member State has a duty to consider the personal circumstances of the taxpayer for tax law purposes, which subsequently frees the host Member State from any obligations of that kind. The Court went on and argued that, in the case at hand, the resident and non-resident taxpayer were, however, in a comparable situation because the taxpayer earned almost all of his income in the host state 'with the result'[250] that he was not able to claim the benefit in the home Member State. Allowing a comparison between the resident and the non-resident taxpayer subsequently forced the host Member State to grant a non-resident taxpayer the benefit to deduct personal expenses. Disallowing such a taxpayer from deducting personal expenses in the host Member State would be discriminatory, as the 'personal and family circumstances are taken into account neither in the State of residence nor in the State of employment'.[251]

245 See also Hey, 'Vorrecht des Quellenstaates' (n 151) 777 et seq.

246 Paul Farmer and Adam Zalasinski, 'General Report' in Xenios L Xenopoulos (ed), *Direct Tax Rules and the EU Fundamental Freedoms: Origin and Scope of the Problem; National and Community Responses and Solutions: FIDE 2006 National Reports* (Theopress 2006) 403.

247 Schön, 'Neutrality and Territoriality' (n 69) 290; Farmer and Zalasinski (n 246) 403.

248 CJEU, 14 March 2019, C-174/18, *Jacobs and Lennertz*, ECLI:EU:C:2019:205, para 38 et seq.

249 CJEU, 14 February 1995, C-279/93, *Schumacker*, ECLI:EU:C:1995:31.

250 ibid para 36.

251 ibid para 38.

From this, it follows that the Court maintains the firm belief that personal and family circumstances have to be taken into account for tax law matters. Generally, the home Member State is obliged to do so. The CJEU establishes a primary responsibility of the home Member State by denying comparability between a resident and a non-resident taxpayer in cases in which the non-resident taxpayer can claim family deductions in the home Member State. The host Member State is required to help only if the home Member State is not capable of taking personal and family circumstances into account because there is simply no income earned within the home Member State.[252] The obligation to consider personal and family circumstances switches from the home to the host Member State,[253] regardless of whether the taxpayer earns all or almost all of his income in the host Member State.[254] The CJEU case law on personal allowances shows that the Court uses the comparability test to follow its own value choice. If the CJEU did not believe that the home Member State is primarily responsible for granting family deductions, the Court would rule on the comparability question based on the aim and purpose of the national rule, which may in most cases allow a comparison of the resident and the non-resident taxpayer.

The Court also extended this logic to negative rent income,[255] meaning that the host Member State must allow a deduction of the negative income if it can only be offset against positive income in the host Member State. In cases where the negative income (or likewise the personal deductions) could be taken into account in more than one host Member State, each host Member State is only required to grant the tax advantage 'in proportion to the share of his income received within each such Member State'.[256] On the contrary, the home Member State is never entitled to reduce the personal deduction in proportion to the share of the income derived within the home state.[257]

[252] García Prats, 'Is It Possible to Set a Coherent System of Rules on Direct Taxation' (n 145) 434 arguing that the CJEU develops 'the right to move for economic reasons into the right to get at least once, or just once (Gschwind) personal and family allowances income tax, whether in the residence State ([in general terms] or in the source State [when certain undetermined conditions are met]'.

[253] However, the host Member State is only required to consider the family circumstances if the taxpayer earns his income in the host Member State for a sufficient time. A taxpayer who first earned his income in the host Member State but then moved to a third country so that he spent three-quarters of the income year in the third county earning his income there was not allowed to deduct his mortgage interest for a house in the home Member State (CJEU, 18 June 2015, C-9/14, *Kieback*, ECLI:EU:C:2015:406). Bart Peeters, 'Kieback: When Schumacker Emigrates …' (2016) 25 EC Tax Review 58, 67 criticising the outcome of the case in the light of the CJEU's earlier case law.

[254] The *Schumacker* doctrine indicates that the host Member State is only responsible if the taxpayer earns all or almost all of his income in the host Member State. However, in *X*, the CJEU forced a Member State to consider personal and family circumstances of a taxpayer who did not earn any taxable income in the home state regardless of the fact that the taxpayer only earned a fraction of his income in that Member State. The Court ruled that this Member State was only required to grant personal allowances on a factual basis; CJEU, 9 February 2017, C-283/15, *X*, ECLI:EU:C:2017:102, para 48; see also Hannelore Niesten, 'Pro Rata Deduction of Negative Income from Income Received in Each Member State' (2018) 58 European Taxation 116, 119.

[255] CJEU, 18 July 2007, C-182/06, *Lakebrink*, ECLI:EU:C:2007:452.

[256] CJEU, 9 February 2017, C-283/15, *X*, ECLI:EU:C:2017:102, para 48.

[257] CJEU, 12 December 2002, C-385/00, *de Groot*, ECLI:EU:C:2002:750.

The case law clearly shows that the CJEU primarily requires the home Member State to take personal and family circumstances into account. The host Member State is not required to grant any tax benefits in this regard as long as the home Member State is capable of granting those benefits. The home Member State cannot free itself from the obligation to recognise personal circumstances[258] even if the host Member States grants a family allowance,[259] which may put the taxpayer in the favourable position of having his personal circumstances recognised twice.[260] However, an agreement between the home and the host Member State can release the home Member State from the obligation to grant all personal and family allowances.[261]

[258] CJEU, 12 December 2013, C-303/12, *Imfeld*, ECLI:EU:C:2013, para 43 'the residence State is responsible under international tax law for taking personal and family circumstances into account'. Peter J Wattel, 'Progressive Taxation of Non-Residents and Intra-EC Allocation of Personal Tax Allowances' (2000) 40 European Taxation 210, 214 et seq, argues that non-income related deductions (eg personal allowances) take the personal ability-to-pay into account and thus are only linked to the person. However, if the home Member State is the only State taking non-income related expenses (eg illness, alimony, children, etc) into account, the expenses do not relate to the total income but to parts of the income. On the negative implication of the prior responsibility of the home Member State to consider personal circumstances in cases in which the taxpayer earns a substantial part of his income in the host Member State, see Peeters, 'Kieback' (n 253) 66; John F Avery Jones, 'A Comment on "Progressive Taxation of Non-Residents and Intra-EC Allocation of Personal Tax Allowances"' (2000) 40 European Taxation 375 arguing that the negative effects can be addressed by a general switch from the exemption method to the credit method allowing the home Member State to take all the income and the personal circumstances into account. In the area of social security benefits, Art 68 of the Regulation 883/2004/EC (Regulation, 29 April 2004, 883/2004/EC, on the coordination of social security systems, OJ, 20 April 2004, L 166, 1) provides for priority rules if a family is entitled to (the 'same') benefits in more than one Member States. However, these rules may not be applied in the field of tax law: CJEU, 24 October 2013, C-177/12, *Lachheb*, ECLI:EU:C:2013:689, para 31: the child bonus of one Member State is 'granted automatically, without any link to the income or tax owed by the applicant' and thus the priority rules can of the secondary EU law can be applied.

[259] CJEU, 12 December 2013, C-303/12, *Imfeld*, ECLI:EU:C:2013, paras 59–60; Isabella de Groot criticises the CJEU's restrictive approach in the field of personal deductions because the Court allows neutralisation in the field of withholding taxes: Isabella M de Groot, 'The CJEU's Conflicting Case Law on Neutralization' (2014) 42 Intertax 721.

[260] Hannelore Niesten, 'Personal and Family Tax Benefits in the EU Internal Market: From Schumacker to Fractional Tax Treatment' (2018) 55 Common Market Law Review 819, 825 highlighting the Court's missed opportunity to analyse the effects of double advantages on the EU internal market. Peeters and Verschueren (n 14) 268 arguing that an unjust enrichment in the form of double allowances may in particular be triggered by Art 7 Subsection 2 of the Regulation 1612/68 on the free movement of workers which explicitly entitles non-national workers to the same tax benefits as nationals. Luca Cerioni, 'Guido Imfeld and Nathalie Garcet v Belgian State: A Continuation of the Schumacker Doctrine?' (2014) British Tax Review 128, 134 criticising that the Court unsystematically changes from an overall perspective to a per-country perspective.

[261] CJEU, 12 December 2013, C-303/12, *Imfeld*, ECLI:EU:C:2013, para 69 et seq. The demand for an agreement between the home and the host Member State to relieve the home Member State from its duties and to prevent the personal circumstances from being taken into account twice equals the need to sign double tax treaties to prevent double taxation: Hannelore Niesten, 'Growing Impetus for Harmonization of Personal and Family Allowances: Current State of Affairs of the Schumacker-Doctrine after Imfeld and Garcet' (2015) 24 EC Tax Review 185, 193; Bruno Peeters, 'Mobility of EU Citizens and Family Taxation: A Hard to Reconcile Combination' (2014) 23 EC Tax Review 118, 199 explicitly on the 'automatic nature' of the loss of the family allowance.

If, however, the taxpayer earns no income or not enough to have his personal circumstances recognised in the home Member State,[262] the host Member State subsequently has to give the tax benefit to a non-resident,[263] but it only has to do so in proportion to the share of income received within this host Member State.[264] It is striking that the Court first assumes that there is a general notion of personal deductions in all the Member States, and secondly, finds that the home Member State is primarily responsible for taking personal and family circumstances into account.

We shall start with the first point of criticism: the Court seems to assume that the tax benefits granted in different Member States are identical or at least similar.[265] This assumption is not, however, in line with the general understanding that every Member State is free to design its tax system.[266] There are no rules on what an income tax system must look like, or which features it must have, and thus the Member States should be free in deciding whether or not they want to apply a tax reduction for personal circumstances.[267] To be fair, the notion of personal allowances has been embedded in all of the Member States' tax laws involved in the cases presented in the above.[268] However, a general claim towards the host or home Member State to consider personal allowances cannot be deduced from the European treaties.

The second point of criticism turns to the fact that there is no part in the EU treaties or secondary EU law that requires the home Member State to bear the entire burden of personal deductions.[269] The Court, however, assumes that every

[262] The host Member State may be obliged to grant personal allowances or a basic allowance even if the taxpayer earns half of his income in the resident Member State (CJEU, 10 May 2012, C-39/10, *Commission v Estonia*, ECLI:EU:C:2012:282, para 54 et seq) or a substantive part of his income in the host Member State but the host Member State may be unable to grant personal allowances or a basic allowance because the taxpayer earns tax-free income (eg a stipend, CJEU, 1 July 2004, C-169/03, *Wallentin*, ECLI:EU:C:2004:403).

[263] CJEU, 11 August 1995, C-80/94, *Wielockx*, ECLI:EU:C:1995:271, paras 20–22; CJEU, 14 September 1999, C-391/97, *Gschwind*, ECLI:EU:C:1999:409, paras 26–27; CJEU, 28. February 2013, C-168/11, *Beker*, ECLI:EU:C:2013:117 para 44.

[264] CJEU, 9 February 2017, C-283/15, *X*, ECLI:EU:C:2017:102, para 48.

[265] Nils Mattsson, 'Does the European Court of Justice Understand the Policy behind Tax Benefits Based on Personal and Family Circumstances?' (2003) 43 European Taxation 186, 188 et seq criticising the Court's approach on the basis that the national provisions may be fundamentally different or that a Member State may be free to not provide personal and family allowances at all.

[266] Axel Cordewener, 'Personal Income Taxation of Non-Residents and the Increasing Impact of the EC Treaty Freedoms' in Dennis Weber (ed), *The Influence of European Law on Direct Taxation: Recent and Future Developments* (Kluwer Law International 2007) 61 et seq.

[267] Schön, 'Neutrality and Territoriality' (n 69) 278.

[268] Since the concept of personal and family allowances is not defined in the European treaties or the double tax treaty, the national concepts vary fundamentally, Alfredo F García Prats, 'Revisiting "Schumacker": Source, Residence and Citizenship in the ECJ Case Law on Direct Taxation' in Isabelle Richelle, Wolfgang Schön, and Edoardo Traversa (eds), *Allocating Taxing Powers within the European Union* (Springer-Verlag 2013) 18; Niesten, 'Personal and Family Tax Benefits in the EU Internal Market' (n 260) 830.

[269] Alfredo F García Prats, 'Subjective Ability to Pay: Schumacker' in Werner Haslehner, Georg Kofler, and Alexander Rust (eds), *Landmark Decisions of the ECJ in Direct Taxation* (Kluwer Law International 2015) 24.

taxpayer has strong ties to the home Member State because of his residency and economic integration,[270] and these ties make it feasible to consider personal and family circumstances for tax law purposes.[271] Requiring the home Member State to take the taxpayer's personal circumstances into account and allowing the host Member State to deny any tax reduction for personal circumstances contradicts the general presumption that EU law neither allocates taxing rights nor distributes obligations among Member States.[272] The allocation of primary and secondary tax obligations is purely driven by the CJEU judiciary's value judgement that personal circumstances have to be considered in order to calculate personal income tax.[273] Such circumstances should not be considered twice or not at all; instead they should be considered exactly once, preferentially in the home Member State.

From a legal and internal market perspective, Member States are required to provide a non-discriminatory tax regime. This requirement should overarch all elements of personal income taxation, from tax rates till allowances. Thus, there is no reason why personal deductions should be treated differently. Applying the fundamental freedoms to personal deduction without following an external value order could allow taxpayers to claim a deduction in more than one Member State, which is however fully in line with the unilateral perspective of the market freedoms.[274]

2. CJEU Case Law and External Value Choice on the Level of Justification

The fact that the CJEU follows, at least in some cases, its ideas on which Member State should be given the superior taxing right, or which Member State is required to allow deductions can also be spotted at the justification stage. The CJEU's jurisprudence on the concept of territoriality and the concept of tax avoidance in particular make it clear that the Court favours source taxation over residence taxation. The Court allows Member States to implement a discriminatory mechanism to ensure taxation of income which is derived within their territory. On the other hand,

[270] The total income of a taxable person 'is concentrated at his place of residence': see for many examples CJEU, 14 February 1995, C-279/93, *Schumacker*, ECLI:EU:C:1995:31, para 32; CJEU, 12 December 2002, C-385/00, *de Groot*, ECLI:EU:C:2002:750, para 98; CJEU, 1 July 2004, C-169/03, *Wallentin*, ECLI:EU:C:2004:403, para 15.

[271] Peeters, 'Mobility of EU Citizens and Family Taxation' (n 261) 119 rightly questions the consistency of the CJEU argument. The State of residence is the best place to assess the taxpayer's personal ability to pay tax because his personal and financial interest are centred there: 'the more the mobility of the EU citizens increases, the more the accuracy of the latter assumption by the Court seems to decrease'.

[272] 'Misunderstanding, misinterpretation and wrong assumptions on the tax law application to the cases have *helped* to develop such doctrine', García Prats, 'Is It Possible to Set a Coherent System of Rules on Direct Taxation' (n 145) 435.

[273] Pasquale Pistone, 'European Direct Tax Law: Quo Vadis?' in Philippe Hinnekens and Luc Hinnekens (eds), *A Vision of Taxes Within and Outside the European Borders: Festschrift in Honor of Prof. Dr. Frans Vanistendael* (n 40) 717 arguing that 'the Court draws from tax treaties principles that they do not actually contain'.

[274] CJEU, 12 December 2013, C-303/12, *Imfeld*, ECLI:EU:C:2013, para 77.

the Court assigns the duty of recognising losses to the Member States in which they occurred.[275] Accordingly, the granting of relief of foreign losses is only required by the CJEU in a very narrow set of circumstances.[276]

The Court's preference for source taxation goes far beyond what is indicated by the principle of territoriality under international law standards. In international law, territoriality refers to the sovereignty of a State over its territory.[277] Transferred to the field of taxation, territoriality refers to a State's ability to tax every person or event on its territory.[278] The international concept of territoriality distributes the right to tax to the source and resident State equally, without granting one priority over the other. In the arena of international tax law, the Member States sign tax treaties which all aim to prevent double taxation (and in recent times also double non-taxation) in cases of cross-border economic activities. Tax treaties lead to an increase in source-based taxation because they generally give the source State a right to tax, as well as forcing the resident State either to credit the foreign tax or exempt the income. A general favouring of source taxation through tax treaties does not rise to a general EU law principle granting the source State a preferential taxing right even though a huge amount of treaties has been signed between the Member States.[279]

This case law clearly shows that the Court follows its understanding of territoriality in tax law matters.[280] Such an understanding is neither triggered by international law nor by the values underlying the national tax law rules. Preferred source taxation is thus clearly, and rather simply, a value choice taken by the judges of the CJEU. The application of the fundamental freedoms along the line of external value choices (CJEU judges' value choices) may demand that Member States change their regulatory regimes in ways which are not in line with their policy

[275] For a detailed overview of the CJEU case law on 'final losses' see Michael Lang, 'Has the Case Law of the ECJ on Final Losses Reached the End of the Line?' (2014) 54 European Taxation 530; Roland Ismer and Harald Kandel, 'A Finale Incomparabile to the Saga of Definitive Losses? Deduction of Foreign Losses and Fundamental Freedoms After Bevola and Sofina' (2019) 47 Intertax 573.

[276] In *Marks & Spencer*, and most recently in *Bevola* and *Holmen*, the CJEU only required the home Member State to recognise foreign losses if those losses are final: CJEU, 13 December 2005, C-446/03, *Marks & Spencer*, ECLI:EU:C:2005:763; CJEU, 12 June 2018, C-650/16, *Bevola*, ECLI:EU:C:2018:424, and if there is a direct link between the parent company and the subsidiary sustaining the loss: CJEU, 19 June 2019, C-608/17, *Holmen*, ECLI:EU:C:2019:511. For an analysis of the entire case law see Lang, 'Case Law of the ECJ on Final Losses' (n 275); Ismer and Kandel (n 275); Axel Cordewener, 'Cross-Border Loss Compensation and EU Fundamental Freedoms: The "Final Losses" Doctrine Is Still Alive!' (2018) 27 EC Tax Review 230.

[277] Malcolm N Shaw, 'Territory in International Law' (1982) Netherlands Yearbook of International Law 61, 61 et seq.

[278] Christian Sternberg, *Die extraterritoriale Besteuerungsgewalt des Staates* (Duncker & Humblot 2019) 198 set seq, 223 et seq.

[279] See in this vein Schön, 'Neutrality and Territoriality' (n 69).

[280] Otto Marres, 'The Principle of Territoriality and Cross-Border Loss Compensation' (2011) 39 Intertax 112, 112 et seq identifying the different meaning of territoriality in international law, international tax law, and the CJEU's case law.

choices, and they may therefore wish to address these conflicts through enhanced cooperation laws.

VI. Conclusions

It is the province and duty of the judicial branch of every legal system to state what the law is; accordingly, this also applies to the CJEU. The task of giving meaning to the words of a rule and embedding it into the spirit of the time has its limits where a Court's ruling would become an act of a political nature.[281] This limit draws a clear line between the judiciary and the legislature and may be seen as a manifestation of the principle of separation of powers.[282] To date, the CJEU has not always lived up to this standard.[283] The Court has further developed the fundamental freedoms and massively extended their scope. The CJEU's interest-driven jurisprudence was, and still is, supposed to be justified by the need 'to overcome the political deadlock that prevented the completion of the internal market'.[284]

The specific European equal treatment rules prohibit both a discriminatory and restrictive tax treatment of foreigners, foreign products, and cross-border economic activities. Despite the extensive widening of the scope of the fundamental freedoms, at heart, they still aim to abolish any national law which is protectionist in nature. The equal treatment rules determine by their scope which situations may, in general, be comparable, but the benchmark for what is comparable in the concrete case is set by the aim and purpose of the national law. Only the aim and purpose of the national law can ascertain its potentially protectionist nature. Likewise, the aim and purpose of the national law shows whether compliance with the domestic regulatory framework establishes a (protectionist) double burden and subsequently imposes market access restrictions or whether the regulatory framework in the home Member State has not sufficiently considered these non-market interests.

Where the Member State was not able to prove the non-protectionist character of the national law at the restriction or comparability level, the Member State may put forward the non-market values it tries to protect on the justification level. Thus far, the Court has acknowledged a wide range of non-market values but has always rejected economic reasons as a ground of justification.

281 Chief Justice Marshall in *Marbury v Madison*, 5 U.S. 1 Cranch 137 137 (1803).

282 ibid.

283 'The evolution of EC Law under the ECJ case law parameters overrides the traditional distinction between creation and interpretation of law', García Prats, 'Is It Possible to Set a Coherent System of Rules on Direct Taxation' (n 145) 436.

284 Lenaerts, 'The Court's Outer and Inner Selves: Exploring the External and Internal Legitimacy of the European Court of Justice' (n 40) 16.

In a number of tax cases, the Court has accepted that the fundamental freedoms are value free and thus have to be filled with national values to judge whether or not the national laws are in line with the free movement guarantees. The national values of the Member States influence the decision on whether the national rule constitutes a restriction of the free movement rights, sets the framework for finding the *tertium comparationis*, and may form a ground of justification. Accordingly, the CJEU considers the Member States' policy preferences (and in particular the prioritisation of some non-market values over market efficiency) at these three levels. The implicit permission granted to single Member States to prioritise non-market values forms the baseline for a group of Member States jointly pursuing non-market values. In other words, if one Member State is allowed to create trade obstacles because some non-market values are capable of outweighing market efficiency, enhanced cooperation law is permitted to establish the same trade obstacle to protect the same non-market values within the group.

However, in several other cases, the Court has filled the fundamental freedoms with external values and standards (these being values and standards which can be deduced from neither national nor European law and are thus values and standards important to CJEU judges), without giving enough weight to what the national legislature wished to achieve. The setting of European tax standards by the Court can equally be seen as an attempt to overcome a lack of European tax harmonisation measures. If the CJEU already implements a favouring of source-based taxation over resident taxation, the case law can steer national tax law rules in one direction without the need to implement secondary EU legislation.[285] Such steering helps to overcome existing obstacles to intra-EU trade even though these obstacles would have to be accepted within the European internal market—an incomplete single market—as long as no European harmonising legislation can be accomplished.

The CJEU may wish to act in the best interests of the European internal market; however, the Court oversteps its competences by applying its own value judgements to the fundamental freedoms. We will return to these questions later and ask whether the Member States are able to address areas not covered by the fundamental freedoms and value judgments of the CJEU through enhanced cooperation law.[286]

[285] The future-oriented concept of EU citizenship may be comparable to the CJEU's favouring of source taxation. The CJEU has long viewed EU citizenship as something that will be subject to transformation by a process of ever closer integration and thus the Court has interpreted citizenship in this light: Ronan McCrea, 'Forward or Back: The Future of European Integration and the Impossibility of the Status Quo' (2017) 23 European Law Journal 66, 70.

[286] In this chapter Part I, subsection E.VIII.

D. The Fundamental Freedoms and Secondary European Union Law

The relationship between primary EU law, in particular the market freedoms, and secondary EU law such as directives and regulations, is subject to debate in academic literature with no definitive and final conclusion.[287] Three different points of view emerge: first, the EU legislature may be bound by primary EU law in the same way as the national legislature. Secondly, the EU legislature may not be bound by primary EU law at all, and thus is fully free in its actions, and thirdly, the EU legislature is bound by primary EU law, but not to the same extent as the national legislature.[288]

The first approach could be supported by the hierarchy of EU law, according to which lower EU law must comply with higher EU law. In other words, the hierarchy of norms may demand that a directive or regulation be in line with the fundamental freedoms.[289] In this vein, the CJEU has ruled that secondary EU law has to be interpreted in the light of the fundamental freedoms,[290] and if the wording of a single provision allows for more than one interpretation, 'preference should be given to the interpretation which renders the provision consistent with the EC Treaty [now the TFEU] rather than to the interpretation which leads to its being incompatible with the Treaty'.[291]

The third approach considers the fact that the European legislature is bound by the fundamental freedoms, but this does not tell us anything about how intensely the fundamental freedoms impact secondary EU law. The CJEU may interpret the fundamental freedoms differently in the context of secondary EU law, as in the

[287] For the difference to the US situation see Michel Waelbroeck, 'The Emergent Doctrine of Community Pre-Emption—Consent and Re-Delegation' in Terrance Sandalow and Eric Stein (eds), *Courts and Free Markets: Perspectives from the United States and Europe*, vol II (Clarendon Press 1982) 550 arguing that 'the Court's attitude has generally been to construe the Treaty provisions prohibiting national barriers to trade as being addressed not only to the Member States but also to the Community institutions. Thus, the power of the Council or the Commission legally to consent to nation measures which would normally be prohibited in the absence of such consent is much more limited than the power of the Congress in the United States'.

[288] For an overview of the literature on those different views see Kamiel Mortelmans, 'The Relationship Between the Treaty Rules and Community Measures for the Establishment and Functioning of the Internal Market - Towards a Concordance Rule' (2002) 39 Common Market Law Review 1303.

[289] CJEU, 7 February 1985, 240/83, *ADBHU*, ECLI:EU:C:1985:59, para 9; Martin Nettesheim, 'Normenhierarchien im EU-Recht' (2006) Europarecht 737, 746 et seq. For a very restrictive approach see Isabella M de Groot, 'The Switch-Over Provision in the Proposal for an Anti-Tax Avoidance Directive and Its Compatibility with the EU Treaty Freedoms' (2016) 25 EC Tax Review 162, 165 et seq. Daniel Blum and Andreas Langer, 'At a Crossroads: Mandatory Disclosure under DAC-6 and EU Primary Law—Part 1' (2019) 59 European Taxation 282 applying the same benchmark to national and secondary EU law.

[290] CJEU, 2 February 1994, C-315/92, *Clinique*, ECLI:EU:C:1994:34, para 12.

[291] CJEU, 13 December 1983, 218/82, *Commission v Council*, ECLI:EU:C:1983:369, para 15; CJEU, 29 June 1995, C-135/93, *Kingdom of Spain v Commission*, ECLI:EU:C:1995:201, para 37; CJEU, 26 June 2007, C-305/05, *Ordre des barreaux francophones et germanophone*, ECLI:EU:C:2007:383, para 28.

context of national laws of the Member States.[292] Such an interpretation would lead to a double standard within the fundamental freedoms, depending on whether they are applied to secondary EU law or to the national laws of the Member States.[293]

The second is a minority approach.[294] It is largely based on the idea that the wording of the fundamental freedoms only addresses the Member States because they alone may act in a protectionist way. Every legislative act at European level, however, leads to a market opening that is not protectionist, which means that there is no longer any need for a market freedom review.

The CJEU case law on the relationship between secondary EU law and primary EU law is relatively limited. This is not because European institutions, Member States, and national courts have not challenged secondary EU laws; it is because of the approach the CJEU uses when reviewing national laws which transpose secondary EU law. In cases in which secondary EU law provides for full harmonisation, the Court only tests the national transposing law against secondary EU law.[295] Thus, both secondary EU law and transposing national law may be interpreted in light of the market freedoms, yet the national law is not directly tested against the market freedoms. If the secondary EU law, however, only provides for partial harmonisation,[296] then the national law is directly tested against the market freedoms[297] because the 'fact that a national measure may be consistent with

[292] Thomas von Danwitz, 'Der Grundsatz der Verhältnismäßigkeit im Gemeinschaftsrecht' (2003) Europäisches Wirtschafts- und Steuerrecht 393, 369; Angelika Emmerich-Fritsche, *Der Grundsatz der Verhältnismäßigkeit als Direktive und Schranke der EG-Rechtsetzung* (Duncker & Humblot 2000) 234.

[293] David Edward refuses such an interpretation, according to his view, '[i]t is the power and duty of the Court to interpret the Treaty in accordance with internationally recognized canons of interpretation in order to "ensure that the law is observed". It is the obligation of the political institutions, including the Parliament, to work within the bounds of that interpretation unless and until the Treaty itself is amended by those who have power to amend it.' From this it follows that according to Edward there is only one interpretation of the fundamental freedoms and the European legislature is bound by it, as the national parliament is. David Edward, 'Will There Be Honey Still for Tea?' (2006) 43 Common Market Law Review 623, 627; Christoph Schönberger, 'Normenkontrollen im EG-Föderalismus: Die Logik gegenläufiger Hierarchisierungen im Gemeinschaftsrecht' (2004) Europarecht 600, 622 arguing that the CJEU does not simply apply a double standard but that the loose hierarchy between primary EU law and secondary EU law requires such an approach. Primary EU law shall prohibit any protectionist measures of the Member States and boost the introduction of secondary EU law.

[294] Guido Perau, *Werbeverbote im Gemeinschaftsrecht: gemeinschaftsrechtliche Grenzen nationaler und gemeinschaftsrechtlicher Werbebeschränkungen* (Nomos 1997) 247 et seq. Urban Scheffer, *Die Marktfreiheiten des EG-Vertrages als Ermessensgrenze des Gemeinschaftsgesetzgebers* (Peter Lang 1997) 132 et seq.

[295] CJEU, 27 February 2019, C-563/17, *Associação Peço a Palavra*, ECLI:EU:C:2019:144, para 49; CJEU, 20 December 2017, C-504/16 and C-613/16, *Deister Holding AG*, ECLI:EU:C:2017:1009, para 45; CJEU, 7 September 2017, C-6/16, *Eqiom and Enka*, ECLI:EU:C:2017:641, para 15; CJEU, 8 March 2017, C-14/16, *Euro Park Service*, ECLI:EU:C:2017:177, para 19; CJEU, 17 November 2015, C-115/14, *RegioPost*, ECLI:EU:C:2015:760, para 57; CJEU, 23 January 2003, C-221/00, *Commission v Austria*, ECLI:EU:C:2003:44, para 42.

[296] Or minimum harmonisation see Steven Peeters, 'Exit Taxation: From an Internal Market Barrier to a Tax Avoidance Prevention Tool' (2017) 26 EC Tax Review 122, 122.

[297] Accordingly, the national rules are tested against the fundamental freedoms if the secondary EU law does not achieve 'exhaustive harmonisation' at EU level: CJEU, 8 March 2017, C-14/16, *Euro Park Services*, ECLI:EU:C:2017:177, para 25; in these cases, a specific aim and purpose of the secondary EU law (which does not exhaustively harmonise a particular field) has to be interpreted in line with CJEU case law: CJEU, 7 September 2017, C-6/16, *Eqiom SAS*, ECLI:EU:C:2017:641, para 30; CJEU, 20

a provision of secondary legislation ... does not have the effect of removing that measure from the scope of the provisions of the Treaty'.[298]

This CJEU ruling has to be read in the context of the specific facts of the case. The relevant secondary EU law, a regulation on the application of social security schemes to employed persons, addressed the reimbursement of medical expenses incurred in another Member State; however, it did so only for specific scenarios, such as cases in which the necessary health treatment could not be provided within a sufficient time in the home Member State. The Court concluded that the regulation does not provide for a final system on the reimbursement for medical expenses incurred in other Member States, and thus the national rules are subject to scrutiny under the fundamental freedoms if the particular rule is not subject to a common agreement between all the Member States manifested in the regulation. If, however, the Member States have agreed on more specific secondary EU laws, such as harmonising measures for public interest concerns in the field of undesirable substances in animal feedstuffs, the fundamental freedoms should no longer apply to national laws. In other words, primary EU law can only apply in the absence of more specific secondary EU law.[299]

When national Member State laws are under scrutiny, the CJEU sometimes rules by way of an *obiter dictum* that secondary EU law is in line with the market freedoms as long as it leaves the Member States a sufficient margin to transpose the directive into national law, which is in line with the primary EU law,[300] or allows for an interpretation that is consistent with primary EU law.[301] Since secondary EU

December 2017, C-504/16 and C-613/16, *Deister Holding and Juhler Holding*, ECLI:EU:C:2017:1009, para 56. In *Clinique*, the Court argued that the Directive on the approximation of the law of the Member States relating to cosmetic products provided 'exhaustively for the harmonization of national rules on the packaging and labelling of cosmetic products'. Nonetheless, the CJEU tested the domestic discretional scope against the fundamental freedoms: CJEU, 2 February 1994, C315/92, *Clinique*, ECLI:EU:C:1994:34, para 11 et seq. Phil Syrpis, 'The Relationship between Primary and Secondary Law in the EU' (2015) 52 Common Market Law Review 461, 464 explaining that in cases of minimum harmonisation 'national provisions must comply with both the "floor" set by secondary legislation and the "ceiling" set by the Treaties'.

[298] CJEU, 28 April 1998, C-120/95, *Decker*, ECLI:EU:C:1998:167, para 27; CJEU, 28 April 1998, C-158/96, *Kohll*, ECLI:EU:C:1998:171, para 25.

[299] CJEU, 5 October 1977, 5/77, *Tedeschi*, ECLI:EU:C:1977:144, para 35 (generally referred to as the Tedeschi principle).

[300] CJEU, 5 May 1982, 15/81, *Schul*, ECLI:EU:C:1982:135, paras 41–44; and even in cases where the secondary EU law offers the possibility of refusing the deduction of costs incurred by parent companies in connection with holdings in the capital of their subsidiaries, the Member States are required to transpose the law into their national law in conformity with the fundamental rights: CJEU, 18 September 2003, C-168/01, *Bosal*, ECLI:EU:C:2003:479, paras 25–26; in this vein see also CJEU, 23 February 2006, C-471/04, *Keller Holding*, ECLI:EU:C:2006:143; for a critical analysis of the strict approach of the CJEU and the subsequent uncertainty for the Member States see Ulrich Forsthoff, 'EuGH versus Europäischer Gesetzgeber—oder Freiheiten über alles?' (2006) Internationales Steuerrecht 222.

[301] CJEU, 13 December 1983, *Commission v Council*, ECLI:EU:C:1983:369, para 15; CJEU, 4 December 1986, 205/84, ECLI:EU:C:1986:463, para 62. Thereby the Court 'solves apparent conflicts between [secondary and primary EU law] by a reconciling interpretation than to have to decide on the compatibility of secondary law with primary law and potentially to have to invalidate incompatible secondary law', Rita Szudoczky, 'The Influence of Primary Law on the Interpretation of Secondary

law only provides for full harmonisation in exceptional cases,[302] the Court hardly feels the need to rule on the validity of the secondary EU law.[303]

The following subsections will briefly elaborate on the CJEU case law concerning the relationship between primary and secondary EU law (see subsection I). Contrary to secondary EU law, national Member State laws trigger a restriction of the fundamental freedoms mostly because of their differences in the regulatory approaches of the Member States, and not because of their regulatory intent. If the Member States harmonise their public interest concerns and eliminate burdensome diversity within the European internal market, the obstacles to intra-EU trade are mostly eliminated (see subsection II). It will be stressed that some secondary EU law acts may introduce trade restrictions (despite harmonisation of the national measures) which have to be justified (see subsection III). The analysis will show that the Court differentiates when applying the fundamental freedoms to secondary EU law, on the one hand, and to national laws of the Member States on the other. Whether, and if so to what extent, the Member State can use secondary EU law to correct or influence the application of the fundamental freedoms by the CJEU will be revealed in subsection IV.

I. CJEU Case Law on the Relationship between Secondary EU Law and Free Movement Rights

In *Ramel*,[304] a secondary EU law provision on the organisation of the market in wine was found to contradict primary EU law because it allowed Member States to deviate from the common system and set up charges whose effect is equivalent to customs duties. The provision was challenged because France relied on this provision and levied a charge on Italian wines to prevent Italian wine from being imported at very low prices. Such imports were possible due to 'the abundant harvest and successive devaluations of the lira'.[305]

Law in the Field of EU Citizenship and Direct Taxation: "Whatever Works" . . . ' in Dennis Weber (ed), *Traditional and Alternative Routes to European Tax Integration: Primary Law, Secondary Law, Soft Law, Coordination, Comitology and Their Relationship* (IBFD 2010) 193.

302 See for example the directive on unfair business-to-consumer commercial practices (2005/29/EG): CJEU, 10 July 2014, C-421/12, *Commission v Belgium*, ECLI:EU:C:2014:2064; CJEU, 9 November 2010, C-540/08, *Mediaprint Zeitungs- und Zeitschriftenverlag GmbH & Co. KG*, ECLI:EU:C:2010:660, para 27; CJEU, 14 January 2010, C-304/08, *Zentrale zur Bekämpfung unlauteren Wettbewerbs e.V.*, ECLI:EU:C:2010:12, para 41.

303 Georg W Kofler, 'Das Verhältnis zwischen primärem und sekundärem Unionsrecht im direkten Steuerrecht' in Michael Lang and Christine Weinzierl (eds), *Europäisches Steuerrecht—Festschrift für Friedrich Rödler* (Linde Verlag 2010) 434 et seq.

304 CJEU, 20 April 1978, 80/77 and 81/77, *Ramel*, ECLI:EU:C:1978:87.

305 ibid para 8.

A similar unilateral measure hindering cross-border trade was tested against the market freedoms in *Lancry*.[306] A decision of the Council allowed the French overseas departments to levy dock dues. These taxes were imposed on all goods, regardless of their country of origin, and thus also included goods coming from mainland France as a result of their entry into the overseas department. Products of the region were not, however, subject to the dock dues, and the dues were therefore levied to raise tax revenue and to encourage local economic activity. The decision did not grant an unlimited allowance to levy such a discriminatory tax; it forced French authorities to take the necessary measures that the dock dues were also levied on regional products by 31 December 1992. The Court ruled that the Council had no right to issue such a decision because it contradicts the free movement within the internal market. The fact that France was also required to ensure the application of the same tax on regional products had no impact on the characterisation of the rule as an obstacle to trade; the obstacle to free movement due to the dock dues on imported goods is no less serious if it is also levied on regional products.[307]

In *Roviello*,[308] the CJEU found that some parts of the Regulation on the application of social security schemes to employed persons, to self-employed persons, and to members of their families moving within the Community is invalid because it contradicts primary EU law. The Regulation referred back to the national law to determine who is entitled to claim insurance benefits in cases of occupational invalidity or incapacity for work. To be entitled to an insurance benefit under the German national law, the worker needed to be subject to compulsory insurance for a certain time and needed to have completed an even longer waiting period. The Court found that these requirements essentially concerned migrant workers and thus infringed on the free movement of workers. Since the Regulation directly referred to this national provision, both the German national law and the Regulation infringed on the market freedom, and therefore this provision of the secondary EU law was invalid.

By contrast, in other cases the Court has not expressed itself so clearly. In most cases, the CJEU has argued that secondary EU law leaves enough room to read these provisions in line with primary EU law. If the Member States have not done so, it is the national law which contradicts the primary EU law, and not secondary EU law.[309]

In this line of argument, the CJEU found that the Regulation on the application of social security schemes to employed persons, to self-employed persons, and

306 CJEU, 9 August 1994, C-363/93, C-408/93, C-409/93, C-410/93, and 411/93, *Lancry*, ECLI:EU:C:1994:315.

307 ibid para 28.

308 CJEU, 7 June 1988, 20/85, *Roviello*, ECLI:EU:C:1988:2805.

309 CJEU, 7 February 1985, 240/83, *ADBHU*, ECLI:EU:C:1985:59; CJEU, 10 March 1983, 172/82, *Inter-Huiles*, ECLI:EU:C:1983:69.

to members of their families moving within the Community, does not contradict primary EU law. The secondary EU law regulates the entitlement to receive emergency treatments in another Member State. In cases of non-emergency treatments, the person, 'who *is authorised* by the competent institution to go to the territory of another Member State to receive there the treatment',[310] is entitled to receive benefits in kind, provided on behalf of the competent institution by the institution of the place of stay or residence and cash benefits provided by the competent institution. According to the CJEU, this provision grants a person 'who is authorised by the competent institution' the right to receive benefits in kind in another Member State, but it does not disallow recovery of the costs of health treatment in non-emergency cases if the person did not ask for authorisation beforehand. Since the market freedoms require such a recovery, it is the national law which infringes on the freedom to provide services and not the Regulation, as the provisions of the Regulation give Member States enough room to regulate cases of unauthorised foreign treatments in a manner consistent with primary EU law.

Besides these two lines of case law, the CJEU has found some secondary EU law provisions to be explicitly justified and others to be implicitly justified. In *Meyhui*,[311] for example, the Directive on the approximation of Member State laws relating to crystal glass was tested against the market freedoms. The Directive required that the categories of crystal glass and crystalline and the description of the product was provided *only* in the language or languages used in the Member State in which the goods may be used.[312] The prohibition on affixing to crystal glass products in some categories their description in a language other than the language or languages used in the Member State in which the products are marketed 'constitutes a barrier to intra-Community trade in so far as products coming from other Member States have to be given different labelling causing additional packaging costs'.[313] The obstacle to trade is, however, justified because it is necessary for the protection of consumers and that aim is expressly laid down in the preamble of the directive. The CJEU used a similar line of justification in *Safety Hi-Tech*,[314] in

[310] Art 22 of the Regulation 1408/71/EEC, OJ, 5 July 1971, L 149, 2–50.

[311] CJEU, 9 August 1994, C-51/93, *Meyhui NV*, ECLI:EU:C:1994:312.

[312] A less restrictive approach can be found in the Directive on the approximation of the laws of the Member States relating to cosmetic products (Directive, 27 July 1976, 76/768/EEC). According to the Directive, cosmetic products can only be marketed if the container and packaging bear certain information in indelible, easily legible, and visible lettering. The Member States can require that the information must be expressed *at least* in their own national or official language or languages. However, if cosmetic products comply with the requirements of this Directive Member States may not refuse, prohibit, or restrict their marketing. The CJEU ruled that the directive 'sought to reconcile the objective of achieving the free movement of cosmetic products and that of safeguarding public health', and that 'the obstacles [national linguistic requirements] are justified by the public interest objective of protecting public health', CJEU, 13 September 2001, C-169/99, *Schwarzkopf*, ECLI:EU:C:2001:439, paras 27 and 40.

[313] ibid para 13.

[314] CJEU, 14 July 1998, C-284/95, *Safety Hi-Tech Srl*, ECLI:EU:C:1998:352.

which measures for protecting the environment were tested against the free movement of goods.

Another example of a justified secondary EU law restriction of the fundamental freedoms is the preferential Value-Added Tax (VAT) treatment of small undertakings. According to the VAT Directive, small undertakings (defined by an individual threshold of the Member States) can provide exempt supplies within the territory of their resident Member State. Accordingly, supplies of goods or services are subject to VAT without exemption (regardless of the national threshold) if the taxable person is not resident within the Member State in which the supply is taxable. Such a rule makes it less attractive for small undertakings to supply goods or services outside the Member State of residence.[315] The CJEU reviewed the rule because it was claimed that the secondary EU law provision contradicts the freedom to provide services. As a justification for the restrictive scope of the small undertaking exemption, the idea that the Member States could only review the transactions which take place within their territory was brought forward. An exchange of information between the Member States on that particular issue would not be possible because small undertakings are subject to quite relaxed reporting standards, and thus the Member States are not capable of delivering the required information under the exchange of information scheme.[316] The CJEU simply accepted the fact that Member States are not in possession of the information and are thus not capable of monitoring whether a non-resident taxable person has exceeded the national threshold for small undertakings. The Court applied a very narrow scope to find alternatives and less invasive measures. That approach allowed the small undertaking scheme to restrict the fundamental freedoms and did not force the Member States to find a way to gather the relevant information, for example from the taxable person.

In cases in which the secondary EU law implements a regulatory framework which does not harm intra-EU trade, the Court does not find the law to contradict the market freedoms even if the regulatory framework imposes a burden on the market players. For example, the Court allowed the implementation of a harmonised system of veterinary and public health inspections which transfers the supervision to the exporting Member State, and which went hand in hand with a

[315] To prevent distortions of the European internal market, the European Commission has issued a proposal to amend the current regime for small undertakings within the VAT system. According to these changes, the small undertaking should be entitled to the VAT exemption even in cross-border cases (Commission, 18 January 2018, Proposal for a Council Directive amending Directive 2006/112/EC on the common system of value added tax as regards the special scheme for small enterprises, COM(2018) 21 final). The proposal was discussed in several Council meetings 'where it became apparent that an appropriate balance should ensure that the modified scheme does not lead to weakened control and increase risks of VAT fraud' (See Report by Tom Vandenkendelaere <https://www.europarl.europa.eu/legislative-train/theme-deeper-and-fairer-internal-market-with-a-strengthened-industrial-base-taxation/file-vat-rules-adapted-for-sme> accessed 3 February 2021). On 8 November 2019, the Council found an agreement: ECOFIN, 9 November 2019, 980.

[316] CJEU, 26 October 2010, C-97/09, *Schmelz*, ECLI:EU:C:2010:632, paras 64–68.

fee imposed on entrepreneurs dealing with animals.[317] The system was based on trust between the Member States. Accordingly, animals which have undergone inspections as laid down in the directive 'must be able to be transported from one Member State to the others *without* additional health and veterinary requirements'.[318] The additional fee the entrepreneurs had to pay for the inspections was found not to infringe the market freedoms because these fees do not constitute charges having an effect equivalent to customs duties.

The following principles emerge from this overview of CJEU case law: first, the market freedoms apply to secondary EU law. Secondly, secondary EU law restrictions of the market freedoms can be justified. Thirdly, the CJEU quite strongly recognises harmonised public interest concerns. Fourthly, the Court has not found secondary EU law provisions which allow Member States to apply unilateral discriminatory measures to be justified. Lastly, a non-discriminatory common regulatory regime does not infringe on the fundamental freedoms even if it imposes (regulatory) burdens on the market players.

II. No Doctrine of 'Economic Due Process' in the European Union

Thus far, the European legislature has used its power to abandon existing obstacles to intra-EU trade which existed because of deviating national regulatory regimes.[319] EU law has not banned regulation as such but has attempted to implement a regime which has no effects or only minor effects on cross-border trade. Accordingly, it is not the European legislature's intention to create an area which guarantees the free play of economic forces unaffected by regulatory interference regardless of the public need.[320] The interests of trade and commerce have their role in building the European internal market, but they are not taken as absolute rights. The European Union is made up of more than trade and economic freedoms, and the CJEU has accepted this idea of an internal market. In *ADBHU* the Court explicitly took a stance on the relationship between the value of economic freedom and other non-market values:

> [T]he principle of *freedom of trade is not to be viewed in absolute terms* but is subject to certain limits justified by the objectives of general interest pursued by the Community provided that the rights in question are not substantively impaired.[321]

[317] CJEU, 25 January 1977, 46/76, *Bauhuis*, ECLI:EU:C:1977:6.
[318] ibid para 39, emphasis added.
[319] See Chapter 4, subsection G.
[320] See Chapter 4, subsection G.II.
[321] CJEU, 7 February 1985, 240/83, *ADBHU*, ECLI:EU:C:1985:59, para 12, emphasis added.

Against this background, it becomes crystal clear that the CJEU never intended to follow an *economic due process* approach such as that taken by the US Supreme Court up until 1937.[322] The roots of this approach can be traced back to the beginning of US jurisprudence, when a firm belief emerged that the main purpose and content of the law is to protect property and personal rights. Following on from this, full market freedom was desired and restrictions, exemptions, and monopolies were attacked.[323] Economic liberty required the nullification of statutory acts aiming to protect workers.[324] The US Supreme Court gave up its economic due process approach in 1937,[325] and now follows an approach which allows state interference into economic freedom.[326]

In contrast, the CJEU never required such a turning point. The Court always found economic freedom to be a main value within the internal market, which, however, is not absolute, and thus does not require every other conflicting value to automatically give way.

As has been revealed,[327] the CJEU accepts some obstacles to intra-EU trade following from national laws if the national measures are justified by an overriding reason of public interest and are proportionate. In its rulings on the laws of Member States, the Court is quite strict, upholding the value of economic freedom. Obstacles to trade which follow from different approaches in the national laws are a particular thorn in the Court's side, and thus, the threshold for justification is very high. The strict application of the market freedoms to national laws does not mean that the Court wants to abandon all regulatory measures. It is quite the opposite. The CJEU allows regulation of the internal market but in a coordinated manner. The Court does not stumble at the regulation per se. However, the Court is concerned with the costs an entity has to bear to comply with the different Member States' regulatory regimes.[328] Even if the Court finds that the market needs to be regulated, it is not in the hands of the CJEU to decide which way to go. To put it differently, it is not within the Court's capacity to rule on which one of the different national measures should be favoured, and thus should prevail over the

[322] Miguel Poiares Maduro, *We the Court: The European Court of Justice and the European Economic Constitution* (Hart Publishing 1998) 77.

[323] 'Resurrecting Economic Rights: The Doctrine of Economic Due Process Reconsidered' (1990) 103 Harvard Law Review 1363, 1368.

[324] For example a statutory act restricting the working hours to a maximum of sixty hours per week and ten hours per day, see Poulson Bany, 'Substantive Due Process and Labor Law' (1982) 6 The Journal of Libertarian Studies 267.

[325] Frank Easterbrook, 'The Constitution of Business' (1988) 53 George Mason University Law Review 53.

[326] Whether the Supreme Court has again ruled towards an 'economic due process' approach, see Want William, 'Economic Substantive Due Process: Considered Dead Is Being Revived by a Series of Supreme Court Land-Use Cases' (2014) 36 University of Hawai'i Law Review 455.

[327] See this chapter Part I, subsection C.III.

[328] See also Peter-Christian Müller-Graff, 'Die Rechtsangleichung zur Verwirklichung des Binnenmarktes' (1989) Europarecht 107, 120–21.

others.[329] The fundamental freedoms do not offer an intrinsic set of values which would enable the Court to find one regime more appropriate than the other.[330] There are as many ways to achieve one regulatory goal as there are roads leading to Rome, and so long as there is no European (harmonised) regulatory approach, the Member States have the competence to choose the road they find most suitable.[331] Consequently, the CJEU case law does not have the effect of carving out a particular scenario from the political process;[332] the Court explicitly plays the ball back to the Member States to find a common measure at European level.[333]

The CJEU makes no secret of the fact that it is seeking uniform guiding principles and unless the Member States come up with a coordinated regulatory system it will apply the plain market freedoms directly to the national laws.[334] A strict application of the market freedoms to the national laws of the Member States may incentivise Member States to find an agreement and to achieve uniform regulation at EU level. However, uniformity should not be taken too literally, as implying that no discretion is left to the Member States. Secondary EU law may allow Member States to set some specific unilateral rules. Despite these unilateral deviations, a common approach is applied which allows the Member States to deviate from the

[329] See in that direction also Christioph Teichmann, 'Überprüfung von Sekundärrecht am Maßstab der Grundfreiheiten' in Peter-Christian Müller-Graff, Stefanie Schmahl, and Vassilios Skouris (eds), *Europäisches Recht zwischen Bewährung und Wandel—Festschrift Dieter H. Scheuing* (Nomos 2011) 753.

[330] See this chapter Part I, subsection C.

[331] The secondary EU law does not necessarily choose the least burdensome regulatory framework. If the Member States agree on a framework which protects public interest even beyond their current national framework, the fundamental freedoms do not prevent the Member States from doing so: Markus Möstl, 'Grenzen der Rechtsangleichung im europäischen Binnenmarkt—Kompetenzielle, grundfreiheitliche und grundrechtliche Schranken des Gemeinschaftsgesetzgebers' (2002) Europarecht 318, 335; for the implications of the subsidiarity principle, see Vasiliki Kosta, 'The Principle of Proportionality in EU Law—An Interest-Based Taxonomy' in Joana Mendes (ed), *EU Executive Discretion and the Limits of Law* (OUP 2019).

[332] 'In many instances the Court has in fact tried to further the progress of Community policies by giving impulses to the political actors [that being the *impulse function* of the CJEU]', Jürgen Basedow, 'The Judge's Role in European Integration - The Court of Justice and Its Critics' in Hans-Wolfgang Micklitz and Bruno de Witte (eds), *The European Court of Justice and the Autonomy of the Member States* (Intersentia 2012) 69.

[333] Accordingly, the CJEU case law on the fundamental *freedoms* is not set in stone, which is very different when it comes to CJEU case law in the field of fundamental *rights*: Armin von Bogdandy, 'Grundrechtsgemeinschaft als Integrationsziel? Grundreche und das Wesen der Europäischen Union' (2001) 56 Juristenzeitung 157, 166; Roland Wacker, 'Zur praktischen Konkordanz von Grundfreiheiten und EU-Richtlinienrecht auf dem Gebiet der direkten Steuern' in Klaus-Dieter Drüen, Johanna Hey, and Rudolf Mellinghoff (eds), *100 Jahre Steuerrechtsprechung in Deutschland 1918–2018: Festschrift für den Bundesfinanzhof* (Dr Otto Schmidt Verlag 2018) 793 et seq.

[334] '[I]n the *absence of harmonization of legislation*, measures of equivalent effect prohibited by Article 30 of the Treaty *include obstacles to the free movement of goods* where they are the consequence of applying rules that lay down requirements to be met by such goods ... to goods from other Member States where they are lawfully manufactured and marketed, *even if those rules apply without distinction to all products*' (emphasis added) CJEU, 26 October 1995, C-51/94, *Commission v Germany*, ECLI:EU:C:1995:352, para 29. See also CJEU, 20 February 1979, 120/78, *Rewe-Zentral AG*, ECLI:EU:C:1979:42, para 8; CJEU, 24 November 1993, C-267/91 and C-268/91, *Keck*, ECLI:EU:C:1993:905, para 15; for the free movement of workers CJEU, 9 March 2006, C-493/04, *Piatkowski*, ECLI:EU:C:2006:167, paras 32–33; for the freedom of establishment CJEU, 11 July 2002, C-294/00, *Gräbner*, ECLI:EU:C:2002:442, para 26; for the free movement of services CJEU, 23 October 2003, C-56/01, *Inizan*, ECLI:EU:C:2003:578, para 17.

common system now and then. Accordingly, a 'potentially uniform' approach is required.[335]

The CJEU has explicitly stressed that it will not question the regulatory measure, implemented by secondary EU law, as such. In other words, the uniform application of regulatory measures is in line with the market freedoms even if those measures hurt the market players[336] because the rules impose burdens upon them.[337] The burden is, however, imposed regardless of a cross-border economic activity of the market player. Harmonised regulations between the Member States may impose a burden on the market player but allows them to make use of the market freedoms, without the need to comply with an additional set of regulatory rules (of another Member State).

III. Harmonised Public Interest and the Need for General or Specific Secondary EU Law Restrictions

By and large, unification of regulatory approaches and their underlying values at a European level erodes trade obstacles between the Member States. The uniform approach applies in all Member States to both domestic and cross-border situations, and thus compliance with the regulatory norm set guarantees free movement within the internal market. However, in rare cases, differentiation (which imposes trade-hampering effects) may be necessary to achieve the harmonised policy objectives, as in *Meyhui* and *Schmelz*.[338] The harmonised public interest concerns—customer protection and effectiveness of fiscal supervision—demanded specific measures in every market of the Member States, and for a differentiation between resident and non-resident taxable persons.

Obstacles created by secondary EU law may be of a general or specific nature. The latter is imposed by one Member State or towards one Member State,[339]

[335] Julian Currall, 'Some Aspects of the Relation between Articles 30–36 and Article 100 of the EEC Treaty, with a Closer Look at Optional Harmonisation' (1984) 4 Yearbook of European Law 169, 194–95.

[336] Within the limits of the fundamental rights.

[337] 'The rules are *common*, applying in a uniform manner across the territory of the entire EU, is necessary to put in place the "level playing field" for commercial activity. That is the economic rationale for harmonisation', Stephen Weatherill, 'The Competence to Harmonise and Its Limits' in Panos Koutrakos and Jukka Snell (eds), *Research Handbook on the Law of the EU's Internal Market* (Edward Elgar Publishing 2017) 84.

[338] CJEU, 9 August 1994, C-51/93, *Meyhui NV*, ECLI:EU:C:1994:312; CJEU, 26 October 2010, C-97/09, *Schmelz*, ECLI:EU:C:2010:632; see this chapter Part I, subsection D.I.

[339] Another example of a specific trade obstacle created by secondary EU is the reduced tax rate for ouzo. The Directive on the harmonization of the structures of exercise duties on alcohol and alcoholic beverages (OJ, 31 October 1992, L 316, 21) grant Greece the possibility to apply a reduced tax rate on 'aniseed flavoured spirit drinks'. The Greek transposing national rule was already subject of an infringement proceeding before the CJEU. The Court did not test the secondary EU law provision against primary EU law because the CJEU could only test the national law within the proceeding and found that the national law complies with the Directive (CJEU, 5 October 2004, C-475/01, *Commission v Hellenic Republic*, ECLI:EU:C:2004:585). For the potential impact of the decision on the relationship between

whereas the former applies equally to all cross-border economic activities within the European internal market. The CJEU's case law shows a clear distinction between the two at the justification stage.

The CJEU is only willing to honour the harmonised European value (the harmonised public interests concern) when secondary EU law imposes general obstacles to intra-EU trade by applying a light-touch justification approach. A light-touch justification approach recognises the Member States' joint approach in two steps: First, the harmonised public interest concern is accepted as an overriding reason of public interest which can be relied upon to justify an unequal treatment or trade restrictions (see subsection 1). Secondly, a light-touch proportionality test is applied to trade restrictions imposed by secondary EU law (see subsection 2).

1. Harmonised Interests as Overriding Reasons of Public Interest

In *Meyhui* and *Schmelz*, the harmonised public interests (consumer protection and effectiveness of fiscal supervision)[340] have already been accepted as overriding general interests (of single Member States) by the CJEU in earlier rulings.[341] This does not change the fact that the CJEU may recognise public interests harmonised at European level as grounds of justification which the Court would not accept if put forward by a single Member State. Harmonising public interests at European level creates European interests. European interests are the manifestation of a concern going far beyond national borders, and thus there is an intrinsic need to give these interests more weight than single Member States' interests.

To date, the CJEU has rejected several grounds of justification put forward by single Member States.[342] For example, the Court did not accept lower taxation in a fellow Member State as a justification for unilateral higher, compensatory taxation.[343] Individuals or legal persons can exercise their rights to free movement 'for

secondary and primary EU law, see Kofler, 'Das Verhältnis zwischen primärem und sekundärem Unionsrecht' (n 303) 439–40.

[340] CJEU, 9 August 1994, C-51/93, *Meyhui NV*, ECLI:EU:C:1994:312, para 15 et seq; CJEU, 26 October 2010, C-97/09, *Schmelz*, ECLI:EU:C:2010:632, para 56 et seq.

[341] For the effectiveness of fiscal supervision CJEU, 20 February 1979, 120/78, *Rewe-Zentral*, ECLI:EU:C:1979:42, para 8; CJEU, 15 May 1997, C-250/95, *Futura Participations and Singer*, ECLI:EU:C:1997:239, para 31; CJEU, 8 July 1999, C-254/97, *Société Baxter*, ECLI:EU:C:1999:368, para 18; CJEU, 11 March 2004, C-9/02, *Hughes de Lasteyrie du Saillant*, ECLI:EU:C:2004:138, para 25; CJEU, 27 January 2009, C-318/07, *Persche*, ECLI:EU:C:2009:33, para 52; for consumer protection (defence of the consumer) CJEU, 20 February 1979, 120/78, *Rewe-Zentral*, ECLI:EU:C:1979:42, para 8; CJEU, 26 June 1980, 788/79, *Gilli*, ECLI:EU:C:1980:171, para 6; CJEU, 16 December 1980, 27/80, *Fietje*, ECLI:EU:C:1980:293, para 10.

[342] See this chapter Part I, subsection C.III.1.

[343] CJEU, 26 October 1999, C-294/97, *Eurowings Luftverkehrs AG*, ECLI:EU:C:1999:524, para 43; CJEU, 3 October 2002, C-136/00, *Danner*, ECLI:EU:C:2002:558, para 56; CJEU, 26 June 2003, *Skandia*, ECLI:EU:C:2003:380, para 52; CJEU, 12 September 2006, C-196/04, *Cadbury Schweppes*, ECLI:EU:C:2006:544, para 49.

the purpose of benefiting from favourable legislation', which does not constitute abuse of that freedom.[344] However, at a European level it may be possible to introduce legal measures which guarantee minimum taxation. We shall assume that the Member States agree on a minimum level of taxation and that the European legislature transposes the OECD global anti-base erosion proposal into secondary EU law.[345] This legislative action establishes a harmonised interest in the form of fair minimum taxation within the European Union. The global anti-base erosion proposal is the second pillar of the Organisation for Economic Co-operation and Development (OECD) initiative on finding solutions to the tax challenges arising from the digitalisation of the economy and consists of two main mechanisms: the income inclusion rule and the tax on base eroding payments. The income inclusion rule shall help the resident State in the fight against base erosion and profit shifting by taxing the income of foreign branches or controlled entities if their income was subject to tax at an effective rate that is below a minimum rate. On the other hand, the tax on eroding payments operates as a denial of deductions in cases in which the payments would be subject to tax at or below a minimum rate in the other State. Within a European context, an income inclusion rule would allow the Member States to tax the income of branches or controlled entities of their resident companies if the income of the branch or entity is taxed below an agreed minimum rate (eg 15%). Different from ordinary CFC rules, the income inclusion approach also applies to real investment in low tax (Member) States, and thus the rule does not only include low-taxed passive income. A tax on base-eroding payments would allow the source Member States to deny tax deductions in cases where the income flows into a low tax jurisdiction.

Transposing the global anti-base erosion proposal into secondary EU law would not harmonise tax rates; however, it would set a floor of minimum taxation. Any Member State can decide—for whatever reason—to tax at a rate below the agreed standard, but it has to face the consequences of the income inclusion rule and the tax on base eroding payments.[346] These consequences (income inclusion of the

[344] CJEU, 25 October 2017, C-106/16, *Polbud—Wykonawstwo sp. z o.o.*, ECLI:EU:C:2017:804, para 40; CJEU, 17 July 2014, C-58/13 and 59/13, *Torresi*, ECLI:EU:C:2014:2088, para 50; CJEU, 12 September 2006, C-196/04, *Cadbury Schweppes*, ECLI:EU:C:2006:544, para 37; CJEU, 30 September 2003, C-167/01, *Inspire Art*, ECLI:EU:C:2003:512, para 96; CJEU, 9 March 1999, C-212/97, *Centros*, ECLI:EU:C:1999:126, para 27.

[345] OECD, 'Programme of Work to Develop a Consensus Solution to the Tax Challenges Arising from the Digitalisation of the Economy' (2019) <https://www.oecd.org/tax/beps/programme-of-work-to-develop-a-consensus-solution-to-the-tax-challenges-arising-from-the-digitalisation-of-the-economy.pdf> accessed 3 February 2021.

[346] These consequences are necessary to ensure minimum taxation between the Member States which have committed themselves to a commonly agreed 'fair' minimum taxation of business profits. If Member States were to transpose the OECD global anti-base erosion proposal into enhanced cooperation law, the income inclusion rule and the tax on base eroding payments applied towards non-participating Member States would constitute a defensive obstacle (see this chapter, Part I, subsection E.VI.2.b)(cc)). The income inclusion and denial of tax deductions are triggered by low taxation in non-participating Member States and are not intrinsic features of the participating Member States' tax system. Moreover, the application of the income inclusion rule and the tax on base eroding payments

resident Member State and denial of tax deductions in the source Member State) constitute trade restrictions as it may be less favourable to invest in a Member State which does not tax at the minimum level.

Against the background of existing CJEU case law, and in particular *Cadbury Schweppes*,[347] one may wonder whether an income inclusion approach which is only triggered by low taxation in the other Member State can be justified on the grounds of public interest. In *Cadbury Schweppes*, the CJEU found that 'a national measure restricting freedom of establishment may be justified where it specifically relates to wholly artificial arrangements aimed at circumventing the application of the legislation of the Member State concerned'.[348] This line of reasoning may not help justify restrictions under the income inclusion rule as it goes far beyond 'wholly artificial arrangements' and applies to real investment, whose income is not taxed at a sufficient rate.

Against the CJEU's reasoning in *Cadbury Schweppes*, it is quite obvious that the income inclusion rule in the form of a unilateral measure of a single Member State would not be allowed to stand, because the free movement rights cannot be restricted to prevent a legal (or natural) person from profiting from tax advantages in a fellow Member State,[349] and the income inclusion rule goes far beyond what is necessary to prevent tax avoidance and evasion. However, if the income inclusion rule were adopted by secondary EU law, the public interest of taxing business profits at a fair minimum rate would be harmonised at European level. The harmonised interest would reflect the Member States' desire to secure minimum taxation of all business profits of companies which are resident within their territory and profit from their public goods. Minimum taxation is predominantly influenced by aspects of justice because it prevents Member States from engaging in harmful tax competition. Ensuring that every Member State taxes income at a level which is considered legitimate does not necessarily answer Member States' budgetary constraints as the secondary EU law does not allocate any income between the Member States. Since all Member States embrace the idea of taxing all business profits at a fair minimum level, the inclusion mechanism is no longer a unilateral measure which aims to compensate taxation in a fellow Member State but is the manifestation of a European interest on fair taxation. Therefore, the harmonised interest of fair (minimum) taxation can be considered an overriding general interest which may be relied upon to justify trade restrictions.

towards non-participating Member States are not necessary to establish a fair minimum taxation of business profits between the Member States which have committed themselves to tax fairly.

[347] CJEU, 12 September 2006, C-196/04, *Cadbury Schweppes*, ECLI:EU:C:2006:544.

[348] ibid para 51.

[349] ibid para 36; CJEU, 11 December 2003, C-364/01, *Barbier*, ECLI:EU:C:2003:665, para 71.

Having said this, there are natural boundaries for the creation of European interests. A European interest can never have protectionist intents.[350] The shielding of a Member State's domestic market from foreign goods, services, persons, and investment can never be aligned with the spirit of the European internal market. A shielding of the Member States' markets would occur, for example, if secondary EU law made pursuing an actual business activity conditional on an entitlement to cross-border conversions. A discussion on the possibility of a secondary EU law ban for cross-border conversions in cases of isolated transfers of registered offices arose within the European Union because of the CJEU's liberal case law. In *Centros*, the CJEU already ruled that it is not an abuse of the right of establishment if a Member State's company law is used to set up a company which does not conduct any business in that Member State.[351] Accordingly, the freedom of establishment allows everyone to choose the Member State's company law which seems to him the least restrictive one.[352] In *Polbud*, the CJEU applied this logic to the mere transfer of the registered office and allowed a company formed in accordance with the legislation of one Member State to convert itself into a company under the law of another Member State even if the company continues to conduct its main business in the first Member State.[353] The CJEU case law allows companies to choose a Member State's company law which best suits their needs. The company's real place of business activity does not influence the choice of company law. However, the Court allowed Member States to restrict the freedom of establishment on a case-by-case basis to protect public interests, such as the protection of creditors, minority shareholders, and employees.[354]

Meanwhile, the European institutions worked on secondary EU law legislation which regulates the procedural framework for cross-border conversions, mergers, and divisions.[355] The Commission's proposal recognised the CJEU case law and did not prohibit cross-border conversions in case of a mere transfer of the registered office.[356] However, the European Parliament proposed amendments according to which '[c]ross-border conversions should be conditional on the company moving its registered office together with its head office in order to carry out a substantial

[350] See in this vein Opinion of Advocate General Jääskinen, 16 April 2013, C-105/12 to 107/12, *Essent Nederland BV, Eneco Holding NV and Delta NV*, ECLI:EU:C:2013:242, para 89.

[351] CJEU, 9 March 1999, C-212/97, *Centros*, ECLI:EU:C:1999, paras 27 and 29.

[352] CJEU, 30 September 2003, C-167/01, *Inspire Art*, ECLI:EU:C:2003:512, para 138.

[353] CJEU, 25 October 2017, C-106/16, *Polbud*, ECLI:EU:C:2017:804, para 38.

[354] CJEU, 25 October 2017, C-106/16, *Polbud*, ECLI:EU:C:2017:804, para 53.

[355] For an overview of the entire legislative procedure see Wolfgang Schön, 'Missbrauchskontrolle im Europäischen Umwandlungsrecht' in Michael Hoffmann-Becking and Peter Hommelhoff (eds), *Festschrift für Gerd Krieger* (Beck Verlag 2020) 879, 892 et seq.

[356] Commission, 25 April 2018, Proposal for a Directive of the European Parliament and of the Council amending Directive (EU) 2017/1132 as regards cross-border conversions, mergers and divisions, COM(2018) 241.

part of its economic activity in the Member State of destination'.[357] The European Parliament might have been of the opinion that the mere transfer of the registered office leads to abusive practices because the amendments to the directive aimed at preventing 'opportunities for abuses related to tax, social security and the rights of different stakeholders'.[358] The final directive includes a compromise which allows for consideration of the intention of the operation, the number of employees, the assets and their location, equipment, and other factors giving information about the movement of the business activity as relevant facts to determine whether the cross-border operation is set up for abusive or fraudulent purposes.[359]

Some scholars argued that the European legislature has the power to prohibit cross-border conversions in case of a mere transfer of the registered office.[360] However, they disregard the fact that such a ban cannot serve a public interest concern but aims to hinder the companies' access to Member States' company laws. Considering the public interest concern, the mere transfer of the registered office hardly has any impact on tax, social security, or labour law issues.[361] These fields are determined by connecting factures other than the place of the registered office. However, the European legislature has the power to harmonise the standards for the protection of creditors, minority shareholders, and employees.[362] Such a harmonised protection threshold would establish Europeanised values. The exclusion of the mere transfer of the registered office from the scope of the right of establishment would not establish such a Europeanised value as it would only serve the purpose of restricting companies' access to Member States' company laws. Such a restriction cannot be aligned with the spirit of the European internal market.

Fiscal interests[363] of the Member States may lie somewhere between purely protectionist claims, understood as the overt aim of protecting industries from

[357] European Parliament, 9 January 2019, on the proposal for a directive of the European Parliament and the Council amending Directive (EU) 2017/1132 as regards cross-border conversions, mergers and divisions (COM(2018)0241–C8-0167/2018–2018/0114(COD)), Amendment 9.

[358] Ibid Amendment 11.

[359] Directive, 27 November 2019, 2019/2121/EU, amending Directive (EU) 2017/1132 as regards cross-border conversions, mergers and divisions, OJ, 12 December 2019, L 321, 1.

[360] Hartmut Wicke, 'Grenzüberschreitender Formwechsel kann ohne Verlegung des Verwaltungssitzes in Zuzugsstaat zulässig sein—Anmerkung zu EuGH, Urt. V. 25.10.2017 C-106/16, Polbud Wykonawstwo sp.zo.o.' (2017) Deutsches Steuerrecht 2684, 2691; Oliver Mörsdorf, 'Der Entwurf einer Richtlinie für grenzüberschreitende Umwandlungen—Meilenstein oder Scheinriese?' (2019) Europäische Zeitschrift für Wirtschaftsrecht 141, 148; for a different view: Walter Bayer and Jessica Schmidt, 'Grenzüberschreitende Mobilität von Gesellschaften: Formwechsel durch isolierte Sitzverlegung' (2017) 39 Zeitschrift für Wirtschaftsrecht 2225, 2233.

[361] Wolfgang Schön, 'Missbrauchskontrolle im Europäischen Umwandlungsrecht' in Michael Hoffmann-Becking and Peter Hommelhoff (eds), *Festschrift für Gerd Krieger* (Beck Verlag 2020) 879, 898 et seq .

[362] See Art 86i, Art 86j, and Art 86k of the Directive 2019/2121/EU.

[363] Jukka Snell, 'Economic Justifications and the Role of the State' in Panos Koutrakos, Niamh Nic Shuibhne, and Phil Syrpis (eds), *Exceptions from EU Free Movement Law: Derogation, Justification and Proportionality* (Hart Publishing 2016) 15 defining the protection of particular undertakings, measures avoiding the loss of revenue and the erosion of the tax base to be the first cluster of justification grounds which the CJEU deems to be purely economic.

competition,[364] and public interests, as public spending is one way of responding to needs and demands of society, and thus the economic nature of the fiscal interest claim may serve a non-economic end.[365] All Member States within the European Union finance their public spending through tax revenue (fiscal state).[366] On a global scale, a loss of revenue has to be followed by a cut in public spending, and thus, any loss of revenue may negatively affect public interests. This finding is as false as it is true. It is true that tax revenue is used for public interests, but it is impossible to allocate one revenue stream directly to one public interest concern. Every tax levied contributes to the Member State's budget, and this entire budget is used to satisfy public interests. Therefore, the loss of revenue does not become an overriding general interest which may be relied upon to justify trade restrictions even if the concern is (partially) harmonised at a European level.[367] The situation would only change if the Member States' budgets were fully harmonised at European level. In such a situation, it may be possible to establish that EU law harmonises public interest concerns because the Member States' budgets reflect their public spending.

2. Light-touch Proportionality Test

The CJEU not only acknowledges the harmonised European interests, the Court also allows the application of a form of light-touch proportionality test to restrictions introduced by secondary EU law. The proportionality test is of a light-touch nature as the secondary EU law restrictions may be considered proportionate, whereas the same trade restriction imposed by a single Member State would not be justified. The Court gives the Member States the possibility of prioritising non-market values over market interests through joint legislation. Accordingly, non-market values have more weight in the balancing act against the values of market integration if all the Member States consider them as public interests worth protecting. In other words, the harmonised public interest concerns are more likely to

[364] In this vein see Sue Arrowsmith, 'Application of the EC Treaty and Directives to Horizontal Policies: A Critical Review' in Sue Arrowsmith and Peter Kunzlik (eds), *Social and Environmental Policies in EC Procurement Law*, vol 13 (CUP 1999) 156 arguing that a general principle of economic interests is too unsophisticated and thus needs to be more nuanced. European treaty 'derogations cannot be used to justify objectives that are "mere" protectionism ... However, other policies that are economic in the sense of affecting industrial development—or, indeed, other financial or commercial interests of the state—should not be caught by a general principle that automatically precludes justification.'

[365] Arrowsmith (n 217) 309, 312; Roth, 'Economic Justifications' (n 219) 37, 39, 51; Snell, 'Economic Aims' (n 219) 78 et seq.

[366] For the development of fiscal states in Europe see Richard Bonney, *The Rise of the Fiscal State in Europe c.1200–1815* (OUP 1999).

[367] For the existing CJEU case law on revenue losses as public interest concerns see CJEU, 16 July 1998, C-264/96, *Imperial Chemical Industries plc (ICI)*, ECLI:EU:C:1998:370, para 28; CJEU, 21 September 1999, C-307/97, *Compagnie de Saint-Gobain*, ECLI:EU:C:1999:438, para 50; CJEU, 6 June 2000, C-35/98, *B.G.M. Verkooijen*, ECLI:EU:C:2000:294, para 59; CJEU, 8 March 2001, C-397/98 and C-410/98, *Metallgesellschaft Ltd and Others*, ECLI:EU:C:2001:134, para 59; CJEU, 21 November 2002, C-436/00, *X*, ECLI:EU:C:2002:704, para 50; CJEU, 11 March 2004, *Hughes de Lasteyrie du Saillant*, ECLI:EU:C:2004:138, para 60; see this chapter subsection C.III.1.

outweigh European internal market needs than public interest concerns of a single Member State.

In the *Schmelz* case, the CJEU restricted the necessity test quite extensively. The Court did not consider whether the Member States could gather the necessary information for extending the exemption for small undertakings to non-resident taxpayers via the taxable person, or whether a separate threshold should be imposed in the host Member State.[368] Likewise, in *Meyhui*, the CJEU did not question whether consumers really only need specific information on the crystal glass in the language of the Member State in which territory the glass is marketed or sold, or whether the use of three or all languages of the European Union would be sufficient to serve the public interest concern.[369]

On the other hand, the CJEU's case law shows that it is hardly impossible to justify restrictions of secondary EU law which expose specific Member States to a less favourable treatment, or which set the ground for a less favourable treatment of one Member State. In *Ramel*,[370] for example, the Court ruled that a regulation provision runs foul of the free movement of goods if it allows Member States to levy a charge which hinders trade between the Member States. In that particular case, one Member State wanted to take actions and shield its market from the entry of goods from the other Member States, or the entry of goods of a specific Member State. Accordingly, it is not a general obstacle but a specific obstacle to intra-EU trade. The same holds true for *Roviello*,[371] in which the CJEU found that some parts of the Regulation on the application of social security schemes to employed persons, to self-employed persons, and to members of their families moving within the Community is invalid because it contradicts primary EU law. The Regulation referred back to the national law to determine who is entitled to claim insurance benefits in cases of occupational invalidity or incapacity for work. Linking the entitlement to claim insurance benefits to the national law allows the individual Member State to set quite a high threshold which would particularly harm foreign workers. Since the threshold is not implemented by the secondary EU law provision, but by each Member State's law, the obstacles to trade are specific and not general. The Court did not consider why the secondary EU law preferred to refer back to the Member States to determine the entitlement to claim insurance benefits. It was enough for the CJEU to find a contradiction between the secondary EU law and the fundamental freedoms.

The case law clearly shows that in cases in which secondary EU law provides for general obstacles to trade which do not impose burdens on specific Member States or the trade between specific Member States, the Court accepts the underlying harmonised public interest concerns of the Member States for justification and does

[368] CJEU, 26 October 2010, C-97/09, *Schmelz*, ECLI:EU:C:2010:632, para 65 et seq.
[369] CJEU, 9 August 1994, C-51/93, *Meyhui* NV, ECLI:EU:C:1994:312.
[370] CJEU, 20 April 1978, 80/77 and 81/77, *Ramel*, ECLI:EU:C:1978:87.
[371] CJEU, 7 June 1988, 20/85, *Roviello*, ECLI:EU:C:1988:2805.

not easily call into question the adequacy and necessity of the measure. If, however, the secondary EU law imposes specific obstacles to intra-EU trade, the CJEU does not allow the light-touch justification.

IV. 'Correction Function' of Secondary Law

In the previous subsection, the application of primary law to secondary law has been examined, and it has been shown that the CJEU is not an enemy of regulation but instead is an enemy of barriers to trade resulting from diversity of regulation in the Member States. Many infringements of fundamental freedoms sanctioned by the CJEU are therefore not to be understood as an attempt to curb regulation. Rather, Member States should be encouraged to find common solutions which may burden the market players but do not burden cross-border economic activities.[372] What is already implied by these remarks should be emphasised once again: the Member States can influence[373] or even correct certain outcomes of the CJEU's case law using secondary legislation.[374]

In this sense, Member States can harmonise public interest concerns at a European level and thereby erode intra-EU trade obstacles. For example, the European legislature may introduce secondary EU law requiring a minimum capital for all limited companies in Europe. This legislative act may be a reaction to the CJEU rulings which found that the requirement of minimum capital in the host Member State for a foreign limited company not being subject to strict regulations in the home Member State contradicts the freedom of establishment.[375] Or secondary EU law may harmonise interests which the Member States may not be able to pursue on an isolated basis, such as the interest in taxing business profits at a fair minimum rate.[376] Moreover, secondary EU law may also be capable of influencing the Court's approach to the balancing acts, for example when fundamental freedoms and fundamental rights clash, as was the case in *Viking*[377] and *Laval*[378].[379]

[372] Amedeo Arena, 'The Doctrine of Union Preemption in the E.U. Internal Market: Between Sein and Sollen' (2010) 17 Columbia Journal of European Law 477, 506 argues that within the scope of secondary EU internal market legislation the 'crux is striking a balance between trade liberalization (thus reaping the benefits of comparative advantage) and an adequate level of protection of non-economic interests (such as human health, consumer protection, environmental concerns, etc.)'.

[373] Gareth Davies, 'Legislative Control of the European Court of Justice' (2014) 51 Common Market Law Review 1579, 1587 arguing that '[a] legislative act that embodies a different understanding than the that of the Court of the legal rules and principles which the Treaty entails would . . . be vulnerable to annulment, but legislative decisions on balancing of interests, consequences, and the necessity of certain measures, for example, would be accorded more leeway'.

[374] Bogdandy (n 333) 166.

[375] CJEU, 9 March 1999, C-212/97, *Centros*, ECLI:EU:C:1999:126; CJEU, 30 September 2003, C-167/01, *Inspire Art*, ECLI:EU:C:2003:512; Teichmann (n 329) 754.

[376] See this chapter, subsection D.III.1.

[377] CJEU, 11 December 2007, C-438/05, *Viking*, ECLI:EU:C:2007:772.

[378] CJEU, 18 December 2007, C-341/05, *Laval*, ECLI:EU:C:2007:809.

[379] The Member States changed the directive on the posting of workers (Directive, 28 June 2018, 2018/957/EU, amending Directive 96/71/EC concerning the posting of workers in the framework of

Accordingly, secondary EU law may function as a correction tool for the Member States,[380] and thus can be used to show the CJEU which direction the European Union should move towards.[381] Of course, secondary EU law cannot introduce specific discriminatory measures within the European internal market, but it can implement regulations which may be found restrictive if imposed at the level of a single Member State. And secondary measures can force the Court to place more weight on non-market values when a balancing act is required.

Allowing the Member States to influence or even correct the CJEU case law is convincing as it can solve a conflict of interest at the legislative and not at the judicative level. The decision on which value should be prioritised over the market freedoms should be taken by the legislature and not the CJEU. This does not mean that the Court should not rule on the infringements of the fundamental freedoms as long as there is no common agreement among the Member States. If, however, the Member States are ready to set regulatory standards or define public interest needs, they should be allowed to do so regardless of existing (and conflicting) CJEU case law. When elucidating secondary EU law, the CJEU may easily deviate from its previous rulings. The situation has changed since the Member States have carried out their obligation of shaping a common regulatory framework where necessary.

the provisions of services, OJ, 7 July 2018, L 173, 16) as a response to the CJEU ruling in *Viking* and *Laval*. Daniel Carter, 'Equal Pay for Equal Work in the Same Place? Assessing the Revision to the Posted Workers Directive' (2018) 14 Croatian Yearbook of European Law & Policy 31, 60 et seq analysing how the Court might interpret the new provisions in the light of the Court's earlier case law; 'From the Board: Towards a Social Europe?' (2018) 45 Legal Issues of Economic Integration 323. See also Vasiliki Kosta, *Fundamental Rights in EU Internal Market Legislation* (Hart Publishing 2015) 233; Phil Syrpis and Tonia Novitz, 'Economic and Social Rights in Conflict: Political and Judicial Approaches to Their Reconciliation' (2008) 33 European Law Review 411, 417.

380 Sacha Garben, 'The Constitutional (Im)Balance between "the Market" and "the Social" in the European Union' (2017) 13 European Constitutional Law Review 23, 37 criticising that the 'political process has been unable to readjust the balance' but the political process is able to 'correct the negative integration resulting from European Court of Justice case law'.

381 Importantly, the CJEU may only accept restrictions of free movement rights through secondary EU law when it is explicit. In *Gerardo Ruiz Zambrano*, concerning residency right protection of third country nationals, secondary EU law granted third country nationals residency rights in cases where a family member, the EU citizen, moves to or resides in a Member State other than that of which he or she is a national. In *Gerardo Ruiz Zambrano*, however, the EU citizen did not move between the Member States and yet the CJEU directed the referring national court to grant a residency right in Belgium to a Colombian father of underage children holding a Belgian nationality (CJEU, 8 March 2011, C-34/09, *Gerardo Ruiz Zambrano*, ECLI:EU:C:2011:124). The 'Court was quick to set aside the legislature's intent, although the Parliament and the Council had deliberately decided to limit the scope of the Citizenship Directive 2004/38/EC to "Union citizens who move to or reside in a Member State other than that of which they are a national, and to their family members ... who accompany or join them"', Kay Hailbronner and Daniel Thym, 'Case Note on Ruiz Zambrano' (2011) 48 Common Market Law Review 1253, 1256; Udo Di Fabio, *Grenzen der Rechtsfortbildung in Europa* (Zentrum für Europäisches Wirtschaftsrecht 2012) 15 referring to this as 'Extensionstendenzen' (extension trends) in the CJEU case law. For an overview of the development of the case law and the reaction of the Member States (in particular Ireland) see Susanne K Schmidt, *The European Court of Justice and the Policy Process: The Shadow of Case Law* (OUP 2018) 182 et seq.

V. Findings

The CJEU applies the fundamental freedoms differently to secondary EU law than to national Member State laws. On the one hand, the different application exists because secondary legislation creates uniformity, and thus barriers to trade resulting from regulatory differences between the Member States' approaches cannot arise. For example, the minimum capital requirement for the establishment of a domestic branch of a foreign limited company which is not subject to any capital regulations may be an obstacle for the freedom to establish a branch in another Member State. If the formation of a company throughout the European Union is linked to the condition of raising a minimum capital, there is no longer any need for protective measures for foreign companies establishing domestic branches, because there are no (foreign) companies without minimum capital. However, the fundamental obligation to raise minimum capital cannot be understood as having a negative impact on the European internal market. Rather, it is a regulatory decision taken at a European level.

On the other hand, the CJEU allows a light-touch justification in cases in which secondary EU law imposes general obstacles to intra-EU trade. Accordingly, the Court accepts the harmonised public interest concern underlying the unified substantive law. If all the Member States give a non-market value more weight than market interests, the Court only follows a plausibility test and thereby asks whether there are any less restrictive, but equally effective measures. Concerning equal effectiveness, the Court relies on the given legal and factual situation, which is entirely different from what the Court does when testing national laws against the fundamental freedoms. Accordingly, the CJEU accepted in *Schmelz*[382] that the Member States do not have the information they would need to treat domestic and foreign small undertakings alike, and thus did not require the Member States to gather the relevant information directly from the undertakings, which the CJEU may have pressed for in a case concerning a single Member State's national tax law rule.

Despite using secondary EU law to implement regulatory measures which the Member States would not be allowed to implement on their own, the Member States may utilise secondary legislation to influence the CJEU's application of the fundamental freedoms. The Member States can employ secondary EU law to give the Court guidance, particularly in cases in which the Court has to balance competing values. This ensures that the political decision upon which values gain priority over each other is taken at the legislative and not judicial level.

[382] CJEU, 26 October 2010, C-97/09, *Schmelz*, ECLI:EU:C:2010:632.

E. The Fundamental Freedoms and Law Enacted under the Enhanced Cooperation Procedure

Thus far, we have learned that the CJEU differentiates between secondary EU law and unilateral measures of Member States when applying the fundamental freedoms. Unlike domestic Member State laws, secondary EU law is subject to softer examination, making it easier to align secondary EU law trade obstacles with free movement rights. The reduced threshold honours the Member States' joint harmonisation efforts. Against this background, the level of integration established between the Member States may be a determining factor for applying the fundamental freedoms to laws enacted under the enhanced cooperation procedure. This would mean that it makes a difference whether the participating Member States can (only) agree on conflict of law rules or whether they can go further and harmonise values underlying the laws.

However, enhanced cooperation not only fosters European integration but also establishes differentiation by dividing the Member States into groups of enhanced cooperators and non-cooperators. The existing CJEU case law on the application of the fundamental freedoms does not exhaustively address grouping issues as neither unilateral measures of Member States nor secondary EU law typically differentiate between groups of Member States. In other words, trade obstacles introduced by secondary EU law usually apply to trade between Member State A and Member State B as well as to trade between Member State C and Member State D. Likewise, unilateral trade obstacles ordinarily hinder the access of the domestic markets for (all) foreign goods, services, or persons regardless of the Member State from which they emigrate. Since the law of enhanced cooperation may differentiate between Member States inside and outside enhanced cooperation, one may wonder whether an integration-based approach truly suits the application of the fundamental freedoms in the field of enhanced cooperation, or whether an approach which reflects the existence of the two groups (group-based approach) would be more appropriate. A group-based approach may not be found in the CJEU case law on the application of the fundamental freedoms to economic activities within the European internal market; however, a group-based approach is not an entirely new concept for the application of one of the fundamental freedoms, the free movement of capital. Free movement of capital is guaranteed within the European internal market and between Member States and third countries. The CJEU's case law reveals that the yardstick for applying the free movement provision may depend on whether intra-EU capital movement or capital movement from or to third countries is at stake.

The following subsection will first give an overview of the CJEU case law on the application of free movement of capital guarantee between Member States and between Member States and third countries (see subsection I). Against this background, it will be argued that the logic underlying this case law cannot be transposed to enhanced cooperation law. Rather, the application of an integration-based approach has to be pursued (see subsection II). In the light of an integration-based approach, the different integration levels of secondary EU law (see subsection III) and their potential trade-hampering effects (see subsection IV) will be revealed. Based on a general analysis of the fields in which enhanced cooperation may be pursued (see subsection V), three concrete categories of enhanced cooperation law are identified. The first one is defined by value-based harmonisation (see subsection VI), the second by trade-favouring rules (see subsection VII), and the third by coordinative attempts (see subsection VIII).

I. Group-based Approach: Intrinsic Differentiation between Participating and Non-participating Member States

Applying the fundamental freedoms to the law enacted under enhanced cooperation is very different from testing laws of a single Member State or ordinary secondary EU law against the market freedoms. This fundamental difference is triggered by intrinsic group building when applying the enhanced cooperation procedure. As soon as enhanced cooperation is established, a natural differentiation between the group of participating Member States and the group of non-participating Member States exists. Only the participating Member States are bound by enhanced cooperation law. The enhanced cooperation procedure and its intrinsic differentiation between the group of participating and the group of non-participating Member States may demand that market freedoms apply a different standard depending on which group of Member States is involved in the cross-border economic activity.

The need to differentiate between two groups of States when applying the market freedoms is not an entirely new claim, as it has been suggested that one should differentiate between Member States and third countries when applying the free movement of capital clause. Unlike the free movement of goods, services, and persons, free movement of capital is guaranteed between Member States and between Member States and third countries (*erga omnes* effect).[383] The exceptionally wide scope of the free movement of capital provisions soon raised the question of whether the European treaties guarantee the free flow of capital between Member States and third countries in exactly the same vein as between Member States, or

[383] Art 63 Subsection 1 of the TFEU: 'all restrictions on the movement of capital between Member States and between *Member States and third countries*' are prohibited [emphasis added]. The *erga omnis* effect of the free movement of capital demand a thorough differentiation between the scope of the free movement of capital clause and all other free movement provisions: see for more details Karoline Spies, *Die Kapitalverkehrsfreiheit in Konkurrenz zu den anderen Grundfreiheiten* (Lexis Nexis 2015); Wolfgang Schön, 'Kapitalverkehrsfreiheit und Niederlassungsfreiheit' in Thomas Ackermann and Johannes Köndgen (eds), *Privat- und Wirtschaftsrecht in Europa: Festschrift für Wulf-Henning Roth zum 70. Geburtstag* (Beck Verlag 2015).

whether differentiation is needed between the group of capital movements between Member States and the group of capital movements between Member States and third countries. Within the group of capital movements from or to third countries, one may further distinguish between States with close ties to the European internal market through substantive treaties, such as the European Economic Area (EEA) Agreement and the Free Trade Agreement between the European Union and Switzerland, and States which are completely separated from the European internal market. The EEA Agreement and the Free Trade Agreement with Switzerland extend the fundamental freedoms to these States which may allow an (almost) equal treatment of these States and Member States of the European Union. If the free movement of capital clause is already familiar with a differentiated application depending on the group (the group of Member States, the group of quasi-Member States, or the group of third countries), it may be possible to use the logic underlying this differentiation to help applying the fundamental freedoms to enhanced cooperation law which may distinguish between participating and non-participating Member States.

1. Free Movement of Capital: Differentiation between Member States and Third Countries

The free movement of capital between Member States and third countries shall be free from restrictions such as the free movement of capital between Member States. The wide scope of the free movement of capital guarantee automatically leads to an opening of the internal market to achieve an efficient allocation of capital far across European borders. The European treaties establish a unilateral (ie not demanding a reciprocal action of third countries) liberalisation of the capital market[384] without[385] defining an explicit exception for particularly sensitive fields, such as the tax treatment of capital movement from or to third countries. From a teleological and systemic point of view, a worldwide efficient allocation of capital goes far beyond the European treaties' aim of opening up markets of all Member States and establishing one European internal market. All other market freedoms

[384] Steffen Hindelang, *The Free Movement of Capital and Foreign Direct Investment: The Scope of Protection in EU Law* (OUP 2009) 24 et seq.

[385] The plain wording of Art 65 Subsection 1(a) of the TFEU demands that the free movement of capital does not prejudice the Member States' right to apply their national tax laws differently to resident taxpayers and domestic investment than to taxpayers who are resident in a third country and third country investment. The national tax laws must not constitute a means of arbitrary discrimination or a disguised restriction on the free movement of capital and payments (Art 65 Subsection 3 of the TFEU). However, the CJEU interprets Art 65 Subsection 1(a) of the TFEU in line with the possibility to justify a restriction of the free movement of capital between two Member States, and thus Art 65 Subsection 1(a) of the TFEU 'has been virtually deprived of its legal substance' (Wolfgang Schön, 'EU Tax Law: An Introduction' (Social Science Research Network 2019) SSRN Scholarly Paper ID 3432273 36 <https://papers.ssrn.com/abstract=3432273> accessed 28 January 2020). For the CJEU case law see in particular CJEU, 6 June 2000, C-35/98, *Verkooijen*, ECLI:EU:C:2000:294, para 44 et seq; CJEU, 10 April 2014, C-190/12, *Emerging Markets Series of DFA Investment Trust Company*, ECLI:EU:C:2014:249, para 54 et seq.

(only) guarantee free movement of goods, services, and persons between Member States. Therefore, doubts have been raised over whether the free movement of capital aims to establish a globalised internal market for capital, or whether the free movement of capital toward and from third countries is only secured to the extent necessary for the functioning of the European internal market.[386]

The plain wording of Art 63 Subsection 1 of the TFEU may not indicate that differentiation between capital movement within the European internal market on the one hand, and capital movement across European borders on the other, is allowed. However, Art 64 of the TFEU clearly differentiates between capital movement between the Member States and capital movement to and from third countries. Subsection 1 allows the Member States to apply to third countries (not to Member States of the European Union)[387] restrictions which exist on 31 December 1993 under national or European Union law 'involving direct investment—including in real estate—establishment, the provision of financial services or the admission of securities to capital markets'. Moreover, Subsection 2 grants the European Parliament and the Council authorisation to 'adopt measures on the movement of capital to or from third countries involving direct investment—including real estate—establishment, the provision of financial services or the admission of securities to capital markets' in accordance with the ordinary legislative procedure. The differentiation in Art 64 of the TFEU already indicates that at least for the standstill clause and the legislative actions of the European Parliament and the Council differentiation between third countries and Member States of the European Union and the EEA is legitimate.

Beyond Arts 63 and 64 of the TFEU, differentiation between Member States and third countries can be achieved at different stages. First, the scope of the free movement clause may depend on whether it is applied between Member States or between Member States and third countries; secondly, on the level of comparability, meaning that the flow of capital between Member States and between Member States and third countries cannot be compared; thirdly, on the justification level certain public interest concerns may justify restrictions of the free movement of capital between Member States and third countries, but not between Member States; and fourthly, the proportionality test may be applied stricter between the Member States as between Member States and third countries.

[386] Wolfgang Schön, 'Der Kapitalverkehr mit Drittstaaten und das internationale Steuerrecht' in Rudolf Gocke, Dietmar Gosch, and Michael Lang (eds), *Körperschaftsteuer, Internationales Steuerrecht, Doppelbesteuerung: Festschrift für Franz Wassermeyer zum 65. Geburtstag* (Beck Verlag 2005) 503–04; René Smits, 'Freedom of Payment and Capital Movement under EMU' in Albrecht Weber (ed), *Währung und Wirtschaft: das Geld im Recht ; Festschrift für Prof. Dr. Hugo J. Hahn zum 70. Geburtstag* (Nomos 1997) 250.

[387] And Member States of the EEA-Agreement: CJEU, 23 September 2003, C-452/01, *Ospelt*, ECLI:EU:C:2003:493, paras 30 and 31; for a different take see Opinion of Advocate General Geelhoed, 10 April 2003, C-452/01, *Ospelt*, ECLI:EU:C:2003:232, para 50. See also Lang, 'Kapitalverkehrsfreiheit' (n 58) 212–13.

a) Scope

Wolfgang Schön[388] has suggested limiting the application of the free movement of capital clause to the extent necessary to establish common external European borders for the flow of capital. Common capital borders would not demand an equal treatment of foreign and domestic capital but would require an unimpeded inflow and outflow of capital towards and from third countries. Such an approach would highlight the interconnection between the free movement of capital and the European internal market: a European internal market cannot be established without common capital borders. However, a European internal market does not demand an equal treatment of all capital movements between Member States and third countries. Contrary to aims of the European treaties, it is convincing to limit the guarantee of a free movement of capital to what is necessary to establish the European internal market; however, the CJEU has not followed this approach. Rather, the Court has applied Art 63 of the TFEU to third country dividend payments in the same way as to dividend payments following from a Member State.[389]

b) Comparability

Within the framework of free movement of capital, differences between Member States and third countries could also be acknowledged at the comparability level. Art 65 of the TFEU may even provide justification for such a differentiated view, as Subsection 1(a) allows tax laws of the Member States to differentiate between investor State and investment State and Subsection 1(b) allows the Member States to take measures required 'to prevent infringements of national law and regulation, in particular in the field of taxation ..., or to take measures which are justified on grounds of public policy or public security'.[390] However, these measures must not arbitrarily discriminate or restrict the free movement of capital.[391] The CJEU has not used Art 65 of the TFEU to differentiate between foreign and domestic investment. To the contrary, the Court interpreted this provision in line with the other market freedoms, meaning that the Member State has to prove that a restriction of the free movement of capital is justified by an overriding public interest concern which is pursued in a manner that does not exceed what is necessary and proportionate to achieve its goal.[392]

Besides the fact that the CJEU has not used Art 65 of the TFEU to differentiate substantially between investor and investment States within and outside the European Union or third-country, intra-EU, and domestic investment, Advocate

[388] Schön, 'Der Kapitalverkehr mit Drittstaaten' (n 386) 506.

[389] CJEU, 10 February 2011, C-436/08 and 437/08, *Haribo and Salinen*, ECLI:EU:C:2011:61, para 50 et seq.

[390] See in this vein CJEU, 18 December 2007, C-101/05, *A*, ECLI:EU:C:2007:804, para 32.

[391] Art 65 Subsection 3 of the TFEU.

[392] CJEU, 6 June 2000, C-35/98, *Verkooijen*, ECLI:EU:C:2000:294, para 43; CJEU, 10 April 2014, C-190/12, *Emerging Markets Series of DFA Investment Trust Company*, ECLI:EU:C:2014:249, para 57 et seq.

General Kokott indicated (without giving a final and definitive answer) that capital movement to or from third countries may not be comparable to capital movements within the European internal market, and thus an equal treatment between these movements may not be required.[393]

Within the framework of free movement of capital, the CJEU has differentiated between European Union Member States and third countries 'because of the degree of legal integration that exists between Member States of the Union, in particular by reason of the presence of Community legislation which seeks to ensure cooperation between national tax authorities'.[394] The Court finds Member States and third countries to be in a different position because the European legal framework ties the Member States close together by ensuring mutual assistance, aligning laws, and establishing common values. The Directive on Mutual Assistance,[395] as cited by the CJEU, is only one piece of the puzzle.[396] Primary and secondary EU law establish a framework between the Member States which allows the equal treatment of purely domestic and intra-EU economic activities. With respect to third countries, the situation is different, as such a framework can only be established through international agreements, which establish bridges between two legal orders, for example through mutual assistance.[397] Such international agreements only exist on an isolated basis and they do not enjoy the characteristics of supranational law, such as direct effect and supremacy[398] which ensure a proper application and enforcement of the law.

[393] Opinion of Advocate General Kokott, 18 March 2004, C-319/02, *Manninen*, ECLI:EU:C:2004:164, para 79.

[394] CJEU, 12 December 2006, C-446/04, *Test Claimants in the FII Group Litigation*, ECLI:EU:C:2006:774, para 170; CJEU, 18 December 2007, C-101/05, *A*, ECLI:EU:C:2007:804, para 37; CJEU, 20 May 2008, *Orange European Smallcap Fund NV*, ECLI:EU:C:2008:289, para 89; CJEU, 4 June 2009, C-439/07, *KBC Bank NV*, ECLI:EU:C:2009:339, para 72; see also Opinion of Advocat General Kokott, 11 November 2010, C-436/08 and C-437/08, *Haribo and Salinen*, ECLI:EU:C:2010:668, para 112.

[395] Directive, 15 February 2011, 2011/16/EU, on administrative cooperation in the field of taxation and repealing Directive 77/799/EEC, OJ, 11 March 2011, L 64, 1.

[396] The outcome that intra-EU movements of capital and cross-EU movements of capital are not comparable cannot be based solely on the Directive on Mutual Assistance; it is the entire European legal framework which makes these two transactions incomparable. Since it is the entire European legal framework which makes the difference, it is convincing that the Court discusses the issue on the comparability level and not on the justification level. In cases where it is not the entire framework which is at stake but a particular aspect of the Directive on Mutual Assistance, that particular element of secondary EU law may serve as a ground of justification, eg the possibility to get information on whether or not a legal entity is a charitable body (CJEU, 27 January 2009, C-318/07, *Persche*, ECLI:EU:C:2009:33, paras 68–70). For a different view, see Lang, 'Kapitalverkehrsfreiheit' (n 58) 218.

[397] In *Emerging Markets Series*, the CJEU asked the referring court to examine whether the exchange of information mechanisms under a particular tax treaty are 'are in fact capable of enabling ... tax authorities [of a Member State] to verify ... the information provided by investment funds established in [a third country]'. In other words, the CJEU wanted to know whether the exchange of information clause in international tax treaties is comparable with mutual assistance under the European Mutual Assistance Directive. CJEU, 10 April 2014, C-190/12, *Emerging Markets Series*, ECLI:EU:2014:249, para 88. See also Ana Paula Dourado, 'The EU Free Movement of Capital and Third Countries: Recent Developments' (2017) 45 Intertax 192, 201.

[398] For an overview of the characteristics of supranationalism see Alan Dashwood and others (eds), Wyatt and Dashwood's European Union Law (6th edn, Hart Publishing 2011) 235 et seq.

From this it already follows that the legal framework established between the Member States is more sophisticated and advanced than the one existing between Member States and third countries. These differences may indicate that Member States and third countries are not in a comparable situation. However, the comparability question has to be asked in the light of the aim and purpose of the national provision which is tested against the free movement of capital clause.[399] Therefore, the sophisticated legal framework between the Member States may only have an impact on the comparability of the movement of capital between Member States and the movement of capital between Member States and third countries if the domestic provision is built on trust and cooperation between two States. However, if the national law is not built on any of this, the movement of capital between Member States and the movement of capital between Member States and third countries may be comparable as there is nothing which demands differentiation.

To sum up, the sophisticated legal framework at a European level influences comparability of the law, as tested against Art 62 of the TFEU, to the extent it builds on solid cooperation between States. If, however, the aim and purpose of the law does not build on trust, cooperation, or assistance between States, which may be influenced by the European legal framework, there is no reason why the movement of capital between Member States and between Member States and third countries should not or cannot be compared.

c) Justification

Differentiation between the Member States of the European Union and third countries can also be established at the justification level. The CJEU has established one-sided equality in that sense that any ground of justification applicable in the relationship between the Member States can '*a fortiori*, be recognised in the Member States' relations with non-member States',[400] but a certain public interest concern which is capable of justifying restrictions of the free movement of capital in the relationship between Member States and third countries may not justify restrictions between Member States of the European Union.[401] In that vein, the CJEU may not allow Member States to rely on certain public interest concerns for justifying a restriction of intra-EU capital movement, since the European legal framework addresses these concerns, but allows these public interest concerns to justify a free movement restriction between Member States and third countries.[402]

[399] See this chapter Part I, subsection C.II.

[400] CJEU, 10 February 2011, C-436/08 and 437/08, *Haribo and Salinen*, ECLI:EU:C:2011:61, para 121.

[401] CJEU, 12 December 2006, C-446/04, *Test Claimants in the FII Group Litigation*, ECLI:EU:C:2006:774, para 171; CJEU, 18 December 2007, C-101/05, *A*, ECLI:EU:C:2007:804, para 37; CJEU, 23 April 2008, C-201/05, *The Test Claimants in the CFC and Dividend Group Litigation*, ECLI:EU:C:2008:239, para 93; CJEU, 20 May 2008, C-194/06, *Orange European Smallcap Fund NV*, ECLI:EU:C:2008:289, para 90; CJEU, 4 June 2009, C-439/07 and C-499/07, *KBC Bank NV and Beleggen, Risicokapitaal, Beheer NV*, ECLI:EU:C:2009:339, para 73.

[402] CJEU, 18 December 2007, C-101/05, *A*, ECLI:EU:C:2007:804, para 37; CJEU, 12 December 2006, C-446/04, *Test Claimants in the FII Group Litigation*, ECLI:EU:C:2006:774, para 171; CJEU, 4 June

It is hardly impossible to differentiate between the CJEU case law claiming that capital movement within the internal market and capital movement between Member States and third countries are not comparable because of the sophisticated legal framework between the Member States,[403] and the CJEU case law finding a ground of justification in the missing enforceable assistance between Member States and third countries[404] .[405] From a systematic point of view, the sophisticated legal framework between Member States is relevant on the comparability level if the main aim and purpose of the law is cooperation and assistance. If this is not the case, the lack of mutual assistance between Member States and third countries may be recognised on the level of justification.

To date, the CJEU has not invented or allowed entirely new grounds of justification for obstacles to the capital movement between Member States and third countries but has interpreted the justification ground more broadly[406] or, as set out above, has allowed some justification grounds to stand which the Court would have rejected in a purely intra-EU setting.

d) Proportionality

When the movement of capital between Member States is at stake, the CJEU puts a great deal of effort into finding a less restrictive measure for achieving the Member State's aim. Where the Mutual Assistance Directive is not applicable, the Court has forced the Member States to gather the relevant information directly from the taxpayer.[407] In contrast, the CJEU has not pursued this alternative route

2009, C-439/07, *KBC Bank NV*, ECLI:EU:C:2009:339, para 73; CJEU, 20 May 2008, C-194/06, *Orange European Smallcap Fund NV*, ECLI:EU:C:2008:289, para 90. However, there may be the possibility that Member States and third countries establish a framework which equals the European one, and thus, a particular public interest concern does no longer justify restrictions of the free movement of capital between Member States and third countries: CJEU, 10 April 2014, C-190/12, *Emerging Markets Series*, ECLI:EU:2014:249, para 88. See also Dourado, 'The EU Free Movement of Capital and Third Countries' (n 397) 201.

403 CJEU, 12 December 2006, C-446/04, *Test Claimants in the FII Group Litigation*, ECLI:EU:C:2006:774, para 170; CJEU, 18 December 2007, C-101/05, *A*, ECLI:EU:C:2007:804, para 37; CJEU, 20 May 2008, *Orange European Smallcap Fund NV*, ECLI:EU:C:2008:289, para 89; CJEU, 4 June 2009, C-439/07, *KBC Bank NV*, ECLI:EU:C:2009:339, para 72; see also Opinion of Advocat General Kokott, 11 November 2010, C-436/08 and C-437/08, *Haribo and Salinen*, ECLI:EU:C:2010:668, para 112.

404 CJEU, 18 December 2007, C-101/05, *A*, ECLI:EU:C:2007:804, para 55 et seq; CJEU, 28 October 2010, *Établissements Rimbaud SA*, ECLI:EU:C:2010:645, para 44; CJEU, 17 October 2013, C-181/12, *Welte*, ECLI:EU:C:2013:662, para 63; CJEU, 24 November 2016, C-464/14, *SECIL—Companhia Geral de Cal e Cimento SA*, ECLI:EU:C:2016:896, para 64; CJEU, 19 July 2012, C-48/11, *A Oy*, ECLI:EU:C:2012:485, para 36 (for the European Economic Area).

405 See already Lang, 'Kapitalverkehrsfreiheit' (n 58) 218.

406 CJEU, 26 February 2019, C-135/17, *X GmbH*, ECLI:EU:C:2019:136, para 84; see for a deeper analysis of the case: Wolfgang Schön, 'Interpreting European Law in the Light of the BEPS Action Plan' (2020) Max Planck Institute for Tax Law and Public Finance Working Paper 24 <https://papers.ssrn.com/sol3/papers.cfm?abstract_id=3522962> accessed 3 February 2021.

407 CJEU, 11 October 2007, C-451/05, *Européenne et Luxembourgeoise d'investissements SA (ELISA)*, ECLI:EU:C:2007:594, para 95; CJEU, 6 June 2013, C-383/10, *Commission v Belgium*,

to minimise obstacles to free movement of capital between Member States and third countries.[408] The CJEU may be of the opinion that the taxpayer may be able to produce evidence demonstrating that the legal conditions are satisfied, but the Member State has no power to verify the information provided by the taxpayer, as the third country may not be obliged under a treaty to provide information or verify it.[409]

However, the CJEU only applies a light proportionality test in cases in which the Member States have to rely on the cooperation of third countries to gather or verify information relevant for the satisfaction of legal conditions, for example conditions for the entitlement to a tax advantage. Where Member States impose obstacles to free capital movement which aim at preventing abuse and tax evasion, they have to meet the same proportionality test regardless of whether the obstacles restrict capital movement between the Member States or between Member States and third countries.[410]

2. Enhanced Cooperation and Group-based Differentiation

The CJEU case law stipulates that free movement of capital applies a different yardstick on the comparability, justification, and proportionality level depending on which States are involved. In the light of the enhanced cooperation procedure, one may wonder whether it is possible to rely on this case law in the relationship between participating and non-participating Member States. If a different free movement yardstick were applied to cases of enhanced cooperation, the free movement guarantees would use different standards depending upon whether participating or non-participating Member States were involved in the cross-border economic activity. Intra-group economic activities would enjoy the full protection of the market freedoms, whereas cross-group economic activities would be subject to a lower level of examination because a different yardstick on the comparability, justification and proportionality level would apply.

Such an attempt has to be rejected on fundamental grounds. Any enhanced cooperation must not have a negative impact on the relationship between the Member States (meaning both participating and non-participating Member

ECLI:EU:C:2013:364, para 54; CJEU, 28 February 2013, C-544/11, *Petersen*, ECLI:EU:C:2013:124, para 51; 23 January 2014, C-296/12, *Commission v Belgium*, ECLI:EU:C:2014:24, para 44.

[408] CJEU, 28 October 2010, C-72/09, *Établissements Rimbaud SA*, ECLI:EU:C:2010:645, para 45 et seq.

[409] CJEU, 26 February 2019, C-135/17, *X GmbH*, ECLI:EU:C:2019:136, paras 91 and 92; if the Member States rely on impossibility to verify or gather information concerning a third country, they have to do so in a consistent manner. Otherwise, a justification may not be possible: CJEU, 17 October 2013, C-181/12, *Welte*, ECLI:EU:C:2013:662, para 65 et seq; CJEU, 4 September 2014, C-211/13, *Commission v Germany*, ECLI:EU:C:2014:2148, para 59.

[410] CJEU, 20 September 2018, C-685/16, *EV*, ECLI:EU:C:2018:743, para 94 et seq; CJEU, 3 October 2013, c-282/12, *Itelcar—Automóveis de aluguer Lda*, ECLI:EU:C:2013:629, para 36 et seq.

States). If, however, the mere existence of enhanced cooperation would differentiate between Member States benefiting from full protection of the fundamental freedoms (Member States inside the group) and Member States enjoying a lower level of internal market protection (Member States outside the group), market integration would be at risk. A differentiation between insiders and outsiders and an automatic changing yardstick in the application of the movement rights would harm the entire European internal market and clearly contradict the constitutional framework of the enhanced cooperation procedure. Since any enhanced cooperation must not negatively affect the relationship between the Member States of the European Union, it is illegitimate to use a different yardstick automatically for the application of the fundamental freedoms to laws enacted under the enhanced cooperation procedure and unilateral measures of a single Member State.

Against the background of unfettered internal market protection for all Member States (regardless of whether or not they participate in enhanced cooperation), the key question for the application of the fundamental freedoms to laws enacted under the enhanced cooperation procedure has to be framed quite differently. One must ask whether the objectives of the enhanced cooperation procedure, as a primary EU law mechanism, enjoy protection from the strict application of purely efficiency-driven market freedoms. The enhanced cooperation procedure aims to deepen integration between a group of Member States without bringing any harm to the European internal market. Therefore, the integration efforts of some Member States are central to the whole procedure. These efforts may demand the law of the group to differentiate between insiders and outsiders of enhanced cooperation. Accordingly, it is not the group-building factor which requires differentiation but the integration efforts of the participating Member States. The integration progress of enhanced cooperation may vary depending on the form and substance of the law. Member States may use the enhanced cooperation procedure to harmonise values and install an entire legal framework among them, but they may also apply the procedure to introduce merely technical agreements which do not provide for a great integrational benefit. These different integrational levels may provide guidance to decide whether or not the law enacted under the enhanced cooperation procedure needs 'more' protection than a unilateral measure of a single Member State. In other words, the integration efforts of some Member States may allow insiders and outsiders of enhanced cooperation to be treated differently to protect the group's integration achievements. The mere fact of belonging to or falling outside a group cannot be the ground for differentiation because enhanced cooperation cannot establish two tiers of Member States which would automatically allow the application of a different yardstick on the comparability, justification, and proportionality level depending on whether participating or non-participating Member States are involved.

II. Integration-based Differentiation as the Optimal Yardstick

Thus far, it has been suggested that the intrinsic differentiation of enhanced cooperation law between participating and non-participating Member States cannot influence the application of the fundamental freedoms. Rather, the deeper integration level established between the participating Member States may demand protection of the joint efforts when applying the fundamental freedoms. The level of integration within enhanced cooperation may vary quite substantially. On one side of the scale lies enhanced cooperation which implements an entire regulatory system between the participating Member States, as would be the case in a European tax on financial transactions. On the other side of the scale are conflict of law rules which 'only' establish a coordinative framework between the legal orders of the Member States. In between these two extremes lies enhanced cooperation which aims to ease cross-border economic activities between the participating Member States in certain fields without establishing system-building principles or common values among them. The different levels of integration have an impact on whether and how to justify a different treatment of intra-group and cross-group situations because the deeper the bond between the participating Member States becomes, the more they differ from non-participating Member States.

The following subsections will first give an overview of the different levels of integration both secondary EU law and enhanced cooperation law are capable of achieving (see subsections III and V) and which trade restrictions these various types of law may create (see subsection IV). The subsequent analysis will be split into three parts: the first will deal with enhanced cooperation law which establishes harmonised values between the participating Member States (see subsection VI). In this context, it will be necessary to examine whether the use of the enhanced cooperation procedure and consequently joint actions of some Member States have an impact on the significance of the public interest concern functioning as a ground of justification. The analysis of the CJEU case law on the application of fundamental freedoms in the field of secondary EU law and national laws of the Member States has shown that a ground of justification which is supported by all Member States weighs more heavily than one which is only supported by a single Member State. Against this background, one may ask whether a joint action of at least nine Member States under the enhanced cooperation procedure allows one to give priority to the harmonised value of the group, and thus allows one to justify restrictions of the fundamental freedoms which may not be able to be justified if a single Member State acts on its own.

The second part analyses enhanced cooperation laws which aim at easing cross-border trade between the Member States (see subsection VII). Cross-border trade can be particularly favoured by extending the resident treatment to non-residents (or the treatment of pure domestic economic activities to cross-border economic activities) when the fundamental freedoms fail to demand equal treatment. The law of a trade-favouring enhanced cooperation does not abide by intrinsic values or principles but by a special reciprocal bond between the participating Member States which may no longer allow a comparison between intra-group and cross-group economic activities.

The third part addresses forms of enhanced cooperation which establish tax coordination between participating Member States (see subsection VIII). Tax coordination allows Member States to fulfil their obligations under the fundamental freedoms jointly but in accordance with their national values and principles. Such a common approach gives the Member States more flexibility and allows them to share the burden equally or in a way which best fits their national tax system. Tax coordination links the national tax treatment of the Member States, which may prohibit a comparison of a purely intra-group and cross-group situation.

III. Different Integration Levels of Secondary European Union Law

Any secondary EU law, including the law of enhanced cooperation, has to improve the European internal market.[411] The law of enhanced cooperation fosters the free movement of goods, services, persons, and capital, most likely not within the entire European internal market but rather between participating Member States by harmonising the law between them. The harmonisation can range from common conflict of law rules to rules which unify the Member States' substantive law.[412] The different mechanism chosen by the Member States determines the level of integration achieved between them.[413] Conflict of law rules provide for certainty, as it becomes quite clear which Member State law has to be applied in a situation which is covered by the law of more than one Member State. On the other hand, unification of the substantive laws of the Member States has to be built on common interests and harmonised values which establish a much deeper bond between the Member States than an agreement on conflict of law rules.

The following subsections will elaborate more specifically on the different integration levels and will ask why the Member States have chosen a particular form of harmonisation, and how these laws influence the relationship between the

[411] For the details of the European internal market competence see Chapter 4, subsection G.

[412] Peter-Christian Müller-Graff, 'Privatrechtsangleichung durch die EG im Schnittfeld von Sachenrecht und Kollisionsrecht' in Ole Lando, Ulrich Magnus, and Monika Novak-Stief (eds), *Angleichung des materiellen und des internationalen Privatrechts in der EU* (Peter Lang 2003).

[413] The different integration levels not only reflect the internal market needs but also the similar or different preferences of the Member States. 'If by contrast member States have diverse preferences regarding the desired policy solutions and appropriate limits of supranational power, the outcome of the decision process in the main arena is likely to be vaguely formulated (an incomplete contract) and/or at the lowest common denominator', Adrienne Héritier, 'Covert Integration of Core State Powers: Renegotiating Incomplete Contracts' in Philipp Genschel and Markus Jachtenfuchs (eds), *Beyond the Regulatory Polity?: The European Integration of Core State Powers* (OUP 2014) 234.

participating Member States on the one hand, and, on the other hand, the relationship between the participating and the non-participating Member States. The relationship between the participating and the non-participating Member States may be particularly influenced by the integration level of the law introduced under enhanced cooperation if the legitimation to protect the common efforts of the participating Member States would depend upon the level of integration they have achieved.

1. Conflict of Law Rules

The phrase 'conflict of law rules' can be used in a very broad or a narrow manner. Understood more broadly, it can refer to the rules on the jurisdictional competence of courts (jurisdiction rules), or to the rules for the cross-border recognition and enforcement of judicial decisions (recognition and enforcement rules).[414] The phrase also possesses a narrower meaning, which is more suitable for the present purpose and that asks for the applicable law.[415] Conflict of law rules are predominantly associated with civil law and they ask which legal order should be applied to a particular situation if the application of more than one State's law is legitimate. Accordingly, the rules identify the proper sphere of applicability of a particular national rule.[416] In taxation, the rationale underlying the conflict of law rules can be found in tax treaties,[417] but the rules are embedded into a wider framework, and thus should be understood as coordination rules.[418]

Conflict of law rules are only required when the law between the Member States is not unified, or when the law applying to cross-border situations is not the same in the relevant States. Rules determining the applicable law become especially important when the law and its underlying principles are very different and when cross-border situations can easily occur, as within the European Union in which the free movement of goods, services, persons, and capital is guaranteed. If the conflict of law rules between the Member States differ from each other, the outcome of their application may be unsatisfactory because it may lead to situations in which no Member State law is applicable or situations in which more than one Member State claims the application of its law. A common approach towards conflict of law rules allows them to be more effective.[419]

414 Katharina Boele-Woelki, *Unifying and Harmonising Substantive Law and the Role of Conflict of Laws* (Martinus Nijhoff Publishers 2010) 36.

415 ibid.

416 René David, 'The Methods of Unification' (1968) 16 The American Journal of Comparative Law 13, 13.

417 Conflict of law rules ask which national laws should be applied; tax treaties ask which treaty partner is entitled to tax.

418 See this chapter Part I, subsection E.III.3.

419 Larry Kramer, 'On the Need for a Uniform Choice of Law Code' (1991) 89 Michigan Law Review 2134, 2137; more critical because of the costs: Toshiyuki Kōno, *Efficiency in Private International Law* (2014) 111.

Within the European Union, conflict of law rules identify the substantive law of one Member State which should be applied to a particular situation or relationship. These rules may follow certain principles and are subject to specific value choices of the Member States.[420] However, the conflict of law rules do not provide for legal consequences; they are imposed by the substantive laws of the Member States.[421] Accordingly, the values and principles underlying the legal consequences are the ones of the Member State whose law is applicable. For example, take a German individual who is married to an Austrian citizen, and who lives with his or her spouse in the Netherlands. If he or she is unhappy with the marriage and wants to divorce, the question of which law should be applied emerges: the law of the Member State in which both are currently living, the law of the Member State in which they married, or the law of Member State of which one of them is a citizen? Conflict of law rules can solve the issue by determining which law is applicable.[422] The rules determining which rules are applicable may be based on some principles defining which connecting factor should have priority, such as residence.[423] However, the rules do not develop any principles or values in the area of divorce law; they merely serve to solve the conflict between the application of different Member States' laws.

From this, it follows that the benefit from unifying the conflict of law rules rests with the certainty of which law will be applied in a cross-border setting. The Member States have, however, not harmonised any of their substantive laws, or at least the principles or values underlying their substantive law. The substantive law of the Member States remain as they are, only the framework for deciding which jurisdiction should have priority over the other is unified among the Member States.

2. Mutual Recognition

The law of enhanced cooperation could go further than simply implementing conflict of law provisions, but without harmonising values among the Member States; it could establish the principle of mutual recognition in particular areas of the law. Mutual recognition is, to some degree, already safeguarded by the fundamental freedoms.[424] Secondary EU law may, however, ensure the recognition of product

[420] Sometimes the principles underlying these rules may be driven by interests of the Member States which do not add any value to the conflict of law rules as such: Peter Mankowski, *Interessenpolitik und europäisches Kollisionsrecht: rechtspolitische Überlegungen zur Rom I- und zur Rom II-Verordnung* (Nomos 2011).

[421] Ralf Michaels and Joost Paulwelyn, 'Conflict of Norms or Conflict of Laws: Different Techniques in the Fragmentation of Public International Law' (2011) 22 Duke Journal of Comparative & International Law 349.

[422] Within the European Union, the Rome III regulation includes conflict of law rules: Council, 20 December 2010, 1259/2010/EU, Regulation implementing enhanced cooperation in the area of the law applicable to divorce and legal separation, OJ, 29 December 2010, L 343, 10.

[423] Konrad Zweigert, 'Some Reflections on the Sociological Dimensions of Private International Law or What Is Justice in Conflict of Laws?' (1972) 44 University of Colorado Law Review 283, 291.

[424] Markus Möstl, 'Preconditions and Limits of Mutual Recognition' (2010) 47 Common Market Law Review 405; for the area of company law see Casper Behme, 'The Principle of Mutual Recognition in

and education standards from fellow participating Member States, notably in cases in which the restrictions of the fundamental freedoms could be justified using public interest concerns.[425] Outside the enhanced cooperation procedure, the recognition of diplomas in some particular fields is an example of the principle of mutual recognition not being claimed based on the fundamental freedoms but (at least partially) based on secondary EU law of the Member States. But the partial implementation of the principle of mutual recognition by secondary EU law does not provide for a standard, for example a standard on the education of lawyers; it merely regulates that the Member States are not allowed to shield their national market and forbid foreign lawyers from entering their markets. The law is, however, a compromise since the host Member State can require the foreign lawyer to be assisted by a local lawyer when representing and defending his clients in a domestic court. After living under the system of another Member State for three years, foreign lawyers acquire the right to the full exercise of their profession.[426]

3. Coordination Rules

Another category of rules which can be implemented through the enhanced cooperation procedure and which are—in some parts—linked to the conflict of law rules is that of coordination rules. These rules coordinate the legal orders, or more precisely the actions of the Member States by restricting the national discretion or requiring Member States to follow a particular route. Like the conflict of law rules, the coordination rules follow certain principles the Member States have agreed upon, but the rules do not change the substantive laws of the Member States or their underlying values. However, the coordination rules go beyond the scope of mere conflict solving and embed the conflict of law rules into a wider framework of coordination.

In tax law, the coordination rules are of particular importance.[427] Conflicts of two or more tax regimes—by way of double taxation or double non-taxation—have not been solved by granting one claim priority over the other,[428] as in the field of private international law,[429] but by restricting the right to tax.[430] Moreover, in

the European Internal Market With Special Regard to the Cross-Border Mobility of Companies' (2016) European Company and Financial Law Review 31, 35 et seq.

[425] Christine Janssens, *The Principle of Mutual Recognition in EU Law* (OUP 2013) 67 et seq.

[426] Directive, 16 February 1998, 98/5/EC, to facilitate practice of the profession of lawyer on a permanent basis in a Member State other than that in which the qualification was obtained, OJ, 14 March 1998, L 77, 36.

[427] 'The scope of the tax systems, taxing both foreign income and foreign taxpayers makes them to interrelate, especially as regards the determination of tax consequences applied to cross-border income', García Prats, 'Is It Possible to Set a Coherent System of Rules on Direct Taxation' (n 145) 432.

[428] Nor would the conflict be solved if the Member State tax systems were the same: Ian Roxan, 'Assuring Real Freedom of Movement in EU Direct Taxation' (2000) 63 Modern Law Review 831, 833 et seq. Wattel, 'Red Herrings' (n 226) 88.

[429] See this chapter Part I, subsection E.III.3.

[430] Helmut Debatin, 'Zum Grundverständnis der Doppelbsteuerungsabkommen' (1988) Recht der Internationalen Wirtschaft 727, 728.

the aftermath of the Base Erosion and Profit Shifting (BEPS) discussion, it would not be sufficient to qualify tax treaties only as a tool for restricting the taxing rights of the contracting States. Now, the treaties also provide tools which ensure one-off taxation of income.[431] Despite the new developments in treaty law, tax treaty rules coordinate the taxing rights between the participating legal orders without changing the underlying substantive law rules. Secondary EU law can work in the same vein if it aims for coordination between the Member States in tax law matters. Take the Parent-Subsidiary Directive as an example. The Directive aims to eliminate economic double taxation[432] on cross-border dividend flows via a ban on withholding taxes on outbound dividends flows and an optional scheme for the taxation of the parent on the dividends, which is either a full exemption from taxation, or full taxation with a credit of the corporate tax of the subsidiary on the profits distributed to the parent. The Directive does not touch on the Member States' national corporate tax systems; it (only) ensures that economic double taxation is prevented in a cross-border situation, as in a purely domestic setting.

A group of Member States could use the enhanced cooperation to coordinate further the tax systems of the Member States in the area of double taxation or double non-taxation; however, they could also use the mechanism to implement other cooperative measures among them without touching on the fundaments of their national tax systems. One area which could benefit from additional coordination between Member States is personal allowances. Among the Member States, there is consensus that the personal situation of a taxpayer should be considered, usually in the form of family deductions.[433] According to CJEU case law, the home Member State is not allowed to reduce the allowances simply because the taxpayer has earned some of his income in another Member State and is subject to tax on that income in the other Member State.[434] But some Member States may find an aliquot allowance (in accordance with the taxing rights) to be more appropriate, and thus agree on a coordinating approach granting each taxpayer family deductions but in accordance with the taxable income in every Member State.[435] Tax coordination in the field of aliquot family allowances does not change the fundaments of the national tax systems. Even if the Member States are required to consider personal circumstances of their taxpayers, because they levy taxes in accordance with the ability to pay principle, they are free to decide to fulfil this obligation using

[431] OECD, 'Model Tax Convention on Income and on Capital: Condensed Version 2017' (2017) Text 11 <https://www.oecd-ilibrary.org/taxation/model-tax-convention-on-income-and-on-capital-condensed-version-2017_mtc_cond-2017-en> accessed 3 February 2021.

[432] But because the Parent-Subsidiary Directive is applied in a cross-border setting, the aim of preventing economic double taxation also has implications on the judicative double taxation.

[433] See for an overview of the different national approaches Cathal O'Donoghue and Holly Sutherland, 'Accounting for the family in European income tax systems' (1999) 23 Cambridge Journal of Economics 565.

[434] CJEU, 12 December 2013, C-303/12, *Imfeld*, ECLI:EU:C:2013.

[435] For a more detailed analysis of whether or not the Member States are allowed to agree on such a system and modify the existing case law in that respect see this chapter Part I, subsection E.VIII.

a one-off allowance in the home Member State or an aliquot allowance in all the Member States in which the taxpayer earns his income.

4. Unifying Substantive Law

Finally, the Member States can use enhanced cooperation to provide for deeper harmonisation among them: the unification of substantive law. The unification of the law is a 'process of providing the same rule for the different countries so that the same solution applies everywhere in France and Germany, and England and Poland'.[436] The importance of unifying substantive Member State laws lies in the harmonisation of the values and principles underlying the law, and not simply in achieving rules in all the Member States using identical wording.[437] Only such a process ensures that the same solution applies in each Member State, regardless of its traditional legal framework.

The Member States can use the enhanced cooperation procedure to unify their substantive law which applies to cross-border situations, or they can unify parts of their substantive laws also covering purely domestic scenarios if this is necessary to achieve harmonisation.[438] In cases in which the Member States only unify the law of cross-border interactions, two sets of law for the domestic and the cross-border setting exist. Take the Societas Europaea as an example. The Member States have agreed on a common company type which is particularly beneficial for those engaging in an economic activity in more than one Member State. The law on the Societas Europaea is built on (partly harmonised) principles and values on which all the Member States have agreed, but the secondary EU law does not change the company law of the Member States in any form. The national company law rules and the law on the Societas Europaea exist in parallel.

On the other hand, Member States can also agree to unify substantive law through secondary EU laws which apply both in a cross-border and a purely domestic setting. Take the European VAT system as an example. The VAT Directive not only unifies the place of supply rules for cross-border transactions to ensure single taxation of consumption within the European Union, it also applies to purely domestic scenarios.

Regardless of whether the unified substantive law measures only apply in a cross-border setting, or whether a purely domestic scenario is also subject to these rules, the law must be built on common, and thus harmonised, values or principles which form the baseline for the law. The development of common principles and values will always require a balance of contradicting fundamental interests[439]

[436] For the context of unified private international law see David (n 416) 15.

[437] Mauro Cappelletti, Monica Seccombe, and Joseph HH Weiler, *Integration Through Law: Europe and the American Federal Experience. Vol. 1: Methods, Tools and Institutions*, vol I (de Gruyter 1986) 42–43.

[438] Otherwise the subsidiarity requirement would not be met: see Chapter 4, subsection G.VI.

[439] For the European legislature's competence: see Chapter 4, subsection G.III.1.

which are either the State's right to intervene and a guaranteed freedom, or two contradicting freedoms (rights) of persons. If the Member States find a common agreement on how these conflicts should be solved, such as by giving one priority over the other, the Member States have achieved more than a simple aligning of the wording of their national rules. They have harmonised the values and principles underlying the law, which allows for a true unification of the laws between the Member States. The unification of the laws establishes a deep bond between the participating Member States, a bond which allows for a true merging of the national markets to form one common market.

The balancing of contradicting freedoms may be quite evident in areas in which the Member States harmonise their public interest concerns. Take creditor protection in the field of corporate law, which finds its expression in the requirements for a capital stock for a limited liability company: the contradicting interests of the freedom to conduct business on the one hand, and the protection of economic exploitation, on the other hand, may be differently weighted by the Member States. Some Member States require such a capital stock for limited liability companies, others allow the founding of limited liability companies without raising any capital.[440] If these Member States were to require a capital stock for every branch of a foreign limited liability company without capital stock, the freedom of establishment would be at risk. But a harmonised capital stock requirement for limited liability companies would harmonise the public interest concerns among the Member States for the benefit of the European internal market.

In tax law, the Member States have to unify their national taxes quite substantively to come to a balancing of freedoms (fundamental rights) of the taxpayers and the Member States' right to intervene. With regards to income taxes, Member States would need to go so deep as to touch on the fundamental principles of taxation, such as the ability to pay principle. The project for a Common Consolidated Corporate Tax Base (CCCTB), for example, has sufficient depth to affect the fundamental principles of income taxation because it determines the tax base. The tax base reveals what should and should not be subject to tax, and thus truly reflects the principles underlying the tax. Beyond income taxation, Member States may want to commonly implement a steering tax, a tax which influences the behaviour of the taxpayers, such as a tax on financial transactions. Such a tax is determined by principles other than the ones underlying income taxation. The Financial Transaction Tax (FTT), for example, intends to prevent financial institutions from engaging in financial transactions which are harmful to the European financial market, such as high-frequency trading. Accordingly, the FTT follows different principles than an income tax would because the factor to raise revenue equally is not the only

[440] For an overview of the different national approaches towards share capital see Dirk van Gerven, *Capital Directive in Europe: The Rules on Incorporation and Capital of Limited Liability Companies* (CUP 2014).

determining factor. From this it follows that in the field of taxation, Member States have either to aim for a deep harmonisation of their national tax laws or to introduce a new tax regime which is independent of the existing national framework, to allow for separate values and principles determining the tax.

5. Findings

It follows that the law of enhanced cooperation can aim at different levels of integration. The secondary EU law established between a group of Member States can favour cross-border economic activities without harmonising the principles and values underlying the regulation like conflict of law rules, the mutual recognition mechanism, or coordination rules between the Member States. These rules favour trade because they defeat uncertainty and costly adjustments; however, the laws are not determined by a harmonised value of the Member States or a fundamental principle, which is capable of establishing a framework which brings to light the balancing of the contradicting interests and the choice the Member States made. The Member States can, however, also harmonise the principles and values underlying their laws and establish a very deep bond between them.

IV. Ways of Harmful Treatment

1. Obstacles to Trade: Restrictions and Discrimination

Setting regulatory standards by way of secondary EU law eliminates different approaches taken by Member States. The uniformity makes cross-border and purely domestic economic activities equally attractive because no additional costs are incurred when accessing another Member State's market. Thus far, the CJEU has not tested the regulatory approach taken by the Member States against the fundamental freedoms if it provides for real uniformity. Accordingly, the Court leaves it up to the Member States to decide which regulatory approach best suits their needs, as long as a free movement of goods, services, persons, and capital within the European internal market is ensured by complying with these rules once. If the regulatory framework is enacted under the enhanced cooperation procedure, the situation is a bit different because some goods, services, persons, and capital of the European internal market may comply with different rules from the ones used in enhanced cooperation. If the members of the enhanced cooperation do not accept the regulatory framework of the non-participating Member States as being equal, barriers to intra-EU trade will still exist. From this it follows that the law of a common regulatory framework implemented by the enhanced cooperation procedure may still contradict the fundamental freedoms because it does not achieve uniformity within the whole European internal market.

Like in the case of ordinary secondary EU law which binds all the Member States, the law of the enhanced cooperation can provide for rules which allow the shielding of the national markets of the Member States by making entry into the market of another Member State less attractive. The trade obstacles created by the law of enhanced cooperation subsequently also hinder the trade between the Member States within the enhanced cooperation.

Besides constituting obstacles to intra-EU trade, the law of enhanced cooperation may discriminate, especially against goods, services, persons, and capital outside the enhanced cooperation. The members of the enhanced cooperation may wish to discriminate to protect their regulatory framework or to prevent outsiders from free-riding.[441] Accordingly, the law of enhanced cooperation may not only establish barriers to trade between the participating and non-participating Member States, but may also (in contrast to ordinary secondary EU law) fundamentally discriminate against outsiders.

2. A Question of Comparison

The law introduced under the enhanced cooperation procedure gives rise to questions on the relevant comparison. Should one compare an intra-group economic activity (the economic activity between two participating Member States) with a cross-group economic activity (the economic activity between a non-participating and a participating Member State)? Or should one only compare the purely domestic economic activity with a cross-border economic activity (which could either be a cross-group or an intra-group economic activity)?

The fundamental aim of the market freedoms is to prevent any protectionist Member State measures. Member States shall not be allowed to protect their nationals or domestic goods, services, and capital from competition, and thus a comparison is traditionally drawn between a purely domestic situation and a cross-border situation.[442] In enhanced cooperation law, protectionist measures in the traditional sense may not be a serious concern for the European internal market as the participating Member States may not want to protect their national markets from goods, services, persons, or capital from another participating Member State, but they may want to protect the enhanced cooperation market from competing goods, services, persons, or capital of non-participating Member States. The law of enhanced cooperation is thus not protectionist in the same manner as a single Member State's national laws but aims to protect the group. From the perspective of both the non-participating Member States and the European internal market, group protectionism may be as harmful as protectionist rules of a single Member State.

The constitutional framework of enhanced cooperation law acknowledges the possibility of trade-hampering group protectionism, and thus in principle allows

[441] See for a detailed analysis this chapter Part I, subsection E.VII.7.

[442] Member States are also prohibited from fragmenting the internal market by differentiating within their national laws between two cross-border situations, see this chapter Part I, subsection C.II.4.b)(cc).

a comparison between intra-group and cross-group economic transactions. Art 326 of the TFEU explicitly forbids enhanced cooperation law from constituting barriers between participating and non-participating Member States, and a comparison between transactions purely within the group and transactions involving non-participating Member States therefore needs to be drawn. The fundaments of enhanced cooperation law lay out that the fundamental freedoms may test enhanced cooperation law based on an intra-group versus cross-group approach, but it does not reveal anything on whether or not the intra-group situation and the cross-group situation are comparable in the concrete setting.[443]

V. Different Categories of Enhanced Cooperation Law

The different levels of integration enhanced cooperation law can achieve and the different ways the law harms cross-border economic activities make it useful to build different categories, which make the interference between enhanced cooperation law and the fundamental freedoms more visible. First, one must distinguish whether the law of enhanced cooperation is built on harmonised principles and values, or whether the law (only) aims to foster intra-group or intra-EU trade, or whether it provides for (tax) coordination without harmonising the values underlying national laws. The Member States follow common values if, within the law-making process, they engage in a real balancing of contradicting interests and take a stand, like the Member States do when harmonising their public interest concerns, for example by setting product standards, a minimum capital for limited liability companies, or by agreeing on common accounting standards. These harmonisation mechanisms also foster trade between the Member States because they provide for uniformity. The positive impact on trade is, however, only a reflex of harmonisation. The guiding principles for designing the law are determined by the harmonised values of the Member States, such as a high priority of customer and creditor protection or the protection of the environment. If the law of enhanced cooperation does not follow any such values but aims to favour intra-group or intra-EU trade, the law will most likely balance the interests of the Member States and establish either tax-coordination or trade-favouring rules.

The category of values-based harmonisation can be divided into different subcategories depending on the obstacles created. On the one hand, the law of enhanced cooperation can establish obstacles which harm intra-group and cross-group economic activities. On the other hand, the obstacles may only hurt outsiders, and thus the law does not establish any obstacles for intra-group trade. The

[443] See this chapter Part I, subsection E.VII.7.

latter category—mere cross-group trade obstacles—is much more likely to occur. The participating Member States may want to establish such obstacles because they want to protect their harmonised values within the group from being exploited by non-participating Member States. The obstacles to cross-group trade may vary in intensity from mere restrictions to hard discrimination.

Where enhanced cooperation establishes mere trade-favouring rules, the law may also establish barriers to cross-group trade to prevent anyone outside the group benefiting from the harmonisation efforts of enhanced cooperation.

In that vein, the following subsections are divided into three main categories: the first category addresses value-based harmonisation within enhanced cooperation and potential obstacles the law may create within the group and towards non-participating Member States. The second set of laws introduced under the enhanced cooperation procedure aims to foster trade between participating Member States ((mere) trade-favouring rules). The third category of rules lays out the possibility to establish a cross-border coordination system between the participating Member States. Such a system grants Member States more flexibility in complying with their European treaty obligations within the group but may conflict with their obligations towards the non-participating Member States.

VI. Value-based Harmonisation: Restrictions and Justification

We shall now address the scenario in which Member States achieve unification of the laws by harmonising the underlying values of the law. The resulting (partial) uniformity favours the trade between the participating Member States. However, the process of unifying laws is shaped by the common values of the Member States and not by aiming to favour trade, which is (only) the reflex of unification.[444] Depending on the underlying principles and values of the law, enhanced cooperation may establish obstacles either to cross-group trade (trade between participating and non-participating Member States) or to both intra-group trade (trade between participating Member States) and cross-group trade.

In the academic literature, it has been argued that enhanced cooperation could and should be the key to grant a group of Member States the possibility of following important non-trade related values without being struck down by market

[444] In taxation, the mere reflex of trade favouring does not prevent the Member States from using Art 115 of the TFEU as a legal basis. As it has been revealed, the main advantage test only has to be applied when there are two contradicting competence clauses. If, however, the European Union does not hold the power in the field of 'main' purpose, the European legislature is still allowed to act based on the EU's internal market competence under the condition that any provision of the secondary EU law enhances the free movement within the European internal market. The fact that the strengthening of the free movement is only a by-product does not prohibit the application of Art 115 of the TFEU because trade fostering rules have been implemented: see Chapter 4, subsections F.III and G.III.3.

freedoms.[445] Such a view allows the law of enhanced cooperation to develop a market-correcting function, as ordinary secondary EU law has,[446] but ignores the very fact that the law does not establish a uniform regulatory approach within the whole European internal market. The lack of Europe-wide uniformity makes it impossible to find the regulatory approach per se compliant with the fundamental freedoms because enhanced cooperation law does not eliminate all the differences within the European internal market with respect to the particular regulatory objective. On the other hand, it should not be ignored that the Member States do not act unilaterally but combine their interests and follow a common approach. The simple fact that a group of Member States wants to pursue the same regulatory approach indicates that the underlying values and principles cannot and should not be easily overlooked.

Against this background, the application of the fundamental freedoms to the law of enhanced cooperation is determined by two peculiarities: first, enhanced cooperation law does not achieve a uniform regulatory standard or system within the European internal market. Second, the law follows values and principles which are shared and harmonised between all participating Member States. The former feature of the law of enhanced cooperation makes it clear that the remaining obstacles to cross-group trade following from the different regulatory approaches of the participating and the non-participating Member States cannot simply be ignored. These differences may constitute a relevant obstacle to trade and may therefore infringe on the fundamental freedoms. The latter feature may demand that trade obstacles created by enhanced cooperation law are treated like obstacles constituted by secondary EU law, and not like obstacles established by national laws of the Member States. If trade obstacles following from the law of enhanced cooperation were treated like secondary EU law trade obstacles, the harmonised values would constitute a ground of justification and, at the proportionality stage, only a light-touch test would apply. A uniform treatment of the obstacles created by secondary EU law and the law of enhanced cooperation presupposes that the obstacles created by enhanced cooperation law can be considered as being general. If they were specific obstacles, uniform treatment would not add any value because the benchmark for justifying specific obstacles following from secondary EU law is the same as the one for justifying obstacles created by national laws of the Member States.[447]

The following subsection will examine the question of whether enhanced cooperation law automatically establishes specific trade obstacles because it always

[445] Scharpf, 'Was man von einer europäischen Verfassung erwarten und nicht erwarten sollte' (n 177); Fritz W Scharpf, 'Legitimate Diversity: The New Challenge of European Integration' (2002) Les Cahiers européens de Sciences Po 1, 29–30.

[446] For a deeper analysis of the market-correcting function of secondary EU law see this chapter Part I, subsection D.IV.

[447] See this chapter Part I, subsection D.III.

(and sometimes only) applies in a setting involving both participating and non-participating Member States. It will further ask whether the obstacles can alternatively be considered general (see subsection 1). After that, the analysis will be split into two parts which recognise the nature of the obstacle constituted by the law of enhanced cooperation: obstacles harming only cross-group economic activities (see subsection 2), and obstacles harming intra-group and cross-group economic activities (see subsection 3).

1. Enhanced Cooperation Law: A Specific Obstacle to Intra-EU Trade?

The basic distinction between specific and general obstacles to intra-EU trade follows from CJEU case law.[448] General obstacles emerge if all cross-border economic transactions are burdened regardless of the Member States involved. If the obstacle only exists towards or from one particular Member State, the obstacle is specific. To date, the Court has allowed the application of a light-touch justification approach only when general obstacles are at stake. Specific obstacles have to be justified as if they were imposed by the law of a single Member State. In the field of enhanced cooperation, the characteristic of specific obstacles is of particular relevance because the law never binds all Member States. It may be the case that only one Member State is outside the enhanced cooperation, but it may also be the case that all except nine Member States are outsiders. Does the intrinsic notion of the enhanced cooperation—never to bind all the Member States—automatically characterise the obstacles created by the law as being specific?

If one examines the CJEU's case law more closely, one can see that the Court developed the notion of specific obstacles to intra-EU trade, in which secondary EU law allowed the Member States a certain leeway to introduce or maintain obstacles. In such cases, the secondary EU law established the foundation for the obstacles which were ultimately created by the law of a single Member State. Thus, the specific obstacle was not borne of the common values and principles underlying secondary EU laws. The unilateral character of the trade obstacle prohibits applying a light-touch justification approach.

In the field of enhanced cooperation, trade obstacles towards non-participating Member States may not be considered specific (even if the trade obstacles do not exist within enhanced cooperation) if the trade obstacles are introduced by enhanced cooperation law. The trade obstacles cannot be attributable to one single participating Member State and are thus general obstacles even if they only apply in a cross-group setting. Of course, it would be possible to design the law of enhanced cooperation in a way which would refer important decisions back to the Member States and would allow imputing the obstacle to a single Member State

[448] See this chapter Part I, subsection D.III.

of the group. However, such obstacles are the result of unilateral measures of the Member States and are not intrinsic to enhanced cooperation law.

2. Obstacles to Cross-Group Trade

In cases in which Member States utilise the enhanced cooperation procedure to harmonise values and principles underlying their laws, the unified laws eliminate trade obstacles within enhanced cooperation because all participating Member States follow a common regulatory approach but may establish protective trade obstacles towards non-participating Member States. We shall assume, for example, that a group of Member States agrees on using the International Financial Reporting Standards (IFRS) as standards for calculating the income tax base. To do so, the Member States have weighed competing interests against each other, being the ability to pay principle and simplification. The former principle is the overarching principle within the tax codes of the participating Member States ensuring equal taxation. Simplification, on the other hand, is an important commodity, allowing the taxpayers to comply easily with their obligations under the national income tax code. A common approach for calculating the tax base within a group of Member States would allow the taxpayers to use the same standards for calculating the tax base in all participating Member States. In the case of a cross-border economic activity, a non-resident taxpayer who is subject to tax with his income in the source Member State would be able to apply the same standards to calculate the tax base in the source Member States as he uses in the home Member State to calculate his worldwide income. However, if the home or the host Member State is not a participating Member State, the taxpayer may be forced to adjust the tax base to comply with the tax rules in both the home and host Member State.

This example clearly shows that enhanced cooperation law eliminates trade obstacles within the group, but obstacles to cross-group economic activities may still exist or may be newly constituted. The harmonising of the standards for calculating the national tax base eliminates trade obstacles within the group. If, however, the participating Member States require taxpayers who are resident in a non-participating Member State to comply with the harmonised standard for calculating the tax base of his source income, obstacles still exist in a cross-group setting.

Trade obstacles to cross-group economic activities may vary in intensity from restrictions to discriminations. Restrictions[449] may apply especially in cases in which the participating Member States force outsiders to comply with their regulatory measures to uphold their harmonised values (see subsection a). The participating Member States may, however, especially wish to discriminate towards outsiders of the group if they wish to cope with (negative) effects of the regulatory regime implemented by enhanced cooperation (see subsection b). The reasons for

[449] As used by the CJEU: see this chapter Part I, subsection C.I.

restriction or discrimination may have a particularly high impact on whether or not to apply a light-touch justification approach.

a) Obstacles to Upholding the Harmonised Values

Member States which have harmonised values among them and established a coherent system in the light of these values may want goods, services, persons, and capital from outside enhanced cooperation to comply with their common regulatory approach to be able to uphold and protect their harmonised values. Protective trade obstacles which shield the markets of the participating Member States may be necessary to protect the harmonised values, but they may clash with the value of market integration.

We shall assume, for example, that the Member States have agreed on a minimum share capital for limited liability companies to protect creditors. The Member States may believe that creditors can only be protected if the share capital is sufficiently high because this threshold prevents companies from being founded hastily and liabilities from being entered into imprudently. The non-participating Member States may not share this view, and thus may not require limited liability companies to have a minimum share capital. If the Member States of the group require foreign companies which do not have a minimum share capital to comply with the minimum share capital rules, the establishing of a branch within the territory of a participating Member States would become less attractive. On the other hand, Member States would not be able to protect creditors as they wish if they allowed companies to circumvent the rules on a minimum share capital by getting incorporated in a non-participating Member State and establish a branch in a participating Member State.

It becomes quite clear that any attempts by participating Member States to extend their regulatory approach towards goods, services, persons, and capital from outside the enhanced cooperation establishes a trade obstacle between the participating and the non-participating Member States. In cases where the CJEU has already denied the possibility of justifying restrictions to the fundamental freedoms on the grounds of certain public interest concerns,[450] or where the CJEU is likely to do so, it becomes especially interesting whether a group of Member States would be able to justify such restrictions based on their harmonised public interests concern. In other words, one must analyse whether protective obstacles to trade between participating and non-participating Member States constituted by enhanced cooperation law are subject to a light-touch justification approach (the benchmark applied to secondary EU law restrictions) or to the same benchmark which is applied to restrictions of the fundamental freedoms by national laws of the Member

[450] For the minimum share capital and creditor protection see CJEU, 30 September 2003, C-167/01, *Inspire Art*, ECLI:EU:C:2003:51.

States. The application of a light-touch justification would allow an honouring of the harmonised values of the group, as is the case when ordinary secondary EU law imposes general obstacles to intra-EU trade.

Following up on the minimum share capital example, the CJEU has already ruled that a minimum share capital is not necessary[451] for the protection of creditors because it is clear that a branch of a foreign company is governed by the law of another Member State, which may provide for different rules (including the protection of the creditors) than the host Member State. The 'potential creditors are put on sufficient notice that it is covered by legislation other than that regulating the formation in the [host Member State] of limited liability companies and, in particular, laying down rules in respect of minimum capital and directors' liability'.[452] If this line of reasoning were applied to enhanced cooperation law introducing a minimum share capital, it would not be possible to justify restrictions of the freedom of establishment (by forcing companies incorporated in a non-participating Member State to comply with the requirements on a minimum share capital) on the ground of creditor protection. On the other hand, secondary EU law implemented the requirement of a minimum share capital for public limited liability companies as early as 1976.[453] The CJEU has not (yet) tested the secondary EU law provisions on the minimum share capital, but the existing case law gives quite a good idea of the potential outcome of such an investigation: the Court would not find any obstacles to intra-EU trade because the rules on the minimum share capital are unified between all Member States. The regulatory decision of all Member States to demand a minimum share capital for public limited liability companies will not be scrutinised under the fundamental freedoms.[454]

The example perfectly demonstrates the difference between uniform actions of all the Member States (causing no obstacles within the European internal market), national regulatory measures (causing obstacles within the European internal market), and regulatory measures implemented under enhanced cooperation (causing no obstacles within the group but between the group members and non-group members).

451 The CJEU did not address the question of whether the minimum share capital is per se capable of protecting the creditor.

452 CJEU, 30 September 2003, C-167/01, *Inspire Art*, ECLI:EU:C:2003:51, para 135.

453 Art 6 of the Second Company Law Directive (13 December 1976, 77/91/EEC, Second Council Directive on coordination of safeguards which, for the protection of the interests of members and others, are required by Member States of companies within the meaning of the second paragraph of Article 58 of the Treaty, in respect of the formation of public limited liability companies and the maintenance and alteration of their capital, with a view to making such safeguards equivalent, OJ, 31 January 1977, L 26, pp 1–13; now Art 45 of the Company Law Directive (14 June 2017, 2017/1132/EU, directive relating to certain aspects of company law, OJ, 30 June 2017, L 169/46.

454 See in that vein Opinion of AG Alber, 30 January 2002, C-167/01, *Inspire Art*, ECLI:EU:C:2003:57, para 140, arguing that 'the Member States have not been able to reach agreement on harmonising their rules relating to minimum capital requirements for limited liability companies. Both Article 44 EC and Article 293 EC entitle them to harmonise those rules.'

(aa) Honouring the Harmonised Values of the Group The question of whether a group of Member States is allowed to implement common trade obstacles which aim to protect harmonised values (protective trade obstacles), but which each of the participating Member States would not be allowed to introduce on a unilateral basis, is a question of whether or not to honour the harmonised values of the group. In this respect, different views can be taken. One may argue that uniformity among all Member States is required to allow secondary EU law to impose a market-correcting function because it equals a change to the scope and impact of the fundamental freedoms which would otherwise demand an amendment of the European treaties. If not exclusively all the Member States, but also a sub-group of Member States, could change the foundation of the European Union by influencing the scope and impact of the fundamental freedoms, the principle of equality of all Member States (a core principle of the European Union) would be harmed.[455]

Such a line of argument misjudges both the aim of the enhanced cooperation procedure and the interpretation of it proposed in this study. It is not and will not be argued that all obstacles to cross-group trade are justified simply because the obstacle is constituted by a group of Member States and not by a single Member State. It will, however, be argued that the enhanced cooperation mechanism is a tool which allows Member States to identify certain values which they find particularly worthy of protecting against market efficiency. At this point in time, the CJEU already allows the Member States (on a unilateral basis) to protect certain public interests, and thus tolerates restrictions of the market freedoms. However, some public interest concerns of Member States are not considered strong enough to outweigh the value of market integration, and thus the national value in the form of a public interest concern has to give way to market efficiency. In the light of this, the enhanced cooperation procedure should be understood as a tool Member States can use to emphasise the importance of certain non-market values by way of joint harmonisation efforts. Harmonising values is, beyond any doubt, the deepest form of European market integration and the most effective way of truly uniting Member States. Participating Member States of value-based enhanced cooperation do not only follow a common path to enhance trade between them, they align their values which allows that their markets merge to one market of common values.

Accordingly, the mechanism of enhanced cooperation is not supposed to provide a group of Member States with a carte blanche to create any obstacle to intra-EU trade they find appropriate; instead, it is supposed to be a tool which can influence the balancing of the market efficiency and contradicting non-market values. In other words, enhanced cooperation should be understood as a tool Member States can utilise to ensure that the CJEU is aware of how important these non-market values are to the participating Member States.

[455] See Art 4 Subsection 2 of the TEU.

From this it follows that any obstacle created by the law of enhanced cooperation should not automatically be justified simply because a group of Member States is acting and not a single Member State. However, the fact that a group of Member States agrees on certain values and principles should be honoured by understanding the enhanced cooperation as a claim of a group of Member States to respect important (harmonised) non-market values. This is achieved by recognising justifications for trade obstacles imposed by enhanced cooperation law to protect or pursue the harmonised values in the same way as trade obstacles created by ordinary secondary EU law; in other words, protective trade obstacles are subject to a light-touch justification approach.

(bb) Applying a Light-touch Justification Approach to Enhanced Cooperation Law Applying a light-touch justification approach to enhanced cooperation law honours the harmonised values of the participating Member States because a light-touch approach accepts the harmonised non-market value as a ground of justification and allows a light-touch proportionality test. Concerning the former argument, the CJEU may recognise public interests harmonised at European level by a group of Member States as grounds of justification which the Court would not accept if put forward by a single Member State. However, these public interest concerns have to be of a non-protectionist and non-group-protectionist nature to be accepted as a ground of justification as otherwise, the European integration process would be at risk.[456] A light-touch proportionality test restricts the scope for finding less restrictive measures quite dramatically as the system introduced by secondary EU law is accepted to a large extent and it is only tested whether the prioritisation of the harmonised value(s) is way out of line.[457]

In the case of the minimum share capital, this would mean the following: the protection of creditors is a legitimate public interest concern. At the appropriateness stage, the CJEU only undergoes a plausibility check of whether the legal measure is capable of achieving the aim. The Court should not touch on conflicting points of view; if it is merely possible that the measure achieves the goal, the measure passes the appropriateness test.

At the next stage, the necessity test, the Court restricts the set of potential alternative measures to those which are allowed by the law of enhanced cooperation. In other words, the CJEU has to consider the whole legal framework in which the restriction is embedded. In *Schmelz*,[458] for example, the CJEU has accepted that the Member States had agreed on a compromise between simplified rules for small undertakings to enhance their competitiveness and full market efficiency. The Court not only accepted the general desire to implement a simplified scheme for

456 See this chapter Part I, subsection D.III.1.
457 See this chapter Part I, subsection D.III.2.
458 CJEU, 26 October 2010, C-97/09, *Schmelz*, ECLI:EU:C:2010:632.

small undertakings, it also accepted the concrete scheme chosen by the Member States, which included a simplified approach for providing information to the authorities. Since the Member States do not hold all the relevant information on the supplies of small undertakings, an exchange of the information is not a less restrictive but equally effective measure according to the CJEU. An exchange of information would—beyond any doubt—be less restrictive than a restriction of the exemption for small undertakings to supplies within their home Member State but would not be equally effective because the small undertakings would be required to fill all their relevant information, which would contradict the aim to simplify the administration of VAT for small undertakings.

Applied to the minimum share capital, this would mean that the search for less restrictive but equally effective measures is determined by the framework chosen by the group of Member States. We shall assume that the Member States have chosen to implement a system of severe creditor protection, including a minimum share capital, a ban on a return of deposits, and a fallback clause which triggers a personal liability of the shareholders if they do not comply with the rules on the minimum share capital. According to the participating Member States, the framework should ensure that for every creditor any limited liability company has to pass a certain monetary threshold which prevents companies from being founded hastily and liabilities from being entered into imprudently. If that particular framework sets the parameters for finding an alternative measure which is less restrictive but equally effective, the measure has to ensure that the founding of companies is not taken lightly by the shareholders, although they do not have to raise any capital and they are not personally liable for the debts of the company. Accordingly, a less restrictive but equally effective measure may look to the founding process itself, whether it involves a notary or any equivalent institutions. Within that framework, a reference to the fact that a foreign company does not hold itself out as a domestic company would not be sufficient to deny the necessity of the measure. The information that a company is founded in another Member State is not equally efficient in ensuring the creditor a certain thoughtfulness and respectability of the shareholders.

The third stage in the justification process—the true balancing act—is normally omitted by the CJEU. If a restrictive measure is suitable to achieve a certain public interest, and if the measure is necessary, the Court finds the measure to be justified. When the light-touch justification is applied to enhanced cooperation law, the third step of the justification process could, however, have an important role in securing and protecting internal market needs. The light-touch justification approach restricts the second step of the justification process by requiring the whole secondary EU law framework to be taken into account for determining equal effectiveness, and thus the group of Member States can heavily influence the necessity of the restrictive measure by adopting a targeted and detailed system. The last step in the justification stage ensures that measures taken for pursing and protecting the harmonised values underlying the law of enhanced cooperation and the restrictions of European internal market interests are not out of proportion.

(cc) Findings In cases in which the Member States use the enhanced cooperation procedure to harmonise values and principles underlying their laws, and thus subsequently to unify their laws, the Member States are allowed to protect their harmonised values. If they protect their harmonised values by forcing outsiders to comply with their regulatory framework, for example to comply with rules on a minimum share capital, the participating Member States constitute trade barriers in the form of restrictions towards non-participating Member States. Since the participating Member States have achieved more than trade favouring by setting common rules, they have achieved an agreement on how to balance contradicting rights or freedoms and have thus contributed to the process of establishing a community of common values. To honour the joint integration efforts of the participating Member States and to allow them to protect their joint achievements, trade obstacles towards non-participating Member States are subject to a so-called light-touch justification approach. The CJEU applies such a justification approach to general trade obstacles imposed by ordinary secondary EU law. The light-touch justification approach is different from the ordinary justification threshold, which obstacles of national rules of the Member States have to pass, insofar as the harmonised non-market values are accepted as grounds of justification, and a light-touch proportionality test is applied.

Within the proportionality test, the suitability level is influenced by the light-touch approach because the question of whether the trade obstacle is capable of protecting or achieving the public interest concern underlying enhanced cooperation law is reduced to a mere plausibility test. It is sufficient that it is plausible that the legal measure is capable of achieving the aim. Contradicting views (even quite convincing ones) can simply be ignored when applying a light-touch proportionality test.

The second stage in the proportionality test, necessity considerations, is also amended by reducing the scope to find a less restrictive but equally effective measure. With regards to effectiveness in particular, the whole framework introduced by the participating Member States has to be considered. This may rule out alternative measures which are less restrictive but cannot fulfil the aim and purpose of the framework the Member States have agreed upon. Thus, at the necessity level, it makes a big difference whether the Member States introduce an entire regulatory system or just certain limited standards among them because a system is much more detailed and its underlying values are clearly defined so that the range of alternative equally effective legal measures is small.

The third and final stage of the justification level, the true balancing act, does not play a big role under existing CJEU case law. However, in cases in which a light-touch justification approach is applied to obstacles constituted by enhanced cooperation law, the third justification stage can ensure that European internal market needs are sufficiently considered and that the obstacles protecting the harmonised values of the group are not disproportionate.

b) Obstacles to Cope with Negative Effects of Enhanced Cooperation

Member States may wish to use the enhanced cooperation procedure to harmonise their national (tax) regimes, but they may also wish to introduce new regimes with no primarily revenue raising objective. If revenue raising is not the primary purpose of the tax regime, the tax may aim for an impact on the behaviour of the taxpayers or follow certain redistributive goals. Taxes which steer taxpayers' behaviour towards a more efficient, more market-friendly, or less harmful (eg to the environment or the financial market) way of acting often impose negative effects upon the (Member) State levying the tax. The negative effects follow from the responsive behaviour of the taxpayers. They are neither willing to pay the tax nor willing to change their behaviour and thus move to a jurisdiction which does not force the taxpayers to change their behaviour and offer them an equal (legal and factual) environment.

The following subsection provides an overview of the different negative effects a (Member) State has to face when levying certain taxes. It will be revealed that a collective action of Member States is one way to address negative effects of taxation. However, finding the right scope of participating Member States is a balancing act between the need to tackle negative locational effects of the tax and the need to restrict the group to like-minded Member States. Otherwise, it may not be possible to find a consensus on the design and scope of the tax. In case the number of participating Member States is not sufficient to avert all negative effects of the tax, the participating Member States may want to introduce defensive measures. Accordingly, the following subsections will also analyse defensive measures under enhanced cooperation and their impact on the fundamental freedoms.

(aa) Negative Effects of Taxation Within the tax environment, fiscal effects describe the responsive behaviour of taxpayers. High taxation on capital may trigger a move of investment to a low or no tax jurisdiction;[459] environmental taxes such as carbon taxes may have an impact on the locational decision of producers.[460]

[459] Thiess Büttner, 'Fiscal Externalities in Local Tax Competition: Empirical Evidence from a Panel of German Jurisdictions' (2011) ZEW Discussion Paper.

[460] For the discussion on the 'race to the bottom' see Katharina Holzinger and Thomas Sommerer, '"Race to the Bottom" or "Race to Brussels"? Environmental Competition in Europe' (2011) 49 Journal of Common Market Studies 315. In the field of US corporate law, the race was won by Delaware, and thus it is often referred to as the 'Delaware effect', see William L Cary, 'Federalism and Corporate Law: Reflections upon Delaware' (1974) 83 The Yale Law Journal 663. For the reverse trend, the 'race to the top', see David Vogel, *Trading Up: Consumer and Environmental Regulation in a Global Economy* (Harvard University Press 2009). For the 'race to the top' in the Californian motor vehicle industry see Ann E Carlson, 'California Motor Vehicle Standards and Federalism: Lessons for the EU' in David

The responsive behaviour of taxpayers to taxation in the form of relocation or transaction shifting can either be addressed by a lowering of the tax burden and joining the harsh competition for domestic investment and national tax bases. The Member States can also try to close down (which would be the optimum but the least likely possibility) the taxpayer's fallback alternatives through collective actions. If the regulatory measure is not applied unilaterally, but within the territory of a significant group of (Member) States, the shifting and relocating may become less attractive.[461] Accordingly, enhanced cooperation itself is already a mechanism to deal with undesired effects caused by the levying of the tax.[462] The mechanism gives the Member State the freedom to act collectively and soften the negative effects,[463] but simultaneously gives them the flexibility to limit the range of co-operators to find an agreement within a group of like-minded actors.[464]

(bb) Inclusiveness and Exclusiveness Decide on Success In the field of taxation, the balance between inclusiveness and exclusiveness becomes particularly challenging. Collective actions in taxation are only as good as the number of Member States joining the action.[465] For tax measures, it would even be desirable to extend the scope to non-EU States to reduce the leeway for responsive behaviour. A larger group of Member States may be able to address the external effect of the tax better, but it is less likely that all Member States will agree on a common approach.

In some cases, the enhanced cooperation may only be the starting point for common regulatory actions. A spreading of the law of enhanced cooperation to other (non-participating Member) States requires a particular set of circumstances.[466] Non-participating Member States need to suffer from (factual) disadvantages to feel encouraged to join enhanced cooperation. In certain regulatory areas, such as product and banking regulation, not being a part of the group which establishes high standards may put the outsiders at a disadvantage. In these fields, market players may derive a competitive advantage if their products are subject to national regulations which assure a high level of protection against health, safety,

Vogel and Johan Swinnen (eds), *Transatlantic Regulatory Cooperation* (Edward Elgar Publishing 2011). For the impact negative integration has on regulatory competition see Scharpf, 'Negative and Positive Integration' (n 26); Fritz W Scharpf, 'The Asymmetry of European Integration, or Why the EU Cannot Be a "Social Market Economy"' (2010) 8 Socio-Economic Review 211.

461 Philipp Genschel and Thomas Plumper, 'Regulatory Competition and International Co-Operation' (1997) 4 Journal of European Public Policy 626, 627.

462 See Chapter 3, subsection D.

463 For an analysis of the sharing of the burden through collective actions see Mancur Olson, *Logic of Collective Action: Public Goods and the Theory of Groups* (Harvard University Press 2009) 10.

464 For a general analysis of inclusiveness and exclusiveness in common regulatory approaches, see Genschel and Plumper (n 461) 634 et seq.

465 Kai Konrad and Tim BM Stolper, 'Coordination and the Fight against Tax Havens' (2016) 103 Journal of International Economics 96.

466 May Elsayyad and Kai A Konrad, 'Fighting Multiple Tax Havens' (2012) 86 Journal of International Economics 295.

or financial risk.[467] This advantage may force other States to set the same standards to achieve a level playing field for their market players.[468] In taxation, a spreading of the law of the enhanced cooperation is less likely to happen, in particular, if the law sets standards for the tax base or the tax rates because the group no longer competes with outsiders for tax bases which puts non-participating Member State in a favourable situation, in particular tax havens. The fewer States a tax haven has to compete with, the better. In other words, 'being a tax haven in a world where every other state is also a tax haven is not very profitable, but being the sole tax haven in an otherwise tax haven-free world is potentially very profitable'.[469]

The argument works not only when tax havens are involved but is also applicable when a non-haven is simply not willing to levy a certain tax because of its domestic market structure; for example the United Kingdom was not willing to embrace an FTT because it already levied a stamp duty and did not want to harm its financial market with a more burdensome tax.[470] From this it follows that a fully fledged cooperative turnaround is unlikely to happen in the field of (regulatory) taxation because the non-participating Member States most likely will not suffer any disadvantages.

In cases where the like-minded group of Member States is too small to prevent a shifting of transactions or relocation of taxpayers and production sites, and where it is unlikely that the measures spread from the small group of participating Member States to virtually all relevant countries, the group has to bear all of the negative implications associated with the implementation of the regulatory tax measure, and thus it is questionable whether they are allowed to introduce defensive measures.

(cc) Defensive Measures Despite the fact that negative effects may be less felt if a group of Member States commonly implements the same tax regime, the Member States may still want to insert safeguards to minimise negative effects. Any defensive measure introduced by enhanced cooperation is a response to the unwillingness of some Member States to join the collective action. The policies of Member States outside the group give the taxpayers enough leeway for responsive behaviour and allow taxpayers to move outside the scope of the regulatory tax measures implemented through the enhanced cooperation procedure. This leeway does not make it legally impossible to follow up on implementing the regulatory tax measure; this will only result in higher costs for the participating Member States.

In the field of FTTs, for example, the Member States may wish to heavily extend the scope of the tax to make it harder for market players to circumvent taxation by

[467] Vogel (n 460). For the 'race to the top' in the Californian motor vehicle industry see Carlson (n 460).

[468] Fritz W Scharpf, 'Introduction: The Problem-Solving Capacity of Multi-Level Governance' (1997) 4 Journal of European Public Policy 520, 522.

[469] Genschel and Plumper (n 461) 637; see also Elsayyad and Konrad (n 466).

[470] An FTT would cause a shift to other financial markets and thus the UK was 'opposed to an FTT unless it is adopted by other G-20 countries', John Vella, Clemens Fuest, and Tim Schmidt-Eisenlohr, 'The EU Commission's Proposal for a Financial Transaction Tax' (2011) British Tax Review 607, 608.

simply shifting the place of trade. The first and second proposal for a common FTT have designed the tax as a burden on financial transactions with an economic substance in the market of the (participating) Member States. To make the tax easier to administer, the scope of the tax was linked to the residency of the parties involved in the transaction.[471] The residency status of the parties to the financial transaction was heavily extended by two principles:[472] the first principle, the counter-party principle, deems financial agents to be resident in a (participating) Member State if they enter into a financial transaction with a financial agent who is actually resident in a (participating) Member State. The second principle, the issuance principle,[473] deems both parties to a financial transaction featuring shares to be resident in the participating Member State in which the shares were originally issued.

Another example of a massive extension of the scope of a tax to deal with the negative effects of the tax would be a carbon tax levied on any motor vehicle newly produced either within or for the market of the participating Member States. Extending the scope of the tax to car producers outside its territory may prevent their domestic car production from moving elsewhere.

A third example of a defensive measure widening the scope of secondary EU law can be found in the C(C)CTB proposal which suggests a Controlled Foreign Corporation (CFC) rule as a specific anti-avoidance measure.[474] A European corporate tax base would include passive income of EU companies and tax the profits at the Member States' standard tax rate. EU companies may engage in tax planning and outsource activities which do not need a lot of infrastructure and manpower to low-tax jurisdictions.[475] The current proposal for a European C(C)CTB includes common anti-abuse rules for situations in which the European C(C)CTB is directly affected.[476] The CFC rule within this proposal reveals the defensive character of the measure best. If a controlled foreign company receives passive income without engaging in any real economic activity in the host State, the undistributed profits are attributed to the European tax base which eliminates any benefits of tax deferral.[477] If we assume that the C(C)CTB proposal were introduced under the

471 Oskar Henkow, 'The Commission's Proposal for a Common System of Financial Transaction Tax: A Legal Appraisal' (2012) 21 EC Tax Review 5, 12 et seq.

472 Cédelle and Vella (n 7) 358 et seq.

473 It has only been introduced by the second Commission's proposal.

474 Art 82 of the first proposal (COM(2011) 121/4 final) and Arts 59 and 60 of the second proposal (COM(2016) 685 final).

475 The elimination of withholding taxes may also trigger tax planning activities: Erik Röder, 'Proposal for an Enhanced CCTB as Alternative to a CCCTB with Formulary Apportionment' (2012) 4 World Tax Journal 125, 140.

476 Commission, 26 March 2008, Common Consolidated Corporate Tax Base Working Group, Anti-abuse rules, CCCTB/WP065\doc\en; Commission, 30 August 2010, Workshop on the Common Consolidated Corporate Tax Base, Anti-Abuse Rules in the CCCTB, CCCTB/RD\004\doc\en.

477 Christiana Panayi, 'The ATAD CFC Rule and Its Impact on the Existing Regimes of EU Member States' in Pasquale Pistone and Dennis Weber (eds), *The Implementation of Anti-BEPS Rules in the EU: A Comprehensive Study* (IBFD 2018) 370 et seq. The idea of the CFC rule within the CC(C)TB proposal has made its way into the ATAD.

enhanced cooperation procedure, the CFC rule would also be applied against controlled foreign companies established within a non-participating Member State to counter any responsive behaviour of the taxpayers within the European internal market.

The examples clearly show that in cases in which the joint action of some Member States is not sufficient to curb negative effects, the Member States may wish to extend the scope of the tax to make it harder for taxpayers to adapt their behaviour to fall outside the tax's scope. However, defensive measures are not per se necessary to achieve the regulatory aim of the tax; they only intend to soften the negative effects which follow from implementing the tax. For example, introducing an FTT without the counter-party and the issuance principles under enhanced cooperation is not legally impossible. However, having only some Member States onboard makes it easier for taxpayers to respond to the tax by shifting financial transactions outside the scope of the FTT, and thus the costs the Member States within the group have to bear (in the form of a loss of domestic financial transactions) increase.[478]

The defensive mechanisms generally work by extending the scope which will, in some cases, be discriminatory because persons, goods, services, or capital are made subject to taxes, which are not comparable to those elements which should be taxed with respect to the aim and purpose of the law. If the defensive mechanisms (in the form of an extension of the tax scope) contradict the fundamental freedoms by imposing restrictions or discriminations against goods, services, persons, or capital from outside the enhanced cooperation, the pertinent provisions of the enhanced cooperation have to be justified.

It has been argued above that Member States of enhanced cooperation are allowed to protect their harmonised values by applying a light-touch justification approach to protective trade obstacles. The light-touch justification approach allows the Member States to use their harmonised values as grounds for justification and apply only a light-touch proportionality test. Whether participating Member States are also allowed to apply the light-touch justification approach to defensive obstacles, meaning trade obstacles which aim at shielding them from negative effects of enhanced cooperation law, for example locational effects, shall be analysed in the following subsections. Before answering the question of whether defensive obstacles should be subject to light-touch justification, we elaborate further on the restrictive or discriminatory nature of defensive mechanisms. Three specific exemplary cases, the counter-party principle of the proposed European FTT, the CFC rule in the C(C)CTB proposal, and a carbon tax on motor vehicles, are used to illustrate the problems resulting from a massive widening of the tax scope.

[478] It was not impossible for Sweden to levy a tax on financial transactions in a unilateral and uncoordinated manner. However, Sweden had to bear the consequences of a dramatic shifting of financial transactions outside its territory: European Commission, 'Impact Assessment Nr. 9—Proposal for a Council Directive on a Common System of Financial Transaction Tax and Amending Directive 2008/7/EC' (2011) SEC(2011) 1102 final 8 et seq.

i) Counter-Party-Principle: A Discrimination of Non-resident Financial Institutions?
The European Commission has issued two proposals for a common FTT. The first aimed for legislative action by all Member States,[479] whereas the second attempted to introduce a tax system on financial transactions by way of enhanced cooperation.[480] Some amendments to the first proposal have been made (eg the adoption of the issuance principle), but the aim and purpose of the tax has not changed. The tax is intended to burden financial institutions by making them contribute to the costs of dealing with the last financial crisis, and by preventing them from engaging in financial transactions which are harmful to the financial market (in particular high-frequency trading). Accordingly, the FTT should not only satisfy the financial needs of the Member States or the European Union[481] but should also steer the behaviour of the financial agents.

At the current stage, there is a third proposal on the table. Olaf Scholz, the German Finance Minister, put forward a new proposal for a European FTT which should be levied on the acquisition of shares of listed company with a market capitalisation above €1 billion and at a minimum standard rate of 0.2%.[482] The proposal has not yet been made public, but Olaf Scholz revealed that the French FTT should serve as a model. If this is the case, taxation depends upon the location of the companies' headquarters, and thus a counter-party principle would no longer be necessary. However, other participating Member States have already rejected Scholz's proposal as 'a common, broad financial transaction tax'[483] is desired. Since the third proposal is not public and since it is not clear whether other participating Member States will support the proposal, the following analysis will use the existing Commission proposals for a European FTT and will identify whether the counter-party principle has a potentially discriminatory nature.

The European Commission has put a lot of thought into the design of the tax, since the high mobility of financial transactions makes it quite likely that the tax triggers delocalisation effects. To prevent such effects, the Commission explicitly rejected the currently existing approaches, such as the British stamp duty, which imposes a tax liability on the transfer of securities of British companies, and the Swedish transaction tax, which applies to 'all equity security trades in Sweden using local brokerage services as well as to stock options'.[484] The Commission's proposal aims for a tax which applies to 'all financial transactions, on the condition

[479] COM(2011) 594 final.

[480] COM(2013) 71 final.

[481] It has been suggested that part of the receipts generated by the FTT shall contribute to the EU budget: Proposal for a Council decision on the system of own resources of the European Union, COM(2011) 510 final, and its amended proposal COM(2011) 739 final.

[482] <https://www.bundesfinanzministerium.de/Content/DE/Standardartikel/Themen/Schlaglichter/Steuergerechtigkeit/2019-12-10-Gesetzesvorschlag-Finanztransaktionsteuer.html> accessed 3 February 2021.

[483] <https://www.bloomberg.com/news/articles/2020-01-21/eu-financial-tax-faces-new-trouble-as-austria-threatens-to-quit> accessed 3 February 2021.

[484] European Commission, 'Impact Assessment Vol. 1—Proposal for a Council Directive on a Common System of Financial Transaction Tax and Amending Directive 2008/7/EC' (n 305) 18.

that at least one party to the transaction is established in the territory of a participating Member State'.[485] The proposal defines financial transactions in its widest possible sense, which includes, for example, the purchase and sale of financial instruments, the conclusion of derivatives, and the exchange of financial instruments.[486] The question of who is established within the territory of a participating Member State is addressed by Art 4 of the Commission's proposal, according to which a financial institution is deemed to be established in the territory of a participating Member State where (a) it has been authorised by the authorities of that Member State to act as such; (b) it is authorised or otherwise entitled to operate, from abroad, as financial institution in regard to the territory of that Member State; (c) it has its registered seat within that Member State; (d) its permanent address or its usual residence is located in that Member State; (e) it has a branch within that Member State; (f) it is party to a financial transaction with another financial institution established in the territory of that Member State according to one of the previous criteria (counter-party principle); it is party to a financial transaction in a certain financial instrument issued within the territory of that Member State. If a financial institute fulfils more than one listed criterion, the first condition fulfilled from the start of the list in descending order shall be relevant for determining the establishment. The proposal also provides for an escape clause, according to which a financial institution shall not be deemed to be established in the territory of a participating Member State if it proves that there is 'no link between the economic substance of the transaction and the territory of any participating Member State'.[487]

From this it follows that the scope of the FTT is determined by financial transactions which have their economic substance within the territory of a participating Member State. The economic substance of a financial transaction is supposed to be within the territory of a Member State if a party to the transaction is established in that particular Member State. If the counter-party principle applies, the non-resident financial institutions are deemed to be established within the territory of the home Member States of the counter party to the financial transaction. At first glance, all financial institutions, whether or not they are established in the territory of a participating Member State, are treated alike, wiping out all claims of unjustified discriminatory treatment. According to CJEU case law, however, discrimination consists not only of the application of different rules to comparable situations but also of the application of the same rules to different situations.[488] The deeming

[485] Art 3 of the proposal COM(2013) 71 final.

[486] Art 2 Subsection 1 Nr. 2 of the Proposal COM(2013) 71 final.

[487] Art 4 Subsection 3 of the proposal COM(2013) 71 final.

[488] CJEU, 14 February 1995, C-279/93, *Schumacker*, ECLI:EU:C:1995:31, para 30; CJEU, 11 August 1995, C-80/94, *Wielockx*, ECLI:EU:C:1995:271, para 17; CJEU, 29 April 1999, C-311/97, *Royal Bank of Scotland*, CJEU, ECLI:EU:C:1999:216, para 26; CJEU, 14 November 2006, C-513/04, *Kerckhaert and Morres*, ECLI:EU:C:2006:713, para 19. Implicitly also applied in *Deutsche Shell*: CJEU, 28 February 2008, C-293/06, *Deutsche Shell*, ECLI:EU:C:2008:129, para 29 et seq; see for more details Lang, 'Recent Case Law of the ECJ in Direct Taxation' (n 128) 99–100.

provision may discriminate, not because it treats comparable situations differently but because it treats non-comparable situations alike. In tax law, the factor distinguishing a comparable and a non-comparable situation is residence, domicile, or place of management. From this perspective, a financial agent resident in a non-participating Member State and a financial agent resident in a participating Member State are not comparable. A change in the general system—this being the fundamental difference between resident and non-resident taxpayers—therefore requires justification.[489]

Despite the question of whether or not the equal treatment of resident and non-resident taxpayers contradicts the fundamental freedoms, the rules factually discriminate against foreign taxpayers. The CJEU found that any national measure which is applicable without any distinction between resident and non-resident taxpayers but whose deterrent effect is much greater for non-resident taxpayers accounts for a restriction under the market freedoms.[490] A deemed resident financial agent only has to comply with all the obligations related to the payment of the FTT and the verification of the payment because the foreign financial agent entered into one contract with a resident financial agent. Resident financial agents will have to comply with the same rules; however, they will engage in many more financial transactions which are subject to the European FTT. Forcing a financial agent which is deemed to be resident in a participating Member State and a financial agent which is truly resident in the Member State to meet the same compliance obligations has a greater deterrent effect on the former.[491]

From this it follows that the counterparty principle as laid down in the proposals for a common European FTT contradicts the fundamental freedoms because it creates obstacles to trade between participating and non-participating Member States by discriminating against certain financial institutions outside the territory of enhanced cooperation.

[489] The Council Legal Service also concludes that the counter-party principle violates the fundamental freedoms (in particular the free movement of capital and the freedom to provide services). According to the Council Legal Service, the principle is discriminatory because it allows one participating Member State to levy the tax twice when a financial transaction takes place between participating and non-participating Member States and only once if the financial transaction takes place between two participating Member States; Council, 6 September 2013, Opinion of the Legal Service on the Proposal for a Council Directive implementing enhanced cooperation in the area of financial transaction tax (FTT), 2013/0045, para 29. Furthermore, the Council Legal Service found that double taxation in cross-border situations is only eliminated within the FTT zone, while double taxation with respect to financial transactions between financial institutions resident in a participating and a non-participating Member States is not eliminated. See for more details on this issue this chapter Part I, subsection E.VII.7. See for more details on this line of arguments Cédelle and Vella (n 7) 373–75.

[490] CJEU, 21 October 2010, C-81/09, *Idrima Tipou*, ECLI:EU:C:2010:622, para 58; CJEU, 9 October 2014, C-326/12, *van Caster*, ECLI:EU:C:2014:2269, para 37.

[491] Pablo Hernández González-Barreda qualifies the high tax burden as restrictive (Hernández González-Barreda, 'On the European Way to a Financial Transaction Tax under Enhanced Cooperation: Multi-Speed Europe or Shortcut?' (2013) 41 Intertax 208, 226). The author rejects such an approach because the CJEU has never found the mere levying of a tax to be restrictive. See for more details see this chapter Part I, subsection C.I.5.

ii) Carbon Tax on Motor Vehicles Produced Within and For the Market of the Participating Member States: A Discrimination under the Market Freedoms?

A carbon tax on motor vehicles is another example which may trigger locational effects. If a group of Member States decides to levy a carbon dioxide tax on any car produced within each of their territories (and the exact amount of the tax would depend upon the anticipated average life and the emission of carbon dioxide), it becomes quite likely that car production plants will relocate to Member States which do not levy such a tax. To minimise locational effects, the Member States participating in enhanced cooperation may wish to extend the scope of the carbon tax as much as possible to make it less attractive for the car-producing industry to move. The Member States could bring the foreign car-producing industry within the tax net, at least in relation to the cars produced for and sold on the domestic market. Accordingly, both the production of cars as well as their sale within the territory (either directly to the customer or via a car dealer) shall be subject to a carbon tax. The carbon tax on imported cars is levied when the car crosses the border of one of the Member States' levying the carbon tax.

The tax on imported cars may run foul of Art 30 or Art 110 of the TFEU. Art 30 of the TFEU applies to any pecuniary charges which are imposed unilaterally on goods which cross a frontier and which are not a customs duty in the strict sense but which have an equal effect. However, if the charge forms part of the Member States' general system of internal dues applied systematically to categories of products based on objective criteria without regard to the origin of the products, the tax measure has to be tested against Art 110 of the TFEU.[492] In this vein, the Court found national car registration taxes to fall within the scope of Art 110 of the TFEU if applied both to domestic and imported cars and not charged by reason of the vehicle crossing the border of the Member State.[493]

In this example, the tax is only levied on imported cars, not on domestic cars. Domestic cars are not subject to tax because the tax was already levied on their production. The tax on imported goods is only tested against Art 110 of the TFEU if the Court finds that the tax on imports and the tax on production forms one coherent tax system.[494] Since the taxes are designed quite differently and since the tax on imported cars is levied based on the crossing of the Member State's borders, the tax runs foul of Art 30 of the TFEU.

[492] CJEU, 2 April 1998, C-213/96, *Outokumpu Oy*, ECLI:EU:C:1998:155, para 20.

[493] CJEU, 7 April 2011, C-401/09, *Tatu*, ECLI:EU:C:2011:219, para 32 et seq; CJEU, 29 April 2004, C-387/01, *Weigel*, ECLI:EU:C:2004:256, para 65 et seq.

[494] In the recent infringement proceedings against Germany, the CJEU was willing to undertake a joint assessment of two national measures because they were sufficiently closely connected. The infrastructure use charge and the relief from motor vehicle tax were introduced on the same date (temporal link) and the application of that relief was dependent on the commencement of collection of that charge (substantive link); CJEU, 18 June 2019, C-591/17, *Austria v Germany*, ECLI:EU:C:2019:504, para 44 et seq. Therefore, it may not be impossible that the CJEU combines two national measures when analysing their effects on the European internal market. However, these measures have to be sufficiently linked.

iii) CFC Rule and the C(C)CTB

In 2001, the European Commission announced a 'strategy for providing companies with a consolidated corporate tax base for their EU-wide activities'.[495] A CCCTB would eliminate trade obstacles within the European internal market and would allow European companies to take full advantage of the European internal market. The Commission's first initiative was fully driven by the idea to improve the European internal market, to foster cross-border trade and to enable the European internal market and European companies to compete against US and the Japanese competitors.[496]

On 16 March 2011, the European Commission published the final proposal for a Council Directive on a Common Consolidated Corporate Tax Base.[497] In line with the initial Commission initiative, the C(C)CTB aimed to reduce administrative burdens and compliance costs for European companies by way of introducing a 'one-stop shop' principle which would allow companies to apply a single set of tax rules across the European Union and deal with only one tax administration.[498] However, the proposed secondary EU law initially failed due to a lack of compromise between Member States. In October 2016, the Commission relaunched the C(C)CTB project. However, the new proposal follows a different methodology and rationale[499] because the new proposal predominantly focuses on fairness, transparency, and anti-avoidance.[500] Now, the C(C)CTB should be the main mechanism to prevent base erosion and profit shifting within the European Union.[501]

Also under the new proposal, the C(C)CTB should provide companies which are established in at least two Member States with the possibility of calculating their group taxable income in accordance with one set of European rules, rather than national rules.[502] The C(C)CTB applies to EU companies (accordingly companies which are established under the law of a Member State)[503] which take one of

[495] Commission, 23 October 2001, COM(2001) 582 final.

[496] Commission, 7 July 2004, Commission Non-Paper to informal Ecofin Council, 10 and 11 September 2004, A Common Consolidated EU Corporate Tax Base.

[497] Commission, 16 March 2011, Proposal for a Council Directive on a Common Consolidated Corporate Tax Base (CCCTB), COM(2011) 121/4 final.

[498] COM(2011) 121/4 final, 5; 'making business easier and cheaper', Press release 16 March 2011, IP/11/319; see also Eric CCM Kemmeren, 'CCCTB: Enhanced Speed Ahead for Improvement' (2011) 20 EC Tax Review 208 ;Johanna Hey, 'CCCTB—Optionality' in Michael Lang and others (eds), *Common Consolidated Corporate Tax Base* (Linde Verlag 2008) 95 et seq.

[499] Shafi U Khan Niazi, 'Re-Launch of the Proposal for a Common Consolidated Corporate Tax Base (CCCTB) in the EU: A Shift in Paradigm' (2017) 44 Legal Issues of Economic Integration 293, 301.

[500] 'Alongside the anti-tax avoidance function of the CCCTB, the re-launched project would *also* retain its features as a corporate tax system which facilitates cross-border trade and investment in the internal market' (emphasis added), Commission, 25 October 2016, Proposal for a Council Directive on a Common Corporate Tax Base, COM(2011) 685 final, 2. See also Jan Lambertus van de Streek, 'Some Introductory Remarks on the Relaunched CCTB/CCCTB Proposals from a Policy Perspective' in Dennis Weber and Jan Lambertus van de Streek (eds), The EU Common Consolidated Corporate Tax Base: Critical Analysis (Kluwer Law International 2018) 4 et seq.

[501] Maarten Floris de Wilde, 'The CCCTB Relaunch: A Critical Assessment and Some Suggestions for Modification' in Pasquale Pistone (ed), *European Tax Integration: Law, Policy and Politics* (IBFD 2018) 38.

[502] Christiana Panayi, 'CFC Rules within the CCCTB' in Michael Lang and others (eds), *Corporate Income Taxation in Europe: The Common Consolidated Corporate Tax Base (CCTB) and Third Countries* (Edward Elgar 2013) 321.

[503] Art 2(1) of the first proposal (COM(2011) 121/4 final).

the forms listed in Annex I to the C(C)CTB proposal and are subject to corporate taxes in a Member State listed in Annex II. The company has to belong to a consolidated group for financial accounting purposes with a total consolidated group revenue exceeding €750,000,000 and the company has to qualify as a parent company or a qualified subsidiary. According to Art 3 of the C(C)CTB proposal, any immediate and lower-tier subsidiary is a qualified subsidiary in which the parent company holds the following rights: (a) it has a right to exercise more than 50% of the voting rights; and (b) it has an ownership right amounting to more than 75% of the subsidiary.

The new tax base was not compulsory in the first Commission proposal. However, this has changed in the second Commission proposal[504] which suggests a mandatory application of the C(C)CTB for at least a subset of firms based on their size. Only micro-enterprises, small, and medium-sized enterprises should be exempt from the application of the C(C)CTB.[505]

After the European Commission announced the initiative for a CCCTB for the first time, a discussion on necessary anti-avoidance measures started. Following the recommendations of these discussions,[506] the first and second C(C)CTB proposals contain both a General Anti-Abuse Rule (GAAR)[507] and specific anti-abuse provisions (in the form of a thin capitalisation rule,[508] a CFC clause,[509] and clauses on hybrid[510] and tax residency mismatches[511]).[512]

The CFC rule may best reveal the creation of defensive obstacles, and thus the following discussion will only focus on this clause. The CFC rule allows the inclusion of the non-distributed income of an entity resident outside the C(C)CTB zone in the tax base if certain conditions are met. First, the EU company itself, or together with its associated enterprises, has to hold a direct or indirect participation of more than 50% of the voting rights, or own directly or indirectly more than 50% of capital, or is entitled to receive more than 50% of the profits of that entity. Secondly, the actual corporate tax paid by the foreign company has to be

504 The change from an option-model to a compulsory CCTB is particularly influenced by the CCTB new aim being to prevent base erosion and profit shifting within the European Union. Wilde (n 501) 38. See Chapter 3, subsection B.IV.

505 Commission, 25 October 2016, Proposal for a Council Directive on a Common Corporate Tax Base, COM(2016) 685 final, p 8.

506 Commission, 26 March 2008, Common Consolidated Corporate Tax Base Working Group, Anti-abuse rules, CCCTB/WP065\doc\en; Commission, 30 August 2010, Workshop on the Common Consolidated Corporate Tax Base, Anti-Abuse Rules in the CCCTB, CCCTB/RD\004\doc\en.

507 Art 80 of the first proposal (COM(2011) 121/4 final) and Art 58 of the second proposal (COM(2016) 685 final).

508 Art 81 of the first proposal (COM(2011) 121/4 final) and 13 of the second proposal (COM(2016) 685 final).

509 Art 82 of the first proposal (COM(2011) 121/4 final) and Arts 59 and 60 of the second proposal (COM(2016) 685 final).

510 Art 61 of the second proposal (COM(2016) 685 final).

511 Art 61a of the second proposal (COM(2016) 685 final).

512 For the relationship between the general and specific anti-abuse rule see Christiana Panayi, 'The Anti-Abuse Rules of the CCCTB' (2012) 66 Bulletin for International Taxation 256.

significantly low. Thirdly, the non-distributed profits consist of passive income (eg interest and royalties).[513]

According to the second proposal, the CFC rule should not apply to controlled foreign companies resident in a Member State or within the EEA and where the controlled foreign company has been set up 'for a valid commercial reason that reflects economic reality'.[514] Economic reality may be supported by commensurate staff, equipment, assets, and premises.[515]

However, we shall assume that a C(C)CTB will be introduced between some but not all Member States under the enhanced cooperation procedure as it has been proposed in the beginning of the CCCTB initiative.[516] In such a situation, the CFC rule would not only apply to third countries but also to non-participating Member States because the participating Member States may want to prevent optimisation practices of EU companies which may be triggered by the wide tax base. If, for example, a consolidated group establishes a financing company in a low-tax non-participating Member State, the group would shift the profits of the financing activity to the low-tax jurisdiction and would benefit from the tax deferral until the financing subsidiary distributes the profits. The CFC rule would eliminate the possibility of tax deferral by attributing the undistributed profits to the group's tax base. From the perspective of the fundamental freedoms, one has to ask whether the denial of the tax deferral penalises the parent company for having invested in a low-tax Member State. If this were the case, the CFC rule applied between Member States may contradict the fundamental freedoms as it burdens both the foreign investment and the establishment of a foreign subsidiary more heavily.

The existing CJEU case law quite clearly sets out the requirements with which domestic CFC rules have to align with the fundamental freedoms. At the outset, however, the different tax treatment of foreign and domestic investment creates a tax disadvantage for the taxable person investing in a foreign company which a priori restricts the fundamental freedoms.[517] If the CFC rule is applied to controlled companies in a non-participating Member State, the discriminatory element would exist. In light of the existing CJEU case law, there is no doubt that a CFC rule implemented within a C(C)CTB enacted under the enhanced cooperation procedure would constitute a restriction of the fundamental freedoms.

(dd) Benchmark for Justifying Defensive Obstacles It is one thing to allow participating Member States to protect their harmonised values, but it is another to

[513] Art 59 Subsection 2 of the second proposal (COM(2016) 685 final).
[514] ibid.
[515] ibid.
[516] Commission, 7 July 2004, Commission Non-Paper to informal Ecofin Council, 10 and 11 September 2004, A Common Consolidated EU Corporate Tax Base, 4; Commission, 23 October 2001, COM(2001) 582 final, 17.
[517] CJEU, 12 September 2012, C-196/04, *Cadbury Schweppes*, ECLI:EU:C:2012:544, para 45; CJEU, 26 February 2019, C-135/17, *X GmbH*, ECLI:EU:C:2019:136, para 57.

allow them to shield themselves from negative effects following from enhanced cooperation law. Obstacles to the European internal market protecting the values of the group are necessary to allow the participating Member States to pursue the values on which they have agreed. Mechanisms to curb negative effects of enhanced cooperation law are, however, not necessary for pursuing and protecting the harmonised values of the group. Taken to the extreme, if all financial transactions moved outside the territory of the participating Member States, the Member States would no longer be able to make the financial sector pay for the costs of the last financial crisis because there would be nobody left paying the tax. But there are no more harmful financial transactions (eg in the form of high-frequency trading) which need to be banned from the financial market to prevent another financial crisis.

The applications of a light-touch justification approach to defensive obstacles cannot be grounded on the same reasons as its application to protecting obstacles because only the latter is necessary to allow the group of Member States to pursue the value(s) on which they have commonly agreed. However, defensive obstacles aim for the best of both worlds: allowing the participating Member States to implement tax measures without having to bear the consequences of levying the tax.

From this it follows that in cases in which the members of the group introduce binding laws among them and thereby create a value which goes beyond the mere value of harmonisation, they are allowed to protect that very value by constituting obstacles to cross-group trade which (only) have to pass a light-touch justification threshold. If, however, the participating Member States decide to implement measures which not (only) protect their harmonised values but also try to shield the Member States from negative effects of enhanced cooperation law, they have to satisfy the ordinary justification threshold, meaning the benchmark that an obstacle created by a single Member State's law has to pass to be allowed to stand.

(ee) Applying the National-obstacle Benchmark to Defensive Obstacles

i) Justifying the Counter-party Principle

The counter-party principle creates obstacles to trade between the participating and the non-participating Member States. These obstacles are not of a protective but of a defensive nature and thus they have to meet the standard a restriction or discrimination of the law of a single Member State has to satisfy to be allowed to stand. There are two potential public interest concerns which may be able to justify the obstacles created by the counter-party principle: the balanced allocation of taxing rights and the aim of preventing tax avoidance.

The Balanced Allocation of Taxing Rights

The CJEU accepts any non-favourable treatment of non-resident taxpayers and cross-border economic transactions if the treatment follows from a balanced allocation of taxing rights. Such a balanced allocation of taxing rights can either be achieved by a bilateral tax treaty or unilateral national tax rules,[518] but may also be achieved by the law of enhanced cooperation. The Court accepts any allocation which follows either the international standards set by the OECD model convention[519] or the narrow concept of territoriality.[520] The latter led to a general acceptance of the exercise of a Member State's tax jurisdiction in relation to activities which are carried out in the Member State's territory.[521] The deeming provisions under the proposal for a European FTT, however, do not allocate the taxing rights between the Member States; these provisions work as mere defence of the domestic tax base from being eroded by switching to financial institutions not established within the territory of a participating Member State or relocating of financial agents.[522] In the light of Art 4 of the FTT proposal,[523] the defensive nature of the provision becomes especially evident because a foreign financial agent shall not in any case be subject to FTT; only if the foreign entity enters into a financial contract with a party which is resident in a participating Member State is the former within the FTT net. Furthermore, Art 4 Subsection 3 of the FTT proposal makes it clear that a financial agent shall not be considered to be established within the territory of a participating Member State if no 'link between the economic substance of the transaction and the territory of any Member State' exists.

Having said this, the wording of Art 4 Subsection 3 of the FTT proposal could also be understood as laying down the benchmark for the allocation of taxing rights. In this case, it would not be the residency of the financial agents which would trigger the tax. All financial transactions would be within the FTT net which have their economic substance linked to the territory of an FTT Member State. Since the deeming provision took its inspiration from the place of supply rules in the VAT Directive,[524] it becomes even more likely that the financial transaction should be subject to FTT if there is a link between the economic substance of the transaction and the territory of an FTT Member State. However, there are two main reasons why the economic substance is not the benchmark for distributing

[518] CJEU, 5 July 2005, C-376/03, *D*, ECLI:EU:C:2005:424, para 52; CJEU, 12 December 2006, C-374/04, *Test Claimants in Class IV of the ACT Group Litigation*; ECLI:EU:C:2006:773, para 52; CJEU, 20 May 2008, C-194/06, *Orange European Smallcap Fund NV*; ECLI:EU:C:2008:289, para 32.

[519] CJEU, 14 February 1995, C-279/93, *Schumacker*, ECLI:EU:C:1995:31, para 32; CJEU, 27 June 1996, C-107/94, *Asscher*, ECLI:EU:C:1996:251, para 42; CJEU, 12 June 2003, C-234/01, *Gerritse*, ECLI:EU:C:2003:340, para 45; CJEU, 15 May, C-414/06, *Lidl Belgium*, ECLI:EU:C:2008:278, para 22; Schön, 'Neutrality and Territoriality' (n 69) 275; Jan Wouters and Maarten Vidal, 'An International Lawyer's Perspective on the ECJ's Case Law Concerning the OECD Model Tax Convention and Its Commentaries' in Philippe Hinnekens and Luc Hinnekens (eds), *A Vision of Taxes Within and Outside the European Borders: Festschrift in Honor of Prof. Dr. Frans Vanistendael* (n 40).

[520] CJEU, 13 December 2005, C-446/03, *Marks & Spencer*, ECLI:EU:C:2005:763, para 45 et. seq; CJEU, 15 May, C-414/06, *Lidl Belgium*, ECLI:EU:C:2008:278, para 31 et seq.

[521] Schön, 'Neutrality and Territoriality' (n 69) 280 et seq.

[522] European Commission, 'Impact Assessment Vol. 1—Proposal for a Council Directive on a Common System of Financial Transaction Tax and Amending Directive 2008/7/EC' (n 305) 43, 47.

[523] COM(2013) 71 final.

[524] European Commission, 'Technical Fiche The "Residence Principle" and the Territoriality of the Tax' (2012) 2.

the taxing powers in the field of FTT. First, VAT is a tax on consumption and should therefore be levied in the place of consumption. If the place of supply is located within a Member State, VAT is due regardless of the residency of the taxable person providing the service. In contrast, the FTT is not supposed to be a consumption tax. The FTT is supposed to burden banks and not their customers.[525] Secondly, the European Commission has explicitly rejected the possibility of implementing a source principle, which would grant each Member State the right to tax if 'the financial transactions are deemed to have taken place in its jurisdiction, regardless of the tax residence of the parties involved in the transaction'.[526] Linking the FTT to factors such as place of settlement or residence of the issuing entity would make the FTT too fragile and would therefore give market players way too many options of avoiding the tax.[527]

From this, it follows that the proposal for a common European FTT does not implement a benchmark for allocating taxing rights between the Member States, which would justify restrictions of the market freedoms by the counter-party principle. And even if one would assume that the proposal does allocate taxing rights between the Member States, the proposal does not do so in a balanced way as required by CJEU case law. The taxing rights of non-participating Member States are ignored because FTT is levied regardless of whether the other Member State imposes an equivalent tax.

Preventing Tax Avoidance

It has been stressed in the above that the massive extension of the scope of the FTT through the deemed residency of the financial agent attempts to fight forms of tax avoidance behaviour. The high mobility of financial transactions makes it especially easy for market players to shift the transactions to lower the tax burden. The question which arises is whether the possibility of circumventing taxation justifies the discriminatory treatment of non-resident financial agents.

First of all, settled CJEU case law provides that market players are free to structure their business in a way which allows them to minimise their tax burden. Accordingly, it is very much in line with the European internal market to consider other factors than resources, labour, and infrastructure when exercising one's rights to move; the national tax burden can also be considered. A structure cannot be considered abusive simply because the taxpayer seeks to profit from a tax benefit in

[525] At this stage, we can leave the question of whether the structure of the FTT is capable of achieving this goal open.

[526] European Commission, 'Impact Assessment Vol. 8—Proposal for a Council Directive on a Common System of Financial Transaction Tax and Amending Directive 2008/7/EC' (2011) SEC(2011) 1102 final 7.

[527] See an overview of all the different approaches States use for taxing the financial market European Commission, 'Impact Assessment Vol. 8—Proposal for a Council Directive on a Common System of Financial Transaction Tax and Amending Directive 2008/7/EC' (n 526).

a Member State.[528] Member States are allowed to compete against each other for investment by using the national tax regime as a locational advantage. Subsequently, the Member States are not allowed to use mechanisms within their national law which address cross-border activities and which are capable of removing tax benefits derived from the tax system of a fellow Member State.[529] Therefore, Member States are neither allowed to increase the national tax base because the economic activity is subject to low taxation in the other Member States,[530] nor are they allowed to widen the scope of the tax in a manner which makes it impossible for taxpayers to benefit from no taxation in another Member State.[531]

The existing case law makes it quite clear that the market freedoms do not prevent market players from structuring their economic activities in a way which minimises their overall tax burden, and the massive enlargement of the scope of the FTT therefore cannot be justified by the fact that non-participating Member States are not levying an equal tax. National tax measures are only justified if these measures address artificial arrangements which lack any economic substance.[532] The counter-party principle goes far beyond what is necessary to prevent wholly artificial arrangements because a financial transaction between financial institutions from which only one is resident in a participating Member State cannot per se be considered artificial.

Findings

From this it follows that the restrictions of the market freedoms by the counter-party principle cannot be justified by an overriding reason of public interest. The regime for taxing financial transactions does not implement a system which balances the taxing rights between participating and non-participating Member States, from which a discriminatory tax treatment of financial institutions established outside the territory of enhanced cooperation has to follow. Neither can the discriminatory treatment of non-resident financial institutions be justified by the attempt to prevent tax avoidance, since the counter-party principle is much too broad to be a measure to fight an abusive behaviour of taxpayers, and thus catches more than just artificial arrangements, which is required under the existing CJEU case law. To summarise, the obstacles to trade between participating and non-participating Member States following from the counter-party principle are not

[528] CJEU, 11 December 2003, C-364/01, *Barbier*, ECLI:EU:C:2003:665, para 71; CJEU, 12 September 2012, C-196/04, *Cadbury Schweppes*, ECLI:EU:C:2012:544, paras 36–38.

[529] CJEU, 28 April 1998, C-118/96, *Safir*, ECLI:EU:C:1998:170, para 34; CJEU, 3 October 2002, C-136/00, *Danner*, ECLI:EU:C:2002:558, para 55; CJEU, 26. June 2003, C-422/01, *Skandia*, ECLI:EU:C:2003:380, paras 51–52.

[530] CJEU, 26 October 1999, C-294/97, *Eurowings*, ECLI:EU:C:1999:524, para 43.

[531] CJEU, 14. October 1999, C-439/97, *Sandoz*, ECLI:EU:C:1999:499, para 19.

[532] See for example CJEU, 12 September 2012, C-196/04, *Cadbury Schweppes*, ECLI:EU:C:2012:544, para 51 et seq; CJEU, 13 March 2007, C-524/04, *Test Claimants in the Thin Cap Group Litigation*, ECLI:EU:C:2007:161, para 81 et seq.

justified by an overriding reason of public interest, and thus the defensive obstacle in the form of the counter-party principle is not allowed to stand.

ii) Justifying the Extensive Scope of the Carbon Tax

A carbon dioxide tax on motor vehicles produced outside a participating Member State's territory is discriminatory because the sale of domestically produced cars is not subject to an equal tax at the time of sale. Accordingly, the rule is only allowed to stand if it is justified by an overriding reason of public interest. There are two grounds which may justify the restriction, which will now be considered.

Coherence

In very rare cases, the CJEU has recognised that restrictions of the fundamental freedoms are justified due to the concept of 'coherence', which can be understood as a consistency claim of the domestic tax system. In other words, the concept of coherence is meant to allow Member States to deny the granting of a tax benefit if the taxpayer is not subject to the corresponding tax disadvantage. The taxpayer shall be allowed to move freely within the internal market, but should be prevented from free-riding

In that vein, the Court has allowed the Member States to deny the deductibility of foreign losses if the Member States have no corresponding right to tax the foreign gains.[533] For the sake of protecting the internal market, the CJEU has been very strict on the requirements for allowing a discriminatory treatment to be justified based on coherence claims. According to the CJEU, coherence of a national tax system requires a direct link between the benefit and the disadvantage, such as a direct link between profits and losses or income and expenditure. The benefit and the disadvantage are only linked if the same taxpayer is exposed to both the benefit and the disadvantage. The requirement to benefit and burden the same entity becomes too narrow when it comes to the cross-border distribution of dividends. It may not be the same person who is subject to a burden or a benefit, but it is the same economic undertaking which is subject to both the tax benefit and the tax disadvantage.[534] Accordingly, the Court extends the concept of coherence to two taxpayers if they are economically alike, as in the case of dividend flows.[535]

Whether or not the concept of coherence is capable of justifying the levying of the carbon dioxide tax on sales of cars produced abroad depends upon the possibility to link the levying of the tax on production and sale. Sales of domestically produced cars are not subject to tax because their production was already subject to the carbon dioxide tax. At first glance, there may be an obvious link between the levying of a tax on sales on foreign-produced cars and the non-levy of a tax

[533] CJEU, 7 November 2013, C-322/11, *K*, ECLI:EU:C:2013:716.

[534] Englisch, 'Fiscal Cohesion' (n 227) 356.

[535] CJEU, 7 September 2004, C-319/02, *Manninen*, ECLI:EU:C:2004:484, para 42 et seq.

on domestically produced cars. However, the tax is imposed on different stages of the production and distribution chain and the person required to pay the tax may differ; in a purely domestic setting it is always the car producer, in a cross-border setting it can be either the car producer or the customer or the car dealer. In *Eurowings*,[536] the CJEU did not allow Germany to take an overall stance and argue that services from foreign taxpayers are not subject to the German trade tax and thus have to be subject to tax at the stage of the resident taxpayer. The fact that the foreign taxpayer was not subject to an equivalent tax in his home state does not justify the discriminatory treatment of foreign services. The same must be true for cars produced abroad. They are only subject to a domestic carbon dioxide tax because the production of these cars was not already subject to the domestic tax at the time of production.

From this it follows that it is rather likely that the CJEU would reject a direct link between the levying of taxes on domestic production and the levying of taxes on the sale of cars produced in another Member State. The linkage is crucial for relying on the coherence claim, and thus, it may not be possible to justify the discriminatory tax based on the concept of coherence.

Pollution Control—Steering Tax

The carbon dioxide tax is levied to steer car producers towards the production of cars with reduced carbon dioxide emissions. The fewer cars emit carbon dioxide, the lower the tax burden becomes. The tax clearly has a public interest aim; however, this does not justify its discriminatory features because a tax on car emissions could also be designed in a non-discriminatory way. Accordingly, the aim of minimising pollution is a valid reason for levying a tax, and it justifies a higher tax on foreign cars if they emit more carbon dioxide than the domestically produced cars. Yet if the link between the tax on the import and the production cannot be established, the aim of reducing pollution cannot, on its own, justify the different tax treatment.

Findings

From this, it follows that a carbon dioxide tax levied on domestic sales of foreign produced cars is not allowed to stand because the discriminatory features of the tax cannot be justified based on overriding reasons of public interest.

iii) Justifying the CFC rule within the C(C)CTB Proposal

A CFC rule may infringe both the freedom of establishment and the free movement of capital as such a rule treats foreign establishments and foreign investment less favourably.[537] However, the CFC rule within the C(C)CTB proposal assumes that

[536] CJEU, 26 October 1999, C-294/97, *Eurowings*, ECLI:EU:C:1999:524.
[537] Schön, 'EU Tax Law' (n 385) 66.

CCCTB taxpayers have a 'definitive influence and control' over their CFCs, and thus only the freedom of establishment should be applicable.[538] If the CFC rule applies because the profits from a passive economic activity are taxed at a very low rate, the undistributed profits are attributed to the CCCTB, and thus the benefit following from a tax deferral is eliminated. According to the existing CJEU case law, there is one main ground of justification which the Court accepts to justify restrictions of the free movement rights through CFC legislation: that being the fight against tax avoidance and tax evasion.

In *Cadbury Schweppes*,[539] the CJEU ruled that restrictions of the freedom of establishment may only be justified based on the fight against tax avoidance if the rules apply to 'wholly artificial arrangements'.[540] If a restriction of the free movement rights between Member States can only be justified based on the wholly artificial arrangement requirement, one may wonder whether the application of the CFC rule to controlled foreign companies which are not set up for 'valid commercial reasons' would satisfy the requirement.[541] In *Cadbury Schweppes*,[542] the CJEU explicitly referred to 'letterbox' or 'front' subsidiaries which do not carry out any genuine economic activity in the territory of the host Member State, and are therefore used to create wholly artificial arrangements.[543] The wording of the C(C)CTB proposal tries to address these 'letterbox' and 'front' subsidiaries with no economic

[538] Commission, 26 March 2008, Common Consolidated Corporate Tax Base Working Group, Anti-abuse rules, CCCTB/WP065\doc\en; Commission, 30 August 2010, Workshop on the Common Consolidated Corporate Tax Base, Anti-Abuse Rules in the CCCTB, CCCTB/RD\004\doc\en, 7.

[539] CJEU, 12 September 2006, C-196/04, *Cadbury Schweppes*, ECLI:EU:C:2006:544, para 51 et seq.

[540] With respect to restrictions of the free movement of capital *X GmbH* (CJEU, 26 February 2019, C-135/17, *X GmbH*, ECLI:EU:C:2019:136, para 84) may have softened the requirement of 'wholly artificial arrangements', at least for a third country situation; Schön, 'Interpreting European Law in the Light of the BEPS Action Plan' (n 406) 24.

[541] Art 59 Subsection 2 of the second proposal (COM(2016) 685 final). In the explanatory note of the ATAD compliance of the CFC rules with the fundamental freedoms is explicitly addressed: 'To comply with the fundamental freedoms, the income categories should be combined with a substance carve-out aimed to limit, within the Union, the impact of the rules to cases where the CFC does not carry on a substantive economic activity' (Council Directive, 12 July 2016, 2016/1164/EU, laying down rules against tax avoidance practices that directly affect the functioning of the internal market, OJ, 19 July 2016, L 193, 1). See in that regard Panayi, 'Anti-Abuse Rules' (n 512) 370 et seq. Werner Haslehner, 'The Controlled Foreign Company Regime' in Dennis Weber and Jan Lambertus van de Streek (eds), *The EU Common Consolidated Corporate Tax Base: Critical Analysis* (Wolters Kluwer Law International 2018) 180 questioning the 'definite influence' requirement following from the CJEU case law.

[542] CJEU, 12 September 2006, C-196/04, *Cadbury Schweppes*, ECLI:EU:C:2006:544, para 68.

[543] Michael Lang, 'Cadbury Schweppes' Line of Case Law from the Member States' Perspective' in Rita de la Féria and Stefan Vogenauer (eds), *Prohibition of Abuse of Law: A New General Principle of EU law?* (OUP 2011) 445; Michael Lang and Sabine Heidenbauer, 'Wholly Artificial Arrangements' in Luc Hinnekens and Frans Vanistendael (eds), *A Vision of Taxes Within and Outside the European Borders: Festschrift in Honor of Prof. Dr. Frans Vanistendael* (n 40) 603 emphasising that the key words within the Cadbury Schweppes ruling are 'economic reality', 'actual establishment', and 'the extent to which the CFC physically exists'. Therefore, the use of the term 'letterbox' can be misleading: one might get the impression that a legal entity that has no premises, staff, or equipment may be described as a letterbox company and thus may, in a cross-border situation, be treated less favourably. However, the requirement imposed by the ECJ that the legal entity 'physically exists in terms of premises, staff and equipment' does not necessarily mean that legal entities without premises, staff, or equipment can be completely ignored.

substance as these companies usually do not have staff or equipment or hold any assets and premises.

From this it follows that a CFC rule which only applies to foreign subsidiaries which are set up for no valid commercial reasons (which may be reflected by the economic reality in the form of a lack of staff, equipment, assets, or premises) fulfils the requirement set by the CJEU case law of restricting the free movement only in cases of wholly artificial arrangements.[544] Accordingly, a CFC rule within a CCCTB enacted under the enhanced cooperation procedure would comply with the free movement rights as a denial of the beneficial tax deferral would only be refused in cases in which the taxpayer aims to avoid taxes in the participating Member States through the establishment of a controlled foreign company with no valid commercial reason in a low tax non-participating Member State.

c) Conclusions

The enhanced cooperation procedure can be used to harmonise values and principles underlying the laws of the Member States which leads to a unification of their laws. The harmonisation of the values requires a thorough balancing of contradictory fundamental rights, as in the case of the minimum share capital, where the Member States have to balance the right to conduct business against creditor protection freely, or, in other words, the right to be protected from exploitation. If the Member States can agree on a common value which balances both contradicting rights, they have achieved more than simply aligning the wording of their laws. They have truly unified their laws. Within the group, the unification also enhances trade because by complying with the regulatory framework in one participating Member State, they automatically comply with the regulatory framework of the other participating Member States. But as has been stressed before, the benefit of unified law goes deeper than merely enhancing the trade between the participating Member States: the participating Member States have established a harmonised value.

In the field of tax law, the establishment of common values between the participating Member States requires one to touch on the fundaments of the national tax system, that is the question of what to tax and why to tax it. The idea of a CCCTB would, for example, go deep enough to allow for the establishment of common values between the participating Member States in the area of income taxation. Outside the scope of fiscal taxes, in the area of steering taxes, it may be easier to establish common values between the Member States, such as by introducing a common tax on financial transactions.

544 Luca Cerioni, 'The Commission's Proposal for a CCCTB Directive: Analysis and Comment' (2011) 65 Bulletin for International Taxation 515, 524 arguing that the definition of the concept of 'genuine economic activities', which is omitted in article 80 [of the first proposal], can be extrapolated from this ECJ ruling.

In the case of unified ordinary secondary EU law which binds all the Member States, the mere burden of regulation does not create an obstacle to intra-EU trade, as all the Member States would follow the same values and would apply the same regulatory approach. If, however, unification is (only) achieved within the enhanced cooperation, the differences between the regulatory approach of the participating and the non-participating Member States may still harm intra-EU trade. Applying the fundamental freedoms to the law of enhanced cooperation raises the question of whether the participating Member States are allowed to protect their commonly established values or whether they bear the same burden for justifying restrictions following from protective measures as a single Member State would bear.

It has been established that enhanced cooperation should be understood as a tool which allows the Member States to emphasise the importance of non-market values, which should not have to give way to market efficiency. Since not all Member States find the value worth fighting for, and some even disagree with its protection, the trade obstacles should not be justified simply because the Member States made use of the enhanced cooperation procedure but should be allowed to apply the same benchmark as required for obstacles imposed by ordinary secondary EU law (light-touch justification approach).

If the obstacles imposed by the law of enhanced cooperation were to curb negative effects following from the responsive behaviour of the taxpayers, such as locational effects, the Member States have to meet the strict justification benchmark (like unilateral measures of a single Member State). Defensive measures to cope with negative effects of the tax or regulatory approach are not necessary to protect the harmonised value of the group. They simply aim to reduce costs for the participating Member States, which does not legitimise the application of light-touch justification.

3. Obstacles to Intra-Group and Cross-Group Trade

The use of the enhanced cooperation procedure to harmonise the values and principles underlying the law achieves a unification of the Member States' laws. Despite being unified, the law of enhanced cooperation may still impose trade obstacles. Both cross-group and intra-group trade may be affected by the obstacles. Intra-group and cross-group obstacles may be triggered by public interest concerns which have to be addressed individually in every Member State's market. Of course, the Member States are not very often exposed to such needs, and thus the law of enhanced cooperation only rarely implies trade obstacles which exist in an intra-group and a cross-group setting. However, *Meyhui*[545] and *Schmelz*[546] show that it is possible.

[545] CJEU, 9 August 1994, C-51/93, *Meyhui NV*, ECLI:EU:C:1994:312.
[546] CJEU, 26 October 2010, C-97/09, *Schmelz*, ECLI:EU:C:2010:632.

In cases where enhanced cooperation law imposes trade obstacles to both intra-group and cross-group situations, the requirement of justifying them has to be revealed from inside and across the group. Intra-group trade obstacles can best be compared with obstacles constituted by ordinary secondary EU law as all participating Member States have agreed on imposing trade obstacles for the sake of a certain public interest concerns, such as consumer, environment, or creditor protection. The participating Member States prioritise the public interest over market efficiency and are thus willing to bear the costs for harming trade between them. On the level of justification, it is quite evident that a light-touch justification approach should apply to intra-group obstacles if the participating Member States follow non-protectionist interests. The European internal market does not guarantee the free play of economic forces unaffected by regulatory interference of the Member States. Since the Member States affected by the trade obstacle share the public interest concern, they should have the chance to follow their regulatory policy decisions.

From this it follows that intra-group trade obstacles imposed by the law of enhanced cooperation are subject to light-touch justification. The affected Member States have agreed on these obstacles and have given priority to a particular public interest concern as all Member States would have done when introducing ordinary secondary EU laws.

VII. (Mere) Trade-favouring Rules

Another category of rules which may be implemented by way of enhanced cooperation is trade-favouring rules. In contrast to the first category, the unification of national laws based on harmonised values, trade-favouring rules are not determined by a common set of values, they merely aim to foster trade between the Member States. Trade-favouring secondary EU laws can range from conflict of law rules to mutual recognition and coordination rules.

Trade-favouring rules apply where the fundamental freedoms are incapable of eliminating trade obstacles. On the one hand, trade obstacles may exist on the European internal market because Member States are able to justify their national measures by overriding reasons of public interest.[547] On the other hand, economic trade obstacles such as inconsistencies between laws of the Member States do not even fall within the scope of the fundamental freedoms.[548] Economic obstacles may, for example, be eliminated through conflict of law rules, which provide certainty that neither multiple nor no legal order claims jurisdiction or coordination rules which, in particular, prevent double taxation. Moreover, Member States may be willing to refrain from holding on to their justified trade-hampering measures

[547] See this chapter Part I, subsection C.III.
[548] See Chapter 4, subsection G.V.1.

because their public interest concerns are addressed by certain actions, a certain behaviour or treatment by or in participating Member State(s). Accordingly, Member States may refuse to impose justified restrictions on the supply of foreign goods within their territory if the goods comply with high product standards of a fellow Member State (mutual recognition measures). Member States may also be willing to recognise losses occurred in other Member States if these Member States are equally willing to recognise losses occurred in the former Member States (co-ordination rules).

Enhanced cooperation law in form of coordination or mutual recognition rules may only eliminate trade obstacles within the group. Trade obstacles towards non-participating Member States may remain as the participating Member States only obtain a *quid pro quo* for their own trade liberalisation within enhanced cooperation. Therefore, trade-favouring enhanced cooperation may be most likely to introduce a differentiation between intra-group and cross-group trade, which may contradict the fundamental freedoms.

The following subsections will first reveal in greater detail under which circumstances the Member States may be willing to grant market efficiency priority over certain public interest concerns, and why exactly the Member States may wish to hold on to trade obstacles in the relationship with non-participating Member States (see subsection 1). The desire of limiting benefits of deeper integration to participating Member States is not uncommon in international trade law. World Trade Organization (WTO) law grants an exception from most-favoured-nation treatment for preferential trade agreements. To understand the notion of preferential trade agreements, the second subsection lays out the requirements for their establishment and the reasons underlying the exception from most-favoured nation treatment (see subsection 2). The analysis of WTO law identifies reciprocity as the main driver for group-based integration (see subsection 3). Within the European integration process, reciprocity has played a fundamental part in tearing down trade walls between Member States, since no member of the European Union is allowed to levy customs or charges with equivalent effects on intra-EU trades. However, under European law, reciprocity has no disciplinary function on the national legislature. Accordingly, Member States do not have to follow the integration efforts of their fellow Member States, and Member States cannot limit their beneficial treatment to domestic economic activities based on a lack of reciprocity (see subsection 4). Reciprocity may not function as a general ground of justification under EU law, but the CJEU honours the Member States' efforts to foster cross-border trade by entering into reciprocal tax treaties. In other words, Member States are allowed to limit tax treaty benefits to the contracting parties (see subsection 5). The CJEU case law on the entitlement to limit tax treaty benefits to contracting Member States and preferential trade agreements is based on the same fundaments (see subsection 6). These fundaments allow for the development of a systemic approach on the denial of the group benefit for cross-group economic activities (see subsection 7) and the limits of such different treatment (see subsection 8).

1. Denying a Non-Group-Member the Group-Benefit

Within the European internal market, obstacles to trade between the Member States still exist, either because the obstacles do not fall within the scope of the fundamental freedoms or because important Member States' interests are capable of justifying a more burdensome treatment of non-resident taxpayers or cross-border economic activities. One example would be the right of every Member State to restrict loss relief of a domestic parent company to domestic group members and domestic permanent establishments.[549] Beyond any doubt, prohibiting foreign loss compensation creates intra-EU trade obstacles because the refusal to recognise losses of foreign subsidiaries and permanent establishments (which would lower the taxable domestic profits of the head company) may prevent the company from locating certain non-profitable business functions outside the home Member State, regardless of the fact that this may achieve efficiency gains.

We shall first elaborate a bit further on the example of foreign loss-compensation rules. Against the background of the current tax treaty rules,[550] Member States will not be able to tax the profits of a foreign subsidiary or permanent establishment even though the losses of these foreign entities can be deducted from domestic profits.[551] The impossibility of taxing a foreign entity's profit may make the Member States hesitant to allow a deduction of their foreign losses from the domestic tax base. However, some Member States may be willing to accept the incoherence of taxing profits and recognising losses of foreign entities if the losses incurred within their territory are equally deductible in the other Member States. The entitlement to deduct foreign losses may be beneficial for the host Member State—the State in which the losses occurred—since the establishment of a branch,

[549] In *Marks & Spencer* and *Bevola* the CJEU found that a restriction is only proportionate if final foreign losses can be deducted (CJEU, 13 December 2005, C-446/03, *Marks & Spencer* ECLI:EU:C:2005:763; CJEU, 12 June 2018, C-650/16, *Bevola*, ECLI:EU:C:2018:424). However, the Member States are allowed to demand a direct link between the parent company and the non-resident subsidiary sustaining the losses: CJEU, 19 June 2019, C-608/17, *Holmen*, ECLI:EU:C:2019:511. For a detailed analysis of the entire CJEU case law on final losses see Lang, 'Case Law of the ECJ on Final Losses' (n 275).

[550] Concerning the profits of a foreign permanent establishment, Art 7 of the OECD Model Tax Convention allocates the primary taxing right to the source country. The resident country may be allowed to tax the profits, in case the contracting parties have not agreed on the exemption method, but the resident State has to eliminate double taxation by credit foreign taxes (taxes levied in the host State).

[551] The CJEU finds that there is a kind of symmetry between restraining from taxing foreign profits and the requirement to grant a foreign tax relief: Claus Staringer, 'Missbrauchsbekämpfung, Aufteilung der Besteuerungsbefugnisse und Kohärenz in der Rechtsprechung des EuGH', *Europäisches Steuerrecht*, vol 41 (Dr Otto Schmidt Verlag 2018) 371 et seq. Member States should, however, not be capable of influencing their obligations under the market freedoms by signing bilateral tax treaties with the consequence of restraining from taxing a particular part of the worldwide income of a resident: Wolfgang Schön, 'Neutralität und Territorialität—Gegensätze oder Grundsätze des Europäischen Steuerrechts?' in Wolfgang Schön and Caroline Heber (eds), *Grundfragen des Europäischen Steuerrechts*, vol 5 (Springer 2015) 139; Schön, 'Neutrality and Territoriality' (n 69) 284.

a subsidiary, or a permanent establishment becomes more attractive from the foreign entity's perspective.

If at least nine Member States can mutually agree on recognising foreign losses, the participating Member States may want to restrict the foreign loss compensation to losses which occurred in a participating Member State. The desire to limit the beneficial treatment to members of the group is linked to the non-participating Member States' decision on how to treat foreign losses (being losses which are occurred in the participating Member States). Taxpayers resident outside the territory of enhanced cooperation are not usually allowed to deduct their losses occurred in a subsidiary or permanent establishment within the territory of a participating Member State.[552]

Another example of eliminating trade obstacles within enhanced cooperation would be the abolition of double taxation by way of recognising taxes already paid in the territory of a participating Member State. To date, the fundamental freedoms are not capable of preventing double taxation because they do not ask for a non-discriminatory treatment of foreign taxes.[553] Under the umbrella of enhanced cooperation, Member States can agree on certain mechanisms to prevent double taxation. They may, for example, agree on tax exemptions. From a single Member State's perspective, intra-group economic activities may be subject to an even more beneficial tax treatment than a purely domestic activity. The willingness to recognise foreign taxes may be driven by the fact that all members of the group recognise taxes levied in participating Member States, and since the foreign taxes are only recognised within enhanced cooperation, the members of the group may want to restrict the beneficial treatment to themselves.

At the outset, trade-favouring enhanced cooperation which aims to restrict the benefits of deeper integration between participating Member States and to maintain trade obstacles in a cross-group setting can be compared with preferential trade agreements under WTO law. Customs Unions and Free Trade Areas are 'voluntary agreements, of closer integration between the economies of the countries parties to such agreements'[554] which aim to foster trade between the contracting parties. The abandonment of trade restrictions is limited to the contracting parties and thus, the trading walls to third countries in the form of customs remain.

Accordingly, there are some fundamental similarities between a Customs Union and a Free Trade Area on the one hand, and enhanced cooperation establishing a

[552] Just to make the point clear, these are not scenarios covered by the Saint-Gabain doctrine (CJEU, 21 September 1999, C-307/97, *Saint-Gabain*, ECLI:EU:C:1999:438) which grants the free-mover treaty benefits. Accordingly, treaty benefits cannot be restricted to nationals of the contracting Member State (For an overview of the relevant case law also outside tax law see Sørensen (n 864) 324 et seq). The group benefit would not be restricted to nationals of the group members (accordingly free-movers can equally benefit) but to the residents or the law may use other determining factors necessary to restrict the benefit to group members.

[553] See this chapter Part I, subsection C.I.2.

[554] Art XXIV para 4 of the GATT.

group benefit on the other hand: for the sake of deeper integration, some Member States (of the WTO or the European Union) are allowed to form a group. The members of a Customs Unions or Free Trade Area are allowed to treat insiders differently from outsiders, and thus the fundamental principle of non-discrimination and most-favoured nation is loosened for the benefit of deeper integration between some Member States. The General Agreement on Tariffs and Trade (GATT) provisions on preferential regional trade agreements provide some safeguards to ensure that these agreements do not hinder trade between the Member States inside the Customs Union or Free Trade Area and the Member States outside these zones. We shall exemplify the design of these safeguarding clauses in WTO law, the reason why the members of the trade agreement are allowed to treat outsiders differently, and whether the rationale underlying preferential trade agreements in WTO law can be applied to the field of enhanced cooperation.

2. Preferential Trade Agreements under WTO Law

a) Non-discrimination and Reciprocity in WTO Law and their Exceptions

WTO law is dominated by the principle of non-discrimination, and thus a most-favoured-nation clause has been enshrined in the GATT, meaning that the Member States cannot distinguish between each other when it comes to tariffs and other trade reductions. The most-favoured-nation clause is of particular importance for small countries which have little power to retaliate. They can claim the same import benefits as important trading partners. Accordingly, trade liberalisation is achieved by both the abandonment of trade restrictions and the abandonment of these restrictions in a non-discriminatory manner.[555]

Despite the general principle of non-discrimination and most-favoured nation, WTO law is governed by a second principle: the principle of reciprocity. In general terms, the principle of reciprocity is a 'basic phenomenon of social interaction and consequently a guiding principle behind the formation and application of law'.[556] Under WTO law, the principle of reciprocity plays a particularly important role within the GATT tariff negotiations. A WTO Member State may only be willing to eliminate trade barriers unilaterally if it receives something in return.[557] In other words, a WTO Member State may only agree to lower its tariffs on a particular item if another WTO Member State is either doing the same or is lowering the tariffs on other goods which is preferential for the former Member State. From this

[555] Martin Wolf, 'An Unholy Alliance: The European Community and Developing Countries in the International Trading System' in LBM Mennes and Jacob Kol (eds), *European Trade Policies and Developing Countries* (Routledge 1988) 39–40.

[556] Bruno Simma, 'Reciprocity' in Rüdiger Wolfrum (ed), *The Max Planck Encyclopedia of Public International Law* (OUP 2008) n 1.

[557] J Michael Finger and L Alan Winters, 'Reciprocity in the WTO' in Bernard M Hoekman and others (eds), *Development, Trade, and the WTO: A Handbook* (World Bank 2002) 50 et seq.

perspective, reciprocity forms the basic principle which aims at 'limiting the scope for free riding that may arise because of the most-favoured-nation rule and the desire to obtain a quid pro quo for own trade liberalization'.[558] From the perspective of each WTO Member State, reciprocity is thus the 'ideal of mutual changes in trade policy which bring about changes in the volume of each country's imports that are of equal value to changes in the volume of its exports'.[559] Accordingly, reciprocity in GATT terms is achieved by an equivalent change in bilateral trade flows.[560]

The notion of reciprocity may expect WTO Member States 'to make similar efforts in undertaking concessions',[561] but a lack of reciprocity does not justify infringements of the most-favoured-nation treatment. In other words, a reciprocal effort to remove trade barriers may influence the tariff negotiation process, but as soon as a WTO Member State decides to lower its import tariffs unilaterally it has to grant the benefit to all States regardless of their endeavours.

Aside from the fact that the GATT wishes to take down all trade restrictions in a non-discriminatory and reciprocal manner, it allows the Member States to enter into trade agreements such as a Customs Union and a Free Trade Area. Under such agreements, Member States are allowed to deviate from the principle of most-favoured nation and thus can only grant the contracting States preferential trading conditions. The closer integration between the economies of the contracting parties should 'facilitate trade between the constituent territories' but should not 'raise barriers to the trade', with other WTO Member States not being part of that trade agreement.[562]

Members of a regional trade agreement are allowed to deviate from the most-favoured-nation clause because their reduction of trade barriers is based on a reciprocal agreement (each member eliminates its trade barriers because the others are doing the same). The lack of reciprocity towards outsiders of the agreement makes the members of the regional trade agreement unwilling to remove trade barriers on a general basis. To protect the special bond of reciprocity between the members of the trade agreement, the most-favoured-nation clause does not apply. In other words, the WTO Member States which are not part of the trade agreement and thus do not eliminate their trade barriers cannot claim the same preferential treatment as the members of the trade agreement.

558 Bernard M Hoekman and Petros C Mavroidis, *The World Trade Organization: Law, Economics, and Politics* (2nd edn, Routledge 2016) 21.

559 Kyle Bagwell and Robert W Staiger, 'The WTO: Theory and Practice' (2009) NBER Working Papers 19.

560 Juan Marchetti, Martin Roy, and Laura Zoratto, 'Is There Reciprocity in Preferential Trade Agreements on Services?' (2012) WTO Staff Working Paper 3. This form of reciprocity was first referred to as 'first-difference reciprocity' by Jagdish Bhagwati, which can be contrasted with full reciprocity, the latter being the elimination of market access barriers to achieve identical market access conditions (Jagdish N Bhagwati, *Protectionism* (MIT Press 1988) 36.).

561 Marchetti, Roy, and Zoratto (n 560) 3.

562 Art XXIV para 4 of the GATT.

The exception from the most-favoured-nation clause in the GATT provisions was a clear reflection of reality.[563] WTO Member States tried to achieve on a regional level what they were not able to accomplish on a multilateral level, and thus preferential trade agreements provide for a second-best world.[564] The deviation from the non-discriminatory abandonment of trade restrictions was not universally seen as the right way to go. Ludwig Erhard, for example, a former German chancellor, challenged the exception from the most-favoured-nation clause for the European Community consisting of its few Member States. In his view, global trade should be desired, since it is the only way of achieving welfare in Europe and around the world. Ludwig Erhard, however, was not in favour of breaking the European Community into pieces. On the contrary, the German chancellor lobbied for a massive enlargement of the Community to achieve at least Europe-wide trade which is unaffected by discriminatory trade restrictions.[565]

In that vein, preferential trade agreements were found to speed up the process towards global free trade. This hypothesis rests on the idea that negotiations on breaking down trade restrictions between a few blocs are more efficient and more promising than negotiations between all (single) WTO Member States.[566] However, a constant fear exists that there are too few blocs, which may have a negative impact on free trade and welfare. A low number of blocs allows each bloc to develop great market power,[567] which automatically leads to an increase of the optimum tariff. According to economic theory, the welfare loss is extreme if there exist just three main blocs.[568] The blocs are only dependent on others and not self-sufficient (which guarantees an optimal tariff near zero), if there is a large number of them.

Regional trade agreements are also seen as a chance to test certain trade policies within a group of States before extending them multilaterally.[569] Another

563 Such arrangements existed and were likely to continue in future: Michael Finger, 'GATT's Influence on Regional Arrangements' in Jaime de Melo and Arvind Panagariya (eds), *New Dimensions in Regional Integration* (CUP 1993) 130.

564 Marise Cremona and others (eds), 'Regional Trade Agreements: "Stepping Stones" or "Stumbling Blocks" of the WTO?' in Richard Senti, *Reflections on the Constitutionalisation of International Economic Law: Liber Amicorum for Ernst-Ulrich Petersmann* (Brill Nijhoff 2013) 441.

565 Erhard's formula—6 (Members of the European Community) + 7 (EFTA-Countries) + 5 (remaining Western European Countries outside a preferential trading agreement) = 1—has become quite famous and best reflects his intention. For an overview of his work and political agenda see Hans-Gert Pöttering, 'Ludwig Erhard und Europa' (2017) Die Politische Meinung.

566 Paul Krugman, 'Regionalism versus Multilateralism: Analytical Notes' in Jaime de Melo and Arvind Panagariya (eds), *New Dimensions in Regional Integration* (CUP 1993) 73.

567 The building of exclusive economic zones which stand side by side without much interaction is referred to as 'block economy', see Mitsuo Matsushita, 'Japanese Policies toward East Asian Free Trade Agreements: Policy and Legal Perspectives' in Ross P Buckley, Vai Io Lo, and Laurence Boulle (eds), *Challenges to Multilateral Trade: The Impact of Bilateral, Preferential and Regional Agreements* (Wolters Kluwer Law & Business 2008).

568 Elhanan Helpman and Assaf Razin (eds), 'Is Bilateralism Bad?' in Paul Krugman, *International Trade and Trade Policy* (MIT Press 1991) 21.

569 Wilfred J Ethier, 'Regionalism in a Multilateral World' (1998) 106 Journal of Political Economy 1214.

argument put forward in favour of regional trade agreements is their threat of punitive actions. If countries outside a trade agreement fear that one trading bloc is obtaining too much market power, they will try to enhance multilateral cooperation.[570]

b) Requirements for Implementing Preferential Trade Agreements

Art XXIV of the GATT grants Member States the possibility of entering into a trade agreement and deviating from the principle of most-favoured nation. To restrict the negative effects of trading blocs, the formation of a Customs Union or Free Trade Area is bound by strict conditions. First, the trade agreement has to facilitate trade and secondly it must not raise (additional) barriers to trade with Member States outside the trade agreement.

(aa) Facilitating Trade The wording of Art XXIV of the GATT indicates that a trade agreement which increases trade between the States is allowed, whereas an agreement which harms trade is prohibited. But how should the effects of such an agreement on the welfare of the world be determined?

Jacob Viner provided the traditional answer in his book *The Customs Union Issue*.[571] He divided the possible effects of a Customs Union into 'trade creation' and 'trade diversion'. To understand this differentiation, we shall assume that Member State A applies a non-discriminatory tariff to all trading partners. We shall further assume that Member State A enters into a Customs Union with Member State B. The elimination of tariffs has the consequence that Member State A now imports all towels from Member State B. To decide whether the Customs Union creates or diverts trade under Viner's theory depends on whether Member State A has previously imported towels from other States or has produced its own towels. The Customs Union only creates trade in the latter scenario because Member State A produces these goods at a higher cost. Producing these goods in Member State A and not importing them from Member State B is only due to the tariffs. In this case, the Customs Union creates trade. If, however, Member State A has always imported towels from other States (eg Member State C), the Customs Union diverts trade. Due to the abolition of tariffs Member State A stopped importing towels from a low-cost producing country (Member State C) and started to import those goods from a country which produces at higher costs (Member State B). Accordingly, there is a shift from a low-cost producer to a high-cost producer, and this causes a decline in the welfare of the Customs Union and the world.

570 Using the example of the European Union and the United States: Kyle Bagwell and Robert W Staiger, 'Multilateral Tariff Cooperation during the Formation of Free Trade Areas' (1997) 38 International Economic Review 291.

571 Jacob Viner, *The Customs Union Issue* (Stevens 1950).

This approach has been criticised as it is almost impossible to consider a regional trading scheme in isolation. The formation of a regional trade agreement may simultaneously have both favourable trade-increasing effects and unfavourable trade-diverting effects.[572] However, the more recent academic literature claims that regional trade agreements have (only) a positive impact on trade and thus are, in any case, trade-favouring.[573]

(bb) No Additional Trade Barriers to Third Countries—But They Have to Accept the Loss Art XXIV of the GATT explicitly states that any regional trade agreement must not raise trade barriers with WTO Member States which are not parties to the preferential trade agreement. Precisely what this means for the tariff has been debated in the literature. Some have asked whether it is in line with this provision if two States enter into a Customs Union and decide to levy a common import tariff of 10%. The new tariff reflects the average of the import tariff both countries levied before they entered into the Customs Union, namely 5% in case of Member State A and 15% in case of Member State B.[574]

Somehow, it seems that the conditions for trade between the Member States inside and outside the regional trade agreement should not be changed so as to have negative effects on the latter after entering into the trade agreement. However, this only concerns the levying of the import tariffs and does not mean that a regional trade agreement may not have negative welfare consequences for countries outside the agreement,[575] in particular in the form of trade diversion.[576]

3. Lesson Learned from Preferential Trade Agreements under WTO Law

WTO law, and in particular the GATT, is based on the fundamental principle of non-discrimination and most-favoured nation. If one WTO Member States lowers its tariffs, it has to do so with respect to all States regardless of their trade liberalising efforts. In other words, Member States of the WTO may only be willing to reduce their trade barriers if other Member States are also lowering their import tariffs because they cannot rely on reciprocity claims at a later stage. As soon as one Member State has liberalised its trade barriers it cannot condition the application of lower trade barriers upon reciprocal endeavour of fellow Member States.

572 Kenneth W Dam, 'Regional Economic Arrangements and the GATT: The Legacy of a Misconception' (1963) 30 The University of Chicago Law Review 615, 625.

573 Andrew K Rose, 'One Money, One Market: The Effect of Common Currencies on Trade' (2000) 15 Economic Policy 08; Robert C Feenstra, James R Markusen, and Andrew K Rose, 'Using the Gravity Equation to Differentiate among Alternative Theories of Trade' (2001) 34 Canadian Journal of Economics; ibid.

574 Dam (n 572) 620 et seq.

575 'World Trade Report 2007 Sixty Years of the Multilateral Trading System: Achievements and Challenges' 312 <https://www.wto.org/english/res_e/publications_e/wtr07_e.htm> accessed 1 April 2021.

576 Finger (n 563) 134.

However, the GATT grants the WTO Member States the possibility of deepened integration based on reciprocal trade liberalising efforts. In other words, WTO Member States may establish Customs Unions or Free Trade Areas. Within these free trade zones, Member States reciprocally eliminate all customs and similar trade obstacles and maintain barriers to trade with WTO Member States not being a part of the preferential trade agreement. Accordingly, Art XXIV of the GATT on regional trade agreements establishes a clear exception from most-favoured-nation treatment under WTO law. The driving factor for allowing group-based integration is reciprocity. Member States are only willing to eliminate their trade obstacles if the other Member States equally eliminate their barriers. Without a reciprocal tearing down of trade walls, none of the Member States would be willing to act and unilaterally demolish trade hampering barriers. Preferential trade agreements are a tool for establishing deeper integration, at least between Member States which are willing to mutually remove trade restrictions and prevent unwilling Member States from free-riding. In other words, preferential trade agreements allow discrimination towards those Member States outside the trade agreement to prevent them from benefitting from the group's trade liberalisation effort without equally contributing.

Preferential trade agreements may by definition establish a different treatment between insiders and outsiders of the free trade zone, but such agreements do not allow trade barriers to be raised against non-members. Trade between members of preferential trade agreement and non-members must not be influenced by the trade agreement, and thus the trade relationship between these WTO Member States has to face the same (or equivalent) trade barriers as before the trade agreement has been put in place. Therefore, trade between non-members and members of a preferential trade agreement may be subject to trade barriers which no longer apply to trade between members of that agreement, but the non-members are not exposed to heavier trade barriers. However, WTO law does not protect non-members of preferential trade agreements from welfare losses following from partial trade diversion. Any losses non-members face because trade within the free trade zone becomes more attractive are in line with WTO law.

To sum up, preferential trade agreements are the result of a reciprocal elimination of trade barriers of some WTO Member States. Preferential trade agreements do not allow their members to punish non-members for not mutually eliminating their trade barriers, and thus trade barriers towards non-members must not be raised, but preferential trade agreements allow their members to prevent non-members from free riding by restricting the integration benefit to the members of the free trade zone.

4. The Principle of Reciprocity in EU Law

The economic provisions of the European treaties building the European Customs Union and subsequently the European internal market are some of the cornerstones of the European Union. The reciprocity concept of general commercial treaties was and still is a driving force within the EU setting because the Member States reciprocally 'maintain a balance between economic pros and cons'.[577] The demolition of customs barriers between the Member States and the requirement of granting national treatment to foreigners and treat cross-border activities like pure domestic activities are economically more beneficial to all Member States than holding on to trade barriers and protectionist measures.[578]

Reciprocity within EU law has, however, no disciplinary function for the national legislature. Member States have to grant national treatment to EU foreigners, but they are not required to provide the same benefits to the taxpayers as other Member States provide.[579] In other words, if some Member States decide unilaterally to grant their nationals and subsequently all EU foreigners a (tax) benefit, other Member States are not bound by the national decision of the former Member State, and thus cannot be compelled to provide for an equally beneficial treatment.[580] They remain entitled to uphold their less favourable national (tax) treatment irrespective of what the other Member States offer.[581]

On the other hand, the Member States aiming to liberalise their national laws and enhance trade are not allowed to make the extension of national treatment to EU foreigners and cross-border activities subject to 'a condition of reciprocity imposed for the purpose of obtaining corresponding advantages'.[582] In this vein, academics have heavily criticised how the market freedoms are applied because they do not recognise the differences between national markets, and thus deregulate them. The deregulatory function of the market freedoms is triggered by the impossibility to justify unilateral trade obstacles based on a lack of reciprocity. In

577 Pär Hallström, 'The European Union—from Reciprocity to Loyalty' (2000) 39 Scandinavian Studies in Law 79, 81.

578 See for the same line of arguments in WTO law Thomas Cottier and Matthias Oesch, 'Direct and Indirect Discrimination in WTO and EU Law' in Sanford E Gaines, Birgitte Egelund Olsen, and Karsten Engsig Sørensen (eds), *Liberalising Trade in the EU and the WTO: A Legal Comparison* (CUP 2012) 153. A momentum of reciprocity can also be seen in the fact that all Member States have to extent their national treatment to EU foreigners and cross-border activities: Georg W Kofler, *Doppelbesteuerungsabkommen und europäisches Gemeinschaftsrecht* (Linde Verlag 2007) 699.

579 CJEU, 30 September 2003, *Colegio de Oficiales de la Marina Mercante Española*, ECLI:EU:C:2003:515, paras 61 and 62; CJEU, 16 May 2002, C-142/01, *Commission v Italy*, ECLI:EU:C:2002:302, para 7. Likewise, Member States cannot infringe their obligations under the European treaties because other Member States are non-compliant either: CJEU, 29 March 2001, *Portugal v Commission*, ECLI:EU:C:2001:189, para 22.

580 This also holds true in the relationship to third countries under free movement of capital: CJEU, 18 December 2007, C-101/05, *A*, ECLI:EU:C:2007:804, para 31; CJEU, 10 February 2011, C-436/08 and C-437/08, *Haribo and Salinen*, ECLI:EU:C:2011:61, para 127.

581 CJEU, 14 July 1981, 155/80, *Oebel*, ECLI:EU:C:1981:177, para 9; CJEU, 14 July 1994, C-379/92, *Peralta*, ECLI:EU:C:1994:296, para 48; CJEU, 10 May 1995, C-384/93, *Alpine Investments*, ECLI:EU:C:1995:126, para 27.

582 CJEU, 28 January 1986, 270/83, *Commission v France*, ECLI:EU:C:1986:37, para 26; CJEU, 1 July 1993, C-20/92, *Hubbard*, ECLI:EU:C:1993:280, para 17; see also Kofler, *Doppelbesteuerungsabkommen* (n 578) 698.

other words, Member States may not be able to justify restrictions on the fundamental freedoms with the argument that a fellow Member State is not providing an equal benefit, and thus they are not allowed to restrict the benefit to their nationals, residents, or domestic economic activities. One of the best examples of a lack of reciprocal granting of benefits exists within the social policy area. Franz Scharpf[583] has shown that the application of the market freedoms in an environment in which some Member States follow a 'Social Market Economy', whereas others apply a 'Liberal Market Economy', and in which reciprocity arguments are rejected, harms one more than the other. Within a social market economy, extensive (social) benefits are provided to those who have contributed to the system. The need to open up these systems to all EU foreigners who have not equally contributed to the system (or to a comparable system in their home Member States, which may allow compensation between the two) destabilises these existing national systems.

On the other hand, liberal market economies provide what is needed for the functioning of the market with respect to property rights, enforcement of private contracts, and undistorted competition, but apart from this the liberal market model leaves it to every individual to seek out a service that fits his needs when it comes to private insurance, investment, and the services market. Accordingly, the fundamental freedoms heavily conflict with the policy choices of the Member States[584] if the Member States' choice and the subsequent lack of reciprocity are not considered on the level of justification. Those who choose to provide social services, transfer payments, and other forms of distributive measures have the choice either to minimise the social protection or allow the exploitation of the system.[585] The differences within the European policy landscape, the straightforward application of the market freedoms and the missing possibility of either claiming a reciprocal granting of benefits[586] from the fellow Member States, or restricting the benefits where a reciprocal granting of benefits does not exist, produces losers. Some Member States will thus feel a need to change their national policies, whereas others are capable of upholding their original system.

In tax law, revenue constraints often force Member States to choose policy changes over an extensive granting of benefits to non-resident taxpayers and

583 Scharpf, 'The Asymmetry of European Integration' (n 460).

584 One example outside taxation would be the Austrian policy decision for open university access, see Floris de Witte, 'Transnational Solidarity and the Mediation of Conflicts of Justice in Europe' (2012) 18 European Law Journal 694.

585 Fritz W Scharpf, 'Weshalb die EU nicht zur sozialen Marktwirtschaft werden kann' (2009) 7 Zeitschrift für Staats- und Europawissenschaften 419, 432; Agustín José Menéndez, 'European Citizenship after Martínez Sala and Baumbast. Has European Law Become More Human but Less Social?' (2009) ARENA Working Papers.

586 For example social and tax benefits.

cross-border economic activities.[587] These policy changes regularly damage the Member State's economy.[588]

From this it follows that a lack of reciprocity does not constitute a general ground of justification for not complying with the principles of non-discrimination under EU law. Member States cannot demand that their fellow Member States pursue liberalisation efforts which are comparable to their endeavours. In that vein, Member States cannot make the extension of national treatment to EU foreigners and cross-border activities subject to a condition of reciprocity. If one Member State decides to grant a (tax) benefit or liberalises its market regulations, it has to apply its laws to both domestic and cross-border situations in an equal manner regardless of the domestic laws of other Member States.

Against this background, the parallel with WTO law becomes clear. In WTO law, the Member States are also not allowed to discriminate against single Member States simply because they are not willing to reduce their trade obstacles equivalently. If one WTO Member State lowers its tariffs, it has to grant this benefit to all WTO Member States and not only to fellow Member States pursuing equal liberalisation endeavours. With that said, WTO Member States may most likely only reduce their tariffs after tariff negotiations which ensure them a reciprocal lowering of the tariffs in fellow Member States. At a European level, the European Commission's recommendations on certain policy issues may be comparable with the WTO tariff negotiations, as the Commission's recommendations aim to align Member States' policies.

From this it follows that WTO and EU law can be compared when it comes to reciprocity claims. Neither EU law nor WTO law allow Member States to condition the granting of their unilaterally decided benefits on fellow Member States' equal endeavours. However, preferential trade agreements establish an exception to the denial of reciprocity claims at WTO level. The following subsection reveals whether EU law also acknowledges reciprocal agreements between Member States with the consequence that these Member States may prevent non-members from benefitting.

587 Rita de la Feria and Clemens Fuest, 'The Economic Effects of EU Tax Jurisprudence' (2016) 41 European Law Review 44, 67; Rita de la Feria and Clemens Fuest, 'The Economic Effects of EU Tax Jurisprudence' in Werner Haslehner, Georg Kofler, and Alexander Rust (eds), *EU Tax Law and Policy in the 21st Century* (Kluwer Law International 2017) 379; Farmer and Zalasinski (n 911) 421, 432; Wolfgang Schön, 'Die Auswirkungen des gemeinschaftsrechtlichen Beihilferechts auf das Steuerrecht' in Österreichischer Jusistentag (ed), *Verhandlungen des Siebzehnten Österreichischen Juristentages*, vol IV/2 (Manz Verlag 2010) 23. See in that vein also Commission, 10 December 2007, Communication from the Commission to the Council, the European Parliament and the European Economic and Social Committee on 'The application of anti-abuse measures in the area of direct taxation—within the EU and in relation to third countries', COM(2007) 785 final, p 6 'In the Commission's view it would be regrettable if, in order to avoid the charge of discrimination, MSs extended the application of anti-abuse measures designed to curb crossborder tax avoidance to purely domestic situations where no possible risk of abuse exists.'

588 Cordewener, Kofler, and Thiel (n 206) 1957.

5. Reciprocity in Tax Treaties and EU Law

Member States of the European Union enter into reciprocal agreements, in particular in tax law to prevent double taxation. Such agreements are negotiated and signed on a bilateral basis and may only entitle residents of the contracting parties to treaty benefits. Within the internal market framework, the question has been raised whether and if so to what extent the market freedoms can demand that tax treaty benefits are extended to residents of Member States who are not party to the treaty.[589] A straightforward application of the internal market non-discrimination principle may not recognise the differences between tax treaty laws and domestic laws of the Member States. Tax treaties are not based on unilateral Member State decisions, but are 'the result of a negotiation process between two states by which the rights and obligations are laid down in a *quid pro quo* deal on the basis of the reciprocity principle, thus creating a balance between benefits and concessions in the closed frame of the bilateral relationship'.[590] The results of the negotiation process manifest themselves in the contracting parties' decision not to tax, to lower the withholding tax rate, or to credit foreign taxes, and are based on equal concessions from both contracting parties.[591]

The CJEU acknowledges that tax treaties are the result of a bilateral negotiation process and that each contracting party is only willing to grant certain benefits because the other party is doing the same.[592] In the language of the Court, non-resident taxpayers which are subject to different tax treaties are not in a comparable situation, and thus the host Member State is allowed to grant a more favourable tax treatment to the residents of Member State A compared to residents of Member State B.[593] A different treatment of two cross-border situations which are each

[589] Since every tax treaty is the result of an individual negotiation process, differences between the treaties even within the European Union is the rule rather than the exception, Georg W Kofler and Clemens P Schindler, '"Dancing with Mr D": The ECJ's Denial of Most-Favoured-Nation Treatment in the "D" Case' (2005) 45 European Taxation 530, 531.

[590] Kofler, 'Most-Favoured-Nation Treatment in Direct Taxation' (n 175) 81; Pasquale Pistone, *The Impact of Community Law on Tax Treaties: Issues and Solutions* (Kluwer Law International 2002) 208 defines tax treaties as 'package deals' which 'contain compromise solutions'.

[591] See also Kofler, *Doppelbesteuerungsabkommen* (n 578) 700 et seq.

[592] CJEU, 30 June 2016, C-176/15, *Riskin and Timmermans*, ECLI:EU:C:2016:488, para 34; CJEU, 20 May 2008, C-194/06, *Orange European Smallcap Fund*, ECLI:EU:C:2008:289, para 63. Most-favoured-nation treatment does not follow from a national treatment which is required under EU law because this would require taxing non-resident taxpayers on a worldwide basis and granting them the same prevention of double taxation as residents: Peter J Wattel, 'Judicial Restraint and Three Trends in the ECJ's Direct Tax Case Law Symposium on Corporate Tax Policy in the European Union: Commentary' (2008) 62 Tax Law Review 205, 213–14; for a different view: Servaas van Thiel, 'The Direct Income Tax Case Law of the European Court of Justice: Past Trends and Future Developments Symposium on Corporate Tax Policy in the European Union' (2008) 62 Tax Law Review 143, 152 et seq.

[593] CJEU, 5 July 2005, C-376/03, *D*, ECLI:EU:C:2005:424, para 61; CJEU, 12 December 2006, C-374/04, *ACT Group Litigation*, ECLI:EU:C:2006:773, para 91. For a fundamental critique of this approach Servaas van Thiel, 'Why the European Court of Justice Should Interpret Directly Applicable Community Law as a Right to Most-Favoured Nation Treatment and a Prohibition of Double Taxation' in Dennis Weber (ed), *The Influence of European Law on Direct Taxation: Recent and Future Developments* (Kluwer Law International 2007) 88 et seq.

subject to a separate and distinct tax treaty honours the specific nature of the tax treaty: the reciprocal deal between two Member States.[594] Non-resident taxpayers from two different Member States are in a non-comparable situation because the Member States involved have signed different tax treaties, granting the residents of these very Member States different rights and obligations. The tax treaties balance these rights and obligations and thus they only apply to residents of one of the contracting Member States and cannot be viewed and applied in an isolated fashion to residents of other Member States.

From this it follows that the Court views any tax treaty as a bargaining deal between the contracting Member States, and it allows the granting of tax treaty benefits to be limited to situations covered by the treaty. Any tax treaty has to be appreciated from an EU law perspective because it enhances cross-border activities, at least between the contracting Member States. The Court respects that, in the absence of secondary EU law, only the Member States have the competence to conclude tax treaties and that it is up to them to decide on the conditions for restricting their taxing rights. Accordingly, the contracting parties are only willing to go further in the integration process on a bilateral basis because they benefit equally from the deal. A contracting party is willing to restrict its taxing rights in a particular situation because the other party also restricts its taxing rights in other situations. Forcing Member States to extend treaty benefits to residents of a Member State which is not a contracting party disregards the reciprocal deal of the two contracting Member States. In other words, extending tax treaty benefits beyond the treaty's scope would ignore the fact that the tax treaty only establishes deeper integration between the contracting parties and that each party is only willing to go further in the integration process because the other party is taking the same steps.[595]

6. Reciprocity within WTO Law and EU Law

The analysis of the principle of reciprocity in WTO and EU law has revealed that neither legal system allows Member States to condition the granting of domestic benefits upon equal trade-favouring endeavours of fellow Member States. If Member States decide unilaterally to reduce trade obstacles within their domestic laws, a lack of reciprocal actions in fellow Member States does not allow one to limit the access to these benefits. However, both WTO and EU law acknowledge that Member States may wish to pursue integration efforts in common. Preferential

[594] Horizontal discrimination following from such a reciprocal deal is different from horizontal discriminations stemming from Member State national tax rules (see this chapter Part I, subsection C.II.4.b)(cc)). Pistone, *The Impact of Community Law on Tax Treaties* (n 1255) 211 arguing that any horizontal discrimination 'affects the internal market and is therefore incompatible with the Community as it stands'.

[595] Kemmeren, 'The Termination of the "most Favoured Nation Cause" Dispute in Tax Treaty Law' (n 186) 148–49; Lehner (n 186) 470.

trade agreements under WTO law allow WTO Member States to tear down their trade walls mutually without being forced by the most-favoured-nation clause to grant these benefits to States which are not party to the agreement. The benefit of eliminating trade barriers can be kept within the free trade zone by allowing a different treatment of members of the preferential trade agreement and non-members. Likewise, the European internal market framework allows Member States of the European Union to enter into bilateral tax treaties and restrict treaty benefits to cross-border situations which only involve the contracting parties. The contracting Member States are willing to go forward in the integration process because they can agree on a deal which allows both parties to benefit mutually. The deeper reciprocal bond between the Member States prohibits a comparison of the cross-border situation subject to a particular tax treaty with any other cross-border situation.

From this it follows that the principle of reciprocity works quite well in a very concrete setting, namely when the Member States can demonstrate that they have only reduced their trade barriers because other Member States have done the same. However, reciprocity claims do not operate as a general disciplinary tool which would force Member States to follow liberalisation attempts of their fellow Member States or would allow Member States to restrict their own liberalisation efforts to fellow Member States pursuing similar endeavours.

7. Findings for Denying a Non-Group Member the Group Benefit

Above, we have seen that the constitutional framework of the enhanced cooperation procedure does in principle allow a comparison between intra-group and cross-group economic transactions.[596] A comparison between intra-group and cross-group economic transactions is needed to identify enhanced cooperation laws which are harmful to the European internal market and, by and large, the entire European integration process because enhanced cooperation law may only introduce rules for intra-group transactions and leave regulatory decisions for purely domestic situations to the Member States. In such a situation, intra-group and cross-group economic transactions have to be compared to identify the group-favouring, and potentially discriminatory character of enhanced cooperation law.

The constitutional framework of enhanced cooperation only determines that cross-group and intra-group economic transactions may, in principle, be compared. However, the constitutional approval to compare these transactions does not mean that they are automatically comparable. Rather, the actual design of enhanced cooperation law may deny comparability of intra-group and cross-group economic transactions. We have seen that comparability of two cross-border situations may be denied in cases in which Member States have

[596] See this chapter Part I, subsection E.IV.2.

conditioned their trade liberalisation measures upon equal endeavours of fellow Member States. The conditioning of own trade liberalisation becomes particularly evident in the case of tax treaties and preferential trade agreements. Each contracting party is only willing to eliminate import tariffs or double taxation (an economic obstacle) by way of refusing to tax or by crediting foreign taxes because of the reciprocal bond.

Trade-favouring enhanced cooperation may show equal features as tax treaties between Member States and preferential trade agreements under WTO law which may influence the comparability of intra-group and cross-group economic transactions. First, trade-favouring enhanced cooperation law aims to tear down national trade barriers which still exist on the European internal market. Secondly, the participating Member States are only willing to proceed with the integration process by eliminating either justified or economic trade obstacles because the other Member States are taking the same integrational steps. In other words, participating Member States are willing to strengthen the European internal market and foster European integration by eliminating trade obstacles, but they are not ready to do so without getting anything in return. Accordingly, the Member States have not introduced trade-favouring legislation on a unilateral basis which may not be open to reciprocity claims but have chosen the enhanced cooperation procedure to link their own liberalisation measures with the ones of the other participating Member States.

Member States outside the group are not bound by the law of the group (enhanced cooperation law, tax treaty law, or the law of preferential trade agreements), and thus, the members of the group cannot demand the granting of an equivalent benefit from non-members. The concept underlying the right to restrict benefits of preferential trade agreements and tax treaty benefits to the contracting parties can be transferred to trade-favouring enhanced cooperation. Extending the benefit of enhanced cooperation to non-participating Member States would be a one-way street, as the latter are not bound by enhanced cooperation law and do not have to grant benefits.

To make the point clear, trade-favouring enhanced cooperation establishes a very close bond between participating Member States. They tear down trade barriers which they are allowed to keep from the perspective of the market freedoms and they do so in a reciprocal manner. Their actions are coordinated and based on each other and none of the participating Member States would pursue the integration efforts through unilateral measures. Therefore, trade-favouring enhanced cooperation establishes deeper integration between the participating Member States which no longer allows a comparison between intra-group and cross-group economic transactions. The participating Member States mutually go beyond that which is required by the market freedoms, and this common and aligned action differentiates the participating Member States from non-participating Member States, and thus prevents a comparison of cross-border activities between participating

Member States on the one hand and participating and non-participating Member States on the other hand.

To conclude, trade-favouring enhanced cooperation establishes a special bond between participating Member States. This bond deepens integration between the participating Member States by imposing reciprocal rights and obligations upon them. Each participating Member State benefits because of the elimination of trade-hampering measures of the other participating Member States, but simultaneously demands equal liberalisation endeavours from the former. The deeper harmonised area consisting of the participating Member States may no longer be comparable with non-participating Member States, and thus the denial of the group benefit to non-participating Member States (eg in the form of a denial of foreign loss compensation) does not infringe the fundamental freedoms. The fundamental freedoms honour the integration efforts of participating Member States and allow them to restrict the trade-favouring benefits of enhanced cooperation to participating Member States. However, each non-participating Member State can join at any time and become part of the group which entitles the joining Member State to enjoy the trade-favouring benefit, but also demands that they grant the group benefit to all other participating Member States.[597]

8. Limits of the Different Treatment

The right to treat cross-group economic transactions differently from intra-group economic transactions has its limits. Enhanced cooperation is not allowed to build a protective fence around its members, which would harm trade between Member States inside and outside enhanced cooperation. Trade conditions between the bloc of participating and the bloc of non-participating Member States should remain as they were before enhanced cooperation has been introduced. Accordingly, non-participating Member States are allowed to rely on the status quo which existed before a group of Member States has established enhanced cooperation. In other words, enhanced cooperation should not and must not place economic activities between insiders and outsiders of enhanced cooperation in a worse position. Under WTO law, the Member States outside a preferential trade agreement also lack the entitlement to claim a reduction of existing tariffs. The trade barriers between those inside the free trade zone and those outside should, however, remain the same as before some Member States entered into the free trade agreement.

The consolidation of the status quo ensures that enhanced cooperation does not harm the European integration process. The non-participating Member States find themselves in the same economic situation as before enhanced cooperation has been introduced. Thus, trade between participating and non-participating Member States remains subject to the same, but not heavier or harsher, trade

[597] See Chapter 4, subsection E.I.

obstacles. However, the elimination of these trade barriers within enhanced cooperation may make trade between participating Member States more attractive than trade between participating and non-participating Member States. Any trade-diverting effects[598] of enhanced cooperation cannot account for a worse treatment under the fundamental freedoms[599] because trade enhancement is a reflex of deeper integration between the participating Member States.[600]

VIII. Establishing Cross-border (Tax) Coordination for More Flexibility

The third category of common actions of Member States under the enhanced cooperation procedure forms the establishment of tax coordination which grants Member States more flexibility to comply with their obligations under the fundamental freedoms in cross-border situations. Member States may seek more flexibility in complying with their obligations under the European treaties where the CJEU has followed its own value set when applying the fundamental freedoms and has ignored the design of national tax systems.[601] Tax coordination may give the Member States the freedom to pursue their domestic policies in a coherent and consistent manner in cross-border situations without harming free movement rights.

The following subsections start by describing what exactly is meant by tax coordination, and what triggers the need for such coordination (see subsection 1). This is followed by an analysis of the CJEU case law on the possibility of neutralising trade obstacles and the question of whether Member States are allowed to introduce trade obstacles to intra-group economic transactions which are compensated by another participating Member State. In other words, the second subsection asks whether Member States can introduce an overall perspective through enhanced cooperation for deciding on infringements of the fundamental freedoms (see subsection 2). The third subsection examines the relationship with non-participating Member States and asks whether benefits (see subsection 3.a) and disadvantages (see subsection 3.b) of enhanced cooperation can or must be applied to cross-group situations.

1. Starting Point: What is Cross-border Tax Coordination?

Following on from what has been stressed in the above chapters, the CJEU has fought national tax rules which hinder intra-EU trade. Both discriminatory and

[598] See this chapter Part I, subsection E.VII.2.b)(aa).
[599] For a protection of non-participating Member States from factual effects, see Chapter 6, subsection E.II.3.
[600] See this chapter Part I, subsection E.VII.2.b)(bb).
[601] See this chapter Part I, subsection C.IV.

restrictive measures are prohibited if they are not justified by a strong national public interest concern. The prohibition against restriction or discrimination only disallows a worse treatment of cross-border economic activities compared to a similar pure domestic action. But negative integration is not capable of achieving any form of coordination or cooperation between Member States. Rather, the framework of the market freedoms inevitably disregards any form of cooperation and coordination between Member States when deciding on the discriminatory or restrictive character of national measures. Accordingly, a Member State may be prohibited from taxing cross-border economic activities even though the tax may be credited in the other Member State and the tax credit ensures no increase of the overall tax burden. This is a generalising statement; however, the equality-in-a-box approach demands a focus of the fundamental freedoms on the national rules when deciding whether the Member State's measure constitutes a prohibited trade obstacle to the European internal market. The progress of deeper market integration may not only provoke harmonisation attempts for the entire European internal market but may also make the Member States willing to cooperate and coordinate their laws on bilateral basis. Tax coordination between Member States may, for example, aim to divide the obligations of European law in a way which allows one Member State to impose a trade obstacle which is subsequently neutralised by another Member State. Such coordination would give the Member States a chance to allocate taxing rights between Member States in a way which fits with their national policies, and simultaneously alleviate double taxation within the European internal market to ensure the one-off taxation of income and assets, and to choose which Member State is responsible for granting a tax benefit to which the taxpayer is entitled.

Take personal deductions and expenses as an example. Within the European Union, it is common practice to grant a taxpayer the right to a basic tax-free allowance as well as a tax deduction of some personal expenses.[602] The thresholds and requirements, of course, vary from Member State to Member State but there is a general understanding that taxes should only be levied when the supply of basic needs is satisfied and that personal and family circumstances have an impact on the personal ability to pay taxes.[603] The general claim to consider family circumstances and to refrain from taxing the subsistence minimum does not say anything about which Member State has the duty to do so if the taxpayer earns income in more than one Member State. The fundamental goal of recognising the personal circumstances of the taxpayer for income taxation can be achieved if one Member State (most likely the home Member State), or all the Member States (on an aliquot

[602] Mathieu Isenbaert, *EC Law and the Sovereignty of the Member States in Direct Taxation* (2010) para 532.

[603] Frans Vanistendael, 'Democracy, Revolution and Taxation' (2017) 71 Bulletin for International Taxation 444, 447.

basis) take the individual circumstances into account. Both options may comply with the fundamental principles underlying the national tax systems.

According to the CJEU case law, however, the home Member State has to consider personal expenses and the threshold of tax-free income because the ties between the taxpayer and the home Member State are particularly strong. The aggregate income and the personal and family circumstances are presumed to be more easily assessable where the personal and financial interests are centred.[604] The host Member State only has to grant these tax benefits if the home Member State is not able to do so due to a lack of taxable income in the home Member State.[605] If the home Member State is, however, able to grant the allowances and tax relief, it has to do so regardless of the fact that a taxable person has earned some of his income in another Member State. In other words, the home Member State is not entitled to restrict the benefits to the proportion of the total income which the taxpayer derives within the home Member State's territory.[606]

Some Member States may prefer to consider the personal and family circumstances, as well as the tax-free allowance, according to the proportion of the income taxable in each Member State, and thus argue for a sharing of the burden between the Member States taxing (parts of) the taxpayer's income.[607] This would still require the home Member State to issue an assessment on the income distribution between the Member States. The harmonisation of the allowances and tax-free thresholds would make it much easier for the Member State to grant the taxpayer an appropriate portion of the tax benefit, but it is not an indispensable requirement. The Member States may still be able to use their thresholds and allowances when it comes to an aliquot granting of tax benefits.

Another policy area where Member States may want to coordinate their actions is the taxation of cross-border dividend flows outside the scope of the Parent-Subsidiary Directive. According to CJEU case law, Member States are required to grant a non-resident taxpayer all mechanisms to avoid economic double taxation which are available to national taxpayers if a Member State decides to tax non-resident taxpayers on their dividends distributed by a resident entity.[608] Granting non-resident taxpayers access to the Member States' tools for eliminating economic double taxation domestically means that if a Member State decides to exempt dividends in a purely domestic situation, the Member State is prohibited

[604] CJEU, 14 February 1995, C-279/93, *Schumacker*, ECLI:EU:C:1995:31, para 32.

[605] CJEU, 14 February 1995, C-279/93, *Schumacker*, ECLI:EU:C:1995:31, para 36; CJEU, 16 October 2008, C-527/06, *Renneberg*, ECLI:EU:C:2008:566, para 61; CJEU, 18 June 2015, C-9/14, *Kieback*, ECLI:EU:C:2015:406, para 25; CJEU, 9 February 2017, C-283/15, *X*, ECLI:EU:C:2017:102, para 33.

[606] CJEU, 12 December 2002, C-385/00, *de Groot*, ECLI:EU:C:2002:750.

[607] Hannelore Niesten, 'Case X v. Staatssecretaris van Financiën: Fractional Allocation of Personal and Family Tax Benefits for EU Resident Individuals with Multi-State Income' (2017) 26 EC Tax Review 201, 211 argues that such a system requires a progression clause for the tax treatment of privileged non-residents to avoid cherry-picking.

[608] CJEU, 14 December 2006, C-170/05, *Denkavit Internationaal*, ECLI:EU:C:2006:783, para 36; CJEU, 8 November 2007, C-379/05, *Amurta*, ECLI:EU:C:2007:655, para 38.

from taxing dividend flows to a non-resident taxpayer. In such cases, Member States may wish to cooperate and coordinate their actions to deviate from the requirements set by CJEU case law. We shall assume, for example, that some Member States find a general agreement according to which non-resident taxpayers should be taxed on their domestic dividends at a particular rate—for example 5%—which is subsequently credited by the home Member State. The agreement between the Member States on the taxation of the non-resident taxpayer in the form of a withholding tax is unrelated to the Member State's decision on how to relieve the pure domestic dividend distribution from an economic double taxation, but the system of taxing non-resident taxpayers may fit more properly into the Member States' tax framework.

A third and probably more recent example for tax coordination would be an agreement between the Member States to levy a common Digital Service Tax (DST) to address weaknesses of their current income tax regimes.[609] A DST could be understood to either form part of the Member States' income tax regime or to constitute an entire new tax regime which is separate and distinct from the Member States' income tax systems.[610] A DST is levied to compensate Member States for not being able to tax foreign companies on their gains attributable to a so-called digital permanent establishment, which suggests that such a tax shall form part of the Member States' income tax system. In this vein, the European Commission explicitly states that a DST should only be an interim solution up until the Member States can implement the notion of a digital permanent establishment within their treaty network. However, a DST exhibits features which may not be in line with the principles underlying the Member States' income tax regimes, and thus these characteristics may indicate that a DST establishes an entirely new and distinct tax regime. For example, a DST is levied on gross revenue of business, which contradicts the fundament of income taxation, this being net taxation. The Commission has attempted to provide the European DST with such non-income tax features to circumvent any tax treaty breaches in relation to third countries.[611]

[609] See for the recent proposal of the European Commission the Proposal for a Council Directive on the common system of a digital service tax on revenue resulting from the provision of certain digital services, 21 March 2018, COM(2018) 148 final. Some Member States have already or are moving to a DST on a unilateral basis until an agreement can be reached at the European level. For the Spanish proposal see Francisco José Nocete Correa, 'The Spanish Digital Services Tax: A Paradigm for the Base Enlargement & Profit Attraction (BEPA) Plan for the Digitalized Economy' (2019) 59 European Taxation 341; for the Austrian response of a revenue-based digital business tax of 5% on online advertising see Gunter Mayr, 'Austria—New Digital Business Tax on Online Advertising in Austria' (2019) 59 European Taxation 350; for the Italian Web Tax, Valente Piergiorgio, 'The Italian Web Tax from a National and International Perspective' (2018) 58 European Taxation 186.

[610] Georg W Kofler and Julia Sinnig, 'Equalization Taxes and the EU's "Digital Services Tax"' in Werner Haslehner and others (eds), *Tax and the Digital Economy: Challenges and Proposals for Reform* (Kluwer Law International 2019).

[611] This practice is also common in other places in the world: see for an overview Daniela Hohenwarter-Mayr and others, 'Qualification of the Digital Services Tax Under Tax Treaties' (2019) 47 Intertax 140, 140–41. For a critical analysis of these taxes see Roland Ismer and Christoph Jescheck,

A thorough analysis of the characteristics and features of the DST falls outside the scope of this study, but four fundamental arguments may suggest that the DST may form a part of the Member States' income tax system and does not establish an entirely new tax regime for the digital economy.[612] First, the fact that the European Commission has based the proposal for a European DST on Art 113 of the TFEU (ie the competence clause for indirect taxes) and not on Art 115 of the TFEU (ie the competence clause for direct taxes) does not automatically exclude the DST from being an income tax.[613] Secondly, the Commission has revealed that levying a DST may lead to 'double taxation where the same revenues are subject to the corporate income tax and DST'. The Commission expects the Member States to 'allow businesses to deduct the DST paid as a cost from the corporate income tax base in their territory, irrespective of whether both taxes are paid in the same Member State or in different ones'.[614] So far, double taxation is understood as an overlap of a tax claim (of the same sort) of two jurisdictions.[615] If the Commission does not have a different understanding of double taxation in mind, the Commission acknowledges that the DST is a form of income tax which may trigger double taxation in combination with the levying of corporate taxes.[616] Thirdly, it is compensation for not being able to tax foreign digital businesses on their domestic source income. Foreign digital businesses cannot be taxed on their domestic source income because of the existing tax treaty network, which is not yet familiar with the notion of a digital permanent establishment.[617] Fourthly, the income tax systems of the Member States occasionally provide for gross taxation, like in the case of dividend and interest taxation, and no-one would claim that the taxation of interests is not part of the Member States' income tax system.[618]

'Taxes on Digital Services and the Substantive Scope of Application of Tax Treaties: Pushing the Boundaries of Article 2 of the OECD Model?' (2018) 46 Intertax 573; Sagar Wagh, 'The Taxation of Digital Transactions in India: The New Equalization Levy' (2016) 70 Bulletin for International Taxation 538.

612 However, there are strong counterarguments: Georg Kofler and Julia Sinnig, 'Equalization Taxes and the EU's "Digital Services Tax"' (2019) 47 Intertax 176, 185 et seq.

613 Council, 8 October 2018, Opinion of the legal service on the proposal for a Council directive on the common system of a digital services tax on revenues resulting from the provision of certain digital services, 12922/18, para 6.

614 Commission, 21 March 2018, Proposal for a Council Directive on the common system of a digital service tax on revenue resulting from the provision of certain digital services, COM(2018) 148 final, point 27 of the preamble.

615 Lang, *Introduction* (n 17) para 12.

616 For a different view see Hohenwarter-Mayr and others (n 611) 143.

617 Carlo Garbarino, 'Permanent Establishments and BEPS Action 7: Perspectives in Evolution' (2019) 47 Intertax 365; Eva Escribano López, 'An Opportunistic, and yet Appropriate, Revision of the Source Threshold for the Twenty-First Century Tax Treaties' (2015) 43 Intertax 6.

618 The following subsections will discuss the discriminatory features of the DST in more detail but only to the extent that it is relevant for the relationship between the participating and the non-participating Member States. General claims of discriminatory treatment of the DST are not discussed. See for such a discussion Ruth Mason and Leopoldo Parada, 'Digital Battlefront in the Tax Wars' (2018) 92 Tax Notes International 1183.

A DST established by way of enhanced cooperation may coordinate the tax systems of the participating Member States as it allocates parts of the income taxable in the home Member State to the source Member State. The DST is the first step towards allowing source Member States to tax digital businesses on the profits they derived through a digital activity within these Member States. The levying of the tax may discriminate on two grounds; first, because it is targeted at big businesses established in some particular Member States, and second, because an equivalent domestic business may not be subject to DST.[619] Within enhanced cooperation, however, Member States may agree that the home Member State credits the foreign DST against the national income tax due. The crediting of the foreign DST would (if certain conditions are satisfied) neutralise the additional layer of taxation in the host Member State, thereby allowing the Member States to coordinate their taxing rights.

These three examples are potential scenarios in which the Member States may wish to establish coordination between each other. Tax coordination may allow the Member States to tax cross-border situations in a way which best fits their domestic policy decisions, and at the same time to comply with the requirements set by the fundamental freedoms. From the perspective of a single Member State, the coordination approach may be seen as discriminatory because the equal treatment in relation to the domestic situation is established only by the other Member State. On the other hand, the Member States of the group may not want to grant the compensation benefit to cross-group situations, which may account for unequal and thus discriminatory treatment.

The following subsections will reveal the different claims of discrimination. First, it will be asked whether one Member State in the group can provide compensation for the wrongdoings of another group member or whether every Member State is required to fulfil its duties imposed by European law in an isolated manner (see subsection 2). Secondly, the different forms of discriminatory treatment towards non-participating Member States will be identified and analysed in the light of the fundamental freedoms (see subsection 3).

2. Discrimination within the Group

In the above, it has been revealed that Member States have a particular interest in entering into agreements with each other as a countermeasure against a harsh application of the fundamental freedoms and CJEU case law which is driven by value choices of the judges.[620] These agreements ensure that cross-border economic activities are not treated more onerously than purely domestic situations. Thus far,

[619] The Commission's current proposal explicitly extends the levying of the tax to a purely domestic situation to avoid any infringements of the fundamental freedoms.

[620] See this chapter Part I, subsection C.IV.

the CJEU has been very hesitant to allow a discriminatory national rule to stand because the discrimination is neutralised by another Member State.[621] However, while the CJEU has rejected a compensation of discrimination in cases in which the Member State did so in accordance with its domestic tax law,[622] the Court seems to take compensatory measures into account if those measures are required by a bilateral tax treaty.[623] From the perspective of the effective tax burden, it may not make a difference whether the discriminatory treatment is neutralised by another Member State because of domestic or tax treaty law. However, it makes a big difference when it comes to the accountability of the Member State discriminating cross-border economic activities.[624] A Member State has no power over the domestic tax regime of a fellow Member State. Thus, whether or not compensation is provided is entirely up to the other Member State's discretion. The CJEU requires more than an accidental relief from the burden. A Member State is only allowed to treat a cross-border economic activity less favourably than a purely domestic undertaking if the Member State takes measures to ensure that the other Member State(s) involved compensate, and if this compensatory treatment can be enforced. In other words, one Member State is only entitled to transfer its obligations under EU law to a fellow Member State in cases in which the rights and obligations of both Member States are linked by an agreement which can be enforced by each party.[625]

Enhanced cooperation law establishes a strong bond between participating Member States since they can use the tools enshrined in the European treaties to demand compliance with enhanced cooperation law. Accordingly, enhanced cooperation law forms a sufficient basis for Member States to coordinate their rights and obligations and thereby transfer their obligations under EU law between each other.

In the academic literature, a huge debate has flared up on the requirements for an effective neutralisation by another Member State. Some scholars claim

[621] See for more details of what neutralisation in the CJEU case law means this chapter Part I, subsection E.VIII.2.

[622] CJEU, 8 November 2007, C-379/05, *Amurta*, ECLI:EU:C:2007:655, paras. 84 and 78; CJEU, 11 September 2008, C-43/07, *Arens-Sikken*, ECLI:EU:C:2008:490, para 66.

[623] CJEU, 19 January 2006, C-265/04, *Margaretha Bouanich*, ECLI:EU:C:2006:51, para 51; CJEU, 12 December 2006, C-374/04, *Test Claimants in Class IV of the ACT Group Litigation*; ECLI:EU:C:2006:773, para 71; CJEU, 14 December 2006, C-170/05, *Denkavit Internationaal*, ECLI:EU:C:2006:783, para 44 et seq; 17 September 2015, C-10/14, C-14/14, and C-17/14, *Miljoen*, ECLI:EU:C:2015:608, para 80. See also CJEU, 8 November 2007, C-379/05, *Amurta*, ECLI:EU:C:2007:655, para 83. 'In the *Bouanich* case, the ECJ invited the national court to take into account the concrete effects of the bilateral convention which was applicable in order to appreciate the consistency of the national tax legislation at issue with the free movement of capital', Lenaerts, 'United in Diversity' (n 40) 633. See also Wattel, Marres, and Vermeulen (n 10) 368.

[624] CJEU, 17 September 2015, C-10/14, C-14/14, and C-17/14, *Miljoen*, ECLI:EU:C:2015:608, para 82; Lang, 'ECJ Case Law on Cross-Border Dividend Taxation' (n 815) 71.

[625] Kofler, 'Tax Treaty "Neutralization"' (n 149) 687.

that neutralisation is only provided if the tax treaty in any case envisages a full tax credit.[626] A full credit not only requires a credit of the foreign tax regardless of whether or not the amount exceeds the tax that would have been levied in the resident state, it also requires a refund of non-creditable foreign taxes.[627] Whether the home Member State grants a full tax credit for cases in which a credit carry-forward is granted is still open to discussion,[628] and different views can be taken.[629] On the one hand, the withholding tax will, at some point, be credited against the national tax due; on the other hand, the time difference between paying the tax and crediting it may be extensive. The delay in obtaining the credit may place the foreign shareholder in a worse position than the resident shareholder.[630]

Some commentators advocate allowing the neutralisation of a discriminatory treatment if the tax treaty only provides for an ordinary credit, but in the individual case, it results in a full credit.[631] This approach would require an individual assessment of each case and would oblige the host Member State to tax the non-resident shareholder in a non-discriminatory manner if a credit is—factually or legally—not available in the resident Member State.

For enhanced cooperation, it would only make sense to implement a robust system which effectively neutralises a discriminatory treatment of a fellow Member State. Otherwise, the Member States would not be allowed to rely entirely on the obligations of the other Member States and would still be required to assess whether the discriminatory treatment is eligible for neutralisation in the other Member State. Accordingly, the enhanced compensation has to ensure that full compensation is provided within the group.

[626] Jaap Bellingwout, 'Amurta: A Tribute to (the Late) Advocate General Geelhoed' (2008) 48 European Taxation 124, 129; Marc Dassesse, 'Belgian Withholding Taxes on Outbound Dividends and Interest: The Challenge of Community Law' (2008) 62 Bulletin for International Taxation 337, 342.

[627] Philippe Martin, 'Dividends and Withholding Taxes' in Guglielmo Maisto (ed), *Taxation of Intercompany Dividends under Tax Treaties and EU Law* (IBFD 2012) 28 arguing that 'the neutralization theory seems to be shrinking: it is accepted in theory, but the requirements for neutralization will seldom be met in practice'.

[628] In light of the recent *Sofina* case, it is quite likely that such a cash-flow disadvantage restricts the free movement rights: CJEU, 22 November 2018, C-575/17, *Sofina*, ECLI:EU:C:2018:943. See also Georg W Kofler, 'Foreign Losses and Territoriality: Did Sofina Revolutionize Source-State Taxation?' in Servaas van Thiel, Piergiorgio Valente, and Stella Raventós-Calvo (eds), *CFE Tax Advisers Europe: 60th Anniversary Liber Amicorum* (IBFD 2019) 156 et seq. Georg W Kofler, 'Grenzüberschreitende Verlustverwertung im Quellenstaat: Stellt Sofina die beschränkte Steuerpflicht auf den Kopf?' in Dietmar Gosch, Arne Schnitger and Wolfgang Schön (eds), *Festschrift für Jürgen Lüdicke* (Beck Verlag 2019) 396 et seq.

[629] Bellingwout (n 626) 129.

[630] Whether or not the difference in timing account for a different treatment of the resident and the foreign shareholder is not entirely clear from the existing CJEU case law. In a very different setting, the Court ruled that full compensation for a discriminatory treatment 'cannot leave out the account factors, such as the effluxion of time, which may in fact reduce its value, and that the award of interest is an essential component of compensation for the purposes of restoring real equality of treatment' (CJEU, 8 March 2001, C-397/98 and C-410/98, *Metallgesellschaft et al*, ECLI:EU:C:2001:134, para 94 referencing CJEU, 2 August 1993, C-271/91, *Marshall*, ECLI:EU:C:1993:335, para 32).

[631] Dick F van Sprundel, 'Analysis of the Netherlands Dividend Withholding Tax on Shares—No Need to Abolish This Tax Yet?' (2008) 48 European Taxation 607, 614.

3. Forms of Discrimination towards Non-participating Member States

If at least nine Member States can agree on the terms of a coordination approach which allows them to neutralise obstacles to trade mutually, the Member States may use the enhanced cooperation procedure to enact laws necessary for a reliable framework between the Member States. The use of enhanced cooperation procedure for placing such a framework into law opens up the possibility of multiple forms of potential discrimination towards outsiders of the group.

First, only participating Member States coordinate their actions. Member States outside the group are not willing to be part of the framework and are therefore unwilling to neutralise any obstacles to trade created by another Member States. The non-participating Member States may uphold their national tax system and only adjust it to the extent required by the market freedoms. The refusal to enter into enhanced cooperation and accept both rights and obligations which are different from what the market freedoms demand also has an impact on the behaviour of the participating Member States. They are unwilling to extend the beneficial group treatment to cross-group situations because the non-participating Member States are not offering a reciprocal benefit. Despite the lack of reciprocity, the market players may not be exposed to the disadvantage in a cross-group situation which would require compensation. Granting the compensation benefit in cross-group situations would not serve its purpose. In other words, participating Member States are not willing to credit a DST or withholding tax on dividends against their resident taxpayers' corporate income tax if a non-participating Member State has levied these taxes in accordance with its national rules. However, if the participating Member States granted taxpayers resident in a non-participating Member State proportional personal allowances, despite the home Member State granting its residents personal allowances in full, the taxpayers would receive a compensation benefit without suffering from a disadvantage which asks for such compensation. Nonetheless, the denial of the compensation benefit may discriminate against market players engaging in economic activities outside enhanced cooperation against market players operating only within the territory of participating Member States.

Secondly, the participating Member States may wish to apply the framework they have agreed upon within enhanced cooperation regardless of whether the other Member State (the host Member State in the case of the personal allowances, and the resident Member State in the case of the DST and the withholding tax on dividends) participates in enhanced cooperation. This would mean that the (participating) Member State, as the host Member State, levies a withholding tax on all dividends flowing outside of its territory and a DST, both of which may not be credited in the (non-participating) home Member State, and, as the home Member State, only grants personal allowances proportionally, but the (non-participating) host Member State does not grant personal allowances proportionally on the income taxable in its territory.

The refusal to deduct personal allowances in full in the residence Member State, as well as the levying of a withholding tax on dividends and a tax on digital services, may constitute discrimination because in a purely domestic setting the deduction of the personal allowances is granted in full, and no withholding tax on dividends or a tax on digital services[632] is applied.

From this it follows that there are two categories of potential discriminations following from coordinative enhanced cooperation: the first category describes a denial of the compensation benefit to non-group members, whereas the second category is defined by the application of the group disadvantage towards the non-participating Member States.

a) Denying the Compensation Benefit

At first glance, the denial of the compensation benefit equates to the denial of the group benefit, as discussed above.[633] However, when examining the details of what is presumed to be the 'benefit' more closely, there are fundamental differences between the compensation benefit and the group benefit. The latter enhances cross-border economic activities because the resident treatment is extended to non-resident taxpayers and cross-border economic activities in cases in which the market freedoms fail to achieve resident treatment. Thus, the (tax) treatment within enhanced cooperation is a real benefit which favours cross-border economic activities within the group. The compensation benefit, on the other hand, does not particularly aim to foster trade between the participating Member States. Rather, the benefit intends to neutralise trade obstacles created by a fellow Member State, and thus taken together with the coordination disadvantage, the compensation benefit only establishes what the fundamental freedoms already demand. In other words, the compensation benefit is not designed to benefit intra-EU trade but to allow Member States to transfer their obligations under EU law to other Member States without any setbacks in the European integration process. However, the granting of the compensation benefit in cross-group situations would allow a gratuitous benefiting. The taxpayer would receive a tax benefit without being subject to a (corresponding) tax disadvantage in the other Member State. Assume, for example, that the source Member State (being a participating Member State) takes proportional personal allowances into account, even though the home Member State (being a non-participating Member State) allows a full deduction of personal

[632] Whether the levying of the DST per se accounts for a discriminatory treatment very much depends on the actual design of the tax. The tax may not be levied in an intra-group setting because the group members have agreed on implementing a digital permanent establishment within their treaties. Or they may have chosen to also levy a digital services tax in a purely domestic setting. The following subsections will examine the question of what truly accounts for a discrimination more deeply.

[633] See this chapter Part I, subsection E.VII.7.

and family expenses; in this case, the taxpayer would be entitled to a full deduction in the home state and a partial deduction in the host state.[634]

The compensation benefit creates a strong bond only between the participating Member States which is even more visible than in the case of the group benefit. Within coordinative enhanced cooperation, Member States establish deeper integration through coordination of their actions. The linkage between measures which on the one hand place burdens on, and on the other hand remove burdens from the intra-group economic transactions introduces a strong framework between the participating Member States, which makes it impossible to compare intra-group with cross-group transactions. As in the case of trade-favouring enhanced cooperation, coordinative enhanced cooperation sets up an integration level between the participating Member States which no longer allows a comparison between intra-group and cross-group economic transactions. Since the deeper integration bond within enhanced cooperation prohibits a comparison between the intra-group and cross-group economic transactions, a denial of the compensation benefit in cross-group situations does not infringe the fundamental freedoms. The participating Member States are allowed to restrict the granting of compensation to the group.

b) Putting Non-participating Member States in a Worse Position

Participating Member States may want to apply the coordination-disadvantage (eg the levying of withholding taxes) even outside enhanced cooperation, an area which is not determined by a coordinating bond with a fellow Member State ensuring that the imposed trade obstacles are neutralised. The levying of a DST or withholding taxes on dividends may be found to be discriminatory because such a tax would not apply in a purely domestic setting, and these taxes are not credited by the home Member State. To overcome potential infringements of the fundamental freedoms, the European Commission's proposal for a European DST[635] explicitly extends the scope of the tax to purely domestic scenarios. However, the aim and purpose of the tax clearly shows that the entire idea of a DST aims to only tax cross-border situations. If Member States opt for a DST which applies both to domestic and cross-border situations, as proposed by the Commission, the CJEU may nonetheless find the tax discriminatory because within a purely domestic setting, the Member States will credit the DST against the national income tax due; whereas in a cross-border situation, the DST will (most likely) not be credited, and the DST therefore happens to be a burden for foreign undertakings. The possibility

[634] The uncoordinated application of national tax rules may grant the free mover a double benefit (see CJEU, 12 December 2013, C-303/12, *Imfeld*, ECLI:EU:C:2013) to ensure an equal treatment, but the free movement rights do not demand a gratuitous benefitting of the free mover.

[635] Commission, 21 March 2018, Proposal for a Council Directive on the common system of a digital service tax on revenue resulting from the provision of certain digital services, COM(2018) 148 final.

of deducting the DST as business expenditure does not alter the picture because the double burden is not entirely eliminated. The Court could, however, also take a very narrow approach and find that the DST applies to both domestic and cross-border situations and thus is not discriminatory, but this is less likely to be the case.

Outside enhanced cooperation, no agreement exists which ensures compensation for trade obstacles between the Member States. Therefore, the Member States are bound by the fundamental freedoms and have to achieve unilateral equal treatment between domestic and cross-border activities. Being part of enhanced cooperation which implements a cooperative system does not change the requirements set by the fundamental freedoms outside enhanced cooperation. Allowing Member States to impose burdens on cross-border activities without having agreed on a neutralisation mechanism with fellow Member States would either harm trade between the two Member States or force the other Member State to absorb the trade obstacle by granting a tax treatment which is similar to the one which a participating Member State has to grant.

Both harming intra-EU trade and forcing non-participating Member States to apply the group tax treatment contradict the European internal market concept, as well as the idea underlying enhanced cooperation. Forcing Member States outside enhanced cooperation to apply a tax treatment to cross-border activities which equals the treatment that participating Member States apply just to uphold the status quo would contradict the idea of enhanced cooperation. The Member States participating in enhanced cooperation would not respect the decision of the fellow Member States to stay out of the group and would not respect what has already been accomplished for enhancing trade between all Member States.

c) Conclusions

Member States can use enhanced cooperation to implement a cooperative system for cross-border economic activities which allows them to transfer their obligations under EU law to other participating Member States. A transfer of these obligations may be necessary if the Member States disagree with the CJEU case law and find an agreement on a more appropriate sharing of obligations. Under the umbrella of enhanced cooperation, Member States are allowed to discriminate or create obstacles to trade if a fellow Member State neutralises these hurdles. Accordingly, Member States may be allowed to levy a withholding tax on cross-border dividends even though they do not levy such a tax in a purely domestic setting if the discriminatory treatment is compensated by another participating Member State. Participating Member States are not required under European free movement law to grant the compensation benefit in cross-group situations because cooperative enhanced cooperation establishes deeper integration between the participating Member States which no longer allows a comparison between intra-group and cross-group economic transactions.

On the other hand, participating Member States have to acknowledge that some Member States have not joined enhanced cooperation, and thus, in a cross-group situation, the participating Member States are bound by the market freedoms. Any less favourable treatment of cross-border situations compared to domestic situations need to be justified. Subsequently, the Member States are not allowed to apply the coordinating disadvantage of enhanced cooperation to cross-group transactions.

IX. Findings

The enhanced cooperation procedure can be used to obtain different levels of integration within the participating Member States. On the one hand, Member States may harmonise values, thereby achieving an entire unification the laws. Value-based harmonisation establishes the deepest form of market integration because it not only fosters trade but also establishes harmonised values for a true community of values. On the other hand, Member States may use the enhanced cooperation procedure to enhance trade between the participating Member States or provide for coordination which grants them more flexibility in sharing the obligations imposed upon them, in particular by the fundamental freedoms. Trade favouring rules and coordinative systems, however, do not touch on the fundaments underlying the national laws.

It has been established that enhanced cooperation should be understood as a tool which gives Member States the chance to emphasise the importance of certain non-market values. If all Member States harmonised the value, the regulatory approach introduced by ordinary secondary EU law would (in most cases) not impose any trade obstacles because, from the perspective of the fundamental freedoms, regulation is not per se a trade-hampering factor. If, however, only a group of Member States can agree on the legislative approach, obstacles to trade may still exist in a cross-group situation. These obstacles cannot be accepted simply because the Member States have used the enhanced cooperation procedure to unify their laws; instead, these obstacles have to be justified.

However, trade obstacles imposed by value-based enhanced cooperation may be necessary to pursue and protect the harmonised values. To honour these harmonised values a light-touch justification approach applies to protective trade obstacles. So far, the CJEU has only applied a light-touch justification approach to trade obstacles imposed by (ordinary) secondary EU law. Such secondary EU law obstacles exist, for example, where the public interest concerns require amendments of every Member State's market (like in *Meyhui*). However, if the obstacles do not protect the harmonised values but soften negative effects following from enhanced cooperation law, the Member States have to meet the ordinary justification threshold (the one an obstacle of a single Member State has to meet) to be allowed to hold on to these obstacles. The higher justification threshold is legitimised by the fact that these obstacles are not necessary to pursue or protect the harmonised values; they should simply reduce negative effects, such as locational effects.

Aside from harmonising values, the enhanced cooperation procedure can be used to foster trade between the participating Member States by extending a national/resident treatment to non-nationals/non-residents or the treatment of a purely domestic scenario to a cross-border one. To prevent double taxation, the participating Member States may even go beyond resident treatment. Enhanced cooperation can, of course, only enhance trade through such an extension where the fundamental freedoms do not already demand it, for example because the discrimination is justified by a public interest concern, or (as in the case of double taxation) because the trade obstacle does not fall within the scope of the fundamental freedoms. Since the constitutional framework of enhanced cooperation in principle allows a comparison between cross-group and intra-group economic activities, one may ask what legitimises a more beneficial treatment of intra-group economic activities. As in the case of preferential trade agreements under WTO law, a restriction of the group benefit to intra-group transactions is based on reciprocity concerns. The Member States inside enhanced cooperation are willing to change their policy concerning cross-border economic activities because the other group members grant an equal benefit. The reciprocal bond between participating Member States establishes deeper integration which no longer allows a comparison between intra-group and cross-group economic transactions, and thus restricting the group benefit to intra-group transactions does not contradict the fundamental freedoms.

The Member States could also use enhanced cooperation to address the CJEU case law on the obligations imposed upon them by the fundamental freedoms. The Member States' obligations under the European treaties may not comply with their policy objectives, and thus the Member States may wish to introduce coordinative measures to share the burden in a way which better suits their tax systems. Coordinating enhanced cooperation law follows an intrinsic logic by linking advantages and disadvantages, but without touching on the values or principles underlying the national laws. In cross-group situations, the granting of a benefit, which—within the coordinating system—compensates a disadvantage, may be demanded based on the fundamental freedoms. Such a claim can be rejected because the coordinative system establishes deeper integration between the participating Member States which no longer allows a comparison between intra-group and cross-group economic activities. On the other hand, the cross-group situation must not be subject to the coordination disadvantage because it would not be neutralised by the non-participating Member States. Accordingly, the fundamental freedoms protect the cross-group economic transactions from a treatment which is worse than the one applied before cooperative enhanced cooperation has been introduced.

Part II: STATE AID LAW

The rules on state aid form the second cornerstone in the European treaties protecting the European internal market through the elimination of distortions of production and location decisions between the Member States.[636] The prohibition on providing selective state benefits to undertakings applies at a stage when the national markets are already opened up and when foreign and domestic market players are competing against each other, which sets the provision on state aid and the market freedoms in a very close context.[637]

Importantly, state aid does not always distort competition harming consumers and companies within the European internal market. In the case of a genuine market failure, state aid may be necessary and justified to limit distortions and negative effects on competition. In economic terms, the market fails when prices are not equal to social costs or benefits.[638] In the case of negative externalities, social costs exceed the prices, such as in the case of pollution, and the prices fall below social benefits in the case of positive externalities, like in the case of research and development.[639] The State has to interfere in cases of positive as well as of negative externalities to stop undertakings from increasing their profits at the expense of society, and to encourage undertakings to invest in certain activities which are more valuable for the society at large than for the single firm.[640]

[636] Leigh Hancher, 'EU State Aid Law—Déja Vu All Over Again?' in Leigh Hancher, Tom Ottervanger, and Pieter J Slot (eds), *EU State Aids* (5th edn, Thomson Reuters 2016) 9.

[637] In some way their relationship is even too close, making it hard to define the limits of their scope and whether they should be applied simultaneously or exclusively: Michael Lang, 'Seminar J: Steuerrecht, Grundfreiheiten und Beihilfeverbot' (2010) Internationales Steuerrecht 570, 574 et seq; Frank Engelen, 'State Aid and Restrictions on Free Movement: Two Sides of the Same Coin?' (2012) 52 European taxation 204; Claire Micheau, 'Fundamental Freedoms and State Aid Rules under EU Law: The Example of Taxation' (2012) 52 European Taxation 210; Juliane Kokott, 'Steuerrecht und unionsrechtlicher Beihilfebegriff' in Michael Lang (ed), *Europäisches Steuerrecht*, vol 42 (2018) 550 et seq; Pierpaolo Rossi-Maccanico, 'Community Review of Direct Business Tax Measures: Selectivity, Discrimination and Restrictions' (2009) 8 European State Aid Law Quarterly 489; Mélanie Staes, 'The Combined Application of the Fundamental Freedoms and the EU State Aid Rules: In Search of a Way Out of the Maze' (2014) 42 Intertax 106; Peter J Wattel, 'Interaction of State Aid, Free Movement, Policy Competition and Abuse Control in Direct Tax Matters' (2013) 5 World Tax Journal 128; Raymond Luja, '(Re)Shaping Fiscal State Aid: Selected Recent Cases and Their Impact' (2012) 40 Intertax 120, 124 et seq; Rita Szudoczky, 'Convergence of the Analysis of National Tax Measures under the EU State Aid Rules and the Fundamental Freedoms' (2016) 15 European State Aid Law Quarterly 357, 363 et seq. Andreas Bartosch, 'Fiscal Aid: Recent Trends and Relationship to Fundamental Freedoms' in Werner Haslehner, Georg Kofler, and Alexander Rust (eds), *EU Tax Law and Policy in the 21st Century* (Kluwer Law International 2017).

[638] Hal R Varian, *Intermediate Microeconomics: A Modern Approach* (9th edn, 2014) 664 et seq; Bernard Salanie, *Microeconomics of Market Failures* (MIT Press 2000).

[639] Varian (n 638) 664 et seq.

[640] The generation of new knowledge generates positive externalities. It may not always be possible to protect the new knowledge, which leads to an underproduction of such knowledge. See for more details Phedon Nicolaides, 'The Economics of Subsidies for R&D: The Intrinsic Difficulty of Determining Optimum Subsidies and Implications for Reform of EU State Aid Rules on R & D' (2013) Bruges European Economic Research Papers 19, 7.

Despite market failure, the granting of aid distorts competition between Member States because the undertakings are released from costs which they would normally have to bear.[641] The European treaties only prohibit the granting of aid which affects trade between Member States. The CJEU has a broad understanding of the element affecting the European internal market since according to the case law any domestic aid may strengthen the position of the beneficiary and competition may be distorted.[642] In that vein, the European Commission is not required to provide any proof that there are competing undertakings.[643]

The primary EU provisions on enhanced cooperation explicitly stress that any enhanced cooperation shall not in any way harm the European internal market. Since the granting of aid outside market failure may be one way of doing so, there is a need to analyse whether and, if so, to what extent the rules on state aid have to be considered when using the enhanced cooperation procedure.

Art 107 of the TFEU states that 'any aid granted by a Member State or through State resources in any form whatsoever which distorts or threatens to distort competition by favouring certain undertakings or the production of certain goods shall, in so far as it affects trade between the Member States, be incompatible with the internal market'. The provision sets out four conditions which all have to be fulfilled to constitute a benefit as prohibited aid.[644] First, intervention by the Member State or through Member State's resources is required; secondly, the intervention must be liable to affect trade between Member States; thirdly, the measure must confer an advantage on the recipient; and fourthly, it must distort or threaten to distort competition between Member States.[645] Art 107 of the TFEU makes it quite clear that competition on the European internal market shall not be distorted by 'favouring certain undertakings or the production of certain goods'.[646]

From the outset, it is far from obvious that the rules on state aid also apply in the field of tax law because taxation is the very opposite of a financial benefit. However,

[641] Marta Villar Ezcurra, 'State Aids and Energy Taxes: Towards a Coherent Reference Framework' (2013) 41 Intertax 340, 343.

[642] Leigh Hancher, 'The General Framework' in Leigh Hancher, Tom Ottervanger, and Pieter J Slot (eds), *EU State Aids* (5th edn, Thomson Reuters 2016) paras 3–149. CJEU, 19 September 2000, C-156/98, *Germany v Commission*, ECLI:EU:C:2000:467, para 30; CJEU, 3 March, C-172/03, *Heiser*, ECLI:EU:C:2005:130, para 55; CJEU, 25 July 2018, C-128/16 P, *Commission v Spain*, ECLI:EU:C:2018:591, para 84.

[643] Kelyn Bacon, 'State Aids and General Measures' (1997) 17 Yearbook of European Law 269, para 2.146.

[644] CJE, 21 March 1990, C-142/87, *Belgium v Commission*, ECLI:EU:C:1990:123, para 25; CJEU, 14 September 1994, C-278/92, C-379/92, and C-380/92, *Spain v Commission*, ECLI:EU:C:1994:325, para 20; CJEU, 16 May 2002, *French Republic v Commission*, ECLI:EU:C:2002:294, para 68; CJEU, 24 July 2003, C-280/00, *Altmark Trans GmbH Regierungspräsidium Magdeburg*, ECLI:EU:C:2003:415, para 74.

[645] CJEU, 30 March 2006, C-451/03, *Servizi Ausiliari Dottori Commercialisti*, ECLI:EU:C:2006:208, para 56; CJEU, 1 July 2008, C-341/06 P and C-342/06 P, *Chronopost and La Poste*, ECLI:EU:C:2008:375, para 122.

[646] European Commission, 'Guidelines for the Examination of State Aid to the Fishery and Aquaculture Sector' (2015) C 217/1 1.

from quite early on[647] the CJEU has ruled that Member States can provide state aid through their national tax laws. In this regard, the aid is not provided by a transfer of public resources to the undertaking. Rather, the undertaking is not required to transfer private funds to the Member State's coffer in the form of tax payments.[648] Accordingly, a selective reduction of the tax burden (eg through reducing the tax base, lowering the tax rate, or providing exemptions) can be qualified as state aid, and thus such national tax rules may run foul of Art 107 of the TFEU.[649]

The first condition of Art 107 of the TFEU—the Member State's intervention—is easily fulfilled if purely national laws are at stake. Tax measures of one Member State are always imputable to this Member State. However, in the field of enhanced cooperation, the situation is not so clear: is the measure imputable to each of the Member States, to the group of Member States, or to the European Union? The requirement of individual actions of Member States reflects the bias that single-handed state actions are very likely to work in favour of the domestic production, market players, and products.

Both the requirement of conferring an advantage on the recipient (advantage test) and the requirement that only some undertakings benefit from the measure (selectivity test) ask for some form of benchmarking. Only if the treatment of some undertakings is compared with the common or average tax treatment it is possible to ascertain the advantage of the treatment,[650] and only if the availability of the beneficial treatment is defined can the selective character of the measure be determined. The special treatment of some undertakings would be quite easy to assess if there were a standard tax treatment within the European Union. Any deviation from the standard in favour of certain taxpayers would then account for an advantage granted selectively. However, in the European Union, Member States are free to design their national tax system. They can decide which economic events should be taxed, what form the tax base should take, and which tax rates they wish to apply. Accordingly, the reference system—the standard—needs to be determined by the tax legislation of the relevant Member State.[651] In the field of enhanced cooperation

[647] In recent times, the CJEU has ruled substantively on the interplay between state aid law and national taxation: Pasquale Pistone, 'The Growing Importance of the Prohibition of State Aids in Tax Matters' (2012) 40 Intertax 84.

[648] Wolfgang Schön, 'Tax Legislation and the Notion of Fiscal Aid: A Review of 5 Years of European Jurisprudence' in Isabelle Richelle, Wolfgang Schön, and Edoardo Traversa (eds), *State Aid Law and Business Taxation*, vol 6 (Springer 2016) 4.

[649] If the selective tax incentive increases the Member State's budget (because taxpayers invest more in that Member State), the tax measure still causes a loss of revenue. Accordingly, positive impacts on the Member State's budget are not taken into account, Joris Luts, 'Compatibility of IP Box Regimes with EU State Aid Rules and Code of Conduct' (2014) 23 EC Tax Review 258, 260.

[650] Recent CJEU case law shows that the selectivity and the advantage requirement 'are not only closely connected but even merge with each other and my eventually be arbitrarily exchanged' Michael Lang, 'State Aid and Taxation: Recent Trends in the Case Law of the ECJ' (2012) 11 European State Aid Law Quarterly 411, 418.

[651] Roland Ismer and Sophia Piotrowski, 'The Selectivity of Tax Measures: A Tale of Two Consistencies' (2015) 43 Intertax 559, 561; Šime Jozipović, *Die Anwendung des EU-Beihilferechts auf*

it may be even harder to determine the reference system: is it the system implemented through the enhanced cooperation procedure, or is it the group-system plus the corresponding national tax rules, or is it only the national laws which are capable of building the standard from which some rules may deviate?

The requirement of a distortion of competition and the interference with the trade between the Member States[652] has undeniable ties to the selectivity and advantage test.[653] To be frank, the requirements of a distortion of competition and an interference with intra-EU trade under Art 107 of the TFEU are fundamentally linked, allowing a joint examination.[654] The European Commission is not required to undergo a market analysis to show that the measure can affect competition or intra-EU trade.[655] It is sufficient for the Commission to establish a link between the measure and the effect on competition and trade.[656] To affect intra-EU trade, it is not necessary that the undertaking receiving the benefit engages in exporting business.[657] The trade between the Member States may also be affected if the beneficiary's market position has become stronger through the aid rendering the import of services and products more difficult.[658]

das internationale Steuerrecht: die wettbewerbs- und handelsrechtlichen Einflüsse auf die staatliche Fiskalsystemgestaltung (Springer 2018) 153.

652 The condition concerning the effect on trade between the Member States intends to define the scope of the European measure and ensures that European state aid law does not conflict with any domestic aid which is exclusively limited to the territory of one Member States and thus is not 'capable of affecting, even indirectly, freedom of intra-Community [intra-EU] trade in a way which could hinder the realization of the single market', Opinion of Advocate General Tesauro, 19 September 1989, C-142/87, *Belgium v Commission*, ECLI:EU:C:1989:335, para 28.

653 Accordingly, the CJEU does not pay much attention to the requirement of distortions of competition in cases where the national tax law provides a selective advantage: Luts (n 649) 268.

654 CJEU, 14 January 2015, C-518/13, *Eventech*, ECLI:EU:C:2015:9, para 65; CJEU, 8 May 2013, C-197/11 and C-203/11, *Libert at al.*, ECLI:EU:C:2013:288, para 76; CJEU, 15 December 2005, C-148/04, *Unicredito Italiano*, ECLI:EU:C:2005:774, para 54; CJEU, 10 January 2006, C-222/04, *Cassa di Risparmio di Firenze et al*, ECLI:EU:C:2006:8, para 140. See for more references to the case law Jacques Derenne and others, 'Recent Developments in State Aid Law' (2014) 5 Journal of European Competition Law & Practice 53, 61.

655 '[I]n certain cases the very circumstances in which the aid is granted are sufficient to show that the aid is capable of affecting trade between the Member States of distorting or threatening to distort competition', CJEU, 13 March 1985, 296/82 and 318/82, *the Netherlands v Commission*, ECLI:EU:C:1985, para 24, see also European Commission, 'Commission Notice on the Notion of State Aid as Referred to in Article 107(1) of the Treaty on the Functioning of the European Union' (2016) C 262/1 para 198. However, the effects on intra-EU trade must not only be hypothetical of presumed, CJEU, 24 July 2003, C-280/00, *Altmark Trans*, ECLI:EU:C:2003:415, para 79.

656 Hancher (n 642) 89.

657 Even if the aid is not designed to strengthen export, the national measure may constitute prohibited aid: Bernadette Zelger, 'The Effect on Trade Criterion in European Union State Aid Law: A Critical Approach' (2018) 17 European State Aid Law Quarterly 28, 30.

658 CJEU, 14 January 2015, C-518/13, *Eventech*, ECLI:EU:C:2015:9, para 66; CJEU, 8 May 2013, C-197/11 and C-203/11, *Libert at al.*, ECLI:EU:C:2013:288, para 77; CJEU, 24 July 2003, C-280/00, *Altmark Trans*, ECLI:EU:C:2003:415, para 78. Cees Dekker, 'The Effect on Trade between the Member States' Criterion: Is It the Right Criterion by Which the Commission's Workload Can Be Managed' (2017) 16 European State Aid Law Quarterly 154.

Before addressing the question of how the advantage test (see subsection D) and the selectivity test (see subsection E) work, and how they should be applied in the case of enhanced cooperation, and when aid affects intra-EU trade, it is necessary to determine whether Art 107 of the TFEU applies to enhanced cooperation law in the first place. To answer this question, the following subsections will reveal how state aid law is applied to secondary EU law (see subsection A). Based on these findings, it will be elaborated whether the same approach should be applied to secondary EU law enacted under the enhanced cooperation procedure (see subsection C). The fact that the law of the enhanced cooperation only binds the participating Member States may have a significant impact on this decision.

A. State Aid: An Aid Granted by One Single Member State

Art 107 of the TFEU explicitly requires a state origin when it refers to aid granted by a Member State or through state resources. The two alternatives demonstrate that no distinction is to be drawn between 'cases where the aid is granted directly by the State and those where it is granted by public or private bodies which the State establishes or designates with a view to administering the aid'.[659] Thus, the provision tries to protect the prohibition on state aid to be circumvented by the Member States through the use of entities granting aid to undertakings from state resources.

Despite the need to finance the aid through state funds, the measure has to be imputable to the Member State. According to the European Commission's opinion, aid measures are not imputable to a Member State 'if the Member State is under an obligation to implement it under Union law without any discretion'.[660] If the secondary EU law does not give the Member States any freedom on how to transpose certain measures into national law,[661] any aid stemming from these measures has been imputable to the European Union. The Commission's view is grounded on the CJEU ruling in *Puffer*,[662] in which the Court had to decide whether the granting of the right to deduct input VAT only to taxable persons providing taxed output supplies can be found to be an aid in the meaning of Art 107 of the TFEU. The CJEU referred to the VAT Directive and its exhaustive provisions on who is entitled to an input VAT credit. Since the Member States are bound to transpose these provisions

[659] CJEU, 16 May 2002, C-482/99, *France v Commission*, ECLI:EU:C:2002:294, para 23 with further references.

[660] European Commission, 'Commission Notice on the Notion of State Aid as Referred to in Article 107(1) of the Treaty on the Functioning of the European Union' (n 655) para 44.

[661] On the question of how to determine whether the beneficial treatment is attributable to the Member States or the European Union see Joachim Englisch, 'State Aid and Indirect Taxation' in Alexander Rust and Claire Micheau (eds), *State Aid and Tax Law* (Kluwer Law International 2013) 79 et seq.

[662] CJEU, 23 April 2009, C-460/07, *Puffer*, ECLI:EU:C:2009:254.

into their national laws without much leeway, 'the condition of intervention by the State is not met', meaning that the rules on state aid do not apply.[663]

With respect to the question of attribution, similarities can be found in the application of the fundamental freedoms. The Court found that a discriminatory national rule cannot be attributed to the Member State if the national law simply transposes an exemption of the VAT Directive, which offers a VAT exemption for small undertakings established within the Member State's territory.[664] Since the Directive exactingly delineates the scope of the exemption—only undertakings established within the territory of the Member State—the Member States have no discretion on which taxable persons are allowed to benefit from providing exempt supplies. The discriminatory design of the provision—restricting the exemption to resident taxpayers—has to be 'attributed' to the European legislature and not the Member States and thus it would be the secondary EU law which infringes the fundamental freedoms and not national provisions.

In the field of state aid, the Court has, however, refused to test secondary EU law against the primary law provisions on state aid; a balancing act of contradicting interests is only required at the level of the European legislature.[665] At first glance, it may seem arbitrary to apply the rules on state aid and the fundamental freedoms to secondary EU law (regardless of the explicit wording of the provisions) differently because both aim to ensure the functioning of the European internal market. However, when examining the systemic and functions of the state aid rules more closely, it becomes apparent why the rules are restricted to Member States' interventions. The rules on state aid relate to the competition between undertakings, which is influenced by the competition between Member States for production and location decisions of these very undertakings.[666] The competitive advantage is, however, removed as soon as all Member States grant the same aid to the same undertakings in their territory. Under such circumstances, the aid has no impact on the competition for investment between Member States because the undertaking would receive the aid in all of the Member States. Of course, it may in theory be possible that secondary EU law restricts the granting of certain benefits to some Member States, which could fuel the competition between Member States. However, since the decision to allow some Member States to grant aid through beneficial taxation is backed by the consent of all Member States,[667] the aid may compensate for some structural weaknesses inherent in the Member States and can be seen as a justified act of European solidarity.[668]

663 ibid para 70; see also CJEU, 5 April 2006, T-351/02, *Deutsche Bahn*, ECLI:EU:C:2006:104, para 102.

664 CJEU, 26 October 2010, C-97/09, *Schmelz*, ECLI:EU:C:2010:632, para 54.

665 CJEU, 21 May 1987, 249/85, *Albako Margarinefabrik Maria von der Linde*, ECLI:EU:C:1987:245, para 16.

666 Hancher (n 636) 9.

667 Ruth Mason, 'A Political-Process Defense of Deutsche Bahn Deference' (2018) Virginia Law and Economics Research Paper, 2.

668 The reduced tax rate for ouzo in the Directive on the harmonization of the structures of exercise duties on alcohol and alcoholic beverages (OJ, 31 October 1992, L 316,21) would be a good example.

European State aid may not influence competition between Member States because it allows all of them to grant the same aid to the same undertakings. However, secondary EU law may have an impact on the competition between undertakings if the law defines the scope of the recipient in a way which does not precisely reflect the competitive context, and thus would carve out some undertakings from the scope of the aid which are effectively competing with those undertakings receiving the aid. Such Union aid must be assessed in light of the general equality principle of the Charter of the Fundamental Rights of the European Union.[669] It is not the aid per se which distorts the competition. Rather, drawing the line between those entitled to aid and those not eligible for the benefit without a proper understanding of the competitive context has a distorting effect.

B. State Aid: An Aid Granted by a Group of Member States

Again, the law enacted under the enhanced cooperation procedure raises the question of whether it needs to be treated as ordinary secondary EU law, leading to the non-application of state aid rules, or whether the law should be imputable to each Member State allowing an unrestrained application of Art 107 of the TFEU. The second approach would honour the fact that not all Member States are bound by the law, and thus the law does not achieve a European level playing field. It would, however, ignore the fact that it is not an act of a single Member State; the law is the result of a compromise between at least nine Member States, which makes it unlikely or virtually impossible that the measures are of a protectionist nature. Despite the lack of protectionist ambitions, competition between Member States—especially those within the group and those outside the group—still exists because a level playing field only exists within the group and not on a Europe-wide basis. Considering that enhanced cooperation law can distort the competition on the European internal market, it becomes quite obvious that the law enacted under the enhanced cooperation procedure needs to be tested against state aid law.

Aside from the impact enhanced cooperation laws have on the internal market level playing field, the competence framework of the European treaties for economic policy-making through approval of aid may demand the application of state aid law to enhanced cooperation laws. The European treaties allocate the competence for economic policy-making through the permission of aid between the European Commission and the Council, and the enhanced cooperation procedure

The directive grants Greece the possibility to apply a reduced tax rate on 'aniseed flavoured spirit drinks'. A reduced tax rate has a serious impact on the competition between the Member States; however, the secondary EU law piece balances the interests of all Member States and the participation of the European Commission safeguards that the effects are minor and justifiable.

[669] See Art 20 of the Charter (18 December 2000, OJ, C 364/3).

must not undermine this framework. Despite the fact that both the Commission and the Council influence state aid law policy, the Commission has the lead as the Commission in principle holds the power to approve Member State aid.[670] We will come back to the competence framework for approving state aid in a later subsection and will question whether compliance with the procedural framework of enhanced cooperation may implicitly incorporate an approval for potential state aid through enhanced cooperation laws.[671]

C. Granting of Selective Benefits through Enhanced Cooperation Law: Baseline of Art 107 of the TFEU

Despite the fact that the law enacted under the enhanced cooperation procedure has a secondary EU law nature, it is still capable of distorting the competition between undertakings within the European internal market. The impact that enhanced cooperation law may have on competition between undertakings within the internal market requires severe testing of the law against Art 107 of the TFEU.

Under the traditional approach, the CJEU discovered the tax benefits by comparing the actual tax burden and the charges an undertaking would normally face.[672] In other words, the Court first identified 'normal' taxation[673] , and every beneficial deviation from the reference system was found to be a tax advantage. Accordingly, the CJEU has used a rule-exception rationale to determine whether or not a national tax rule grants a relevant benefit. It goes without saying that it is far from easy to determine normal taxation under the national law of a Member State and that an exception may not be a benefit but may instead reflect a Member State's decision on what to tax.[674]

The exception to the general rule approach leads to a very wide definition of the benefit. On a stand-alone basis, the advantage test would bring (too) many state measures into the net of Art 107 of the TFEU.[675] Accordingly, the selectivity test should narrow the scope of prohibited state aid to an amount which is consistent with the spirit and purpose of Art 107 of the TFEU. The CJEU has developed the notion of 'general measures'[676] to refute state aid suspicion by distinguishing tax

[670] Art 108 of the TFEU.
[671] See this chapter Part II, subsection H.
[672] CJEU, 23 February 1961, 30–59, *De Gezamenlijke Steenkolenmijnen in Limburg v High Authority of the European Coal and Steel Community*, ECLI:EU:C:1961:2, S. 19.
[673] CJEU, 6 September 2006, C-88/03, *Portuguese Republic v Commission*, ECLI:EU:C:2006:511, para 56.
[674] CJEU, 28 June 2018, C-203/16 P, *Dirk Anders*, ECLI:EU:C:2018:505, para 92 et seq.
[675] Edouard Fort, 'EU State Aid and Tax: An Evolutionary Approach' (2017) 57 European Taxation 14, 375 arguing that the notion of an advantage must be understood in a very wide manner to equal the term subsidy.
[676] See for a general analysis Bacon (n 643).

incentives which are available to all economic operators from benefits which are restricted to certain enterprises or certain sectors.[677] Only the latter may constitute prohibited state aid. The general measure test allows one to single out tax incentives from the state aid assessment if they follow an economic or socio-political intention.[678]

In other cases, the Court has used a more case-by-case approach and analysed the distinguishing criteria. If those differentiating factors were not triggered by the nature or general scheme of the system, the measure was considered selective.[679] In this line of case law, general distinctive factors such as the percentage of female employees[680] had already been considered sufficient to identify a selective national measure.[681] In defining whether or not national measures are selective, the Court does not consider their causes or objectives; only their effects matter.[682]

The CJEU does not hold on to a clear distinction between the advantage test on the one hand and the selectivity test on the other hand as soon as the Court starts to test the national law against Art 107 of the TFEU and stops its general remarks on what is prohibited under state aid law. A three-step approach defines whether a particular tax measure grants selective aid. The test starts by identifying the 'reference system'. Setting the reference system also implies a determination of which undertakings are in a similar legal and factual position in the light of the objects of the reference system. Second, it needs to be identified whether the tax measure at hand derogates from the reference system and allows for a different (tax) treatment.[683] If both requirements are met, the national measure is prima facie selective.[684] The third step allows one to justify an a priori selective measure on the grounds of the 'nature or general scheme' of the reference system.[685]

[677] CJEU, 15 November 2011, C-106/09 P and C-107/09 P, *Gibraltar*, ECLI:EU:C:2011:732, para 73; CJEU, 29 March 2012, C-417/10, *3M Italia*, ECLI:EU:C:2012:184, para 39; CJEU, 18 July 2013, C-6/12, *P Oy*, ECLI:EU:C:2013:525, para 18; CJEU, 9 October 2014, C-522/13, *Navantia*, ECLI:EU:C:2014:2262, para 23; CJEU, 21 December 2016, C-20/15 P and C-21/15 P, *World Duty Free*, ECLI:EU:2016:981, para 56; CJEU, 19 December 2018, C-374/17, *A-Brauerei*, ECLI:EU:C:2018:1024, para 23.

[678] Wolfgang Schön, 'Selektivität schlägt Souveränität' (2019) 183 Zeitschrift für das gesamte Handelsrecht und Wirtschaftsrecht 393 arguing that the general measure test should be retained.

[679] CJEU, 2 July 1974, 173–73, *Italian Republic v Commission*, ECLI:EU:C:1974:71, para 33; CJEU, 26 September 2002, C-351/98, *Kingdom of Spain v Commission*, ECLI:EU:C:2002:530, para 42; Michael Lang, *Die Auswirkungen des gemeinschaftsrechtlichen Beihilferechts auf das Steuerrecht: Gutachten* (2009) 24.

[680] CJEU, 14 July 1983, 203/82, *Commission v Italian Republic*, ECLI:EU:C:1983:218.

[681] Chiara Balbinot, *Beihilfeverbot und Rechtsformneutralität: Zugleich ein Beitrag zur Auslegung des Beihilfeverbots im Steuerrecht* (Dr Otto Schmidt Verlag 2018) 21–22; Franz Philipp Sutter, *Das EG-Beihilfenverbot und sein Durchführungsverbot in Steuersachen* (Linde Verlag 2005) 89 et seq.

[682] CJEU, 29 February 1996, C-56/93, *Kingdom of Belgium v Commission*, ECLI:EU:C:1996:64, para 79; CJEU, 26 September 1996, C-241/94, *French Republic v Commission*, ECLI:EU:C:1996:353, para 20; CJEU, 13 February 2003, C-409/00, *Kingdom of Spain*, ECLI:EU:C:2003:92, para 46.

[683] CJEU, 8 September 2011, C-78/08, 79/08 and 80/08, *Paint Graphos Soc.*, ECLI:EU:2011:550, para 45; CJEU, 8 December 2011, C-81/10 P, *France Télécom SA*, ECLI:EU:C:2011:811, para 16.

[684] CJEU, 8 November 2001, C-143/99, *Adria-Wien Pipeline*, ECLI:EU:C:2001:598, para 41.

[685] CJEU, 21 June 2012, C-452/10 P, BNP Paribas, ECLI:EU:C:2012:366, para 101; CJEU, 6 September 2006, C-88/03, *Portuguese Republic v Commission*, ECLI:EU:C:2006:511, para 52; CJEU, 22 December 2008, C-487/06 P, *British Aggregates Association*, ECLI:EU:2008:757, para 83; CJEU, 15 November 2011, C-106/09 P and C-107/09 P, *Gibraltar*, ECLI:EU:C:2011:732, para 145.

Under the more recent approach, the CJEU deviates from the traditional approach insofar as the beneficial treatment and its selectivity are no longer determined by a rule-exception rationale but are summarised in a kind of non-discrimination examination.[686] More precisely the Court asks whether a state measure favours '"certain undertakings or the production of certain goods" in comparison with others which, in the light of the objective pursued by the system in question, are in a comparable legal and factual situation'.[687] Under this approach, the aim and purpose of the law is crucial in determining comparability but is no longer needed to define 'normal taxation'. However, under a comparison approach, the measure may also be 'justified by the nature or general scheme of the system of which it is part'.[688]

The comparison approach contrasts privileged with non-privileged undertakings in light of the aim and purpose of the national measure, and thus the objective of the national measure must be identified in a first step. Then, it must be established whether the national measure treats comparable undertakings in an unequal manner which 'boils down to a non-discrimination test'.[689] One the one hand, the new approach is highly appreciated in the literature because the comparison test overcomes the weakness of the traditional approach: the finding of normal taxation.[690] On the other hand, the new approach is found to be too broad and fails to sufficiently emphasise *certain* undertakings (accordingly, a very specific and isolated group of undertakings),[691] which threatens Member State sovereignty and allows the European Commission to fight any national low-tax regime attracting foreign investment.[692]

686 CJEU, 9 December 1997, C-353/95 P, *Tiercé Ladbroke SA v Commission*, ECLI:EU:C:1997:596, para 33 et seq; CJEU, 8 November 2001, C-143/99, *Adria-Wien Pipeline and Wietersdorfer & Peggauer Zementwerke*, ECLI:EU:C:2001:598, para 41; CJEU, 29 April 2004, C-308/01, *GIL Insurance*, ECLI:EU:C:2004:252, para 68; CJEU, 3 March 2005, C-172/03, Heiser, ECLI:EU:C:2005:130, para 40; CJEU, 6 September 2006, C-88/03, *Portuguese Republic v Commission*, ECLI:EU:C:2006:511, para 54; Axel Cordewener, 'Asymmetrical Tax Burdens and EU State Aid Control' (2012) 21 EC Tax Review 288.

687 ibid.

688 CJEU, 8 November 2001, C-143/99, *Adria-Wien Pipeline and Wietersdorfer & Peggauer Zementwerke*, ECLI:EU:C:2001:598, para 42; CJEU, 3 March 2005, C-172/03, *Heiser*, ECLI:EU:C:2005:130, para 43.

689 Cordewener, 'Asymmetrical Tax Burdens' (n 686) 288.

690 Michael Lang, 'State Aid and Taxation: Selectivity and Comparability Analysis' in Isabelle Richelle, Wolfgang Schön, and Edoardo Traversa (eds), *State Aid Law and Business Taxation* (Springer 2016); Werner Haslehner, 'Double Taxation Relief, Transfer Pricing Adjustments and State Aid Law' in Isabelle Richelle, Wolfgang Schön, and Edoardo Traversa (eds), *State Aid Law and Business Taxation* (Springer 2016) 139 emphasising that the comparison approach is also tied to the reference system because the aim and purpose of the reference system determines comparability.

691 Opinion of Advocate General Saugmandsgaard Øe, 19 September 2018, C-374/17, *A-Brauerei*, ECLI:EU:C:2018:741, para 68; Rita Szudoczky and Jan van de Streek, 'Revisiting the Dutch Interest Box under the EU State Aid Rules and the Code of Conduct: When a "Disparity" Is Selective and Harmful' (2010) 38 Intertax 260, 264.

692 Cees Peters, 'Tax Policy Convergence and EU Fiscal State Aid Control: In Search of Rationality' (2019) 28 EC Tax Review 6 analysing the nature of EU fiscal state aid control and the Commission's current application. Emily Forrester, 'Is the State Aid Regime a Suitable Instrument to Be Used in the Fight Against Harmful Tax Competition?' (2018) 27 EC Tax Review 19, 29 et seq.

To date, the CJEU has not abandoned the traditional approach. An analysis of which rules form the reference system can also be found in recent case law.[693] The European Commission also maintains a strict separation between the 'benefit' and the 'selectivity' requirement in its guidelines on Art 107 of the TFEU.[694]

It is suggested that a strict distinction between the advantage test and the selectivity test is the right path to take. Such a division is required both by the wording of Art 107 of the TFEU and by their different aim and purpose. Art 107 of the TFEU explicitly refers to the aid granted by a Member State or through state resources (being the benefit requirement) and requires that the aid is only granted to certain undertakings or certain products (being the selectivity requirement). Since EU law does not provide any standards on how to tax and what to tax, the question of whether a tax benefit exists because of non-taxation or low taxation can, by its very nature, only be determined with reference to the national tax framework. Without a benchmark, it is virtually impossible to determine whether the treatment of a specific economic event is beneficial or not. However, the granting of a tax benefit does not say anything about whether the benefit favours certain undertakings or certain sectors. This must be determined by the selectivity requirement. And neither the benefit nor the selectivity requirement say anything on the competitive advantages the national tax rule may offer some undertakings. The competitive advantage plays a role when assessing whether or not a selective advantage distorts intra-EU trade.[695]

Having said this, the non-discriminatory approach which brings together the advantage test and the selectivity test with the effects of the selective benefit on trade in state aid matters would not sufficiently value the requirement set by Art 107 of the TFEU, according to which the benefit has to be granted through the *use* of state resources. In the case of direct subsidies, the use of state resources becomes most evident because money is directly transferred from the State's pockets to certain undertakings. In the field of taxation, an equal transfer of state resources has to take place which does not require a positive transfer, but (at least) the foregoing of state revenue.[696] If the existence of state aid could only be determined by a discriminatory tax treatment, the requirement of a financial loss or shortfall would not, in all cases, be fulfilled.[697]

From this it follows that the advantage test and the selectivity test should remain separate. The starting point of the subsequent subsection is an analysis of the advantage test (see subsection D) which requires one to define the reference system.

[693] CJEU, 14 December 2018, C-374/17, *A-Brauerei*, ECLI:EU:C:2018:1024, para 20, however, the Court turns to a non-discrimination approach at para 33.

[694] European Commission, 'Commission Notice on the Notion of State Aid as Referred to in Article 107(1) of the Treaty on the Functioning of the European Union' (n 655).

[695] Schön, 'Tax Legislation and the Notion of Fiscal Aid' (n 648) 17.

[696] European Commission, 'Commission Notice on the Notion of State Aid as Referred to in Article 107(1) of the Treaty on the Functioning of the European Union' (n 655) para 51.

[697] Wolfgang Schön, 'State Aid in the Area of Taxation' in Leigh Hancher, Tom Ottervanger, and Pieter J Slot (eds), *EU State Aids* (5th edn, Thomson Reuters 2016) 408–09.

Finding the reference system may become particularly hard when enhanced cooperation law is at stake: is it purely the national laws which define what normal taxation is, or does enhanced cooperation law have an impact on the benchmark? After the benefit test, the selectivity test (see subsection E) will be analysed. When applying the notion of selectivity to enhanced cooperation law, it has to be determined whether the selectivity requirement is automatically satisfied if the ones inside enhanced cooperation are entitled to a benefit whereas the ones outside are not. Both subsections set the benchmark for the application of these tests to national laws at first. Their application to the special field of enhanced cooperation law will then be addressed. The findings of what constitutes a selective benefit in the field of enhanced cooperation law are summarised in the subsequent subsection (see subsection F). To complete the picture, it will be revealed whether special charges on some undertakings imposed by enhanced cooperation law can have equally distorting effects as state aid and thus have to be prohibited under Art 107 of the TFEU (see subsection G). On a procedural level, it will be suggested that the constitutional framework of the enhanced cooperation procedure already includes a form of automatic notification as defined in Art 108 of the TFEU (see subsection H).

D. The Advantage Test

I. The Reference System

1. Basic Principles

Defining the reference system[698] is important in order to determine whether a certain tax measure confers an advantage on the recipient.[699] Since EU law does not provide a standard tax system model, it is up to the Member States to decide on the taxpayer, the tax event, the tax base, and the tax rate. The regulatory technique chosen by the Member State does not reveal what the rule is and what is the exception.[700] Rather, the substance of the tax regime determines 'normal' taxation.[701]

[698] Marek Szydło, 'Differential Tax Burdens of Undertakings And Internal Market Law: The Way Forward after "ANGED"' (2019) 56 Common Market Law Review 1093, 1107 arguing that 'it would be wrong to think that there is always only one correct reference system for a given tax measure, or that an error in determining the system necessarily vitiates the selectivity analysis as a whole'.

[699] From a purely systematic approach, the reference system shall identify whether a benefit is granted. However, the CJEU often uses the reference system to determine whether a Member States grants a selective advantage (CJEU, 28 June 2018, C-203/16 P, *Dirk Anders*, ECLI:EU:C:2018:505, para 76) and thus the reference system is often understood to be part of the selectivity test: Luc de Broe, 'The State Aid Selectivity-Test in Corporate Tax Matters: CJEU Applies Common Sense in Its Judgments on the German 'Sanierungs'-Clause, but Do We Have All Pieces of the Puzzle Now?' (2018) 27 EC Tax Review 285.

[700] Luts (n 649) 267.

[701] CJEU, 15 November 2011, C-106/09 P and C-107/09 P, *Commission v Gibraltar*, ECLI:EU:C:2011:732, para 88 et seq; CJEU, 28 June 2018, C-203/16 P, *Dirk Anders*, ECLI:EU:C:2018:505,

Within the European Union, it is generally accepted that the Member States levy their fiscal taxes[702] in accordance with the ability to pay principle,[703] and thus it is proposed that this broad concept, and not a single statutory tax provision, may function as a reference system.[704] From a systemic point of view, it is necessary to view the bigger picture of the tax burden and not restrict the reference system to the rule from which the one at hand forms an exception.[705] However, Member States are free to organise their tax system without reference to the ability to pay principle. A half-hearted attempt by a Member State to distance its tax system from this core principle will of course not change the reference system.[706] However, this does not mean that it is virtually impossible for a Member State to design its tax system without following the ability to pay principle. Such a system may raise questions of equality and fairness, but as stressed earlier, the European Union, as it stands today, does not have a say in defining the tax base, the tax rate, or the tax events of a Member State.

Even though Member States are free to choose what they want to tax, they are bound by EU law, and more precisely by the general principle of non-discrimination, to implement a tax system which is not per se discriminatory. Requiring a non-discriminatory tax system is different from requiring a tax system which follows the ability to pay principle. A non-discriminatory system does not say anything about what should be taxed or why it should be taxed. It takes the decision of the Member States on what to tax (including the underlying values) as a starting point and asks whether each rule reflects it coherently.[707]

If the reference system contains recourse to the *one* substantive principle of national taxation (eg the ability to pay principle), it becomes easier to deal with special tax regimes for certain branches, such as the insurance or the oil and gas industries. The special regimes could be seen as a self-sufficient and self-coherent system, and thus do not raise any concerns under state aid law. On the other hand, the systems

para 92 et seq; John Temple Lang, 'The Gibraltar State Aid and Taxation Judgment—A Methodical Revolution' (2012) 11 European State Aid Law Quarterly 805, 807.

702 Taxes which merely aim to raise revenue.

703 Frans Vanistendael, 'Ability to Pay in European Community Law' (2014) 23 EC Tax Review 121 argues that there is even a notion of ability to pay in European tax law; Eric CCM Kemmeren, 'The CJEU and the Internal Market Concept in Direct Taxation' in Werner Haslehner, Georg Kofler, and Alexander Rust (eds), *EU Tax Law and Policy in the 21st Century* (Kluwer Law International 2017) 10–11.

704 Schön, 'State Aid' (n 697) 418–19; for an overview of the scope of the advantage: Raymond Luja, 'Do State Aid Rules Still Allow European Union Member States to Claim Fiscal Sovereignty?' (2016) 25 EC Tax Review 312, 313 et seq.

705 CJEU, 28 June 2018, C-209/16 P, *Germany v Commission*, ECLI:EU:C:2018:507, para 97–98; for a different view see Roland Ismer and Alexandra Karch, 'Das Referenzsystem bei der beihilferechtlichen Überprüfung nationaler Steuervergünstigungen' (2014) Internationales Steuerrecht 130, 134.

706 CJEU, 15 November 2011, C-106/09 P and C-107/09 P, *Commission v Gibraltar*, ECLI:EU:C:2011:732; Wolfgang Schön, 'Steuerliche Beihilfen' in Christian Koenig and Ulrich Ehricke (eds), *Aktuelle Fragen des EG-Beihilfenrechts* (Verlag Recht und Wirtschaft 2001) 119–20.

707 Jozipović (n 651) 169.

can be regarded as a deviation from the standard indicator that the Member State chose to tax (eg a tax on the profit of an entity), and thus may run foul of Art 107 of the TFEU, if indeed the systems confer an advantage to certain undertakings.[708]

From this it follows that the reference system is determined by the substance of taxation and what the Member State chose to tax (eg income, wealth, consumption, pollution, or certain economic transactions), without too much weight placed on the small details of the design techniques of the national law.

2. The Reference System: A Domestic or an International System?

It has been stressed above that the reference system asks for the big picture and not a detailed one. But how big does the picture need to be? Should the reference system include rules in response to external systems or standards of international taxation or should it only cover the purely domestic setting? On a bilateral basis, Member States may want to sign tax treaties between each other in order to address the negative effects of double taxation on cross-border economic activities stemming from the application of two uncoordinated national tax regimes. These treaties fragmentarily build bridges between the two national systems by allocating taxing rights between the contracting parties. On a unilateral basis, the Member States may also implement measures to prevent double taxation, to foster international trade and investment, or Member States may perhaps create specific rules for cross-border economic activities in response to the allocation of taxing rights through tax treaties. Prohibitions on foreign loss compensation in the home Member State are often an example of a response to an exclusive taxing right of the Member State where the permanent establishment is sourced.

To define the reference system, are the rules which specifically address cross-border economic activities and may deviate from what is laid down for pure domestic activities, part of the reference system, or should they not influence the reference system at all, or do these rules form a separate reference system?

As is clear from the above, the reference system is determined by the system-building factors both for residence and source taxation. If the national provisions which address cross-border economic activities, such as issues of double taxation, were to form part of the reference system, the principle of one-off taxation would have to be a guiding principle for the whole system.[709] The same must be true for national provisions responding to the allocation of taxing rights. If the national provision prohibiting compensation of foreign losses (because the foreign gains from this source, eg a permanent establishment, are exclusively taxed at source) were part of the reference system, a notion of symmetry between the taxation of

[708] Schön, 'Steuerliche Beihilfen' (n 1371) 119–20.

[709] Pierpaolo Rossi-Maccanico, 'Fiscal State Aids, Tax Base Erosion and Profit Shifting' (2015) 24 EC Tax Review 63, 66 arguing that any tax system is 'consistent with some well-established principles, including the Single-Tax Principle, the Benefit Principle and the Non-Discrimination Principle'.

profits and the deduction of losses would need to be a principle of the national tax system.

Both unilateral and bilateral rules to prevent double taxation build on the national tax system and accept that other States may tax the same income, profits, wealth, or economic transactions leading to a heavy tax burden. The allocation of taxing rights between the contracting parties of a tax treaty, or the unilateral denial to tax on a piecemeal approach does not change the national substance of taxation. Tax treaties do not provide for an intrinsic systemic logic which spills over to the national tax regime and has an impact on its coherence. This does not change the fact that tax treaties themselves follow a coherent logic when it comes to the allocation of taxing rights: source taxation is accepted in some scenarios because purely resident taxation prevails in other cases. Accordingly, the coherence of a tax treaty refers to the well-balanced deal of taxing rights between the contracting parties.[710] In contrast, the coherence of the national tax system refers to the substance of taxation: the fundamental decision of States on the principles of taxation. If the bilateral or unilateral provisions on preventing double taxation have no impact on the fundaments of national taxation, these provisions are not part of the reference system. Their fragmentary character and the fact that they build on the contracting parties' national tax system, and are thereby not self-sufficient, does not allow a classification of these rules as a separate and distinct reference system. Therefore, only the purely national framework for taxation builds the reference system.

From this it follows that the reference system needs to be defined through the substance of national taxation which cannot be changed or amended by tax treaties or unilateral measures addressing forms of double taxation.[711] Thus, tax treaties and unilateral measures have no impact on 'normal' taxation. Rather, they constitute a deviation from the national standard.[712] The same holds true for national provisions denying foreign taxpayers net taxation and requiring them to account on a gross amount instead. The standard is set by net taxation. Gross taxation may be justified but is a deviation from normal taxation in the first place.

3. Recognising the Autonomy of Local and Regional Authorities

In the past, the CJEU was confronted with the question of whether the law of regional or local authorities contradicts Art 107 of the TFEU, simply because the law is not applied to all undertakings in one Member State, and thus provides a benefit

[710] Lang, *Introduction* (n 17) 32 et seq.

[711] For a different view see European Commission, 3 December 2015, Alleged aid to McDonald's, C(2015) 8343 final, para 72.

[712] Luc De Broe, 'Can Tax Treaties Confer State Aid?' (2017) 26 EC Tax Review 228, 228 arguing that the restriction of a Member State's right to tax constitutes a benefit but does not define a reference system for the benefit test.

to certain (regionally definable) undertakings. This line of case law is of particular importance for identifying the reference system of enhanced cooperation laws because the CJEU has in these cases set out its requirements for accepting the regional or local legal system as an independent and distinct reference system. To answer the question of whether state aid law allows qualifying regions as separate and distinct areas of Member State with their own tax rules, the Court has placed special emphasis on the autonomy of the regional or local authority:

> [I]n order that a decision taken in such circumstances can be regarded as having been adopted in the exercise of sufficiently autonomous powers, that decision must, first of all, have been taken by a regional or local authority which has, from a constitutional point of view, a political and administrative status separate from that of the central government. Next, it must have been adopted without the central government being able to directly intervene as regards its content. Finally, the financial consequences of a reduction of the national tax rate for undertakings in the region must not be offset by aid or subsidies from other regions or central government. It follows that political and fiscal independence of central government which is sufficient as regards the application of Community rules on State aid presupposes ... that the infra-State body not only has powers in the territory within its competence to adopt measures reducing the tax rate, regardless of any considerations related to the conduct of the central State, but that in addition it assumes the political and financial consequences of such a measure.[713]

The concept of sufficient autonomy of the region establishes a 'reasonable balance' between the national identity of each Member State and the need to protect the European treaties from being circumvented by reference to the national constitutional order.[714] Despite being a Member of the European Union, any Member State is free to decide on its own constitutional order, which includes the decision to form a centralist or federal state. Accordingly, it is up to each Member State to decide whether it wishes power to only be distributed at a federal level or whether it wishes to delegate some competences to local and regional authorities.[715] On the other hand, the constitutional order of a Member State must not justify the failure to comply with the obligations under European Union law. If a local or regional authority is endowed with autonomous power and has to bear the consequences

[713] CJEU, 6 September 2006, C-88/03, *Portuguese Republic v Commission*, ECLI:EU:C:2006:511, paras 67–68.

[714] Opinion of Advocate General Kokott, 8 May 2008, C-428/06 to C-434/06, *UGT-Rioja*, ECLI:EU:C:2008:262, paras 54–57.

[715] Art 4 subparagraph 2 of the TEU; see also Lang, *Die Auswirkungen des gemeinschaftsrechtlichen Beihilferechts auf das Steuerrecht* (n 1344) 39; Franz Philipp Sutter, 'The Influence of the European State Aid Rules on National Tax Policy' in Krister Andersson, Eva Eberhartinger, and Lars Oxelheim (eds), *National Tax Policy in Europe: To Be or Not To Be?* (Springer 2007) 131 et seq.

of granting preferential tax treatments, in the form of low tax rates or a small tax base, it can be ensured that the granting of the benefit does not have to be attributed to the federal level. Without sufficient autonomy, federal authorities would impose the tax treatment on the local or regional authority and would, if necessary, cross-finance the shortfalls. In such a case, the Member States would be able to hide behind their constitutional order and circumvent their obligations under the European treaties.

Both Advocate General Geelhoed and Advocate General Kokott have defined the requirement of autonomy in their opinions in quite some detail, and these views have influenced the European Commission.[716] According to Advocate General Geelhoed, the authority has to be institutionally, procedurally, and economically autonomous, in order to be truly independent. Institutional autonomy requires an authority which has its own 'constitutional, political and administrative status separate from that of the central government'.[717] An authority is procedurally autonomous if the central government has no power to intervene in the legislative procedure. In that regard, Advocate General Kokott has emphasised that procedural autonomy is not jeopardised if the local or regional authorities merely consult with the central government on their legislative attempts. Their autonomy would, however, be jeopardised if the federal authority were given veto power or the power to assure the competence for the act, or if the law were to require approval by a central authority.[718] The last criterion for an authority to be truly autonomous is economic autonomy. This prism of autonomy requires the authorities to bear the economic consequences of their actions,[719] meaning that any lowering of the tax rates or tax bases needs to impact authorities' budgets. The tax measure must not be cross-financed by the central government. Accordingly, a tax cut must lead to a cut in public spending,[720] or cross-financing of other (newly implemented or newly extended) revenue streams.

If a local or regional authority can claim true autonomy from the central government, it is capable of implementing its own tax rules and has to bear their consequences. In the case of true autonomy, the law of the European Union has to respect the federal structure of the Member State and power of the local and regional authorities. In the field of state aid law, the recognition of local and regional authorities requires that their rules have their own reference system and are not benchmarked against national normal taxation. In a federal system with truly

[716] European Commission, 'Commission Notice on the Notion of State Aid as Referred to in Article 107(1) of the Treaty on the Functioning of the European Union' (n 655) para 142 et seq.

[717] Opinion of Advocate General Geelhoed, 20 October 2005, C-88/03, *Portuguese Republic v Commission*, ECLI:EU:C:2005:618, para 54.

[718] Opinion of Advocate General Kokott, 8 May 2008, C-428/06 to C-434/06, *UGT-Rioja*, ECLI:EU:C:2008:262, paras 85–86.

[719] Opinion of Advocate General Geelhoed, 20 October 2005, C-88/03, *Portuguese Republic v Commission*, ECLI:EU:C:2005:618, para 54.

[720] Lang, *Die Auswirkungen des gemeinschaftsrechtlichen Beihilferechts auf das Steuerrecht* (n 1344) 44.

independent local and regional authorities, two reference systems exist: first, the national reference system determining normal taxation on a national level and, second, the local or regional reference system determining normal taxation on a local or regional level.

4. The Impact of Enhanced Cooperation Law on 'Normal' Taxation

The question of whether or not enhanced cooperation law provides its own reference system to judge the state aid implications of the law depends upon the aim and purpose of the law. It has been stressed that there are different categories of enhanced cooperation. The first category is determined by harmonised values of the participating Member States.[721] The integration progress may be extensive when the members of enhanced cooperation have established common values by thoroughly weighing conflicting (fundamental) rights against each other. These values may, but do not necessarily have to form the ground for an entire legal system. In case of an agreement on a minimum share capital, the participating Member States have established a common value which, however, (only) forms one value of the Member States' national company law system. In the case of the FTT, however, the value(s) established between the Member States form the foundation of an entire system on the taxation of financial transactions.

The second field of potential grouping covers trade-favouring rules in the form of a reciprocal granting of beneficial national or resident treatment which cannot already be forced upon the Member States by the fundamental freedoms.[722] In the light of state aid law, a commitment under enhanced cooperation which, at macro-level, treats intra-group economic transactions more favourably than the comparable purely domestic transaction to establish a resident treatment at micro-level may be of particular relevance. In other words, one should look to enhanced cooperation, which attempts to prevent double taxation (micro level), because in these cases the Member States grant a tax treatment to a cross-border economic activity which is more beneficial than the taxation of a purely domestic activity (macro level). The participating Member State is willing to grant such a treatment because it acknowledges taxation of the same activity in the fellow Member State. The overall tax burden (the tax burden of both Member States: micro level) is equivalent to the tax burden in a purely domestic activity in one Member State.

The third group of common actions under enhanced cooperation is hallmarked by the willingness of Member States to address obligations which are imposed upon them by the European treaties and subsequent CJEU case law.[723] Coordinating enhanced cooperation links benefits and disadvantages and allows the participating

[721] See this chapter Part I, subsection E.VI.
[722] See this chapter Part I, subsection E.VII.
[723] See this chapter Part I, subsection E.VIII.

Member States to comply with their obligations under the European treaties within a more flexible framework.

In the following subsections, the different forms of enhanced cooperation will be analysed with respect to their system-building character. As the reference system is only determined by principles setting the fundaments of the tax system, the law of enhanced cooperation can only have an impact on the reference system if it has some system-building features.

a) A (National) System-adjusting Enhanced Cooperation

Neither of the second and third categories of enhanced cooperation law implement an entirely new tax system from scratch. The law builds on the existing national tax regimes and adjusts them in certain cross-border situations. For example, enhanced cooperation law, which guarantees foreign loss compensation between participating Member States, adjusts the existing national systems by extending resident treatment within enhanced cooperation. If under domestic law, however, the deduction of losses is not allowed (even not in a purely domestic setting), the enhanced cooperation would go beyond resident treatment and would treat intra-group transactions more beneficial than a purely domestic one. In any case, the law of enhanced cooperation builds on the participating Member States' existing tax framework.

An exemption for certain cross-border economic activities from taxation in one Member State due to taxation in a fellow Member State would be another example of a tax treatment going beyond resident treatment. In a purely domestic setting, the income stream or economic transaction would be taxed, but because of the cross-border situation and the tax imposed in another Member State, the Member State refuses to levy a tax.

Another example of system-adjusting enhanced cooperation would be a sharing of the obligations imposed by the European treaties between the Member States. Under cooperative enhanced cooperation one Member State would be allowed to treat cross-border economic activities differently from purely domestic ones because a fellow Member State neutralises any negative implications. The neutralising act may force a more favourable treatment of the intra-group economic activity than for the comparable purely domestic situation. In other words, two Member States may comply with their obligations under the European treaties if they treat intra-group economic activities differently from their purely domestic economic activities. One example would be the levying of a discriminatory withholding tax in one participating Member State and a corresponding full tax credit in the other participating Member State.

From the perspective of the national tax system, there is no difference between enhanced cooperation law providing for coordination between the tax regimes of the participating Member States and a tax treaty. Both build on the existing legal framework of the Member States and both provide for a linking of two or more national tax regimes in the sense that one Member State is required to do something because of the actions of a fellow Member State.

Where the law introduced under the enhanced cooperation procedure adjusts the national tax system of the participating Member States, the national tax system, without any impact of enhanced cooperation law, remains the reference system. The law of enhanced cooperation has no system-building features. Rather, it builds on the systemic grounds of the tax systems of the participating Member States and provides for some adjustments through coordination. These adjustments do not touch on the fundamentals of national law, irrespective of their intrinsic logic, and thus they cannot have an impact on the defining of the reference system. To clarify, the fact that the law of enhanced cooperation has no impact on the basic principles of the national tax system does not mean that the law of enhanced cooperation cannot follow an intrinsic logic. In fact, to the contrary, the coordinating measures of enhanced cooperation may follow an intrinsic rational, but nonetheless the fundamental principles of taxation are determined by the national law of the Member States.

b) A (New) System-building Enhanced Cooperation

Value-based enhanced cooperation may go far beyond the creation of isolated coordination of Member States' tax regimes; it may establish an independent tax regime, for example for the financial sector or environmental taxes. These systems may not only follow the purpose of raising revenue, they may also have a regulatory goal, for example the reduction of harmful emissions or the containment of high-frequency trading. Such tax regimes are established without reference to Member States' national tax systems and go beyond a balancing of taxing rights and obligations. Such systems are therefore capable of building a reference system which is separate and distinct from the national tax system.

To date, the CJEU has used a national and, under certain circumstances, a local or regional reference system to determine whether the law grants aid to certain undertakings or certain goods. Enhanced cooperation law as the reference system would be very different from both previously used systems. First, the law of enhanced cooperation is not delivered by an authority explicitly responsible for this territory. The law is crafted by the institutions of the European Union in accordance with the special rules on enhanced cooperation laid down in the European treaties. Thus, the authorities are sufficiently distinguishable from the central government; however, the authorities have no sovereign or referred power to rule over the relevant territory in a certain field of the law. Only when the Member States have a common understanding and follow the enhanced cooperation procedure are the European institutions allowed to enact laws binding for that particular territory. Secondly, the legislative process at a European level has to be distinguished from the Member States' legislature. However, members of the national government are represented in the Council, allowing each Member State to veto every legislative action, at least in tax law matters. Thirdly, any revenue effects of harmonisation measure taken by the European institutions in the area of tax law will only affect the budget of each single Member State.

From the perspective of existing CJEU case law, one would argue for employing the national tax system (the individual tax system of each Member State) as a reference system for the law enacted under the enhanced cooperation procedure, since enhanced cooperation does not establish a truly autonomous authority. This approach would be misguided as it would not recognise the differences between the law of enhanced cooperation and the law of a local or regional authority. An essential difference between the two lies in the fact that a regional deviation from standard taxation within a Member State may allow the Member State to grant a certain group of undertakings aid, which would be prohibited if granted on a national level. Therefore, one must ensure that the local or regional authority is acting autonomously when granting a beneficial tax treatment. An entirely new system of taxation, such as the taxation of the financial sector, may be enacted under the enhanced cooperation procedure, but may also be taken as a unilateral action by one Member State. In contrast to a local or regional legislative action, a common action of Member States under enhanced cooperation is not per se suspicious from a state aid law perspective. Furthermore, if the Member States aim to implement an entirely new tax regime for economic transactions or other economic events which they have not explicitly taxed before, what should determine normal taxation?

From this it follows that in cases in which enhanced cooperation law implements an entirely new tax regime among the participating Member States, the reference system should be determined in accordance with the aim and purpose of enhanced cooperation. Accordingly, there is no *national* reference system, but *normal* taxation under enhanced cooperation law.

II. The Advantage

Determining whether the law grants an advantage is straightforward once the reference system has been established. Each deviation from the system which leads to a reduction of the national or normal tax burden accounts for an advantage. In cases in which the reduction of the national or normal tax burden is intended to avoid or minimise double taxation, one may argue that no advantage is granted. Such exemptions or reductions simply recompense for taxes paid both in the home and in the host Member State, and thus put the taxpayer on an equal footing with a domestic taxpayer.[724] This line of reasoning calls for a systematic equivalence

[724] Schön, 'State Aid' (n 697) 426. The European Commission may also take the view that there is no differentiation to be made between the taxation of the gain of a taxpayer by the source or by the resident State (For a different view see European Commission, 3 December 2015, Alleged aid to McDonald's, C(2015) 8343 final, para 92).

between taxes paid abroad and domestic taxes,[725] as well as a shift in perspective. A purely national perspective is taken when determining the reference system because it is based on the guiding principles of the national tax system and external factors have no impact at all. Taking the foreign paid tax into account, to determine whether the deviation from the national reference system is beneficial to the taxpayer or not would require an overall (and not just a purely domestic) perspective. Since there are no legitimate reasons for the shift in perspective, any deviation from normal taxation reducing the national tax burden qualifies as an advantage under Art 107 of the TFEU. Whether or not the aid granted is also prohibited under the European treaties depends upon the selective nature of the measure.

Considering the second category of potential enhanced cooperation projects, the traditional group benefit does not grant any aid. A group benefit aims to extend the national or resident treatment to non-nationals or non-resident taxpayers. Accordingly, the tax treatment is fully in line with the reference system, and thus no deviation occurs.

Within the third category (cooperative enhanced cooperation), a participating Member State neutralises a discriminatory tax treatment of a fellow Member State. The neutralising act may require a treatment which is more beneficial than the tax treatment applied to a purely domestic situation. Accordingly, the compensation benefit may confer an advantage if the reference system does not offer the same compensation mechanism in a purely domestic setting. Again, the fact that the Member State 'only' compensates taxation of a fellow Member State does not establish a legitimate reason to deny the existence of an advantage. A purely domestic perspective has to be taken and from this view, the taxpayer is granted a tax treatment, for example a tax exemption, for which the reference system does not provide.

In terms of the first category, there are multiple ways in which the new tax regime can be designed, and thus there are multiple options of a granting an advantage. Accordingly, a standard scenario cannot be provided for that particular category.

E. Selectivity

I. Status Quo

Once it has been established that the tax measure confers an advantage to a recipient, the next step to be taken in determining whether the aid is prohibited under Art 107 of the TFEU is to examine whether the measure is selective. It has

[725] Jozipović (n 651) 176.

already been stressed that the CJEU is not consistent in its case law when it comes to examining a measure on the grounds of selectivity. Sometimes, the Court finds a national tax measure to be selective if the measure deviates from normal taxation,[726] and the derogation leads to a differentiation between operators who, in the light of the objective pursued by the ordinary tax system, are in a comparable factual and legal situation,[727] and the differentiation is not justified by the general structure of that national tax system.[728] This three-step approach conflates the two separate and distinct requirements of an advantage and the granting of this advantage on a selective basis. The advantage test and the selectivity test are not only mingled but fully merged when the Court seeks to find a selective benefit based on a discrimination examination without reference to normal taxation.[729] With the full support of some academics,[730] the CJEU sought favourable selective tax treatment in relation to the treatment accorded to competitors who are in the same legal and factual position. Yet the more recent approach also allows one to justify a prima facie selective measure because of the systemic of the tax system.

[726] For an overview the CJEU case law on the identification of the policy objectives to identify normal taxation see Conor Quigley, 'Direct Taxation and State Aid: Recent Developments Concerning the Notion of Selectivity' (2012) 40 Intertax 112, 115 et seq. CJEU, 26 April 2018, C-233/16, *ANGED*, ECLI:EU:C:2018:280, para 28 (however, in para 30 the Court switches to a discrimination examination without a reference system).

[727] Lang, 'State Aid and Taxation' (n 1315) 418. If selectivity is determined with reference to the objects of the national regime, the Member States are able to influence which undertakings are in a comparable situation and thus influence the decision on whether a national rule constitutes state aid, et seq. Juan Jorge Piernas Lopez, 'Revisiting Some Fundamentals of Fiscal Selectivity: The ANGED Case - Case Law Annotations by Juan Jorge Piernas López' (2018) 17 European State Aid Law Quarterly 274, 277; Begona Perez-Bernabeu, 'Refining the Derogation Test on Material Tax Selectivity: The Equality Test' (2017) 16 European State Aid Law Quarterly 582, 589; European Commission, 'Commission Notice on the Notion of State Aid as Referred to in Article 107(1) of the Treaty on the Functioning of the European Union' (n 655) para 129 trying to tackle this problem by examining the boundaries of the system. Moreover, if a narrow view is taken on the selectivity test according to which the objects of the system equals the aim and purpose of the national law, the scope of European state aid law and the fundamental freedoms overlap extensively (ibid 594). However, such an approach does not sufficiently take into account the competition aspect of state aid law.

[728] CJEU, 8 November 2001, C-143/99, *Adria-Wien Pipeline*, ECLI:EU:C:2001:598, para 41; CJEU, 28 July 2011, C-403/10 P, *Mediaset SpA*, ECLI:EU:C:2011:533, para 36; CJEU, 14 January 2015, C-518/13, *Eventech Ltd*, ECLI:EU:C:2015:9, paras 53–55, CJEU, 11 November 2011, C-106/09 P and C-107/09 P, *Commission v Gibraltar*, ECLI:EU:C:2011:732, para 75; CJEU, 21 December 2016, C-20/15 P and C-21/15 P, *World Duty Free*, ECLI:EU:C:2016:981, para 54; CJEU, 26 April 2018, C-233/16, *ANGED*, ECLI:EU:C:2018:280, para 38.

[729] CJEU, 9 December 1997, C-353/95 P, *Tiercé Ladbroke SA v Commission*, ECLI:EU:C:1997:596, para 33; CJEU, 22 December 2008, C-487/06 P, *British Aggregates Association*, ECLI:EU:C:2008:757, para 82; CJEU, 8 September 2011, C-279/08 P, *Commission v the Netherlands*, ECLI:EU:C:2011:551, para 62; CJEU, 14 January 2015, C-518/13, *Eventech Ltd*, ECLI:EU:C:2015:9, para 55, CJEU, 11 November 2011, C-106/09 P and C-107/09 P, *Commission v Gibraltar*, ECLI:EU:C:2011:732, para 91; CJEU, 21 December 2016, C-20/15 P and C-21/15 P, *World Duty Free Group SA*, ECLI:EU:C:2016:981, para 57 (explicit reference to the Commission's examination on the reference system), 58, 60; CJEU, 14 December 2018, C-374/17, *A-Brauerei*, ECLI:EU:C:2018:1024, para 22 (however, the Court first refers to the notion of a general measure: para 20).

[730] For an explicit discrimination approach see Lang, 'State Aid and Taxation' (n 1355) 29 et seq; Cordewener, 'Asymmetrical Tax Burdens' (n 686) 288; Pierpaolo Rossi-Maccanico, 'EU Review of Direct Tax Measures: Interplay between Fundamental Freedoms and State Aid Control' (2013) 22 EC Tax Review 19, 21.

Both approaches follow a non-discriminatory path and neither is capable of providing a coherent and persuasive analysis of all the requirements set by Art 107 of the TFEU. Only the traditional general measure approach truly values the autonomy of both requirements: the advantage test and the selectivity test. Unlike the discrimination test (with or without using the reference system), the general measure test reveals whether the favourable tax treatment is 'of *general availability*',[731] and therefore does not grant *certain* undertakings or *certain* goods a tax benefit.[732] The general availability in this sense does not require that *all* undertakings benefit from the measure ('actual enjoyment test'), but that *all* undertakings may benefit from the tax measure ('availability test').[733] Accordingly, it is not the factual situation which matters, it is the possibility that counts.

II. Efficient Allocation of Resources between Business Sectors as a Measure for General Availability

The phrase 'available to all undertakings' certainly sounds simple but at the same time undefinable. When is a tax measure truly general? Does it mean that the law must not attach any strings or requirements to the granting of the benefit, or is it allowed to use some? And if so, what requirement shifts national tax measures from the corner of general measures to the corner of the selective measures?

The aim and purpose of the European state aid rules may give some guidance on how to deal with the question of selectivity. The aim of state aid law is the protection of the European internal market from Member States' interference leading to an ineffective market because of a hampered free play of economic forces.[734] State aid has an impact on the efficient allocation of resources, even without granting targeted support to one individual undertaking; it also has an impact on the efficiency of the market when aid is granted for specific sectors. We shall assume that one Member State (Member State A) has no shoe production in its country because the qualified labour in the Member State A is much too expensive. We shall further assume that another Member State (Member State B) is very rich in the shoe-production business due to a high amount of qualified and cheap labour. If Member State A wishes to attract shoe-production businesses, it has to offer tax benefits to compensate for the natural resources setting. If Member State B imposes a high tax burden on the shoe-production business, the tax benefit granted

[731] Opinion of Advocate General Saugmandsgaard Øe, 19 September 2018, C-374/17, *A-Brauerei*, ECLI:EU:C:2018:741, para 91.

[732] Opinion of Advocate General Saugmandsgaard Øe, 19 September 2018, C-374/17, *A-Brauerei*, ECLI:EU:C:2018:741, paras 66 and 67; slightly in this vein also Opinion of Advocate General Kokott, 12 June 2019, *Vodafone*, ECLI:EU:C:2019:492, para 152.

[733] Opinion of Advocate General Saugmandsgaard Øe, 19 September 2018, C-374/17, *A-Brauerei*, ECLI:EU:C:2018:741, para 94.

[734] This presupposes that there is no market failure.

in Member State A may make some undertakings to move their production from Member State B to Member State A. Such a move is only triggered by the unsystematic tax cut[735] in Member State A, distorting the efficient allocation of resources within the European internal market.

Against the background of an efficient allocation of resources, any aid which affects neutrality within the European internal market and causes a situation in which goods are used in places (either as factors of production or consumer items) where they are not of the greatest benefit must be considered selective. Under such a view, tax measures may only be selective if the beneficial treatment is related to the business activity.[736] All other requirements (requirements which do not have any relation to the business activity) set by the national law for the entitlement to benefit have no impact on the efficient allocation of resources, but on how the entrepreneurs (and how the Member State may want them to) structure their business activity. Requirements which do not touch on sector specifics but on the structure of an undertaking are, for example, the size[737] of a company (eg number of employees or turnover),[738] the legal form of an entity and time of market presence (eg start-ups). The use of such requirements does not make tax measures selective, as understood under Art 107 of the TFEU. Tax benefits for specific research and development,[739] for industries requiring a great deal of manual labour, or for the banking sector are linked to the business activity of the undertaking. Such a linkage has an impact on the neutrality of the European internal market, and thus such tax measures are selective in the meaning of Art 107 of the TFEU.

III. Selectivity and Enhanced Cooperation Law

Enhanced cooperation law triggers a fundamental question concerning selectivity: is the law enacted under the enhanced cooperation procedure per se selective because any benefit of enhanced cooperation law may be restricted to

[735] If the tax system of Member State A were beneficial for all undertakings and not only for the shoe production industry, the question of tax competition within the European internal market would be at stake, see for this discussion Schön, 'Tax Competition in Europe' (n 521).

[736] Wolfgang Schön, 'Taxation and State Aid Law in the European Union' (1999) 36 Common Market Law Review 911, 933; Schön, 'State Aid' (n 697) paras 13–090.

[737] The CJEU has ruled that subsidies based on size may infringe Art 107 of the TFEU: CJEU, 26 September 2002, C-351/98, *Spain v Commission*, ECLI:EU:C:2002:530, para 40; see also Ruth Mason and Leopoldo Parada, 'Company Size Matters' (2019) British Tax Review 610.

[738] CJEU, 26 September 2002, C-351/98, *Kingdom of Spain v Commission*, ECLI:EU:C:2002:530, para 40 finding the beneficial treatment of small and medium entrepreneurs to be selective; in this vein see also Opinion of Advocate General Wathelet, 28 July 2016, C-20/15 P and 21/15 P, *World Duty Free*, ECLI:EU:C:2016:624, para 83.

[739] However, general incentives for research and development would account for a general measure and thus would not constitute prohibited aid, Schön, 'Tax Legislation and the Notion of Fiscal Aid' (n 648) 16; Luts (n 649) analysing the different tax incentives for R&D under the more restrictive approach of the CJEU.

undertakings resident within the territory of Member States participating in enhanced cooperation or economic transactions linked to the territory of a participating Member State?

1. Applying the General Measure Approach

Three main forms of enhanced cooperation have been identified above.[740] The second and third categories have one thing in common: benefits are granted. These benefits are permitted either generally within the group, meaning from the participating Member States to their taxpayers (group benefit), or on the basis of the systematic commitment of each participating Member State (compensation benefit). It became quite clear from the analysis that the group members are willing to grant tax benefits to intra-group economic activities either to foster trade within the group[741] or to allow for a deviation from the standard set by CJEU case law without infringing the market freedoms.[742] The desire to restrict the benefit (ie the group benefit or the compensation benefit) to the group and not extend it to cross-group economic activities arises from the lack of reciprocity and the lack of a linked disadvantage in the other Member State.

In state aid law, enhanced cooperation law may always form an a priori selective tax measure because only a restricted group of undertakings—such as undertakings resident within the territory of enhanced cooperation—is entitled to the benefit.

Applying the general measure or general availability rationale[743] to the law enacted under the enhanced cooperation procedure would demand a deeper analysis of the differentiation factor. Accordingly, the factor which divides undertakings into the group of eligible entities and the group of non-eligible entities has to be examined with respect to its impact on the (natural) distribution of resources. Only if the factor is capable of having an impact on the neutrality of the European internal market, may the tax measures be considered selective. The dividing factor which is at stake in the field of enhanced cooperation refers to undertakings or economic transactions which are within or outside enhanced cooperation. In tax law, the question of which entity is within and which entity is outside enhanced cooperation is most likely to be determined by residence. Taken in isolation, the resident factor has no link to the trade or business carried on by the beneficiary, and thus the factor is not capable of negatively impacting on the neutrality of the European internal market as required by Art 107 of the TFEU.

From this it follows that the general distinction between insiders and outsiders (being either the taxpayer resident/non-resident within the territory of a

[740] See this chapter Part I, subsection E.V–E.VIII.
[741] See this chapter Part I, subsection E.VII.7.
[742] See this chapter Part I, subsection E.VIII.
[743] See this chapter Part I, subsection E.II.

participating Member States or the intra-group/cross-group economic activities) of enhanced cooperation is not sufficient to classify the law as selective. A different tax treatment trigged by residency or economic nexus is a general measure since it does not take any recourse on the trade or business carried out by the group of beneficiaries.

2. Applying the Non-discrimination Approach

From the perspective of the CJEU case law, the analysis would not give a complete picture if it stopped here. The application of the general availability rationale is certainly the appropriate and best tool to measure whether or not the law is selective. But the CJEU's case law also applies other methods to decide on selectivity concerns, as stressed in the above.[744] In each of these alternative mechanisms, the CJEU asks whether the eligible group is in the same legal and factual situation as the non-eligible group. The Court tries to find the *tertium comparationis* with respect to (the aim and purpose of) the reference system. In a subsequent step, however, the Court allows justifying a priori selective measures based on the intrinsic systemic of the national system.

Applying the non-discrimination approach in the field of trade-favouring and cooperative enhanced cooperation requires one to determine whether insiders (taxpayers resident within the territory of a participating Member States or an economic transaction linked to the territory of a participating Member State) and outsiders (taxpayers not resident within the territory of a participating Member States or an economic transaction not linked to the territory of a participating Member State) of enhanced cooperation are in a comparable factual and legal situation, and whether the intrinsic concept of differentiation underlying enhanced cooperation may justify an a priori selective group or compensation advantage. Appling the non-discrimination approach to value-based enhanced cooperation is hardly possible on an abstract basis, because the factor differentiating between the group entitled to benefits and the group not entitled to benefits depends upon the aim and purpose of enhanced cooperation law.

a) Group Benefit and Compensation Benefit

(aa) The Comparability Test The framework to identify comparability is set by (the aim and purpose of) the reference system.[745] In case of trade-favouring rules and cross-border tax coordination, it is the national tax system which has

[744] See this chapter Part II, subsection E.I.

[745] The reference system is a key element in finding of selectivity for both the comparability approach and the derogation approach. 'Under the first approach, this requires the definition of the relevant system in light of whose objectives differently treated taxpayers might be comparable; under the second approach, it requires the definition of the relevant system from which a measure derogates', Haslehner (n 1355) 139.

to determine whether or not taxpayers or economic transactions targeted by enhanced cooperation are comparable with taxpayers or economic transactions outside the scope of enhanced cooperation. A good starting point for approaching the question of whether the general distinction between insiders (falling within the scope) and outsiders (falling outside the scope) of enhanced cooperation accounts for selectivity is the case law of the CJEU on the question of whether the distinction between domestic and foreign investment or resident and non-resident taxpayers within the national law is selective.[746] To date, the CJEU is very strict and classifies national laws as selective if the levying of an environmental tax on stopovers of aircrafts and recreational crafts depends upon the residence of the taxpayer[747] or if the tax amortisation of financial goodwill is restricted to foreign shareholding acquisitions[748] .[749] Accordingly, a distinction between domestic and foreign investment or resident and non-resident taxpayers may be sufficient to find a tax measure a priori selective. For example, an environmental tax on air traffic which excludes resident aircraft operators from the tax would—a priori—be selective. The emission triggers taxation and resident and non-resident taxpayer are comparable with respect to their emissions (both equally pollute the environment) but are treated differently.[750]

The group benefit rules place the intra-group economic transactions and non-resident taxpayers on an equal footing with domestic economic transactions and resident taxpayers.[751] However, in some cases—in particular when double taxation should be eliminated—the group benefit provides the insider with a treatment which is more beneficial than the treatment of domestic transactions or resident taxpayers. Of course, from an overall perspective the purely domestic transaction and the resident taxpayer are treated equally to the intra-group transaction and the resident taxpayer of another participating Member State. But from a single Member State's perspective, the treatment is more beneficial.

The compensation benefit may often lead to a more beneficial treatment of the intra-group transaction or the resident taxpayer of another participating Member State. The law of enhanced cooperation distinguishes between the group entitled

[746] For the comparability of resident and non-resident taxpayers in the field of the fundamental freedoms see CJEU, 14 February 1995, C-279/93, *Schumacker*, ECLI:EU:C:1995:31 (personal deduction); CJEU, 12 June 2003, C-234/01, *Arnoud Gerritse*, ECLI:EU:C:2003:340 (deduction of business expenses); CJEU, 1 July 2004, C-169/03, *Wallentin*, ECLI:EU:C:2004:403 (basic allowance); CJEU, 27 June 1996, C-107/94, *Asscher*, ECLI:EU:C:1996:251 (tax rates).

[747] CJEU, 17 November 2009, C-169/08, *Presidente del Consiglio dei Ministri*, ECLI:EU:C:2009:709.

[748] CJEU, 21 December 2016, C-20/15 P and C-21/15 P, *World Duty Free Group SA*, ECLI:EU:C:2016:981.

[749] See for a different view GC, 7 November 2014, T-219/10, *Autogrill España*, ECLI:EU:T:2014:939; Opinion of Advocate General Kokott, 16 April 2015, C-66/14, *Finanzamt Linz*, ECLI:EU:C:2015:242, para 100 et seq.

[750] CJEU, 17 November 2009, C-169/08, *Presidente del Consiglio dei Ministri*, ECLI:EU:C:2009:709, paras 36–37 and 63.

[751] Which does not fulfil the requirement of granting a benefit.

to the benefit and the group not so entitled on the basis of residence or economic nexus. The demarcation between non-resident taxpayers of the group and resident taxpayers, or domestic transactions and intra-group transactions is triggered by the aim and purpose of enhanced cooperation, but not by the aim and purpose of the national tax system of the Member States: the reference system. Since the national reference system does require more beneficial treatment of intra-group transactions or non-resident taxpayers of the group, the CJEU may find the tax measure of enhanced cooperation to be a priori selective.

(bb) Justifying a Selective Tax Measure As a final hurdle, the selectivity of the tax measure may be justified by the nature and general structure of the system.[752] According to CJEU case law and the European Commission, such a justification is at stake when a measure derives directly from the basic or guiding principles of the reference system (the national tax system) or when the derogation is the result of inherent mechanisms necessary for the functioning and effectiveness of the system.[753] Intrinsic principles of the tax system are capable of justifying selective measures, but only if those principles are no guiding principles of the reference system. Otherwise, the principle would have already influenced the comparability test, and thus, the insiders and outsiders of enhanced cooperation would not be in a factual and legal comparable situation.[754] However, the principles may not be external policy objectives.[755] What remains are principles which are not per se system building, but which support and improve the system, such as the fight against tax fraud and tax evasion, or administrative manageability.

(cc) Differentiation within Enhanced Cooperation as a Structural Element under State Aid Law In the field of enhanced cooperation, the fundamental question is whether the intrinsic differentiation between participating and non-participating Member States is recognised as a systemic element of enhanced

[752] CJEU, 2 July 1974, 173/73, *Italian Republic v Commission*, ECLI:EU:C:1974:71, para 33; CJEU, 17 June 1999, C-75/97, *Belgium v Commission*, ECLI:EU:C:1999:311, para 33; CJEU, 29 April 2004, *GIL Insurance*, ECLI:EU:C:2004:252, para 72; CJEU, 22 December 2008, *British Aggregates Association*, ECLI:EU:C:2008:757, para 88; CJEU, 6 September 2006, C-88/03, *Portugal v Commission*, ECLI:EU:C:2006:511, para 56 et seq; CJEU, 8 September 2011, C-78/08 to C-80/08, *Paint Graphos and others*, ECLI:EU:C:2011:550, para 69 and 70.

[753] CJEU, 8 September 2011, C-78/08 to 80/08, *Paint Graphos et al*, ECLI:EU:C:2011:550, para 69; European Commission, 'Commission Notice on the Notion of State Aid as Referred to in Article 107(1) of the Treaty on the Functioning of the European Union' (n 655) para 138.

[754] For a different view see Franz Philipp Sutter, 'Die abkommensrechtliche Verteilung der Besteuerungsrechte zwischen Ansässigkeits- und Quellenstaat aus beihilfenrechtlicher Sicht' in Wolfgang Gassner and others (eds), *Die Verteilung der Besteuerungsrechte zwischen Ansässigkeits- und Quellenstaat im Recht der Doppelbesteuerungsabkommen* (Linde Verlag 2005) 93.

[755] CJEU, 6 September 2006, C-88/03, *Portugal v Commission*, ECLI:EU:C:2006:511, para 81; CJEU, 8 September 2011, C-279/08 P, *Commission v Netherlands*, ECLI:EU:C:2011:551; CJEU, 22 December 2008, C-487/06 P, *British Aggregates v Commission*, ECLI:EU:C:2008:757; CJEU, 18 July 2013, C-6/12, *P Oy*, ECLI:EU:C:2013:525, para 27 et seq.

cooperation law which may justify restricting the granting of an advantage to the group. The differentiating factor of enhanced cooperation depends upon the substantive law. In some cases, differentiation between insiders and outsiders needs to be based on residence. In other cases, economic nexus determines who is entitled to a group or compensation advantage.

The justification level within the discrimination-based approach of the selectivity test does not constitute a traditional form of justification. In fact, justification within the selectivity test establishes the possibility of recognising the coherence of the legal system which has nothing to do with traditional justification endeavours. Within a traditional justification approach, market efficiency would be balanced with contradicting overriding reasons of public interest. Under state aid law, however, an a priori selective benefit can be justified based on the system and design of the law and its demand to grant a beneficial treatment to certain undertakings or certain goods. The aim and purpose underlying the law is not considered to justify an a priori selective benefit. Against this background it is clear that the differentiating nature of enhanced cooperation cannot function as a ground of justification in the field of the fundamental freedoms,[756] but may justify an a priori selective advantage under state aid law.

Thus far, the CJEU has used principles to justify deviations from standard taxation which are not system building but which are within the DNA of each provision. The best example may be the fight against tax avoidance and tax evasion.[757] The aim of making a tax system fraud-proof may not be a guiding principle for deciding what to tax but may be important for deciding how to tax or whom to levy the tax on. The same is true for the aim of preventing double taxation. Any bilateral or unilateral measure to prevent double taxation does not influence the reference system, since the principle of one-off taxation is not a system-building principle. However, there can be no doubt that the Member States are keen on eliminating double taxation to foster trade, and thus the aim of preventing double taxation is embedded in the national tax system without having an impact on the fundaments of national taxation.[758]

Likewise, the European flexibility mechanism brings about a natural distinction between participating and non-participating Member States. The participating Member States can agree on common legislation, but the non-participating Member States do not want to join this action. Enhanced cooperation law necessarily restricts its scope to participating Member States in the form of residents of or an economic linkage to participating Member States. Like the principle of

[756] Within the field of fundamental freedoms, a traditional justification approach is applied, see this chapter Part I, subsection C.III.

[757] CJEU, 29 April 2004, *GIL Insurance*, ECLI:EU:C:2004:252, para 72 et seq; European Commission, 'Commission Notice on the Notion of State Aid as Referred to in Article 107(1) of the Treaty on the Functioning of the European Union' (n 655) para 139.

[758] Jozipović (n 651) 213–14.

one-off taxation or the aim of preventing tax avoidance and evasion, the differentiation between participating and non-participating Member States does not influence the reference system but forms a guiding principle on defining the scope of the law.

However, a collective benefiting of outsiders or cross-border activities with non-participating Member States cannot be supported by the idea of enhanced cooperation. It must therefore follow that only collective acts which provide for the granting of advantages within the group can be justified by the system of enhanced cooperation. An advantage for non-participants of the group (either in the form of residence in a non-participating Member State or economic nexus of transactions to the territory of a non-participating Member State) can never be justified by the notion of enhanced cooperation. An example of a non-justifiable advantage would be a tax exemption for the return from an investment in a non-participating Member State.

From this it follows that a (tax) measure of enhanced cooperation is not selective simply because it differentiates between insiders and outsiders of the system. Such a differentiation is intrinsic to enhanced cooperation because the European flexibility mechanism enables a group of Member States to cooperate more closely and to achieve deeper market integration between them. The implementation of tax measures preventing double taxation or measures coordinating the taxing rights and obligations between participating Member States fosters trade between these Member States and leads to a closer merging together of their national markets. Therefore, the intrinsic differentiation between participating and non-participating Member States within the enhanced cooperation procedure allows one to justify the granting of the group benefit and the compensation benefit only within the group (in other words, the a priori selective advantage). However, a common Member State action which does not foster intra-group trade but grants a benefit to cross-group transactions or resident taxpayers of a non-participating Member State would not be in line with the notion of enhanced cooperation, and thus the fact that the enhanced cooperation procedure has been used does not help justify such a selective tax advantage.

b) The New Tax Regime of Enhanced Cooperation

When Member States use the enhanced cooperation procedure to implement an entirely new tax regime among them, such as a tax system on financial transactions or a tax scheme on the emission of carbon dioxide, the Member States are free to design and structure the tax. As already described above, the law of enhanced cooperation builds its reference system, since the new regime does not build on existing national laws, and thus it is separate and distinct from them. The question on the selectivity issue cannot be addressed without having regard to a particular framework because there can be multiple ways of differentiating. In the field of the FTT, for example, one could envisage an exemption for certain entities like clearing parties[759] or some hand-picked banks.[760] Whether or not such an exemption from the tax is selective depends upon the substance of the entire FTT regime.

F. Findings on the Interplay between the Enhanced Cooperation Law and State Aid Law

It was first necessary to demonstrate that the provisions of European state aid law also apply to laws adopted under the enhanced cooperation procedure. At the outset, one may be hesitant to apply Art 107 of the TFEU to enhanced cooperation law because the basic definition of state aid concerns aid granted by a Member State or through state resources. The law enacted under the enhanced cooperation procedure is, however, not an act of a single Member State and may therefore not be imputable to one single Member State. However, the analysis has revealed that the enhanced cooperation law and secondary EU law, which binds all Member States is different when it comes to the prohibition of state aid because the former may still have an impact on the neutrality of the European internal market.

In terms of the benefit and the reference system, the analysis has shown that it is necessary to distinguish between enhanced cooperation which adjusts the tax systems of the participating Member States and enhanced cooperation which builds an entirely new tax system. The former set of rules builds on the national tax systems of the Member States and establishes bridges between them. These bridges help overcome trade obstacles following from the differences between the laws and provide for special coordination of rights and obligations between the Member States to establish a tax system according to the wishes of the Member States and their obligations under the European treaties. Since trade-favouring and cooperative (system-adjusting) enhanced cooperation lack a system-building character, the national tax law system establishes the reference system. In contrast, where the enhanced cooperation establishes an entirely new tax regime, for example for the taxation of financial transactions, the law shows system-building features, and thus the enhanced cooperation law establishes its reference system.

Any deviation from the reference system in favour of the taxpayer accounts for an advantage. In case of system-adjusting enhanced cooperation, any deviation from national taxation to avoid double taxation is an advantage because the tax burden imposed in another Member State is not considered to determine the benefit. System-building enhanced cooperation may deviate in various forms from its reference system, like by implementing exemptions from taxation.

[759] Which is likely to be selective because the exemption is linked to the activity of the entity but will be justified by the entire regulatory system of which the FTT is a part.

[760] Which is quite likely to be selective without having the possibility of justification.

Even if the law of enhanced cooperation satisfies the advantage test, the aid is only prohibited under the European treaties if it is also selective. According to the existing CJEU case law, there are different ways to test selectivity. The traditional approach begs the question of whether the law provides an advantage to *certain* undertakings or *certain* goods, or whether it is a general measure, and thus available to all undertakings. The general availability test in particular examines whether the law harmfully distinguishes on the basis of the trade or business carried on by the beneficiary. Or whether the law distinguishes based on other features which do not have an impact on the neutrality of the European internal market, such as a distinction based on the legal form of the entity. Only the differentiation on the basis of the business activity is harmful to the European internal market, and thus only such a differentiation determines that the measure is selective. When applying the general availability test to the law of enhanced cooperation, the general and intrinsic distinction between insiders and outsiders of enhanced cooperation is not selective.

The non-discrimination approach taken by the CJEU in determining selectivity is based on a three-step approach. At the very heart of the approach lies a comparability test which questions whether or not two differently treated undertakings are in a comparable situation. In the final stage, however, an a priori selective measure may be justified by the nature and general structure of the system. If a three-step approach is applied to the law of enhanced cooperation, the general structure of enhanced cooperation is capable of justifying the selective granting of benefits within the group or to intra-group transactions. If the benefit is, however, granted to outsiders of the group, the notion of enhanced cooperation is not capable of justifying selectivity implications.

G. Special Charges: A Form of State Aid?

It has been shown that Art 107 of the TFEU prohibits the granting of aid to certain undertakings or certain goods. In tax law, a tax cut or any other form of preferential treatment of some taxpayers may account for prohibited state aid, because the Member State foregoes tax revenue in favour of one or some taxable persons. But what if the Member State does not grant favourable tax treatment for some taxpayers but imposes a special charge on some taxpayers? A special charge is similar to aid because it also leads to a deviation from standard taxation, but it does not do so by mitigating normal taxation, but by charging over and above normal taxation. Such additional charges may also hurt the European internal market because they distort competition.[761] But does Art 107 of the TFEU cover a more burdensome

[761] Opinion of Advocate General Geelhoed, 18 September 2003, C-308/01, *Gil Insurance*, ECLI:EU:C:2003:481, para 65.

treatment of some taxpayers, such as an additional tax burden on the digital services industry by way of a digital service tax? Or does Art 107 of the TFEU only fight national tax measures which provide benefits for certain undertakings or certain goods?

The following subsections will elucidate whether special charges are covered by the ban on state aid. At first, the impact of special charges on the internal market will be revealed and compared with a favourable tax treatment (see subsection I). Secondly, it will be analysed whether there are reasons for not covering special charges by Art 107 of the TFEU (see subsection II). Thirdly, it will be revealed whether other measures of EU law can apply to special charges, such as the fundamental freedoms (see subsection III). And fourthly, it will be proposed to apply Art 107 of the TFEU analogously to special charges, with the consequence that unjustified special charges are incompatible with EU law (see subsection IV). The last subsection concludes with examples of special charges in enhanced cooperation law (see subsection V).

I. Special Charges and Their Impact on the Internal Market

The burdening of certain economic operators or certain goods by way of special charges has negative effects on the efficient allocation of resources on the European internal market. An additional charge on certain undertakings or certain goods will make it unattractive for them to engage in that particular activity despite the fact that the natural resource setting would require one to continue. We shall assume, for example, that one Member State (Member State A) does not produce shoes in its country because the cost of qualified labour in Member State A is too expensive. Let us further assume that another Member State (Member State B) is very successful in the shoe-production business because it has a large amount of qualified and cheap labour. If Member State B imposes a special charge on the production of shoes, some undertakings may move to Member State A in order to escape the burdensome treatment, in spite of a less favourable environment of resources. Such a move would only be triggered by unsystematic charges in Member State B confounding the efficient allocation of resources within the European internal market. The example highlights the fact that the special charge operates in reverse to the beneficial tax treatment and provides for the same negative effects for the efficient allocation of resources, and subsequently for the European internal market.

Therefore, it is hardly surprising that the TFEU's forerunner, the Treaty of the European Coal and Steel Community, explicitly banned subsidies, aids, and special charges.[762] A special charge was considered to distort the competition on the

[762] For a deeper analysis of the provisions of the ECSC Treaty see Wolfgang Schön, 'Special Charges—A Gap in European Competition Law' (2006) 5 European State Aid Law Quarterly 494, 395–96.

European market in an equally negative way as aid does: subsidies and aids create artificial advantages in competition, and special charges eliminate natural advantages.[763] It is therefore questionable why the explicit wording on special charges has not been included in the later European treaties.

II. Special Charges: The Reverse of State Aid?

One may argue that special charges and aid represent the flip side of the coin. If some undertakings are burdened with a special charge (eg a tax on the production of shoes), some undertakings (all undertakings except the ones producing shoes) are exempt from the tax.[764] Accordingly, one may be tempted to just flip the coin and describe the problem as a tax benefit for some undertakings.[765] But is defining a special charge in reverse and argue that some—but in reality almost all—undertakings are granted a beneficial (tax) treatment the same? The answer is no. As soon as the non-taxation of some undertakings is considered to be a beneficial tax treatment to some undertakings and thus the exception, the special charge becomes part of normal taxation. Accordingly, the additional burdening of some undertakings, which reflects a clear deviation from standard taxation, suddenly reflects normal taxation.

From the perspective of the internal market, however, the additional burden needs to be eliminated because this particular burden brings some undertakings into a less competitive situation. The flipping of the coin may, at first glance, have the same impact on the competition between undertakings because all of them are now exposed to the additional tax. Yet the true aim and purpose of the competition rules is to eliminate national measures which contradict the level playing field, and

[763] Opinion of Advocate General Roemer, 23 April 1956, 7 and 9/54 (in case 7/54), *Groupement des industries sidérurgiques Luxembourgeoises*, ECLI:EU:C:1956:1, p 220.

[764] The CJEU has also flipped the coin in *Ferring* (22 November 2011, C-53/00, ECLI:EU:C:2001:627) and *Laboratoires Boiron* (7 September 2006, C-526/04, ECLI:EU:C:2006:528). In both cases, a tax on direct sales of medicine was levied. The tax was supposed to compensate wholesalers for the obligation of keeping a permanent stock of medicinal products sufficient to ensure a month's supply. The Court did not rule on the additional burden imposed on the companies engaging in a direct supply of medical products but ruled on the exemption of the wholesalers of the tax on direct sales (*Ferring*, para 18). See also Ruth Mason and Leopoldo Parada, 'Digital Battlefront in the Tax Wars' (2018) 92 Tax Notes International 1183, 1191; Antonis Metaxas, 'Selectivity of Asymmetrical Tax Measures and Distortion of Competition in the Telecoms Sector: An Analysis on the Legality of the Duty Imposed in Greece on Mobile Network Operators' Subscribers under EU State Aid Rules' (2010) 9 European State Aid Law Quarterly 771, 773, 776 et seq; Phedon Nicolaides and Antonis Metaxas, 'Asymmetric Tax Measures and EU State Aid Law' (2014) 13 European State Aid Law Quarterly 51, 56; Conor Quigley, *European State Aid Law and Policy* (3rd edn, 2015) 136 et seq.

[765] Raymond Luja asks whether the majority of undertakings is burdened or not taxed in order to decide whether the tax is a burden or an advantage (Raymond Luja, 'Group Taxation, Sectoral Tax Benefits and De Facto Selectivity in State Aid Review' (2009) 8 European State Aid Law Quarterly 473, 482 et seq. Raymond Luja, 'Revisiting the Balance between Aid, Selectivity and Selective Aid in Respect of Taxes and Special Levies' (2010) 9 European State Aid Law Quarterly 161. Such an approach fails to identify the key of state aid law: normal taxation.

not to extend unsystematic and incoherent taxes to all undertakings just for the sake of an equal burden. The unsystematic extension of the tax burden would be the result of qualifying the non-taxation of some undertakings as an advantage.

From this it follows that, from the perspective of Art 107 of the TFEU, aid and special charges are not just different sides of the same coin. If this were the case, any special charge on some undertakings could easily be described as a benefit to all the other undertakings not subject to tax. Such an understanding of special charges under Art 107 of the TFEU would lead to an extending of the tax and not—as would be required—to an elimination of the additional charge.

III. Special Charges and other Provisions of the European Treaties

It has been shown that selective special charges have an equally negative impact on the European internal market as selective tax benefits, and thus there is a need to prevent Member States from implementing selective deviations from their tax systems. A ban on such deviations or the requirement of a special justification does not touch on the tax sovereignty of the Member States. They are still allowed to freely decide on the tax base, the tax event, and the tax rates. However, they are not allowed to deviate from their standards without good reasons for doing so.

If special charges are not covered by Art 107 of the TFEU, they may be prohibited by other provisions of the European treaties such as the fundamental freedoms. Part I of this chapter[766] has been devoted to deal with the fundamental freedoms and their application to enhanced cooperation law. The fundamental freedoms aim to fight national measures which are protectionist, and thus they require Member States to treat cross-border economic activities in the same way as they treat purely domestic activities. The intrinsic notion of the fundamental freedoms requires some form of cross-border activity—within a purely domestic setting, they cannot apply.[767] This is hugely different from state aid law. Art 107 of the TFEU also applies to subsidies and aids which are only provided in a purely domestic setting.[768] The application of state aid law in a purely domestic setting is justified because purely domestic subsidies and aids still have an impact on the European internal

[766] See above, Part I.

[767] For the free movement of goods: 'restriction on *import/export* shall be prohibited *between the Member States*' (Art 34 and Art 35 of the TFEU); for the freedom to provide services: 'restrictions on the freedom to provide services *within the Union* shall be prohibited' (Art 56 subsection 1 of the TFEU); for the freedom of establishment: 'freedom of establishment of nationals *of a Member State in the territory of another Member State*' (Art 49 Subsection 1 of the TFEU); for the free movement of capital: 'restrictions on the movement of capital *between Member States and between Member States and third countries* shall be prohibited' (Art 63 of the TFEU).

[768] Hancher (n 642) paras 3–149.

market.[769] The requirement of a cross-border element clearly shows that the fundamental freedoms are not capable of preventing Member States from implementing (all) special charges which harm the European internal market, because purely domestic burdens also affect the efficient allocation of resources.

Despite the application of the fundamental freedoms, harmonisation at a European level may also be a way of removing distortions of competition on the European internal market. However, applying Art 115 of the TFEU to special charges has significant shortcomings and secondary EU law may not be able to facilitate the functioning of the internal market. In special charges, the distortion of competition follows from the additional burden and not from the different application of the charge in the Member States.[770] Harmonising national tax measures at a European level, however, requires that the differences between the national charges lead to a distortion of competition. The harmonisation of the special charges may not mitigate the distortion; it will only secure an equally distortive application of the charge in every Member State.

IV. Applying Art 107 of the TFEU Analogous to Special Charges

Wolfgang Schön has put forward the idea of an analogous application of the rules on state aid law when it comes to special charges.[771] This idea allows special charges (on one undertaking) not to be seen as an advantage for all others, and yet still to be able to apply state aid law. Thus, the basis for the distortion (the special charge) can be eliminated. The elimination of the additional burden allows one to combat the problem at the root and does not require an artificial application of the charge to all undertakings to achieve an equal level playing field.

In recent times, the CJEU has had the chance to rule on the application of Art 107 of the TFEU on special charges. Germany levied a special tax only on the energy production of nuclear fuel. Accordingly, the extraction of energy from coal, wind, water, and gas was not taxed. The CJEU did not rule on the issue of whether the special charge itself contradicted state aid law. Rather it asked whether the non-burdening of other energy producers accounts for a selective advantage.[772] However, this view was also triggered by the questions referred upon the Court. In the end, the CJEU rejected the claim and concluded that the German nuclear fuel

[769] Chad Damro, 'EU State Aid Policy and the Politics of External Trade Relations' (2013) 13 Journal of Industry, Competition and Trade 159, 162.

[770] Schön, 'Special Charges' (n 762) 499.

[771] ibid 502 et seq.

[772] CJEU, 4 June 2015, C-5/14, *Kraftwerk Lippe Ems*, ECLI:EU:C:2015:354, paras 76–77; Opinion of Advocate General Szpunar, 3 February 2015, C-5/14, *Kraftwerk Lippe Ems*, ECLI:EU:C:2015:51, para 74.

tax represents a self-standing regime, which is based on the notion of the 'polluter-pays principle'.[773]

V. Example for Special Charges in the Area of Enhanced Cooperation

In the aftermath of the BESP project and the certainty that not all existing problems in international law can be addressed by the proposed measures, the Member States of the European Union are keen on implementing new taxes safeguarding their slice of the 'tax cake'. Such a measure would, in particular, be a tax on digital services, as proposed by the European Commission.[774] It is already foreseeable that the project will not be supported by all Member States and that there will be no directive binding on all members of the European Union. However, it would be possible to launch this project using enhanced cooperation.

A DST would tax undertakings which are not resident in the relevant Member State and which exceed a certain minimum turnover threshold on the gross amount of their digital services provided within the relevant Member State.[775] The application of the tax requires different criteria to be met: first, the undertaking has to provide digital services and second, the undertaking has to be of a certain size to exceed the relevant threshold. The applying of an additional charge on some undertakings for some services may run foul of Art 107 of the TFEU. Importantly, neither the benefit of not taxing small undertakings with their digital services nor undertakings with non-digital services are under scrutiny; the artificial application of an additional layer of tax will be measured against state aid law.

Accordingly, it is not necessary to ask for an advantage or benefit granted to some undertakings; it is necessary to ask whether there is a deviation from standard taxation through the imposition of an additional burden. Following the European Commission's proposal, the tax is supposed to be an indirect tax and thus the Commission proposes to use Art 113 of the TFEU as a legal basis.[776] The legal basis may, however, be incapable of giving meaningful insights into the true nature of the tax. The Commission's proposal clearly shows that the levying of a DST should only be an interim solution until the Member States are allowed to levy an (income) tax based on the significant digital presence of foreign taxpayers. Accordingly, the DST should only compensate for the current lack of a digital

[773] CJEU, 4 June 2015, C-5/14, *Kraftwerk Lippe Ems*, ECLI:EU:C:2015:354, para 78.

[774] Commission, 21 March 2018, Proposal for a Council directive laying down rules relating to the corporate taxation of a significant digital presence, COM(2018) 147 final.

[775] To comply with the fundamental freedoms, it is supposed that the same tax should also be levied on resident undertakings, which is, however, not covered by the aim and purpose of the tax.

[776] Proposal for a Council Directive on the common system of a digital service tax on revenue resulting from the provision of certain digital services, 21 March 2018, COM(2018) 148 final, p 5.

permanent establishment and the consequent lack of a right to tax under the current tax treaty network. Furthermore, the Commission argues that the tax should not burden customers[777] but rather large foreign tech companies. The DST has the feature of a compensation tax in not taxing foreign digital service providers on their income generated through customers resident within the territory of the Member States. It is supposed that the Commission argues that the DST is an indirect tax and not an income tax to allow the levying of the DST without making the Member States breaching their obligations under the existing tax treaties with third countries.[778]

The DST, as proposed by the Commission, raises many substantive questions, for example whether the customer base is a valid reason for taxing foreign companies on their profits or whether the value added by the use of local customers should only be covered by the VAT.[779] Furthermore, it is unclear whether the DST can be considered as 'income' or 'elements of income' as referred to in Art 2 of the OECD Model.[780] However, these questions fall outside the scope of this study. For the forthcoming analysis, it will be assumed that the levying of the DST is legitimate from the perspective of international law, and the purpose of income and consumption taxation.

As long as the DST is not fully credited by the home Member State of the digital service provider, it does not make a difference for the purpose of state aid law whether the DST accounts for an additional layer of income taxation or an additional charge. In both cases, the DST leads to a special burden of the qualified digital service provider.

With regards to selectivity, the scope of the DST provides for two restrictions. First, only large companies with a turnover of €750 million and a 'significant digital footprint'[781] shall be covered by the DST. Secondly, the DST only covers the provision of digital services and no other forms such as telecommunication services. It has already been argued that only such dividing factors which touch on the business activity are capable of providing for selective advantages or burdens.[782] If this rationale is applied to the DST, the tax is not selective because it only

777 European Commission, 21 March 2018, Fact Sheet: Questions and Answers on a Fair and Efficient Tax System in the EU for the Digital Single Market, Memo/18/2141: 'Will consumers have to bear the cost of new tax measures for the digital economy? There is no reason why this should happen, provided that companies behave responsibly towards their customers.'

778 Fred van Horzen and Andy van Esdonk, 'Proposed 3% Digital Services Tax' (2018) 25 International Transfer Pricing Journal 267, 270.

779 Wolfgang Schön, 'Ten Questions About Why and How to Tax the Digitalized Economy' (2018) 72 Bulletin for International Taxation 287, 284 et seq.

780 Hohenwarter-Mayr and others (n 611) arguing that the DST does not fall within the scope of Art 2 of a tax treaty.

781 Proposal for a Council Directive on the common system of a digital service tax on revenue resulting from the provision of certain digital services, 21 March 2018, COM(2018) 148 final, p 10.

782 See this chapter Part II, subsection E.II.

burdens big companies,[783] but it may run foul of Art 107 of the TFEU because of its sector-specific limitations. The fact that the size specification does not trigger selectivity implications of the state aid law rules does not tell one anything about whether or not it may account for discrimination under the fundamental freedoms.[784] However, from the perspective of state aid law, only the sector-specific restrictions—levying the tax only on digital services and not on all services—makes the law selective.

Not much attention is usually given to the question of whether the selective tax measure distorts the competition and affects trade between the Member States. In the case of a DST, it can be seriously doubted because the provision of digital services to customers in the Member State imposing the tax does not trigger additional costs for the service provided. In other words, there are no severe additional costs for large online search engines to provide access to their website from all around the world. On the contrary, blocking the websites for specific countries or regions (geo-blocking) imposes additional costs. Since the cost structure is different to ordinary business and since any new customer increases the value of the services (network effects), it may well be that digital service providers are less affected by additional charges than one would assume in the case of an ordinary service provider. However, to conclude the example, let us assume that the DST distorts the competition and affects the trade between Member States.

Based on the various assumptions, one can conclude that the DST is an additional burden on some specific undertakings, and it distorts competition and affects trade between Member States. The additional burden contradicts with the internal market and not the non-burdening of all other undertakings. Accordingly, enhanced cooperation law contradicts state aid law with the consequence that all participating Member States have to stop levying the tax and pay back the additional charge to ensure an equal level playing field. The constitutional framework of enhanced cooperation may allow the invalidation of enhanced cooperation law which contradicts state aid law.[785] But enhanced cooperation law does not become invalid by itself (*ipso iure*), this would require constitutive action by the CJEU.[786]

[783] This line of arguments contradicts with the Commission's view. See in that regard the Polish tax on the retail sector, which the Commission found ran foul of Art 107 of the TFEU. Currently, the issue is pending before the Court of first instance: T-624/17, *Poland v Commission*, and T-836/16 *Poland v Commission*.

[784] See for a deeper analysis of the company-size issue in the area of the fundamental freedom Mason and Parada, 'The Illegality of Digital Services Taxes' (n 618).

[785] Art 326 of the TFEU.

[786] According to existing CJEU case law, secondary EU law 'must be deemed to be valid until such time as it is declared invalid' (CJEU, 28 February 1989, 201/87, *Cargill*, ECLI:EU:C:1989:100, para 21). See this chapter Part III, subsection E.

H. Automatic Notification within the Enhanced Cooperation Procedure: A Possible Way to Go?

Enhanced cooperation law may fulfil the substantive conditions under Art 107 of the TFEU and thus may constitute prohibited aid, or it may, at the outset, not be entirely clear whether the aid provided is prohibited under Art 107 of the TFEU. One way of providing some certainty among Member States engaging in enhanced cooperation would be to combine the notion of state aid notification with the law-making process of enhanced cooperation. Until now, Member States have had to undergo the notification procedure if they fear that their national laws contradict state aid law. An extension of this procedure to the law of enhanced cooperation would require some serious amendments, but the notion of a preliminary testing of the law by the European Commission would remain the same. Before examining the details of how the notification procedure could be embedded into the procedural framework for introducing enhanced cooperation, it is necessary to first provide an overview of how the notification process under Art 108 of the TFEU works.

I. The Notification Procedure under Art 108 of the TFEU

The starting point for an analysis of the notification procedure is Art 108 Subsection 3 of the TFEU which states that the

> Commission shall be informed, in sufficient time to enable it to submit its comments, of any plans to grant or alter aid. If it considers that any such plan is not compatible with the internal market having regard to Article 107, it shall without delay initiate the procedure provided for in Paragraph 2. The Member State concerned shall not put its proposed measures into effect until this procedure has resulted in a final decision.

This provision establishes a system of prior control.[787] Any Member State planning to grant aid is required to notify the European Commission beforehand. Importantly, a Member State has only to undergo the notification procedure if all the requirements of Art 107 of the TFEU are satisfied.[788] Accordingly, the scope of the notification obligation is identical to what Art 107 of the TFEU describes as prohibited aid. This has not always been the case. Before the adoption of the procedural regulation, the Commission was of the opinion that the notification

[787] Dashwood and others (n 398) 867.

[788] Art 1 of Council Regulation 2015/1589/EU, 13 July 2015, laying down detailed rules for the application of Article 108 of the Treaty on the Functioning of the European Union, OJ, 24 September 2015, L 248/9.

obligation is wider in scope[789] to bring every potential state aid to the attention of the Commission and not allow any Member State to escape state aid control easily.[790] Such a view introduces the obligation to notify the Commission of any potential aid which may contradict the Commission's effective and efficient work. On the other hand, restricting the scope of the notification procedure to aid fulfilling all the requirements set by Art 107 of the TFEU creates uncertainty because of the different views the Member States and the Commission may have on whether or not a measure is selective or is capable of distorting the competition between the Member States. In any case, if there is a sufficient likelihood that the national measure involves state aid, Member States are better off notifying the Commission of the measure, since if the Commission classifies grey zone cases to be incompatible with state aid law, recovery has to follow subsequently.

If a Member State notifies the European Commission of its measures, there are three possible outcomes of the Commission's preliminary investigation. First, the Commission may find that the notified measure does not constitute aid. Secondly, the Commission may decide that the measure fulfils all the criteria set by Art 107 Subsection 1 of the TFEU, but it falls within the scope of an exception of Art 107 Subsection 2 and 3 of the TFEU. Thirdly, the Commission could raise doubts on the comparability of the aid with the European internal market. If the latter occurs, the Commission widens the investigations and commences the formal procedure under Art 108 Subsection 2 of the TFEU.[791]

The outcome of the preliminary examination that the notified measure does not constitute aid has to be recorded by way of a decision.[792] Likewise, the European Commission has to come to a decision which ends the formal investigation procedure. Under the formal procedure, the Commission makes a positive decision, stating that the notified aid does not constitute a prohibited aid under Art 107 Subsection 1 of the TFEU.[793] The Commission may also issue a conditional decision, meaning that the aid may be considered comparable with the internal market when complying with certain obligations.[794] Lastly, the Commission may conclude that the notified aid under no circumstances complies with the European internal market, and thus the aid should not be put into effect (negative decision).[795]

[789] European Commission, 'Competition Law in the European Communities: Explanation of the Rules Applicable to State Aid' (1997) Volume II B 27; Adinda Sinnaeve, 'State Aid Procedures: Developments since the Entry into Force of the Procedural Regulation' (2007) 44 Common Market Law Review 965, 967.

[790] Adinda Sinnaeve and Piet Jan Slot, 'The New Regulation on State Aid Procedures' (1999) 36 Common Market Law Review 1153, 1163.

[791] Dashwood and others (n 398) 867–68.

[792] Art 4 subsection 2 of Council Regulation 2015/1589/EU, 13 July 2015, laying down detailed rules for the application of Article 108 of the Treaty on the Functioning of the European Union, OJ, 24 September 2015, L 248/9.

[793] Art 10 Subsections 2 and 3 of Council Regulation 2015/1589/EU.

[794] Art 10 Subsection 4 of Council Regulation 2015/1589/EU.

[795] Art 10 Subsection 5 of Council Regulation 2015/1589/EU.

The Member State granting the aid, the beneficiary, other Member States, and competitors of the beneficiary may have a different take on whether or not the aid satisfies the conditions of being prohibited aid. To give interested parties, that is 'any person, undertaking or association of undertakings whose interests might be affected by the granting of aid',[796] a say in the procedure, they are allowed to comment on the preliminary assessment of the European Commission.[797] These parties are also allowed to challenge the Commission's decision when disagreeing with the outcome.[798]

II. The Baseline for Embedding a Notification Procedure into the Enhanced Cooperation Procedure

Within the enhanced cooperation procedure, the European Commission plays a key role and is vested with quite some power.[799] In this vein, it would be consistent to allow the Commission to decide on the aid implication of the planned enhanced cooperation.[800] Such a decision could be made both implicitly and explicitly. An implicit approval of enhanced cooperation under state aid law considerations could be seen in the fact that the Commission submitted a proposal to the Council. The Commission would not entrust the Council with a vote on a proposal which obviously contradicts with the European internal market because it contains prohibited aid. An explicit approval, on the other hand, would require a more detailed discussion of potential state aid implications, which the Commission could set out in the recitals to secondary legislation or in supplementary materials.

The possibility of approving a legislative act on its state aid implications in an implicit manner should be rejected on two grounds. First, the European Commission's decision to entrust the Council with the matter and to allow the Council to authorise the establishment of enhanced cooperation does not include a detailed analysis of the potential law, nor does the Commission know, at this point, what the substance of enhanced cooperation law is going to look like. The fact that there is still room for participating Member States to shape the law after establishing

[796] Art 1 lit. h of Council Regulation 2015/1589/EU.
[797] Art 6 Subsection 1 of Council Regulation 2015/1589/EU.
[798] For the question of who is entitled to challenge the decision of the European Commission on the preliminary investigation and the decision on the formal investigation procedure depends on the actual effect of the measure on the party, see for more details Gabriela von Wallenberg and Michael Schütte, 'Art. 108' in Eberhard Grabitz, Meinhard Hilf, and Martin Nettesheim (eds), *Das Recht der Europäischen Union* (64th edn, 2018) para 42 et seq.
[799] See Chapter 4, subsection B.
[800] From a mere practical point of view, different directorates are involved. For the proposal of a directive in the field of taxation, the Directorate-General for Taxation and Customs Unions is in charge; whereas the Directorate-General for Competition is responsible for testing the law against Art 107 of the TFEU. Despite the fact that these are two separate branches within the European Commission, a form of cooperation in this matter should be possible.

enhanced cooperation becomes particularly evident when considering the legal nature of the Council's authorisation for establishing enhanced cooperation. The CJEU has ruled that the Council's authorisation to establish enhanced cooperation does not give a reliable prospect of the law of the potential enhanced cooperation. The law is still subject to a negotiation process between the participating Member States, and thus enhanced cooperation law may, at least in some parts, look different from what was on the table at the time when the Council authorised the proposal.[801] In that vein, the Commission does not yet know how the law of enhanced cooperation will look, and thus the approval on the state law implications cannot be definitive at this stage. Second, the Commission's decision on the state aid implications may be challenged by parties affected by the decision. On the one hand, willing Member States may want to fight the Commission's decision if they are not allowed to establish enhanced cooperation; on the other hand, third parties such as competitors who are affected by the law of enhanced cooperation may want to challenge the decision.

With regards to the willing Member States, in blatant cases the European Commission may already inform the Member States on state aid law implications based on Art 329 of the TFEU. According to this provision, the Commission has to inform the Member States of the reasons for not submitting a proposal for enhanced cooperation to the Council. The European treaties do not provide any defence mechanisms allowing the Member States to fight the Commission's negative decision. If the Commission recorded its findings on state aid implications of the law, the European legal order would require that any person affected by the act could ask for judicial review.

In the past, it has become clear that the European Commission's policy is far from defeating any legislative intent of the Member States. On the contrary, the Commission engages in a dialogue with the Member States and gives them a guiding hand on how to shape their national tax rules to comply with state aid law.[802] This will not change in the field of enhanced cooperation. If the Member States aim to implement certain rules among them which grant selective benefits to certain undertakings, the Commission may work on the proposal in coordination with the participating Member States to find a solution which does not contradict state aid law rules.

From this it follows that the negative decision of the European Commission will not be of major concern. However, the Commission's decision to submit a proposal to the Council and the question of whether this includes a positive decision on all state aid law concerns requires deeper investigation concerning the possibility of

[801] See for more details and the leeway the participating Member States have when acting based on the Council's authorisation for a particular legislative action Chapter 4, subsection C.

[802] European Commission, 'Code of Best Practices for the Conduct of State Aid Control Procedures' (2018) C(2018) 4412 final.

third parties to challenge the decision. Within the European legal framework, natural or legal persons may take actions against acts of European institutions which are 'of direct and individual concern to them'.[803] In the field of state aid law, the aid beneficiary's competitors may fulfil the requirements and are thus allowed to challenge the (positive) decision of the Commission before the CJEU. If this logic is applied to the enhanced cooperation procedure, natural and legal persons directly and individually concerned must be given the right to oppose the Commission's decision on the state aid law implications of enhanced cooperation law before the CJEU.

As already stressed, the European Commission's decision to entrust the Council with the matter may not be a sufficient ground for third parties to challenge the Commission's decision on potential state aid law implications. Thus, the only act of the Commission which can truly function as an approval of potential state aid implications of enhanced cooperation law, and which forms a sufficient ground to be challenged by third parties, is the Commission's proposal for enhanced cooperation law. As for any other legislative act, the Commission engages in preparatory work and issues a proposal for the secondary EU law act under enhanced cooperation. That particular proposal includes both an outline of the aim and purpose of the law and the wording of the provision, which allows the Commission to test the provisions against Art 107 of the TFEU. Therefore, such a proposal should not only be understood as the Commission's view of the law the participating Member States may be likely to agree on; such a proposal has to also be perceived as the Commission's view on how the legislative attempt can be shaped and designed to comply with the European treaties.

Within the law-making process it may likely be that the participating Member States change the proposal issued by the European Commission during negotiations within the Council. The Commission has to monitor any amendments made by the Council.[804] If the amended proposal no longer meets the substantive conditions set by the European treaties and if the participating Member States are not willing to undo their changes or find an agreement which complies with the primary EU legal framework, the Commission has the power to withdraw the proposal. The Commission derives the power of withdrawal from the power of legislative initiative. Within the enhanced cooperation procedure, the Member States' right of initiative does not change the Commission's power of withdrawal.[805]

Having said this, the Commission's power to withdraw does not vest the Commission with a general veto power.[806] Any withdrawal must be based on

[803] Art 263 Subsection 4 of the TFEU.

[804] According to Art 291 Subsection 1 of the TFEU, whereby the Council acts on a proposal from the Commission, the Council may amend the proposal by acting unanimously. In enhanced cooperation, the provision has to be applied in an analogous manner, meaning that the participating Member States within the Council can amend the proposal from the Commission.

[805] See for more details Chapter 4, subsection B.II.4.

[806] CJEU, 14 April 2015, C-409/13, *Council v Commission*, ECLI:EU:C:2015:217, para 75.

objective grounds which are subject to judicial review.[807] Accordingly, if the amendments to the proposal by the Council do not satisfy European state aid law standards, the Commission is entitled to withdraw its proposal. The Commission's monitoring power and power to withdraw ensure that any legislative act which is not entirely based on the initial proposal has the Commission's blessing.

Besides the Commission's blessing, the outline on state aid implications of the law may be less detailed and specific as a positive decision of the Commission ending the formal investigation process under Art 108 Subsection 2 of the TFEU. But nonetheless, the proposal reveals the reasons why the Commission finds a need for a deviation from the standard or other forms of a beneficial treatment compliant with state aid law.

If the third parties were given a chance to fight the European Commission's decision before the CJEU, they would challenge the Commission's proposal and not the decision of the Council to allow some Member States to establish enhanced cooperation. The decision of which party is entitled to bring the decision of the Commission before the CJEU should be taken according to the same standards that are applicable to Commission decisions under the ordinary notification procedure of Art 108 of the TFEU.

At first sight, it may seem rather odd to give competitors the right to challenge the European Commission's proposal for enhanced cooperation law. On closer inspection, however, it is only logical. Because if the law adopted under enhanced cooperation has certain measures which fulfil the conditions of aid under Art 107 of the TFEU, the legal positions of the parties affected by that measure must not be diminished. They can only exercise their rights if they are allowed to have the Commission's decision reviewed by the CJEU. Within the enhanced cooperation procedure, the parties affected by enhanced cooperation law in the meaning of Art 263 Subsection 4 of the TFEU must be granted the right to challenge the Commission's proposal before the CJEU.

III. Findings on Linking the Notification and the Enhanced Cooperation Procedure

The analysis has set out the possibility of implementing the notion of the notification procedure within the enhanced cooperation procedure. It is fair to say that the European Commission has thought deeply about the state aid implications of the law it proposes within the enhanced cooperation law-making process and may only issue a proposal if the law does not distort the competition or the trade between Member States. If, however, it is assumed that the proposal

[807] ibid para 76.

for a directive in tax law matters submitted to the Council (consisting of the representatives of the participating Member States) includes a positive decision on all state aid law implications, the relevant parties affected by the aid must be given the right to bring the Commission's decision to review before the CJEU. Accordingly, any natural or legal person may challenge the Commission's proposal under the proceeding of Art 263 of the TFEU if the law is of direct and individual concern to them.

IV. Conclusions

Enhanced cooperation law forms a hybrid in the European legal framework. It is not the law of a single Member State or secondary EU law binding all Member States. The hybrid character of the law introduced under the enhanced cooperation procedure raises the question of whether or not the law should be tested against European state aid law. Art 107 of the TFEU, the key rule to define state aid, demands that the aid is granted by a Member State or through State resources. If a single Member State's law forms the basis for the aid, the requirement of granting aid via a Member State or through State resources is satisfied. If the legal basis for the aid is to be found in European Union law, the requirement is not satisfied because the legal measure cannot be imputable to a single Member State. However, the law of enhanced cooperation does not entirely fit into one of these categories. Against the background of the aim and purpose of state aid law, it becomes clear that enhanced cooperation law has to be treated like the law of a single Member State. Unlike ordinary secondary EU law, the law of enhanced cooperation is capable of affecting the efficient allocation of resources, and thus may harm competition on the European internal market.

The CJEU's case law is not entirely consistent on the application of state aid law. Although the Court initially attempted to test the benefit and the selectivity requirement separately, the Court has recently combined these two elements in the form of a discrimination test. The analysis has revealed that the latter approach has severe shortcomings, and thus it is necessary to test both the benefit and the selectivity requirement separately. The benefit requirement asks for a benchmarking, that is, a comparison with the 'normal' tax burden. If the law of enhanced cooperation establishes an entire (tax) system based on harmonised values, enhanced cooperation law may build its own reference system. If, however, the law of enhanced cooperation only supplements existing Member State laws without having an impact on the underlying values of the law, the national (tax) system forms the reference system without reference to enhanced cooperation law.

Within trade-favouring or coordinative enhanced cooperation, the law may grant an advantage because the (tax) treatment of intra-group transactions may be more beneficial than the (tax) treatment of the pure domestic equivalent. The group and compensation benefits may only account for an advantage if the (tax) treatment within the fellow Member State is not considered. However, the application of a purely national reference system demands such an approach.

The wide understanding of the benefit under state aid law puts a particular emphasis on the selectivity test. According to the primary EU law provisions, the aid is only prohibited if it is granted to *certain* undertakings or to the production of *certain* goods. The analysis has made it clear that a tax benefit is selective if the benefit is granted to a distinct group, and the differentiating factor for being entitled is based on the business activity. Other distinguishing factors which are not linked to the business activity, such as the legal form or size of the business,[808] may be used by the law because such differentiation does not establish selectivity in the meaning of state aid law. Therefore, the differentiation between participating and non-participating Member States is not selective within the meaning of Art 107 of the TFEU. If one wants to apply a more discrimination-oriented approach, the intrinsic differentiation between participating and non-participating Member States within enhanced cooperation may justify an a priori selective measure.

Enhanced cooperation law may not only conflict with the provisions on state aid law because it grants certain undertakings or the production of certain goods a tax benefit, but it may also infringe state aid law if the law of the group imposes special charges upon some undertakings or the production of some goods. The unsystematic burdening of some but not all undertakings equally affects the efficient allocation of resources and subsequently the European internal market. Importantly, if a special charge is levied, one may not demand that all undertakings be subject to the tax and thus disadvantaged, but one may instead demand a repeal of the special charge. In other words, a special charge should not be addressed by applying the tax to all who are not in the tax net, but those upon which the tax is imposed should be freed from the burden.

The study has also revealed that the notification procedure in state aid law should be adjusted in order to fit in with the procedural framework of enhanced cooperation. In other words, the European Commission's proposal for secondary EU law of enhanced cooperation should be perceived as an approval on state aid law implications. As in any other ordinary Commission assessment, the third parties affected by the state aid law implications of enhanced cooperation law are allowed to ask for judicial review.

[808] The CJEU has ruled that subsidies based on size may infringe Art 107 of the TFEU: CJEU, 26 September 2002, C-351/98, *Spain v Commission*, ECLI:EU:C:2002:530, para 40

Part III: INTERNAL LEGAL COHERENCE

A. Complying with Existing and Future Secondary EU Law

Aside from complying with the fundamental freedoms and state aid law, Art 326 of the TFEU demands that any enhanced cooperation complies with the European treaties and Union law (including secondary EU laws). Any secondary EU law has to comply with primary EU law, and thus in this regard, Art 326 of the TFEU only sets out what the hierarchy of EU law already demands.[809] With respect to secondary EU law, however, Art 326 of the TFEU may set out a relationship between (ordinary) secondary EU law and enhanced cooperation law which is different from the relationship between (ordinary) secondary EU legislation.[810] Art 326 of the TFEU requires that enhanced cooperation law must prevent any conflicts with (ordinary) secondary EU laws, whereas conflicts between two secondary EU law acts may be resolved by applying the *lex specialis* or the *lex posterior* principle,[811] or at least the notion underlying these principles within the interpretation process, as no hierarchical relationship between regulations, directives and decisions exists.[812] It seems as if Art 326 of the TFEU defines enhanced cooperation law as a form of second-class secondary EU law which has to comply with both primary and (ordinary) secondary EU laws.

Conflicts between secondary EU laws arise where legal provisions overlap and both provisions have different legal consequences. In the vast majority of cases, the legal provisions' scope only partially overlaps as some circumstances are covered either only by one or only by the other provision.[813] The partial overlap of two legal norms may best be described as two intersecting circles. Only the situations within the intersection are subject to both legal rules and it is only in these situations that a conflict between the legal provisions can be established.[814]

[809] The hierarchy of EU law only demands that lower EU law has to comply with higher EU law, CJEU, 5 October 1978, 26/78, *Antonio Viola*, ECLI:EU:C:1978:172, para 9; see also Nettesheim (n 289) 746; Ana Paula Dourado, 'The Relationship between Primary and Secondary EU Law in Tax Law: The Legitimacy of Different Interpretation Criteria Applied to EU and National Legal Sources' in Dennis Weber (ed), *Traditional and Alternative Routes to European Tax Integration: Primary Law, Secondary Law, Soft Law, Coordination, Comitology and Their Relationship* (IBFD 2010) 171. For more details, see this chapter Part I, subsection D.

[810] The fact that enhanced cooperation law has to comply with secondary EU law is even more obvious when considering the initial primary EU law provisions introduced by the Treaty of Amsterdam: Art K.15 Subsection 1(e) demanded that any enhanced cooperation 'does not affect the *acquis communautaire*'.

[811] Szudoczky, *The Sources of EU Law* (n 1) 68; Meurs (n 1) 81 with further references.

[812] On the missing hierarchy between legal forms mentioned in Art 288 of the TFEU, Bieber and Salomé (n 2) 917.

[813] See for example CJEU, 19 December 2013, C-174/12, Hirmann, ECLI:EU:C:2013:856; Kaspar Krolop, 'European Company Law' in Karl Riesenhuber (ed), *European Legal Methodology* (Intersentia 2017) 477.

[814] Michael Lang, 'Normenkonflikte zwischen den Vorschriften des nationalen Steuerrechts und der Doppelbesteuerungsabkomme' in Dietmar Gosch, Arne Schnitger, and Wolfgang Schön (eds), *Festschrift für Jürgen Lüdicke* (Beck Verlag 2019) 441.

At the current stage, it is not possible to say whether the CJEU wants the *lex specialis* or the *lex posterior* principle to apply automatically as soon as a conflict between two legal provisions arises or whether the Court would use the notion underlying the *lex specialis* or the *lex posterior* principle within its systematic interpretation to solve conflicts between legal provisions.[815] If the *lex specialis* or the *lex posterior* principle were applied automatically, the older or more general rule would correspondingly become invalid automatically. However, the CJEU case law rejects an automatic invalidation of European laws.

The following subsections will first set out how conflicts between secondary EU laws have to be resolved (see subsection B). In the course of this subsection it will be demonstrated that not every conflict between secondary EU laws can be resolved by directly applying the *lex specialis* or the *lex posterior* principle or by using the notion underlying these principles when interpreting the potentially conflicting provisions. The European legislature uses its power to renew or specify its previous legislation in cases in which the European legislature considers and balances the same interests and comes to a different outcome. Only in these cases is the application of the *lex specialis* or *lex posterior* rule or its underlying notion allowed (see subsection B.II). If the European legislature weighs different interests, a conflict between the laws has to be resolved by balancing both Europeanised values, allowing them to coexist with each other (see subsection B.I). The second subsection defines the leeway given to Member States in the case of existing secondary EU law legislation to follow public interests which have not influenced law-making at European level (see subsection C). This subsection discusses the pre-emption doctrine (see subsection C.I) and how it is possible to determine the scope of existing secondary EU laws (see subsection C.II). The third subsection uses the constitutional framework of the enhanced cooperation procedure and the logic of conflict solving, elaborated in subsections B and C, to define the legislative freedom of enhanced cooperation with regard to existing secondary EU laws (see subsection D.I) and the impact secondary EU law legislation has on existing enhanced cooperation laws (see subsection D.II). The fourth subsection discusses the enforcement of invalidity claims (see subsection E), before the fifth subsection provides a conclusion based on three examples (see subsection F).

B. Conflicts between Secondary EU Laws

Except for the relationship between basic regulations and implementing regulations,[816] the European treaties do not set out any hierarchical order between

[815] ibid 442 et seq in favour of solving conflicts by way of law interpretation.

[816] Implementing regulations do not find their legal basis directly in the European treaties, but rather in an act of secondary EU law (Jürgen Bast, 'On the Grammar of EU Law: Legal Instruments' in Armin von Bogdandy and Joseph HH Weiler (eds), *European Integration: The New German Scholarship* (2003)

secondary EU legislation, and thus the European constitutional framework may not provide any intrinsic conflict of law rules.[817] Due to the missing hierarchical relationship, most commentators want to resolve a conflict arising between secondary EU laws by the application of the *lex specialis* or the *lex posterior* principle.[818] The *lex specialis* or the *lex posterior* principle can either be applied directly, or the notion underlying this principle (that being the legislature's freedom) can be embedded into the Court's systematic interpretation of the legal provisions. A direct application of the principle would lead to a certain automatism in the resolution of norm conflicts because the younger or more specific rule would invalidate[819] the older or the more general law automatically.[820] However, an application of the notion underlying the *lex specialis* or the *lex posterior* principle within the interpretation process would only recognise the legislature's power to amend existing laws as one of many other factors. The interpretative approach may also allow granting one legal provision precedence over the other without declaring the latter invalid. Either way, the lack of European conflict of law rules does not automatically allow solving *any* conflict between secondary EU legislation based on basic derogation rules or allow the *lex specialis* or the *lex posterior* principle to influence the interpretation process, as these general rules may undermine the European law-making process.

At a European level, the European legislature weighs the values of market integration against other public interests such as consumer and health protection, fairness, or neutrality of funding.[821] The outcome of these considerations, the harmonised European interest, is manifested in the secondary EU law act.[822] For

23 < https://jeanmonnetprogram.org/archive/papers/03/030901-05.pdf > accessed 3 February 2021.). Thus, the implementing regulation has to be understood in the sense of the basic regulation: CJEU, 10 March 1971, 38/70, ECLI:EU:C:1971:24, para 9; CJEU, 18 June 1996, C-303/94, *Parliament v Council*, ECLI:EU:C:1996:238. See also Alina Kaczorowska-Ireland, *European Union Law* (4th edn, Routledge 2016) 146.

[817] Koen Lenaerts and Marlies Desomer, 'Towards a Hierarchy of Legal Acts in the European Union? Simplification of Legal Instruments and Procedures' (2005) 11 European Law Journal 744, 745 et seq.

[818] Szudoczky, *The Sources of EU Law* (n 1) 68.

[819] Derogation refers to the repeal of force of a rule by another rule. In other words, derogation invalidates the norm, and thus it is no longer part of the legal system: Lang, 'Normenkonflikte' (n 814) 445.

[820] ibid 442.

[821] Carsten Herresthal, 'Die Ablehnung einer primärrechtlichen Perpetuierung des sekundärrechtlichen Verbraucherschutzniveaus' (2011) Europäische Zeitschrift für Wirtschaftsrecht 328, 329; Werner Schroeder, 'Die Sicherung eines hohen Schutzniveaus für Gesundheits-, Umwelt- und Verbraucherschutz im europäischen Binnenmarkt' (2002) Deutsches Verwaltungsblatt 213, 215.

[822] Any secondary EU law act balances the different (conflicting) interests and thereby establishes harmonised European interests (a European value). The CJEU has recognised this balancing act because the Court did not oblige the European legislature to establish a common approach in the form of adopting the highest level of protection which can be found in a particular Member State. The European legislature is free to balance internal market interests and non-economic interest which may, from the perspective of a single Member State, lead to a higher or lower protection of certain public interest concerns, but the secondary EU law must achieve a considerable improvement in the protection of non-economic interests within the European Union, CJEU, 13 May 1997, C-233/94, *Germany v European Parliament and Council*, ECLI:EU:C:1997:231, para 48; see also Isidora Maletič, *The Law and Policy of Harmonisation in Europe's Internal Market* (2013) 23.

example, secondary EU laws may include precise and detailed prohibitions on economic operators if the European legislature has emphasised consumer protection (in contrast to competition and freedom of contract). The process of weighing conflicting interests against each other establishes a European hierarchy of interests and subsequently a European order of values.[823] Secondary EU law can only manifest a hierarchy of those interests which have influenced the law-making process. In other words, interests which have not been considered by the European legislature are not Europeanised and thus do not form a part of the European value order. For example, European legislation pursuing consumer protection may balance this goal with competition and freedom of contract, while possibly ignoring public health or environmental issues.[824] It makes a difference for the process of conflict solving whether a conflict arises between secondary EU laws balancing the same interests, but with different outcomes (see subsection II), or whether conflicting secondary EU legislation is based on a balance of different interests (see subsection I).

I. Conflict of Laws Balancing different Interests

Secondary EU laws may clash if the European legislature weighs interests of European market integration against public interests in different legislative acts without establishing a clear balance between the non-economic values (the public interest concerns).[825] These conflicting secondary EU law acts may, but do not necessarily have to be based on the same competence clause. In cases where the internal market competence (Art 114 and Art 115 of the TFEU) is the legal basis,[826] the European harmonisation measure should already provide a high level of health, safety, consumer and environmental protection.[827] However, if the Member States

[823] See for more details, this chapter Part I, subsection D.III.

[824] Opinion of Advocate General Bobek, 7 March 2019, C-2/18, *Lietuvos Respublikos Seimo nariu grupė*, ECLI:EU:C:2019:180, para 39.

[825] Under Art 114 and Art 115 of the TFEU, the European legislature is allowed not only to pursue the non-market goals included in Art 114 Subsection 3 of the TFEU, but also other values or policy objectives which are not expressly 'mainstreamed' by the European treaties, Bruno de Witte, 'A Competence to Protect—The Pursuit of Non-Market Aims through Internal Market Legislation' in Phil Syrpis (ed), *The Judiciary, the Legislature and the EU Internal Market* (CUP 2012) 32.

[826] The aim of European legislation based on Art 114 or Art 115 of the TFEU is not limited to the elimination of distortion of competition, it may also pursue other aims. For a different view: Opinion of Advocate General Sharpston, 17 December 2009, C-518/08, *Fundació Gala-Salvador Dalí*, ECLI:EU:C:2009:799, para 65.

[827] See Art 114 Subsection 3 of the TFEU. Art 115 of the TFEU does not explicitly refer to the need for a high level of protection of consumers, health, safety, and environment, but Art 115 of the TFEU demands unanimous voting in the Council, which ensures that any legislative act does not go beneath a level of protection every Member State finds necessary. For the historical development of Art 114 Subsection 3 of the TFEU in the light of the majority voting requirement see Opinion of Advocate General Tesauro, 26 January 1994, C-41/93, *France v Commission*, ECLI:EU:C:1994:196, para 4; Claus-Dieter Ehlermann, 'The Internal Market Following the Single European Act' (1987) 24 Common

find that the secondary EU law does not sufficiently protect certain public interests, and if they have made use of the possibility of maintaining national provisions on the grounds of major public interest concerns,[828] the European legislature may harmonise these concerns on the basis of Art 114 Subsection 1 of the TFEU either by amending the initial secondary EU law act or by issuing additional legislation. Accumulating legislation would focus more closely on the public interest concerns which the initial secondary EU law act has not already (sufficiently) considered.

Secondary EU law may, for example, balance market integration interests and public safety by setting out requirements a motor vehicle has to fulfil with respect to the installation of lighting and light-signalling devices. These road safety standards may define the colours which have to be used for the light-signalling device and the range of headlights, but they may not prohibit the use of particular lightings (xenon, halogen, etc). Every motor vehicle complying with these requirements can be traded on the entire European internal market. In a separate and distinct secondary EU law act, the European legislature may balance market integration and environmental interests with the result of secondary EU law forbidding the use of xenon headlights because of its enormous use of environmentally harmful mercury. Considering both secondary EU law acts, it is no longer possible to sell motor vehicles on the European internal market which only comply with one of these acts. Despite the fact that compliance with both legislative acts may be possible, a conflict of secondary EU norms exists because the first legislative act (weighing of internal market interests and public safety) *permits* the marketing of all motor vehicles which comply with its requirements (colours and range). The second European legislative act (weighing of internal market interests and environmental concerns) *prohibits* the use of particular lighting devices (xenon headlights). Compliance with both legal acts can only be reached if priority is given to the stricter norm (the prohibition on the use of xenon headlights) and thereby reducing the scope of the permission to market legally all motor vehicles which comply with the colour and range requirements. The overlap between the *prohibition* on the use of xenon headings and the *permission* to use xenon lights complying with the colour and range requirements leads to a conflict of secondary EU law norms.[829]

The European legislature can avoid conflicts of secondary EU law norms by setting out a clear hierarchical order between the non-economic values, as the

Market Law Review 361, 389; James Flynn, 'How Will Article 100(4) Work? A Comparison with Article 93' (1987) 24 Common Market Law Review 689.

[828] Art 114 Subsection 4 of the TFEU.

[829] Joost Pauwelyn, *Conflict of Norms in Public International Law: How WTO Law Relates to Other Rules of International Law* (CUP 2008) 170–71; however, some authors may only find a conflict of norms if two norms impose mutually exclusive obligations: C Wilfred Jenks, 'The Conflict of Law-Making Treaties' (1953) British Year Book of International Law 401, 426 arguing that '[a] conflict in the strict sense of direct incompatibility arises only where a party to the two treaties cannot simultaneously comply with its obligations under both treaties'.

European legislature did for the relationship between the Capital Duty Directive and the Directive on a European Financial Transaction Tax.[830] A financial transaction tax, aiming for financial market regulation and a fair contribution of the banking sector to the costs of the last financial crisis,[831] can be applied either to transactions both on the primary and secondary financial market or only to transactions on the secondary financial market. Burdening both the primary and secondary financial market may establish funding neutrality for small and large undertakings,[832] but at the same time, may burden the raising of capital which may hamper investment. The Capital Duty Directive[833] explicitly prohibits the levying of indirect taxes on the raising of capital to foster investment, regrouping and development of undertakings,[834] and more generally economic growth.[835] The proposal of a European Financial Transaction Tax clearly prioritises unrestricted raising of capital, as the proposed tax on financial transactions only applies to the secondary financial market,[836] and thereby preventing conflicts between the Capital Duty Directive and a European FTT.[837]

[830] European Commission, 'Impact Assessment Vol. 4—Proposal for a Council Directive on a Common System of Financial Transaction Tax and Amending Directive 2008/7/EC' (2011) SEC(2011) 1102 final para 212; European Commission, 'Impact Assessment Vol. 8—Proposal for a Council Directive on a Common System of Financial Transaction Tax and Amending Directive 2008/7/EC' (n 526) 3.

[831] Explanatory Memorandum, COM(2011) 594 final, 2.

[832] See for more details 'Financial Sector Taxation: The IMF's Report to the G-20 and Background Material' (International Monetary Fund 2010) 172 <https://www.imf.org/external/np/seminars/eng/2010/paris/pdf/090110.pdf> accessed 3 February 2021.

[833] Council, 12 February 2008, Directive 2008/7/EC, concerning indirect taxes on the raising of capital, OJ, 21 February 2008, L 46, 11.

[834] Council, 12 February 2008, Directive 2008/7/EC, concerning indirect taxes on the raising of capital, OJ, 21 February 2008, L 46, 11, recital 4.

[835] Commission, 4 December 2006, Press Release, Indirect taxation: the European Commission proposes to abolish capital duty on the raising of capital, IP/06/1673.

[836] Art 1 Subsection 4 (a) of the Commission's Proposal, and Subsection 3.3.4. of the explanatory memorandum ('The provisions of Council Directive 2008/7/EC of 12 February 2008 concerning indirect taxes on the raising of capital continue to be in principle fully applicable. This entails for instance that the primary issue ... of shares or other securities of the same type, or of certificates representing such securities, debentures ... or other negotiable securities relating to loans is not subject to FTT in the EU'), COM(2011) 594 final.

[837] Some authors have found that any European financial transaction tax (also a transaction tax restricted to the secondary financial market) conflicts with the Capital Duty Directive because Art 5 Subsection 2 of the Directive prohibits any form of indirect taxation on dealings in stocks, shares, or other securities and the exception allowing to charge duties and taxes on the transfer of securities only applies to capital duties, accordingly the primary financial market (CJEU, 9 October 2014, C-299/13, *Gielen*, ECLI:EU:C:2014:2266, para 28). The first proposal for a common financial transaction tax addressed these concerns by amendments to the Capital Duty Directive (COM(2011) 594 final). See for more details on the critique, in particular with respect to the second proposal for a financial transaction tax under the enhanced cooperation procedure, Joachim Dahm and Rolfjosef Hamacher, 'Finanztransaktionssteuern anderer Länder—(taugliche) Muster für die grenzüberschreitende Steuererhebung?' (2013) Internationales Steuerrecht 123, 128 et seq; Joachim Dahm and Rolfjosef Hamacher, 'Verstärkte Zusammenarbeit für FTT mit Kapitalansammlungsrichtlinie vereinbar?' (2015) Internationales Steuerrecht Länderbericht 29, 29; Jan Liepe, Hendrik Pielka and Nina Malaviya, 'Der aktuelle Richtlinienentwurf zur Finanztransaktionssteuer im Lichte des europäischen

Against this background, it becomes clear that the application of the traditional derogation rules (*lex specialis* or the *lex posterior*) or an impact of their underlying notion on the interpretation process cannot satisfactorily solve a conflict arising between two secondary EU laws which balance different interests. The traditional conflict of law rules are a manifestation of the legislature's power to specify general and amend outdated laws.[838] A changing social and political environment may require giving more weight to some interests and less weight to others. The outcome of the new balancing of these interests has to invalidate laws which are based on the old or more general balancing act[839] or should at least allow the setting aside of the older or more general laws if the notion of the *lex specialis* or the *lex posterior* principle is considered when interpreting the potentially conflicting secondary EU law rules. However, a conflict between two secondary EU law acts balancing different interests has to be solved in a way which allows both Europeanised values to take as much effect as possible. It is not an all or nothing decision as it would be in case of a direct application of the *lex specialis* or the *lex posterior* rule; it is the finding of a balance which allows both Europeanised values to coexist in the most fruitful manner.[840]

We shall return to the example of secondary EU laws concerning motor vehicles. One secondary EU law act balances public safety interests and internal market interests and the other secondary EU law legislation balances environmental and internal market interests. The former legislative rules intend to set standards for the use of colours (ie red for the brake and yellow for the blinker light) and the range of headlights (ie they have to illuminate at least 25 metres of the road), whereas the other tries to prohibit the use of substances which are particularly harmful to the environment. Giving full effect to the prohibition on xenon headlights does not weaken the Europeanised safety standards but limits the tradability of motor vehicles. The internal market interests have been considered within the balancing act of secondary EU legislation prohibiting xenon lightings, and thus the balancing

Rechts' (2013) Zeitschrift für Wirtschafts- und Bankrecht, 1344, 1350–51; Thomas Ihering, 'Die Finanztransaktionssteuer im Rahmen der verstärkten Zusammenarbeit' (2013) Zeitschrift für das gesamte Kreditwesen 612, 614; for a different view: Franz C Mayer and Christian Heidfeld, 'Europarechtliche Aspekte einer Finanztransaktionsteuer' (2011) Europäische Zeitschrift für Wirtschaftsrecht 373, 377–78.

[838] See in that vein Erich Vranes, 'Lex Superior, Lex Specialis, Lex Posterior—Zur Rechtsnatur der „Konfliktlösungsregeln"' (2005) Zeitschrift für ausländisches öffentliches Recht und Völkerrecht 391, 397 et seq.

[839] See this chapter Part III, subsection B.II.

[840] The approach may be compared with the German constitutional law principle '*praktische Konkordanz*' (practical concordance) which attempts to balance conflicting equal-ranking constitutional norms. None of these norms should derogate the other one, but both should take as much effect as possible. The principle of practical concordance also cannot be compared with the principle of reciprocity, as the latter defines the limit of tolerance whereas the former tries to optimise both norms in the best way possible, Marcus Schladebach, 'Praktische Konkordanz als verfassungsrechtliches Kollisionsprinzip: Eine Verteidigung' (2014) 53 Der Staat 263, 272.

of both harmonised interests may allow to give full effect to the prohibition of the use of substances particularly harmful to the environment and thereby limiting the tradability of motor vehicles as supposed by secondary EU law on the colour and range of lightings.

II. Conflict of Laws Balancing Identical Interests

The picture is different where two secondary EU laws conflict and both norms balance the same underlying interests, but with a different outcome. The outcome may be different because the legislature now finds the need to give more weight to one particular interest because the political and social circumstances have changed. In these cases, the legislature holds the power to amend existing laws allowing them to reflect societal values in the best way possible. Conflicts between old and new or general and specific laws need to be solved by the *lex specialis* and the *lex posterior* rules as they are based on the legislature's freedom to renew, amend, or specify existing laws.[841] But again, the *lex specialis* or the *lex posterior* principle can be applied directly, which may lead to a certain automatism in the resolution of norm conflicts,[842] or the notion underlying this principle (the legislature's freedom) may be embedded into the interpretation process. If the conflict of law rules are directly applied, they invalidate laws which should have been explicitly repealed by the legislature[843] as they no longer reflect the right balancing outcome.[844] If a mere interpretative approach is applied, the conflicting laws would be set aside, as these laws would remain in force and applicable if *lex posterior* or the *lex specialis* are, for whatever reason, repealed.

C. Conflict between Secondary EU Law and National Laws

Within the field of shared policy-making competences, secondary EU law holds precedence over national conflicting laws,[845] meaning that EU law 'provisions and measures not only by their entry into force render automatically inapplicable any conflicting provision of current national law but ... also preclude the valid

841 See in that vein Vranes (n 838) 397 et seq.

842 Lang, 'Normenkonflikte' (n 814) 442.

843 In this vein see Sebastian AE Martens, *Methodenlehre des Unionsrechts* (Mohr Siebeck 2013) 426.

844 Bernd Rüthers, Christian Fischer, and Axel Birk, *Rechtstheorie: mit juristischer Methodenlehre* (10th edn, 2018) para 772. For the enforcement issue: see this chapter Part III, subsection E.

845 Here, we shall only focus on the relationship between secondary EU law and national laws from a European perspective, Monica Claes, 'The Primacy of EU Law in European and National Law' in Anthony Arnull and Damian Chalmers (eds), *The Oxford Handbook of European Union Law* (OUP 2015) 179 arguing that 'a complete understanding of the actual relationship between national and European law as it operates in practice thus requires an inquiry both into the EU and the national perspective'.

adoption of new national measures to the extent to which they would be incompatible with Community provisions'.[846] Accordingly, newly introduced secondary EU law may render existing national laws inapplicable,[847] and existing secondary EU law may prohibit Member States from introducing conflicting national laws or may even hinder Member States from taking any legislative actions at all.

Concerning the inapplicability of national laws, primary and secondary EU law can only supersede national legislation to the extent the national law conflicts with EU law.[848] The inapplicable national law is still valid and applies to situations not covered by secondary EU law (eg a purely domestic situation).[849] Setting aside national laws in case they conflict with EU law without invalidating them protects Member State sovereignty.

Moreover, secondary EU law can also set limits on the Member States' legislative freedom.[850] Member States are no longer free to regulate a particular policy area if it is already occupied by secondary EU law, meaning that in this field 'it is the duty of the Community to fill and regulate'.[851] First and foremost, it is necessary to distinguish between policy fields in which the Member States are (only) precluded from enacting national legislation contradictory to the law of the European Union, and fields in which they are pre-empted from taking any action at all.[852] The first constraint is a manifestation of the doctrine of supremacy.[853] The Member

[846] CJEU, 9 March 1978, 106/77, *Simmenthal*, ECLI:EU:C:1978:49, para 17. For more details on the principle of precedence see Dashwood and others (n 398) 270 et seq.

[847] Michael Dougan, 'Primacy and the Remedy of Disapplication' (2019) 56 Common Market Law Review 1459, 1460 et seq. Most national legal orders accept the primacy of EU law over national legislation, including (parts of) the national constitution. For an overview of the 'Solange' jurisprudence ('a story about national constitutional courts resisting a straightforward surrender of national legal sovereignties': Wojciech Sadurski, '"Solange, Chapter 3": Constitutional Courts in Central Europe—Democracy—European Union' (2008) 14 European Law Journal 1; see also Mehrdad Payandeh, 'Constitutional Review of EU Law after Honeywell Contextualizing the Relationship between the German Constitutional Court and the EU Court of Justice' (2011) 48 Common Market Law Review 9.

[848] Koen Lenaerts and Tim Corthaut, 'Of Birds and Hedges: The Role of Primacy in Invoking Norms of EU Law' (2006) 31 European Law Review 287, 289 et seq on the lack of a clear differentiation between primacy and direct effects Michael Dougan, 'When Worlds Collide! Competing Visions of the Relationship between Direct Effect and Supremacy' (2007) 44 Common Market Law Review 931, 933.

[849] For a thorough distinction between *Geltungsvorrang* and *Anwendungsvorrang* see Claes (n 845) 182.

[850] Eugene Daniel Cross, 'Pre-Emption of Member State Law in the European Economic Community: A Framework for Analysis' (1992) 29 Common Market Law Review 447, 455 et seq defines four categories for the relationship between European legislation and Member State law: express pre-emption, express saving, occupation of the field pre-emption, and conflict pre-emption.

[851] Samuel Krislov, Claus-Dieter Ehlermann, and Joseph HH Weiler, 'The Political Organs and the Decision-Making Process in the United States and the European Community' in Mauro Cappelletti, Monica Seccombe, and Joseph HH Weiler (eds), *Integration Through Law: Europe and the American Federal Experience*, vol 1 (Walter de Gruyter & Co 1985) 90.

[852] Joseph HH Weiler, 'The Community System: The Dual Character of Supranationalism' (1981) 1 Yearbook of European Law 267, 277; for a different interpretation: Robert Schütze, 'Supremacy without Pre-Emption? The Very Slowly Emergent Doctrine of Community Pre-Emption' (2006) 43 Common Market Law Review 1023, 1039 arguing that 'pre-emption' represents a relative doctrine: 'the question to be asked is not whether Community legislation pre-empts national law but to what degree is national legislation pre-empted'.

[853] Robert Schütze, 'The Morphology of Legislative Power in the European Community: Legal Instruments and the Federal Division of Powers' (2006) 25 Yearbook of European Law 91, 117 et seq

States are allowed to enact national legislation as long as it does not clash with (primary and secondary) EU law. Here, the problem is how to identify 'whether or not the exercise by Member States of their powers is contrary to rules adopted by the Community'.[854] The second constraint goes much further and precludes Member States from taking any action at all. The following subsections address the exclusivity claim of secondary EU law (see subsection I) and the question of how to determine the scope of exhaustive secondary EU law (see subsection II) in more detail.

I. Pre-emption Doctrine—Exclusivity as a Limit on Legislative Action

A total pre-emption of national law-making powers can follow from either vesting the European Union with exclusive competence[855] (such as the customs union)[856] or the exhaustive exercise of a shared competence by the European legislature.[857] In the latter case, secondary EU law provides for an exhaustive regulatory framework leaving no room for any legislative actions of the Member States, not even for measures likely to support the policy of the European legal act.[858] In that vein, the CJEU found that the Regulation on the Community system of protection of geographical indications and of designations of origin for agricultural products and foodstuffs[859] provides a 'uniform and exhaustive system of protection' of consumer expectations of products coming from a particular geographical area.[860] Centralising the instruments of protection at a European level precludes the application of a system

arguing that the obligation of national authorities to refrain from enacting national measures contradicting the letter or spirit of the European law forms part of the pre-emption doctrine.

[854] Waelbroeck (n 287) 551.

[855] See for example for the European Union's power to set tariffs CJEU, 18 February 1970, 40/69, *Bollmann*, ECLI:EU:C:1970:12, para 4: 'To the extent to which Member States have transferred legislative powers in tariff matters with the object of ensuring the satisfactory operation of a common market in agriculture they no longer have the power to adopt legislative provisions in this field'. In this vein see also, CJEU, 17 December 1970, C-34/70, *Syndicat national du commerce extérieur des céréales and others*, ECLI:EU:C:1970:119.

[856] See Art 3 of the TFEU.

[857] For the distinction between 'constitutional pre-emption' and 'legislative pre-emption' see Arena (n 372) 483 et seq. For the field of shared competence, the Protocol No. 25 on the exercise of shared competence lays down that 'when the Union has taken action in a certain area, the scope of this exercise of competence only covers those elements governed by the Union act in question and therefore does not cover the whole area', OJ, 9 May 2008, 115, 307. Michel Waelbroeck has referred to the total ban of Member States' legislative action as the 'conceptualist-federalist approach': Waelbroeck (n 287) 551 et seq.

[858] CJEU, 14 October 2004, C-173/02, *Spain v Commission*, ECLI:EU:C:2004:617, para 19.

[859] Regulation, 20 March 2006, 510/2006/EC, OJ, 31 March 2006, L 93, 12; now Regulation, 21 November 2012, 1151/2012/EU, on quality schemes for agricultural products and foodstuffs, OJ, 14 December 2012, L 343, 1.

[860] CJEU, 8 September 2009, C-478/07, *Budweiser*, ECLI:EU:C:2009:521, paras 111, 114.

of protection laid down by agreements between two Member States.[861] Likewise, the Directive harmonising the Member States' laws relating to the installation of lighting and light-signalling devices on motor vehicles,[862] prohibited the United Kingdom from setting additional equipment requirements ('dim-dip' lighting devices) as a condition for sale of vehicles in the United Kingdom. The secondary EU law framework introduced an exhaustive system so that a Member State could not 'unilaterally require manufacturers who have complied with [the requirements set by the European Directive] to comply with a requirement not provided for by that directive, since motor vehicles complying with the technical requirements laid down therein must be able to move freely within the common market'[863].[864]

European internal market legislation harmonises national product standards and other requirements Member States impose for trading goods and services legally within the European Union. Such legislation weighs internal market interests against other non-economic interests and establishes a European standard for a particular policy area. This European standard may most commonly serve as both a floor and a ceiling of regulation,[865] as the free movement of goods, services, persons, and capital may demand uniform standards prohibiting Member States from demanding to comply with additional requirements. The CJEU recognises the balancing act and the establishment of harmonised values, as the Court has not obliged the European legislature to establish a common approach in the form of

[861] ibid para 129.

[862] Directive, 27 July 1976, 76/756/EEC, on the approximation of the laws of the Member States relating to the installation of lights and light-signalling devices on motor vehicles and their trailers, OJ, 27 September 1976, L 262, 1; now Regulation, 13 July 2009, 661/2009/EC, concerning type-approval requirements for the general safety of motor vehicles, their trailers and systems, components, and separate technical units intended therefore, OJ, 31 July 2009, L 200, 1.

[863] CJEU, 12 July 1988, 60/88, *Commission v United Kingdom*, ECLI:EU:C:1988:382, paras 11–12.

[864] There are various other examples of exhaustive European secondary EU law. The Directive 98/5/EC facilitating practice of the profession of lawyer on a permanent basis in a Member State other than that in which the qualification was obtained carries out a complete harmonisation of requirements which need to be fulfilled to allow European lawyers to practise on a permanent basis in any other Member State under the professional title which they enjoy in their home Member State. Additional language tests which are not set out in the Directive contradict the aim and purpose of the Directive. The European 'legislature sought to put an end to the differences in national rules on the conditions for registration with the competent authorities which gave rise to inequalities and obstacles to free movement' (CJEU, 19 September 2006, C-506/04, *Wilson*, ECLI:EU:C:2006:587, paras 64, 66, 77). Moreover, the CJEU has constantly ruled that the European Union holds the exclusive competence to enter into international agreements with third countries in cases in which the content of the treaty falls within the scope of secondary EU law (implied powers doctrine; CJEU, 31 March 1971, 22/70, *Commission v Council*, ECLI:EU:C:1971:31; CJEU, 14 July 1976, 3/76, 4/76, and 6/76, *Kramer*, ECLI:EU:C:1976:114; Opinion of the CJEU, 19 March 1993, 2/91, ECLI:EU:C:1993:106; Opinion of the Court, 7 February 2006, ECLI:EU:C:2006:81); see for example Koen Lenaerts, 'Les répercussions des compétences de la Communauté européenne sur les compétences externes des États membres et la question de "preemption"' in Paul Demaret (ed), *Relations extérieures de la Communauté Européenne et marché intérieur: aspects juridiques et fonctionnels* (Story-Scientia 1988); Joseph HH Weiler, 'The External Legal Relations of Non-Unitary Actors: Mixity and the Federal Principle' in David O'Keeffe and Henry G Schermers (eds), *Mixed Agreements* (Kluwer Law and Taxation Publishers 1983) 46 et seq.

[865] Meaning that the secondary EU law introduces measures of maximum harmonisation: Weatherill, *The Internal Market* (n 4) 210.

adopting the highest level of protection which can be found in a particular Member State.[866] The European legislature is free to balance internal market interests and non-economic interests which may, from the perspective of a single Member State, lead to a higher or lower protection of certain public interest concerns, but the Europeanised standard must achieve a considerable improvement in the protection of non-economic interests within the European Union.[867]

A directive harmonising the installation of lightings and light-signalling devices in motor vehicles, for example, focuses, in particular, on a balance between road safety concerns and internal market interests. Furthermore, Art 114 Subsection 3 of the TFEU demands that any legislative act which is based on European internal market competence has also to consider other interests which may not be obvious in the light of the aim and purpose of the secondary EU law. Considering these public interests on a standardised basis allows internal market legislation to provide for a high level of health, safety, and environmental and consumer protection. The European legislature is bound to consider a wide range of public interests as exhaustive secondary EU law does not allow the Member States to maintain trade hampering national measures which provide for higher protection. Exhaustive secondary EU law legislation precludes a recourse to the fundamental freedoms,[868] and thus Member States can no longer justify trade obstacles based on public interest concerns: exhaustive secondary EU law is supposed to satisfy all public interest claims.[869]

According to CJEU case law, the question of whether or not secondary EU law establishes an exhaustive system has to be answered with respect to the objectives of the law and the substance of the provisions.[870] In cases in which the secondary EU law aims to smooth intra-EU trade through the harmonisation of product standards or standards for providing services, it is very likely that secondary EU

[866] See also Maletič (n 822) 23.

[867] CJEU, 13 May 1997, C-233/94, *Germany v European Parliament and Council*, ECLI:EU:C:1997:231, para 48.

[868] CJEU, 5 October 1977, 5-77, *Tedeschi*, ECLI:EU:C:1977:144, para 35 (generally referred to as the Tedeschi principle). See this chapter Part I, subsection D.

[869] To balance the majority voting requirement of Art 114 of the TFEU and Member States' public interest concerns, a Member State may be allowed to maintain national provision providing for a higher standard of protection as laid out by secondary EU law if the Member State deems it necessary, Art 114 Subsection 4. See for example Opinion of Advocate General Tesauro, 26 January 1994, C-41/93, *France v Commission*, ECLI:EU:C:1994:196, para 4; Ehlermann, 'The Internal Market' (n 827) 389; Flynn (n 827). However, the Member State has to follow the procedure laid out in Art 114 of the TFEU.

[870] CJEU, 30 October 1974, 190/73, *van Haaster*, ECLI:EU:C:1974:113, para 7; CJEU, 24 November 2011, C-468/10 and C-469/10, *Asociación Nacional de Establecimientos Financieros de Crédito (ASNEF) and Federación de Comercio Electrónico y Marketing Directo (FECEMD)*, ECLI:EU:C:2011:77, para 30; CJEU, 21 December 2016, C-203 and C-698/15, *Tele2 Sverige AB*, ECLI:EU:C:2016:970, para 90; Amedeo Arena, 'The Twin Doctrines of Primacy and Pre-Emption' in Robert Schütze and Takis Tridimas (eds), *The European Legal Order*, vol 1 (OUP 2018) 33x, arguing that 'comprehensive and detailed regulatory schemes are more likely to be regarded as exhaustive. That is certainly the case for EU legislation that "contains a set of provisions specifically devoted" to the same aspect the national measure seeks to regulate.'

law establishes full harmonisation, since an undistorted movement within the internal market can only be guaranteed if no single Member State is capable of imposing additional requirements for the sale of goods or the performance of services.[871] Apart from internal market legislation, European secondary EU law may often (only) establish minimum harmonisation[872] in the field of environmental protection and health and public safety, allowing the Member States to introduce or retain higher standards[873] or introduce a parallel regulatory scheme aiming for the same objective as the secondary EU law. In case of minimum harmonisation or safeguard clauses within secondary EU law permitting derogations from the Europeanised regime, primary EU law is applicable. In other words, if national laws go beyond what secondary EU law provides as the minimum floor or if the national legislature derogates from secondary EU law framework, the law has to comply with the market freedoms.[874]

In *Gallaher*, for example, the Court found a British rule which required that health warnings on tobacco products have to cover 6% of the label surface to be in line with secondary EU law legislation which only demanded a coverage of 'at least 4%' of the surface.[875] According to the CJEU, it is up to Member States to decide 'that the indications and warnings are to cover a greater surface area in view of the level of public awareness of the health risks associated with tobacco

[871] CJEU, 30 January 1974, 159/73, *Hannoversche Zucker AG*, ECLI:EU:C:1974:9, para 4: 'The rules of the common organization of the market in sugar must be regarded as forming a *complete system in the sense that it does not leave the Member States the power to fill [gaps]* by resorting to their national law' (emphasis added); CJEU, 30 October 1974, 190/73, *van Haaster*, ECLI:EU:C:1974:113, para 8 et seq, even if the secondary EU law system only covers explicit rules for the marketing, the aim and purpose of EU law (freedom of commercial transactions under conditions of genuine competition shall stabilise the quality of products) may have an impact on the production of goods, and thus, may prohibit Member States from imposing restrictions on production; CJEU, 23 January 1975, *Galli*, ECLI:EU:C:1975:8; CJEU, 24 November 2011, C-468/10 and C-469/10, *Asociación Nacional de Establecimientos Financieros de Crédito (ASNEF) and Federación de Comercio Electrónico y Marketing Directo (FECEMD)*, ECLI:EU:C:2011:77, paras 30–32 (conditions for the processing of personal data); CJEU, 19 October 2016, C-582/14, *Breyer*, ECLI:EU:C:2016:779, para 57 (conditions for the processing of personal data); CJEU, 22 June 2017, C-549/15, *E.ON Biofor Sverige AB*, ECLI:EU:C:2017:490, para 32 (Member States are not allowed to demand additional sustainability criteria for bioliquids than those provided by secondary EU law); CJEU, 4 October 2018, C-242/17, *Legatoria Editoriale Giovanni Olivotto (L.E.G.O.)*, ECLI:EU:C:2018:804, paras 29–33 (Member States are not allowed to demand additional sustainability criteria for bioliquids than those provided by secondary EU law).

[872] Minimum harmonisation cannot pre-empt Member States from any legislative actions, Armin von Bogdandy and Jürgen Bast, 'The European Union's Vertical Order of Competences: The Current Law and Proposals for Its Reform' (2002) 39 Common Market Law Review 227, 243.

[873] CJEU, 10 March 2016, C-235/14, *Safe Interenvíos SA*, ECLI:EU:C:2016:154 (on money laundering and terrorist financing); CJEU, 15 March 2018, C-104/17, *SC Cali Esprou SRL*, ECLI:EU:C:2018:188, para 35 (on packaging waste and the recovery and recycling of waste); CJEU, 7 September 2016, C-121/15, *Association nationale des opérateurs détaillants en énergie (ANODE)*, ECLI:EU:C:2016:637, para 50 (public service obligations).

[874] For the derogation allowance within secondary EU law see CJEU, 6 November 2003, C-101/01, *Bodil Lindqvist*, ECLI:EU:C:2003:596, para 97. Weatherill, *The Internal Market* (n 4) 210.

[875] Directive, 13 November 1989, 89/622/EEC, on the approximation of the laws, regulations and administrative provisions of the Member States concerning the labelling of tobacco products, OJ, 8 December 1989, L 359, 1 (no longer in force).

consumption'.[876] Since secondary EU law on the packaging of tobacco products does not establish an exhaustive framework for health and safety issues related to smoking, a Member State would be allowed to demand that the telephone number of a domestic help line needs to be printed on the surface of any tobacco product. The setting up of a help line for smokers willing to quit constitutes a parallel initiative to counteract the extensive tobacco use.

From this it follows that the exclusivity claim of secondary EU law concerns the question of whether or not the Member States are allowed to set national measures to achieve objectives already subject to secondary EU legislation. If secondary EU law lays out exhaustive rules, the Member States are prohibited from taking any legislative actions. Exhaustive secondary EU law considers all public interest claims, and thus national legislation cannot protect any seemingly forgotten interests.

II. The Scope of the Existing Secondary EU Law as a Limit on Legislative Action

The scope of secondary EU law is determined by both its wording and its objective. The CJEU has placed particular emphasis on the latter and, by way of interpretation, considered facts and situations to be covered by provisions of secondary EU law because the aim and purpose of the law would require one to go beyond the meaning of the rules' wording. In other words, the Court applied provisions of secondary EU laws to situations and circumstances which would not have been covered by these provisions if the Court had restricted itself to the literal wording of these rules.[877] Most of these cases concern equal treatment issues[878] within the

[876] CJEU, 22 June 1993, C-11/92, *Gallaher*, ECLI:EU:C:1993:262, para 20.

[877] 'Application of a provision by analogy, with regard to an economic operator, is possible where the legal rules applicable, on the one hand, are very similar to those which it is sought to have applied by analogy and, on the other hand, contain an omission which is incompatible with a general principle of Community law and which can be remedied by application by analogy of those other rules.' CJEU, 11 November 2010, C-152/09, *Grootes*, ECLI:EU:C:2010:671, para 41. The CJEU has ruled that the VAT Directive does not provide for specific rules, eg relating to the adjustment by the issuer of the invoice of VAT which has been improperly invoiced (CJEU, 19 September 2000, C-454/98, *Schmeink & Cofreth*, ECLI:EU:C:2000:469, para 48; CJEU, 6 November 2003, C-78/02, C-79/02 and C-80/02, *Dimosio*, ECLI:EU:C:2003:604, para 49) or relating to the methods or criteria which have to be applied to determine the apportionment of input VAT paid according to whether the relevant expenditure relates to economic or non-economic activities (CJEU, 13 March 2008, C-437/06, *Securenta*, ECLI:EU:C:2008:166, para 33). However, the Court required the Member States to fill this gap with respect to the fundamental principles of the VAT Directive. Thus, the secondary EU law does not provide for any explicit rules on the particular matter but requires the application of the fundaments of the secondary EU law.

[878] The question of equal treatment is answered against the background of the harmonised principles and values. In the *Sturgeon* case, for example, the CJEU analysed the objectives of the Regulation 261/2004, a secondary EU law measure harmonising the compensation and assistance to passengers in the event of flight cancellation and delays, to determine whether compensation must only be provided in case of cancellation. The wording of the Regulation only asked for compensation in case of cancellation but in accordance with the objectives of the Regulation and the principle of equal treatment the Court found that passengers booked on a delayed flight and passengers booked on a cancelled flight must

scope of secondary EU law (eg the question of whether VAT exempt 'public postal services' can also be provided by private undertakings,[879] or whether a reduced rate for printed books also has to be applied to electronic books[880]).[881] The extension of exemption provisions or other derogation clauses (but also the restriction of such clauses)[882] do not extend the scope of secondary EU law which would limit the Member States' ability to regulate. Rather, the CJEU has rejected claims to widen the personal[883] or material scope[884] of secondary EU law preventing an increase in the Member States' obligations.

III. Conclusions

Conflicts between secondary EU laws and national laws are not solved by the *lex specialis* or the *lex posterior* principle because a hierarchical relationship exists between national and EU laws. The conflict is solved by setting aside national laws which conflict with EU law, as the latter holds precedence. The national law remains valid,[885] but must only be applied outside the scope of conflicting EU law.

not be treated differently with respect to compensation. They suffer similar losses and there are no objective grounds to justify different treatment (CJEU, 19 November 2009, C-402 and C-432/07, *Sturgeon*, ECLI:EU:C:2009:716, para 44 et seq. For a different view see Opinion of Advocate General Sharpston, 2 July 2009, C-402 and C-432/07, *Sturgeon*, ECLI:EU:C:200):416, para 97 'I do not think that the underlying problem can be "fixed" by interpretation.'

[879] CJEU, 23 April 2009, C-357/07, *TNT Post UK Ltd*, ECLI:EU:C:2009:248.

[880] CJEU, 5 March 2015, C-502/13, *Commission v Luxembourg*, ECLI:EU:C:2015:143.

[881] The CJEU's approach has been criticised, as secondary EU law and European Union law in general only establish a partial legal order and thus have no conclusive character which would allow to apply the law to situations not covered by the law's wording. See for the discussion Konrad Walter, *Rechtsfortbildung durch den EuGH: eine rechtsmethodische Untersuchung ausgehend von der deutschen und französischen Methodenlehre* (Duncker & Humblot 2009) 76 et seq. See also Hans Christoph Grigoleit, 'Der Verbraucheracquis und die Entwicklung des Europäischen Privatrechts' (2010) 210 Archiv fuer die civilistische Praxis 354, 391 et seq; Katja Langenbucher, 'Argument by Analogy in European Law' (1998) 57 The Cambridge Law Journal 481, 500 et seq arguing for a restrictive application of the argument by analogy to protect the division of powers between the Member States and the European Union. Explicitly for directives, see Grigoleit 378, 391 et seq; Axel Adrian, *Grundprobleme einer juristischen (gemeinschaftsrechtlichen) Methodenlehre* (2009) 447; Clemens Höpfner and Bernd Rüthers, 'Grundlagen einer europäischen Methodenlehre' (2009) 209 1, 12.

[882] Based on a coherent application of the principles underlying the secondary EU law: Horsley (n 35) 947; Michael Dougan, 'Judicial Activism or Constitutional Interaction? Policymaking by the ECJ in the Field of Union Citizenship' in Hans-Wolfgang Micklitz and Bruno de Witte (eds), *The European Court of Justice and the Autonomy of the Member States* (Intersentia 2012).

[883] CJEU, 1 October 2009, C-247/08, *Gaz de France—Berliner Investissement SA*, ECLI:EU:C:2009:600, para 34 et seq.

[884] CJEU, 22 December 2008, C-48/07, *État belge—Service public fédéral Finances*, ECLI:EU:C:2008:758, para 44; for a critical analysis see Schön, 'Die Analogie' (n 817) 168 arguing that the aim and purpose of the Parent-Subsidiary Directive does not differentiate between holding of the shares with full title and holding of shares in usufruct.

[885] The CJEU has no power to invalidate laws of Member States. According to Art 267 of the TFEU the Court has jurisdiction to rule on 'the *validity* and interpretation of *acts of the institutions*, bodies, offices or agencies of the Union' (emphasis added). See also Koenraad Lenaerts and Piet Van Nuffel, European Union Law (3rd edn, Sweet & Maxwell 2011) ss 22–009. For the German constitutional

Secondary EU law legislation guards against conflicts with Member States' laws by prohibiting any national legislative action in case of exhaustive secondary EU legislation. The CJEU has strictly prohibited Member States from law-making in the field of exhaustive secondary EU laws, as the Court does not even allow national legislation fostering the aim and purpose of EU legislation. However, the Court is reluctant to extend the scope of secondary EU laws to circumstances not explicitly covered by law. The Member States' legislative freedom shall only be restricted to the extent to that the European legislature has used its power and has introduced exhaustive secondary EU legislation.

D. Conflicts between Secondary EU Law and Enhanced Cooperation Law

So far, we have learned that a conflict between secondary EU legislation balancing different interests has to be solved not by way of invalidation but by balancing both Europeanised values and allowing them to take as much effect as possible. A conflict between secondary EU laws can only be resolved by applying the *lex specialis* or *lex posterior* rule or by allowing the underlying notion of the principle to influence the interpretation process if the secondary EU law rules balance identical interests. The relationship between secondary EU law and national laws is determined by the principle of precedence which allows one to set aside conflicting national laws without ruling on their validity and existing secondary EU law precludes the national legislature from introducing conflicting laws. Exhaustive secondary EU laws restrict the legislative freedom of the national legislature even further as an exhaustive regulatory framework prohibits any national legislative action.

Now we have to ask how conflicts between secondary EU law and enhanced cooperation law are to be resolved. Should a group of Member States be allowed to enact enhanced cooperation law which conflicts with existing secondary EU law, meaning that either enhanced cooperation law invalidates secondary EU law or harmonised values of both secondary EU law and enhanced cooperation law have to be balanced in a way which gives them the widest possible effect? Or should a group of Member States be restricted in its legislative freedoms as any national legislature would be (see subsection I)? And which effects does enhanced cooperation law have on the European legislature: may the law of a group of Member States be able to prevent the European legislature from introducing contradictory secondary EU law which is binding for all Member States (see subsection II)?

framework see Matej Avbelj, 'Supremacy or Primacy of EU Law—(Why) Does It Matter?' (2011) 17 European Law Review 744, 751; for the German constitutional framework Nettesheim (n 289) 737.

I. The Impact of Existing Secondary EU Law on the Group's Legislative Freedom

As in the field of conflicting (ordinary) secondary EU laws, a conflict between existing secondary EU law and enhanced cooperation law can arise either because a group of Member States is unsatisfied with the current European legal framework and wants to introduce a new set of rules or because a group of Member States is eager to introduce a regulatory framework for a particular field, such as the financial market, which conflicts with more general secondary EU law. Conflicts of the first categories arise because (at least some) Member States find the existing secondary EU laws to be ineffective or inefficient, and thus, they want to amend these laws. In the vast majority of cases, the ineffectiveness or inefficiency of the law follows from being outdated and incapable to deal with new economic realities. It is quite natural for laws to become outdated or lose their ability to deal sufficiently with new legal and factual challenges. Laws are designed and crafted against the background of existing economic and social realities. Sometimes the European legislature examines the future and provides its laws with the tools needed to apply to a factually changing environment. Since the future is unpredictable, the factual, but also the legal environment in the Member States may change other than expected, and thus the European laws may no longer be capable of sufficiently addressing the problem, or may even backfire, as in the case of the Directive on cross-border interest and royalty payments.[886]

The VAT Directive may provide a perfect example for (partially) outdated secondary EU law. The roots of the conceptual framework of the entire European VAT system go back to the beginning of VAT harmonisation in the mid- and late-1960s. Up until today, the taxable amount has been determined by the consideration received for one's supply.[887] Under the European VAT system, consideration is a subjective value and not estimated by objective criteria.[888] The subjective element in determining the tax base has raised several issues, especially when the supplier has accepted a consideration below production costs,[889] but overall the provisions were administrable in the old economy. Now, at a time at which customers provide social media platforms with their data in order to be granted access to that service, it is impossible to determine the subjective value to tax the service. To determine the subjective value of the consideration, one would have to answer questions such as whether a social media platform would grant anyone access without getting any

[886] Wolfgang Schön, 'Facilitating Entry by Facilitating Exit: New Paths in EU Tax Legislation' (2018) 46 Intertax 339.

[887] Art 73 of the VAT Directive.

[888] CJEU, 23 November 1988, 230/87, *Naturally Yours Cosmetics*, ECLI:EU:C:1988:508, para 16; CJEU, 2 June 1994, C-33/93, *Empire Stores*, ECLI:EU:C:1994:225, para 18-19; CJEU, 3 July 2001, C-380/99, *Bertelsmann*, ECLI:EU:C:2001:372, para 22; CJEU, 19 December 2012, C-310/11, *Gratten*, ECLI:EU:C:2012:822, para 22.

[889] CJEU, 20 January 2005, C-412/03, *Scandic*, ECLI:EU:C:2005:47.

data in return, and whether someone would pay 'real money' for social media services. The issue may only be solved by amending the VAT Directive and allowing the introduction of objective criteria to determine the consideration and subsequently the tax base for certain supplies. To date, Member States cannot agree on an amendment of the VAT Directive, and thus they are stuck with rules designed for the old economy and have to try solving the related problems with unsystematic approaches outside of the VAT world.[890]

Legislative amendments to outdated secondary EU laws are based on the balancing of the same interests which already influenced the initial law-making. However, the outcome of the balancing act differs from the initial outcome leading to legislative changes. If these changes were based on the consent of all Member States, the outdated law would have been replaced. In the absence of an explicit act of the European legislature, the *lex posterior* rule would either apply automatically or its underlying notion would influence the interpretation process. A direct application of the *lex posterior* rule would invalidate the older law and grant the more recent legislation full effect.[891] If one wishes to recognise the *lex posterior* rule's underlying notion only within the interpretation process, the legislature's freedom to renew and amend existing laws would allow a setting aside of the conflicting legal provision.

However, the constitutional framework of the enhanced cooperation procedure explicitly prohibits the application of the *lex specialis* and the *lex posterior* rule in cases where enhanced cooperation laws conflict with secondary EU law so as to protect the integration level already established between all Member States.[892] Primary EU law grants primacy to secondary EU law, which binds all Member States regardless of its problematic content or impracticability and regardless of how preferential, practical, thoughtful, and systematic enhanced cooperation law may be. Considering outdated VAT law, a group of Member States is not allowed to use the enhanced cooperation procedure to amend the VAT Directive in a way which would allow the Member States to better deal with the taxation of the digital economy.

At first glance, the outcome seems to be highly unsatisfactory. But viewed from the perspective of the unwilling Member States (the Member States which do not want to amend the law, and thus, do not join enhanced cooperation), the outcome is justified. The judgment of whether the secondary EU law is outdated or does not fulfil its aims and objectives would rest with a group of at least nine Member States

[890] Schön, 'Ten Questions' (n 779) 286; Wolfgang Schön, 'Der digitale Steuer-Irrweg' Frankfurter Allgemeine Zeitung (6 April 2018) 16.

[891] See this chapter Part III, subsection B.

[892] In this vein see also Ulrich Becker, 'Differenzierungen der Rechtseinheit durch "abgestufte Integration"' in Jürgen Schwarze and Peter-Christian Müller-Graff (eds), *Europäische Rechtseinheit durch einheitliche Rechtsdurchsetzung* (Nomos 1998) 53; Veronika Grieser, *Flexible Integration in der Europäischen Union: neue Dynamik oder Gefährdung der Rechtseinheit?* (Duncker & Humblot 2003) 125; Sebastian Reinhard Johannes Cloppenburg, *Eine Finanztransaktionssteuer im 'kleinen Kreis'* (Peter Lang 2018) 738 et seq.

if enhanced cooperation were a suitable mechanism to refrain from the obligations imposed by secondary EU law. As has been stressed above,[893] there are other tools to ensure that Member States are not unsuitably bound to secondary EU laws.[894] The enhanced cooperation procedure is, however, not a tool which is capable of overriding existing secondary EU laws binding among all Member States. It may only function as a fallback option if the secondary EU law grants the Member States an exit route, but some Member States want to retain the law and thus pursue it under the heading of enhanced cooperation.[895]

The second set of conflicts between secondary EU law and enhanced cooperation law may arise where a group of Member States pursues different interests than those harmonised by existing secondary EU law. Secondary EU law may, for example, prohibit imposing any capital duties and other indirect taxes on dealings in stocks, shares, or other securities fostering the process of raising capital by companies and governments as well as free movement of capital within the European internal market. Despite the secondary EU law guarantee of not taxing the process of raising capital, a group of Member States may wish to introduce a tax on financial transactions on both the primary and secondary financial market. The financial transaction tax is supposed to regulate the financial market and making the financial sector to contribute to the costs of the last financial crisis. If this conflict arose between ordinary secondary EU laws, it would not be solved by way of invalidation but by finding a way which allows both Europeanised values to take as much effect as possible. Such a balancing act may aim to undermine the legal effects of secondary EU laws as little as possible, but it still limits the scope of both conflicting laws to an extent which allows both laws to apply alongside each other. Balancing the harmonised interest of secondary EU law and the harmonised interest of enhanced cooperation law may reduce the scope of all binding secondary EU law, and thus, affect the *acquis communautaire.* Such effects would contradict the constitutional framework of enhanced cooperation.

From this it follows that existing secondary EU law limits the legislative freedom of enhanced cooperation in the same way as the law-making power of a single Member State. A group of Member States is prohibited from introducing laws under the enhanced cooperation procedure which conflict with existing (ordinary) secondary EU laws. Differences to the law-making of a single Member State exist, however, in cases where (ordinary) secondary EU law only provides for minimum harmonisation and a group of Member States commonly agrees to go beyond the protection provided by existing EU laws. Under these circumstances, laws of

[893] See Chapter 2, subsection A.IV.
[894] Schön, 'Facilitating Entry by Facilitating Exit' (n 886); Wolfram Richter, 'Mehrheitsbeschlüsse in der europäischen Steuerpolitik?' (2019) Ökonomenstimme <https://www.oekonomenstimme.org/artikel/2019/05/mehrheitsbeschluesse-in-der-europaeischen-steuerpolitik/> accessed 3 February 2021 .
[895] See Chapter 2, subsection A.IV.

enhanced cooperation, like the laws of single Member States, have to comply with the fundamental freedoms,[896] and it may make a difference to aligning with the free movement guarantees of the European treaties whether a particular rule pursues a harmonised interest of a group of Member States or whether the law (only) reflects an interest of a single Member State.[897]

II. The Impact of Existing Enhanced Cooperation Law on the European Legislature's Freedom

The intention of Art 326 of the TFEU, to protect the level of integration already established between all Member States does not change in the reverse case, meaning when enhanced cooperation law already exists and (ordinary) secondary EU law is later introduced. The enhanced cooperation procedure is designed as an alternative for willing Member States to cooperate if some Member States are not ready or willing to join the legislative initiative. Differentiated integration within the European Union is a response to an increased diversity among Member States of the European Union and the European treaties' preference of common group actions of Member States vis-à-vis unilateral law-making of single Member States.[898] The common action of some Member States deepens integration between them and fosters the functioning of the European internal market, as enhanced cooperation law erodes trade hampering legislative differences, at least between some Member States. However, the constitutional framework of enhanced cooperation gives primacy to an EU-wide integration process even if integration between all Member States is slower. Against the constitutional foundation of the enhanced cooperation procedure and the European integration process, the *lex specialis* or the *lex posterior* rule and its underlying notion do not help to solve a conflict between existing enhanced cooperation law and (ordinary) secondary EU law[899] because these conflict of law rules reflect the legislature's freedom to amend and change existing laws.[900] However, the European legislature is not entirely free within the enhanced cooperation procedure. Rather, the European legislature is bound by both existing and future (ordinary) secondary EU law, and thus the conflict of law rule to be applied has to recognise the different scope of integration (all Member States

[896] Weatherill, *The Internal Market* (n 4) 210; Nadja Braun Binder, *Rechtsangleichung in der EU im Bereich der direkten Steuern: Analyse der Handlungsformen unter besonderer Berücksichtigung des Soft Law* (Mohr Siebeck 2017) 60.

[897] See this chapter Part I, subsections C and E.

[898] See Chapter 4, subsection G.I.

[899] Becker, 'Differenzierungen der Rechtseinheit' (n 892) 53; Grieser (n 892) 126 arguing that the *lex posterior* rule should apply in case ordinary secondary EU law constitutes the latter law-making; in this vein see also Cloppenburg (n 892) 741. However, some authors want to apply the *lex posterior* rule when ordinary secondary EU law has later been enacted: Grieser (n 892) 126; Cloppenburg (n 892) 741.

[900] Vranes (n 841) 397.

versus a group of Member States) and invalidate the rules with the lower integration threshold. In other words, *lex uniformis derogat legi particulari.*

Conflict of law rules aiming to solve a conflict between enhanced cooperation law and (ordinary) secondary EU laws are allowed to invalidate enhanced cooperation law, as the conflicting laws are both the result of European law-making.[901] One may counter that the European legislature's introduction of (ordinary) secondary EU laws and enhanced cooperation laws are only identical if unanimous voting is required in the Council, as the Member States which voted on the (ordinary) secondary EU law have only voted on the law of enhanced co-operation in those cases. Such an understanding of European law-making would reduce the European legislature to an accumulation of the Member States' unilateral opinions.[902] Majority voting in the Council goes far beyond an enforcement of national interests of the majority of Member States and an inferiority of national interests of a minority of Member States. The European legislature establishes European values which are borne by all Member States, and thus a derogation of enhanced cooperation law to the extent it conflicts with ordinary secondary EU law is, from a methodological and constitutional point of view, the only legitimate approach.

To conclude, a conflict arising between existing enhanced cooperation law and later introduced secondary EU law has to be resolved by conflict of law rules recognising the constitutional framework of the enhanced cooperation procedure, in particular Art 326 of the TFEU. These conflict of law rules have to invalidate laws with the least integrational scope, which will always be the law of enhanced cooperation as it only establishes deeper integration between a group of Member States.

E. Enforcement of the Invalidity Claim

I. Overview of the Enforcement Tools

Derogation rules solve a conflict between laws by way of invalidation. The conflicting law may either become invalid by itself (*ipso iure*) or it may need a constitutive action by the CJEU to invalidate the law. CJEU case law on the invalidity claim of secondary EU laws points towards the need for a Court's decision, as secondary EU law 'must be deemed to be valid until such time as it is declared invalid'.[903] Granting the CJEU the monopoly to interpret and (if necessary)

[901] Which excludes the precedence doctrine applied to conflicts between secondary EU law and national legislation, see above in this chapter Part III, subsection C. For a different view on the legislature see Cloppenburg (n 892) 739.
[902] In that negative vein, ibid.
[903] CJEU, 28 February 1989, 201/87, *Cargill*, ECLI:EU:C:1989:100, para 21.

invalidate EU laws[904] ensures the uniform application of EU laws, as the requirement of uniformity is particularly imperative when the validity of EU law is in question.[905]

Concerning the procedure available to bring conflicting secondary EU laws before the CJEU, one has to distinguish between derogation clauses reflecting the European constitutional framework with which the European legislature has to comply, and derogation clauses expressing the constitutional freedom of the European legislature. The first category consists of the *lex superior derogat legi inferiori* and the *lex uniformis derogat legi particulari* rule. Both rules find their justification within the European constitutional framework, as secondary EU law has to comply with primary EU law[906] and enhanced cooperation law has to comply with both primary and secondary EU law.[907] The European constitutional framework prohibited the European legislature from introducing (ordinary) secondary EU law conflicting with primary EU law as well as enhanced cooperation law conflicting with (ordinary) secondary EU laws.[908] Both the *lex superior derogat legi inferiori* and the *lex uniformis derogat legi particulari* rule may therefore be enforced by an action of annulment under Art 263 of the TFEU.

The second category covers the *lex posterior derogat legi priori* and the *lex specialis derogat legi generali* rule. These rules manifest the European legislature's power to introduce new or more specific European legislation and offer solutions to overcome problems related to the legislature's neglected duty to determine the relationship between the laws (eg through repealing previous laws). The invalidity of the conflicting rules may not follow from an infringement of the European constitutional framework but from the European constitutional framework itself. Since the European legislature did not infringe European constitutional law, there is no need to allow conflicting (and therefore derogated) secondary EU laws to be brought before the CJEU under Art 263 of the TFEU. In the course of applying the laws, questions on how to solve conflicts between secondary EU laws may arise, which can be brought before the Court under Art 267 of the TFEU.

[904] CJEU, 10 January 2006, C-344/04, *International Air Transport Association and European Low Fares Airline Association*, ECLI:EU:C:2006:10, para 27; CJEU, 21 March 2000, C-6/99, *Association Greenpeace France*, ECLI:EU:C:2000:148, para 54; CJEU, 21 February 1991, C-143/88 and C-92/89, *Zuckerfabrik Süderdithmarschen AG*, ECLI:EU:C:1991:65, para 17; CJEU; 18 July 2007, C-119/05, *Lucchini SpA*, ECLI:EU:C:2007:434, para 53.

[905] CJEU, 22 October 1987, 314/85, *Foto-Frost*, ECLI:EU:C:1987:452, para 15; CJEU, 22 June 2010, C-188/10 and C-189/10, *Aziz Melki and Sélim Abdeli*, ECLI:EU:C:2010:363, para 54; see also Paul Craig, 'The Classics of EU Law Revisited: CILFIT and Foto-Frost' in Miguel Poiares Maduro and Loïc Azoulai (eds), *The Past and Future of EU Law: The Classics of EU Law Revisited on the 50th Anniversary of the Rome Treaty* (Hart Publishing 2010) 190.

[906] Dourado, 'The Relationship between Primary and Secondary EU Law in Tax Law' (n 809).

[907] Art 326 of the TFEU.

[908] In those cases, the irregularity may not be 'of such manifest seriousness that it could not be tolerated by the Community legal order' and may therefore be a non-existent act (CJEU, 29 June 1995, C-135/93, *Spain v Commission*, ECLI:EU:C:1995:201, para 18; see also CJEU, 5 October 2004, C-475/01, *Commission v Hellenic Republic*, ECLI:EU:C:2004:585, para 19).

II. Annulment of Enhanced Cooperation Law

Following this reasoning, any enhanced cooperation law conflicting with (ordinary) secondary EU laws remains valid until the Court declares otherwise. However, any Member State (whether participating or non-participating) as well as the European Parliament, European Commission, and the Council are entitled to demand annulment of these laws before the CJEU under Art 263 of the TFEU. Moreover, domestic courts of participating Member States can refer the validity question of enhanced cooperation law to the CJEU[909] in cases in which the domestic court needs to apply enhanced cooperation law and has doubts regarding its validity.

We shall return to the possibility of demanding an annulment of enhanced cooperation law under Art 263 of the TFEU. According to Art 263 of the TFEU, the CJEU 'shall review the legality of legislative acts', and '[i]f the action is well founded, the Court … shall declare the act concerned to be void'.[910] Under these proceedings, each Member State is a privileged applicant, meaning that the applicant does not have to demonstrate any legal interest whatsoever in order to raise proceedings.[911] In that regard, the proceedings under Art 263 of the TFEU have the function of an objective legitimacy review, allowing the CJEU to deprive the legal effects of enhanced cooperation law conflicting with secondary EU laws.

The action of annulment is subject to a two-month time bar,[912] starting with the publication of the measure, or the notification of the measure to the plaintiff. In absence of a publication or notification, the two-month period begins with the day on which it came to the knowledge of the plaintiff. So far, the CJEU has strictly enforced the grace period,[913] ensuring that the legal positions are clear and certain.[914]

[909] Under Art 267 of the TFEU.

[910] Art 264 Subsection 1 of the TFEU.

[911] CJEU, 26 March 1987, 45/86, *Commission v Council*, ECLI:EU:C:1987:163, para 3; CJEU, 23 February 1988, 131/86, *United Kingdom*, ECLI:EU:C:1988:86, para 6; CJEU, 21 January 2003, C-378/00, *Commission v Parliament*, ECLI:EU:C:2003:42, para 28; CJEU, 13 October 2011, C-463/10 P and C-475/10 P, *Deutsche Post AG*, ECLI:EU:C:2011:656, para 36; CJEU, 5 September 2012, C-355/10, *Parliament v Council and Commission*, ECLI:EU:C:2012:516, para 37; see also David Edward and Robert Lane, *Edward and Lane on European Union Law* (Edward Elgar Publishing 2013) para 5.74.

[912] Art 263 Subsection 6 of the TFEU.

[913] CJEU, 9 July 2019, T-254/19, *AlpaSuri GbR Barbara Bruns & Wolfgang Stamp*, ECLI:EU:T:2019:486, para 7 et seq; CJEU, 12 October 2018, T-416/18, *Hungary Restaurant Company Kereskedelmi és Szolgáltató Kft.*, ECLI:EU:T:2018:705, para 5 et seq; CJEU, 21 March 2002, T-218/01, *Laboratoire Monique Rémy SAS*, ECLI:EU:T:2002:86, para 9 et seq; see in this vein see also Edward and Lane (n 911) para 5.67.

[914] CJEU, 12 July 1984, 227/83, *Sophie Moussis*, ECLI:EU:C:1984:276, para 12; CJEU, 7 May 1986, 191/84, *Jean-Pierre Barcella*, ECLI:EU:C:1986:197, para 12; CJEU, 23 January 1997, C-246/95, *Myrianne Coen*, ECLI:EU:C:1997:33, para 21; CJEU, 1 April 2011, T-468/10, *Joseph Doherty*, ECLI:EU:T:2011:133, para 12; CJEU, 16 June 2016, T-124/16, *Laurenz Ferdinand Eigner*, ECLI:EU:T:2016:387, para 6; CJEU, 4 July 2018, T-294/18, *Lackmann Fleisch- und Feinkostfabrik*, ECLI:EU:T:2018:415, para 6; CJEU, 12 October 2018, T-416/18, *Hungary Restaurant Company Kereskedelmi és Szolgáltató Kft.*, ECLI:EU:T:2018:705, para 6; CJEU, 14 March 2019, C-700/18 P, *Hungary Restaurant Company Kft.*, ECLI:EU:C:2019:215, para 4; CJEU, 9 July 2019, T-254/19, *AlpaSuri GbR Barbara Bruns & Wolfgang Stamp*, ECLI:EU:T:2019:486, para 8. In this vein, the parties entitled to bring infringements proceedings

Bringing infringement proceedings before the CJEU within two months after the enhanced cooperation law's publication may only be possible if secondary EU law already exists and the group of Member States went beyond its legislative freedom. However, if conflicting secondary EU laws were introduced at a later stage, accordingly after enhanced cooperation has already been established, Member States may no longer be allowed to bring infringement proceedings before the CJEU, as the two-month period may already have elapsed. Considering the aim and purpose of the two-month time bar, establishing legal certainty and clarity and ensuring equal treatment, it may be possible to argue that in cases in which (ordinary) secondary EU law is introduced after enhanced cooperation law has already been enacted, the Member States are only able to recognise the conflict and the infringement of Art 326 of the TFEU after secondary EU law is in place. Therefore, the two-month period should commence with the publication of the secondary EU law act which allows one to recognise the conflict and the infringement of Art 326 of the TFEU. Such a reading of the provision does not extend the two-month period but allows the clock to start ticking at a time when it is possible for the Member States and the European institutions to recognise infringements of the European constitutional framework.

F. Illustrative Cases

Three examples may best explain how existing secondary EU laws may or may not limit the Member States' freedom to enact laws under the enhanced cooperation procedure. The first case will be a fictitious European air passenger tax which may conflict with the European emission trading scheme (see subsection I). The second example elaborates on the European Commission's proposal for a financial transaction tax and potential conflicts between such a tax and the Capital Duty Directive (see subsection II). The last example will deal with a financial activity tax compensating for VAT undertaxation caused by the VAT exemption for certain financial services (see subsection III).

I. Air Passenger Tax

Assume that there is sufficient political support to introduce an air passenger tax at European Union level under the enhanced cooperation procedure between at least nine Member States. The European air passenger tax is supposed to 'encourage

under Art 263 of the TFEU are not allowed to demand judicial review under Art 267 of the TFEU, at a point when the two-month period (Art 263 Subsection 6 of the TFEU) is over: Lorna Woods and others, *Steiner & Woods EU Law* (13th edn, OUP 2017) 285.

environmentally friendly behaviour' and should apply to any departure or arrival of a passenger in one of the participating Member States. Passenger flights departing from or arriving in one of the Member States would therefore be subject to tax. The tax debtor shall be the operating air carrier. The tax liability is calculated per passenger and flight distance. To allow the participating Member States to remain competitive, air freight transport shall be excluded from the tax. The aim of the air passenger tax is clearly to reduce greenhouse gas emissions, but the secondary EU law will also harmonise all participating Member States' existing taxes in that field. To identify the relevant competence clause, the main purpose and content of the EU air passenger tax has to be determined.[915] Accordingly, it has to be determined whether the primary aim of the tax is to harmonise existing national taxes, the differences between which constitute a barrier to the European internal market, or whether the European air passenger tax is primarily intended to influence people's behaviour, leading to a reduction of CO_2 emissions. If tax harmonisation is sought with a view to the functioning of the European internal market, Art 115 of the TFEU may be the appropriate rule; however, if the European air passenger tax predominately aims to reduce CO_2 emissions, the European environmental competence of Art 192 of the TFEU[916] has to form the legal ground for any legislative action.

We shall further assume that it follows from Member States' submissions that the purpose of the air passenger tax shall be to meet the standards of the Paris Agreement.[917] This aim is also reflected in the tax base, which depends on the flight distance, which in turn indirectly identifies the level of polluting emissions. The harmonisation of national taxes would only be a reflex of secondary EU law, but not its main purpose.[918] Against this background, it is now necessary to ask whether there is any secondary EU law which could block a new European initiative to reduce greenhouse emissions. The European emissions trading scheme is the current European mechanism to reduce harmful emissions (also) from air traffic and comply with the Kyoto Protocol, and now additionally to comply with the Paris Agreement.

The European emission trading scheme could prevent the participating Member States from introducing an air passenger tax under the enhanced cooperation procedure if the scheme exhaustively regulates the control of harmful emissions within the European Union. The European emissions trading scheme is based on a European directive which aims to meet the EU's commitment under the Kyoto Protocol through an efficient European market for greenhouse gas emission

[915] See Chapter 4, subsection F.III.

[916] Provisions with a primary fiscal nature require a unanimous vote in the Council, Art 192 Subsection 2 of the TFEU.

[917] Paris Agreement, <https://unfccc.int/sites/default/files/english_paris_agreement.pdf> accessed 3 February 2021.

[918] For more details see this chapter subsections F and G.

allowances.[919] Aircraft operators have also been included in the third phase of European emissions trading.[920] Initially, it was restricted to flights within Europe, but from 2017 onwards, all flights from and into the European Union fall within the scope of the European emissions trading scheme.

Emissions trading aims to reduce greenhouse gas emissions by ensuring that the volume of greenhouse gases emitted is covered by sufficient certificates. Issuers are initially allocated certificates free of charge on the primary market and can also purchase them at auctions. If these certificates are not sufficient to cover the issues, certificates must be purchased on the secondary market, that is, in trading with other issuers. The demand thus determines the price of these certificates. If there is a shortage, it will be cheaper for emitters to invest in technologies or processes that reduce greenhouse gas emissions.

Accordingly, the European air passenger tax and the European emission trading scheme have the same aim, namely a reduction of greenhouse gasses. In terms of whether both mechanisms can coexist, it is necessary to determine whether the emissions trading scheme constitutes a closed and exhaustive system for regulating greenhouse gas emissions, in particular in the area of air traffic. The question of whether or not secondary EU law establishes an exhaustive system has to be answered with respect to the objectives of the law and the substance of the provisions.[921] According to recital 23 in the preamble to the Directive, emissions trading is 'part of a comprehensive and coherent package of policies and measures implemented at Member State and Community level'.[922] Additionally, for activities covered by the trading scheme, Member States may examine the impact of regulatory, fiscal, and other measures aimed at the same objectives. The recital 24 adds that '[t]he instrument of taxation can be a national policy to limit emissions from installations temporarily excluded'.

The recitals of the Directive state that the European emissions trading scheme does not constitute an exhaustive regulation on the control of harmful emissions within the European Union. In addition to emissions trading (the floor of common regulation),[923] Member States are free to take unilateral fiscal measures

919 Directive, 13 October 2003, 2003/87/EC, establishing a system for greenhouse gas emission allowanced trading within the Union and amending Council Directive 96/61/EC, OJ, 25 October 2003, L 275, 32, in the version of Directive, 14 March 2018, 2003/87/EC, to enhance cost-effective emission reductions and low-carbon investments, and Decision (EU) 2015/1814, OJ, 19 March 2018, L 76, 3.

920 Art 3c of the ETS Directive.

921 CJEU, 30 October 1974, 190/73, *van Haaster*, ECLI:EU:C:1974:113, para 7; CJEU, 24 November 2011, C-468/10 and C-469/10, *Asociación Nacional de Establecimientos Financieros de Crédito (ASNEF) and Federación de Comercio Electrónico y Marketing Directo (FECEMD)*, ECLI:EU:C:2011:77, para 30; CJEU, 21 December 2016, C-203 and C-698/15, *Tele2 Sverige AB*, ECLI:EU:C:2016:970, para 90; Arena (n 870) 33x arguing that 'comprehensive and detailed regulatory schemes are more likely to be regarded as exhaustive. That is certainly the case of EU legislation that "contains a set of provisions specifically devoted" to the same aspect the national measure seeks to regulate.' See this chapter Part I, subsection D.

922 Directive, 13 October 2003, 2003/87/EC, establishing a scheme for greenhouse gas emission allowance trading within the Community and amending Council Directive 96/61/EC, OJ, 25 October 2003, L 275, 32.

923 Weatherill, *The Internal Market* (n 4) 210.

or introduce enhanced cooperation law to achieve the objective of reducing greenhouse gas emissions. However, any legal measure taken by a single Member State or a group of Member States going beyond European (minimum) harmonisation (eg introduction of a European air passenger tax) has to respect the ceiling set out by 'the broader legal rules of the internal market, most of all those governing non-discrimination and free movement'.[924]

II. Financial Transaction Tax

The European Commission already issued two proposals for a European financial transaction tax.[925] The first proposal aimed for an EU-wide harmonisation of transaction taxes in the financial sector;[926] the second proposal recognised the resistance of some Member States and aimed for a harmonised approach within enhanced cooperation.[927] Both proposals aim for a transaction tax on the secondary financial market, covering a broadly determined range of financial institutions and transactions. The first proposal also included changes to the Capital Duty Directive,[928] preventing conflicts between existing secondary EU law and a common financial transaction tax.[929] The Capital Duty Directive is a measure of exhaustive harmonisation.[930] Thus, it prohibits the introduction of new indirect taxes on the raising of capital and only allows Member States to maintain[931] such taxes under certain circumstances.[932] Indirect taxes on the raising of capital hamper investment, regrouping and development of undertakings,[933] and more generally economic

[924] ibid. For the interaction between enhanced cooperation law and the European internal market see this chapter Part I and Part II.

[925] Now, there is a third proposal on the table. However, the details have not yet been made public, and thus the following discussion will focus on the Commission's first and second proposal.

[926] Commission, 28 September 2011, Proposal for a Council Directive on a common system of financial transaction tax an amending Directive 2008/7/EC, COM(2011) 594.

[927] Commission, 14 February 2013, Proposal for a Council Directive implementing enhanced cooperation in the area of financial transaction tax, COM(2013) 71 final.

[928] Council, 12 February 2008, Directive 2008/7/EC, concerning indirect taxes on the raising of capital, OJ, 21 February 2008, L 46, 11.

[929] The proposal wanted to introduce Art 6a into the Capital Duty Directive laying out that the Capital Duty Directive 'shall be without prejudice to Council Directive' introducing the European financial transaction tax.

[930] CJEU, 19 October 2017, C-573/16, *Air Berlin*, ECLI:EU:C:2017:772, para 27; for the Directive 69/335/EEC (Council, 17 July 1969, directive concerning indirect taxes on the raising of capital, OJ, 3 October 1969, L 249, 25) which was recast by the Capital Duty Directive 2008/7/EC: CJEU, 7 June 2007, C-178/05, *Commission v Greece*, ECLI:EU:C:2007:317, para 31; CJEU, 1 October 2009, C-569/07, *HSBC Holdings*, ECLI:EU:C:2009:594, para 25.

[931] The Member State must have charged the capital duty on 1 January 2006, Art 7 of the Capital Duty Directive.

[932] Arts 8–14 of the Capital Duty Directive.

[933] Council, 12 February 2008, Directive 2008/7/EC, concerning indirect taxes on the raising of capital, OJ, 21 February 2008, L 46, 11, recital 4.

growth,[934] and thus they are banned within the European internal market. Despite any amendments to the Capital Duty Directive, the Commission argued that a conflict between the Capital Duty Directive and a European financial transaction tax may not arise because the proposed financial transaction tax shall only apply to secondary financial market transactions.[935] The Commission's proposal for a European financial transaction tax under enhanced cooperation does not include any amending provisions for the Capital Duty Directive but explicitly sets out that the 'provisions of Council Directive 2008/7/EC continue to be fully applicable'.[936] The Commission proposal grants the Capital Duty Directive primacy, as to the extent the Directive 'prohibits or could prohibit the imposition of taxes on certain transactions, ... they should not be subject to FTT'.[937]

However, it has been argued that the granting of clear primacy of the Capital Duty Directive within the proposal for a common financial transaction tax under enhanced cooperation is not enough to comply with existing secondary EU law, as Art 5 Subsection 2 of the Capital Duty Directive prohibits the imposition of any form of indirect tax whatsoever on dealings in stocks, shares or other securities. The wording of this provision is not restricted to dealings on the primary financial market, and thus it is argued that the levying of indirect taxes on dealings in stocks, shares, and securities both on the primary and secondary EU market are prohibited.[938] Some authors want to apply Art 6 of the Capital Duty Directive, an exception to the prohibition on levying capital duties, to all taxes on the secondary financial market.[939] Others claim, based on CJEU case law,[940] that Art 6 of the Capital Duty Directive allows Member States to levy taxes with the same characteristics as capital duty on the transfer of securities. Accordingly, Art 6 of the Capital Duty Directive shall only provide an exception for the taxation of transactions on the primary financial market.[941] If the Capital Duty Directive prohibited any tax on dealings in stocks, shares, and securities on the secondary financial market, and if Art 6 Subsection 1 (a) of the Capital Duty Directive does not apply to dealings on the secondary financial market, any financial transaction tax would contradict existing secondary EU law. At a European level, Member States are able to introduce

[934] Commission, 4 December 2006, Press Release, Indirect taxation: the European Commission proposes to abolish capital duty on the raising of capital, IP/06/1673.

[935] European Commission, 'Impact Assessment Vol. 4—Proposal for a Council Directive on a Common System of Financial Transaction Tax and Amending Directive 2008/7/EC' (n 830) para 212.

[936] Recital 9 of the Commission's proposal, COM(2013) 71 final.

[937] ibid.

[938] Mayer and Heidfeld (n 837) 377; Dahm and Hamacher, 'Finanztransaktionssteuern' (n 837) 128; Dahm and Hamacher, 'Verstärkte Zusammenarbeit' (n 837) 29.

[939] Mayer and Heidfeld (n 837) 377–78; Christoph Gröpl, 'Steuerrecht' in Manfred A Dauses and Markus Ludwigs (eds), *Handbuch des EU-Wirtschaftsrechts* (44th edn, Beck Verlag 2018) para 641.

[940] CJEU, 9 October 2014, C-299/13, *Gielen*, ECLI:EU:C:2014:2266, para 28; see also CJEU, 19 April 2013, C-443/09, *Grillo Star Srl*, ECLI:EU:C:2012:213, para 28.

[941] Dahm and Hamacher, 'Finanztransaktionssteuern' (n 837) 128 et seq; Liepe, Pielka, and Malaviya (n 837) 1350–51; Ihering (n 837) 614.

a European financial tax when, at the same time, changes to the Capital Duty Directive are made. However, by way of enhanced cooperation, a group of Member States cannot change existing secondary EU laws, as the group's legislative freedom is restricted[942] and any enhanced cooperation law is invalid to the extent it conflicts with (ordinary) secondary EU law.[943]

A closer look at Art 5 Subsection 2 (a) of the Capital Duty Directive reveals that the prohibition on tax dealings in stocks, shares, or other securities only addresses the primary financial market. According to Art 1 of the Capital Duty Directive, defining its substantive scope, the Directive regulates the levying of indirect taxes in respect of contributions of capital to capital companies, restructuring operations involving capital companies, and the issue of certain securities and debentures. None of these elements includes dealings on the secondary financial market. Moreover, recital 2 lays out that 'indirect taxes on the raising of capital, namely the capital duty (the duty chargeable on contributions of capital to companies and firms), the stamp duty on securities, and duty on restructuring operations, … give rise to discrimination, double taxation and disparities which interfere with the free movement of capital'. The scope and purpose of the Capital Duty Directive show that it was never intended to regulate dealings on the secondary financial market.[944] Art 5 Subsection 2 (a) of the Capital Duty Directive prohibits the levying of taxes on dealings in stocks, shares, and securities not with the intention to prohibit taxation on dealings on the secondary financial market but prevent the possibility that the prohibition of capital duties is denied practical effect. Member States' financial regulations may demand that clearing parties or other authorities in the process of issuing shares are involved. To ensure that the entire issuing process (including all acquisitions of securities between (clearing) parties which have to be involved) remains untaxed,[945] Art 5 Subsection 2 (a) of the Capital Duty Directive prohibits indirect taxation on the 'creation, issue, admission to quotation on a stock exchange, making available on the market or dealing in stocks, shares or other securities'.

From this it follows that the Capital Duty Directive does not prohibit the taxation of transactions on the secondary financial market. Art 5 of the Capital Duty Directive is drafted in a very broad manner to ensure that the issuing process is not taxed regardless of how many interim steps and persons are involved to comply with financial regulations. The aim and purpose of the Directive does not go beyond a ban on capital duties, and thus a financial transaction tax, which does not apply to the issuing of securities and which does not tax the restructuring of capital companies, complies with the Capital Duty Directive. In other words, a group of Member States is free to introduce a financial transaction tax for the secondary

[942] See this chapter Part III, subsection D.I.

[943] See in this chapter Part III, subsection D.II.

[944] Daniel Weyde and others, 'Der Kommissionsvorschlag zur Einführung einer Finanztransaktionssteuer in elf EU-Mitgliedstaaten' (2013) Deutsche Steuer-Zeitung 495, 503.

[945] CJEU, 19 October 2017, C-573/16, *Air Berlin*, ECLI:EU:C:2017:772, paras 40–41.

financial market, which does not burden the restructuring of capital companies under enhanced cooperation.

III. Financial Activity Tax Compensating for VAT Undertaxation

The European VAT system widely exempts financial services, meaning that the granting of a credit and the managing of that credit are not subject to VAT,[946] but any input VAT levied on (input) transactions necessary to provide these exempt output transactions is not deductible. Depending on the amount of input VAT, the exemption may either be beneficial or unfavourable for the non-business recipient of the services because the taxable person (the service provider) will pass the VAT burden onto the recipient. Since the unrecoverable input VAT is also passed onto the business recipient, business use of financial services tends to be overtaxed and this leads to cascading effects. However, in any case, the value added by the financial service provider is not taxed under the European VAT system.

According to the explanatory memorandum, VAT exemptions were introduced into the VAT Directive for services 'related to the fields, such as insurance, provision of credit and dealings in currency and stock exchange, *where they are justified for reasons of general policy common to all the Member States*'.[947] From this it follows that the European legislature did not pursue a specific and autonomous policy objective when introducing exemptions for financial services into the VAT Directive. Rather, exemptions for the financial sector were a common practice in the Member States because it was assumed to be impossible to determine the consideration for the supply.[948] Therefore, the VAT exemption in the financial sector is triggered by practical considerations and not by system-building features.

Some Member States may wish to address the potential undertaxation of financial services by imposing on the financial sector a specific addition-based tax. Since the net VAT (the difference between the VAT charged on sales and the VAT paid on purchases) equals the sum of profits and wages, an alternative approach for taxing the financial sector would be a tax levied on the sum of profits and wages.[949] An

[946] Art 135 Subsection 1 (b) and (c) of the VAT Directive.

[947] Commission, 20 June 1973, Proposal for a sixth Council Directive on the harmonization of Member States concerning turnover taxes, COM(73) 950 final, Bulletin of the European Communities, Supplement 11/73, 15.

[948] Alan Schenk and Howell Zee, 'Treating Financial Services under a Value-Added Tax: Conceptual Issues and Country Practices' (2001) 22 Tax Notes International 3309; Oskar Henkow, *Financial Activities in European VAT: A Theoretical and Legal Research of the European VAT System and the Actual and Preferred Treatment of Financial Activities* (Kluwer Law International 2008) 6 et seq. However, today, modern GST/VAT system overcame these problems: Satya Poddar, 'VAT on Financial Services, Searching for a Workable Alternative' in Richard E Krever and David Ian White (eds), *GST in Retrospect and Prospect* (Thomson Brookers 2007).

[949] This approach is called the 'addition method', see Lorey Hoffman, Satya Poddar, and John Whalley, 'Taxation of Banking Services under a Consumption Type, Destination Basis VAT' (1987)

addition-based tax for the financial sector allows taxing the value added of any margin-based transactions.[950]

Member States may be prohibited from levying an addition-based tax if the European VAT system provides an exhaustive framework for taxing value added within the European Union. In other words, the Member States are pre-empted from taking any action on indirectly taxing the value added by financial services if the European VAT system establishes full harmonisation this field. Art 401 of the VAT Directive states that the Member States are free to maintain or introduce 'taxes on insurance contracts, taxes on betting and gambling, excise duties, stamp duties or, more generally, any taxes, duties or charges which cannot be characterised as turnover taxes'. To put it differently, Member States are precluded from introducing turnover taxes,[951] meaning taxes which have the same characteristics as the European VAT. The CJEU has ruled that the European VAT follows four essential characteristics,

> namely that VAT applies generally to transactions relating to goods or services, it is proportional to the price charged by the taxable person in return for the goods and services which he has supplied, it is charged at each stage of the production and distribution process, including that of retail sale, irrespective of the number of transactions which have previously taken place, and the amounts paid during the preceding stages of the production and distribution process are deducted from the VAT payable by a taxable person, with the result that that tax applies, at any given stage, only to the value added at that stage and the final burden of that tax rests ultimately with the consumer.[952]

The ban on introducing turnover taxes which have the same characteristics as the European VAT aims to protect the harmonisation efforts at European level and prevent trade hampering effects following from a second layer of national value-added taxation. An addition-based tax for the financial sector would not undermine the EU's harmonisation efforts but would correct some of the VAT Directive's shortcomings. Moreover, an addition-based tax would have a completely different tax base. Profits and wages would be subject to tax and not the consideration for the

40 National Tax Journal 547, 551; Liam P Ebrill and others, *The Modern VAT* (International Monetary Fund 2001) 20.

[950] See for more details 'Financial Sector Taxation: The IMF's Report to the G-20 and Background Material' (n 832) 118 et seq.

[951] See Art 401 of the VAT Directive; CJEU, 12 June 2019, C-185/18, *Oro Efectivo SL*, ECLI:EU:C:2019:485, para 21; CJEU, 7 August 2018, C-475/17, *Viking Motors and Others*, ECLI:EU:C:2018:636, para 27.

[952] CJEU, 12 June 2019, C-185/18, *Oro Efectivo SL*, ECLI:EU:C:2019:485, para 23; see also CJEU, 27 November 2008, C-151/08, *Renta*, ECLI:EU:C:2008:662, para 32, 45; CJEU, 20 March 2014, C-139/12, *Caixa d'Estalvis I Pensions de Barcelona*, ECLI:EU:C:2014:174, para 29.

supply. Since such a tax would neither share all the relevant characteristics of the European VAT nor undermine the European harmonisation efforts, the Member States are free to use the enhanced cooperation procedure to enact an addition-based tax for the financial sector.

Part IV: CONCLUSIONS

The procedural framework of the primary EU law provisions on the establishment of enhanced cooperation protects the European internal market. Any enhanced cooperation shall not only 'comply with the Treaties and the law of the Union' but shall also 'not constitute a barrier to or discrimination in trade between Member States' or 'distort competition between them'.[953] The wording of the provisions is relatively familiar to every lawyer specialised in EU law because non-discrimination, free competition, and internal legal coherence are the backbones of the European internal market. In the traditional setting, the special non-discrimination provisions, the fundamental freedoms, as well as competition law prevent the national legislature from introducing laws of a protectionist nature. In other words, the fundamental freedoms and competition law prohibit national laws which shield the national markets from foreign goods, services, persons, and capital. A shielding of the national markets prevents free movement within and competition on the European internal market, which has a negative effect on the efficient allocation of resources. Despite the efficiency claims, the European internal market allows Member States to prioritise certain (national) values over market neutrality. Accordingly, the European internal market is not a clean single market, but a market consisting of the individual markets of the Member States.

The application of the fundamental freedoms and competition law, in particular state aid law, to (tax) laws of a single Member State raised multiple issues which are extensively addressed by the CJEU's case law. When it comes to the application of the fundamental freedoms and state aid law to enhanced cooperation law, the logic underlying this case law may not be entirely applicable. Enhanced cooperation law represents the will and intention of at least nine Member States and its law-making process involves several European institutions. Therefore, enhanced cooperation law cannot be considered as the law of a single Member State. Contrary to the interplay between the fundamental freedoms and Member State national laws, only a few CJEU rulings exist on the application of the fundamental freedoms to secondary EU law. Even though there are some Court rulings on how the fundamental freedoms have to be applied to secondary EU law, the rationale underlying these cases may not be applicable to enhanced cooperation law because it is

[953] Art 326 of the TFEU.

different from ordinary secondary EU law as it does not bind all the Member States. Regulatory harmonisation at European level defeats the trade-hampering effect through uniformity and since the European internal market does not prohibit regulation per se, a uniform regulatory approach is in line with the fundamental freedoms. However, if certain public interest concerns demand adjustments of goods and services on the market of every single Member State, secondary EU law may create trade obstacles within the European internal market, obstacles which need to be justified. In any case, enhanced cooperation is only capable of establishing uniformity within the group, and thus trade-hampering diversity may always exist in the relationship between participating and non-participating Member States.

The hybrid character of enhanced cooperation law makes it particularly hard to apply the fundamental freedoms. On the one hand, it is necessary to honour the integration efforts of the participating Member States, but on the other there is still no uniformity on the entire European internal market. It has been shown that three categories of enhanced cooperation law can be identified based on the participating Member States' integration efforts.

The first group, value-based harmonisation, accounts for the deepest form of integration because the Member States establish harmonised values and unify their laws based on these values. To honour the integration efforts, participating Member States should be allowed to protect the harmonised group values from being exploited by non-participating Member States, but participating Member States should not be allowed to protect themselves from any negative effects following from enhanced cooperation law. In other words, participating Member States are allowed to justify protective obstacles based on a so-called light-touch justification approach, but defensive obstacles have to meet the ordinary justification threshold. The CJEU has developed the light-touch justification approach for general restrictions and discriminations imposed by secondary EU law. Under a light-touch justification approach, the harmonised value may establish a ground of justification and the proportionality test is limited to a plausibility check at the suitability level and a reduced scope for finding a less restrictive but equally effective measure at the necessity level.

The second set of rules enacted under the enhanced cooperation procedure are trade-favouring rules. Trade-favouring applies where the fundamental freedoms are not of any help in smoothening cross-border intra-EU trade. The fundamental freedoms may not be capable of eliminating trade obstacles where the Member States can justify restrictions or a discriminatory treatment based on overriding reasons of public interest or where the trade obstacles do not fall within the scope of the fundamental freedoms. In case of justified restrictions to the fundamental freedoms, the Member States may be willing to grant national or resident treatment to non-nationals or non-residents if the home Member States of these taxpayers grant the same beneficial treatment to the residents or nationals of the former Member State. In other words, Member States may be willing to eliminate 'justified' trade obstacles in a reciprocal manner. In cases where the obstacle does not even fall within the scope of the fundamental freedoms, the Member States may have to go beyond pure resident treatment to remove the obstacle, like in the case of preventing double taxation. Since the participating Member States are only willing to establish resident treatment because the other participating Member States are doing the same, the members of the group may want to restrict the beneficial treatment (the group benefit) to intra-group transactions. It becomes evident that within trade-favouring enhanced cooperation, cross-group economic transactions may be treated less favourably than intra-group economic transactions. The constitutional framework of enhanced cooperation may in principle allow a comparison between intra-group and cross-group economic activities when testing enhanced cooperation laws against the fundamental freedoms, but under trade-favouring enhanced cooperation, a strong reciprocal bond is established between the participating Member States which places intra-group and cross-group economic transactions in a non-comparable situation. A lack of actual comparability of intra-group and cross-group economic transactions allows a less favourable treatment of the latter within the European internal market.

The third category of legal provisions that may be introduced under the enhanced cooperation procedure may establish cross-border tax coordination. Cross-border tax coordination aims to introduce a framework between the participating Member States which allows them to comply with their European treaty obligations in conformity with their national values and standards. A coordination system may, in particular, be needed when the fundamental freedoms do not (sufficiently) consider the Member States' tax framework, and thus force the Member States to apply a tax treatment to non-resident taxpayers or cross-border economic activities which is not in conformity with their national principles. In those fields, the Member States may cooperate and establish a system which allows them to comply with the obligations under the European treaties on the one hand, and on the other hand to have the flexibility to regulate the cross-border situations in a way which is consistent with their national values and the national tax framework. Generally speaking, a framework for cross-border tax coordination consists of both disadvantages and benefits, which neutralise each other. The Member States within enhanced cooperation are not required to grant the compensation benefit to cross-group transactions because the coordinative framework establishes a deeper bond between the participating Member States which no longer allows a comparison between intra-group and cross-group transactions. However, the fundamental freedoms protect cross-group economic transactions insofar as the coordinative disadvantage must only apply within enhanced cooperation.

These three forms of cooperation and in particular the possibility of limiting the group and compensation benefits to intra-group economic transactions and protecting the harmonised value reveal how much flexibility enhanced cooperation grants the Member States to newly define their values but also their European obligations. Against these categories, one may ask whether granting a benefit within enhanced cooperation which goes beyond pure resident or national treatment complies with state aid law. State aid law applies to enhanced cooperation law because such aid may distort competition on the European internal market, just like aid granted by a single Member State, but unlike aid granted by all Member States under (ordinary) secondary EU law.

It has been suggested that it is necessary to separately examine whether the law of enhanced cooperation, first provides a (tax) benefit and second does so in a selective manner. The advantage test requires some form of benchmarking, and thus a comparison to 'normal' taxation needs to be drawn to identify a particular treatment as being beneficial. If enhanced cooperation law only supplements the national system, which is the case when a group benefit is granted, or cross-border tax coordination is established, the law does not influence the national tax system and subsequently the reference system. However, if the participating Member States have agreed on a common value and have based an entire and self-sufficient tax system upon it, as it would be the case in the field of a European FTT, then the law of enhanced cooperation is capable of determining its reference system. Identifying the benefit is straightforward once the reference system is determined. Any deviation from normal taxation for the benefit of the taxpayer creates a benefit under state aid law.

Since the advantage test is straightforward, ignoring any disadvantages suffered in the other Member States, the group benefit and the compensation benefit are a benefit in the meaning of state aid law if they go beyond resident treatment. However, any benefit only constitutes prohibited aid if the advantage is granted selectively.

The selectivity test asks whether the benefit is available to all undertakings, and thus whether all undertakings are allowed to benefit from the tax measure. Against the aim and purpose of state aid law, it becomes clear that not all deviating factors contradict general availability. Factors linked to the business activity are prohibited because the restricted entitlement to benefits negatively affects the efficient allocation of resources. Factors not linked to trade or business, such as business form and business size,[954] are not prohibited. Accordingly, if the law of enhanced cooperation is not designed for a particular business branch or sector, the group- and compensation benefits may not be selective. If the general measure test is not used, the non-discrimination approach is applied to the law of enhanced cooperation to determine whether the law is selective, the fundamental differentiation between intra-group and cross-group economic transactions is likely to establish a priori selectivity. However, the a priori selectivity is justified by the nature and

[954] The CJEU has ruled that subsidies based on size may infringe Art 107 of the TFEU: CJEU, 26 September 2002, C-351/98, *Spain v Commission*, ECLI:EU:C:2002:530, para 40; see also Mason and Parada, 'Company Size Matters' (n 737).

general structure of the law: the differentiation between participating and non-participating Member States is in the DNA of enhanced cooperation law and thus cannot establish selectivity.

On a procedural level, it may be wise to combine both the notification process for state aid and the procedure to establish enhanced cooperation. Embedding the notification procedure into the law-making process of enhanced cooperation law would allow the European Commission's proposal to be characterised as approval for all state aid law implications. The efficiency consideration must, however, not lower the ability of third parties affected by the aid, and thus these parties are allowed to demand judicial review of the Commission's decision.

Aside from satisfying the fundamental freedoms and state aid law demands, Art 326 of the TFEU requires that any enhanced cooperation law complies with secondary EU laws. In this regard, the constitutional framework of the enhanced cooperation procedure clearly shows that the scope of integration (all Member States versus a group of Member States) has to be considered in solving a conflict between overlapping enhanced cooperation law and ordinary secondary EU law. The laws with the lower integrational scope have to be invalidated to give the law with the higher integrational scope primacy (*lex uniformis derogat legi particulari*). In cases in which ordinary secondary EU law already exists, the European legislature is bound from introducing conflicting enhanced cooperation laws, and in cases in which conflicting secondary EU law is newly introduced, the enhanced cooperation law has to be invalidated.

6

The Rights and Obligations of Non-participating Member States

The Principle of Tolerance as a Fundament of Enhanced Cooperation

A. Setting the Scene

Art 327 of the Treaty on the Functioning of the European Union (TFEU) provides a safety net for non-participating Member States because it demands that any enhanced cooperation respects the competences, rights, and obligations of non-participating Member States. However, it is far from clear what Art 327 of the TFEU demands from enhanced cooperation law in order to respect the competences, rights, and obligations of non-participating Member States. The existing scholarship on Art 327 of the TFEU is very limited and only argues that participating Member States are obliged to take the interests of non-participating Member States into account.[1] This line of argument is as vague as the wording of the provision itself. To date, there is also no CJEU case law which may help define what Art 327 of the TFEU requires the participating Member States to do.

The lack of experience in using the enhanced cooperation procedure and the consequential missing CJEU guidance may require looking for other forms of State cooperation and learning from these fields what it may mean to respect rights, competences and obligations. State cooperation can in particular be found in federally organised (Member) States because States, regions, or cantons are mostly explicitly or implicitly granted the right to cooperate under the constitution. In that respect, it is not argued that the European Union is a federal State; however, enhanced cooperation between some, but not all Member States within the EU framework reveals substantial similarities to closer cooperation between some, but not all States within a federation. In both cases, there are some States outside the cooperation

[1] See for example Hermann-Josef Blanke, 'AEUV Art. 327 AEUV' in Eberhard Grabitz, Meinhard Hilf, and Martin Nettesheim (eds), *Das Recht der Europäischen Union* (67th edn, 2019) para 1; Matthias Pechstein, 'Art. 327 AEUV' in Rudolf Streinz (ed), *EUV/AEUV Vertrag über die Europäische Union, Vertrag über die Arbeitsweise der Europäischen Union, Charta der Grundrechte der Europäischen Union* (3rd edn, Beck Verlag 2018) para 1; Matthias Ruffert, 'Art. 327 AEUV' in Matthias Ruffert and Christian Calliess (eds), *Das Verfassungsrecht der Europäischen Union mit Europäischer Grundrechtecharta* (5th edn, Beck Verlag 2016) para 1.

Enhanced Cooperation and European Tax Law. Caroline Heber, Oxford University Press. © Caroline Heber 2021.
DOI: 10.1093/oso/9780192898272.003.0006

which are nonetheless related to the cooperating States under the overarching umbrella of EU law or the federal constitution,[2] and thus there should be some form of loyal behaviour between cooperating and non-cooperating Member States. Some federal constitutions explicitly provide safeguarding clauses which aim to protect the interests of non-cooperating States, regions, or cantons. These constitutional safeguarding clauses are of particular interest for the current analysis as they set an additional safety net to the constitutional and international law framework which may be comparable with Art 327 of the TFEU.

Having said that, for any cooperation under federal constitutional law and EU law, international law builds the outer framework, or at least a fallback alternative if the specific scheme does not provide for an effective protection of the non-participating Member States.

The following subsections will first set out whether European law and in particular enhanced cooperation is bound by international law (see subsection B). If this is the case, the principle of non-intervention, the *pacta tertiis* principle, and the international law rules on *inter se* agreements form the outer limits for enhanced cooperation. Then, more specific safeguarding clauses enshrined in the constitutional framework of federal states, in particular the United States and Switzerland, are laid out to show the context of what these clauses are aiming to prevent (see subsection C). Against this background, the principle of tolerance underlying the entire enhanced cooperation framework is drawn out (see subsection D). The principle of tolerance manifests itself in the non-participating Member States' freedom to abstain from enhanced cooperation (see subsection E) and the participating Member States' freedom to be part of enhanced cooperation (see subsection F).

B. International Law—Outer Boundaries

International law provides three principles which may limit the impact of closer cooperation on non-participating (Member) States: the principle of non-intervention, the principle *pacta tertiis nec nocent nec prosunt*, and the rules on *inter se* agreements. The principle of non-intervention protects every sovereign State from another State's interference with its sovereignty,[3] the principle *pacta tertiis nec nocent nec prosunt* prohibits an international agreement from imposing legal obligations or bestowing legal rights upon third parties. Both principles form

[2] See in this vein for the European umbrella David O'Keeffe and others (eds), '"If I'd Wanted You to Understand I Would Have Explained It Better": What Is the Purpose of the Provisions on Closer Co-Operation Introduced by the Treaty of Amsterdam?', *Legal Issues of the Amsterdam Treaty* (Bloomsbury Publishing PLC 1999) 25.

[3] Maziar Jamnejad and Michael Wood, 'The Principle of Non-Intervention' (2009) 22 Leiden Journal of International Law 345, 346; James Crawford, *Brownlie's Principles of Public International Law* (OUP 2019) 370.

part of customary international law,[4] and the rules on *inter se* agreements specify whether and under what circumstances two or more parties to a multilateral treaty are allowed to conclude an agreement to modify the treaty as between themselves alone.[5]

International law can only establish the outer boundaries for enhanced co-operation laws if the European legislature is bound by sources of international law when organising the cooperation between the Member States within the European Union. The CJEU case law on the European law's autonomy[6] from international law may raise doubts on whether international law can influence European law-making. The following section will set out the relationship between EU law and international law and will define how autonomous the European legal order is.

I. Autonomy of the European Legal Order

The founding Member States chose age-old instruments (namely international treaties) to establish new forms of European cooperation. The Organisation for European Economic Co-Operation (OEEC), the Council of the Europe, and the European Coal and Steel Community were all created as international organisations based on international treaties.[7] Likewise, the founding treaties, accession treaties, and amending treaties are an expression of an old-fashioned approach to European integration. Despite the nature of the foundation of the European Union, the Court of Justice of the European Union (CJEU) proposed that EU law is a 'new legal order' that is distinct from international law.[8] The claim of autonomy of the European Union raises the question of how EU law interacts with international law. Is the European Union bound through customary international law or international treaties?

The autonomy of the European legal order from the surrounding international legal environment may mean two rather different things: either European law establishes a specialised international legal order which 'deviates' from the general rules of international law, or EU law 'fails to comply' with specific international obligations by way of giving priority to its internal rules.[9] Accordingly, when dealing

[4] The *pacta tertiis* principle is also set out in the Vienna Convention on the Law of Treaties, see this chapter subsection B.III.

[5] Art 41 VCLT.

[6] From very early on, the CJEU has repeatedly stated that the European treaties have created their 'own legal system' (CJEU, 19 November 1991, C-6/90 and C-9/90, *Francovich*, ECLI:EU:C:1991:428, para 31) and 'a new legal order of international law' (CJEU, 5 February 1963, 26–62, *van Gend & Loos*, ECLI:EU:C:1963:1).

[7] Bruno de Witte, 'European Union Law: How Autonomous Is Its Legal Order?' (2010) Zeitschrift für öffentliches Recht 141, 143.

[8] CJEU, 5 February 1963, 26–62, *van Gend & Loos*, ECLI:EU:C:1963:1; CJEU, 19 November 1991, C-6/90 and C-9/90, *Francovich*, ECLI:EU:C:1991:428, para 31: 'own legal system'.

[9] Witte, (n 7) 'How Autonomous Is Its Legal Order?' 151.

with the autonomy question, it is necessary to distinguish between the two different roles international law plays for the European Union. First, international law may be used to organise intra-EU relations (the relationship between Member States). Secondly, international law may be used as a tool to shape the EU's relationship with third counties.[10]

1. Autonomy of the European Legal System to Regulate the Relationship between the Member States

The first idea of autonomy concerns the establishment of special rules which are better suited to deal with particular issues and thus set aside rules of general international law.[11] Despite the fact that the European treaties do not mention the significance of general international law, there cannot be any doubt that the European Union is bound by legal rules which address every subject of international law, that being customary international law.[12] Except for peremptory norms of general international law (*jus cogens*)[13] these default rules can be set aside by the European treaties establishing a legal framework for the interaction between the Member States.[14] In this case, the European constitutional framework creates new subjects of law which endow the European Union with autonomy to which the Member States entrust the task of realising common goals.[15] The amount and degree of specificity of European rules is much higher than can be found in any other international organisation, 'but the umbilical cord linking EU law to general international law is not severed by any of its autonomous characteristics'.[16] In other words, the particular regime of European law is connected with general international law[17] and

[10] Bruno de Witte, 'International Law as a Tool for the European Union' (2009) 5 European Constitutional Law Review 265.

[11] For a definition of general international law: Christian Tomuschat, 'General International Law: A New Source of International Law?' in Riccardo Pisillo Mazzeschi and Pasquale De Sena (eds), *Global Justice, Human Rights and the Modernization of International Law* (Springer International Publishing 2018).

[12] CJEU, 16 June 1998, C-162/96, *Racke*, ECLI:EU:C:1998:293, para 45; Frank Hoffmeister, 'The Contribution of EU Practice to International Law' in Marise Cremona (ed), *Developments in EU External Relations Law* (OUP 2008) 55 explaining that the Court may find customary international law binding on the European Union without any need of formal incorporation by reference to a general principle of European law common to the Member States. For the relationship between customary international law and international organisations in general see Michael Wood, 'International Organizations and Customary International Law' (2015) 48 Vanderbilt Journal of Transnational Law 609, 613.

[13] See for a definition Malcolm N Shaw, *International Law* (8th edn, CUP 2017) 92 et seq.

[14] Karl Matthias Meessen, 'The Application of Rules of Public International Law within Community Law' (1976) 13 Common Market Law Review 485, 487; Anne Peters, 'The Position of International Law within the European Community Legal Order Focus Section: Recent Developments in the Application of International Law in Domestic and European Community Law' (1997) 40 German Yearbook of International Law 9, 37.

[15] More generally for all international organisations see ICJ, Advisory Opinion of 8 July 1996, Legality of the Use by a State of Nuclear Weapons in Armed Conflicts, para 19.

[16] Witte, 'How Autonomous Is Its Legal Order?' (n 7) 151.

[17] Georges Abi-Saab, 'Fragmentation or Unification: Some Concluding Remarks Symposium Issue: The Proliferation of International Tribunals: Piecing Together the Puzzle' (1998) 31 New York

if need arises, general international law remains a valid legal measure to 'enhance the effectiveness, the effet utile of the rules' of the European legal system.[18] In this vein, the CJEU has repeatedly ruled that a Member State cannot rely on a possible infringement of EU law by another Member State in order to justify its own default. The European legal system sets out procedures and legal remedies which have to be used in case of EU law infringements. Member States are not allowed to adopt corrective or defensive measures.[19] However, in an exceptional scenario of continuous violation of EU law, a fallback on general international law rules may be promoted.[20]

A fallback on general international law denies the EU law's self-contained character or the existence of truly self-contained regimes on a more general basis. Self-contained regimes intend to exclude in total the application of general international law as these regimes embrace a full, exhaustive, and definitive set of secondary rules.[21] The European legal system may seem to establish a complete and exhaustive system which may not need to fall back on general international law. However, the CJEU has never read EU law in clinical isolation from public international law.[22]

The possibility to deviate from the general rules of international law is only reserved for primary EU law. Secondary EU law has to comply with customary international law[23] except for those legislative acts which are based on deviating European treaty law. In other words, if the European constitutional framework deviates from international law and allows the European institutions to introduce secondary EU law in that particular field, the secondary EU laws have to comply with the deviating primary EU law and may not need to comply with general international law.

University Journal of International Law and Politics 919, 926 arguing that however autonomous and particular a special regime may be, 'there cannot be a totally self-contained regime within the legal order. If the special regime is to remain part of the legal order, some relationship, however tenuous, must subsist between the two. Otherwise, if all links are severed, the special regime becomes a legal order unto itself—a kind of legal Frankenstein, or Kelsen's "gang of robbers"—and no longer partakes in the same basis of legitimacy and formal standards of pertinence.'

[18] B Simma and Dirk Pulkowski, 'Of Planets and the Universe: Self-Contained Regimes in International Law' (2006) 17 European Journal of International Law 483, 510.

[19] CJEU, 25 September 1979, 232/78, *Commission v French Republic*, ECLI:EU:C:1979:215, para 9; CJEU, 14 February 1984, C-325/82, *Commission v Germany*, ECLI:EU:C:1984:60, para 11; CJEU, 9 July 1991, C-146/89, *Commission v UK*, ECLI:EU:C:1991:294, para 47; CJEU, 23 May 1996, C-5/94, *Hedley Lomas*, ECLI:EU:C:1996:205, para 20; CJEU, 20 October 2005, C-111/03, *Commission v Sweden*, ECLI:EU:C:2005:619, para 66.

[20] Simma and Pulkowski (n 18) 517.

[21] ibid 493.

[22] EGC, 22 January 1997, T-115/94, *Opel Austria*, ECLI:EU:T:1997:3, para 30; CJEU, 24 November 1992, C-286/90, *Poulsen and Diva Navigation Corp.*, ECLI:EU:C:1992:453, para 9.

[23] Hoffmeister (n 12) 55.

2. Autonomy of the European Legal System to Define the Relationship with Third Countries

The second meaning of autonomy refers to the capacity of a legal system to give priority to its internal rules 'over and above external international obligations'.[24] This form of autonomy shows how the European constitutional framework aligns international law obligations following from international agreements with internal European rules. The European Union may conclude international agreements which may conflict with primary or secondary EU law. The relationship between international rules and EU law may be answered differently from the perspective of international law and from a European law perspective.

Within the European legal order, it depends on whether the European system follows a monist or a dualist approach. If the European system follows a monist model, EU law and international law would only be different elements of one universal body, whereas a dualist conception would understand EU law and international law as two separate legal systems because they have 'different sources, different contents, and different subjects'.[25] The European constitutional framework does not explicitly answer the question of how international agreements are incorporated into the European law framework, as Art 216 Subsection 2 of the TFEU only states that '[a]greements concluded by the Union are binding upon the institutions of the Union and its Member States'. Further, the practice of the European institutions does not draw a clear picture on whether transformation is needed for international agreements as the practice changed between simple resolutions and resolutions carrying the agreement's text.[26] The case law of the CJEU shows that the Court does not attach any weight to the concrete legal act incorporating the international agreements into the European system and recognises any international agreement concluded by the European Union as a part of the European legal order.[27] This line of case law may allow international agreements to be part of European Union law without the need for formal transformation.[28]

A different question concerns the hierarchy of European and international legal rules, which in particular becomes relevant when a conflict arises where they meet. The international law perspective on the hierarchy of norms may be different than the European law perspective. Except for the superiority of *jus cogens* (peremptory norm of general international law),[29] the international legal order only provides general principles to solve conflicts of international law, for example a conflict between international treaties. However, the international legal order

[24] Witte, 'How Autonomous Is Its Legal Order?' (n 7) 152.
[25] Peters, 'The Position of International Law within the European Community Legal Order Focus Section' (n 14) 18.
[26] For an detailed overview see ibid 22 et seq.
[27] ibid.
[28] Witte, 'How Autonomous Is Its Legal Order?' (n 7) 153.
[29] Codified in Arts 53 and 64 of the VCLT.

does not dictate which hierarchical structure the European Union should apply to international law within its internal legal system.[30] On the international plane, customary international law prevails over both primary and secondary EU law and any international treaty binds the European Union regardless of conflicts with (primary and secondary) EU law rules.[31]

The EU system follows a different hierarchy which only allows *jus cogens* to prevail over the European constitutional framework. International treaties and general international law rank below primary EU law, but influence European law-making. In other words, general international law and international treaties concluded by the European Union prevail over secondary EU law.[32] In *Germany v Council* and *Kadi*, the CJEU granted the European constitutional framework priority over international law obligations. *Germany v Council* concerned the inapplicability of an agreement on bananas within the European Union. The agreement has validly been concluded between the parties, but it was in breach of the general principle of non-discrimination as it harmed the interests of particular categories of banana importers disproportionally.[33] In *Kadi*, the CJEU followed the same approach but felt the need to justify further the prevalence of the European treaties over international law obligations based on the autonomy of the European legal system. In this case, the Court invalidated a regulation which implemented a Security Council resolution because it was not in line with the fundamental rights,[34] accordingly, EU law of a primary EU law nature.[35] The *Kadi* case let scholars believe that EU law is no longer part of international law and thus promotes a strong dualist approach in the relation between EU law and international law.[36] A robustly dualist understanding of the relationship between EU law and international law demands the separateness and autonomy of EU law from any other legal system (including international law) and the priority of the EU's rules. However, this is not the case, as the *Kadi* case 'only' reflects what we already know from the European case law: that

[30] For the rank of customary international law and treaty law in the sphere of municipal law see Ignaz Seidl-Hohenveldern, 'Transformation or Adoption of International Law into Municipal Law' (1963) 12 International & Comparative Law Quarterly 88, 89–90; Luzius Wildhaber and Stephan Breitenmoser, 'The Relationship between Customary International Law and Municipal Law in Western European Countries' (1988) 48 Zeitschrift für ausländisches öffentliches Recht und Völkerrecht 163, 178–79.

[31] Peters, 'The Position of International Law within the European Community Legal Order Focus Section' (n 14) 36.

[32] Witte, 'How Autonomous Is Its Legal Order?' (n 7) 153.

[33] CJEU, 10 March 1998, C-122/95, *Germany v Council*, ECLI:EU:C:1998:94, para 75.

[34] Jan Klabbers, 'The Reception of International Law in the EU Legal Order' in Robert Schütze and Takis Tridimas (eds), *The European Union Legal Order* (OUP 2018) 1232 arguing that the 'EU is bound to respect its own commitment to human rights'.

[35] CJEU, 3 September 2008, C-402/05 P and C-415/05 P, *Yassin Abdullah Kadi and Al Barakaat International Foundation*, ECLI:EU:C:2008:461.

[36] Katja S Ziegler, 'Strengthening the Rule of Law, but Fragmenting International Law: The Kadi Decision of the ECJ from the Perspective of Human Rights Recent Developments' (2009) 9 Human Rights Law Review 288, 293.

the European treaties prevail over any international law obligation[37] regardless of its impact on the international community.

The CJEU case law on World Trade Organization (WTO) law does not change the picture on the hierarchy of legal rules because the question of direct effects of international rules is independent from their rank within the legal system.[38] Some international rules may be superior to secondary EU law, but if the rules of an international agreement do not have direct legal effects and consequences for contrary EU law, 'the validity of [secondary EU legislation] cannot be affected by [these rules]'.[39]

3. Conclusions for the Impact of International Law on Enhanced Cooperation Law-making

The foregoing analysis has shown that EU law is not entirely isolated from surrounding international law. The European treaties established a legal order which complies with the peremptory norms of general international law, but at the same time, deviates from non-binding general international law. The European constitutional framework protects the European constitutional principles,[40] values, and rights by granting primary EU law supremacy over general international law and international treaty law. Thus, the European treaties cannot be prejudiced by any international law obligations,[41] and any international agreements which contradict with the fundamental rights or the principle of non-discrimination must not be applied within the European internal order. The internal constraints do not exonerate the European Union from its international law obligations; they are binding on the plane of international law. The non-application of international agreements within the European Union's internal order renders the European Union liable for breach of contractual obligations under international law.[42]

The constitutional framework of enhanced cooperation sets a framework for the protection of non-participating Member States which may or may not deviate from general international law. In any case, the primary EU law framework enjoys supremacy over general international law. But if the protection of non-participating

[37] Except for *jus cogens*.

[38] For an explanation why the CJEU denied WTO law direct effects see Marco Bronckers, 'From "Direct Effect" to "Muted Dialogue": Recent Developments in the European Courts' Case Law on the WTO and Beyond' (2008) 11 Journal of International Economic Law 885, 886. See in that vein CJEU, 23 November 1999, C-149/96, *Portuguese Republic v Council*, ECLI:EU:C:1999:574, para 42 et seq.

[39] CJEU, 12 December 1972, 21–72 to 24–72, *International Fruit Company*, ECLI:EU:C:1972:115, para 28.

[40] Christiaan Timmermans, 'The EU and Public International Law' (1999) European Foreign Affairs Review 181, 182.

[41] CJEU, 3 September 2008, C-402/05 P and C-415/05 P, *Yassin Abdullah Kadi and Al Barakaat International Foundation*, ECLI:EU:C:2008:461, para 285.

[42] Peters, 'The Position of International Law within the European Community Legal Order Focus Section' (n 14) 36.

Member States is entirely ineffective, a fallback to general international law may be discussed.

The following subsections set out the protection international law offers to non-participating (Member) States to understand from which threshold of protection the constitutional framework of enhanced cooperation may deviate. Subsection II defines the principle of non-intervention and subsection III analyses the protection which international law offers third countries, those which are not party to an international agreement. The scope of protection requires a differentiation between legally enforceable rights and obligations imposed on third countries, and factual effects. Subsection IV lays out the limits for *inter se* agreements.

II. Principle of Non-intervention

Unlike the prohibition of force, the principle of non-intervention is not expressly set out in the UN Charter. However, the principle of non-intervention can be deduced from the general principle of sovereign equality of all States as laid down in Art 2 Subsection 1 of the UN Charter.[43] According to the International Court of Justice, State sovereignty includes 'the choice of political, economic, social and cultural systems, and the formation of foreign policy'.[44] Against this wide definition of State sovereignty, one may argue that any action of one State interfering with another State's political, economic, social, and cultural choices may infringe the principle of non-intervention. However, this is not the case, as the Court only considers interventions of one State wrongful when it uses 'methods of coercion, particularly force, either in the direct form of military action or in the indirect form of support for subversive activities in another State'.[45]

From this it follows that the principle of non-interference only offers protection from substantial intervention that puts the State's sovereignty at risk.[46] The exercised force of one State has to influence the political, economic, social, and cultural choices of another State in a way that the latter is no longer free to decide.[47] However, the legislative action of Member States under the enhanced cooperation procedure may not be strong enough to deprive the other State of its control over a subject matter.

[43] See for example Malcolm Shaw, *International Law* (8th edn, CUP 2017) 168 et seq; Knut Ipsen, *Völkerrecht*, 1073 (6th edn, Beck Verlag2014); Andreas von Arnould, *Völkerrecht* (4th edn, C.f. Müller Verlag 2019) 155.

[44] ICJ 27 June 1986, Report of Judgments, *Nicaragua Case—Nicaragua v United States of America*, p 108.

[45] ibid.

[46] ICJ, 27 June 1986, *Case Concerning Military and Paramilitary Activities in and against Nicaragua*, Merits, ICJ Reports, 1986, S. 14 et seq; Jamnejad and Wood (n 3) 369 et seq. Christian Sternberg *Die extraterritoriale Besteuerungsgewalt des Staates* (Duncker & Humblot 2019) 60 et seq.

[47] Sternberg (n 46) 61, 233 et seq.

III. The *Pacta Tertiis* Principle

International treaties and conventions may affect the position of third countries, meaning countries not being a party to the agreement or convention, in various forms and various levels of intensity. However, according to a fundamental principle of customary international law[48] '*pacta tertiis nec nocent nec prosunt*',[49] an international treaty between two or more powers cannot impose legal obligations or bestow legal rights upon third parties.[50] This fundamental principle of customary international law dates back to Roman law[51] and is enshrined in the Vienna Convention on the Law of Treaties (VCLT). The European Union is a party to neither the 1969 Convention on the Law of Treaties between States nor to the 1986 Vienna Convention on the Law of Treaties between States and International Organizations or between International Organizations of which only the former has entered into force.[52] However, the CJEU has often applied rules which are enshrined in the 1969 Convention.[53] More recent case law shows that the Court only applies the Conventions insofar as their provisions have already become part of customary international law.[54]

According to the *pacta tertiis* rule, a treaty can only provide an obligation for a third party if the State, not party to the treaty or convention, expressly accepts the obligation in writing. If the treaty or convention provides for a right for the third party, the third party (only) has to assent. The *pacta tertiis* rule only regulates the transfer of legal rights and legal obligations on non-treaty partners. However, a third country may also be affected by an international treaty if the treaty threatens the introduction or maintenance of a value by the third party.[55] Such a threat may be provided by a treaty between State A and State B, requiring State A to buy certain goods exclusively from State B in the future. Such an agreement will, beyond any doubt, affect State C if it were the main supplier of these goods to State A. The treaty between State A and State B does not impose any legally enforceable rights

[48] Alexander Proelss, 'Article 34—General Rule Regarding Third States' in Oliver Dörr and Kirsten Schmalenbach (eds), *Vienna Convention on the Law of Treaties: A Commentary* (Springer 2018) para 4.

[49] In *Brita*, the CJEU ruled that the European Union has to respect the *pacta tertiis* principle, a principle of general international law: CJEU, 25 February 2010, C-386/08, *Brita*, ECLI:EU:C:2010:91, para 44.

[50] See Art 34 of the VCLT.

[51] Alexander Proelss, 'The Personal Dimension: Challenges to the Pacta Tertiis Rule' in Christian Tams, Antonios Tzanakopoulos, and Andreas Zimmermann (eds), *Research Handbook on the Law of Treaties* (Edward Elgar 2014) 223.

[52] Pieter Jan Kuiper, 'Case C-386/08, Brita GmbH v. Hauptzollamt Hamburg-Hafen Judgment of the European Court of Justice of 25 February 2010' (2010) 37 Legal Issues of Economic Integration 241, 248.

[53] Hoffmeister (n 12) 57; Jed Odermatt, 'The Use of International Treaty Law by the Court of Justice of the European Union' (2015) 17 Cambridge Yearbook of European Legal Studies 121.

[54] CJEU, 25 February 2010, C-386/08, *Brita*, ECLI:EU:C:2010:91, para 42; Kuiper (n 52) 249.

[55] Christine M Chinkin, *Third Parties in International Law* (Clarendon Press 2015) 20.

or obligations on State C; nonetheless, the treaty may interfere with State C's interests.[56] Hard international law only prohibits direct legal effects of treaties on third parties. Any other—indirect or incidental—effect a treaty may have on strangers is subsequently in line with international law standards.[57]

On the other hand, third parties have a general duty not to interfere with international treaties which do not violate international law or their legal rights.[58] The duty to respect treaties even exists if the third parties have to suffer economic damages. As long as their interests are not legally recognised, any damages that affect them cannot prevent a treaty from entering into force. The international law protection from damages in the field of legally not protected interests corresponds with what is common practice in English tort law: *damnum absque injuria*.[59] This principle states that a natural or legal person who causes a damage or a loss to another, without legally injuring them (accordingly without infringing any laws), is not required to compensate them for the respective damage or loss.[60] An obvious example is the opening of a cocktail bar near another bar causing the latter a loss of customers, but without granting it a cause of action.

From this it follows that international law distinguishes between legal rights and legal obligations which can be enforced by another party, and incidental effects which may be favourable or unfavourable for third parties. A treaty can only force legally enforceable obligations on third parties if the third party explicitly agrees to it in writing. If an international treaty does not create obligations for a non-treaty party but harms its factual position (eg revenue losses because of a move of tax bases), the third party has no legal right to redress the treaty. Accordingly, any factual effects which international treaties cause third parties are allowed and have to be accepted by the non-contracting parties.

Applying these standards to the law of enhanced cooperation, enhanced cooperation cannot impose legal obligations upon non-participating Member States and must respect the legal rights of non-participating Member States, such as the European internal market guarantees. However, any factual effects (being either positive or negative) on non-participating Member States, such as revenue losses or dislocation of taxpayers, have to be accepted. Accordingly, if the constitutional framework of enhanced cooperation does not sufficiently protect the non-participating Member States from factual effects, a fallback to international law

56 Incidentally favourable and incidentally unfavourable: Gerald Sir Fitzmaurice, 'Law of Treaties—Fifth Report by Special Rapporteur Sir Gerald Fitzmaurice' (1960) DOCUMENT A/CN.4/130 74.

57 Ralf Günter Wetzel, *Verträge zugunsten und zu Lasten Dritter nach der Wiener Vertragsrechtskonvention* (Inst für Völkerrecht 1973) 8 et seq.

58 Ronald Francis Roxburgh, *International Conventions and Third States; a Monograph* (Longmans, Green and Co 1917) 32.

59 Edward P Weeks, *The Doctrine of Damnum Absque Injuria Considered in Its Relation to the Law of Torts* (Sumner Whitney 1879).

60 Thomas A Street, *The Theory and Principles of Tort Law* (Beard Books 1999) 492.

would not help, as it also allows the exposure of non-participating Member States to factual effects.

IV. *Inter se* Agreements

The rules for *inter se* agreements laid out in the VCLT may also limit the impact of enhanced cooperation on non-participating Member States. Art 41 of the VCLT sets out the circumstances under which it is admissible that states parties of a multilateral agreement modify the treaty as between themselves alone. If the treaty allows such modifications, the states parties can enter into *inter se* agreements from a purely international point of view. However, if the treaty does not explicitly prohibit modifications, *inter se* agreements are allowed under two circumstances. First, the modification must not affect the enjoyment by the other parties of their rights under the treaty or the performance of their obligations. Secondly, the modification must not relate to a provision, derogation from which is incompatible with the effective execution of the object and purpose of the treaty as a whole. In light of these two conditions, it has been argued that one has to distinguish between treaties imposing obligations of a reciprocal, an independent, or an integral nature.[61] As the legal effects of an *inter se* agreement are limited to its parties, modifications may only be permissible in the case of reciprocal treaties.[62] States parties to an *inter se* agreement remain bound by the original treaty 'and must continue to observe it in their relations with the other parties as if the *inter se* agreement did not exist'.[63]

In the field of EU law, *inter se* agreements are explicitly allowed in the form of enhanced cooperation. Accordingly, the strict international law benchmark, according to which the relationship between parties of an *inter se* agreement and states parties which did not want to modify the treaty must remain as if the *inter se* agreement does not exist, does not apply in the EU context. Since group formation is explicitly allowed within the European treaties, the relationship between participating and non-participating Member States also has to be determined by European treaty law excluding a fallback on the general rule of Art 41 of the VCLT.

[61] Kerstin von der Decken, 'Art. 41—Agreements to Modify Multilateral Treaties between Certain of the Parties Only' in Oliver Dörr and Kirsten Schmalenbach (eds), *Vienna Convention on the Law of Treaties: A Commentary* (Springer 2018) para 18.

[62] ibid.

[63] The international Law commission S. 740

C. Closer Cooperation within Federally Structured States and the Protection of Non-cooperating States

The willingness and ability of States to cooperate within a federation is the rule rather than the exception. The subject areas which are the focus of a joint initiative by some States depend substantively on the distribution of powers between the federal and the state level. Thus, the practices of federal States do not allow one to deduce any statement on which areas of the law are traditionally dealt within closer cooperation of States.

The vast majority of federal States do not provide for any explicit rules within their constitution allowing or encouraging cooperation between States.[64] Under such a constitutional setting, States are generally allowed to enter into inter-State agreements with each other.[65] These agreements are conducted on a federal level, and thus they have to meet the constitutional requirements, such as human rights, and principles of international law are applied analogously.[66] Since the constitutional framework does not determine how States should cooperate, protection of the non-participating States' interests can only be deduced from general constitutional principles such as loyalty to the federal government. Such a legal environment could be compared with an international treaty between some Member States of the European Union (ie a partial agreement).[67] Member States are not obliged to consider the interests of non-treaty partners because of an explicit provision within the European treaties, but they are bound by the general principle of sincere cooperation, enshrined in Art 4 Subsection 3 of the TEU.

[64] For an overview see Christian Starck and Michael Bothe (eds), 'Zusammenarbeit der Gliedstaaten im Bundesstaat', *Zusammenarbeit der Gliedstaaten im Bundesstaat* (Nomos 1988). For a discussion of the concept of cooperative federalism see Frank R Strong, 'Cooperative Federalism Symposium on Cooperative Federalism' (1937) 23 Iowa Law Review 459.

[65] For intra-federal treaties, the German Basic Law contains provisions on treaties on the reclassification of Länder (Art 29 Subsection 8 of the Basic Law). These are agreements between the Länder for which the approval of the federal government is explicitly required by law (Art 29 Subsection 8 sentence 6 of the Basic Law). In addition, the Basic Law provides that the federal government and the Länder may cooperate on the basis of agreements in the field of research promotion (Art 91b Subsection 1 of the Basic Law) and the determination of the efficiency of the education system in an international comparison (Art 91b Subsection 2 of the Basic Law) as well as within the framework of cooperation in information technology systems (Art 91c Subsection 2 sentence 3 of the Basic Law). For Austria, Felix Ermacora, *Föderalismus in Österreich* (Europa Verlag 1970). For Australia, Robert French, 'Co-Operative Federalism in Australia—an Intellectual Resource for Europe? I' (2006) 65 Amicus Curiae 9. For Canada, WR Lederman, 'Some Forms and Limitations of Co-Operative Federalism' (1967) 45 Canadian Bar Review 409; Richard Simeon, *Federal-Provincial Diplomacy: The Making of Recent Policy in Canada* (University of Toronto Press 1972).

[66] For Germany, Bernd Grzeszick, 'Art. 20' in Theodor Maunz and others (eds), *Grundgesetz: Kommentar* (85. Ergänzungslieferung, November 2018, Beck Verlag 2018) para 154; for Switzerland, Thomas Fleiner-Gerster, 'Zusammenarbeit der Gliedstaaten im Bundesstaat' in Christian Starck (ed), *Zusammenarbeit der Gliedstaaten im Bundesstaat: Landesberichte und Generalbericht der Tagung für Rechtsvergleichung 1987 in Innsbruck* (Nomos 1988) 143.

[67] See Chapter 2, subsection A.I.1.

However, Art 327 of the TFEU explicitly protects the interests, rights, and obligations of non-participating Member States, and thus the protection of non-participating Member States may go beyond the general European principle of sincere cooperation.[68] In light of the explicit protection of non-participating Member States it is necessary to seek guidance from a federal jurisdiction which also explicitly provides safeguarding measures for non-participating States. The most prominent examples of a constitutionally enshrined cooperation framework outside the European Union are to be found in Switzerland and in the United States.

The following subsections analyse the Swiss and US constitutional provisions which allow States or cantons to cooperate, and simultaneously compel the closer cooperating group to respect the interests of non-participating States or cantons. The practical experience derived from these provisions may provide some guidance on how to interpret the requirement to respect the competences, rights, and obligations of non-participating Member States as set out by the European treaties.

I. The Swiss Constitutional Basis for Closer Cooperation between Cantons

The Swiss constitution explicitly states in Art 48 Subsection 1 that '[t]he cantons may conclude agreements with each other and create joint organisations and institutions.[69] In particular, they may jointly carry out tasks of regional interest'.[70] The Confederation is allowed to participate in any of these agreements signed between the cantons.[71] The interests of both the Confederation and the non-participating cantons are protected by a safeguarding clause in the Swiss constitution, according to which any '[a]greements between cantons may not conflict with the law and the interests of the Confederation or with the laws of other cantons. They shall be brought to the attention of the Federation.'[72] The plain wording of the provision requires that any cooperation between a sub-group of cantons respects the law of

[68] For a different view see Chloe Lignier and Anton Geier, 'Die Verstärkte Zusammenarbeit in der Europäischen Union—Politischer Hintergrund, Bestandsaufnahme und Zukunftsperspektiven' (2015) 79 Rabels Zeitschrift für ausländisches und internationales Privatrecht (RabelsZ) 546, 561.

[69] For an overview of the different types of agreements see Christian Roos, 'Möglichkeiten und Grenzen interkantonaler Vereinbarungen unter besonderer Beriicksichtigung des Konkordates fiber das offentliche Beschaffungswesen' (1995) 6 LeGes 23, 29 et seq.

[70] '*Die Kantone können miteinander Verträge schliessen sowie gemeinsame Organisationen und Einrichtungen schaffen. Sie können namentlich Aufgaben von regionalem Interesse gemeinsam wahrnehmen.*'

[71] Art 48 Subsection 2 of the Swiss Constitution—'*Der Bund kann sich im Rahmen seiner Zuständigkeiten beteiligen.*'

[72] Art 48 Subsection 3 of the Swiss Constitution—'*Verträge zwischen Kantonen dürfen dem Recht und den Interessen des Bundes sowie den Rechten anderer Kantone nicht zuwiderlaufen. Sie sind dem Bund zur Kenntnis zu bringen.*'

the Confederation and other non-participating cantons. Only the Confederation's interests are explicitly protected by the Swiss constitution. However, the duty to uphold the interests of other non-participating cantons already follows from the constitutional principle of loyalty.[73] The principle of loyalty does not mean that no competition between the Confederation and cantons, and between different cantons can exist, and thus the cooperating cantons may not place their interests before those of the Confederation or other cantons. Accordingly, the interests of the Confederation, the non-participating cantons, and the participating canton can remain on an equal footing.[74] However, any agreement between some cantons must not interfere with the federal government and other cantons in the performance of their duties, and must not harm the federal balance.[75] The cantons must therefore behave loyally among themselves and towards the Confederation.[76] An example of non-compatibility with federal loyalty includes, for example, situations in which a canton insists on an inter-cantonal agreement, although this is disproportionate to the interest of the canton wishing to deviate from it.[77] From this it follows that despite the explicit safeguarding clause enshrined in the Swiss constitution, the procedure of cooperation between cantons is determined by constitutional loyalty to the Confederation and the other cantons.[78] Accordingly, the explicit protection of the outsiders and the Confederation does not create additional protection.

Against the background of the Swiss interpretation of the special safeguarding clause, one may ask whether the explicit protection of non-participating Member States in the context of enhanced cooperation under EU law also stops at the principle of loyalty (ie principle of sincere cooperation). If Art 327 of the TFEU had no independent and distinct value, non-participating Member States would (only) be protected by the fundamental principle of sincere cooperation,[79] which 'is a reflection of the principle of "federal good faith"'.[80] The principle of sincere cooperation has no direct effects in itself, but can serve as an additional argument where the Member States are 'alleged to have breached an unconditional and sufficiently precise obligation'.[81] Before addressing that particular question, the US framework is

[73] The principle of loyalty is deduced from the general principle of allegiance to the federal government, see Blaise Knapp, 'Art. 44' in Bernhard Ehrenzeller and others (eds), *Die schweizerische Bundesverfassung: St. Galler Kommentar, Band I* (3rd edn, Dike Schulthess 2014) para 14 et seq.

[74] ibid 18.

[75] Roos (n 69) 34–35.

[76] Knapp (n 73) para 15.

[77] Rainer J Schweizer and Ursula Abderhalden, 'Art. 48' in Bernhard Ehrenzeller and others (eds), *Die schweizerische Bundesverfassung: St. Galler Kommentar, Band I* (3rd edn, Dike Schulthess 2014) para 44.

[78] Tobias Jaag, '§ 14 Zusammenarbeit zwischen Bund und Kantonen sowie zwischen Kantonen' in Giovanni Biaggini, Thomas Gächter, and Regina Kiener (eds), *Staatsrecht* (Dike Verlag 2011) 154; Denise Buser, *Kantonales Staatsrecht: Eine Einführung für Studium und Praxis* (Helbing & Lichtenhahn Verlag 2004) 83.

[79] Art 4 Subsection 3 of the TEU.

[80] Koenraad Lenaerts and Piet Van Nuffel, *European Union Law* (3rd edn, 2011) ss 7–042; Armin Hatje, *Loyalität als Rechtsprinzip in der Europäischen Union* (Nomos 2001) 11.

[81] Lenaerts and Nuffel, (n 80) paras 7–042.

analysed to identify whether it is a common approach to protect interests of non-cooperating States explicitly, but in truth reducing it to the constitutional principle of a friendly consideration of their interests.

II. The US Compact Clause

Establishing differentiation between States is also allowed under the US constitution, which grants some States the possibility of cooperating in groups under the so-called compact clause. According to this clause, a State is allowed to enter into both agreements and compacts, either with another State or a foreign power, with the consent of Congress.[82] In any case, the States are prohibited from entering into a treaty, alliance, or confederation with each other, regardless of Congress' potential blessing. Both the prohibition of certain forms of State cooperation, but also the high threshold—the consent of Congress—for any other form of cooperation which is not per se prohibited have been introduced to the US constitution to fight any threats of dissolution through sedition and secession, which States are 'more likely to commit collectively than individually'.[83]

Under a plain reading of the provision, no agreement between two or more States could be signed without Congress' *ex-ante* or at least *ex-post* blessing. The relaxed interpretation of the provision by the US Supreme Court, which some critics suggest means the Court has held that the 'Compact Clause cannot possibly mean what it says',[84] has allowed some agreements between States to be found exempt from the congressional consent requirement.[85] Agreements between States should not be rendered impossible by the compact clause; the clause should (only) protect federal interests, and thus should prevent any accretion of power that encroaches upon the unity and supremacy of the federal government.[86] A 'federal supremacy' test[87] is, beyond any doubt, much narrower than what the compact clause truly requires: Congress' consent for any agreement or compact between States. Any agreement violating federal supremacy may already be unconstitutional irrespective of the compact clause.[88] In *Steel Corp. v Multistate Tax Commission*, the

[82] 'No State shall, without the consent of the Congress ... enter into any Agreement or Compact', Art I, section 10, clause 3 of the US Constitution.
[83] Michael S Greve 'Compacts, Cartels, and Congressional Consent' (2003) 68 Missouri Law Review 285, 296.
[84] ibid 287.
[85] Matthew Pincus, 'When Should Interstate Compacts Require Congressional Consent?' (2009) 42 Columbia Journal of Law & Social Problems 511, 517.
[86] Supreme Court, 3 April 1893, *Virginia v Tennessee*, 148 U.S. 503, 519 (1893).
[87] Duncan B Hollis, 'Unpacking the Compact Clause' (2009) 88 Texas Law Review 741, 763.
[88] For a critical view: 'The Power of the States to Make Compacts' (1922) 31 The Yale Law Journal 635. Michael Greve criticised the federal supremacy test on two grounds: first, the test only views the compact clause in its *vertical* (State-to-federation) dimension and is silent on the *horizontal* (State-to-State) effects, and second, the test renders the compact clause a virtual nullity because any agreement

US Supreme Court further elaborated on the federal supremacy test and found that even if a compact between States increases their bargaining power vis-à-vis industries, their bargaining power vis-à-vis the federal government does not increase. Of course, this assumes that a compact does not authorise States to exercise powers which they would not be able to exercise in the absence of the treaty, and that the compact does not transpose sovereign powers to an institution established by the compact, and that each participating State is free to withdraw from the compact.[89] As long as bargaining power vis-à-vis the federal government is not increased, the federal supremacy test is satisfied.

Despite the liberal interpretation of the compact clause for inter-State compacts, the Supreme Court has not softened the requirements in case of involvement of foreign powers. Any agreement or compact between one or more States and a foreign nation requires Congress' blessing.[90]

In a pure inter-State setting, abandoning the onerous requirement of constitutional consent was seen as a strengthening of the potential of inter-State agreements to deal with 'overwhelming difficulties confronting modern society'.[91] Indeed, the States have used the agreements and compacts[92] more frequently and in various fields, such as boundaries and cession of territory, control of natural resources, utility of regulation, and taxation.

Before attempting to compare the protection of non-participating Member States under the compact clause and non-participating Member States under enhanced cooperation, it is necessary to elucidate some differences between those two mechanisms of flexibility. It has been argued that the difference is supposed to rest on the aim and purpose of the flexibility mechanism, which is open in the case of the US compact clause, and thus the clause can be used for a variety of functions. In contrast, the enhanced cooperation procedure aims to foster and advance integration within the European Union.[93] In other words, the enhanced cooperation procedure can only be used to promote the European integration process, whereas the US compact clause can also be used to determine legal circumstances for a matter only relevant for a limited number of States, such as water regulations for a particular lake or river flowing through two or three States. Purely inter-State problems that are not of interest to or do not concern the whole European Union

encroaching on the federal supremacy would violate the ordinary rules of federal supremacy, and thus would be unconstitutional with or without the compact clause: Greve (n 83) 301–02.

89 US Supreme Court, 21 February 1978, *United States Steel Corp. v Multistate Tax Comm'n*, 434 U.S. 452, 553 (1978).

90 For an explanation along the line of the 'one voice' rational see Greve (n 83) 298.

91 Felix Frankfurter and James M Landis, 'The Compact Clause of the Constitution. A Study in Interstate Adjustments' (1925) 34 The Yale Law Journal 685, 729.

92 For a deeper analysis of the classic indicia of a compact see Hollis (n 87) 766.

93 Federico Fabbrini, 'Enhanced Cooperation under Scrutiny: Revisiting the Law and Practice of Multi-Speed Integration in Light of the First Involvement of the EU Judiciary' (2013) 40 Legal Issues of Economic Integration 197, 205–06.

are not explicitly excluded from the framework of enhanced cooperation, but several provisions of the European treaties ensure alignment of the European Union's policies and any enhanced cooperation. Purely inter-State issues, such as the construction of a tunnel providing for better transit between two States, or the protection of fish species in a river being contiguous to two Member States, would not overcome the threshold of being in the EU's interest, and would also not meet the basic requirements set by the European treaties. The US compact clause can, however, also be used for matters beyond a purely two-State problem, such as the alignment of laws,[94] and come quite close to enhanced cooperation law's aims. In particular, those fields in which the law of the group is not naturally restricted to the group members, issues on the treatment of non-participating (Member) States equally arise within the context of the compact clause and the enhanced cooperation procedure because both the US federal law and the European Union establish a framework between the (Member) States which must not be destroyed by establishing rivalling groups. Thus, both the US compact clause and the European enhanced cooperation procedure must provide for provisions protecting the (Member) States outside the group.

With regards to the protection of non-participating States, the US compact clause introduces a very strict safeguarding clause: it requires Congress' consent. However, the Supreme Court has refrained from enforcing this onerous requirement in purely inter-state matters, reducing the States' protection from the group's externalities. In the literature, it has been argued that the possibility of States cooperating without the requirement Congress' consent would not sufficiently protect the outsiders from exploitation, because without competition, a group of States may create a monopoly exploiting non-participating States.[95]

Despite the claims that Congress' consent protects outsiders from an overly powerful group of States, the Supreme Court has not changed its restrictive interpretation of the compact clause. In the field of purely inter-State agreements, only the federal competences are truly protected. The interests of non-participating States are not by any means protected.

III. Lesson Learned from Other Constitutionally Enshrined Closer Cooperation Mechanisms

If the constitution of a federally organised State explicitly allows regions, States, or cantons to cooperate, the constitutional framework may explicitly protect non-participating regions, States, or cantons against any exploitation by the group. Both the Swiss and the US examples show, however, that the safeguarding clauses are

[94] Which is, however, predominantly achieved by the US Uniform Law Commission.
[95] Greve (n 83) 325.

reduced to a minimum protection which could already be deduced from general constitutional principles. The restrictive interpretation of safeguarding clauses has been criticised in the literature since cooperation of some regions, States, or cantons may have negative legal or factual effects on non-participating regions, States, or cantons.

In the context of enhanced cooperation, one may wonder whether Art 327 of the TFEU which explicitly protects the 'competences, rights and obligations' of non-participating Member States, only demands that any enhanced cooperation to be loyal to Member States not participating in it and that enhanced cooperation not infringe on the non-participating Member States' internal market guarantees (ie the market freedoms). In such a case, Art 327 of the TFEU would not establish a safety net which goes beyond the fundamental freedoms and Art 4 Subsection 3 of the TEU, the demand for sincere cooperation within the European Union.[96]

The following sections reveal that the restrictive approach reflected in Switzerland and the US has to be rejected for Art 327 of the TFEU. The finding that Art 327 of the TFEU goes beyond a mere demand for loyal cooperation between participating and non-participating Member States and a protection of legally protected market rights of non-participating Member States is grounded on objective and systemic reasons. Art 327 of the TFEU establishes a safety net for both participating and non-participating Member States to allow the willing Member States to cooperate, and the non-participating Member States to remain outside enhanced cooperation.

D. The Principle of Tolerance: More Than Mere Lip Service

Enhanced cooperation gives the Member States both a way in and a way out of enhanced cooperation. On the one hand, Member States which can agree on certain terms are allowed to move forward with their legislative attempt. On the other hand, Member States which do not share the policy agenda are free to stay outside enhanced cooperation. Accordingly, every Member State is free to decide whether it joins enhanced cooperation and becomes part of a group of Member States strengthening the harmonisation of their legal systems or whether the Member State wants to stay out of the group.

The intrinsic logic of enhanced cooperation requires serious tolerance between the two groups of Member States, as a result of every Member State's right to choose

[96] Nathalie Wittock, 'The Influence of the Principle of Union Loyalty in Tax Matters' (2014) 23 EC Tax Review 171, 171 arguing that the principle of loyalty (principle of sincere cooperation) applies 'where the Treaty itself offered no solution'. Applying this line of argument to the primary EU law framework of the enhanced cooperation procedure: Art 327 of the TFEU explicitly states that any enhanced cooperation has to respect the competences, rights, and obligations of the non-participating Member States and thus the principle of sincere cooperation does not have to apply.

whether to join or to abstain and the subsequent building of two blocs, consisting of the participating Member States, on the one hand, and the non-participating Member States on the other hand. The framework of enhanced cooperation cannot work if the group of participating Member States punishes non-participating Member States for not becoming a part of enhanced cooperation and if the non-participating Member States can look for ways to undermine what the participating Member States mutually have accomplished.

The following subsections argue that enhanced cooperation is built on the principle of tolerance which goes far beyond mere loyalty claims, as enshrined in Art 4 Subsection 3 of the TEU. Enhanced cooperation demands tolerance from non-participating Member-States towards Member States within enhanced cooperation, and tolerance from participating Member States towards Member States outside enhanced cooperation.

E. Freedom to Abstain from Enhanced Cooperation

Each Member State is free to decide whether to become a member of enhanced cooperation or to abstain from joining. The commitment to every Member State's free choice would, however, be worthless if enhanced cooperation law could force the consequences of being within enhanced cooperation upon non-participating Member States. Non-participating Member States are explicitly protected by the constitutional framework of enhanced cooperation because any enhanced cooperation 'shall respect the competences, rights and obligations' of non-participating Member State. Therefore, primary EU law defends both the European internal market[97] and (on a separate basis) non-participating Member States.

Regardless of the clear constitutional differentiation between the protection of the European internal market on the one hand, and non-participating Member States on the other, Art 327 of the TFEU may be read in a way which (only) demands a protection of the Member States' internal market guarantees. In other words, a guarantee that all the rights, obligations, and competences which Member States hold within the legal framework of the European Union remain unaffected. If this were the case, non-participating Member States would not gain any more from the guarantees enshrined in Art 327 of the TFEU than what is already required by other provisions of the European treaties, the requirement that any enhanced cooperation does not undermine the European internal market.[98]

[97] The fundamental freedoms and state aid law protect the internal market by prohibiting Member States from using the enhanced cooperation procedure as a legal basis for establishing a cartel and work against what the European Union as a whole has already accomplished, see Chapter 5.

[98] See Chapter 5, Part I and Part II.

Therefore, Art 327 of the TFFEU should be understood as a protection of non-participating Member States that goes beyond the Member States' internal market guarantees and otherwise legally protected interests. Such a promise goes far beyond the standards of international law, which only protects non-treaty countries from legally enforceable obligations, and the standard set by the principle of sincere cooperation, which (only) emphasises the Member States' obligations under the European treaties, and in particular, the internal market guarantees, as the principle of sincere cooperation does not have direct effect in itself.[99] If Art 327 of the TFEU were read as a fundamental protection of non-participating Member States, Art 327 of the TFEU would allow non-participating Member States to fight factual effects of enhanced cooperation threatening their (national) values.

The following sections will first define the scope of 'rights, competences and obligations' (see subsection I). The outcome of this subsection will show that Art 327 of the TFEU guarantees non-participating Member States the freedom to act. In other words, enhanced cooperation law must not affect non-participating Member States in a way which no longer allows them to regulate the objectives underlying enhanced cooperation law in accordance with their policy decisions (see subsection II). The question of how much impact enhanced cooperation law is allowed to have on non-participating Member States, in particular in the form of negative factual (not legal) effects, leads us to the central discussion of tax and regulatory competition between Member States because the fiscal or regulatory framework of one Member State has factual effects on other Member States like enhanced cooperation law may have factual effects on non-participating Member States.

Two concepts developed in the area of regulatory competition (the beggar-thy-neighbour and the beggar-thyself theory) categorise the law based on its internal and external effects (see subsection II.1). The beggar-thy-neighbour theory aims for an internal economic benefit at the expense of another (Member) State (negative external effects). The beggar-thyself policy may also affect other (Member) States negatively, but economic costs are also created at home because other competing non-economic policy objects dominate (see subsection II.1.a). Based on these two concepts it will be possible to identify which competitive environment may encourage Member States to establish enhanced cooperation and which policy goals may require unilateral actions (see subsection II.1.b). Against the background of policy areas particularly open to enhanced cooperation, it will be suggested that non-participating Member States need enhanced protection against negative effects imposed on them by enhanced cooperation law, because non-participating Member States may not be able to fight such negative effects imposed by a stable united front of Member States (enhanced cooperation) in the same way as negative effects imposed upon them by unilateral measures of Member States

[99] Koenraad Lenaerts and Piet Van Nuffel, (n 80) paras 7–042.

(see subsection II.2). Art 327 of the TFEU may set out the basis for an enhanced protection (protection of the non-participating Member States' non-legally guaranteed rights and interests), but the constitutional framework of enhanced cooperation does not say anything about how to balance the non-participating Member States' freedom to abstain from enhanced cooperation and to be unaffected by factual effects of enhanced cooperation law, and the participating Member States' right to establish enhanced cooperation. The principle of proportionality may help to identify whether the burden imposed on non-participating Member States by enhanced cooperation law may be disproportionate, meaning that enhanced cooperation law could not stand (see subsection II.3).

I. Rights, Competences and Obligations—A Collective or Three Separate Categories?

Art 327 of the TFEU protects the competences, rights, and obligations of non-participating Member States; however, the European treaties do not provide any further explanation of these terms. Thus, one may ask whether 'competences, rights, and obligations' form a collective bundle of guarantees for non-participating Member States, or whether each of them has a separate and distinct meaning, and can therefore be infringed on an isolated basis by enhanced cooperation law. To answer the question of whether 'competences, rights and obligations' form a collective or three separate categories or guarantees, it is first necessary to define them in isolation, in order to identify whether they complement each other, or are even based on each other which may allow arguing that Art 327 of the TFEU establishes a specific form of guarantee for non-participating Member States.

Beginning with rights, the basic definition of rights[100] reveals the idea that rights constitute duties of (other) people rather than claims.[101] In that vein, Joel Feinberg has categorised the various duties that may correlate with rights of other people.[102] The duty of respect, as he calls one of these categories, may be of particular relevance for the current analysis. Feinberg describes the duty of respect with regard to one's property. The exclusive possession and control of one's property impose a duty of non-interference on others.[103] Transferring the duty of respect to enhanced cooperation, it may not be the right to exclusive possession and control of property which is at stake, but it may be the decision of non-participating Member States to abstain from enhanced cooperation. The right to choose to be within or outside

[100] Jonathan Law, 'Right' in Jonathan Law (ed), *A Dictionary of Law* (OUP 2018).

[101] The view on rights would only be different if rights are understood as constituting claims against the world, see for that view William James, 'The Moral Philosopher and the Moral Life' (1891) 1 International Journal of Ethics 330.

[102] Joel Feinberg, 'Duties, Rights, and Claims' (1966) 3 American Philosophical Quarterly 137.

[103] ibid 139.

enhanced cooperation triggers the duty of participating Member States to respect the choice of non-participating Member States of not joining the group.

The second term—competences—is particularly coined by the European treaties as it refers to the division of powers between the European Union and its Member States.[104] Accordingly, in an EU law setting, holding the competence refers to the power of either the European Union or the Member States to set the legal (regulatory) framework in a particular area.[105] Art 327 of the TFEU refers to the competence of non-participating Member States, that is their sovereign power to regulate a particular area in the law (either actively through legislation, or passively through non-regulation, allowing the free play of market forces). Against this background, the requirement that any enhanced cooperation has to respect the competences of non-participating Member States demands that the law of enhanced cooperation does not restrict the non-participating Member States' power to regulate and, in particular, to regulate the area determined by the law of enhanced cooperation.

Thirdly, Art 327 of the TFEU requires participating Member States to respect the obligations of non-participating Member States. An obligation is nothing other than a legal duty.[106] The non-participating Member States may face legal obligations towards third countries based on international treaties, towards a party with whom the non-participating Member States have entered into a private law contract, but also towards their citizens. Every member of the European Union follows a democratic legal order,[107] and thus it is the people who rule. The political entities within a Member State are the representatives of the people who have to act, not in their own individual interests, but in the interests of the very people they represent. Accordingly, enhanced cooperation law has to give non-participating Member States enough room to fulfil all of their obligations on an international and domestic level, but also their obligations towards their people. The last set of obligations, the obligation towards their people, demands that any Member State possess the freedom to decide not to join enhanced cooperation because the legal (regulatory) framework of enhanced cooperation cannot be aligned with their national policy choices. The Member States or, more precisely, the representatives of the people, need to have the freedom to take necessary measures to ensure a coherent pursuit of the will of the people.

The analysis of the three separate terms 'rights', 'competences', and 'obligations' shows that they build on each other. The decision of non-participating Member States not to join enhanced cooperation must be respected by the participating Member States. The respect and acceptance of the decision of non-participating Member States is expressed by the freedom of non-participating Member States

104 Art 2 of the TFEU.

105 Art 5 Subsections 1 and 2 of the TEU.

106 Jonathan Law and Elizabeth A Martin (eds), *Oxford Dictionary of Law* (7th edn, OUP 2013) 375.

107 Which is also a fundamental principle of the European Union: Preamble of the TEU, Art 10 and Art 21 of the TEU.

to regulate freely and fulfil all their obligations towards third parties and their people.[108] The non-participating Member States are only capable of fulfilling their duties towards their people if they have the freedom and power to act. Otherwise, the non-participating Member States would not be able to pursue the policy choices taken by the people.

From this, it follows that Art 327 of the TFEU purports to grant non-participating Member States the power to act unaffected by the law of enhanced cooperation. In other words, Art 327 of the TFEU guarantees non-participating Member States the right to pursue their policies without interference, and thus Art 327 of the TFEU imposes the duty of non-interference upon participating Member States.

II. The Duty of Non-interference

So far, it has been stressed that Art 327 of the TFEU can be read as a guarantee of the freedom to act for non-participating Member States. Non-participating Member States should retain their freedom to regulate the objects of enhanced cooperation law in accordance with their policy decisions. It may well be that the national policy is opposed to that for which enhanced cooperation law is providing. We shall assume, for example, that the participating Member States want to regulate the financial sector through taxation of financial transactions. A tax on each transaction may reduce high-frequency trading which is assumed to harm the financial market. The non-participating Member States may, however, be of the opinion that high-frequency trading is not harmful to the financial market, and thus need not be curbed. Alternatively, even if the non-participating Member States qualify high-frequency trading as harmful to the financial market, they may think that a tax on financial transactions is not capable of preventing these harmful transactions as assumed by the participating Member States. Perhaps non-participating Member States may not wish to tax the financial sector at all, disregarding the steering implications of the tax, simply because they want to strengthen their financial hubs.

At first glance, one may ask: what is the issue here? Allowing non-participating Member States to pursue their policy agenda is pretty straightforward; they are free to make their own laws or abstain from implementing a regulatory or legal framework in that particular area. This may be true in areas which do not provide for external effects, such as divorce law, land zoning regulations, or the law

[108] So also Council, 6 September 2013, Opinion of the Legal Service on the Proposal for a Council Directive implementing enhanced cooperation in the area of financial transaction tax (FTT), 2013/0045, para 35: 'By virtue of Article 327 TFEU, the competences, rights and obligations of non participating Member States must be respected by any enhanced cooperation. This entails the protection of the right of non participating Member States to maintain or adopt their own tax system, while respecting Union law of general application but without being made subject to an obligation to amend or complement their national rules in order to make them compatible with provisions adopted in the framework of an enhanced cooperation to which they are not a party.'

on the domestication of pets. These areas of the law may reflect the social values of a Member State, but they have no impact on decisions of consumption or production, and thus the law of one or some Member States does not affect the legislative actions of other Member States. In contrast, tax laws, financial regulation, or the setting of product standards have effects on whether, what, and where to produce.[109] Thus, the decision to regulate the financial market in one country may have an impact on another country in the form of locational effects. The locational decisions of businesses may be favourable (attracting businesses) or unfavourable (making businesses leave) for Member States depending on the regulatory approach chosen.[110] These effects automatically have a spillover effect on other Member States. If the law attracts businesses, it will make them leave another Member State. The same holds true for incentives to invest.

Returning to the baseline international law draws between lawful and unlawful effects of an international agreement on third countries,[111] the entrepreneurs' decisions which respond to enhanced cooperation law (eg in the form of locational decisions) may be considered as purely factual with no legal implications, and thus the law does not contradict international law standards. In other words, the international law framework would not prohibit enhanced cooperation laws which imposed factual effects upon non-participating Member States in the form of businesses leaving.

Despite the hesitance of international law to address factual effects, these effects may be highly demanding on third parties. We shall assume, for example, that a country decides to implement no financial regulations and not to levy taxes on financial transactions, the country may turn out to be the new financial hub leaving no business to other financial markets. Of course, in reality, there will never be a situation where all financial transactions are only executed on one financial market because various factors influence the decision on where to trade. However, one State's decision on taxation and regulation may have a serious (factual) impact on another State. And in cases where a group of States comes together and jointly implements a regulatory or tax framework, the effects on a non-group member may be even more intense. These factual effects on non-participating Member States may not change the fact that they are allowed to set their legal and regulatory framework. If, however, there is hardly anything left which needs to be regulated or

[109] Stephen Weatherill, 'Flexibility or Fragmentation: Trends in European Integration' in John A Usher (ed), *The state of the European Union: structure, enlargement and economic union* (Pearson Education 2000) 10 argues more broadly that '[t]he thickening patterns of mutual interdependence among the Members States makes it implausible that [enhanced] cooperation between some will not affect the others in some form'.

[110] See for the argument of a competitive advantage of the group in the US context US Supreme Court, 21 February 1978, *United States Steel Corporation v Multistate Tax Commission*, 434 U.S. 452, 495 (1978).

[111] See this chapter subsection B.III.

which can be taxed, the promise that non-participating Member States are allowed to set their regulatory framework and their tax laws independently is a sham.

The analysis leads us to the central discussion of tax and regulatory competition between Member States because the fiscal or regulatory framework of one State has factual (not legal) effects on all other States requiring the latter to act. There is no doubt that competition between Member States may unleash positive effects, as Member States have to budget properly to offer taxpayers public goods at 'fair prices'.[112] Otherwise, taxpayers are likely to move to States which offer them a better deal.[113] However, there is a turning point when competition becomes harmful, and this is when the use of a Member State's public goods and the payment of taxes diverge.

The following subsections examine the question of what can be learned from the experience of (factual) effects of (harmful) tax and regulatory competition for the duty of non-interference. Which competitive environment may encourage Member States to join forces and which policy goals may require unilateral actions by Member States? The following subsections use two concepts developed in the field of regulatory competition (the beggar-thy-neighbour and the beggar-thyself theory) to identify the fields in the law which may be open for enhanced cooperation. Based on these findings, the subsequent subsections reveal whether joint actions by some Member States in those particular fields of the law harm non-participating Member States more deeply, and thus require enhanced protection, protection beyond the legal (market) rights of non-participating Member States.

1. Beggar-Thy-Neighbour and Beggar-Thyself Policies as a Way to Identify Fields of Enhanced Cooperation

a) *The Two Concepts*

The beggar-thy-neighbour concept has been extensively used to describe policy decisions of States in the field of regulatory and tax competition which allow a State to derive an economic benefit at the expense of other States.[114] In trade policy,

[112] Geoffrey Brennan and James M Buchanan, 'Towards a Tax Constitution for Leviathan' (1977) 8 Journal of Public Economics 255,258 et seq; Jeremy Edwards and Michael Keen, 'Tax Competition and Leviathan' (1996) 40 European Economic Review 113; Geoffrey Brennan and James M Buchanan, *The Power to Tax: Analytical Foundations of a Fiscal Constitution* (CUP 2006) 15 et seq.

[113] There is a vast choice of literature on the public finance theory and taxation: David E Wildasin, 'Public Expenditures Determined by Voting with One's Feet and Public Choice' (1977) 79 The Scandinavian Journal of Economics 326; Michael Keen and Kai Konrad, 'The Theory of International Tax Competition and Coordination' in Alan J Auerbach and others (eds), *Handbook of Public Economics*, vol 5 (Elsevier 2013).

[114] James A Brander and Barbara J Spencer, 'Tariff Protection and Imperfect Competition' in Gene M Grossman (ed), *Imperfect Competition and International Trade* (MIT Press 1992) 107; Joel Slemrod, 'Competitive Tax Policy' in Kevin A Hassett (ed), *Rethinking Competitiveness* (AEI Press 2012) 34; Edward Iacobucci, 'The Interdependence of Trade and Competition Policies' (1997) 21 World Competition 5. The work of the OECD revealed factors to identify harmful tax practices of States already in 1998. OECD, Harmful Tax Competition—An Emerging Global Issue (1998) https://www.oecd-ilibrary.org/taxation/harmful-tax-competition_9789264162945-en accessed 3 February 2021.

for example, Germany is currently blamed for following a beggar-thy-neighbour policy because it supports export-led growth.[115] Given the sluggish growth in demand across the globe, such a policy creates jobs and thereby increases employment, but may negatively affect other nations, especially in terms of job creation. In tax law, the beggar-thy-neighbour policy can easily be described with reference to a tax haven. A tax haven gains an economic advantage at the expense of other nations because the haven attracts deposits and capital from abroad by taxing the capital at a very low rate. The haven can offer low taxation because there is no need to provide an investor with substantial public goods. The environment needed for the economic activity has already been used in another State. A beggar-thy-neighbour policy of a State not only consciously accepts the damages and losses of other States; such expenses are clearly also the basis of such policy.

In contrast to beggar-thy-neighbour policy there exists beggar-thyself policy. The latter policy approach leads to the creation of economic costs at home.[116] The policy decision may still impact other States. However, the economic costs are primarily borne at home. The important difference between the two policy streams is that in the case of a beggar-thyself policy there may be efficiency losses, but the policy is 'deployed not to extract advantages from other nations, but because other competing policy objects at home—such as distributional, administrative, public health or other political concerns—dominate the economic motives'.[117] Accordingly, the State may choose a different approach if it wishes to increase economic efficiency. Since the policy serves a broader social purpose, the policy pursued may not be optimal from a worldwide or Europe-wide (economic) perspective, but optimal from the perspective of the particular State.[118]

Examples of a beggar-thyself policy are European subsidies in the farming sector,[119] a ban on genetically modified organisms, and in tax law, a tax on financial transactions. All of these mechanisms follow a social and regulatory goal rather than a pure economic efficiency-oriented policy. The subsidies are the price for sustaining rural farming in Europe,[120] the ban on genetically modified organisms accounts for its health risks, and a tax on financial transactions may strengthen the stability of the financial market in order to prevent another financial crisis.[121]

[115] Nick Johnson, 'Beggar-Thy-Neighbour, and Thyself?' (The Political Economy of Development, 29 March 2017) <https://peofdev.wordpress.com/2017/03/29/beggar-thy-neighbour-and-thyself/> accessed 15 December 2019.

[116] Panagiotis E Petrakis, Pantelis C Kostis, and Dionysis G Valsamis, *European Economics and Politics in the Midst of the Crisis: From the Outbreak of the Crisis to the Fragmented European Federation* (Springer Science & Business Media 2014) 243.

[117] Jeffry A Frieden, Michael Pettis, and Dani Rodrik (eds), *After the Fall: The Future of Global Cooperation* (International Center for Monetary and Banking Studies (ICMB) 2012) 55.

[118] ibid.

[119] Dani Rodrik, *Straight Talk on Trade: Ideas for a Sane World Economy* (Princeton University Press 2019) 220.

[120] Frieden, Pettis, and Rodrik (n 117) 55.

[121] ibid.

All of these policies also have a spillover effect to other countries because of their economic inefficiencies. The losses and disadvantages the States have to suffer are, however, the result of prioritising competing goals and not a result of deliberately harming other nations for one's economic advantage. The pursuit of non-economic goals also undermines the pursuing States' economic gain.

Now perhaps one could argue that taxing capital at a very low rate is a valid policy choice, and thus a tax haven may not fit into the category of beggar-thy-neighbour policy. If, however, a State were truly of the opinion that a very low tax rate is the 'correct' policy choice, the State would tax domestic capital equally at a low rate. Pure tax havens, however, only apply the beneficial tax treatment to foreign investment and not to a domestic situation. The restricted application of the tax benefits highlights the harmful effects on other States and makes it evident that the State does not simply follow a policy decision that it finds correct.

Accordingly, the crucial factor in distinguishing between the beggar-thy-neighbour policy and the beggar-thyself policy is not the intensity of the loss or disadvantage on the other States but the reason for pursuing an inefficient and harming policy. If the policy of one State is intended to harm other nations, the State pursues a beggar-thy-neighbour policy. By contrast, States follow a beggar-thyself policy when prioritising non-economic goals leading to an (accidental) hurting of other States.

b) Beggar-Thy-Neighbour and Beggar-Thyself Policies and Joint Actions

On a stand-alone basis, Member States may follow both inefficient policy streams: the beggar-thy-neighbour and the beggar-thyself policy. Within the European Union, some Member States offer preferential tax treatments for interest, royalties from research and development (patent boxes), or for gains from passive income streams, which—depending on their actual design—may follow a beggar-thy-neighbour policy.[122] Other Member States levy environmental taxes to steer their taxpayers towards environmentally friendly behaviour,[123] levy a tax on financial transactions to—amongst other things—stop high-frequency trading,[124] and impose a progressive income tax to allow for redistribution.[125] All of these taxes may cause losses in efficiency, but they are necessary to achieve non-market goals. But which of these policies would Member States like to pursue jointly?

[122] Daniel J Wilson, 'Beggar Thy Neighbor? The In-State, Out-of-State, and Aggregate Effects of R&D Tax Credits' (2009) 91 The Review of Economics and Statistics 431, 435.

[123] For a detailed overview of all the different environmental taxes levied in the European Union: European Environment Agency, 'Environmental Taxation and EU Environmental Policies' (2016) 17 64 et seq. For a statistic of all the environmental tax revenues collected in each Member State between 2008 and 2017, see <http://appsso.eurostat.ec.europa.eu/nui/show.do?dataset=env_ac_tax&lang=en> accessed 3 February 2021

[124] Lena Hiort af Ornäs and Magnus Wiberg, 'Beskattning av finanssektorn, ett ämne på den internationella agendan' (2011) Kkattenytt 497, 510–11.

[125] Marc Bourgeois, 'Constitutional Framework of the Different Types of Income' in Bruno Peeters (ed), *The concept of tax* (IBFD 2005) 175.

Within the beggar-thy-neighbour policy, a common approach by a group of Member States is very unlikely. An exploitative policy can best be pursued when acting alone. A tax haven, for example, will not cooperate with other havens.[126] It competes with other havens and its policy goal—attracting capital and investment from non-resident taxpayers—will only be achieved if it is more attractive than others. Accordingly, it is quite unlikely that enhanced cooperation would pursue a beggar-thy-neighbour policy because such a strategy is more effective when pursued by the Member State on a unilateral basis as opposed to as part of a broader coalition.

Within the beggar-thyself policy category, Member States have two particular reasons for cooperating. First, Member States may wish to form a coalition if the goals underlying the law cannot be achieved unilaterally. For example, the more States agree to fight emissions of carbon dioxide, such as through the levying of a tax on such emissions, the more likely it is that the emission of carbon dioxide gases will be reduced. A carbon dioxide tax increases the production prices and thus reduces the labour demand leading to efficiency losses. The efficiency loss is, however, accepted because the Member States prioritise the reduction of carbon dioxide emissions over market efficiency.

Secondly, Member States may wish to cooperate to counter negative factual effects of a beggar-thyself policy. The diversity in the landscape of taxation may encourage taxpayers to move from one Member State to a fellow Member State which offers a less burdensome treatment. Such movements may be addressed by reducing diversity between Member States. In other words, if a group of Member States levies a tax on highly mobile factors, such as financial transactions, the locational effects may decrease. Reducing diversity between Member States by taxing financial transactions in all the relevant Member States means that the costs of moving to a State following a different approach (not taxing the financial transactions) will increase. The increased costs will render a move to other jurisdictions less likely and thus will reduce the negative (factual) effects of the tax for the Member States.

Reducing diversity between Member States to address negative (factual) effects of a tax can be described as a sort of cartel. Member States do not want to expose themselves to competition, and thus they align their tax policies and wipe out diversity. If, for example, a Member State implements a tax on carbon dioxide emissions, plants which heavily emit carbon dioxide may move to another Member State which offers the same infrastructure but does not tax emissions in the same burdensome way. Taxpayers may, however, be prevented from moving if Member States with equal market conditions tax carbon emissions in a similar manner and

[126] Philipp Genschel and Thomas Plumper, 'Regulatory Competition and International Co-Operation' (1997) 4 Journal of European Public Policy 626637; Kai Konrad and Tim Stolper, 'Coordination and the Fight against Tax Havens' (2016) 103 Journal of International Economics 96 .

taxation can only be circumvented by moving to a Member State with different market conditions.

From this it follows that establishing of enhanced cooperation may be common in the field of a beggar-thyself policy, in order to cope better with negative effects following from the policy decision, for example in the case of a financial transaction tax (FTT), but also to achieve a better policy outcome, as in the case of environmental taxes. The Member States will, however, refrain from forming a coalition if they wish to pursue a beggar-thy-neighbour policy because such a strategy is more effective when pursued unilaterally.

2. Enhanced Protection against Enhanced Cooperation Laws

In the area of a beggar-thyself policy, the Member States may come closer to achieving the aim and purpose of the law and cope with negative effects of the law in a better way if they act jointly. Accordingly, a beggar-thyself policy in the area of taxation raises clear incentives for Member States to join forces and to address a specific issue collectively. It is clear from the outset that any Member State would be allowed to pursue the policy goal unilaterally and none of the other Member States would be able to influence the policy decision or prevent the fellow Member State from pursuing these policy objects. No Member State, and not even the European Union, has a tool to challenge steering taxes which are supposed to be either ineffective or disproportionate. As long as these taxes do not discriminate cross-border economic activities or contradict state aid law, these laws are permitted to stand. If, however, Art 327 of the TFEU were read in a way that gave non-participating Member States the chance to fight any (tax) measures which expose them to unfavourable factual effects, non-participating Member States would be able to protect themselves from negative factual effects of enhanced cooperation law, which the Member States would not be able to do if the negative effects were imposed by international treaties or by unilateral measures of Member States. From the participating Member States' perspective, enhanced protection of non-participating Member States may prevent them from implementing laws under enhanced cooperation which they may be allowed to introduce on a purely unilateral basis.

But is there truly a need for enhanced protection of non-participating Member States in cases in which some Member States establish enhanced cooperation? In other words, are common actions of some Member States more dangerous to the interests of non-participating Member States than the unilateral actions of one Member State,[127] and does the European treaty framework want to address this threat through Art 327 of the TFEU?

[127] For the US context on the compact clause, 'Group action, in itself, may be more influential than independent actions by the States.' However, the Supreme Court refused to distinguish externalities on non-participating States created by the compact clause differently from the ordinary tax competition

a) *The Intensity of the Impact—A United Front*

First, collective actions by some Member States may be considered as having a greater impact on the interests of non-cooperating Member States than a unilateral action of one Member State. We shall assume, for example, that one Member State levies a tax on the sale of high-heeled shoes because they are harmful to muscles within a foot. The tax on high-heeled footwear leads to an increase in prices, which in turn has a negative impact on the sale of these shoes. The decline in sales has an impact beyond the borders of the Member State because as the fixed costs remain constant in the short run, but fewer shoes are sold, the costs and therefore the price of a pair of shoes also increase in other Member States. If not one sole Member State but a group of Member States levied a tax on the sale of high-heeled shoes, the impact on the price would increase.

One could object that the impact on Member States not levying a tax on high-heeled shoes depends on the number of States imposing such a tax, but the intensity of the impact does not change because of a common or unilateral approach of the States. In other words, the Member States not levying a tax on high-heeled shoes are affected by a tax on high-heeled shoes imposed by other Member States regardless of whether the latter Member States levy the tax based on a unilateral approach or based on enhanced cooperation law. The only relevant factor would be the number of Member States imposing a tax on high-heeled shoes.

However, that is only partly true. As long as the group is stable, that is as long as there are sufficient coercive measures to prevent deviation, there is no possibility of non-participating Member States gaining compensation on a bilateral basis. In other words, the non-participating Member States would have to convince the entire group of participating Member States to change their policy approach and not just one Member State at the time. To change the policy choices of a united front needs much more leverage, and thus, there is a factual difference between pursuing certain policies on a unilateral basis as opposed to as part of enhanced cooperation.

From this it follows that the possibility of joining forces and cooperating on a particular policy issue may have a bigger impact on non-cooperating Member States. The non-participating Member States are facing a united front and cannot use individual leverage to push for their interests. The change of circumstances gives rise to a need for a deeper level of protection of non-participating Member States, in case legislative initiatives are pursued within enhanced cooperation and not on a unilateral basis.

between the States. US Supreme Court, 21 February 1978, *United States Steel Corporation v Multistate Tax Commission*, 434 U.S. 452, 473, and 478 (1978); Pincus (n 85) 527.

b) *Extraterritorial Application of the Law as a Requirement to Pursue Policy Objectives of Enhanced Cooperation*

It is quite difficult to meet the beggar-thyself policy objectives if the measures implemented under the enhanced cooperation procedure can easily be circumvented. In tax law, this would mean that it is difficult for the group to levy a burdensome tax on events which may easily be shifted outside the scope of the tax. Accordingly, the more mobile the factors are (in other words, the cheaper it is to move assets or transactions) which are subject to tax, the more likely it is that taxpayers try to circumvent taxation. Above,[128] it has already been stressed that joint actions under enhanced cooperation are already one way of addressing negative effects following from a responsive behaviour of economic players, and thus it is very likely that some Member States would pursue a beggar-thyself policy jointly. Sometimes, however, a joint action may not be enough to reduce negative factual effects if the (Member) States not imposing an equal burdensome treatment are still a viable alternative for economic operators. Accordingly, as long as not all States with an equal offer of public goods join the group, economic operators may still have an incentive to move if the market conditions are acceptable in the other States which do not levy an equally burdensome tax. To reduce negative effects even further, the participating Member States may wish to extend the scope of the tax through an extraterritorial application of the law. An extraterritorial reach may make it less easy to circumvent taxation, and thus it may be less attractive for taxpayers to leave.

Sometimes, the extraterritorial application of the law to prevent negative factual effects may reach the level of being discriminative or imposing market access restrictions. Such defensive obstacles imposed by enhanced cooperation law have to be justified like any other restriction of the fundamental freedom by unilateral measures of Member States.[129]

Despite protecting the group of Member States from negative effects of the beggar-thyself policy, the law's objectives may demand an extraterritorial reach. Take taxes aiming to protect the global environment, and in particular dolphins, as an example. A tax on the sale of tuna fished locally with non-dolphin-friendly techniques asks for an application of the tax also to imported non-dolphin-friendly tuna. The protection of the dolphin population requires an extension of the measures to fishing and resources outside the territorial jurisdiction of the enacting Member States.

From this it follows that there are policy objectives which can only be satisfied if the law is applied to persons, assets, or acts that are located beyond a State's territory (extraterritorial application of the law). Such an application clearly extends

[128] See this chapter section E.II.1.b.

[129] See Chapter 5, Part I, subsection E.VI.2.b.

the scope of the law, and therefore increases the factual effects on the Member States pursuing different policy objectives.

In the following two subsections, a brief overview of the legal restrictions on extraterritorial laws, both from the perspective of international and EU law, will be given. Only the laws which can satisfy the requirements set by international and EU law are allowed to stand and can be analysed further with regard to their factual effects.

(aa) Restrictions under EU Law EU law does not impose any specific restrictions on the extraterritorial application of the law. Therefore, general international law principles apply to the relationship between Member States. However, general principles of EU law such as the principle of non-discrimination, either in its specific form of the fundamental freedoms or the general anti-discrimination clause, and the principle of proportionality can limit the room for extraterritorial application of the law. The principle of non-discrimination, especially in the form of the fundamental freedoms, requires that foreign elements which are brought within the scope of the national law are placed in an equal situation as domestic elements. Foreign and domestic elements can only be treated equally without discrimination if they are both in an equivalent situation.[130]

(bb) Restrictions of International Law International law sets limits on an extraterritorial application of the law. According to the prevailing opinion, an extraterritorial application of the law is lawful if the foreign elements that are subject to national laws have a minimum connection to the personal or territorial jurisdiction.[131] In the academic literature, the minimum connection is generally described as a genuine link or sufficient connection between the state levying the tax and the foreign elements that are brought within the scope of national laws.[132] Accordingly, a minor connecting factor may be sufficient to allow an extraterritorial reach of the law, from the perspective of international law. The Member States may, however,

[130] For more details on the legal issues of an extraterritorial application of the law, see Chapter 5, Part I, subsection E.VI.2.b)(cc)i.

[131] Manfred Mössner, 'Source versus Residence—an EU Perspective' (2006) 60 Bulletin for International Taxation 501; Rutsel S Martha, *The Jurisdiction to Tax in International Law: Theory and Practice of Legislative Fiscal Jurisdiction* (Kluwer Law International 1989) 46 et seq. Cees Peters, *On the Legitimacy of International Tax Law*, vol 31 (IBFD 2014) para 3.3.1; Michael Lang, 'The Marks & Spencer Case—The Open Issues Following the ECJ's Final Word' (2006) 60 Bulletin for International Taxation 54, 57; Michael Lang, 'Doppelbelastung und Doppelbefreiung im grenzüberschreitenden Steuerrecht' in Ulrich Becker and Fredrik Andersson (eds), *Steuer- und Sozialstaat im europäischen Systemwettbewerb* (Mohr Siebeck 2005) 215 et seq.

[132] See for more details Stjepan Gadžo, 'The Principle of "Nexus" or "Genuine Link" as a Keystone of International Income Tax Law: A Reappraisal' (2018) 46 Intertax 194; Caroline Heber and Christian Sternberg, 'The Extraterritorial Reach of the German Progression Clause in Income Tax Law in the Light of International Law' (2017) 45 Intertax 254; Juliane Kokott, 'The "Genuine Link" Requirement for Source Taxation in Public International Law' in Werner Haslehner and others (eds), *Tax and the Digital Economy: Challenges and Proposals for Reform* (Kluwer Law International 2019).

wish to have a quite strong territorial nexus to allow the law to be enforced. If there is only a minor link between the jurisdiction of the Member States and the foreign elements, it may be quite impossible first to identify that the taxable event has occurred, and second to enforce the payment of the tax.

c) *Conclusions*

The intrinsic characteristics of enhanced cooperation—the joint action of some Member States without the possibility of unilaterally deviating from the common effort—already require enhanced protection of non-participating Member States. Non-participating Member States face a united front and may be unable to demand compensation as they may do in the case of unilateral measures of Member States.

If Member States decide to pursue a beggar-thyself policy through enhanced cooperation, they may apply the law extraterritorially to achieve certain objectives or to minimise negative effects following from enhanced cooperation law. Extraterritorially applied enhanced cooperation law increases factual effects on non-participating Member States which makes the need for enhanced protection even more evident. The following subsections will set out what an enhanced protection of the non-participating Member States may look like.

3. The Burden on Outsiders as an Argument for (Dis-)Proportionate Laws

It has been established that the characteristics of enhanced cooperation demand intensive protection of non-participating Member States which is, in principle, provided by the constitutional framework of enhanced cooperation. Art 327 of the TFEU guarantees non-participating Member States the right to pursue their policies without interference from enhanced cooperation law. Aside from the general primary EU law protection of the non-participating Member States' legally unprotected interests, the constitutional framework of enhanced cooperation does not explain how to balance the participating Member States' duty of non-interference and their right to establish enhanced cooperation when it comes to factual effects of enhanced cooperation law. In other words, the constitutional framework of enhanced cooperation does not give specific guidance on deciding to which burdens enhanced cooperation law can legitimately expose non-participating Member States. Prohibiting any factual effects on non-participating Member States may make it impossible to establish enhanced cooperation in most areas of the law because any regulatory legislative approach may have some impact on non-participating Member States. Therefore, a balance is required between the participating Member States' right to enact enhanced cooperation laws on the one hand, and the non-participating Member States' right not to be affected by these laws on the other hand. In the absence of more specific principles, the principle of proportionality, a fundamental principle of European Union law, may allow one to identify certain factual effects on non-participating Member States as a disproportionate burden, and thus may give rise to a claim that enhanced cooperation law is unlawful.

a) Scope of the European Principle of Proportionality

The notion of proportionality requires that an action is proportionate to its objectives.[133] The idea of proportionality goes back to ancient times, but as a general principle of law in modern legal systems it is influenced by the ideas of liberal democracy and in particular the protection of the individual against the State.[134] The German and the French legal systems in particular developed the proportionality principle and it also influenced the European legal system from early on.[135] The CJEU found that the principle of proportionality is a general principle of EU law.[136] The heart of the principle of proportionality applies when the pursuit of a legitimate objective is not in question,[137] but the measures taken to achieve it conflict with other interests. Accordingly, proportionality always requires a set of conflicting interests that need to be 'balanced',[138] and thus it always requires a 'weighted' test.[139]

To date, the principle of proportionality acquired particular importance in three fields: first, it forms a standard for determining the comparability of national rules restricting free movement rights with EU law.[140] Secondly, the principle of proportionality also supplements the principle of subsidiarity and thus protects Member State sovereignty against expanding EU competences.[141] Thirdly, the principle of proportionality protects the fundamental rights of individuals.[142] In all scenarios,

[133] Takis Tridimas, 'The Principle of Proportionality in Community Law: From the Rule of Law to Market Integration Modern Jurisprudence' (1996) 31 Irish Jurist 83, 83.

[134] Tridimas, 'The Principle of Proportionality in Community Law' (n 133) 65.

[135] Nicholas Emiliou, *The Principle of Proportionality in European Law: A Comparative Study* (Kluwer Law International 1996) 23 et seq. Wolf Sauter, 'Proportionality in EU Law: A Balancing Act?' (2013) 15 Cambridge Yearbook of European Legal Studies 439, 442.

[136] For example CJEU, 11 June 2009, C-170/08, *Nijemeisland*, ECLI:EU:C:2009:369, para 41; Tor-Inge Harbo, 'The Function of the Proportionality Principle in EU Law' (2010) 16 European Law Journal 158, 159.

[137] It is sometimes argued that the principle of proportionality follows a four-step approach, which covers at the first step the legitimacy of the policy objective. So far, the Court has granted the legislature wide discretion to decide whether it is necessary to implement certain policies, see Juliane Kokott and Christoph Sobotta, 'The Evolution of the Principle of Proportionality in EU Law—Towards an Anticipative Understanding?' in Stefan Vogenauer and Stephen Weatherill (eds), *General Principles of Law: European and Comparative Perspectives* (2017) 168 et seq.

[138] Vasiliki Kosta, 'The Principle of Proportionality in EU Law—An Interest-Based Taxonomy' in Joana Mendes (ed), *EU Executive Discretion and the Limits of Law* (OUP 2019) 199.

[139] Sauter (n 135) 441.

[140] Takis Tridimas, 'The Principle of Proportionality' in Robert Schütze and Takis Tridimas (eds), *Oxford Principles of European Union Law*, vol I: The European Union Legal Order (OUP 2018) 243–44.

[141] ibid 244.

[142] Günter Hirsch, *Das Verhältnismäßigkeitsprinzip im Gemeinschaftsrecht* (Zentrum für Europäisches Wirtschaftsrecht 1997) 14 arguing that the principle of proportionality has been linked to fundamental rights from the beginning of the CJEU jurisprudence; Eric Engle, 'The History of the General Principle of Proportionality: An Overview' (2012) 10 Dartmouth Law Journal 1, 274.

it is quite clear that the application of the principle of proportionality involves the reconciliation of two premises. In fundamental rights, it is the right of the individual on the one hand, and the policy objective on the other, which need to be balanced against each other. If a conflict of powers between the European Union and the Member States is at stake, the principle of proportionality attempts to reconcile the interests of both power levels. Lastly, if national measures conflict with free movement rights, the aim and purpose of the national rule has to be reconciled with the needs of the European internal market. This shows that the principle of proportionality has no intrinsic value; instead it refers to a 'relationship between other specific and possible competing substantive interests'.[143]

The Maastricht Treaty already enshrined the principle of proportionality as a fundamental principle of EU law into the European constitutional framework,[144] but it was only after the Lisbon Treaty that the principle of proportionality has formally been named as a European legal concept.[145] Today, Art 5 Subsection 4 of the TEU requires that 'the content and form of Union action shall not exceed what is necessary to achieve the objectives of the Treaties'. Some scholars have argued that Art 5 Subsection 4 of the Treaty on European Union (TEU) and its predecessor did not add to the pre-existing case law,[146] and thus the primary EU law provision 'only' codified the unwritten general EU law principle. However, this is not the case. Art 5 Subsection 4 of the TEU has a narrower scope than the unwritten general principle of proportionality as it only addresses acts of the European Union[147] and prevents them from imposing certain disproportionate burdens. The second protocol to the Lisbon Treaty on the application of the principles of subsidiarity and proportionality suggests, with reference to the proportionality test, that any European action 'shall take account of the need for any burden, whether financial or administrative, falling upon the Union, national governments, regional or local authorities, economic operators and citizens, to be minimized and commensurate with the objective to be achieved'.[148] Accordingly, the proportionality test seeks to minimise the burden on economic operators, authorities, and citizens[149]

[143] Gráinne de Búrca, 'The Principle of Proportionality and Its Application in EC Law' (1993) 13 Yearbook of European Law 105, 106.

[144] 'Any action by the Community shall not go beyond what is necessary to achieve the objectives of this Treaty'—Art 3b Subsection 3 of Maastricht Treaty, OJ, 29 July 1992, C 191, 6.

[145] Art 5 Subsection 4 of the TEU; Johannes Saurer, 'Der kompetenzrechtliche Verhältnismäßigkeitsgrundsatz im Recht der Europäischen Union' (2014) 69 Juristenzeitung 281, 285.

[146] Takis Tridimas, 'Proportionality' (n 140) 246; Angelika Emmerich-Fritsche, *Der Grundsatz der Verhältnismäßigkeit als Direktive und Schranke der EG-Rechtsetzung* (Duncker & Humblot 2000) 275; Takis Tridimas, 'Proportionality in Community Law: Searching for the Appropriate Standard of Scrutiny' in Evelyn Ellis (ed), *The Principle of Proportionality in the Laws of Europe* (Hart Publishing 1999) 80.

[147] Accordingly, Art 5 Subsection 4 of the TEU does not cover the proportionality test for obstacles to the fundamental freedoms.

[148] Consolidated version of the Treaty on European Union—Protocol No 2 on the application of the principle of subsidiarity and proportionality, OJ, 9.5.2008, 115, pp 206–09.

[149] See in that vein CJEU, 4 May 2016, C-477/14, *Pillbox*, ECLI:EU:C:2016:324, para 48; CJEU, 21 July 2011, C-15/10, *Etimine SA*, ECLI:EU:C:2011:504, para 124; CJEU, 8 July 2010, C-343/09,

because any of these legal subjects may 'plead infringement of Art 5(4) TEU where the Union unreasonably affects their interests'.[150]

At first glance, the constitutional promise to be free from any disproportionate burdens has a very wide scope and may cover interferences with fundamental rights[151] and the protection of the Member States' power.[152] However, a closer look at the constitutional framework shows that the rights-based proportionality test sits with Art 51 Subsection 1 of the Charter of the fundamental rights. The CJEU has never answered the question of a disproportionate interference of a European action with the fundamental rights of individuals based on Art 5 Subsection 4 of the TEU or its predecessor in the Maastricht Treaty. The Court either referred to the general principle of proportionality or, after the Charter of fundamental rights became legally binding, the CJEU has based the proportionality exercise on Art 52 Subsection 1 of the Charter.[153] Likewise, the Member States' power does not need protection by Art 5 Subsection 4 of the TEU as the principle of subsidiarity already 'embodies a specific application of the principle of proportionality with a view to protecting the residual powers of the Member States'.[154]

If the rights-based and the subsidiarity-based proportionality tests are not covered by Art 5 Subsection 4 of the TEU what does the burden-based proportionality test cover and what does burden on the national governments, regional, or local authorities, economic operators and citizens mean? The following sections will define the burden-based proportionality test by differentiating its scope from the rights-based and subsidiarity-based proportionality tests.

(aa) Burden-based Proportionality Test versus Subsidiarity-based Proportionality Test We shall start with the relationship between the subsidiarity-based and the burden-based proportionality test. The first difference between these two proportionality tests is that only the one enshrined in Art 5 Subsection 4 of the TEU applies to the field which falls within the exclusive competence of the European Union. The second difference is that Art 5 Subsection 4 of the TEU also

Afton Chemical Limited, ECLI:EU:C:2010:419, para 45; CJEU, 9 March 2010, C-379/08 and C-380/08, *Raffinerie Mediterranee*, ECLI:EU:C:2010:127, para 86; CJEU, 12 July 2001, C-189/01, *Jippes*, ECLI:EU:C:2001:420, para 81; CJEU, 5 October 1994, C-133/93, C-300/93 and C-362/93, *Crispoltoni*, ECLI:EU:C:1994:364, para 41; CJEU, 13 November 1990, C-331/88, *Fedesa*, ECLI:EU:C:1990:391, para 13 ('when there is a choice between several appropriate measures recourse must be had to the least onerous').

[150] Lenaerts and Van Nuffel (n 80) paras 7–040.

[151] Any limitation of a personal freedom may also qualify as a burden.

[152] Any limitation of Member States' power may also be understood as a burden on national governments, regional and local authorities.

[153] For the application of Art 51 Subsection 1 of the Charter see CJEU, 8 April 2014, C-293/12 and C-594/12, *Digital Rights Ireland and Kärntner Landesregierung*, ECLI:EU:C:2014:238, para 38; CJEU, 22 January 2013, C-283/11, *Sky Österreich*, ECLI:EU:C:2013:28, para 47; CJEU, 17 October 2013, C-101/12, *Schaible*, ECLI:EU:C:2013:661, para 27.

[154] Lenaerts and Van Nuffel (n 80) ss 7–039.

refers to burdens on the European Union, which is the reverse of the subsidiarity-based proportionality test. These two differences touch on the scope of the proportionality test, whereas the third difference between the subsidiarity-based and the burden-based proportionality tests is more substantive and requires further explanation.

The subsidiarity-based proportionality test aims to restrict the actions of the European Union to that which is strictly necessary to achieve the objective of the European Union. The less regulation the European Union provides the more freedom remains with the Member States. Accordingly, the subsidiarity-based proportionality test balances the European policy objective with the Member States' freedom to regulate. The burden-based proportionality test, however, does not ask how much of the regulatory space can be occupied by the European Union. Rather, it looks at the measure taken to achieve the policy objective and asks whether it would be possible to reach the same results with less burdensome tools.[155] Think of the implementation of a Europe-wide harmonised wealth tax. If the different and uncoordinated approaches within the Member States imposing such a tax is harmful to the internal market, it is beyond question that the European Union has the power to enact a directive for a harmonised European wealth tax.[156] Such a tax would require harmonised valuation standards. Accordingly, the European Union is allowed to choose between different standards, for example, an annual evaluation of the property of the taxpayers or the use of the valuation of the last year adjusted by the average value increase. The latter option may not be as precise as the former, however, it would not burden the Member States as heavily as the former, but both methods would be capable of achieving the redistributive objective. It is true that such a tax not only burdens the Member States but also the taxpayers (in other words the economic operators) because they may have to value their assets in a first step. Nevertheless, the Member States are obliged to verify the accuracy of the information and must therefore at least carry out a plausibility check. Accordingly, the burden-based proportionality test may identify the proportionate valuation method by a balancing of the capability of each of these methods on achieving the policy objective and the burden that method imposes on the Member States. If the policy objective may be achieved with minor limitations by following the value adjustment method, the implementation of a much more burdensome measure may be disproportionate. The subsidiarity-based proportionality test may not be able to achieve the same outcome because the subsidiarity principle only asks whether an EU action for determining the valuation method is required. If a common approach on the valuation method is required to achieve the objectives, the principle of subsidiarity would grant the European legislature the power to choose freely between the annual valuation and the adjusted valuation method.

[155] Kosta, 'The Principle of Proportionality in EU Law' (n 138) 205.
[156] Based on Art 115 of the TFEU, see Chapter 4, subsection G.

Aside from actual burdens imposed on the national governments, regional or local authorities, the Member States may face (negative) factual effects, such as locational effects, following from EU law. Factual effects can easily be described as burdens on Member States: The emigration of businesses, for example, leads to an economic loss, and thus burdens the Member States' revenues. A burdening of the Member States through factual effects may also be at stake when the newly imposed law requires a more intense exchange of information.[157] The burdens imposed on the Member States are legal obligations under the Directives for a Europe-wide exchange of information,[158] but from the perspective of the newly imposed law, the increased obligations for an exchange of information and the gathering of information, which the Member States may not already have, is purely factual.

From this it follows that not only direct burdens imposed by law are subject to scrutiny under the burden-based proportionality test but also the factual effects following from the law.

(bb) Burden-based Proportionality Test versus Rights-based Proportionality Test We shall now turn to the relationship between the rights-based and the burden-based proportionality tests: the protocol of the Lisbon Treaty refers to administrative and financial burdens on economic operators and citizens. But how is the requirement to minimise burdens on economic operators and citizens different from infringing on their fundamental rights, such as the right to conduct business?[159] Any burden on the economic operators or citizen can easily be described as an infringement of their fundamental rights.[160] A withholding tax on dividends, for example, may be qualified as disproportionate because it heavily burdens banks and companies which distribute dividends (the economic operators), but it may also qualify as a disproportionate infringement of the economic operators' right

[157] That line of argument was also raised by the United Kingdom against the FTT. The United Kingdom argued that the FTT 'will also be a source of costs for the non-participating Member States, because of the application of the Council Directive 2010/24/EU of 16 March 2010 concerning mutual assistance for the recovery of claims relating to taxes, duties and other measures', and that a recovery of the costs cannot be claimed based on the current European framework on mutual assistance. However, the United Kingdom did not argue that the costs are disproportionate, and thus infringe their 'competences, rights and obligations' as protected by Art 327 of the TFEU, but argued that Art 332 of the TFEU was infringed. This demands that any expenditure resulting from implementation of the enhanced cooperation be borne by the participating Member States (CJEU, 30 April 2014, C-209/13, *United Kingdom of Great Britain and Northern Ireland v Council*, ECLI:EU:C:2014:282, paras 22–23). However, the Council, Austria, Portugal and the European Commission mandate that the financial guarantee 'concerns solely operational expenditure to be borne by the European Union budget in relation to measures establishing enhanced cooperation' (CJEU, 30 April 2014, C-209/13, *United Kingdom of Great Britain and Northern Ireland v Council*, ECLI:EU:C:2014:282, para 28).

[158] Directive, 15 February 2011, 2011/16/EU, on administrative cooperation in the field of taxation and repealing Directive 77/799/EEC, OJ, 11 March 2011, L 64, 1, in the amended version of Directive, 25 May 2018, 2018/822/EU, on amending Directive 2011/16/EU as regards mandatory automatic exchange of information in the field of taxation in relation to reportable cross-border arrangements, OJ, 5 June 2018, L 139, 1.

[159] Art 16 of the Charter of Fundamental Rights of the European Union.

[160] Kosta, 'The Principle of Proportionality in EU Law' (n 138) 203 et seq.

to freely conduct their business. A fundamental differentiating factor may, however, be found with respect to the right to challenge burdensome EU laws. In other words, does Art 5 Subsection 4 of the TEU grant each legal subject a right to challenge European Union law measures on the grounds of proportionality concerns as fundamental rights do? Or does Art 5 Subsection 4 of the TEU empower the Member States to demand European legislation which does not burden their economic operators and citizens in a disproportionate manner. In the latter case, the Member States would not assert the rights of their economic operators and citizens but would have their own legal position allowing them to protect their economic operators and citizens from excessive burdens of European law.[161] Such a view of the burden-based proportionality test would fundamentally differentiate it from the rights-based proportionality test, granting the Member States an individual right to protect their economic operators and citizens.

b) Conclusion for the Proportionality Test and Enhanced Cooperation Laws

From all of this it follows that Art 5 Subsection 4 of the TEU only reflects a particular aspect of the general principle of proportionality. Art 5 Subsection 4 of the TEU demands that burdens on the Member States and individuals following from European acts are proportionate. These burdens are different from any fundamental right interferences and limitations of Member States' power. Moreover, they do not only cover a deterioration of the individual's or Member States' legal position, the burden-based proportionality test also recognises negative implications of factual effects as relevant burdens. Therefore, Art 5 Subsection 4 of the TEU does not ask for a form of 'light touch regulation' or 'as little regulation as possible'.[162] The burden-based proportionality test, however, requires European institutions to consider the effects that the European law has on authorities, economic operators, and citizens.

For the purpose of this study, negative factual effects are of particular relevance because infringements of the non-participating Member States' legally protected rights are already taken care of by other provisions of the enhanced cooperation's constitutional framework. Therefore, the following analysis will only focus on Art 5 Subsection 4 of the TEU and will not refer to the European general principle of proportionality. Art 5 Subsection 4 of the TEU is more relevant when it comes to factual effects and thus enjoys precedence over the general principle of proportionality.

[161] For a different view see Lenaerts and Van Nuffel (n 80) paras 7–040.

[162] See for a different view Vasiliki Kosta, '"Free-Standing Proportionality" in EU Law: Exploring Ambiguities and Tracing Its Contours' (Emile Noël/Hauser Global Fellows Forum, Jean Monnet Center NYU School of Law, 24 October 2017).

c) Proportionality in Three Steps

Under judicial review, the principle of proportionality is tested by a three-step approach. First, the 'acts of the EU institutions [must] be appropriate for attaining the legitimate objectives pursued by the legislation at issue'; second the acts must 'not exceed the limits of what is necessary in order to achieve those objectives', and 'the disadvantages caused must not be disproportionate to the aims pursued'.[163]

The first step simply asks whether the measure taken by the European institutions is per se suitable to achieve the policy objectives. The suitability requirement covers, but goes beyond, what is known as the requirement set by international law that each State must not act arbitrarily. In the context of legislative actions, arbitrariness would be at stake if there is no internal connection between the provision imposed and the purpose pursued.[164] In other words, a legislative act is arbitrary if there is no intrinsic connection between the policy objective and the measures implemented because the measures can in no way be suitable to achieve the policy objectives. The ban on arbitrary actions in international law is wider than the requirement of suitability because the former only requires some linkage between the measures imposed and the objectives pursued whereas the latter asks for some form of proof that the objectives can be achieved by the measure imposed.

The second step, the necessity requirement, demands staying within the limits of what is necessary to achieve the policy objectives. The European institutions have to go for the least invasive measures which are sufficient to achieve the policy objective. Especially in the field of taxation, there are different ways of designing the tax. The tax base, for example, may be defined in a very precise way, requiring a costly valuation of assets (eg in case of a wealth tax), or allowing the use of proxies. Depending on the policy objective, it may be enough to utilise indicators which are easier to grasp, and thus the use of more burdensome measures would fail the necessity test.

The third step of the proportionality test is the true balancing act: the harm caused by the European action must outweigh its benefits.[165] Such a balancing act always includes underlying subjective values because at some point one has to decide what is more important: the precise levying of the tax and the achieving of the policy objective or the relevant fundamental right, the sovereignty of the Member States or the freedom from burdens.[166]

[163] CJEU, 4 May 2016, C-477/14, *Pillbox*, ECLI:EU:C:2016:324, para 48 with further references.

[164] Gerhard Leibholz, 'Das Verbot der Willkür und des Ermessensmißbrauches im völkerrechtlichen Verkehr der Staaten' (1929) 1 Zeitschrift für ausländisches öffentliches Recht und Völkerrecht 77, 78; Sternberg (n 46) 308 et seq.

[165] Dominik Freyer, 'The Proportionality Principle under EU Tax Law: General and Practical Problems Caused by Its Extensive Application—Part 1' 57 European Taxation 384, 385 arguing that the notion of 'harm caused' does not fit well with EU law, as there is no real harm or disadvantage involved and therefore the 'ECJ searches for a balance between two theoretically equal Treaty objectives'.

[166] Sauter (n 135) 447 arguing that 'only a mild form of balancing is applied at the EU level'.

d) The Burden-based Proportionality Test in the field of Enhanced Cooperation

Thus far, it has been demonstrated that Art 5 Subsection 4 of the TEU allows examining European law on its effects on authorities, economic operators, and citizens. In case of enhanced cooperation law, accordingly in the case where the law only binds some Member States, the question arises whether, and if so to what extent non-participating Member States are allowed to rely on Art 5 Subsection 4 of the TEU and challenge enhanced cooperation law which imposes burdens upon them. In other words, does Art 5 Subsection 4 of the TEU only protect legal subjects within the scope of enhanced cooperation law (ie participating Member States and economic operators resident within a participating Member State) or are all legal subjects of the European internal market allowed to rely on Art 5 Subsection 4 of the TEU and claim that enhanced cooperation law must only impose proportionate burdens upon them.

To answer the question of whether or not non-participating Member States can rely on Art 5 Subsection 4 of the TEU and fight disproportionate burdens of enhanced cooperation law, a comparison between non-EU States and non-participating Member States must not be drawn. Ordinary secondary EU law may have factual effects on States outside the European Union and non-EU States are not entitled to rely on Art 5 Subsection 4 of the TEU,[167] but the principle of non-interference, as enshrined in Art 327 of the TFEU, explicitly demands protection of non-participating Member States. Therefore, Art 327 of the TFEU forms the legal basis for extending the principle of proportionality to the Member States not subject to the law of enhanced cooperation, granting them the chance to fight disproportionate burdens imposed upon them by enhanced cooperation laws.

e) Applying the Burden-based Proportionality Test to Enhanced Cooperation Law

The first step, the suitability test, is not specific to the burden-based proportionality test. As long as the (tax) measure introduced under the enhanced cooperation procedure is per se capable of achieving the policy objective, the law will pass the first hurdle of the proportionality test.

The second step, the necessity requirement, demands the use of a measure which is sufficient to achieve the policy objectives, and which is the least invasive one for the authorities, economic operators, and citizens of the internal market (accordingly, legal subjects of the participating and non-participating Member States). In other words, if the European legislature within the enhanced cooperation law-making process has to choose between two measures which are both suitable to

[167] An extension of the scope of the European treaties to third parties can only be claimed where the European treaties explicitly provide for it, such as in the case of Art 63 of the TFEU; the third countries can only rely on international law. However, international law does not protect third countries from negative factual effect: see this chapter subsection B.III.

achieve the policy goal, but one is less invasive, the one imposing the least burdens on the Member States, businesses or citizens has to be pursued.

As already described,[168] the third step of the proportionality test is the true balancing act: the benefits of enhanced cooperation law must outweigh the burdens on the authorities, economic operators, and citizens of non-participating Member States. The third step of the proportionality test boils down to a balancing of the harmonised interests of enhanced cooperation law and the interests of the non-participating Member States. Only if the interests (in the form of the policy objectives) of enhanced cooperation prevail over the interests (freedom from burdens) of non-participating Member States is the law of enhanced cooperation proportionate and allowed to stand.

f) Examples

We shall assume that some Member States can reach an agreement on the implementation of a horizontal monitoring regime, a regime which allows (big) taxpayers to closely cooperate with the tax authorities.[169] Such a regime allows a continuous dialogue between taxpayers and tax authorities, timely responses by tax authorities to taxpayers' tax structures, and a sensible use of the tax authorities' resources because they can pool their resources to monitor non-cooperative taxpayers.[170] The tax authorities within enhanced cooperation share the information on taxpayers having permanent establishments or subsidiaries in two or more participating Member States, pursue—if necessary—joint audits, and coordinate their evaluation methods, in particular, in the field of transfer pricing. Such a system may be attractive for (big) taxpayers since they are able to receive information from the tax authorities in a timely manner, they have an immediate certainty on their tax outcome without having to wait for the final tax audit, and cross-border transactions will not suffer double taxation because of the use of different evaluation methods in transfer prices adjustment cases. Therefore, enhanced cooperation may trigger locational effects: taxpayers may move from non-participating Member States which do not offer horizontal monitoring to participating Member States. Are non-participating Member States entitled to fight negative effects imposed upon them by enhanced cooperation law?

[168] This chapter subsection E.II.3.c.

[169] For the general framework see the work of the OECD: OECD, 'Study into the Role of Tax Intermediaries' (2008) <http://www.oecd.org/tax/administration/39882938.pdf> accessed 3 February 2021; OECD, 'Co-Operative Compliance: A Framework—From Enhanced Relationship to Co-Operative Compliance' (2013) <https://www.oecd.org/publications/co-operative-compliance-a-framework-9789264200852-en.htm> accessed 3 February 2021; for the Austrian approach, Janina Enachescu and others, 'Horizontal Monitoring in Austria: Subjective Representations by Tax Officials and Company Employees' (2019) 12 Business Research 75; for the Dutch approach, Esther Huiskers-Stoop and Hans Gribnau, 'Cooperative Compliance and the Dutch Horizontal Monitoring Model' (2019) 5 Journal of Tax Administration 66.

[170] Huiskers-Stoop and Gribnau (n 169) 20.

First of all, enhanced cooperation law imposes a financial burden on non-participating Member States in the form of a loss of taxable substance. If economic operators leave, the Member States lose the right to tax those entities on their worldwide income, and thus the Member States may suffer revenue losses. Since enhanced cooperation law neither discriminates any cross-group transactions against any intra-group transactions[171] nor imposes market access restrictions, the law is in line with the fundamental freedoms and the factual effects in the form of locational effects can only be examined under the burden-based proportionality test.

The first step, the suitability test, is quite vague and looks to the aim and purpose of the law of enhanced cooperation. The implementation of a group-wide horizontal monitoring regime aims to lower costs both for tax authorities and taxpayers. Such a regime would allow tax authorities to pool their resources and monitor especially non-compliant taxpayers and would give cooperative taxpayers certainty over their tax structures before the final tax audit. Without going into too much detail on horizontal monitoring, there is enough work from the Organisation for Economic Co-operation and Development (OECD),[172] and state practice (eg the Netherlands)[173] to assume that such a regime is capable of achieving the aims, also when introduced between Member States.

The second step of the burden-based proportionality test, the necessity requirement, asks whether the least burdensome way has been chosen to implement a regime which achieves the relevant aims. In cases in which a whole regime rather than a single measure is at stake, the political freedom of the Member States—even in the form of enhanced cooperation—needs to be emphasised. It is almost impossible for the Court to decide whether the entire regime at hand or a mere hypothetical regime is less burdensome. Such an analysis may work for a single measure of the regime—for example how the information between the Member States is exchanged, or which requirements have to be met to be eligible for the horizontal monitoring program—but it may not work for the entire regime.

From this it follows that the first and second steps of the burden-based proportionality test are quite vague, especially when an entirely new (tax) regime is at stake. Only if the regime as such is in no way suitable to achieve the proposed aim and purpose may the law fail the first steps of the proportionality test. Since the first and second stages of the test can only prevent absolutely unsuitable and exaggerated (tax) regimes, the emphasis is on the third stage, which balances both the

[171] If one argues that the coordinative approach between participating Member States in particular in the field of transfer pricing may lead to a more favourable treatment of intra-group economic transactions (because in case of transfer pricing adjustments, both participating Member States adjust equally), one may counter that such a more favourable treatment does not infringe on the fundamental freedoms because the reciprocal bond between the participating Member States no longer allows a comparison between intra-group and cross-group economic activities; see Chapter 5, Part I, subsection E.VII.7.

[172] See fn 169.

[173] See fn 169.

interests of non-participating and participating Member States. At this stage, the objective of enhanced cooperation must be weighed against the interests of non-participating Member States.

Where there exists a horizontal monitoring regime, the interest in maintaining the tax substrate would have to be balanced against the interest of some Member States in creating a new and innovative procedural standard in tax matters. Thus far, the loss of revenue has not been a public interest concern according to the CJEU case law, and therefore in the field of the fundamental freedoms, the aim of preventing any revenue losses has not allowed the Member State to retain restrictive or discriminatory tax rules.[174] Every Member State is committed to fostering the functioning of the European internal market, and thus each Member State has freely accepted that for the sake of the free movement of goods, services, persons, and capital, and subsequently for an efficient allocation of resources, they may lose some of their revenue claims. At the level of the burden-based proportionality test, however, any burden on the Member States may be considered, and thus, the interest of Member States (freedom from burdens) does not necessarily have to meet the threshold of public interest concerns which would justify one-sided discrimination. Any burden, regardless of whether it is of a financial or administrative nature, can be considered under burden-based proportionality, but not on the justification level when restrictions of the fundamental freedoms are at stake. In other words, in the case of enhanced cooperation law, non-participating Member States are not committed to deeper integration, and thus their revenue losses may be held against the interest of enhanced cooperation.

The outcome of the balancing act is determined by the predicted revenue loss which the European Commission identifies as part of its impact assessment, and the benefits of enhanced cooperation law. In cases in which the enhanced cooperation law pursues legitimate policy objectives and does not steer the negative effects of taxation towards non-participating Member States (defensive obstacles),[175] and the revenue losses of the non-participating Member States are minor, it is very likely that the Court weighs the integration progress as being more important than the reflex following from the law of enhanced cooperation—the revenue loss—is harmful to non-participating Member States. But still, the revenue loss of non-participating Member States is a legitimate interest to be considered on the level of the burden-based proportionality test.

The law of enhanced cooperation may also burden non-participating Member States with active obligations, such as the exchange of information. The obligation to exchange information is a legal obligation under the Mutual Assistance

[174] CJEU, 26 April 1988, 352/85, *Bond van Adverteerders*, ECLI:EU:C:1988:196, para 34; CJEU, 25 July 1991, C-288/89, *Stichting Collectieve Antennevoorziening Gouda*, ECLI:EU:C:1991:323, para 11; CJEU, 14 November 1995, C-484/93, *Svensson and Gustavsson*, ECLI:EU:C:1995:379, para 15.

[175] See Chapter 5, Part I, subsection E.VI.2.b)(cc).

Directive,[176] but may also be a reflex of enhanced cooperation law. A request for information which is not already covered by the existing exchange of information is not restrictive or discriminatory but burdensome for non-participating Member States, especially in cases in which the Member States do not themselves need and are not in the possession of the information which is requested.

We shall assume, for example, that the Member States of enhanced cooperation want to encourage the use of public transport, and thus tax company cars on every 100 kilometres driven.[177] To prevent cars from being registered in subsidiaries established in non-participating Member States, any of these cars used by an employee resident or employed by a subsidiary resident in a participating Member State should equally be taxed, but any environmental taxes already imposed on the cars shall be credited. Non-participating Member States would be required to exchange information on the actual number of kilometres travelled. Since the tax is suitable to encourage people to use public transport, and since Member States do not want to put a general blame on company cars (because there may still be rural areas which are not accessible by public transport), the proportionality decision lies (again) at the third step: balancing the interests of non-participating Member States and enhanced cooperation. What weighs more heavily—the burden of collecting information and exchanging it with participating Member States or the objective of enhanced cooperation law—the reduction of pollution by an increase in the use of public transport?

Within the law-making process, the European Commission has to engage in a balancing act and decide whether it is of the opinion that the interest of enhanced cooperation weighs more heavily, and thus should be pursued further. The decision may be subject to judicial review because Art 327 of the TFEU grants non-participating Member States the right to fight disproportionate burdens imposed upon them by enhanced cooperation law. In such a case, the CJEU has to engage in a balancing act and decide whether the interests of enhanced cooperation law outweigh the interests of non-participating Member States. Such balancing decisions are part of the day-to-day business of the Court, and thus no-one should be hesitant to entrust the CJEU with the final decision on the legitimacy of burdens imposed upon non-participating Member States by enhanced cooperation laws.

[176] Directive, 15 February 2011, 2011/16/EU, on administrative cooperation in the field of taxation and repealing Directive 77/799/EEC, OJ, 11 March 2011, L 64, 1, in the amended version of Directive, 25 May 2018, 2018/822/EU, on amending Directive 2011/16/EU as regards mandatory automatic exchange of information in the field of taxation in relation to reportable cross-border arrangements, OJ, 5 June 2018, L 139, 1.

[177] To allow harmonising measures under Art 115 of the TFEU, one has to assume further that the Member States have already introduced different steering measures aiming to reduce the use of company cars, and the differences of these measures harm the European internal market; see Chapter 4, subsection G.

4. Conclusions

The principle of tolerance, in its form of the non-participating Member States' freedom to abstain from enhanced cooperation, has to be understood as a duty of non-interference. Member States outside enhanced cooperation must retain their power to enact a legal and regulatory framework in accordance with their policy choices. Therefore, non-participating Member States are allowed to fight legal effects of enhanced cooperation law which undermine their European internal market guarantees. In other words, non-participating Member States are allowed to fight any infringements of the fundamental freedoms or state aid rules. Enhanced cooperation law may, however, also impose factual effects upon non-participating Member States, such as locational effects, which may also interfere with the non-participating Member States' freedom to determine their legislative and regulatory framework.

The standards of international law, which may form a fallback option in case the European constitutional framework does not provide sufficient protection, do not help non-participating Member States in the fight against factual effects of enhanced cooperation law because international law only prohibits international agreement from imposing legally enforceable obligations on third countries. The constitutional framework of enhanced cooperation goes beyond international law standards and gives non-participating Member States the chance to fight factual effects of enhanced cooperation law because these effects may be more burdensome than factual effects of unilateral legal measures of Member States.

The analysis has revealed that Member States are only willing to cooperate and establish enhanced cooperation in cases of a beggar-thyself policy, and will generally prefer to act in isolation when pursuing a beggar-thy-neighbour policy. The latter policy stream provides an economic benefit to the State but at the expense of other States. The best example of such a beggar-thy-neighbour policy is a tax haven. A haven does not want to cooperate with other tax havens, they compete with each other, and thus such a strategy is more effective when pursued by the State in isolation as opposed to as part of a broader coalition. In contrast, a beggar-thyself policy leads to the creation of economic costs at home. These costs arise because of the prioritisation of non-market values and may be reduced if the Member States act jointly.

Factual effects on non-participating Member States in the form of financial and administrative burdens on economic operators, authorities, and citizens of non-participating Member States have to be considered under the proportionality test. In terms of burdens on entities of non-participating Member States, the test ensures that enhanced cooperation law follows the least burdensome approach to achieve the policy objective and that the benefits of enhanced cooperation law outweigh unfavourable effects on non-participating Member States. If burdens imposed on economic operators, authorities, and citizens of non-participating Member States are incommensurate with the benefits of enhanced cooperation law, the law would be disproportionate and would not be allowed to stand.

F. The Freedom to be Part of Enhanced Cooperation

The principle of tolerance, as embedded in the enhanced cooperation procedure, not only requires tolerance from enhanced cooperation towards the non-participating Member States but also demands tolerance from the non-participating Member States towards enhanced cooperation. In this vein, Art 327 of the TFEU states that non-participating Member States 'shall not impede' the implementation of enhanced cooperation by the participating Member States. The requirement not to impede the implementation of enhanced cooperation is a lesser obligation than the obligation to facilitate the joint legislative initiative.[178] Yet even if non-participating Member States have no duty to help enhanced cooperation law to succeed, they have to refrain from any actions that would undermine enhanced cooperation laws.

It sounds rather convincing and intuitive that non-participating Member States have to respect and tolerate the establishment of enhanced cooperation, and thus have to refrain from any actions which would impede the implementation of enhanced cooperation. But what does it mean to 'impede' the implementation of the enhanced cooperation? In an area such as environmental regulation, including taxes on the emission of carbon dioxide, one could argue that the tolerance of pollution above the level set within enhanced cooperation law already jeopardises the objects of the joint initiative because if Member States do not all pull together in the area of steering taxes, it is almost impossible to achieve the policy objectives. Such an extensive interpretation has to be rejected because it would force the policy decision of the participating Member States upon the non-participating Member States, and thus would not respect their freedom of non-interference. In contrast, it would also be plausible to apply a higher threshold to the meaning of 'impeding the implementation' of enhanced cooperation, whereby the non-participating Member States would only impede the implementation of enhanced cooperation if they influence the European institutions to complicate or delay the implementation of enhanced cooperation.[179] The high threshold interpretation also has to be rejected because the prohibition on distracting the European institutions would not grant the participating Member States sufficient protection.

[178] Giorgio Gaja, 'How Flexible Is Flexibility under the Amsterdam Treaty?' (1998) 35 Common Market Law Review 855, 868.

[179] Ulrich Becker, 'Art. 327' in von der Groeben, Schwarze and Hatje (eds), *Europäisches Unionsrecht* (7th edn, Nomos 2015) para 6.

The following subsections will set out the concept of an overexploitation of a competitive advantage which is prohibited by Art 327 of the TFEU. The concept will be developed based on the possible responsive behaviour of non-participating Member States and its harm on enhanced cooperation (see subsection I). Based on this foundation the elements of a competitive advantage (see subsection 1) and its overexploitation (see subsection 2) will be defined in more detail. The subsection ends with conclusions (see subsection II).

I. Overexploiting a Competitive Advantage

The plausible responsive behaviour of non-participating Member States may reveal the aim and purpose of the protection of participating Member States under Art 327 of the TFEU. Non-participating Member States may be dissatisfied because they cannot fight any enhanced cooperation which has been authorised by the Council,[180] complies with the further procedural and substantial framework enshrined in the European treaties, and is proportionate. The fact that the non-participating Member States have to accept any legitimate enhanced cooperation may incentivise non-participating Member States to create countermeasures aiming to harm participating Member States. The constant harm may force the participating Member States to dissolve enhanced cooperation. To allow the participating Member States to retain to their joint actions, the non-participating Member States must be prevented from hurting and harming enhanced cooperation.

The distinction between a legitimate policy decision of non-participating Member States that may be directly opposed to enhanced cooperation and a constant undermining of enhanced cooperation may be based on the regulatory or legislative decision of the non-participating Member States. In cases in which the regulatory or legislative decision has a substantial link to the effects or consequences of enhanced cooperation law, the law of the non-participating Member States may aim to harm participating Member States. Thus, any prohibited action of non-participating Member States has to be linked to the effects of enhanced cooperation law, being beneficial for the non-participating Member States and harmful to the participating Member States. In particular, deliberate actions of non-participating Member States, which take advantage of not being part of the joint initiative, fulfil these requirements.

The principle of tolerance prevents non-participating Member States from overexploiting the competitive advantage of being outside of the legal and regulatory framework of enhanced cooperation. The prohibited behaviour consists of two parts: first an advantage which the non-participating Member States derive

180 For the procedural law implications see Chapter 4.

because of not joining enhanced cooperation, and secondly an activity of the non-participating Member States which leads to an increase of the favourable effects.

1. Competitive Advantage for the Non-participating Member States

Non-participating Member States may have a competitive advantage over participating Member States in particular where enhanced cooperation implements a regulatory or legal framework which imposes financial or administrative burdens on the economic operators. A steering tax, for example, which should influence the behaviour of businesses may either lead to a heavy tax burden or, from the perspective of the economic operator, less preferable (because costlier) behaviour. Burdens on economic operators render the Member States inside enhanced cooperation less attractive. The Member States may only be able to avoid negative factual effects in the form of locational effects (leaving of businesses) if their offer of public goods and their imposed overall burdens are still a well-balanced deal for economic operators. Imposing an additional burden on economic operators may force participating Member States to compensate for it if they want to remain competitive. In reverse, not being a member of enhanced cooperation and subsequently being free to determine a less burdensome legal and regulatory framework or to abstain from implementing any legal or regulatory measures grants the non-participating Member States a serious competitive advantage. The less burdensome treatment may attract businesses, and thus the non-participating Member States may enjoy positive factual effects.

There is no harm or blame in enjoying a positive factual effect. The factual effects come with the decision to not be a member of enhanced cooperation and the wish to pursue the policy objectives through different measures or to follow different policy objectives and reject the ones participating Member States pursue jointly. Thus, non-participating Member States are by no means required to fight positive factual effects. Any competitive advantage non-participating Member States gain because of not joining can be enjoyed without hesitation.

2. Overexploitation of Advantages

The non-participating Member States may not only enjoy the factual benefits of being outside enhanced cooperation, they may also take actions which facilitate the benefit. Such actions would aim to increase the positive effects on non-participating Member States and the negative effects on participating Member States. The effects on both the Member States inside and the Member States outside enhanced cooperation are augmented in cases in which the non-participating Member States implement or abolish rules for the sake of making themselves even more attractive for businesses.

We shall assume, for example, that enhanced cooperation implements a tax on financial transactions, which may cause negative effects for the participating Member States because financial transactions may no longer be traded within the territory of the participating Member States. Further, it may cause market players to move their business to other Member States, which are not participating in enhanced cooperation, to avoid being within the net of the FTT. If a non-participating Member State would like to encourage economic operators even more to leave the participating Member State in which they are currently resident, and establish their business within its territory, the Member State would offer additional benefits, such as low or no taxation of bonus payments to bankers or low social security contributions for the banking sector. Of course, such beneficial tax treatments have to comply with state aid law. However, in the case of such radical tax benefits we evidently see an overexploiting action.

However, not all tax incentives of non-participating Member States are particularly harmful to enhanced cooperation. The next subsections will elaborate on the different criteria which are needed to identify which tax incentives of non-participating Member States are overexploitative, and thus harm enhanced cooperation, and which measures are simply part of fair tax competition.

a) Time Linkage

First of all, a certain tax measure may only qualify as a deliberate response to enhanced cooperation which is supposed to increase the negative effects on participating Member States and the positive effects on non-participating Member States if there is a serious proximal temporal ratio. It may not always be possible to implement tax measures the day after enhanced cooperation law comes into force; however, a certain time link must exist. In that regard, it may be necessary to consider the average time the individual Member State usually needs to implement legislative initiatives. The average time for passing the law, of course, can only indicate which legislative initiatives have been taken in response to enhanced cooperation.

b) Substantive Linkage

Much more important than the time link is the substantive connection between the law of enhanced cooperation and the law of the non-participating Member State. A substantive connection between enhanced cooperation law and the legislative action of non-participating Member States does not demand that the latter concerns the same tax or the same regulatory framework. In other words, if enhanced cooperation law implements a legal and regulatory framework in the fields of financial transactions, carbon emissions, or consumption behaviour, the non-participating Member States may amend specific provisions of their income or corporate tax rules and thereby increase the effects of enhanced cooperation on both themselves and the participating Member States. Therefore, the substantive connection does demand that the law of the non-participating Member States and the law of enhanced cooperation is objectively on the same subject matter. The linkage requires that both laws intend to influence the same behaviour, the same economic transaction, or the same undertakings.

Whether the law of the non-participating Member State aims to increase the negative factual effects on participating Member States can best be answered through the lens of the taxable person who bears the tax burden. If, for example, enhanced cooperation law implements a framework for a tax on carbon dioxide, the opinion of the carbon-emitting entity is crucial. The carbon-emitting entity has to decide whether to change its production, for example through the use of plants emitting less carbon dioxide, or to bear the tax burden, or to move to a non-participating Member State which does not tax carbon emissions in the same burdensome way. Only if the carbon-emitting entity concludes that the new tax incentives of a non-participating Member State makes the last of the three options (the move from a participating Member State to a non-participating Member State, which is a proxy for the negative factual effect of enhanced cooperation) even more plausible, is the tax incentive likely to be overexploitative.

Aside from specific incentives, non-participating Member State may introduce more general tax or regulatory benefits. General advantages in the tax law or regulation area may also have an impact on the effects of enhanced cooperation laws because tax incentives on research and development or favourable tax treatment for all bonus payments may influence the decisions of the taxpayers on (which are exposed to the burdens of enhanced cooperation law) whether to leave or to stay within the territory of a participating Member State. However, the fact that the incentive is open to all taxpayers and not simply to those which are burdened by enhanced cooperation law reflects the policy choice of the non-participating Member States. Each Member State outside enhanced cooperation has the right to follow its own policy agenda, which may be contrary to the one chosen by the participating Member States, or which may even have an impact on enhanced co-operation. The non-participating Member States, however, have the duty to follow their policy decisions coherently and consistently, which means that they are not permitted to tailor their benefits to taxpayers which are burdened by the law of enhanced cooperation and 'hide' behind their freedom to choose different policy objectives. A true policy decision of a non-participating Member State is reflected in the design and structure of the entire tax or regulatory (or some may even say legal) system. For example, if a Member State is of the firm belief that capital should be taxed at a low tax rate to encourage people to save, or the conviction that tax incentives for research and development have positive spillover effects for the entire economy of the Member State, the low tax rate and the incentive for research and development have to be open to all taxpayers and not simply to some which happen to be burdened by enhanced cooperation law. Policy decisions and their subsequent regulatory or tax incentives may still increase the effects of enhanced cooperation law, but the measures do not intend to overexploit the competitive advantage following from being outside enhanced cooperation.

The need to identify whether the non-participating Member States legitimately follow their right to pursue different policy objectives, and thus offer certain regulatory and tax incentives, or whether the non-participating Member States aim to increase the negative effects of enhanced cooperation law on the participating Member States and thereby overexploit their competitive advantage, requires that both the law of enhanced cooperation and the law of the non-participating Member States target a particular economic transaction, a particular branch, a particular behaviour, or a particular group of taxpayers. If the law of enhanced cooperation is of a general nature, such as in the case of a fixed tax rate for domestic and foreign capital gains, or a Common (Consolidated) Corporate Tax Base, the competitive advantage the non-participating Member States gain is too general to be exploited by specific national rules, which do not reflect the general policy decisions of the non-participating Member States.

From this it follows that a general tax incentive does not suffice in specifically exploiting the competitive advantage of not having to apply the legal or regulatory framework of enhanced cooperation. Only an advantage which is closely tailored to the taxpayers burdened by enhanced cooperation law may overexploit the competitive advantage. The overexploited advantage can either flow from reduced market regulations or a specific tax benefit. If a non-participating Member State tempts taxpayers with tax benefits, they have to first comply with state aid law.[181] Accordingly, the tax benefits have to be general enough to pass the selectivity test but specific enough to establish a substantive linkage between the law of enhanced cooperation and the national tax benefit.

The requirement of the substantive linkage and the selectivity element under state aid law have a different aim, and thus what is considered general for Art 107 of the TFEU does not necessarily fail to be specific for establishing a substantive linkage. Under state aid law, a benefit is predominantly selective if the favourable treatment is tied to a particular business activity.[182] If a certain business activity is favoured, the beneficial treatment influences the efficient allocation of resources, which shall be prohibited by Art 107 of the TFEU. Other deviating factors which do not touch on the business activity but on the structure of an undertaking, such as the size of a company, the legal form of an entity, or time of market presence (eg start-ups), are allowed when it comes to state aid law, but may still be sufficient to identify a substantive linkage between the law of enhanced cooperation and the law of a non-participating Member State.[183]

We shall assume, for example, that under enhanced cooperation participating Member States levy a tax on companies providing digital services. The tax is imposed on the gross amount of income generated within the participating Member

[181] See Chapter 5, Part II, subsection E.

[182] See Chapter 5, Part II, subsection E.II.

[183] The CJEU has ruled that subsidies based on size may infringe Art 107 of the TFEU: CJEU, 26 September 2002, C-351/98, *Spain v Commission*, ECLI:EU:C:2002:530, para 40; see also Ruth Mason and Leopoldo Parada, 'Company Size Matters' (2019) British Tax Review 610. See Chapter 5, Part II, subsection E.II.

States due to digital services such as online advertising. If the companies are resident in a participating Member State, all services are subject to tax. If, however, the supplier is resident in a non-participating Member State or a third country, only the services provided to a taxpayer resident in a participating Member State are subject tax. The tax may provide an incentive for companies to relocate if they provide digital services to a large amount to taxpayers outside the territory of enhanced cooperation. We shall assume further that these companies have their headquarters based in the United States and have been in the market for no longer than five years. The non-participating Member States may increase the locational effects of enhanced cooperation law if they provide for a specific tax cut for branches and subsidiaries of foreign start-ups (being defined as companies which have been in the market for no longer than ten years). An alternative to this example would be a tax cut for all domestic subsidiaries and permanent establishments of foreign companies which have an annual turnover of more than €10 million. In the latter case, the substantive linkage would be even more visible if the tax on digital services were only levied if the non-resident taxpayers would exceed a threshold of €10 million of supplied services. As discussed in Chapter 5,[184] the tax cut may not qualify as prohibited state aid because it is not selective. However, the benefit is specific enough to allow linking it and its effects with the tax levied under enhanced cooperation. The tax cut increases the negative locational effects for the participating Member States, and thus the non-participating Member States providing the specific tax cut overexploit their competitive advantage. Such an overexploitative tax cut would not be in line with the concept of Art 327 of the TFEU.

II. Conclusions

The principle of tolerance prohibits non-participating Member States from introducing a legislative or regulatory framework which would make it impossible for the participating Member States to pursue enhanced cooperation any further. The overexploitation of the competitive advantage of the non-participating Member States is harmful to any enhanced cooperation and may force the participating Member States to dissolve the joint legislative act. Having said this, not every legislative or regulatory decision of the non-participating Member States strengthening their competitive position must be characterised as being overexploitative. Rules introducing general tax or regulatory benefits to economic operators are not overexploitative since they reflect the policy decision taken by the non-participating Member States. However, a unilateral rule no longer only reflects the purely domestic policy decision if the rule is specifically favouring those economic

[184] Part II, subsection E.III.1.

operators, economic transactions, or economic activities which are exposed to a burden under enhanced cooperation law. Thus, tailor-made tax benefits for economic operators which are subject to burdens under the law of enhanced cooperation may cause an unlawful overexploitation of the non-participating Member States' competitive advantage. A timely and substantive linkage between the law of enhanced cooperation and the unilateral measure of a non-participating Member State helps to distinguish between general policy decisions and rules aiming to undermine enhanced cooperation.

G. Findings

Within federally structured States, the entitlement of States, regions, or cantons to cooperate is the rule, rather than the exception. Some constitutions explicitly reveal the framework to be pursued for the establishment of inter-State cooperation. The US and the Swiss constitutions provide rules of inter-State or inter-cantonal cooperation and demand that the interests of the non-participating States or cantons must not be infringed. The US Supreme Court case law and the Swiss practice have revealed that the claim to protect the non-participating States or cantons is reduced to a mere allegiance to the federal government. Thus, the explicit protection of the non-participating States or cantons is not given any separate and distinct meaning. Against this background, Art 327 of the TFEU may be interpreted as a mere claim for sincere cooperation ensuring the non-participating Member States their internal market guarantees. However, the analysis shows that the proper functioning of the enhanced cooperation mechanism requires more than mere loyalty between the participating and the non-participating Member States guaranteeing them both their legally enforceable rights.[185] The enhanced cooperation procedure is built on the principle of tolerance, enshrined in Art 327 of the TFEU.

The principle of tolerance sets limits both for the participating and for the non-participating Member States. The participating Member States have to accept that some Member States are outside enhanced cooperation and thus follow their own policy decisions in that area. At the same time, the non-participating Member States have to respect that some Member States join forces and pursue certain policy objectives jointly.

Concerning the tolerance of participating Member States towards non-participating Member States, Art 327 of the TFEU requires to respect the 'competences, rights and obligations' of Member States which are not party to enhanced

[185] Alberto Miglio, 'Differentiated Integration and the Principle of Loyalty' (2018) 14 European Constitutional Law Review 475, 483 et seq. argues that a 'loyalty-driven rationale is most evident in the symmetric obligations imposed by Article 327 TFEU'. However, it seems that the author does not distinguish between the principle of loyalty enshrined in Art 4 Subsection 3 of the TFEU and the obligations imposed by Art 327 of the TFEU.

cooperation. The analysis of the provision clearly shows that the European treaties grant the non-participating Member States specific guarantees which go beyond the European internal market guarantees. The specific bundle of guarantees also protects the non-participating Member States from certain factual effects. The need to grant the outsiders protection beyond the international and European framework lies in the fact that enhanced cooperation builds a united front of Member States, making it much harder for non-participating Member States to claim compensation or a policy change than if it were a unilateral measure of a single Member State. Despite the characteristic of group action, the policies pursued under enhanced cooperation (beggar-thyself policy) may typically require a wide scope increasing the factual effects on the non-participating Member States.

The principle of tolerance allows the non-participating Member States to rely on the fundamental European principle of proportionality. The principle of proportionality, as enshrined in Art 5 Subsection 4 of the TEU, does not aim to balance invasive actions and fundamental rights, and the division of powers between the European Union and the Member States, but to protect from burdensome European actions. The burden-based proportionality test allows considering all burdens economic operators and non-participating Member States have to suffer from the law of enhanced cooperation. If the burdens outweigh the benefits of enhanced cooperation, the law is unconstitutional and is not allowed to stand.

With regard to the tolerance of non-participating Member States towards participating Member States, Art 327 of the TFEU prevents the non-participating Member States from impeding the implementation of enhanced cooperation. The ban on impeding the establishment of enhanced cooperation of some Member States does not go so far as to force non-participating Member States to facilitate enhanced cooperation laws, but they are prevented from overexploiting their competitive advantage following from not joining enhanced cooperation. The non-participating Member States may overexploit the competitive advantage by granting specific tax benefits or by relaxing certain regulatory standards. It is important that the benefits granted by the non-participating Member States have a sufficient nexus to the burdens imposed by enhanced cooperation laws. Only if a substantive and timely linkage between the burdens of enhanced cooperation laws and the benefits of the law of the non-participating Member State can be established, may the Member State overexploit the advantage it has already gained by not joining enhanced cooperation, and thus act against the duty of not impeding the establishment of enhanced cooperation.

7
Conclusions and Outlook

A. Observations

Taxation is essential for the functioning of society and is also a key instrument for pursuing public policies.[1] The raising of revenue has long ceased to be the sole purpose of taxation. Taxes are a tool to steer people's behaviour, reflect societal values, and pursue policy decisions. The multiple faces of taxation are one reason for constantly changing laws—new realities need new laws. In a globalised and digitalised world, unilateral tax measures are supposedly not sufficient anymore: a multilateral (tax) response is needed to address problems following from cross-border economic activities.[2] Within the European Union, where the free movement of goods, services, persons, and capital is ensured, even more cross-border economic activities take place and the unilateral tax laws of the Member States constantly have to deal with these situations. The unilateral approach in taxation not only raises problems for the tax administrations but also for the economic operators. They have to comply with different national rules and are exposed to double taxation. The negative impact on the European internal market and the inability to deal properly with multilateral tax phenomenon are the reasons for a constant demand for more European tax law.

At the EU level, the national tax laws of the Member States may be harmonised if the differences between the laws harm the European internal market. Accordingly, the European Union has the power to provide for a European response to multinational economic activities. However, any legislative action in the area of taxation requires the consent of all Member States. In other words, European taxation is bound by unanimous voting in the Council. The onerous requirement of establishing consent between all Member States paralyses the law-making process in taxation at the European level. Given the need for common actions of the Member States in the area of taxation and the hurdle of unanimity, which is difficult

[1] Commission, 15 January 2019, Communication from the Commission to the European Parliament, the European Council and the Council—Towards a more efficient and democratic decision making in the EU tax policy, COM(2019) 8 final, 1.

[2] The OECD's BEPS-initiative is a perfect example: OECD, 'Addressing Base Erosion and Profit Shifting' (2013) <https://www.oecd.org/tax/addressing-base-erosion-and-profit-shifting-9789264192744-en.htm> accessed 3 February 2021; OECD, 'Action Plan on Base Erosion and Profit Shifting' (2013) <https://www.oecd.org/ctp/BEPSActionPlan.pdf> accessed 3 February 2021.

Enhanced Cooperation and European Tax Law. Caroline Heber, Oxford University Press. © Caroline Heber 2021.
DOI: 10.1093/oso/9780192898272.003.0007

to overcome, a demand to move from unanimous to qualified majority voting has repeatedly been put forward.

The whole discussion on moving towards a qualified majority voting system in taxation is dominated by effectiveness claims: some Member States block certain legislative attempts on the EU level, and thus proposals such as the one for a Common Consolidated Corporate Tax Base or other major projects have been lying on the European Commission's table for years. Qualified majority voting should give the law-making process at the European level more flexibility to find compromises, and if necessary, to outvote a small blocking minority. However, the proponents of majority voting in taxation ignore two important facts. First, taxation is very different from pure regulation. The national tax framework determines the Member State's revenue, and accordingly determines the size of financial means the Member State has to fulfil its commitments towards its people. Beyond revenue implications, the national tax framework is an important tool to pursue policy decisions and to reflect societal values. Thus, taxation is not a purely technical area of the law which can be harmonised over the Member States' heads. Taxation is a very sensitive policy area which should not allow for the outvoting of some Member States, since the promised effectiveness and efficiency of the European Union may easily turn into a dangerous instability.[3] Such instability follows from uniform laws which are dictated to some Member States, eliminating diversity in a particularly sensitive area.

The discussion of the lack of effectiveness in the European Union is not new. Throughout the EU's entire expansion process, it has been claimed that the diversity of Member States may hinder legislative actions at the EU level. Diversity in that respect referred in particular to the different economic development of the members of the European Union, but also had the social differences between the Member States in mind. The discussion did not end without a solution. On the contrary, the Member States decided to introduce differentiated integration within the EU framework, and thus the European integration model allows for differentiation.

The discussion on the lack of effectiveness and efficiency in the European legislative process in the context of taxation circles around the wrong question: it should not be asked how to move from unanimity to qualified majority voting but how the existing mechanism for differentiated integration can effectively be used in the area of taxation.

Since the mechanism for differentiated integration in the European Union has been introduced by the Amsterdam Treaty, it has hardly been used. The Member States have refrained from using the enhanced cooperation procedure to implement common legal measures within a group of Member States because

[3] See in this vein also Wolfram Richter, 'Mehrheitsbeschlüsse in der europäischen Steuerpolitik?' (2019) Ökonomenstimme <https://www.oekonomenstimme.org/artikel/2019/05/mehrheitsbeschluesse-in-der-europaeischen-steuerpolitik/> accessed 3 February 2021.

the requirements set by the European treaties are vague and because interested Member States fear being less competitive than the Member States outside enhanced cooperation. In other words, Member States are afraid to be bound by the law of enhanced cooperation and be exploited by the non-participating Member States who could use their freedom to implement legislation which provides them with an additional competitive advantage.

In taxation, differentiated integration is a valid way of overcoming a legislative deadlock in the Council and of establishing deeper integration between some Member States. In taxation, however, it is particularly important to protect both the insiders from the outsiders and the outsiders from the insiders. The vague wording of the provisions in the European treaties and the lack of experience in using enhanced cooperation are not of any help. To foster the use of enhanced cooperation it is necessary to provide more certainty. This book has revealed that the enhanced cooperation procedure already provides sufficient safeguarding measures both for the non-participating Member States and the participating Member States, but they are not immediately evident when reading the plain provisions on the enhanced cooperation procedure in the European treaties.

A step forward in European taxation calls for a robust framework for the establishment of enhanced cooperation. Both participating and non-participating Member States must, ultimately, not fear exploitation because of their decision to be inside or outside enhanced cooperation.

B. Safeguarding Measures—Linchpin of Success

This book has revealed that the existing enhanced cooperation procedure grants protection to both the Member States inside and outside enhanced cooperation. With regard to the insiders, the willing Member States may be hesitant to establish deeper integration between them if any measures set to protect their harmonised value against the outsiders constitute unjustified trade barriers. A common approach by some Member States towards creditor protection in the field of limited liability companies may not have the intended success, if the participating Member States are not allowed to demand compliance with the standard (eg minimum share capital) from limited liability companies established outside of the territory of participating Member States. To ensure that fundamental freedoms do not become an obstacle to integration, the jointly harmonised value is protected by the possibility of using the value as a ground of justification and by applying a form of light-touch proportionality test to restrictions or discriminations imposed by enhanced cooperation laws. The CJEU has developed this form of light-touch justification for hurdles which have emerged from secondary EU law. The light-touch justification approach allows a balancing act of market efficiency needs with the non-market values important to the Member States. In this vein, the application of light-touch justification to trade obstacles, following from the law of enhanced cooperation, allows one to respect the value created by a group of Member States and the protection of the European internal market.

If the willing Member States do not want to go so far as to harmonise the values underlying their laws but are able to agree on harmonised rules fostering trade between them, the participating Member States may fear that they also have to grant the favourable treatment to economic operators of non-participating Member States to comply with the fundamental freedoms. The analysis has clearly shown that the principle of reciprocity is familiar to EU law, but thus far, there has been no need to develop its notion and scope. In the field of a trade favouring enhanced cooperation, however, the reciprocity claim becomes an important tool for restricting the beneficial tax treatment to intra-group economic transactions.

The Member States can use the enhanced cooperation procedure also to comply with their obligations under the European treaties but in a manner which fits the aim and purpose of their national tax systems rather better. Enhanced cooperation allows Member States to establish a robust framework between them as a basis for dealing with discrimination and subsequent compensation. The deeper integrational bond between the participating Member States allows one to reject any claims from a granting of the compensation benefit to cross-group economic transactions.

Aside from the participating Member States' possibility of protecting their common achievements from being exploited by economic operators of non-participating Member States, participating Member States are also protected from being exploited by a responsive behaviour of non-participating Member States. Any non-participating Member State may derive a competitive benefit from not being a member of enhanced cooperation. For example, not being part of enhanced cooperation imposing a financial transaction tax may provide an advantage in the competition between the financial markets of the Member States. The competitive advantage reflects the policy decisions of the non-participating Member States and no measures must be taken to deprive the non-member of the advantage. However, non-participating Member States are prohibited from introducing legislation which only aims to harm enhanced cooperation by way of overexploiting the existing competitive advantage.

In terms of the so-called outsiders, the current legislative framework for the establishment of enhanced cooperation ensures that the non-participating Member States are not put in a worse position than before enhanced cooperation was introduced. The freezing of the status quo is guaranteed if enhanced cooperation is used to implement trade-favouring rules and cross-border tax coordination. Thus, the non-participating Member States need not fear that their economic operators will be treated less favourably than before. Despite efficiency concerns, the non-participating Member States are protected from disproportionate factual effects following from enhanced cooperation laws. Factual effects are capable of preventing non-participating Member States from following their own policy decision which would contradict their choice of not becoming a member of the enhanced cooperation group and pursuing their own legislative path.

The safeguarding measures, both for the insiders and the outsiders, allow willing Member States to pursue certain policies jointly, as well as granting the non-participating Member States enough freedom to pursue these policy objectives on their own.

C. Proposal for Improvement

The current enhanced cooperation procedure already provides for a safety net, both for the participating and the non-participating Member States; however, the plain wording of the provisions of the European treaties may not make its scope entirely clear. Since the safeguarding measures are the linchpin for the success of the enhanced cooperation mechanism, it is necessary to make the Member States familiar with the limits for a common action under the procedure, but also with the possibility of protecting their common achievements. This subsection outlines some changes to the European treaties which would make the use of the enhanced cooperation procedure easier and would grant the participating Member States more certainty in applying the mechanism.

Clarification of the legal framework for the establishment of enhanced cooperation is also on the agenda of the European Parliament as it recently called on the European Commission to propose a regulation based on Art 352 of the TFEU which could simplify and unify the legal framework for the establishment of enhanced cooperation.[4] Any attempts to flesh out the primary EU law provisions on the enhanced cooperation procedure through secondary EU law based on Art 352 of the Treaty on the Functioning of the European Union (TFEU) should be rejected. Art 352 of the TFEU aims to authorise the European Union to adopt European legislation in an area in which the European treaties do not vest the European Union with the necessary powers, but European action proves to be necessary to attain one of the objectives set out in the European treaties. In other words, Art 352 of the TFEU allows the European Union to seize competences which (under the ordinary division of powers) rest with the Member States. In the case of secondary EU law aiming to specify primary EU law, the European Union does not lack competence. On the contrary, the European treaties set out the procedure for establishing differentiated integration within the European Union. Thus, any specifying secondary EU law does not precisely lack competence but interferes with the division of powers within the European legal framework because the primary EU law rules

4 European Parliament, 28 January 2019, on the implementation of the Treaty provisions concerning enhanced cooperation, 2018/2112(INI).

on the enhanced cooperation mechanism do not grant the European legislature the right to specify the primary EU law framework through secondary EU law. According to Art 267 of the TFEU, the Court of Justice of the European Union (CJEU) enjoys exclusive competence in the interpretation of European Union law, and thus the Court should interpret the primary EU law provisions on the enhanced cooperation procedure. Any secondary EU law act specifying the provisions on the enhanced cooperation procedure would not sufficiently respect the competences of the CJEU and the competences of the European legislature. The enhanced cooperation framework could only be specified by secondary EU law if the primary EU law rules on enhanced cooperation vested the European legislature with that competence. From this it follows that it would require amendments to the European treaties to specify the enhanced cooperation procedure concerning the safeguarding measures.

Despite the need to specify the safeguarding measures for the participating and the non-participating Member States, it would be wise to regulate the withdrawal or expulsion of a participating Member State. If enhanced cooperation allows the participating Member States a way out, the Member States may be willing to 'test' the law for a certain time. At this stage, the Member States are free to implement sunset clauses within the legal framework of enhanced cooperation, and thus make the law expire after a certain time or at a particular date. A standardised exit route would not make the testing of the law optional, but it would become an integral part of the enhanced cooperation procedure. A guaranteed way out would not make the procedure any less severe, but much more flexible.

Another important clarification would be required with respect to the aim and purpose of any enhanced cooperation. As Art 20 of the TEU stands right now, it requires that any enhanced cooperation shall 'aim to further the objectives of the Union, protect its interests and reinforce its integration process'. Taken together with all the other provisions on the enhanced cooperation procedure, it is clear that the need to further the objectives of the European Union, to protect the interests of the European Union, and to reinforce the European integration process is the baseline for interpreting the requirements for establishing enhanced cooperation; however, the need to foster the European integration process is not a legal requirement. The legal requirements set by the European treaties establish a sufficient safety net for the protection of the achievements of European integration and to ensure that any enhanced cooperation is not an instrument of exclusion or division of the Member States. In the past, the supposedly required improvement of the integration process raised several concerns since enhanced cooperation is only capable of establishing deeper integration between the participating Member States. However, the Member States have agreed on a European integration model which allows for differentiation. Thus, within the European integration process it is permitted that some Member States follow a different path. Hard laws may ensure certainty that complying with the true legal requirements set by the European treaties already guarantees that enhanced cooperation fosters the European integration process.

The following sets out amendments to the European treaties specifying the legal framework for the establishment of enhanced cooperation. As already stressed above, none of these amendments, except for the amendments for the withdrawal of a Member State, would change the current scope and notion of the enhanced cooperation procedure. However, they would certainly help to make the procedure work by eliminating all ambiguities.

Amendments to Art 20 of the TEU would address three concerns. First, changes to Subsection 1 would make it clear that any enhanced cooperation which complies with the legal requirements set by the relevant provisions furthers the European integration process. Secondly, as regards the time frame for the opening of the enhanced cooperation procedure, a reasonable period can be specified. The European Parliament recently criticised the vague wording and found that it might be the reason why the establishment of enhanced cooperation took so long in the past. To overcome the lengthy process, the European Parliament proposed that the requirement of the last resort measure is fulfilled 'if during a period covering two consecutive Council presidencies, no substantive progress has been made in the Council'.[5] Although it is quite unlikely that such a concrete timeframe would be introduced into the European treaties, it may boost the use of differentiated integration. Thirdly, the possibility for a Member State to withdraw from enhanced cooperation may be introduced into the procedural framework. The amended article might read as follows:

Article 20

(1) Member States which wish to establish enhanced cooperation between themselves within the framework of the Union's non-exclusive competences may make use of the Union's institutions and exercise those competences by applying the relevant provisions of the Treaties, subject to the limits and in accordance with the detailed arrangements laid down in this Article and Articles 326 to 334 of the Treaty on the Functioning of the European Union.
Any enhanced cooperation established in accordance with the detailed arrangements set out in this Article and Articles 326 to 334 of the Treaty on the Functioning of the European Union is deemed to further the objectives of the Union, protect its interests and reinforce its integration process. Such cooperation shall be open at any time to all Member States, in accordance with Article 328 of the Treaty on the Functioning of the European Union.

[5] ibid.

Any participating Member State may withdraw from enhanced cooperation in accordance with Article 328 of the Treaty on the Functioning of the European Union.

(2) The decision authorising enhanced cooperation shall be adopted by the Council as a last resort, when it has established that the objectives of such cooperation cannot be attained within a reasonable period by the Union as a whole, *which may be the case if no fundamental progress has been made over two consecutive Council Presidencies. Any enhanced cooperation requires the participation of at least nine Member States.* The Council shall act in accordance with the procedure laid down in Article 329 of the Treaty on the Functioning of the European Union.

(3) All members of the Council may participate in its deliberations, but only members of the Council representing the Member States participating in enhanced cooperation shall take part in the vote. The voting rules are set out in Article 330 of the Treaty on the Functioning of the European Union.

(4) Acts adopted in the framework of enhanced cooperation shall bind only participating Member States. They shall not be regarded as part of the acquis which has to be accepted by candidate States for accession to the Union.

Art 326 of the TFEU is key in the protection of the European internal market from enhanced cooperation laws. Amendments to this provision should clarify that the European internal market can be infringed if the law of enhanced cooperation establishes trade barriers between the Member States (meaning between the participating and the non-participating Member States but also between the participating Member States) or distorts the competition between the Member States (again between the participating and the non-participating Member States but also between the participating Member States). Both obstacles to trade and a distortion of competition would prevent an efficient allocation of resources. Despite mere clarification, Art 326 of the TFEU should indicate the participating Member States' right to protect their common achievements from being exploited. The common achievements of the group are at risk if the application of the fundamental freedoms would ignore the harmonised values of enhanced cooperation (deeper integration claim) or the deeper integration bond between the participating Member States which is built on the reciprocal granting of benefits within enhanced cooperation (reciprocity claim), or the coordination of benefits and disadvantages within the enhanced cooperation (coordination claim).

Article 326

Any enhanced cooperation shall comply with the Treaties and Union law.

Such cooperation shall not undermine the internal market or economic, social and territorial cohesion by establishing trade barriers between the Member States or by distorting competition between them. The participating Member States shall not be prohibited from taking measures to prevent the exploitation of the cooperation.

Amendments to Art 327 of the TFEU would allow protecting the non-participating Member States not only from infringements of the European internal market guarantees but also from disproportionate burdens in the form of factual effects following from enhanced cooperation laws. Furthermore, the changes should also establish that the non-participating Member States are required to refrain from any actions which would undermine the enhanced cooperation, and this would in particular cover the need to abstain from introducing laws only aiming to harm enhanced cooperation.

Article 327

Any enhanced cooperation shall respect the competences, rights and obligations of those Member States which do not participate in it. *Those Member States shall not be exposed to disproportionate burdens.*

Member States not participating in enhanced cooperation shall refrain from any action which would undermine that cooperation or impede its implementation by the participating Member States.

Amendments to Art 328 and Art 331 of the TFEU on the withdrawal of a Member State from enhanced cooperation would change the current enhanced cooperation framework which does not grant the Member States that much flexibility. The possibility of leaving enhanced cooperation would relax the decision of the Member States to become part of the group, especially when the Member States are not entirely sure whether the law of the enhanced cooperation works in their favour or against them.

Article 328

(1) When enhanced cooperation is being established, it shall be open to all Member States, subject to compliance with any conditions of participation laid down by the authorising decision. It shall also be open to them at any

other time, subject to compliance with the acts already adopted within that framework, in addition to those conditions.

The Commission and the Member States participating in enhanced co-operation shall ensure that they promote participation by as many Member States as possible.

(2) *Any participating Member States may withdraw from enhanced cooperation, subject to an authorisation decision by the Commission.*

(3) The Commission and, where appropriate, the High Representative of the Union for Foreign Affairs and Security Policy shall keep the European Parliament and the Council regularly informed regarding developments in enhanced cooperation.

Article 331

(1) Any Member State which wishes to participate in enhanced cooperation in progress in one of the areas referred to in Article 329(1) shall notify its intention to the Council and the Commission.
The Commission shall, within four months of the date of receipt of the notification, confirm the participation of the Member State concerned. It shall note where necessary that the conditions of participation have been fulfilled and shall adopt any transitional measures necessary with regard to the application of the acts already adopted within the framework of enhanced cooperation.
However, if the Commission considers that the conditions of participation have not been fulfilled, it shall indicate the arrangements to be adopted to fulfil those conditions and shall set a deadline for re-examining the request. On the expiry of that deadline, it shall re-examine the request, in accordance with the procedure set out in the second subparagraph. If the Commission considers that the conditions of participation have still not been met, the Member State concerned may refer the matter to the Council, which shall decide on the request. The Council shall act in accordance with Article 330. It may also adopt the transitional measures referred to in the second subparagraph on a proposal from the Commission.

(2) *Any Member State which wishes to withdraw from enhanced cooperation shall notify its intention to the Commission and its reasons for that withdrawal. The Commission shall grant authorisation to withdraw by setting the date on which the Member State shall no longer participate in enhanced cooperation. If enhanced cooperation does not comply with the participation requirement of Article 20 of the Treaty of the European Union, the Commission shall set the exact date on which the enhanced cooperation shall be terminated.*

(3) Any Member State which wishes to participate in enhanced cooperation in progress in the framework of the common foreign and security policy shall

notify its intention to the Council, the High Representative of the Union for Foreign Affairs and Security Policy and the Commission.

The Council shall confirm the participation of the Member State concerned, after consulting the High Representative of the Union for Foreign Affairs and Security Policy and after noting, where necessary, that the conditions of participation have been fulfilled. The Council, on a proposal from the High Representative, may also adopt any transitional measures necessary with regard to the application of the acts already adopted within the framework of enhanced cooperation. However, if the Council considers that the conditions of participation have not been fulfilled, it shall indicate the arrangements to be adopted to fulfil those conditions and shall set a deadline for re-examining the request for participation.

For the purposes of this paragraph, the Council shall act unanimously and in accordance with Article 330.

D. Final Remark

This book seeks to provide an analysis of the European flexibility mechanism: the enhanced cooperation procedure. Despite the vague wording of the provisions of the European treaties, the existing framework allows for differentiated integration and protects both the participating and the non-participating Member States. These safeguarding mechanisms are essential to prevent division between the Member States. Ultimately, the decision of whether or not to establish enhanced cooperation between some Member States is a purely political one and rests in the hands of the Member States. Even if the European treaties precisely define the rights and limits of the participating and the non-participating Member States, and the law thereby does not give rise to any ambiguities, some Member States will still have to be willing to engage in enhanced cooperation. In other words, it is not the most precise drafting of the mechanism's legal provisions which will make the mechanism a success, but rather, the willingness of the Member States to utilise enhanced cooperation.

Bibliography

Abi-Saab G, 'Fragmentation or Unification: Some Concluding Remarks Symposium Issue: The Proliferation of International Tribunals: Piecing Together the Puzzle' (1998) 31 New York University Journal of International Law and Politics 919

Adler-Nissen R, 'The Diplomacy of Opting Out: A Bourdieudian Approach to National Integration Strategies' (2008) 46 Journal of Common Market Studies 663

Adrian A, *Grundprobleme einer juristischen (gemeinschaftsrechtlichen) Methodenlehre* (Duncker & Humblot 2009)

Almond GA, 'Comparative Political Systems' (1956) 18 The Journal of Politics 391

Alter KJ, *The European Court's Political Power: Selected Essays* (OUP 2009)

Amtenbrink F and Kochenov D, 'Towards a More Flexible Approach to Enhanced Cooperation' in Andrea Ott and Ellen Vos (eds), *50 Years of European Integration: Foundations and Perspectives* (Asser 2009)

Andeweg RB, 'Consociational Democracy' (2000) Annual Review of Political Science 509

Antokolskaia M, 'Objectives and Values of Substantive Family Law' in Johan Meeusen and others (eds), *International Family Law for the European Union* (Intersentia 2007)

Antoniolli L, '"United in Diversity"? Differentiated Integration in an Ever Diverse European Union' in Luisa Antoniolli, Luigi Bonatti, and Carlo Ruzza (eds), *Highs and Lows of European Integration: Sixty Years After the Treaty of Rome* (Springer International Publishing 2019)

Apeldoorn B van, *Transnational Capitalism and the Struggle over European Integration* (Routledge 2009)

Arena A, 'The Doctrine of Union Preemption in the E.U. Internal Market: Between Sein and Sollen' (2010) 17 Columbia Journal of European Law 477

Arena A, 'The Twin Doctrines of Primacy and Pre-Emption' in Robert Schütze and Takis Tridimas (eds), *The European Legal Order*, vol 1 (OUP 2018)

Armstrong K, 'Mutual Recognition' in Catherine Barnard and Joanne Scott (eds), *The Law of the Single European Market: Unpacking the Premises* (Hart 2002)

Arrow KJ and Debreu G, 'Existence of an Equilibrium for a Competitive Economy' (1954) 22 Econometrica 265

Arrowsmith S, 'Application of the EC Treaty and Directives to Horizontal Policies: A Critical Review' in Sue Arrowsmith and Peter Kunzlik (eds), *Social and Environmental Policies in EC Procurement Law*, vol 13 (CUP 1999)

Arrowsmith S, 'Rethinking the Approach to Economic Justifications under the EU's Free Movement Rules' (2015) 68 Current Legal Problems 307

Asen E, 'Where Is Carbon Taxed in Europe?' (Tax Foundation, 14 November 2019) <https://taxfoundation.org/carbon-taxes-in-europe-2019/> accessed 14 December 2019

Aujean M, 'The CCCTB Project and the Future of European Taxation' in Michael Lang and others (eds), *Common Consolidated Corporate Tax Base* (Linde Verlag 2008)

Avbelj M, 'Supremacy or Primacy of EU Law—(Why) Does It Matter?' (2011) 17 European Law Review 744

Avery Jones JF, 'A Comment on "Progressive Taxation of Non-Residents and Intra-EC Allocation of Personal Tax Allowances"' (2000) 40 European Taxation 375

Baarsma NA, *The Europeanisation of International Family Law* (TMC Asser Press 2011)

Bach M, 'The Enlargement Crisis of the European Union: From Political Integration to Social Disintegration?' in Maurizio Bach, Christian Lahusen, and Georg Vobruba (eds), *Europe in Motion: Social Dynamics and Political Institutions in an Enlarging Europe* (Nomos 2006)

Bacon K, 'State Aids and General Measures' (1997) 17 Yearbook of European Law 269

Bagwell K and Staiger RW, 'Multilateral Tariff Cooperation during the Formation of Free Trade Areas' (1997) 38 International Economic Review 291

Bagwell K and Staiger RW, 'The WTO: Theory and Practice' (2009) NBER Working Papers

Balbinot C, *Beihilfeverbot und Rechtsformneutralität: Zugleich ein Beitrag zur Auslegung des Beihilfeverbots im Steuerrecht* (Verlag Dr Otto Schmidt 2018)

Bammens N, *The Principle of Non-Discrimination in International and European Tax Law* (IBFD 2012)

Bany P, 'Substantive Due Process and Labor Law' (1982) 6 The Journal of Libertarian Studies 267

Barents R, 'Charges of Equivalent Effect to Customs Duties' (1978) 15 Common Market Law Review 415

Barents R, 'The Internal Market Unlimited: Some Observations on the Legal Basis of Community Legislation' (1993) 30 Common Market Law Review 85

Barnard C, 'Flexibility and Social Policy' in Gráinne de Búrca and Joanne Scott (eds), *Constitutional Change in the EU: From Uniformity to Flexibility?* (Hart Publishing 2000)

Barnard C, 'Derogations, Justifications and the Four Freedoms: Is State Interest Really Protected?' in Catherine Barnard (ed), *The Outer Limits of European Union Law* (Hart Publishing 2009)

Barnard C, *The Substantive Law of the EU: The Four Freedoms* (6th edn, OUP 2019)

Barnard C and Deakin S, 'Market Access and Regulatory Competition' in Catherine Barnard and Joanne Scott (eds), *The Law of the Single European Market: Unpacking the Premises* (Bloomsbury Publishing PLC 2002)

Bartosch A, 'Fiscal Aid: Recent Trends and Relationship to Fundamental Freedoms' in Werner Haslehner, Georg Kofler, and Alexander Rust (eds), *EU Tax Law and Policy in the 21st Century* (Kluwer Law International 2017)

Basedow J, 'The Judge's Role in European Integration—The Court of Justice and Its Critics' in Hans-Wolfgang Micklitz and Bruno de Witte (eds), *The European Court of Justice and the Autonomy of the Member States* (Intersentia 2012)

Bassini M, 'Rise of Populism and the Five Star Movement Model: An Italian Case Study' (2017) Jean Monnet Working Paper, https://jeanmonnetprogram.org/wp-content/uploads/JMWP-04-Marco-Bassini-1.pdf

Bast J, 'On the Grammar of EU Law: Legal Instruments' in Armin von Bogdandy and Joseph HH Weiler (eds), *European Integration: The New German Scholarship* (2003) Jean Monnet Working Paper 9/03 <https://jeanmonnetprogram.org/archive/papers/03/030901-05.pdf>

Bayer W and Schmidt J, 'Grenzüberschreitende Mobilität von Gesellschaften: Formwechsel durch isolierte Sitzverlegung' (2017) 39 Zeitschrift für Wirtschaftsrecht 2225

Beck H, *Abgestufte Integration im Europäischen Gemeinschaftsrecht unter besonderer Berücksichtigung des Umweltrechts: Bestandsaufnahme und Perspektiven* (Peter Lang 1995)

Becker U, 'Differenzierungen der Rechtseinheit durch "abgestufte Integration"' in Jürgen Schwarze and Peter-Christian Müller-Graff (eds), *Europäische Rechtseinheit durch einheitliche Rechtsdurchsetzung* (Nomos 1998)

Becker U, *EU-Erweiterung und differenzierte Integration: zu beitrittsbedingten Übergangsregelungen am Beispiel der Arbeitnehmerfreizügigkeit* (Nomos 1999)

Becker U, 'Art. 20 EUV' in Hans von der Groeben, Jürgen Schwarze, and Armin Hatje (eds), *Europäisches Unionsrecht* (7th edn, Nomos 2015)
Becker U, 'Art. 327' in Hans von der Groeben, Jürgen Schwarze, and Armin Hatje (eds), *Europäisches Unionsrecht* (7th edn, Nomos 2015)
Behme C, 'The Principle of Mutual Recognition in the European Internal Market With Special Regard to the Cross-Border Mobility of Companies' (2016) European Company and Financial Law Review 31
Beier F-K, 'Stand und Aussichten der europäischen Rechtsvereinheitlichung auf dem Gebiete des gewerblichen Rechtsschutzes' (1969) Gewerblicher Rechtsschutz und Urheberrecht Internationaler Teil 145
Bellingwout J, 'Amurta: A Tribute to (the Late) Advocate General Geelhoed' (2008) 48 European Taxation 124
Bendiner R, *Obstacle Course on Capitol Hill* (McGraw-Hill 1964)
Bentil JK, 'EEC Commercial Law and "Charges Having Equivalent Effect to Customs Duties"' (1975) 9 Journal of World Trade 458
Bérénice L, 'Rome III Regulation: Getting Divorced in Europe' in Thomas Giegerich, Desirée Schmitt, and Sebastian Zeitzmann (eds), *Flexibility in the EU and Beyond: How Much Differentiation can European Integration Bear?* (Nomos 2017)
Beretta G, 'The Brisal and KBC Finance Decision: Once Again the CJEU Assesses the Compatibility with EU Law of Gross Withholding Taxation of Non-Residents' (2017) 26 EC Tax Review 193
Bermann GA, 'Taking Subsidiarity Seriously: Federalism in the European Community and the United States' (1994) 94 Columbia Law Review 331
Bermann GA, 'Proportionality and Subsidiarity' in Catherine Barnard and Joanne Scott (eds), *The Law of the Single European Market: Unpacking the Premises* (Hart Publishing 2002)
Bernard N, 'The Future of European Economic Law in the Light of the Principle of Subsidiarity' (1996) 33 Common Market Law Review 633
Bernard N, 'La libre circulation des marchandises, des personnes et des services dans le Traité CE sous l'angle de la compétence' (1998) 34 Cahiers de droit européen 11
Bernard N, 'Flexibility in the European Single Market' in Catherine Barnard and Joanne Scott (eds), *The Law of the Single European Market: Unpacking the Premises* (Hart Publishing 2002)
Besselink LFM, 'Does EU Law Recognise Legal Limits to Integration? Accommodating Diversity and Its Limits' in Thomas Giegerich, Oskar Josef Gstrein, and Sebastian Zeitzmann (eds), *The EU between 'An Ever Closer Union' and Inalienable Policy Domains of Member States*, vol 80 (Nomos 2014)
Bhagwati JN, *Protectionism* (MIT Press 1988)
Bhambra GK, 'The Current Crisis of Europe: Refugees, Colonialism, and the Limits of Cosmopolitanism' (2017) 23 European Law Journal 395
Bieber R, 'Schlußbetrachtung: Schengen als Modell zukünftiger Integration?' in Alberto Achermann and others (eds), *Schengen und die Folgen: der Abbau der Grenzkontrollen in Europa* (Stämpfli [u.a] 1995)
Bieber R and Salomé I, 'Hierarchy of Norms in European Law' (1996) 33 Common Market Law Review 909
Blanke H-J, 'Art. 20' in Hermann-Josef Blanke and Stelio Mangiameli (eds), *The Treaty on European Union (TEU)—A Commentary* (Springer 2013)
Blanke H-J, 'AEUV Art. 327 AEUV' in Eberhard Grabitz, Meinhard Hilf, and Martin Nettesheim (eds), *Das Recht der Europäischen Union* (67th edn, Beck Verlag 2019)

Blum D and Langer A, 'At a Crossroads: Mandatory Disclosure under DAC-6 and EU Primary Law—Part 1' (2019) 59 European Taxation 282

Blumann C, 'L'Europe des citoyens' (1991) Revue du Marche commun et de l'Union européenne 283

Boeger N, 'Minimum Harmonisation, Free Movement and Proportionality' in Phil Syrpis (ed), *The Judiciary, the Legislature and the EU Internal Market* (CUP 2012)

Boele-Woelki K, 'To Be, Or Not to Be: Enhanced Cooperation in International Divorce Law within the European Union Wider Perspectives' (2008) 39 Victoria University of Wellington Law Review 779

Boele-Woelki K, *Unifying and Harmonising Substantive Law and the Role of Conflict of Laws* (Martinus Nijhoff Publishers 2010)

Bogdandy A von, 'Der rechtliche Rahmen der Zugangsregeln' in Eberhard Grabitz, Armin von Bogdandy, and Martin Nettesheim (eds), *Europäisches Außenwirtschaftsrecht: der Zugang zum Binnenmarkt: Primärrecht, Handelsschutzrecht und Außenaspekte der Binnenmarktharmonisierung* (Beck Verlag 1994)

Bogdandy A von, 'Grundrechtsgemeinschaft als Integrationsziel? Grundreche und das Wesen der Europäischen Union' (2001) 56 Juristenzeitung 157

Bogdandy A von and Bast J, 'The European Union's Vertical Order of Competences: The Current Law and Proposals for Its Reform' (2002) 39 Common Market Law Review 227

Bogdandy A von and Bast J, 'The Federal Order of Competence' in Armin von Bogdandy and Jürgen Bast (eds), *Principles of European Constitutional Law* (2nd edn, Hart Publishing 2010)

Bogdandy A von and Schill S, 'Die Achtung der nationalen Identität unter dem reformierten Unionsvertrag: Zur unionsrechtlichen Rolle nationalen Verfassungsrechts und zur Überwindung des absoluten Vorrangs' (2010) 70 Zeitschrift für ausländisches öffentliches Recht und Völkerrecht 701

Bogdandy A von and Schill S, 'Overcoming Absolute Primacy: Respect for National Identity under the Lisbon Treaty' (2011) 48 Common Market Law Review 1417

Bonadio E, 'The EU Embraces Enhanced Cooperation in Patent Matters: Towards A Unitary Patent Protection System' (2011) 2 European Journal of Risk Regulation 416

Bonney R, *The Rise of the Fiscal State in Europe c.1200–1815* (OUP 1999)

Böttner R, 'The Treaty Amendment Procedures and the Relationship between Article 31(3) TEU and the General Bridging Clause of Article 48(7) TEU' (2016) 12 European Constitutional Law Review 499

Böttner R, 'Eine Idee lernt laufen—zur Praxis der Verstärkten Zusammenarbeit nach Lissabon' (2016) 19 Zeitschrift für europarechtliche Studien 501

Bourgeois M, 'Constitutional Framework of the Different Types of Income' in Bruno Peeters (ed), *The Concept of Tax* (IBFD 2005)

Brander JA and Spencer BJ, 'Tariff Protection and Imperfect Competition' in Gene M Grossman (ed), *Imperfect Competition and International Trade* (MIT Press 1992)

Braun Binder N, *Rechtsangleichung in der EU im Bereich der direkten Steuern: Analyse der Handlungsformen unter besonderer Berücksichtigung des Soft Law* (Mohr Siebeck 2017)

Breier S, 'Der Streit Um Die Richtige Rechtsgrundlage in Der Rechtsprechung Europäischen Gerichtshofes' (1995) Europarecht 46

Brennan G and Buchanan JM, 'Towards a Tax Constitution for Leviathan' (1977) 8 Journal of Public Economics 255

Brennan G and Buchanan JM, *The Power to Tax: Analytical Foundations of a Fiscal Constitution* (CUP 2006)

Bribosia H, 'De la Subsidiarité à la Coopération Renforcée' in Yves Lejeune (ed), *Le traité d'Amsterdam: espoirs et déceptions* (Bruylant 1998)

Brighouse H and Fleurbaey M, 'Democracy and Proportionality' (2010) 18 Journal of Political Philosophy 137

Broe L de, 'The State Aid Selectivity-Test in Corporate Tax Matters: CJEU Applies Common Sense in Its Judgments on the German "Sanierungs" Clause, but Do We Have All Pieces of the Puzzle Now?' (2018) 27 EC Tax Review 285

Broe L de and Bammens N, 'Truck Center: Belgian Withholding Tax on Interest Payments to Non-Resident Companies Does Not Violate EC Law: A Critical Look at the ECJ's Judgment in Truck Center' (2009) 18 EC Tax Review 131

Broe LD, 'Can Tax Treaties Confer State Aid?' (2017) 26 EC Tax Review 228

Bronckers M, 'From "Direct Effect" to "Muted Dialogue": Recent Developments in the European Courts' Case Law on the WTO and Beyond' (2008) 11 Journal of International Economic Law 885

Brownlie I, *Principles of Public International Law* (6th edn, OUP 2003)

Búrca G de, 'The Principle of Proportionality and Its Application in EC Law' (1993) 13 Yearbook of European Law 105

Búrca G de, 'The Principle of Subsidiarity and the Court of Justice as an Institutional Actor' (1998) 36 Journal of Common Market Studies 217

Búrca G de, 'Differentiation within the Core: The Case of the Common Market' in Gráinne de Búrca and Joanne Scott (eds), *Constitutional Change in the EU: from Uniformity to Flexibility?* (Hart Publishing 2000)

Buser D, *Kantonales Staatsrecht: Eine Einführung für Studium und Praxis* (Helbing & Lichtenhahn Verlag 2004)

Buttlar C von, 'Rechtsprobleme der "verstärkten Zusammenarbeit" nach dem Vertrag von Nizza' (2011) Zeitschrift für Europarechtliche Studien 649

Büttner T, 'Fiscal Externalities in Local Tax Competition: Empirical Evidence from a Panel of German Jurisdictions' (2011) ZEW Discussion Paper

Cappelletti M, Seccombe M, and Weiler JHH, *Integration Through Law: Europe and the American Federal Experience. Vol. 1: Methods, Tools and Institutions*, vol I (de Gruyter 1986)

Carlson AE, 'California Motor Vehicle Standards and Federalism: Lessons for the EU' in David Vogel and Johan Swinnen (eds), *Transatlantic Regulatory Cooperation* (Edward Elgar Publishing 2011)

Caron PL and Repetti JR, 'Occupy the Tax Code: Using the Estate Tax to Reduce Inequality and Spur Economic Growth' (2012) 40 Pepperdine Law Review 1255

Carter D, 'Equal Pay for Equal Work in the Same Place? Assessing the Revision to the Posted Workers Directive' (2018) 14 Croatian Yearbook of European Law & Policy 31

Cary WL, 'Federalism and Corporate Law: Reflections upon Delaware' (1974) 83 The Yale Law Journal 663

Cass DZ, 'The Word That Saves Maastricht? The Principle of Subsidiarity and the Division of Powers within the European Community' (1992) 29 Common Market Law Review 1107

Cédelle A, 'Enhanced Cooperation: A Way Forward for Tax Harmonization in the European Union?' in Joachim Englisch (ed), *International Tax Law: New Challenges to and from Constitutional and Legal Pluralism* (IBFD 2016)

Cédelle A, 'Double Taxation and the Internal Market: No Simple Fix?' in Pasquale Pistone (ed), *European Tax Integration: Law, Policy and Politics* (IBFD 2018)

Cédelle A and Vella J, 'Differentiated Integration in the EU: Lessons from the Financial Transaction Tax' in Panos Koutrakos and Jukka Snell (eds), *Research Handbook on the Law of the EU's Internal Market* (Edward Elgar Publishing 2017)

Cerioni L, 'The Possible Introduction of Common Consolidated Base Taxation via Enhanced Cooperation: Some Open Issues' (2006) 46 European Taxation 187

Cerioni L, 'The Commission's Proposal for a CCCTB Directive: Analysis and Comment' (2011) 65 Bulletin for International Taxation 515

Cerioni L, 'Guido Imfeld and Nathalie Garcet v Belgian State: A Continuation of the Schumacker Doctrine?' (2014) British Tax Review 128

Cerioni L, *European Union and Direct Taxation: A Solution for a Difficult Relationship* (Routledge 2015)

Chaltiel PF, 'Le traité d'Amsterdam et la coopération renforcée' (1998) Revue du Marche commun et de l'Union européenne 289

Chinkin CM, *Third Parties in International Law* (Clarendon Press 2015)

Claes M, 'The Primacy of EU Law in European and National Law' in Anthony Arnull and Damian Chalmers (eds), *The Oxford Handbook of European Union Law* (OUP 2015)

Clift B and Woll C, 'Economic Patriotism: Reinventing Control over Open Markets' (2012) 19 Journal of European Public Policy 307

Cloots E, *National Identity in EU Law* (OUP 2015)

Cloppenburg SRJ, *Eine Finanztransaktionssteuer im 'kleinen Kreis'* (Peter Lang 2018)

Constantinesco V, 'Les clauses de "coopération renforcée". Le protocole sur l'application des principes de subsidiarité et de proportionnalité' (1997) 33 Revue trimestrielle de droit europeen 751

Cordewener A, *Europäische Grundfreiheiten und nationales Steuerrecht: 'Konvergenz' des Gemeinschaftsrechts und 'Kohärenz' der direkten Steuern in der Rechtsprechung des EuGH* (Dr Otto Schmidt Verlag 2002)

Cordewener A, 'The Prohibitions of Discrimination and Restrictions within the Framework of the Fully Integrated Internal Market' in Frans Vanistendael (ed), *EU Freedoms and Taxation* (IBFD 2006)

Cordewener A, 'Personal Income Taxation of Non-Residents and the Increasing Impact of the EC Treaty Freedoms' in Dennis Weber (ed), *The Influence of European Law on Direct Taxation: Recent and Future Developments* (Kluwer Law International 2007)

Cordewener A, 'Asymmetrical Tax Burdens and EU State Aid Control' (2012) 21 EC Tax Review 288

Cordewener A, 'Cross-Border Loss Compensation and EU Fundamental Freedoms: The "Final Losses" Doctrine Is Still Alive!' (2018) 27 EC Tax Review 230

Cordewener A, Kofler GW, and van Thiel S, 'The Clash Between European Freedoms and National Direct Tax Law: Public Interest Defences Available to the Member States' (2009) 46 Common Market Law Review 1951

Cottier T and Oesch M, 'Direct and Indirect Discrimination in WTO and EU Law' in Sanford E Gaines, Birgitte Egelund Olsen, and Karsten Engsig Sørensen (eds), *Liberalising Trade in the EU and the WTO: A Legal Comparison* (CUP 2012)

Craig P, 'The Classics of EU Law Revisited: CILFIT and Foto-Frost' in Miguel Poiares Maduro and Loïc Azoulai (eds), *The Past and Future of EU Law: The Classics of EU Law Revisited on the 50th Anniversary of the Rome Treaty* (Hart Publishing 2010)

Craig P, 'Subsidiarity: A Political and Legal Analysis' (2012) 50 Journal of Common Market Studies 72

Craig P, *The Lisbon Treaty: Law, Politics, and Treaty Reform* (OUP 2013)

Craig P, 'Pringle and Use of EU Institutions Outside the EU Legal Framework: Foundations, Procedure and Substance' (2013) 9 European Constitutional Law Review 263

Craig PP and Búrca G de, *EU Law: Text, Cases, and Materials* (6th edn, 2015 OUP)

Crawford J, *Brownlie's Principles of Public International Law* (OUP 2019)

Cremer H-J, 'Art. 48' in Christian Calliess and Matthias Ruffert (eds), *EUV/AEUV* (5th edn, Beck Verlag 2016)

Cremona M and others (eds), 'Regional Trade Agreements: "Stepping Stones" or "Stumbling Blocks" of the WTO?' in Richard Senti, *Reflections on the Constitutionalisation of International Economic Law: Liber Amicorum for Ernst-Ulrich Petersmann* (Brill Nijhoff 2013)

Cross ED, 'Pre-Emption of Member State Law in the European Economic Community: A Framework for Analysis' (1992) 29 Common Market Law Review 447

Cullen H and Charlesworth A, 'Diplomacy by Other Means: The Use of Legal Basis Litigation as a Political Strategy by the European Parliament and Member States' (1999) 36 Common Market Law Review 1243

Currall J, 'Some Aspects of the Relation between Articles 30–36 and Article 100 of the EEC Treaty, with a Closer Look at Optional Harmonisation' (1984) 4 Yearbook of European Law 169

Curtin D, 'Emerging Institutional Parameters and Organised Difference in the European Union' in Bruno de Witte, Dominik Hanf, and Ellen Vos (eds), *The Many Faces of Differentiation in EU Law* (Intersentia nv 2001)

Dahm J and Hamacher R, 'Finanztransaktionssteuern anderer Länder—(taugliche) Muster für die grenzüberschreitende Steuererhebung?' (2013) Internationales Steuerrecht 123

Dahm J and Hamacher R, 'Verstärkte Zusammenarbeit für FTT mit Kapitalansammlungsrichtlinie vereinbar?' (2015) Internationales Steuerrecht Länderbericht 29

Dam KW, 'Regional Economic Arrangements and the GATT: The Legacy of a Misconception' (1963) 30 The University of Chicago Law Review 615

Damro C, 'EU State Aid Policy and the Politics of External Trade Relations' (2013) 13 Journal of Industry, Competition and Trade 159

Danwitz T von, 'Der Grundsatz der Verhältnismäßigkeit im Gemeinschaftsrecht' (2003) Europäisches Wirtschafts- und Steuerrecht 393

Dashwood A, 'The Limits of European Community Powers' (1996) 21 European Law Review 113

Dashwood A, 'The Relationship between the Member States and the European Union' (2004) 41 Common Market Law Review 355

Dashwood A and others (eds), *Wyatt and Dashwood's European Union Law* (6th edn, Hart Publishing 2011)

Dassesse M, 'Belgian Withholding Taxes on Outbound Dividends and Interest: The Challenge of Community Law' (2008) 62 Bulletin for International Taxation 337

David R, 'The Methods of Unification' (1968) 16 The American Journal of Comparative Law 13

Davies G, 'Subsidiarity: The Wrong Idea, in the Wrong Place, at the Wrong Time' (2006) 43 Common Market Law Review 63

Davies G, 'Internal Market Adjudication and the Quality of Life in Europe' (2014) Columbia Journal of European Law 289

Davies G, 'Legislative Control of the European Court of Justice' (2014) 51 Common Market Law Review 1579

Davies G, 'The Competence to Create an Internal Market: Conceptual Poverty and Unbalanced Interests' in Sacha Garben and Inge Govaere (eds), *The Division of Competences between the EU and the Member States: Reflections on the Past, the Present and the Future* (Hart Publishing 2017)

Deakin S, 'Legal Diversity and Regulatory Competition: Which Model for Europe?' (2006) 12 European Law Journal 440

Debatin H, 'Zum Grundverständnis der Doppelbsteuerungsabkommen' (1988) Recht der Internationalen Wirtschaft 727

Dehousse R, 'Integration v. Regulation? Social Regulation in the European Community' (1992) EUI Working Paper LAW
Dekker C, 'The Effect on Trade between the Member States' Criterion: Is It the Right Criterion by Which the Commission's Workload Can Be Managed' (2017) 16 European State Aid Law Quarterly 154
Denza E, 'Art. 48' in Hermann-Josef Blanke and Stelio Mangiameli (eds), *The Treaty on European Union (TEU)—A Commentary* (Springer 2013)
Derenne J and others, 'Recent Developments in State Aid Law' (2014) 5 Journal of European Competition Law & Practice 53
Derpa U, *Die verstärkte Zusammenarbeit im Recht der Europäischen Union: Dogmatik Interpretation und Praxis eines alternativen Integrationskonzeptes* (Boorberg Verlag 2003)
Di Fabio U, *Grenzen der Rechtsfortbildung in Europa* (Zentrum für Europäisches Wirtschaftsrecht 2012)
Di Fabio U, 'Europa am Wendepunkt: Wirtschaftsregierung oder Subsidiarität' in Handwerkskammer Düsseldorf (ed), *Welche Chancen hat Subsidiarität in Europa?*, vol 5 (Verlagsanstalt Handwerk 2014)
Donnelly SW, *The Regimes of European Integration: Constructing Governance of the Single Market* (OUP 2010)
Dougan M, 'Minimum Harmonization and the Internal Market' (2000) 37 Common Market Law Review 853
Dougan M, *National Remedies before the Court of Justice: Issues of Harmonisation and Differentiation* (Hart Publishing 2004)
Dougan M, 'When Worlds Collide! Competing Visions of the Relationship between Direct Effect and Supremacy' (2007) 44 Common Market Law Review 931
Dougan M, 'Judicial Activism or Constitutional Interaction? Policymaking by the ECJ in the Field of Union Citizenship' in Hans-Wolfgang Micklitz and Bruno de Witte (eds), *The European Court of Justice and the Autonomy of the Member States* (Intersentia 2012)
Dougan M, 'Primacy and the Remedy of Disapplication' (2019) 56 Common Market Law Review 1459
Douma S, 'The Three Ds of Direct Tax Jurisdiction: Disparity, Discrimination and Double Taxation' (2006) 46 European Taxation 522
Douma S, 'Non-Discriminatory Tax Obstacles' (2012) 21 EC Tax Review 67
Douma S and Engelen F, 'Non-Discriminatory Tax Obstacles to Free Movement' in Michael Lang and Christine Weinzierl (eds), *Europäisches Steuerrecht—Festschrift für Friedrich Rödler* (Linde Verlag 2010)
Dourado AP, 'The Relationship between Primary and Secondary EU Law in Tax Law: The Legitimacy of Different Interpretation Criteria Applied to EU and National Legal Sources' in Dennis Weber (ed), *Traditional and Alternative Routes to European Tax Integration: Primary Law, Secondary Law, Soft Law, Coordination, Comitology and Their Relationship* (IBFD 2010)
Dourado AP, 'The EU Free Movement of Capital and Third Countries: Recent Developments' (2017) 45 Intertax 192
Dourado AP, 'The Commission Proposal to Replace Unanimity with a Qualified Majority in the Case of Tax Matters' (2019) 47 Intertax 341
Dunne N, 'Liberalisation and the Pursuit of the Internal Market' (2018) 43 European Law Review 803
Easterbrook F, 'The Constitution of Business' (1988) 11 George Mason University Law Review 53
Ebrill LP and others, *The Modern VAT* (International Monetary Fund 2001)

'Editorial Comments: Enhanced Cooperation: A Union à Taille Réduite or à Porte Tournante?' (2011) 48 Common Market Law Review 317

'Editorial: What Do We Want? "Flexibility! Sort-of . . ." When Do We Want It? "Now! Maybe . . ."' (2013) 50 Common Market Law Review 673

Edward D, 'Will There Be Honey Still for Tea?' (2006) 43 Common Market Law Review 623

Edward D and Lane R, *Edward and Lane on European Union Law* (Edward Elgar Publishing 2013)

Edwards J and Keen M, 'Tax Competition and Leviathan' (1996) 40 European Economic Review 113

Ehlermann C-D, 'How Flexible Is Community Law? An Unusual Approach to the Concept of "Two Speeds"' (1984) 82 Michigan Law Review 1274

Ehlermann C-D, 'The Internal Market Following the Single European Act' (1987) 24 Common Market Law Review 361

Ehlermann C-D, 'Differenciation, flexibilite, cooperation renforcee: les nouvelles dispositions du traite d'Amsterdam' (1997) Revue du Marche Unique Europeen 53

Ehlermann C-D, 'Engere Zusammenarbeit nach dem Amsterdamer Vertrag: Ein neues Verfassungsprinzip?' (1997) Europarecht 362

Elsayyad M and Konrad KA, 'Fighting Multiple Tax Havens' (2012) 86 Journal of International Economics 295

Elwes S, 'The Internal Market versus the Right of Member States to Levy Direct Tax-A Clash of Fundamental Principles' (2013) 41 Intertax 15

Emiliou N, *The Principle of Proportionality in European Law: A Comparative Study* (Kluwer Law International 1996)

Emmerich-Fritsche A, *Der Grundsatz der Verhältnismäßigkeit als Direktive und Schranke der EG-Rechtsetzung* (Duncker & Humblot 2000)

Enachescu J and others, 'Horizontal Monitoring in Austria: Subjective Representations by Tax Officials and Company Employees' (2019) 12 Business Research 75

Engel A, *The Choice of Legal Basis for Acts of the European Union: Competence Overlaps, Institutional Preferences, and Legal Basis Litigation* (Springer 2018)

Engelen F, 'State Aid and Restrictions on Free Movement: Two Sides of the Same Coin?' (2012) 52 European Taxation 204

Engle E, 'The History of the General Principle of Proportionality: An Overview' (2012) 10 Dartmouth Law Journal 1

Englisch J, 'Fiscal Cohesion in the Taxation of Cross-Border Dividends (Part Two)' (2004) 44 European Taxation 355

Englisch J, *Wettbewerbsgleichheit im grenzüberschreitenden Handel: mit Schlussfolgerungen für indirekte Steuern* (Mohr Siebeck 2008)

Englisch J, 'State Aid and Indirect Taxation' in Alexander Rust and Claire Micheau (eds), *State Aid and Tax Law* (Kluwer Law International 2013)

Englisch J, 'Comment on ECJ 17.7.2014 (Nordea Bank)' (2014) Highlights & Insights on European Taxation 10

Englisch J, 'Nordea Bank—ein weiterer Meilenstein der EuGH-Judikatur' (2014) Internationales Steuerrecht 561

Englisch J, 'Dividend Taxation: Outbound and Inbound (Verkooijen and ACT Group Litigation)' in Werner Haslehner, Georg Kofler, and Alexander Rust (eds), *Landmark Decisions of the ECJ in Direct Taxation* (Kluwer Law International 2015)

Englisch J, 'Grundfreiheiten: Vergleichbarkeit, Rechtfertigung und Verhältnismäßigkeit', *Europäisches Steuerrecht*, vol 41 (Dr Otto Schmidt Verlag 2018)

Englisch J, Vella J, and Cédelle A, 'The Financial Transaction Tax Proposal under the Enhanced Cooperation Procedure: Legal and Practical Considerations' (2013) British Tax Review 223

Epiney A, 'Das zweite Schengener Abkommen: Entstehung, Konzept und Einbettung in die Europäische Union' in Alberto Achermann and others (eds), *Schengen und die Folgen: der Abbau der Grenzkontrollen in Europa* (Beck Verlag 1995)

Ermacora F, *Föderalismus in Österreich* (Europa Verlag 1970)

Escribano López E, 'An Opportunistic, and yet Appropriate, Revision of the Source Threshold for the Twenty-First Century Tax Treaties' (2015) 43 Intertax 6

Ethier WJ, 'Regionalism in a Multilateral World' (1998) 106 Journal of Political Economy 1214

Everling U, 'Zur Mehrheit und Einstimmigkeit in der verfaßten Europäischen Union' in Reinhard Hendler, Martin Ibler, and José Martínez Soria (eds), *Für Sicherheit, für Europa: Festschrift für Volkmar Götz zum 70. Geburtstag* (Vandenhoeck & Ruprecht 2005)

Ezcurra MV, 'State Aids and Energy Taxes: Towards a Coherent Reference Framework' (2013) 41 Intertax 340

Fabbrini F, 'Enhanced Cooperation under Scrutiny: Revisiting the Law and Practice of Multi-Speed Integration in Light of the First Involvement of the EU Judiciary' (2013) 40 Legal Issues of Economic Integration 197

Fabbrini F, 'The Enhanced Cooperation Procedure: A Study in Multispeed Integration' Centro Studi Sul Federalismo—Research Paper, http://www.csfederalismo.it/en/publications/research-papers/998-the-enhanced-cooperation-procedure-a-study-in-multispeed-integration-2

Farmer P, 'Striking a Proper Balance between the National Fiscal Interests and the Community Interest - a Perpetual Struggle?' in Dennis Weber (ed), *The Influence of European Law on Direct Taxation: Recent and Future Developments* (Kluwer Law International 2007)

Farmer P, 'Direct Taxation and the Fundamental Freedoms' in Anthony Arnull and Damian Chalmers (eds), *The Oxford Handbook of European Union Law* (OUP 2015)

Farmer P and Zalasinski A, 'General Report' in Xenios L Xenopoulos (ed), *Direct Tax Rules and the EU Fundamental Freedoms: Origin and Scope of the Problem; National and Community Responses and Solutions: FIDE 2006 National Reports* (Theopress 2006)

Farrell JE, *The Interface of International Trade Law and Taxation* (IBFD 2013)

Feenstra RC, Markusen JR, and Rose AK, 'Using the Gravity Equation to Differentiate among Alternative Theories of Trade' (2001) 34 Canadian Journal of Economics

Feinberg J, 'Duties, Rights, and Claims' (1966) 3 American Philosophical Quarterly 137

Feria R de la and Fuest C, 'The Economic Effects of EU Tax Jurisprudence' (2016) 41 European Law Review 44

Feria R de la and Fuest C, 'The Economic Effects of EU Tax Jurisprudence' in Werner Haslehner, Georg Kofler, and Alexander Rust (eds), *EU Tax Law and Policy in the 21st Century* (Kluwer Law International 2017)

Finger JM and Winters LA, 'Reciprocity in the WTO' in Bernard M Hoekman and others (eds), *Development, Trade, and the WTO: A Handbook* (World Bank 2002)

Finger M, 'GATT's Influence on Regional Arrangements' in Jaime de Melo and Arvind Panagariya (eds), *New Dimensions in Regional Integration* (CUP 1993)

Fiorini A, 'Rome III—Choice of Law in Divorce: Is the Europeanization of Family Law Going Too Far' (2008) 22 International Journal of Law, Policy and the Family 178

Fitzmaurice GS, 'Law of Treaties—Fifth Report by Special Rapporteur Sir Gerald Fitzmaurice' (1960) DOCUMENT A/CN.4/130

Fleiner-Gerster T, 'Zusammenarbeit der Gliedstaaten im Bundesstaat' in Christian Starck (ed), *Zusammenarbeit der Gliedstaaten im Bundesstaat: Landesberichte und Generalbericht der Tagung für Rechtsvergleichung 1987 in Innsbruck* (Nomos 1988)

Flynn J, 'How Will Article 100(4) Work? A Comparison with Article 93' (1987) 24 Common Market Law Review 689

Forrester E, 'Is the State Aid Regime a Suitable Instrument to Be Used in the Fight Against Harmful Tax Competition?' (2018) 27 EC Tax Review 19

Forsthoff U, 'EuGH versus Europäischer Gesetzgeber—oder Freiheiten über alles?' (2006) Internationales Steuerrecht 222

Fort E, 'EU State Aid and Tax: An Evolutionary Approach' (2017) 57 European Taxation 14

Fortuin A, 'Denkavit Internationaal: The Procedural Issues' (2007) 47 European Taxation 239

Frankfurter F and Landis JM, 'The Compact Clause of the Constitution. A Study in Interstate Adjustments' (1925) 34 The Yale Law Journal 685

French R, 'Co-Operative Federalism in Australia—an Intellectual Resource for Europe? I' (2006) 65 Amicus Curiae 9

Frey BS, 'European Unification Based on Flexibility and Diversity' (2019) 75 FinanzArchiv 93

Freyer D, 'The Proportionality Principle under EU Tax Law: General and Practical Problems Caused by Its Extensive Application—Part 1' (2017) 57 European Taxation 384

Frieden JA, Pettis M, and Rodrik D (eds), *After the Fall: The Future of Global Cooperation* (International Center for Monetary and Banking Studies (ICMB) 2012)

Friese A, *Rechtsformwahlfreiheit im Europäischen Steuerrecht* (Dr Otto Schmidt Verlag 2010)

'From the Board: Towards a Social Europe?' (2018) 45 Legal Issues of Economic Integration 323

Gadžo S, 'The Principle of "Nexus" or "Genuine Link" as a Keystone of International Income Tax Law: A Reappraisal' (2018) 46 Intertax 194

Gaja G, 'How Flexible Is Flexibility under the Amsterdam Treaty?' (1998) 35 Common Market Law Review 855

Gammie M, 'The Compatibility of National Tax Principles with the Single Market' in Frans Vanistendael (ed), *EU Freedoms and Taxation* (IBFD 2006)

Gammie M, 'Non-Discrimination and the Taxation of Cross-Border Dividends' (2010) 2 World Tax Journal 162

Gammie M and Brannan G, 'EC Law Strikes at the UK Corporation Tax—The Death Knell of UK Imputation?' (1995) 23 Intertax 389

Garbarino C, 'Harmonization and Coordination of Corporate Taxes in the European Union' (2016) 25 EC Tax Review 277

Garbarino C, 'Permanent Establishments and BEPS Action 7: Perspectives in Evolution' (2019) 47 Intertax 365

Garben S, 'The Constitutional (Im)Balance between "the Market" and "the Social" in the European Union' (2017) 13 European Constitutional Law Review 23

García Prats AF, 'Is It Possible to Set a Coherent System of Rules on Direct Taxation under EC Law Requirements?' in Philippe Hinnekens and Luc Hinnekens (eds), *A Vision of Taxes Within and Outside the European Borders: Festschrift in Honor of Prof. Dr. Frans Vanistendael* (Kluwer Law International 2008)

García Prats AF, 'Revisiting "Schumacker": Source, Residence and Citizenship in the ECJ Case Law on Direct Taxation' in Isabelle Richelle, Wolfgang Schön, and Edoardo Traversa (eds), *Allocating Taxing Powers within the European Union* (Springer-Verlag 2013)

García Prats AF, 'Subjective Ability to Pay: Schumacker' in Werner Haslehner, Georg Kofler and Alexander Rust (eds), *Landmark Decisions of the ECJ in Direct Taxation* (Kluwer Law International 2015)

Genschel P and Plumper T, 'Regulatory Competition and International Co-Operation' (1997) 4 Journal of European Public Policy 626

Genscher H-D, *Erinnerungen* (2nd edn, Siedler 1995)

Gerven D van, *Capital Directive in Europe: The Rules on Incorporation and Capital of Limited Liability Companies* (CUP 2014)

Giegerich T, 'Introduction: Trying to Fathom the Shallows of European Unification' in Thomas Giegerich, Oskar Josef Gstrein, and Sebastian Zeitzmann (eds), *The EU between 'An Ever Closer Union' and Inalienable Policy Domains of Member States*, vol 80 (Nomos 2014)

Goetz KH, 'The Temporal Dimension' in Kenneth Dyson and Angelos Sepos (eds), *Which Europe? Differentiated Integration* (Palgrave Macmillan 2010)

Golub J, 'In the Shadow of the Vote? Decision Making in the European Community' (1999) 53 International Organization 733

Gordon D, *Steering a New Course: Transportation, Energy, and the Environment* (Island Press 1991)

Grabitz E, 'Community Law and Differentiation between the Member States' in Asser Instituut Colloquium Europees Recht (ed), *Gedifferentieerde integratie en Gemeenschapsrecht* (TMC Asser Instituut 1985)

Grabitz E and Langeheine B, 'Legal Problems Related to a Proposed "Two-Tier System" of Integration within the European Community' (1981) 18 Common Market Law Review 33

Graetz MJ and Warren AC Jr, 'Dividend Taxation in Europe: When the ECJ Makes Tax Policy' (2007) 44 Common Market Law Review 1577

Granat K, *The Principle of Subsidiarity and Its Enforcement in the EU Legal Order: The Role of National Parliaments in the Early Warning System* (Hart Publishing 2018)

Granger M-P and Irion K, 'The Court of Justice and the Data Retention Directive in Digital Rights Ireland: Telling off the EU Legislator and Teaching a Lesson in Privacy and Data Protection' (2014) 39 European Law Review 835

Greve MS, 'Compacts, Cartels, and Congressional Consent' (2003) 68 Missouri Law Review 285

Grieser V, *Flexible Integration in der Europäischen Union: neue Dynamik oder Gefährdung der Rechtseinheit?* (Duncker & Humblot 2003)

Grigoleit HC, 'Der Verbraucheracquis und die Entwicklung des Europäischen Privatrechts' (2010) 210 Archiv fuer die civilistische Praxis 354

Griller S and others, *The Treaty of Amsterdam: Facts, Analysis, Prospects* (Springer 2000)

Groot IM de, 'The CJEU's Conflicting Case Law on Neutralization' (2014) 42 Intertax 721

Groot IM de, 'The Switch-Over Provision in the Proposal for an Anti-Tax Avoidance Directive and Its Compatibility with the EU Treaty Freedoms' (2016) 25 EC Tax Review 162

Gröpl C, 'Steuerrecht' in Manfred A Dauses and Markus Ludwigs (eds), *Handbuch des EU-Wirtschaftsrechts* (44th edn, Beck Verlag 2018)

Grzeszick B, 'Art. 20' in Theodor Maunz and others (eds), *Grundgesetz: Kommentar* (85. Ergänzungslieferung, November 2018, Beck Verlag 2018)

Gutmann D, 'Some Theoretical Thoughts on Judicial Power and Tax Law—with a Particular Focus on the ECJ' in Philippe Hinnekens and Luc Hinnekens (eds), *A Vision of Taxes Within and Outside the European Borders: Festschrift in Honor of Prof. Dr. Frans Vanistendael* (Kluwer Law International 2008)

Gutmann D, 'How to Avoid Double Taxation in the European Union?' in Isabelle Richelle, Wolfgang Schön, and Edoardo Traversa (eds), *Allocating Taxing Powers within the European Union* (Springer 2013)

Hailbronner K and Thym D, 'Case Note on Ruiz Zambrano' (2011) 48 Common Market Law Review 1253
Hall B, 'How Flexible Should Europe Be?' (2000) Centre for European Reform Working Paper, London
Hallström P, 'The European Union—from Reciprocity to Loyalty' (2000) 39 Scandinavian Studies in Law 79
Hamran L and Szabova E, 'European Public Prosecutor's Office—Cui Bono? The Future of Prosecution after Lisbon' (2013) 4 New Journal of European Criminal Law 40
Hancher L, 'EU State Aid Law—Déja Vu All Over Again?' in Leigh Hancher, Tom Ottervanger, and Pieter J Slot (eds), *EU State Aids* (5th edn, Thomson Reuters 2016)
Hancher L, 'The General Framework' in Leigh Hancher, Tom Ottervanger, and Pieter J Slot (eds), *EU State Aids* (5th edn, Thomson Reuters 2016)
Hanf D, 'Flexibility Clauses in the Founding Treaties, from Rome to Nice' in Bruno de Witte, Dominik Hanf, and Ellen Vos (eds), *The Many Faces of Differentiation in EU Law* (Intersentia nv 2001)
Hanf D, '"Reverse Discrimination" in EU Law: Constitutional Aberration, Constitutional Necessity, or Judicial Choice?' (2011) 18 Maastricht Journal of European and Comparative Law 29
Harbo T-I, 'The Function of the Proportionality Principle in EU Law' (2010) 16 European Law Journal 158
Haslehner W, 'Double Taxation Relief, Transfer Pricing Adjustments and State Aid Law' in Isabelle Richelle, Wolfgang Schön, and Edoardo Traversa (eds), *State Aid Law and Business Taxation* (Springer 2016)
Haslehner W, 'The Controlled Foreign Company Regime' in Dennis Weber and Jan Lambertus van de Streek (eds), *The EU Common Consolidated Corporate Tax Base: Critical Analysis* (Wolters Kluwer Law International 2018)
Hatje A, *Loyalität als Rechtsprinzip in der Europäischen Union* (Nomos 2001)
Heber C, 'Die Kompetenzverteilung Im Rahmen Der Austrittsverhandlungen Nach Art. 50 EUV Unter Besonderer Berücksichtigung Bestehenden Sekundärrechts' (2017) 52 Europarecht 581
Heber C and Sternberg C, 'Over-the-Counter Derivative Markets in the Light of EMIR Clearing Obligations and the Financial Transaction Tax' (2014) 16 Derivatives & Financial Instruments 107
Heber C and Sternberg C, 'Market Infrastructure Regulation and the Financial Transaction Tax' (2016) 8 World Tax Journal 3
Heber C and Sternberg C, 'The Extraterritorial Reach of the German Progression Clause in Income Tax Law in the Light of International Law' (2017) 45 Intertax 254
Hedemann-Robinson M, 'The Area of Freedom, Security and Justice with Regard to the UK, Ireland and Denmark: The "Opt-in Opt-Outs" under the Treaty of Amsterdam' in David O'Keeffe and Patrick Twomey (eds), *Legal Issues of the Amsterdam Treaty* (Hart Publishing 1999)
Heidenbauer S, *Charity Crossing Borders: The Fundamental Freedoms' Influence on Charity and Donor Taxation in Europe* (Kluwer Law International 2011)
Helpman E and Razin A (eds), 'Is Bilateralism Bad?' in Paul Krugman, *International Trade and Trade Policy* (MIT Press 1991)
Henkow O, *Financial Activities in European VAT: A Theoretical and Legal Research of the European VAT System and the Actual and Preferred Treatment of Financial Activities* (Kluwer Law International 2008)
Henkow O, 'The Commission's Proposal for a Common System of Financial Transaction Tax: A Legal Appraisal' (2012) 21 EC Tax Review 5

Héritier A, *Policy-Making and Diversity in Europe: Escape from Deadlock* (CUP 1999)
Héritier A, 'Covert Integration of Core State Powers: Renegotiating Incomplete Contracts' in Philipp Genschel and Markus Jachtenfuchs (eds), *Beyond the Regulatory Polity? The European Integration of Core State Powers* (OUP 2014)
Hernández González-Barreda PA, 'On the European Way to a Financial Transaction Tax under Enhanced Cooperation: Multi-Speed Europe or Shortcut?' (2013) 41 Intertax 208
Herolf G (ed), 'Enlargement and Flexibility—Recurrent Items on the Agenda', *EU Enlargement and Flexibility* (Utrikespolitiska Institute 1998)
Herresthal C, 'Die Ablehnung einer primärrechtlichen Perpetuierung des sekundärrechtlichen Verbraucherschutzniveaus' (2011) Europäische Zeitschrift für Wirtschaftsrecht 328
Hey J, *Harmonisierung der Unternehmensbesteuerung in Europa* (Verlag Dr Otto Schmidt 1997)
Hey J, 'CCCTB—Optionality' in Michael Lang and others (eds), *Common Consolidated Corporate Tax Base* (Linde Verlag 2008)
Hey J, 'Vorrecht des Quellenstaates und binnenmarktkonforme Besteuerung von Kapitalgesellschaften in der Europäischen Union' in Wolfgang Spindler, Klaus Tipke, and Thomas Rödder (eds), *Steuerzentrierte Rechtsberatung: Festschrift für Harald Schaumburg zum 65. Geburtstag* (Dr Otto Schmidt Verlag 2009)
Hillgruber C, '§ 61 Mehrheitsprinzip' in Hanno Kube and others (eds), *Die Leitgedanken des Rechts in der Diskussion: Symposion aus Anlass des 70. Geburtstages von Professor Dr. Dr. h.c. mult. Paul Kirchhof, Band I* (CF Müller Wissenschaft 2013)
Hillion C and Wessel RA, 'Competence Distribution in EU External Relations after ECOWAS: Clarification or Continued Fuzziness?' (2009) 46 Common Market Law Review 551
Hindelang S, *The Free Movement of Capital and Foreign Direct Investment: The Scope of Protection in EU Law* (OUP 2009)
Hinnekens L, 'Basis and Scope of Public Interest Justification of National Tax Measures Infringing Fundamental Treaty Freedoms' in Frans Vanistendael (ed), *EU Freedoms and Taxation* (IBFD 2006)
Hiort af Ornäs L and Wiberg M, 'Beskattning av finanssektorn, ett ämne på den internationella agendan' (2011) Kkattenytt 497
Hirsch G, *Das Verhältnismäßigkeitsprinzip im Gemeinschaftsrecht* (Zentrum für Europäisches Wirtschaftsrecht 1997)
Hoekman BM and Mavroidis PC, *The World Trade Organization: Law, Economics, and Politics* (2nd edn, Routledge 2016)
Hoffman L, Poddar S, and Whalley J, 'Taxation of Banking Services under a Consumption Type, Destination Basis VAT' (1987) 40 National Tax Journal 547
Hoffmeister F, 'The Contribution of EU Practice to International Law' in Marise Cremona (ed), *Developments in EU External Relations Law* (OUP 2008)
Hohenwarter-Mayr D, *Verlustverwertung im Konzern* (LexisNexis Verl ARD ORAC 2010)
Hohenwarter-Mayr D, 'Qualification of the Digital Services Tax Under Tax Treaties' (2019) 47 Intertax 140
Hollis DB, 'Unpacking the Compact Clause' (2009) 88 Texas Law Review 741
Holzinger K and Sommerer T, '"Race to the Bottom" or "Race to Brussels"? Environmental Competition in Europe' (2011) 49 Journal of Common Market Studies 315
Höpfner C and Rüthers B, 'Grundlagen einer europäischen Methodenlehre' (2009) 209 1
Horsley T, 'Reflections on the Role of the Court of Justice as the "Motor" of European Integration: Legal Limits to Judicial Lawmaking' (2013) 50 Common Market Law Review 931

Horzen F van and Esdonk A van, 'Proposed 3% Digital Services Tax' (2018) 25 International Transfer Pricing Journal 267

Hügel H, 'Grenzüberschreitende Umgründungen, Sitzverlegung und Wegzug im Lichte der Änderung der Fusionsrichtlinie und der neueren EuGH-Judikatur' in Elisabeth König and Walter Schwarzinger (eds), *Körperschaften im Steuerrecht: Festschrift für Werner Wiesner zum 65. Geburtstag* (Linde Verlag 2004)

Huiskers-Stoop E and Gribnau H, 'Cooperative Compliance and the Dutch Horizontal Monitoring Model' (2019) 5 Journal of Tax Administration 66

Hvidsten AH and Hovi J, 'Why No Twin-Track Europe? Unity, Discontent, and Differentiation in European Integration' (2015) 16 European Union Politics 3

Iacobucci E, 'The Interdependence of Trade and Competition Policies' (1997) 21 World Competition 5

Ihering T, 'Die Finanztransaktionssteuer im Rahmen der verstärkten Zusammenarbeit' (2013) Zeitschrift für das gesamte Kreditwesen 612

Immenga U and others (eds), 'Über Privatrechtsvereinheitlichung und Marktintegration', *Festschrift für Ernst-Joachim Mestmäcker: zum siebzigsten Geburtstag* (Nomos 1996)

Ipsen K, Völkerrecht (6th edn, Beck Verlag 2014)

Isenbaert M, *EC Law and the Sovereignty of the Member States in Direct Taxation* (IBFD 2010)

Ismer R and Jescheck C, 'Taxes on Digital Services and the Substantive Scope of Application of Tax Treaties: Pushing the Boundaries of Article 2 of the OECD Model?' (2018) 46 Intertax 573

Ismer R and Kandel H, 'A Finale Incomparabile to the Saga of Definitive Losses? Deduction of Foreign Losses and Fundamental Freedoms After Bevola and Sofina' (2019) 47 Intertax 573

Ismer R and Karch A, 'Das Referenzsystem bei der beihilferechtlichen Überprüfung nationaler Steuervergünstigungen' (2014) Internationales Steuerrecht 130

Ismer R and Piotrowski S, 'The Selectivity of Tax Measures: A Tale of Two Consistencies' (2015) 43 Intertax 559

Jaag T, '§ 14 Zusammenarbeit zwischen Bund und Kantonen sowie zwischen Kantonen' in Giovanni Biaggini, Thomas Gächter, and Regina Kiener (eds), *Staatsrecht* (Dike Verlag 2011)

Jacqué J-P, 'The Principle of Institutional Balance' (2004) 41 Common Market Law Review 383

Jaeger T, 'The EU Patent: Cui Bono et Quo Vadit?' (2010) 47 Common Market Law Review 63

James W, 'The Moral Philosopher and the Moral Life' (1891) 1 International Journal of Ethics 330

Jamnejad M and Wood M, 'The Principle of Non-Intervention' (2009) 22 Leiden Journal of International Law 345

Janssens C, *The Principle of Mutual Recognition in EU Law* (OUP 2013)

Jenks CW, 'The Conflict of Law-Making Treaties' (1953) British Year Book of International Law 401

Jimeno-Bulnes M, 'The Proposal for a Council Framework Decision on Certain Procedural Rights in Criminal Proceedings throughout the European Union' in Elspeth Guild and Florian Geyer (eds), *Security Versus Justice? Police and Judicial Cooperation in the European Union* (Ashgate Publishing, Ltd 2008)

Johnson N, 'Beggar-Thy-Neighbour, and Thyself?' (The Political Economy of Development, 29 March 2017) <https://peofdev.wordpress.com/2017/03/29/beggar-thy-neighbour-and-thyself/> accessed 15 December 2019

Jopp M and others (eds), 'Entscheidungseffizienz und Handlungsfähigkeit nach Nizza: die neuen Anwendungsfelder für Mehrheitsentscheidungen', *Das Vertragswerk von Nizza und die Zukunft der Europäischen Union* (Europa Union 2001)

Jozipović Š, *Die Anwendung des EU-Beihilferechts auf das internationale Steuerrecht: die wettbewerbs- und handelsrechtlichen Einflüsse auf die staatliche Fiskalsystemgestaltung* (Springer 2018)

Juncker J-C, 'State of the Union Address 2017' (European Parliament, Brussels, 12 September 2017) <http://europa.eu/rapid/press-release_SPEECH-17-3165_en.htm> accessed 3 February 2021

Jung S, 'Need for a New Approach in European Company Law?—The European Foundation as a Turning Point' (2015) 21 Trusts & Trustees 625

Kaczorowska-Ireland A, *European Union Law* (4th edn, Routledge 2016)

Kaddous C, 'The European Union's Common Values and National Identities: Convergence or Contradiction?' in Thomas Giegerich, Oskar Josef Gstrein, and Sebastian Zeitzmann (eds), *The EU between 'An Ever Closer Union' and Inalienable Policy Domains of Member States*, vol 80 (Nomos 2014)

Kamm FM, 'Equal Treatment and Equal Chances' (1985) 14 Philosophy & Public Affairs 177

Keen M and Konrad K, 'The Theory of International Tax Competition and Coordination' in Alan J Auerbach and others (eds), *Handbook of Public Economics*, vol 5 (Elsevier 2013)

Kemmeren E, 'The Termination of the "most Favoured Nation Cause" Dispute in Tax Treaty Law and the Necessity of a Euro Model Tax Convention' (1997) 6 EC Tax Review 146

Kemmeren ECCM, 'The Internal Market Approach Should Prevail over the Single Country Approach' in Luc Hinnekens and Philippe Hinnekens (eds), *A Vision of Taxes Within and Outside the European Borders: Festschrift in Honor of Prof. Dr. Frans Vanistendael* (Kluwer Law International 2008)

Kemmeren ECCM, 'Sources of EU Law for European Tax Integration: Well-Known and Alternative Legal Instruments' in Dennis Weber (ed), *Traditional and Alternative Routes to European Tax Integration: Primary Law, Secondary Law, Soft Law, Coordination, Comitology and Their Relationship* (IBFD 2010)

Kemmeren ECCM, 'CCCTB: Enhanced Speed Ahead for Improvement' (2011) 20 EC Tax Review 208

Kemmeren ECCM, 'Double Tax Conventions on Income and Capital and the EU: Past, Present and Future' (2012) 21 EC Tax Review 157

Kemmeren ECCM, 'Sopora: A Welcome Landmark Decision on Horizontal Comparison' (2015) 24 EC Tax Review 178

Kemmeren ECCM, 'The CJEU and the Internal Market Concept in Direct Taxation' in Werner Haslehner, Georg Kofler, and Alexander Rust (eds), *EU Tax Law and Policy in the 21st Century* (Kluwer Law International 2017)

Kemmeren ECCM, 'Gross Withholding Taxes: Is the Court of Justice of the European Union Back on Track with Regard to Deductible Expenses?' (2017) 26 EC Tax Review 2

Kersbergen K van and Verbeek B, 'The Politics of International Norms: Subsidiarity and the Imperfect Competence Regime of the European Union' (2007) 13 European Journal of International Relations 217

Kiiver P, *The Early Warning System for the Principle of Subsidiarity: Constitutional Theory and Empirical Reality* (Routledge 2012)

Kingston S, 'The Boundaries of Sovereignty: The ECJ's Controversial Role Applying Internal Market Law to Direct Tax Measures' (2007) 9 Cambridge Yearbook of European Legal Studies 287

Klabbers J, 'The Reception of International Law in the EU Legal Order' in Robert Schütze and Takis Tridimas (eds), *The European Union Legal Order* (OUP 2018)

Knapp B, 'Art. 44' in Bernhard Ehrenzeller and others (eds), *Die schweizerische Bundesverfassung: St. Galler Kommentar, Band I* (3rd edn, Dike Schulthess 2014)
Kofler G and Sinnig J, 'Equalization Taxes and the EU's "Digital Services Tax"' (2019) 47 Intertax 176
Kofler GW, 'Most-Favoured-Nation Treatment in Direct Taxation: Does EC Law Provide for Community MFN in Bilateral Double Taxation Treaties?' (2005) 5 Houston Business and Tax Law Journal 1
Kofler GW, *Doppelbesteuerungsabkommen und europäisches Gemeinschaftsrecht* (Linde Verlag 2007)
Kofler GW, 'Das Verhältnis zwischen primärem und sekundärem Unionsrecht im direkten Steuerrecht' in Michael Lang and Christine Weinzierl (eds), *Europäisches Steuerrecht—Festschrift für Friedrich Rödler* (Linde Verlag 2010)
Kofler GW, 'Double Taxation and European Law: Analysis of the Jurisprudence' in Alexander Rust (ed), *Double Taxation within the European Union* (Kluwer Law International 2011)
Kofler GW, 'Tax Treaty "Neutralization" of Source State Discrimination under the EU Fundamental Freedoms?' (2011) 65 Bulletin for International Taxation 684
Kofler GW, 'Foreign Losses and Territoriality: Did Sofina Revolutionize Source-State Taxation?' in Servaas van Thiel, Piergiorgio Valente, and Stella Raventós-Calvo (eds), *CFE Tax Advisers Europe: 60th Anniversary Liber Amicorum* (IBFD 2019)
Kofler GW, 'Grenzüberschreitende Verlustverwertung im Quellenstaat: Stellt Sofina die beschränkte Steuerpflicht auf den Kopf?' in Dietmar Gosch, Arne Schnitger, and Wolfgang Schön (eds), *Festschrift für Jürgen Lüdicke* (Beck Verlag 2019)
Kofler GW and Mason R, 'Double Taxation: A European Switch in Time' (2007) 14 Columbia Journal of European Law 63
Kofler GW and Schindler CP, '"Dancing with Mr D": The ECJ's Denial of Most-Favoured-Nation Treatment in the "D" Case' (2005) 45 European Taxation 530
Kofler GW and Sinnig J, 'Equalization Taxes and the EU's "Digital Services Tax"' in Werner Haslehner and others (eds), *Tax and the Digital Economy: Challenges and Proposals for Reform* (Kluwer Law International 2019)
Kokott J, 'Steuerrecht und unionsrechtlicher Beihilfebegriff' in Michael Lang (ed), *Europäisches Steuerrecht*, vol 42 (Dr Otto Schmidt Verlag 2018)
Kokott J, 'The "Genuine Link" Requirement for Source Taxation in Public International Law' in Werner Haslehner and others (eds), *Tax and the Digital Economy: Challenges and Proposals for Reform* (Kluwer Law International 2019)
Kokott J and Ost H, 'Europäische Grundfreiheiten und nationales Steuerrecht' (2011) Europäische Zeitschrift für Wirtschaftsrecht 496
Kokott J and Sobotta C, 'The Evolution of the Principle of Proportionality in EU Law - Towards an Anticipative Understanding?' in Stefan Vogenauer and Stephen Weatherill (eds), *General Principles of Law: European and Comparative Perspectives* (Hart Publishing 2017)
Kōno T, *Efficiency in Private International Law* (Hague Academy of International Law 2014)
Konrad K and Stolper TBM, 'Coordination and the Fight against Tax Havens' (2016) 103 Journal of International Economics 96
Konstadinides T, *Division of Powers in European Union Law: The Delimitation of Internal Competence between the EU and the Member States* (Kluwer Law International 2009)
Korte S, 'AEUV Art. 115' in Christian Calliess and Matthias Ruffert (eds), *EUV/AEUV* (5th edn, Beck Verlag 2016)
Kortenberg H, 'Closer Cooperation in the Treaty of Amsterdam' (1998) 35 Common Market Law Review 833

Kosta V, *Fundamental Rights in EU Internal Market Legislation* (Hart Publishing 2015)
Kosta V, 'The Principle of Proportionality in EU Law—An Interest-Based Taxonomy' in Joana Mendes (ed), *EU Executive Discretion and the Limits of Law* (OUP 2019)
Köster T, 'Subsidarität als Lebenselixier für Europa—Statement' in Handwerkskammer Düsseldorf (ed), *Welche Chancen hat Subsidiarität in Europa?*, vol 5 (Verlagsanstalt Handwerk 2014)
Kramer L, 'On the Need for a Uniform Choice of Law Code' (1991) 89 Michigan Law Review 2134
Krislov S, Ehlermann C-D, and Weiler JHH, 'The Political Organs and the Decision-Making Process in the United States and the European Community' in Mauro Cappelletti, Monica Seccombe, and Joseph HH Weiler (eds), *Integration Through Law: Europe and the American Federal Experience*, vol 1 (Walter de Gruyter & Co 1985)
Kroll DA and Leuffen D, 'Enhanced Cooperation in Practice. An Analysis of Differentiated Integration in EU Secondary Law' (2015) 22 Journal of European Public Policy 353
Krolop K, 'European Company Law' in Karl Riesenhuber (ed), *European Legal Methodology* (Intersentia 2017)
Krugman P, 'Regionalism versus Multilateralism: Analytical Notes' in Jaime de Melo and Arvind Panagariya (eds), *New Dimensions in Regional Integration* (CUP 1993)
Kube H, Reimer E, and Spengel C, 'Tax Policy: Trends in the Allocation of Powers Between the Union and Its Member States' (2016) 25 EC Tax Review 247
Kuiper PJ, 'Case C-386/08, Brita GmbH v. Hauptzollamt Hamburg-Hafen Judgment of the European Court of Justice of 25 February 2010' (2010) 37 Legal Issues of Economic Integration 241
Kuipers J-J, 'The Law Applicable to Divorce as Test Ground for Enhanced Cooperation' (2012) 18 European Law Journal 201
Lamers K and Schäuble W, 'Reflections on European Policy' (1994) European Documents 1895/96
Lamping M, 'Enhanced Cooperation—A Proper Approach to Market Integration in the Field of Unitary Patent Protection?' (2011) 42 International Review of Intellectual Property and Competition Law 879
Lang JT, 'The Gibraltar State Aid and Taxation Judgment—A Methodical Revolution' (2012) 11 European State Aid Law Quarterly 805
Lang M, 'Das EuGH-Urteil in der Rechtssache D. —Gerät der Motor der Steuerharmonisierung ins Stottern?' (2005) Steuer und Wirtschaft International 356
Lang M, 'Doppelbelastung und Doppelbefreiung im grenzüberschreitenden Steuerrecht' in Ulrich Becker and Fredrik Andersson (eds), *Steuer- und Sozialstaat im europäischen Systemwettbewerb* (Mohr Siebeck 2005)
Lang M, 'Eine Wende in der Rechtsprechung des EuGH zu den direkten Steuern?' in Michael Hebig, Wilhelm H Wacker and Peter Bareis (eds), *Aktuelle Entwicklungsaspekte der Unternehmensbesteuerung: Festschrift für Wilhelm H. Wacker zum 75. Geburtstag* (Erich Schmidt Verlag 2006)
Lang M, 'The Marks & Spencer Case—The Open Issues Following the ECJ's Final Word' (2006) 60 Bulletin for International Taxation 54
Lang M, 'Limitation of the Temporal Effects of Judgments of the ECJ' in Dennis Weber (ed), *The Influence of European Law on Direct Taxation: Recent and Future Developments* (Kluwer Law International 2007)
Lang M, 'ECJ Case Law on Cross-Border Dividend Taxation—Recent Developments' (2008) 17 EC Tax Review 67
Lang M, *Die Auswirkungen des gemeinschaftsrechtlichen Beihilferechts auf das Steuerrecht: Gutachten* (Manz Verlag 2009)

Lang M, 'Recent Case Law of the ECJ in Direct Taxation: Trends, Tensions, and Contradictions' (2009) 18 EC Tax Review 98
Lang M, 'Seminar J: Steuerrecht, Grundfreiheiten und Beihilfeverbot' (2010) Internationales Steuerrecht 570
Lang M, 'Cadbury Schweppes' Line of Case Law from the Member States' Perspective' in Rita de la Féria and Stefan Vogenauer (eds), *Prohibition of Abuse of Law: A New General Principle of EU Law?* (OUP 2011)
Lang M, 'Kapitalverkehrsfreiheit, Steuerrecht und Drittstaaten' (2011) Steuer und Wirtschaft 209
Lang M, 'State Aid and Taxation: Recent Trends in the Case Law of the ECJ' (2012) 11 European State Aid Law Quarterly 411
Lang M, *Introduction to the Law of Double Taxation Conventions* (2nd edn, Linde Verlag 2013)
Lang M, 'Has the Case Law of the ECJ on Final Losses Reached the End of the Line?' (2014) 54 European Taxation 530
Lang M, 'State Aid and Taxation: Selectivity and Comparability Analysis' in Isabelle Richelle, Wolfgang Schön, and Edoardo Traversa (eds), *State Aid Law and Business Taxation* (Springer 2016)
Lang M, 'There Is Life in the Old Dog Yet: Horizontal Comparability and the Establishment of the Internal Marke' in Reuven S Avi-Yonah and Michael Lang (eds), *Comparative Fiscal Federalism* (2nd edn, Kluwer Law International 2016)
Lang M, 'Totgesagte leben länger: Horizontale Vergleichbarkeit und die Verwirklichung des Binnenmarkts' (2016) 26 Steuer und Wirtschaft International 118
Lang M, 'Normenkonflikte zwischen den Vorschriften des nationalen Steuerrechts und der Doppelbesteuerungsabkomme' in Dietmar Gosch, Arne Schnitger, and Wolfgang Schön (eds), *Festschrift für Jürgen Lüdicke* (Beck Verlag 2019)
Lang M, 'Direct Taxation: Is the ECJ Heading in a New Direction?' (2006) 46 European Taxation 421
Lang M and Heidenbauer S, 'Wholly Artificial Arrangements' in Luc Hinnekens and Frans Vanistendael (eds), *A Vision of Taxes Within and Outside the European Borders: Festschrift in Honor of Prof. Dr. Frans Vanistendael* (Kluwer Law International 2008)
Langeheine B, 'Abgestufte Integration' (1983) Europarecht 227
Langenbucher K, 'Argument by Analogy in European Law' (1998) 57 The Cambridge Law Journal 481
Law J, 'Right' in Jonathan Law (ed), *A Dictionary of Law* (OUP 2018)
Law J and Martin EA (eds), *Oxford Dictionary of Law* (7th edn, OUP 2013)
Lederman WR, 'Some Forms and Limitations of Co-Operative Federalism' (1967) 45 Canadian Bar Review 409
Lehner M, 'The Influence of EU Law on Tax Treaties from a German Perspective' (2000) 54 Bulletin for International Taxation 461
Leibholz G, 'Das Verbot der Willkür und des Ermessensmißbrauches im völkerrechtlichen Verkehr der Staaten' (1929) 1 Zeitschrift für ausländisches öffentliches Recht und Völkerrecht 77
Leino P, 'The Politics of Efficient Compromise in the Adoption of EU Legal Acts' in Marise Cremona and Claire Kilpatrick (eds), *EU Legal Acts: Challenges and Transformations*, vol XXV/4 (1st edn, OUP 2018)
Lenaerts K, 'Les répercussions des compétences de la Communauté européenne sur les compétences externes des États membres et la question de "preemption"' in Paul Demaret (ed), *Relations extérieures de la Communauté Européenne et marché intérieur: aspects juridiques et fonctionnels* (Story-Scientia 1988)

Lenaerts K, 'The Principle of Subsidiarity and the Environment in the European Union: Keeping the Balance of Federalism' (1993) 17 Fordham International Law Journal 846
Lenaerts K, 'Die gemeinschaftsrechtliche Umrahmung der direkten Besteuerung', *Verhandlungen des 66. Deutschen Juristentages*, vol II/1 (Beck Verlag 2006)
Lenaerts K, '"United in Diversity"—Also in Fiscalibus?' in Luc Hinnekens and Frans Vanistendael (eds), *A Vision of Taxes Within and Outside the European Borders: Festschrift in Honor of Prof. Dr. Frans Vanistendael* (Kluwer Law International 2008)
Lenaerts K, 'The Court's Outer and Inner Selves: Exploring the External and Internal Legitimacy of the European Court of Justice' in Maurice Adams and others (eds), *Judging Europe's Judges: The Legitimacy of the Case Law of the European Court of Justice* (Hart Publishing 2013)
Lenaerts K and Corthaut T, 'Of Birds and Hedges: The Role of Primacy in Invoking Norms of EU Law' (2006) 31 European Law Review 287
Lenaerts K and Desomer M, 'Towards a Hierarchy of Legal Acts in the European Union? Simplification of Legal Instruments and Procedures' (2005) 11 European Law Journal 744
Lenaerts K and Van Nuffel P, *European Union Law* (3rd edn, Sweet & Maxwell 2011)
Liepe J, Pielka H, and Malaviya N, 'Der aktuelle Richtlinienentwurf zur Finanztransaktionssteuer im Lichte des europäischen Rechts' (2013) Zeitschrift für Wirtschafts- und Bankrecht, 1344
Ligeti K and Simonato M, 'The European Public Prosecutor's Office: Towards a Truly European Prosecution Service?' (2013) 4 New Journal of European Criminal Law 7
Lignier C and Geier A, 'Die Verstärkte Zusammenarbeit in der Europäischen Union – Politischer Hintergrund, Bestandsaufnahme und Zukunftsperspektiven' (2015) 79 Rabels Zeitschrift für ausländisches und internationales Privatrecht (RabelsZ) 546
Lijphart A, 'Consociational Democracy' (1969) 21 World Politics 207
Lijphart A, 'The Power-Sharing Approach' in Joseph V Montville (ed), *Conflict and Peacemaking in Multiethnic Societies* (Lexington Books 1990)
Lijphart A, 'Consensus and Consensus Democracy: Cultural, Structural, Functional, and Rational-Choice Explanations' (1998) 21 Scandinavian Political Studies 99
Linde R van der, 'Some Thoughts on Most-Favoured-Nation Treatment within the European Community Legal Order in Pursuance of the D Case' (2004) 13 EC Tax Review 10
Lively J, *Democracy* (Blackwell 1975)
López FJQ, 'Análisis de las reformas en el Espacio de Libertad, Seguridad y Justicia en el Tratado de Niza' (2007) Revista de Derecho Comunitario Europeo 117
Lüdicke J, 'European Tax Law, Quo Vadis?' (2008) 62 Bulletin for International Fiscal Documentation 8
Luja R, 'Group Taxation, Sectoral Tax Benefits and De Facto Selectivity in State Aid Review' (2009) 8 European State Aid Law Quarterly 473
Luja R, 'Revisiting the Balance between Aid, Selectivity and Selective Aid in Respect of Taxes and Special Levies' (2010) 9 European State Aid Law Quarterly 161
Luja R, '(Re)Shaping Fiscal State Aid: Selected Recent Cases and Their Impact' (2012) 40 Intertax 120
Luja R, 'Do State Aid Rules Still Allow European Union Member States to Claim Fiscal Sovereignty?' (2016) 25 EC Tax Review 312
Lustick I, 'Stability in Deeply Divided Societies: Consociationalism versus Control' (1979) 31 World Politics 325
Luther KR and Müller WC, *Politics in Austria: Still a Case of Consociationalism?* (Psychology Press 1992)
Luts J, 'Compatibility of IP Box Regimes with EU State Aid Rules and Code of Conduct' (2014) 23 EC Tax Review 258

Lyal R, 'Non-Discrimination and Direct Tax in Community Law' (2003) 12 EC Tax Review 68

Lyons C, 'Flexibility and the European Court of Justice' in Gráinne de Búrca and Joanne Scott (eds), *Constitutional Change in the EU: From Uniformity to Flexibility?* (Hart Publishing 2000)

Maduro MP, 'Reforming the Market or the State Article 30 and the European Constitution: Economic Freedom and Political Rights' (1997) European Law Journal 55

Maduro MP, *We the Court: The European Court of Justice and the European Economic Constitution* (Hart Publishing 1998)

Maletič I, *The Law and Policy of Harmonisation in Europe's Internal Market* (Edward Elgar Publishing 2013)

Manin B, 'On Legitimacy and Political Deliberation' (1987) 15 Political Theory 338

Mankowski P, *Interessenpolitik und europäisches Kollisionsrecht: rechtspolitische Überlegungen zur Rom I- und zur Rom II-Verordnung* (Nomos 2011)

Marchetti J, Roy M, and Zoratto L, 'Is There Reciprocity in Preferential Trade Agreements on Services?' (2012) WTO Staff Working Paper

Marchgraber C, *Double (Non-)Taxation and EU Law* (Kluwer Law International 2018)

Markakis M, 'Can Governments Control Mass Layoffs by Employers? Economic Freedoms vs Labour Rights in Case C-201/15 AGET Iraklis' (2017) 13 European Constitutional Law Review 724

Marquardsen M, *Einstimmigkeit in Steuerfragen—Reformbedarf?* vol 534 (ifst-Schrift 2020)

Marres O, 'The Principle of Territoriality and Cross-Border Loss Compensation' (2011) 39 Intertax 112

Martenczuk B, 'Die differenzierte Integration nach dem Vertrag von Amsterdam' (1998) Zeitschrift für Europarechtliche Studien 447

Martens SAE, *Methodenlehre des Unionsrechts* (Mohr Siebeck 2013)

Martha RS, *The Jurisdiction to Tax in International Law: Theory and Practice of Legislative Fiscal Jurisdiction* (Kluwer Law International 1989)

Martin P, 'Dividends and Withholding Taxes' in Guglielmo Maisto (ed), *Taxation of Intercompany Dividends under Tax Treaties and EU Law* (IBFD 2012)

Mason R, 'Flunking the ECJ's Tax Discrimination Test' (2007) 46 Columbia Journal of Transnational Law 72

Mason R, 'A Political-Process Defense of Deutsche Bahn Deference' (2018) Virginia Law and Economics Research Paper No. 201

Mason R and Knoll MS, 'What Is Tax Discrimination' (2011) 121 Yale Law Journal 1014

Mason R and Knoll MS, 'A Brief Sur-Reply to Professors Graetz and Warren' <https://www.yalelawjournal.org/forum/a-brief-sur-reply-to-professors-graetz-and-warren> accessed 15 December 2019

Mason R and Parada L, 'Digital Battlefront in the Tax Wars' (2018) 92 Tax Notes International 1183

Mason R and Parada L, 'Company Size Matters' (2019) British Tax Review 610

Matsushita M, 'Japanese Policies toward East Asian Free Trade Agreements: Policy and Legal Perspectives' in Ross P Buckley, Vai Io Lo, and Laurence Boulle (eds), *Challenges to Multilateral Trade: The Impact of Bilateral, Preferential and Regional Agreements* (Wolters Kluwer Law & Business 2008)

Mattera A, 'The Principle of Mutual Recognition and Respect for National, Regional and Local Identities and Traditions' in Fiorella Kostoris Padoa Schioppa (ed), *The Principle of Mutual Recognition in the European Integration Process* (Palgrave Macmillan 2005)

Mattsson N, 'Does the European Court of Justice Understand the Policy behind Tax Benefits Based on Personal and Family Circumstances?' (2003) 43 European Taxation 186

Maurer A, 'Reformziel Effizienzsteigerung und Demokratisierung: Die Weiterentwicklung der Entscheidungsmechanismen' in Mathias Jopp and Otto Schmuck (eds), *Die Reform der Europäischen Union—Analysen, Positionen, Dokument* (Bundeszentrale für politische Bildung 1996)

Mayer FC and Heidfeld C, 'Europarechtliche Aspekte einer Finanztransaktionsteuer' (2011) Europäische Zeitschrift für Wirtschaftsrecht 373

Mayr G, 'Austria—New Digital Business Tax on Online Advertising in Austria' (2019) 59 European Taxation 350

McCrea R, 'Forward or Back: The Future of European Integration and the Impossibility of the Status Quo' (2017) 23 European Law Journal 66

McLure CE Jr, 'Legislative, Judicial, Soft Law, and Cooperative Approaches to Harmonizing Corporate Income Taxes in the US and the EU' (2007) 14 Columbia Journal of European Law 377

Meessen KM, 'The Application of Rules of Public International Law within Community Law' (1976) 13 Common Market Law Review 485

Meij AWH and Winter JA, 'Measures Having an Effect Equivalent to Quantitative Restrictions' (1976) 13 Common Market Law Review 79

Menéndez AJ, 'European Citizenship after Martínez Sala and Baumbast. Has European Law Become More Human but Less Social?' (2009) ARENA Working Papers https://www.sv.uio.no/arena/english/research/publications/arena-working-papers/2001-2010/2009/WP11_09_Online.pdf

Metaxas A, 'Selectivity of Asymmetrical Tax Measures and Distortion of Competition in the Telecoms Sector: An Analysis on the Legality of the Duty Imposed in Greece on Mobile Network Operators' Subscribers under EU State Aid Rules' (2010) 9 European State Aid Law Quarterly 771

Meurs C, *Normenhierarchien im europäischen Sekundärrecht* (Mohr Siebeck 2012)

Meussen GTK, 'Denkavit Internationaal: The Practical Issues' (2007) 47 European Taxation 244

Meussen GTK, 'Horizontal Discrimination and EU Law: The Sopora Case' (2014) 54 European Taxation 322

Meuwese ACM, *Impact Assessment in EU Lawmaking* (Kluwer Law International BV 2008)

Michaels R and Paulwelyn J, 'Conflict of Norms or Conflict of Laws: Different Techniques in the Fragmentation of Public International Law' (2011) 22 Duke Journal of Comparative & International Law 349

Micheau C, 'Fundamental Freedoms and State Aid Rules under EU Law: The Example of Taxation' (2012) 52 European Taxation 210

Miglio A, 'Differentiated Integration and the Principle of Loyalty' (2018) 14 European Constitutional Law Review 475

Moran B, 'Wealth Redistribution and the Income Tax' (2009) 53 Howard Law Journal 319

Mörsdorf O, 'Der Entwurf einer Richtlinie für grenzüberschreitende Umwandlungen—Meilenstein oder Scheinriese?' (2019) Europäische Zeitschrift für Wirtschaftsrecht 141

Mortelmans K, 'The Relationship Between the Treaty Rules and Community Measures for the Establishment and Functioning of the Internal Market—Towards a Concordance Rule' (2002) 39 Common Market Law Review 1303

Mössner M, 'Source versus Residence—an EU Perspective' (2006) 60 Bulletin for International Taxation 501

Möstl M, 'Grenzen der Rechtsangleichung im europäischen Binnenmarkt—Kompetenzielle, grundfreiheitliche und grundrechtliche Schranken des Gemeinschaftsgesetzgebers' (2002) Europarecht 318

Möstl M, 'Preconditions and Limits of Mutual Recognition' (2010) 47 Common Market Law Review 405

Mulder J, 'Responsive Adjudication and the "Social Legitimacy" of the Internal Market: Social Legitimacy of EU Free Movement Adjudication' (2016) 22 European Law Journal 597

Müller M, *Systemwettbewerb, Harmonisierung und Wettbewerbsverzerrung: Europa zwischen einem Wettbewerb der Gesetzgeber und vollständiger Harmonisierung* (Nomos 2000)

Müller-Graff P-C, 'Die Rechtsangleichung zur Verwirklichung des Binnenmarktes' (1989) Europarecht 107

Müller-Graff P-C, 'Privatrechtsangleichung durch die EG im Schnittfeld von Sachenrecht und Kollisionsrecht' in Ole Lando, Ulrich Magnus, and Monika Novak-Stief (eds), *Angleichung des materiellen und des internationalen Privatrechts in der EU* (Peter Lang 2003)

Müller-Graff P-C, 'Differenzierte Integration: Konzept mit sprengender oder unitarisierender Kraft für die Europäische Union?' (2007) 30 Integration 129

Müller-Graff P-C and Weidenfeld W, 'Die Kompetenzen in der Europäischen Union', *Europa Handbuch: Band I: Die Europäische Union—Politisches System und Politikbereiche* (4th edn, Verlag Bertelsmann Stiftung 2006)

Murphy DT, 'Closer or Enhanced Cooperation: Amsterdam or Nice' (2003) 31 Georgia Journal of International and Comparative Law 265

Murphy L and Nagel T, *The Myth of Ownership: Taxes and Justice* (OUP 2002)

Nanclares JMYPD, 'La flexibilidad en el Tratado de Amsterdam: especial referencia a la noción de cooperación reforzada' (2007) Revista de Derecho Comunitario Europeo 205

Nanz K-P, 'Das Schengener Übereinkommen: Personenfreizügigkeit in integrationspolitischer Perspektive' (1994) Integration 92

Naurin D, 'The Councils of the EU: Intergovernmental Bargaining in a Supranational Polity' in Jeremy Richardson and Sonia Mazey (eds), *European Union: Power and Policy-making* (4th edn, Routledge 2015)

Nettesheim M, 'Normenhierarchien im EU-Recht' (2006) Europarecht 737

Nettesheim M, 'Kompetenzen' in Armin von Bogdandy and Jürgen Bast (eds), *Europäisches Verfassungsrecht: theoretische und dogmatische Grundzüge* (2nd edn, Springer 2009)

Neyt R and Peeters S, 'Balanced Allocation and Coherence: Some Thoughts in Light of Argenta and K' (2014) 23 EC Tax Review 64

Niazi SUK, 'Re-Launch of the Proposal for a Common Consolidated Corporate Tax Base (CCCTB) in the EU: A Shift in Paradigm' (2017) 44 Legal Issues of Economic Integration 293

Nicolaides P, 'The Economics of Subsidies for R&D: The Intrinsic Difficulty of Determining Optimum Subsidies and Implications for Reform of EU State Aid Rules on R & D' (2013) Bruges European Economic Research Papers 19

Nicolaides P and Metaxas A, 'Asymmetric Tax Measures and EU State Aid Law' (2014) 13 European State Aid Law Quarterly 51

Niesten H, 'Growing Impetus for Harmonization of Personal and Family Allowances: Current State of Affairs of the Schumacker-Doctrine after Imfeld and Garcet' (2015) 24 EC Tax Review 185

Niesten H, 'Case X v. Staatssecretaris van Financiën: Fractional Allocation of Personal and Family Tax Benefits for EU Resident Individuals with Multi-State Income' (2017) 26 EC Tax Review 201

Niesten H, 'Personal and Family Tax Benefits in the EU Internal Market: From Schumacker to Fractional Tax Treatment' (2018) 55 Common Market Law Review 819

Niesten H, 'Pro Rata Deduction of Negative Income from Income Received in Each Member State' (2018) 58 European Taxation 116

Niglia L, 'Eclipse of the Constitution {Europe Nouveau Siècle}' (2016) 22 European Law Journal 132

Nocete Correa FJ, 'The Spanish Digital Services Tax: A Paradigm for the Base Enlargement & Profit Attraction (BEPA) Plan for the Digitalized Economy' (2019) 59 European Taxation 341

Noriega AE de, *The EU Principle of Subsidiarity and Its Critique* (OUP 2002)

Norris P, 'Stable Democracy and Good Governance in Divided Societies: Do Powersharing Institutions Work?' (2005) Harvard University Faculty Research Working Papers Series https://www.hks.harvard.edu/publications/stable-democracy-and-good-governance-divided-societies-do-power-sharing-institutions

Novak S, 'Qualified Majority Voting from the Single European Act to Present Day: An Unexpected Permanence' Notre Europe—Research Paper https://institutdelors.eu/wp-content/uploads/2018/01/etud88_en-qualifiedmajority-voting-novak.pdf

Odermatt J, 'The Use of International Treaty Law by the Court of Justice of the European Union' (2015) 17 Cambridge Yearbook of European Legal Studies 121

O'Donoghue C and Sutherland H, 'Accounting for the Family in European Income Tax Systems' (1999) 23 Cambridge Journal of Economics 565

Olson M, *Logic of Collective Action: Public Goods and the Theory of Groups* (Harvard University Press 2009)

Ooik R van, 'Cross-Pillar Litigation before the ECJ: Demarcation of Community and Union Competences' (2008) 4 European Constitutional Law Review 399

Ost N, 'Flexibilitat des Gemeinschaftsrechts—Vom Notantrieb zum Vertragsprinzip?' (1997) Die Öffentliche Verwaltung 495

Osterloh-Konrad C, 'Zur Legitimation steuerlicher Umverteilung' (2017) Steuer und Wirtschaft 305

Osterloh-Konrad C, Heber C, and Beuchert T, *Anzeigepflichten für Steuergestaltungen in Deutschland: verfassungs- und europarechtliche Grenzen sowie Überlegungen zur Ausgestaltung* (Springer 2017)

Panayi C, 'The Anti-Abuse Rules of the CCCTB' (2012) 66 Bulletin for International Taxation 256

Panayi C, 'CFC Rules within the CCCTB' in Michael Lang and others (eds), *Corporate Income Taxation in Europe: The Common Consolidated Corporate Tax Base (CCTB) and Third Countries* (Edward Elgar 2013)

Panayi C, *European Union Corporate Tax Law* (CUP 2013)

Panayi C, 'The EU's Financial Transaction Tax, Enhanced Cooperation and the UK's Challenge—IBFD' (2013) 53 European Taxation 358

Panayi C, 'The ATAD CFC Rule and Its Impact on the Existing Regimes of EU Member States' in Pasquale Pistone and Dennis Weber (eds), *The Implementation of Anti-BEPS Rules in the EU: A Comprehensive Study* (IBFD 2018)

Papp M, 'Member State Interests and EU Internal Market Law' in Marton Varju (ed), *Between Compliance and Particularism: Member State Interests and European Union Law* (Springer 2019)

Pauwelyn J, *Conflict of Norms in Public International Law: How WTO Law Relates to Other Rules of International Law* (CUP 2008)

Payandeh M, 'Constitutional Review of EU Law after Honeywell Contextualizing the Relationship between the German Constitutional Court and the EU Court of Justice' (2011) 48 Common Market Law Review 9

Pechstein M, 'Art. 327 AEUV' in Rudolf Streinz (ed), *EUV/AEUV Vertrag über die Europäische Union, Vertrag über die Arbeitsweise der Europäischen Union, Charta der Grundrechte der Europäischen Union* (3rd edn, Beck Verlag 2018)

Peers S, 'The Constitutional Implications of the EU Patent' (2011) 7 European Constitutional Law Review 229

Peers S, 'The Future of EU Treaty Amendments' (2012) 31 Yearbook of European Law 17

Peers S, 'Towards a New Form of EU Law?: The Use of EU Institutions Outside the EU Legal Framework' (2013) 9 European Constitutional Law Review 37

Peers S, 'Enhanced Cooperation: The Cinderella of Differentiated Integration' in Bruno de Witte, Andrea Ott, and Ellen Vos (eds), *Between Flexibility and Disintegration—The Trajectory of Differentiation in EU Law* (Edward Elgar 2017)

Peeters B, 'Mobility of EU Citizens and Family Taxation: A Hard to Reconcile Combination' (2014) 23 EC Tax Review 118

Peeters B, 'EUCIT: For How Much Longer Will Political Objections Outweigh the Advantages?' (2015) 24 EC Tax Review 128

Peeters B, 'Kieback: When Schumacker Emigrates . . .' (2016) 25 EC Tax Review 58

Peeters B and Verschueren H, 'The Impact of European Union Law on the Interaction of Members States' Sovereign Powers in the Policy Fields of Social Protection and Personal Income Tax Benefits' (2016) 25 EC Tax Review 262

Peeters S, 'Exit Taxation: From an Internal Market Barrier to a Tax Avoidance Prevention Tool' (2017) 26 EC Tax Review 122

Pelkmans J, 'Mutual Recognition in Goods and Services: An Economic Perspective' (2003) European Network of Economic Policy Research Institutes Working Paper No 16 <https://www.ceps.eu/publications/mutual-recognition-goods-and-services-economic-perspective> accessed 18 March 2018

Perau G, *Werbeverbote im Gemeinschaftsrecht: gemeinschaftsrechtliche Grenzen nationaler und gemeinschaftsrechtlicher Werbebeschränkungen* (Nomos 1997)

Perez-Bernabeu B, 'Refining the Derogation Test on Material Tax Selectivity: The Equality Test' (2017) 16 European State Aid Law Quarterly 582

Peters A, 'The Position of International Law within the European Community Legal Order Focus Section: Recent Developments in the Application of International Law in Domestic and European Community Law' (1997) 40 German Yearbook of International Law 9

Peters C, *On the Legitimacy of International Tax Law*, vol 31 (IBFD 2014)

Peters C, 'Tax Policy Convergence and EU Fiscal State Aid Control: In Search of Rationality' (2019) 28 EC Tax Review 6

Petite M, 'The Treaty of Amsterdam' (1998) Harvard Jean Monnet Chair Working Paper <www.jeanmonnetprogram.org/archive/papers/98/98-2-.rtf> accessed 3 February 2021

Petrakis PE, Kostis PC, and Valsamis DG, *European Economics and Politics in the Midst of the Crisis: From the Outbreak of the Crisis to the Fragmented European Federation* (Springer Science & Business Media 2014)

Philippart E, 'Un nouveau mécanisme de coopération renforcée pour l'Union européenne élargie' (2003) Notre Europe <https://institutdelors.eu/wp-content/uploads/2020/08/etud22-fr.pdf>

Philippart E and Edwards G, 'The Provisions on Closer Co-Operation in the Treaty of Amsterdam: The Politics of Flexibility in the European Union' (1999) 37 Journal of Common Market Studies 87

Piergiorgio V, 'The Italian Web Tax from a National and International Perspective' (2018) 58 European Taxation 186

Piernas Lopez JJ, 'Revisiting Some Fundamentals of Fiscal Selectivity: The ANGED Case - Case Law Annotation by Juan Jorge Piernas López' (2018) 17 European State Aid Law Quarterly 274

Piketty T, *Le capital au XXIe siècle* (Éditions du Seuil 2013)

Piketty T, *Capital in the Twenty-First Century* (Harvard University Press 2014)

Pila J, 'The European Patent: An Old and Vexing' (2013) 62 International & Comparative Law Quarterly 917

Pincus M, 'When Should Interstate Compacts Require Congressional Consent?' (2009) 42 Columbia Journal of Law & Social Problems 511

Piris J-C, *The Future of Europe: Towards a Two-Speed EU?* (CUP 2011)

Pistone P, *The Impact of Community Law on Tax Treaties: Issues and Solutions* (Kluwer Law International 2002)

Pistone P, 'Expected and Unexpected Developments of European Integration in the Field of Direct Taxes' (2007) 35 Intertax 70

Pistone P, 'European Direct Tax Law: Quo Vadis?' in Luc Hinnekens and Frans Vanistendael (eds), *A Vision of Taxes Within and Outside the European Borders: Festschrift in Honor of Prof. Dr. Frans Vanistendael* (Kluwer Law International 2008)

Pistone P, 'The Growing Importance of the Prohibition of State Aids in Tax Matters' (2012) 40 Intertax 84

Pistone P, 'A Plea for Qualified Majority Voting and the Ordinary Legislative Procedure in European Tax Law' in Servaas van Thiel, Piergiorgio Valente, and Stella Raventós-Calvo (eds), *CFE Tax Advisers Europe: 60th Anniversary Liber Amicorum* (IBFD 2019)

Poddar S, 'VAT on Financial Services, Searching for a Workable Alternative' in Richard E Krever and David Ian White (eds), *GST in Retrospect and Prospect* (Thomson Brookers 2007)

Pollack MA, 'The End of Creeping Competence? EU Policy-Making since Maastricht' (2000) 38 Journal of Common Market Studies 519

Portuese A, 'Principle of Proportionality as Principle of Economic Efficiency' (2013) 19 European Law Journal 612

Pötgens FPG and others, 'The Compatibility of Exit Tax Legislation Applicable to Corporate Taxpayers in France, Germany, Italy, The Netherlands, Portugal, Spain and The United Kingdom with the EU Freedom of Establishment—Part 1' (2016) 44 Intertax 163

Pötgens FPG and others, 'The Compatibility of Exit Tax Legislation Applicable to Corporate Taxpayers in France, Germany, Italy, The Netherlands, Portugal, Spain and The United Kingdom with the EU Freedom of Establishment—Part 2' (2016) 44 Intertax 247

Pöttering H-G, 'Ludwig Erhard und Europa' (2017) Die Politische Meinung, https://www.kas.de/de/web/die-politische-meinung/artikel/detail/-/content/ludwig-erhard-und-europa1

Proelss A, 'The Personal Dimension: Challenges to the Pacta Tertiis Rule' in Christian Tams, Antonios Tzanakopoulos, and Andreas Zimmermann (eds), *Research Handbook on the Law of Treaties* (Edward Elgar 2014)

Proelss A, 'Article 34 - General Rule Regarding Third States' in Oliver Dörr and Kirsten Schmalenbach (eds), *Vienna Convention on the Law of Treaties: A Commentary* (Springer 2018)

Quigley C, 'Direct Taxation and State Aid: Recent Developments Concerning the Notion of Selectivity' (2012) 40 Intertax 112

Quigley C, *European State Aid Law and Policy* (3rd edn, Hart Publishing 2015)

Rädler A, 'Tax Treaties and the Internal Market', Report of the Committee of independent experts on company taxation (Ruling Report), Annex 6 (1992) https://op.europa.eu/en/publication-detail/-/publication/0044caf0-58ff-4be6-bc06-be2af6610870

Rädler A, 'Most-Favoured-Nation Clause in European Tax Law?' (1995) 4 EC Tax Review 66

Raepenbusch S van and Hanf D, 'Flexibility in Social Policy' in Bruno de Witte, Dominik Hanf, and Ellen Vos (eds), *The Many Faces of Differentiation in EU Law* (Intersentia 2001)

Raible M, *Protektionismusverbote im Recht der Wirtschaftsintegration: eine vergleichende Untersuchung der Regelung des Freihandels im Recht der USA, der EU und der WTO* (Nomos 2006)

Reich N, 'How Proportionate Is the Proportionality Principle? Some Critical Remarks on the Use and Methodology of the Proportionality Principle in the Internal Market Case Law of the ECJ' in Hans-Wolfgang Micklitz and Bruno de Witte (eds), *The European Court of Justice and the Autonomy of the Member States* (Intersentia 2012)

Reimer E, 'Taxation—an Area without Mutual Recognition?' in Isabelle Richelle, Wolfgang Schön, and Edoardo Traversa (eds), *Allocating Taxing Powers within the European Union* (Springer 2013)

Richter W, 'Mehrheitsbeschlüsse in der europäischen Steuerpolitik?' (2019) Ökonomenstimme <https://www.oekonomenstimme.org/artikel/2019/05/mehrheitsbeschluesse-in-der-europaeischen-steuerpolitik/> accessed 3 February 2021

Riedeberger A, *Die EU zwischen einheitlicher und differenzierter Integration* (Springer 2016)

Risse M, 'Arguing for Majority Rule' (2004) 12 Journal of Political Philosophy 41

Röder E, 'Proposal for an Enhanced CCTB as Alternative to a CCCTB with Formulary Apportionment' (2012) 4 World Tax Journal 125

Rodrik D, *Straight Talk on Trade: Ideas for a Sane World Economy* (Princeton University Press 2019)

Roos C, 'Möglichkeiten und Grenzen interkantonaler Vereinbarungen unter besonderer Beriicksichtigung des Konkordates fiber das offentliche Beschaffungswesen' (1995) 6 LeGes 23

Rosas A, 'The Status in EU Law of International Agreements Concluded by EU Member States' (2010) 34 Fordham International Law Journal 1304

Rose AK, 'One Money, One Market: The Effect of Common Currencies on Trade' (2000) 15 Economic Policy 08

Rosenfeldt H and Würdemann A, 'Schöpfer des Binnenmarktes im Käfig der Verträge—Die grundfreiheitliche Bindung des EU-Gesetzgebers' (2016) Europarecht 453

Rosengarten U, *Die Genscher-Colombo-Initiative: Baustein für die Europäische Union* (Nomos 2008)

Rossi-Maccanico P, 'Community Review of Direct Business Tax Measures: Selectivity, Discrimination and Restrictions' (2009) 8 European State Aid Law Quarterly 489

Rossi-Maccanico P, 'EU Review of Direct Tax Measures: Interplay between Fundamental Freedoms and State Aid Control' (2013) 22 EC Tax Review 19

Rossi-Maccanico P, 'Fiscal State Aids, Tax Base Erosion and Profit Shifting' (2015) 24 EC Tax Review 63

Roth E, 'The Rule of Reason Doctrine in European Court of Justice Jurisprudence on Direct Taxation' (2008) 56 Canadian Tax Journal 67

Roth W-H, 'Economic Justifications and the Internal Market' in Mielle K Bulterman and others (eds), *Views of European Law from the Mountain: Liber Amicorum Piet Jan Slot* (Wolters Kluwer Law International 2009)

Roth W-H, 'Die Niederlassungsfreiheit zwischen Beschränkungs- und Diskriminierungsverbot' in Wolfgang Schön (ed), *Gedächtnisschrift für Brigitte Knobbe-Keuk* (Dr Otto Schmidt Verlag 1997)

Roxan I, 'Assuring Real Freedom of Movement in EU Direct Taxation' (2000) 63 Modern Law Review 831

Roxburgh RF, *International Conventions and Third States; a Monograph* (Longmans, Green and Co 1917)

Ruffert M, 'Rechtserzeugung und Rechtsdurchsetzung im Europäischen Raum' in Eva Schumann (ed), *Hierarchie, Kooperation und Integration im Europäischen Rechtsraum: 17. Symposion der Kommission 'Die Funktion des Gesetzes in Geschichte und Gegenwart'* (Walter de Gruyter 2015)

Ruffert M, 'Art. 327 AEUV' in Matthias Ruffert and Christian Calliess (eds), *Das Verfassungsrecht der Europäischen Union mit Europäischer Grundrechtecharta* (5th edn, Beck Verlag 2016)

Rust A, 'Double Taxation' in Alexander Rust (ed), *Double Taxation within the European Union* (Kluwer Law International 2011)

Rust A, 'Equality and Non-Discrimination in European Tax Law' in Werner Haslehner, Georg Kofler, and Alexander Rust (eds), *EU Tax Law and Policy in the 21st Century* (Kluwer Law International 2017)

Rüthers B, Fischer C, and Birk A, *Rechtstheorie: mit juristischer Methodenlehre* (10th edn, Beck Verlag 2018)

Sacchetto C, 'Member States Tax Sovereignty: Between the Principle of Subsidiarity and the Necessity of Supranational Coordination' in Philippe Hinnekens and Luc Hinnekens (eds), *A Vision of Taxes Within and Outside the European Borders: Festschrift in Honor of Prof. Dr. Frans Vanistendael* (Kluwer Law International 2008)

Sadurski W, *Equality and Legitimacy* (OUP 2008)

Sadurski W, '"Solange, Chapter 3": Constitutional Courts in Central Europe—Democracy—European Union' (2008) 14 European Law Journal 1

Salanie B, *Microeconomics of Market Failures* (MIT Press 2000)

Saunders B, 'Democracy, Political Equality, and Majority Rule' (2010) 121 Ethics 148

Saurer J, 'Der kompetenzrechtliche Verhältnismäßigkeitsgrundsatz im Recht der Europäischen Union' (2014) 69 Juristenzeitung 281

Sauter W, 'Proportionality in EU Law: A Balancing Act?' (2013) 15 Cambridge Yearbook of European Legal Studies 439

Sauter W and Schepel H, *State and Market in European Union Law: The Public and Private Spheres of the Internal Market before the EU Courts* (CUP 2009)

Scharpf FW, 'Introduction: The Problem-Solving Capacity of Multi-Level Governance' (1997) 4 Journal of European Public Policy 520

Scharpf FW, 'Negative and Positive Integration in the Political Economy of European Welfare States' in Martin Rhodes and Yves Mény (eds), *The Future of European Welfare: A New Social Contract?* (Palgrave Macmillan 1998)

Scharpf FW, 'Legitimate Diversity: The New Challenge of European Integration' (2002) Les Cahiers européens de Sciences Po 1

Scharpf FW, 'Was man von einer europäischen Verfassung erwarten und nicht erwarten sollte' (Darmstadt, 7 November 2002)

Scharpf FW, 'Weshalb die EU nicht zur sozialen Marktwirtschaft werden kann' (2009) 7 Zeitschrift für Staats- und Europawissenschaften 419

Scharpf FW, 'The Asymmetry of European Integration, or Why the EU Cannot Be a "Social Market Economy"' (2010) 8 Socio-Economic Review 211

Scharrer H-E, 'Abgestufte Integration—Eine Einführung' in Eberhard Grabitz (ed), *Abgestufte Integration: Eine Alternative zum herkömmlichen Integrationskonzept* (NP Engel Verlag 1984)

Scheffer U, *Die Marktfreiheiten des EG-Vertrages als Ermessensgrenze des Gemeinschaftsgesetzgebers* (Peter Lang 1997)

Schenk A and Zee H, 'Treating Financial Services under a Value-Added Tax: Conceptual Issues and Country Practices' (2001) 22 Tax Notes International 3309

Schladebach M, 'Praktische Konkordanz als verfassungsrechtliches Kollisionsprinzip: Eine Verteidigung' (2014) 53 Der Staat 263

Schmidt S, 'Mutual Recognition as a New Model of Governance' (2007) 14 Journal of European Public Policy 667

Schmidt SK, *The European Court of Justice and the Policy Process: The Shadow of Case Law* (OUP 2018)

Schmitter PC and Karl TL, 'What Democracy Is... and Is Not' (1991) 2 Journal of Democracy 75

Schön W, 'Taxation and State Aid Law in the European Union' (1999) 36 Common Market Law Review 911

Schön W, 'Tax Competition in Europe—the Legal Perspective' (2000) 9 EC Tax Review 89

Schön W, 'Steuerliche Beihilfen' in Christian Koenig and Ulrich Ehricke (eds), *Aktuelle Fragen des EG-Beihilfenrechts* (Verlag Recht und Wirtschaft 2001)

Schön W, 'The Free Choice between the Right to Establish a Branch and to Set-up a Subsidiary—a Principle of European Business Law' (2001) 2 European Business Organization Law Review 339

Schön W, 'Tax Issues and Constraints on Reorganizations and Reincorporations in the European Union' (2004) 34 Tax Notes International 197

Schön W, 'Der Kapitalverkehr mit Drittstaaten und das internationale Steuerrecht' in Rudolf Gocke, Dietmar Gosch, and Michael Lang (eds), *Körperschaftsteuer, Internationales Steuerrecht, Doppelbesteuerung: Festschrift für Franz Wassermeyer zum 65. Geburtstag* (Beck Verlag 2005)

Schön W, 'Playing Different Games? Regulatory Competition in Tax and Company Law Compared' (2005) 42 Common Market Law Review 331

Schön W, 'Special Charges—A Gap in European Competition Law' (2006) 5 European State Aid Law Quarterly 494

Schön W, 'International Tax Coordination for a Second-Best World (Part I)' (2009) 1 World Tax Journal 67

Schön W, 'Die Auswirkungen des gemeinschaftsrechtlichen Beihilferechts auf das Steuerrecht' in Österreichischer Jusistentag (ed), *Verhandlungen des Siebzehnten Österreichischen Juristentages*, vol IV/2 (Manz Verlag 2010)

Schön W, 'Taxing Multinationals in Europe' in Bettina Banoun, Ole Gjems-Onstad, and Arvid Aage Skaar (eds), *Høyt skattet: festskrift til Frederik Zimmer på 70-årsdagen 28. Mars 2014* (Universitetsforl 2014)

Schön W, 'Kapitalverkehrsfreiheit und Niederlassungsfreiheit' in Thomas Ackermann and Johannes Köndgen (eds), *Privat- und Wirtschaftsrecht in Europa: Festschrift für Wulf-Henning Roth zum 70. Geburtstag* (Beck Verlag 2015)

Schön W, 'Neutralität und Territorialität—Gegensätze oder Grundsätze des Europäischen Steuerrechts?' in Wolfgang Schön and Caroline Heber (eds), *Grundfragen des Europäischen Steuerrechts*, vol 5 (Springer 2015)

Schön W, 'Neutrality and Territoriality—Competing or Converging Concepts in European Tax Law?' (2015) 69 Bulletin for International Taxation 271

Schön W, 'State Aid in the Area of Taxation' in Leigh Hancher, Tom Ottervanger, and Pieter J Slot (eds), *EU State Aids* (5th edn, Thomson Reuters 2016)

Schön W, 'Tax Legislation and the Notion of Fiscal Aid: A Review of 5 Years of European Jurisprudence' in Isabelle Richelle, Wolfgang Schön, and Edoardo Traversa (eds), *State Aid Law and Business Taxation*, vol 6 (Springer 2016)

Schön W, 'Die Analogie im Europäischen (Privat-)Recht' in Marietta Auer and others (eds), Carsten Herresthal, *Privatrechtsdogmatik im 21. Jahrhundert: Festschrift für Claus-Wilhelm Canaris zum 80. Geburtstag* (de Gruyter 2017)

Schön W, 'Ten Questions About Why and How to Tax the Digitalized Economy' (2018) 72 Bulletin for International Taxation 287

Schön W, 'Der digitale Steuer-Irrweg' *Frankfurter Allgemeine Zeitung* (6 April 2018) 16

Schön W, 'Facilitating Entry by Facilitating Exit: New Paths in EU Tax Legislation' (2018) 46 Intertax 339

Schön W, 'Selektivität schlägt Souveränität' (2019) 183 Zeitschrift für das gesamte Handelsrecht und Wirtschaftsrecht 393

Schön W, 'EU Tax Law: An Introduction' (Social Science Research Network 2019) SSRN Scholarly Paper ID 3432273 <https://papers.ssrn.com/abstract=3432273> accessed 28 January 2020

Schön W, 'Interpreting European Law in the Light of the BEPS Action Plan' (2020) Max Planck Institute for Tax Law and Public Finance Working Paper <https://papers.ssrn.com/sol3/papers.cfm?abstract_id=3522962> accessed 3 February 2021

Schön W, 'Missbrauchskontrolle im Europäischen Umwandlungsrecht' in Michael Hoffmann-Becking and Peter Hommelhoff (eds), *Festschrift für Gerd Krieger* (Beck Verlag 2020) 879

Schönberger C, 'Normenkontrollen im EG-Föderalismus: Die Logik gegenläufiger Hierarchisierungen im Gemeinschaftsrecht' (2004) Europarecht 600

Schroeder W, 'Die Sicherung eines hohen Schutzniveaus für Gesundheits-, Umwelt- und Verbraucherschutz im europäischen Binnenmarkt' (2002) Deutsches Verwaltungsblatt 213

Schütze R, 'The Morphology of Legislative Power in the European Community: Legal Instruments and the Federal Division of Powers' (2006) 25 Yearbook of European Law 91

Schütze R, 'Supremacy without Pre-Emption? The Very Slowly Emergent Doctrine of Community Pre-Emption' (2006) 43 Common Market Law Review 1023

Schütze R, 'EC Law and International Agreements of the Member States—An Ambivalent Relationship?' (2007) 9 Cambridge Yearbook of European Legal Studies 387

Schütze R, *Cooperative Federalism Constitutionalized* (OUP 2009)

Schütze R, 'Subsidiarity after Lisbon: Reinforcing the Safeguards of Federalism?' (2009) 68 The Cambridge Law Journal 525

Schütze R, *European Union Law* (CUP 2015)

Schwartz IE, *EG-Kompetenzen für den Binnenmarkt: exklusiv oder konkurrierend/subsidiär?* (Zentrum für Europäisches Wirtschaftsrecht 1995)

Schweizer RJ and Abderhalden U, 'Art. 48' in Bernhard Ehrenzeller and others (eds), *Die schweizerische Bundesverfassung: St. Galler Kommentar, Band I* (3rd edn, Dike Schulthess 2014)

Seer R, 'The Jurisprudence of the European Court of Justice: Limitation of the Legal Consequences?' (2006) 46 European Taxation 470

Seidl-Hohenveldern I, 'Transformation or Adoption of International Law into Municipal Law' (1963) 12 International & Comparative Law Quarterly 88

Shaw J, 'The Treaty of Amsterdam: Challenges of Flexibility and Legitimacy' (1998) 4 European Law Journal 63

Shaw J, 'Constitutionalism and Flexibility in the EU: Developing a Relational approach' in Gráinne de Búrca and Joanne Scott (eds), *Constitutional Change in the EU: From Uniformity to Flexibility?* (Hart Publishing 2000)
Shaw J, 'Flexibility in a "Reorganized" and "Simplified" Treaty' (2003) 40 Common Market Law Review 279
Shaw MN, 'Territory in International Law' (1982) Netherlands Yearbook of International Law 61
Shaw MN, *International Law* (8th edn, CUP 2017)
Shuibhne NN and Maci M, 'Proving Public Interest: The Growing Impact of Evidence in Free Movement Case Law' (2013) 50 Common Market Law Review 965
Sideri K, 'The European Commission and the Law-Making Process: Compromise as a Category of Praxis' (2005) 1 International Journal of Law in Context 155
Sieyès E-J, *Préliminaire de la Constitution françoise* (1789) <https://gallica.bnf.fr/ark:/12148/bpt6k41690g/f6.image.texteImage> accessed 13 May 2019
Simader K, *Withholding Taxes and the Fundamental Freedoms* (Kluwer Law International 2013)
Simeon R, *Federal–Provincial Diplomacy: The Making of Recent Policy in Canada* (University of Toronto Press 1972)
Simma B, 'Reciprocity' in Rüdiger Wolfrum (ed), *The Max Planck Encyclopedia of Public International Law* (OUP 2008)
Simma B and Pulkowski D, 'Of Planets and the Universe: Self-Contained Regimes in International Law' (2006) 17 European Journal of International Law 483
Simma B, Weiler JHH, and Zöckler MC, *Kompetenzen und Grundrechte: Beschränkungen der Tabakwerbung aus der Sicht des Europarechts* (Duncker & Humblot 1999)
Sinnaeve A, 'State Aid Procedures: Developments since the Entry into Force of the Procedural Regulation' (2007) 44 Common Market Law Review 965
Sinnaeve A and Slot PJ, 'The New Regulation on State Aid Procedures' (1999) 36 Common Market Law Review 1153
Sion-Tzidkiyahu M, 'Comparing Opt-Outs: How Different Is Differentiated Integration' in Thomas Giegerich, Desirée Schmitt, and Sebastian Zeitzmann (eds), *Flexibility in the EU and Beyond: How Much Differentiation can European Integration Bear?* (Nomos 2017)
Skouris V, 'Fundamental Rights and Fundamental Freedoms: The Challenge of Striking a Delicate Balance' (2006) 17 European Business Law Review 225
Slemrod J, 'Competitive Tax Policy' in Kevin A Hassett (ed), *Rethinking Competitiveness* (AEI Press 2012)
Smit DS, 'The 150km Requirement under the Dutch 30% Wage Tax Facility C-512/03 (Sopora)' in Michael Lang and others (eds), *ECJ—Recent Developments in Direct Taxation 2013* (Linde Verlag 2014)
Smits R, 'Freedom of Payment and Capital Movement under EMU' in Albrecht Weber (ed), *Währung und Wirtschaft: das Geld im Recht; Festschrift für Prof. Dr. Hugo J. Hahn zum 70. Geburtstag* (Nomos 1997)
Smulders B and Eisele K, 'Reflections on the Institutional Balance, the Community Method and the Interplay between Jurisdictions after Lisbon' (2012) 31 Yearbook of European Law 112
Snell J, 'Economic Aims as Justification for Restrictions on Free Movement' in Annette Schrauwen (ed), *Rule of Reason: Rethinking Another Classic of EC Legal Doctrine* (Europa Law Publishing 2005)
Snell J, 'Non-Discriminatory Tax Obstacles in Community Law' (2007) 56 International & Comparative Law Quarterly 339

Snell J, 'Notion of Market Access: A Concept or a Slogan, The' (2010) 47 Common Market Law Review 437

Snell J, 'The Legitimacy of Free Movement Case Law: Process and Substance' in Maurice Adams and others (eds), *Judging Europe's Judges: The Legitimacy of the Case Law of the European Court of Justice* (Hart Publishing 2013)

Snell J, 'Economic Justifications and the Role of the State' in Panos Koutrakos, Niamh Nic Shuibhne, and Phil Syrpis (eds), *Exceptions from EU Free Movement Law: Derogation, Justification and Proportionality* (Hart Publishing 2016)

Snell J, 'Still United despite Diversity?' (2018) 43 European Law Review 801

Soares AG, 'Pre-Emption, Conflicts of Powers and Subsidiarity' (1998) 23 European Law Review 132

Sørensen KE, 'Enhanced Free Movement: Opportunities and Limits for EU Member States Entering into Bilateral Agreements' (2019) 44 European Law Review 319

Sousa PC de, 'Negative and Positive Integration in EU Economic Law: Between Strategic Denial and Cognitive Dissonance?' (2012) 13 German Law Journal 979

Sousa PC de, *The European Fundamental Freedoms: A Contextual Approach* (OUP 2015)

Spaventa E, 'The Outer Limit of the Treaty Free Movement Provisions: Some Reflections on the Significance of Keck, Remoteness and Deliège' in Catherine Barnard and others (eds), *The Outer Limits of European Union Law* (Bloomsbury Publishing 2009)

Spies K, *Die Kapitalverkehrsfreiheit in Konkurrenz zu den anderen Grundfreiheiten* (Lexis Nexis 2015)

Spindler-Simader K, 'Dividend Withholding Taxes after Miljoen, X and Société Générale' (2016) 25 EC Tax Review 70

Sprundel DF van, 'Analysis of the Netherlands Dividend Withholding Tax on Shares—No Need to Abolish This Tax Yet?' (2008) 48 European Taxation 607

Staes M, 'The Combined Application of the Fundamental Freedoms and the EU State Aid Rules: In Search of a Way Out of the Maze' (2014) 42 Intertax 106

Starck C and Bothe M (eds), 'Zusammenarbeit der Gliedstaaten im Bundesstaat', *Zusammenarbeit der Gliedstaaten im Bundesstaat* (Nomos 1988)

Staringer C, 'Missbrauchsbekämpfung, Aufteilung der Besteuerungsbefugnisse und Kohärenz in der Rechtsprechung des EuGH' in Michael Lang (ed), *Europäisches Steuerrecht*, vol 41 (Dr Otto Schmidt Verlag 2018)

Staringer C and Schneeweiss H, 'Tax Treaty Non-Discrimination and EC Freedoms' in Michael Lang, Josef Schuch, and Claus Staringer (eds), *Tax Treaty Law and EC Law* (Linde Verlag 2007)

Stark J, *Law for Sale: A Philosophical Critique of Regulatory Competition* (OUP 2019)

Sternberg C, *Die extraterritoriale Besteuerungsgewalt des Staates* (Duncker & Humblot 2019)

Stone Sweet A, 'The European Court of Justice' in Paul P Craig and Gráinne de Búrca (eds), *The Evolution of EU Law* (2nd edn, OUP 2011)

Streek JL van de, 'Some Introductory Remarks on the Relaunched CCTB/CCCTB Proposals from a Policy Perspective' in Dennis Weber and Jan Lambertus van de Streek (eds), *The EU Common Consolidated Corporate Tax Base: Critical Analysis* (Kluwer Law International 2018)

Street TA, *The Theory and Principles of Tort Law* (Beard Books 1999)

Strong FR, 'Cooperative Federalism Symposium on Cooperative Federalism' (1937) 23 Iowa Law Review 459

Stubb AC-G, 'A Categorization of Differentiated Integration' (1996) 34 Journal of Common Market Studies 283

Stubb AC-G, *Negotiating Flexibility in the European Union—Amsterdam, Nice and Beyond* (Palgrave Macmillan 2002)

Suteu S, 'The Populist Turn in Central and Eastern Europe: Is Deliberative Democracy (Part of) the Solution?' (2017) Jean Monnet Working Paper, https://jeanmonnetprogram.org/wp-content/uploads/JMWP-06-Silvia-Suteu.pdf

Sutter FP, *Das EG-Beihilfenverbot und sein Durchführungsverbot in Steuersachen* (Linde Verlag 2005)

Sutter FP, 'Die abkommensrechtliche Verteilung der Besteuerungsrechte zwischen Ansässigkeits- und Quellenstaat aus beihilfenrechtlicher Sicht' in Wolfgang Gassner and others (eds), *Die Verteilung der Besteuerungsrechte zwischen Ansässigkeits- und Quellenstaat im Recht der Doppelbesteuerungsabkommen* (Linde Verlag 2005)

Sutter FP, 'The Influence of the European State Aid Rules on National Tax Policy' in Krister Andersson, Eva Eberhartinger, and Lars Oxelheim (eds), *National Tax Policy in Europe: To Be or Not To Be?* (Springer 2007)

Swann D, *The Economics of the Common Market* (4th edn, Penguin Books 1981)

Syrpis P, 'Theorising the Relationship between the Judiciary and the Legislature in the EU Internal Market' in Phil Syrpis (ed), *The Judiciary, the Legislature and the EU Internal Market* (Intersentia 2012)

Syrpis P, 'The Relationship between Primary and Secondary Law in the EU' (2015) 52 Common Market Law Review 461

Syrpis P and Novitz T, 'Economic and Social Rights in Conflict: Political and Judicial Approaches to Their Reconciliation' (2008) 33 European Law Review 411

Szudoczky R, 'The Influence of Primary Law on the Interpretation of Secondary Law in the Field of EU Citizenship and Direct Taxation: "Whatever Works" . . .' in Dennis Weber (ed), *Traditional and Alternative Routes to European Tax Integration: Primary Law, Secondary Law, Soft Law, Coordination, Comitology and Their Relationship* (IBFD 2010)

Szudoczky R, *The Sources of EU Law and Their Relationships: Lessons for the Field of Taxation: Primary Law, Secondary Law, Fundamental Freedoms and State Aid Rules* (IBFD 2014)

Szudoczky R, 'Convergence of the Analysis of National Tax Measures under the EU State Aid Rules and the Fundamental Freedoms' (2016) 15 European State Aid Law Quarterly 357

Szudoczky R and van de Streek J, 'Revisiting the Dutch Interest Box under the EU State Aid Rules and the Code of Conduct: When a "Disparity" Is Selective and Harmful' (2010) 38 Intertax 260

Szydło M, 'Differential Tax Burdens of Undertakings and Internal Market Law: The Way Forward after "ANGED"' (2019) 56 Common Market Law Review 1093

Taschner HC, *Richtlinie oder internationale Übereinkommen?: Rechtsinstrumente zur Erreichung der Ziele der Europäischen Union* (Zentrum für Europäisches Wirtschaftsrecht 1996)

Taschner HC, *Schengen: die Übereinkommen zum Abbau der Personenkontrollen an den Binnengrenzen von EU-Staaten* (Nomos 1997)

Teichmann C, 'Überprüfung von Sekundärrecht am Maßstab der Grundfreiheiten' in Peter-Christian Müller-Graff, Stefanie Schmahl, and Vassilios Skouris (eds), *Europäisches Recht zwischen Bewährung und Wandel—Festschrift Dieter H. Scheuing* (Nomos 2011)

Tenore M, 'Trends and Facts in European Tax Integration: Harmonization and Coordination' in Pasquale Pistone (ed), *European Tax Integration: Law, Policy and Politics* (IBFD 2018)

Thömmers O, 'Corporate Taxation in the European Union in the Year 2002—A Single Currency and Fifteen Different Tax Jurisdictions' (2002) 30 Intertax 123

Thun-Hohenstein C, *Der Vertrag von Amsterdam: die neue Verfassung der EU* (Manz Verlag 1997)

Thym D, 'The Schengen Law: A Challenge for Legal Accountability in the European Union' (2002) 8 European Law Journal 218

Thym D, *Ungleichzeitigkeit und europäisches Verfassungsrecht* (Nomos 2004)

Thym D, 'Flexible Integration: Garant oder Gefahr für die Einheit und die Legitimation des Unionsrechts?' (2013) Europarecht Beiheft

Thym D, 'Competing Models for Understanding Differentiated Integration' in Bruno de Witte, Andrea Ott, and Ellen Vos (eds), *Between Flexibility and Disintegration: The Trajectory of Differentiation in EU Law* (Edward Elgar 2017)

Tiberi G, '"Uniti nella diversita`": l'integrazione differenziata e le cooperazioni rafforzate nell'Union europea' in Franco Bassanini and Giulia Tiberi (eds), *Le nuove istituzioni europee. Commento al trattato di Lisbona* (Il Mulino 2010)

Timmermans C, 'The EU and Public International Law' (1999) European Foreign Affairs Review 181

Tinbergen J, *International Economic Integration* (2nd edn, Elsevier 1965)

Tindemans L, 'Report on the European Union' (1976) 9 Bulletin of the European Communities 11

Tomuschat C, 'General International Law: A New Source of International Law?' in Riccardo Pisillo Mazzeschi and Pasquale De Sena (eds), *Global Justice, Human Rights and the Modernization of International Law* (Springer International Publishing 2018)

Trachtman, 'Trade And ... Problems, Cost-Benefit Analysis and Subsidiarity' (1998) 9 European Journal of International Law 32

Traversa E and Pirlot A, 'The UK Brexit Referendum: A Catalyst to Reform the European Union Institutional Architecture in Tax Matters?' (2016) 44 Intertax 878

Traversa E and Vintras B, 'The Territoriality of Tax Incentives within the Single Market' in Isabelle Richelle, Wolfgang Schön, and Edoardo Traversa (eds), *Allocating Taxing Powers within the European Union* (Springer 2013)

Tridimas T, 'The Principle of Proportionality in Community Law: From the Rule of Law to Market Integration Modern Jurisprudence' (1996) 31 Irish Jurist 83

Tridimas T, 'Proportionality in Community Law: Searching for the Appropriate Standard of Scrutiny' in Evelyn Ellis (ed), *The Principle of Proportionality in the Laws of Europe* (Hart Publishing 1999)

Tridimas T, 'The Rule of Reason and Its Relation to Proportionality and Subsidiarity' in Annette Schrauwen (ed), *Rule of Reason: Rethinking Another Classic of EC Legal Doctrine* (Europa Law Publishing 2005)

Tridimas T, 'The Principle of Proportionality' in Robert Schütze and Takis Tridimas (eds), *Oxford Principles of European Union Law*, vol I: The European Union Legal Order (OUP 2018)

Tryfonidou A, 'Reverse Discrimination in Purely Internal Situations: An Incongruity in a Citizens' Europe' (2008) 35 Legal Issues of Economic Integration 43

Tryfonidou A, *Reverse Discrimination in EC Law* (Kluwer Law International 2009)

Tuytschaever F, *Differentiation in European Union Law* (Hart Publishing 1999)

Ullrich H, 'Patent Protection in Europe: Integrating Europe into the Community or the Community into Europe?' (2002) 8 European Law Journal 433

Vadi V, 'Proportionality, Reasonableness, and Standards of Review in I Treaty Arbitration' in Andrea K Bjorklund (ed), *Yearbook on International Investment Law & Policy, 2013–2014* (OUP 2015)

Raad K van, 'Non-Residents—Personal Allowances, Deduction of Personal Expenses and Tax Rates' (2010) 2 World Tax Journal 154

van Thiel S, 'Why the European Court of Justice Should Interpret Directly Applicable Community Law as a Right to Most-Favoured Nation Treatment and a Prohibition of Double Taxation' in Dennis Weber (ed), *The Influence of European Law on Direct Taxation: Recent and Future Developments* (Kluwer Law International 2007)

van Thiel S, 'The Direct Income Tax Case Law of the European Court of Justice: Past Trends and Future Developments Symposium on Corporate Tax Policy in the European Union' (2008) 62 Tax Law Review 143

Vanistendael F, 'A Personal View' in Ary Lans Bovenberg and others (eds), *Harmonization of Company Taxation in the European Community: Some Comments on the Ruding Committee Report* (Kluwer Law International 1992)

Vanistendael F, 'Comments on the Ruding Committee Report' (1992) 1 EC Tax Review 3

Vanistendael F, 'The Compatibility of the Basic Economic Freedoms with the Sovereign National Tax Systems of the Member States' (2003) 12 EC Tax Review 136

Vanistendael F, 'General Report on the Fundamental Freedoms and National Sovereignty in the European Union' in Frans Vanistendael (ed), *EU Freedoms and Taxation* (IBFD 2006)

Vanistendael F, 'Ability to Pay in European Community Law' (2014) 23 EC Tax Review 121

Vanistendael F, 'Democracy, Revolution and Taxation' (2017) 71 Bulletin for International Taxation 444

Vanistendael F, 'On Democratic Legitimacy of European Tax Law and the Role of the European Parliament' in Pasquale Pistone (ed), *European Tax Integration: Law, Policy and Politics* (IBFD 2018)

Varian HR, *Intermediate Microeconomics: A Modern Approach* (9th edn, Norton 2014)

Vella J, Fuest C, and Schmidt-Eisenlohr T, 'The EU Commission's Proposal for a Financial Transaction Tax' (2011) British Tax Review 607

Verhofstadt G, 'A Vision of Europe' (Brussels, 21 September 2000) <https://www.cvce.eu/content/publication/2005/7/22/e1570f15-55ae-4b60-b9e7-861ccc6876ad/publishable_en.pdf> accessed 3 February 2021

Vilaça JL da C and Piçarra N, *Are There Material Limits to the Revision of the Treaties on the European Union?: Referat Im Rahmen Der Vortragsreihe 'Das Wirtschaftsrecht Der Europäischen Union', Bonn, 17. Oktober 1994* (Zentrum für Europäisches Wirtschaftsrecht 1995)

Viner J, *The Customs Union Issue* (Stevens 1950)

Vobruba G, *Die Dynamik Europas* (Springer 2007)

Vogel D, *Trading Up: Consumer and Environmental Regulation in a Global Economy* (Harvard University Press 2009)

von Arnould A, Völkerrecht (4th edn, C.f. Müller Verlag 2019)

von der Decken K, 'Art. 41—Agreements to Modify Multilateral Treaties between Certain of the Parties Only' in Oliver Dörr and Kirsten Schmalenbach (eds), *Vienna Convention on the Law of Treaties: A Commentary* (Springer 2018)

von Wallenberg G and Schütte M, 'Art. 108' in Eberhard Grabitz, Meinhard Hilf, and Martin Nettesheim (eds), *Das Recht der Europäischen Union* (64th edn, Beck Verlag 2018)

von Weizsäcker R, Dehaene J-L, and Simon D, 'The Institutional Implications of Enlargement—Report to the European Commission' (1999) https://www.cvce.eu/content/publication/2005/1/24/4162db7c-7710-459b-929d-3318d38d0075/publishable_en.pdf

Vooren BV, *EU External Relations Law and the European Neighbourhood Policy: A Paradigm for Coherence* (Routledge 2012)

Vranes E, 'Lex Superior, Lex Specialis, Lex Posterior—Zur Rechtsnatur der „Konfliktlösungsregeln"' (2005) Zeitschrift für ausländisches öffentliches Recht und Völkerrecht 391
Vranes E, 'The Dynamics of European Economic Integration: A Legal Perspective' in Harald Badinger and Volker Nitsch (eds), *Routledge Handbook of the Economics of European Integration* (Routledge 2016)
Wacker R, 'Zur praktischen Konkordanz von Grundfreiheiten und EU-Richtlinienrecht auf dem Gebiet der direkten Steuern' in Klaus-Dieter Drüen, Johanna Hey, and Rudolf Mellinghoff (eds), *100 Jahre Steuerrechtsprechung in Deutschland 1918-2018: Festschrift für den Bundesfinanzhof* (Dr Otto Schmidt Verlag 2018)
Waelbroeck M, 'The Emergent Doctrine of Community Pre-Emption - Consent and Re-Delegation' in Terrance Sandalow and Eric Stein (eds), *Courts and Free Markets: Perspectives from the United States and Europe*, vol II (Clarendon Press 1982)
Wagh S, 'The Taxation of Digital Transactions in India: The New Equalization Levy' (2016) 70 Bulletin for International Taxation 538
Wagner W, 'Negative and Positive Integration in EU Criminal Law Co-Operation' (2011) 15 European Integration Online Papers
Wallace H, 'Flexibility: A Tool of Integration or a Restraint on Disintegration?' in Karlheinz Neunreither and Antje Wiener (eds), *European Integration After Amsterdam: Institutional Dynamics and Prospects for Democracy* (OUP 2000)
Walter K, *Rechtsfortbildung durch den EuGH: eine rechtsmethodische Untersuchung ausgehend von der deutschen und französischen Methodenlehre* (Duncker & Humblot 2009)
Wassermeyer F, 'Does the EC Treaty Force the Member States to Conclude a Multilateral Tax Treaty?', in Michael Lang and others (eds), *Multilateral Tax Treaties* (Kluwer Law International 1998)
Wattel PJ, 'Progressive Taxation of Non-Residents and Intra-EC Allocation of Personal Tax Allowances' (2000) 40 European Taxation 210
Wattel PJ, 'Red Herrings in Direct Tax Cases before the ECJ' (2004) 31 Legal Issues of Economic Integration 81
Wattel PJ, 'Judicial Restraint and Three Trends in the ECJ's Direct Tax Case Law Symposium on Corporate Tax Policy in the European Union: Commentary' (2008) 62 Tax Law Review 205
Wattel PJ, 'Non-Discrimination à la Court: The ECJ's (Lack of) Comparability Analysis in Direct Tax Cases' in Guglielmo Maisto, Pasquale Pistone, and Dennis Weber (eds), *Non-discrimination in Tax Treaties: Selected Issues from a Global Perspective* (IBFD 2016)
Wattel PJ, 'Interaction of State Aid, Free Movement, Policy Competition and Abuse Control in Direct Tax Matters' (2013) 5 World Tax Journal 128
Wattel PJ, Marres O, and Vermeulen H (eds), *Terra/Wattel European Tax Law*, vol I General Topics and Direct Taxation (7th edn, Kluwer Law International 2018)
Weatherill S, 'Beyond Preemption? Shared Competence and Constitutional Change in the European Community' in David O'Keeffe and Patrick Twomey (eds), *Legal Issues of the Maastricht Treaty* (Chancery Law Pub 1994)
Weatherill S, '"If I'd Wanted You to Understand I Would Have Explained It Better": What Is the Purpose of the Provisions on Closer Co-Operation Introduced by the Treaty of Amsterdam?' in David O'Keeffe and Patrick Twomey (eds), *Legal Issues of the Amsterdam Treaty* (Bloomsbury Publishing PLC 1999)
Weatherill S, 'Flexibility or Fragmentation: Trends in European Integration' in John A Usher (ed), *The State of the European Union: Structure, Enlargement and Economic Union* (Pearson Education 2000)

Weatherill S, 'Pre-Emption, Harmonisation and the Distribution of Competence to Regulate the Internal Market' in Catherine Barnard and Joanne Scott (eds), *The Law of the Single European Market: Unpacking the Premises* (Hart Publishing 2002)

Weatherill S, 'The Limits of Legislative Harmonization Ten Years after Tobacco Advertising: How the Court's Case Law Has Become a Drafting Guide' (2011) 12 German Law Journal 827

Weatherill S, 'Viking and Laval: The EU Internal Market Perspective' in Mark R Freedland and Jeremias Prassl (eds), *Viking, Laval and Beyond* (Hart Publishing 2014)

Weatherill S, 'The Competence to Harmonise and Its Limits' in Panos Koutrakos and Jukka Snell (eds), *Research Handbook on the Law of the EU's Internal Market* (Edward Elgar Publishing 2017)

Weatherill S, *The Internal Market as a Legal Concept*, vol XXV/1 (OUP 2017)

Weatherill S, 'The Principle of Mutual Recognition: It Doesn't Work Because It Doesn't Exist' (2018) 43 European Law Review 224

Weber D, 'In Search of a (New) Equilibrium Between Tax Sovereignty and the Freedom of Movement Within the EC' (2006) 34 Intertax 585

Weber D, 'An Analysis of the Past, Current and Future of the Coherence of the Tax System as Justification' (2015) 24 EC Tax Review 43

Weeks EP, *The Doctrine of Damnum Absque Injuria Considered in Its Relation to the Law of Torts* (Sumner Whitney 1879)

Weiler JHH, 'The Community System: The Dual Character of Supranationalism' (1981) 1 Yearbook of European Law 267

Weiler JHH, 'The External Legal Relations of Non-Unitary Actors: Mixity and the Federal Principle' in David O'Keeffe and Henry G Schermers (eds), *Mixed Agreements* (Kluwer Law and Taxation Publishers 1983)

Weiler JHH, 'The Transformation of Europe' (1991) 100 The Yale Law Journal 2403

Weiler JHH, 'The Constitution of the Common Market Place: Text and Context in the Evolution of the Free Movement of Goods' in Paul P Craig and Gráinne de Búrca (eds), *The Evolution of EU Law* (OUP 1999)

Weiler JHH, 'Mutual Recognition, Functional Equivalence and Harmonization in the Evolution of the European Common Market and the WTO' in Fiorella Kostoris Padoa Schioppa (ed), *The Principle of Mutual Recognition in the European Integration Process* (Palgrave Macmillan 2005)

Weiler JHH, 'Epilogue: Judging the Judges - Apology and Critique' in Maurice Adams and others (eds), *Judging Europe's Judges: The Legitimacy of the Case Law of the European Court of Justice* (2013)

Wessels W, 'Verstärkte Zusammenarbeit: Eine neue Variante flexibler Integration' in Mathias Jopp, Andreas Maurer, and Otto Schmuck (eds), *Die Europäische Union nach Amsterdam. Analysen und Stellungnahmen zum neuen EU-Vertrag* (Europa Union Verlag 1998)

Westlake M, *The European Union beyond Amsterdam: New Concepts of European Integration* (Routledge 1998)

Wetzel RG, *Verträge zugunsten und zu Lasten Dritter nach der Wiener Vertragsrechtskonvention* (Inst für Völkerrecht 1973)

Weyde D and others, 'Der Kommissionsvorschlag zur Einführung einer Finanztransaktionssteuer in elf EU-Mitgliedstaaten' (2013) Deutsche Steuer-Zeitung 495

Wicke H, 'Grenzüberschreitender Formwechsel kann ohne Verlegung des Verwaltungssitzes in Zuzugsstaat zulässig sein—Anmerkung zu EuGH, Urt. v. 25.10.2017 C-106/16, Polbud Wykonawstwo sp. zo. o.' (2017) Deutsches Steuerrecht 2684

Wiedmann T, 'Der Vertrag von Nizza—Genesis einer Reform' (2001) Europarecht 185

Wildasin DE, 'Public Expenditures Determined by Voting with One's Feet and Public Choice' (1977) 79 The Scandinavian Journal of Economics 326
Wilde MF de, 'The CCCTB Relaunch: A Critical Assessment and Some Suggestions for Modification' in Pasquale Pistone (ed), *European Tax Integration: Law, Policy and Politics* (IBFD 2018)
Wildhaber L and Breitenmoser S, 'The Relationship between Customary International Law and Municipal Law in Western European Countries' (1988) 48 Zeitschrift für ausländisches öffentliches Recht und Völkerrecht 163
William W, 'Economic Substantive Due Process: Considered Dead Is Being Revived by a Series of Supreme Court Land-Use Cases' (2014) 36 University of Hawai'i Law Review 455
Wilson DJ, 'Beggar Thy Neighbor? The In-State, Out-of-State, and Aggregate Effects of R&D Tax Credits' (2009) 91 The Review of Economics and Statistics 431
Witte B de, 'Old-Fashioned Flexibility: International Agreements between Member States of the European Union' in Gráinne de Búrca and Joanne Scott (eds), *Constitutional Change in the EU: From Uniformity to Flexibility?* (Hart Publishing 2000)
Witte B de, 'Chameleonic Member States: Differentiation by Means of Partial and Parallel International Agreements' in Bruno de Witte, Dominik Hanf, and Ellen Vos (eds), *The Many Faces of Differentiation in EU Law* (Intersentia nv 2001)
Witte B de, 'Non-Market Values in Internal Market Legislation' in Niamh Nic Shuibhne (ed), *Regulating the Internal Market* (Edward Elgar Publishing 2006)
Witte B de, 'International Law as a Tool for the European Union' (2009) 5 European Constitutional Law Review 265
Witte B de, 'European Union Law: How Autonomous Is Its Legal Order?' (2010) Zeitschrift für öffentliches Recht 141
Witte B de, 'A Competence to Protect - The Pursuit of Non-Market Aims through Internal Market Legislation' in Phil Syrpis (ed), *The Judiciary, the Legislature and the EU Internal Market* (CUP 2012)
Witte B de and Martinelli T, 'Treaties between EU Member States as Quasi-Instruments of EU Law' in Marise Cremona and Claire Kilpatrick (eds), *EU Legal Acts: Challenges and Transformations*, vol XXV/4 (OUP 2018)
Witte F de, 'Sex, Drugs & EU Law: The Recognition of Moral and Ethical Diversity in EU Law' (2013) 50 Common Market Law Review 1545
Witte F de, 'Transnational Solidarity and the Mediation of Conflicts of Justice in Europe' (2012) 18 European Law Journal 694
Wittock N, 'The Influence of the Principle of Union Loyalty in Tax Matters' (2014) 23 EC Tax Review 171
Wolf M, 'An Unholy Alliance: The European Community and Developing Countries in the International Trading System' in LBM Mennes and Jacob Kol (eds), *European Trade Policies and Developing Countries* (Routledge 1988)
Wollenschläger F, *Grundfreiheit ohne Markt: die Herausbildung der Unionsbürgerschaft im unionsrechtlichen Freizügigkeitsregime* (Mohr Siebeck 2007)
Wood M, 'International Organizations and Customary International Law' (2015) 48 Vanderbilt Journal of Transnational Law 609
Woods L and others, *Steiner & Woods EU Law* (13th edn, OUP 2017)
Wouters J and Vidal M, 'An International Lawyer's Perspective on the ECJ's Case Law Concerning the OECD Model Tax Convention and Its Commentaries' in Luc Hinnekens and Philippe Hinnekens (eds), *A Vision of Taxes Within and Outside the European Borders: Festschrift in Honor of Prof. Dr. Frans Vanistendael* (Kluwer Law International 2008)

Wyatt D, 'Is the Commission a Lawmaker? On the Right of Initiative, Institutional Transparency and Public Participation in Decision-Making: ClientEarth' (2019) 56 Common Market Law Review 825

Zalasiński A, 'Tax Rules Applicable without Distinction and the EU Internal Market Freedoms—An Analysis of Recent Case Law Regarding Taxation of Investment Income' 57 European Taxation 11

Zelger B, 'The Effect on Trade Criterion in European Union State Aid Law: A Critical Approach' (2018) 17 European State Aid Law Quarterly 28

Zepter B, 'Zukunft und Aufgaben der Europäischen Kommission' (2000) 23 Integration 260

Ziegler KS, 'Strengthening the Rule of Law, but Fragmenting International Law: The Kadi Decision of the ECJ from the Perspective of Human Rights Recent Developments' (2009) 9 Human Rights Law Review 288

Ziller J, 'Flexibility in the Geographical Scope of EU Law: Diversity and Differentiation in the Application of Substantive Law on Member States' Territories' in Gráinne de Búrca and Joanne Scott (eds), *Constitutional Change in the EU: From Uniformity to Flexibility?* (Hart Publishing 2000)

Zimmer F, 'Withholding Taxes in the EU and the EEA' (2008) 52 Tax Notes International 667

Zimmerl I, *Joint Tax Audits als Ausgangspunkt zur Effektuierung des Verständigungsverfahrens - Eine Analyse möglicher dogmatischer Entwicklungen unter besonderer Berücksichtigung der deutsch-italienischen Verwaltungszusammenarbeit* (2019)

Zweigert K, 'Some Reflections on the Sociological Dimensions of Private International Law or What Is Justice in Conflict of Laws?' (1972) 44 University of Colorado Law Review 283

Index

For the benefit of digital users, indexed terms that span two pages (e.g., 52–53) may, on occasion, appear on only one of those pages.